"In this absorbing book, Gillian Gill shows how the royal couple counterpoised their partnership—and their passion—for twenty-one years while bearing the weight of the world on their shoulders."
—DANIEL MARK EPSTEIN, author of *The Lincolns: Portrait of a Marriage*

"A lively, perceptive, impressively researched biography."
—*Publishers Weekly*

"This is a more compassionate look into the lives of Victoria and Albert, in which they become people to whom we can relate—the stuffed shirts get sent to the laundry and a much softer fabric is returned!"
—ANNE PERRY, author of the Pitt and Monk Victorian mystery series

"Gill's dual bio offers juicy new details about the demure yet decisive monarch who defined an era."
—*Good Housekeeping*

"Intimate and delicious. Gill has a gift for finding the telling details which bring the royal couple to life, and she has created a fascinating study of a woman negotiating her supreme power in a male-dominated society and a traditional marriage. The push and pull between Albert, who is a complicated mixture of rigidity and softness, and Victoria, reluctant mother of nine and natural sovereign, makes a great story."
—SUSAN QUINN, author of *Marie Curie: A Life*

"Gill depicts a remarkable relationship at the pinnacle of power in the nineteenth century, in which husband and wife shared an unstoppable ambition along with a longing for intimacy."
—The Daily Beast

"*We Two* is a thought-provoking look at an era starting to grapple with issues that shed light on recent history."
—CAROLYN BURKE, author of *Lee Miller: A Life*

"Gill grippingly recounts the tensions and negotiations between Victoria and Albert, both in politics and in intimate and domestic life. Victoria set about creating an enduring legend of her marriage and inevitably emerged as both heroine and victor. Gill skillfully shows exactly how she did it."
—STELLA TILLYARD, author of *A Royal Affair* and *The Aristocrats*

ALSO BY GILLIAN GILL

Nightingales

WE TWO

BALLANTINE

BOOKS

TRADE

PAPERBACKS

NEW YORK

We Two

...

VICTORIA AND ALBERT:

Rulers, Partners, Rivals

...

GILLIAN GILL

2010 Ballantine Books Trade Paperback Edition

Published in the United States by Ballantine Books,
an imprint of The Random House Publishing Group,
a division of Random House, Inc., New York.

BALLANTINE and colophon are registered
trademarks of Random House, Inc.

Originally published in hardcover in the United States by Ballantine Books,
an imprint of The Random House Publishing Group,
a division of Random House, Inc., in 2009.

LIBRARY OF CONGRESS CATALOGING-IN-PUBLICATION DATA

Gill, Gillian.
We two : Victoria and Albert Rulers, partners, rivals / Gillian Gill.
p. cm.
Includes bibliographical references and index.
ISBN 978-0-345-52001-2
1. Victoria, Queen of Great Britain, 1819–1901—Marriage.
2. Albert, Prince Consort of Victoria, Queen of Great Britain, 1819–1861—Marriage.
3. Queens—Great Britain—Biography.
4. Princes—Great Britain—Biography. I. Title.
DA554.G55 2009
941.081092'2—dc22
[B]   2009008919

Printed in the United States of America

www.ballantinebooks.com

2 4 6 8 9 7 5 3 1

Frontispiece and pages 15, 89, and 145: Art features details from
Modern Times at Windsor Castle by Sir Edwin Landseer.
The Royal Collection © 2008 Her Majesty Queen Elizabeth II.

Book design by Barbara M. Bachman

For Rose

WHO LIVES ON IN MY DREAMS

and For All My Grandchildren

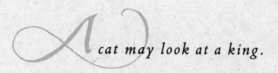 *cat may look at a king.*

—OLD ENGLISH PROVERB

Contents

WE TWO

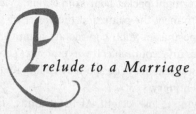

Prelude to a Marriage

WINDSOR CASTLE,
OCTOBER 10, 1839

ALL AFTERNOON QUEEN VICTORIA HAD BEEN EXPECTING THE AR-
rival of her cousin Albert, and she was getting edgier by the minute. Louis
XIV had never had to wait, yet here she was, monarch to an empire that put
the Sun King's France to shame, cooling her heels until some third-rank
German princes arrived and she could go in for dinner. As all the courts of
Europe knew, Albert of Saxe-Coburg and Gotha, dutifully chaperoned by
his elder brother, Ernest, was coming to Windsor so that the Queen of Great
Britain and Ireland could look him over and decide if she wanted to marry
him. How dare that young man be late?

Victoria had in fact been waiting for her Coburg cousins for more than a
week, and she was no longer accustomed to interference with her schedule.
People nowadays waited for her, and she for her part made a point of being
punctual. It was true that her initial invitation to the Coburg cousins had
been less than gracious, and then, at the last minute, she had written
asking them not to come until after the September meeting of her Privy
Council. This request was a shade peremptory, perhaps, but more than reasonable, given the weight of her ceremonial and constitutional duties.
However, the cousins had taken it badly. Albert replied in a huff that he and
his brother could not see their way to leaving Coburg before October 3.
Thereupon the princes crept north through Germany, lingered at the court
of their uncle King Leopold in Brussels, and dallied again at the Belgian
coast, waiting in vain for a calm day to embark. Victoria knew that for her

male Coburg relatives, Calais and Dover might just as well be called Scylla and Charybdis, but she had little sympathy with their dread of the sea. She herself was hardly ever sick.

On finally receiving word from Uncle Leopold that Albert and Ernest were taking the overnight packet boat from Ostend, Victoria at once dispatched equerries to meet the princes at the Tower of London and bring them to Windsor posthaste. Such considerate arrangements made their lateness all the more unaccountable. It was now after seven in the evening. The Coburg party still had not been spotted heading up to Windsor Castle, and the Queen was hungry.

Victoria was trying to lose weight. At 125 pounds, she was heavy for a tiny, small-boned young woman, and she was not feeling her best. Over a stressful summer, her complexion had lost its glow and an ugly sty broke out on her eye. Her dressers were kept busy letting out the new gowns sent over from Paris by Victoria's elegant French aunt, Queen Louise of the Belgians. The royal doctors were recommending that Her Majesty limit lunch to a light broth, while Prime Minister Lord Melbourne urged the Queen to take more exercise.

Such advice made the Queen testy with maids and ministers alike. Always ready to get out for a good, brisk canter on one of her beloved horses, Victoria hated to walk. Pebbles kept getting into her shoes, she complained. As for food, her appetite reminded old men at court of her uncle King George IV, a legendary trencherman of vast girth. The Queen could put away three plates of soup before tucking into her regular menu of fish, fowl, and meat dishes, vegetables, fruits, pies, cakes, jellies, nuts, and ices. In 1836 when the Duc de Nemours, the tall, dainty second son of the French king Louis Philippe, came to Windsor with an eye to marrying the then Princess Victoria, he was shocked at the way she lit into her lamb chops. Nemours made a rapid exit, and Victoria did not regret him.

■

NEMOURS WAS ONLY ONE of the royal gentlemen who had recently come to England to woo its queen. At twenty, Victoria had seen a great many suitors. Given her druthers, she would probably have married one of the many young English aristocrats who danced attendance on her at court. Some, like Lord Elphinstone and Lord Alfred Paget, were handsome; many could trace their ancestry back to the Norman Conquest; some were so rich they could have bought the duchy of Coburg out of pocket change. But unfortunately, not one of these delightful young Englishmen was eligible. English political tradition had long decreed that no monarch could marry a subject.

connoisseur of female flesh. He did not fancy his cousin Vic, as he was known to refer to the heir presumptive. She was short, she was plain, and she showed signs of wanting her own way.

Disappointed in his nephews, King William IV then brought over the sons of the Prince of Orange from the Netherlands, a Protestant kingdom with dynastic links to England. Unfortunately, they were ugly, awkward, and glum, and Victoria was barely civil to them. At last, in desperation, the King trotted out his notorious German cousin the Duke of Brunswick as a possible suitor. That gentleman in his time had certainly charmed enough women, to say nothing of men, and Victoria seemed rather fascinated by him. But her mother was not, so that was that.

William also sounded out the heir to the throne of Prussia, Frederick William Hohenzollern, another Protestant prince. Through the English minister in Berlin, this prince explained that men of his family did not undertake matrimonial scouting expeditions. He would deign to cross the English Channel only upon a written assurance that the Princess Victoria would marry him. On this prince, Victoria and her mama were, for once, entirely in agreement. Their answer was a diplomatically expressed, unequivocal, unexpected, and bitterly resented no.

And so it came about that, in the fall of 1839, by elimination, the chief contender for the hand of the Queen of England was her first cousin Albert of Saxe-Coburg and Gotha.

*

ALBERT COBURG WAS born on August 26, 1819, three months after his English cousin, and their grandmother, the dowager Duchess of Saxe-Coburg, was envisaging a marriage between the two while both were in the cradle. However, the two young people were brought together for the first time only in May 1836. The Duchess of Kent invited her brother, Duke Ernest of Saxe-Coburg and Gotha, and his two sons, Ernest and Albert, to come and celebrate her daughter Victoria's seventeenth birthday.

This invitation caused a minor diplomatic furor. William IV did all in his power to keep the Coburg party out of England. The King went so far as to allege that it was highly improper for the Duchess of Kent to invite two young men to sleep under the same roof as her maiden daughter. Uncle Leopold in Brussels, who took lessons in hypocrisy and prudery from no one, was furious in turn. "I am really *astonished* at the conduct of your old Uncle the King," wrote King Leopold to the Princess Victoria. "Now that slavery is even abolished in the British colonies, I do not comprehend *why*

At twenty, Victoria was almost on the shelf, and conscious of it. Most princesses of her time were married off as soon as they reached puberty. She herself had been officially entered in the royal marriage market at the age of fifteen when her confirmation was celebrated. If her maternal and paternal relations had not been at daggers drawn over the choice of a bride-groom for her, she might well have been married in her midteens, while still merely the heir presumptive to the English throne.

William IV, Victoria's paternal uncle, who succeeded his brother George IV to the throne in 1830, was elderly, obese, and afflicted with gout, asthma, and congestive heart failure. He knew he had not long to live and was anx-ious to see his niece and heir safely married to a man of his choice. The King was determined that man would not be a Coburg. He distrusted the ambi-tions of the Coburg family, which, in the German social hierarchy, was far inferior to his own Guelph-Brunswick-Hanover line. In Leopold, the king of Belgium, the most redoubtable of the Coburgs, William saw only the jumped-up ruler of a silly, fake nation. As for his Coburg sister-in-law the Duchess of Kent, Victoria's mother, William IV positively loathed her.

William IV's preferred candidate for Victoria's husband was her first cousin George Cumberland, the son of the King's brother the Duke of Cum-berland. This youth would have been a popular as well as royal choice: One English newspaper was already touting the marriage when the prospective bride and groom were nine years old. The Duke of Cumberland was heir presumptive to the Guelph family's hereditary German domain of Hanover, just as Victoria was heir presumptive to the kingdom of Great Britain and Ireland. Married, Victoria Kent and her cousin George Cumberland could, in the fullness of time, reunite the kingdoms. But George Cumberland, though handsome and engaging, was born with sight in only one eye, and when he was fourteen, an accident with a swinging curtain pull destroyed his good eye. Given the risk of hereditary blindness, as well as the difficulties of public life for a blind man, George Cumberland was ruled out as a suitor for Victoria Kent.

However, William IV had another nephew called George, the son of his youngest brother, the Duke of Cambridge. George Cambridge led Victoria Kent out to the dance at the few state occasions her mother allowed her to attend. He was a tall, strong young man who seemed to promise well as a sire of kings. He, or his mother, was assiduous in sending gifts and expres-sions of affection when Victoria celebrated her birthday. But once his par-ents pressured him to go a-wooing at Windsor, George Cambridge took off for Gibraltar, supposedly on military service, and remained abroad. Young Cambridge had a distressing case of acne, but he prided himself on being a *your lot alone should be to be kept, a little white slavey in England,* for the pleasure of the Court."

In the end, the Coburg party defied King William's wrath and set sail for England. The Duchess of Kent, flush with parliamentary funds as mother to the heir presumptive, put on an impressive program of excursions, dinners, parties, and balls for her relatives. The Princess Victoria, who at this time was a virtual prisoner in her own home, was extremely happy to see her Coburg cousins so she could have some fun. On the surface, the ducal visit was a success. As Victoria energetically underlined in diary entries that she knew her mother would read with special attention, she found Ernest and Albert *very* pleasant and interesting. In affectionate letters calculated to assuage her uncle Leopold's wrath, Victoria assured him that she found Albert, so handsome and amiable, *very* much to her taste. But she did not beg to marry the Coburg cousin at once, she did not threaten elopement, she did not even make promises for the future. No *coup de foudre* had taken place. King Leopold had miscalculated, and the ducal party returned crestfallen to Brussels to thrash out what had gone wrong. It was not hard.

Victoria at seventeen was already a young woman, charming if not pretty, full of vitality, eager to flirt if given half a chance. Albert was a chubby, self-absorbed, pedantic boy who had no interest at all in girls. Things had gone badly from the outset. After a rough Channel crossing, Albert was a quivering heap. He then spent days in bed with a bilious complaint. His riding habit was not well cut, his seat was very bad, and he did not even care much for the sport—all conspicuous faults in the eyes of such a keen equestrienne as Victoria Kent. Albert was an excellent musician and sketched well, two talents that endeared him to his English cousin. But he was not at all fond of dancing and liked to be in bed by nine, just when, in Victoria's opinion, the evening was getting amusing. After one state dinner, Albert vomited. At his last English ball, he slipped on the dance floor and fell over backward. Victoria took his hand, sat out with him for a while, and was very kind when he said he must go to bed, he felt so unwell. But she was not impressed. Cousin Albert at sixteen and three quarters was not the stuff of which girlish dreams are made.

Victoria was not a romantic, nor was she controlled by her hormones. As perhaps the greatest heiress in the world, the princess saw marriage as the most important business transaction of her life. It behooved her to be cautious and guard her interests intelligently. Certainly she was very unhappy at home and longed for independence. But with her majority only a year away, the health of her uncle king visibly failing, and the throne of

England within her grasp, Victoria in mid-1836 was neither desperate nor willing to take chances.

One year later, following her accession, Victoria was even less inclined to send for Cousin Albert and name the day. She threw herself into the pleasures and duties of being queen. When it came time to send out the invitations to her coronation, she conspicuously failed to invite her cousins of Coburg. But the wild exhilaration of accession did not last. After eighteen months, Victoria began to feel lonely, insecure, and confused. In June 1839, Grand Duke Alexander, heir to the tsar of Russia, came to visit, and he and the Queen had a brief romantic idyll. They spoke to one another in French, he introduced her to the pleasures of dancing the mazurka, and when he left, she felt very low. Marrying the tsarevitch was quite impossible, but the pleasure she had found in Alexander's company had given her a yen to be married. What she needed could no longer be supplied by a governess, a doctor, an uncle, or a prime minister.

As she agonized over the pros and cons of marriage, Victoria turned to her supremely charming prime minister, Lord Melbourne. In his midfifties, he was now her dearest friend. The Queen faithfully recorded their conversations on the subject of marriage in her journal each night. She told Melbourne that she had no wish to marry now, perhaps never. Using the third-person form that was de rigueur in all communications with monarchs, the prime minister replied that Her Majesty need consult only her own wishes. On the whole, women did like to marry, and Her Majesty probably would too, but there was no rush. The country, as he understood the country, was in no urgency for the Queen to marry. Indeed, when one looked at the list of possible suitors, not one of them stood out, and the English press would take pleasure in attacking them all. Yes, Prince Albert was perhaps the front-runner, but marriages between first cousins were often not sound, and Germans, especially Coburgs, were not popular with Englishmen.

The Queen told Lord Melbourne of the pressure from her mother, from her uncle Duke Ernest, and from her uncle King Leopold to allow a visit from the Coburg cousins. By inviting Albert to her home, was she not committing herself to a marriage that, one day—who knew?—might suit her, but as of now was not at all what she desired?

Lord Melbourne advised the Queen to see the projected visit as her chance to look the young man over. She should invite the two princes to come but, in kindness, explain to Albert that he was coming, as it were, on approval. The decision on marriage was entirely Her Majesty's, said Lord Melbourne. She need not fear that if she married Albert, she would no longer have her way. English monarchs, whether men or women, were subject only to the English Constitution.

Reassured by this urbane advice, Victoria carefully drafted a letter to her uncle Leopold, knowing that it would be copied and redirected posthaste to Coburg. She had fond memories of her cousins Ernest and Albert, she said. Like all her beloved German relatives, they would be welcome in England. However, she presently felt no desire to rush into marriage. Albert must come to England only if he understood that his cousin Victoria committed herself to nothing.

•

THE TWO CARRIAGES sent to carry Victoria's cousins to Windsor were finally reaching their destination. As the castle's magnificent gray crenellated bulk loomed ahead in the dusk, Prince Albert looked anxiously across at his brother. Ernest had felt distinctly unwell even before the rigors of the English Channel. He would have to make great efforts this evening to stay up late and be agreeable. Even worse, in the hullabaloo of disembarking onto the quay at Dover, the groggy Coburgers had lost track of the baggage containing their evening clothes. This meant that they would be unable to take dinner with the Queen. What bad luck to arrive not only late but without the fashionable new outfits Uncle Leopold had paid for!

Albert refused to panic. He had given a great deal of thought to this English visit, and his course of action was clear. For years he had been encouraged to imagine himself consort to England's queen. King Leopold and his chief adviser, Baron Christian Stockmar, had dedicated Albert's late adolescence to the task of winning Victoria. They filled his mind with the information and wisdom that would allow him to become Victoria's principal adviser—King of England in fact if not in name. After much walking, riding, swimming, and fencing, Albert's body had grown strong and supple. In the salons of Paris, Brussels, and Rome, his manners had been refined and his drawing room talents developed. All these worldly graces shone now, without for a moment detracting from that moral purity that the Queen of England required. Conscientiously, Albert had transformed himself into the image of Victoria's desire.

Marriage to a queen was still by far Albert's best career option. His plan was to become king consort in England, as his cousin Ferdinand was in Portugal. This position would offer a suitably broad arena for the political and diplomatic talents he felt within him. Beneath his mask of calm and compliance, Prince Albert of Saxe-Coburg and Gotha was fiercely ambitious and competitive.

But Albert was not in the least in love with Victoria and in general had no regard for the female sex. He remembered his English cousin with little affection, and of late he had come to disapprove of her. He felt that the Queen of England's young head had been turned by the adulation that greeted her on her accession. She liked late nights and dancing rather more than was proper. According to the grim doctrine that Stockmar had inculcated in him, Albert viewed marriage to Victoria less as a pleasure in store than as a burden to bear out of duty to his family, his caste, and his beloved Germany. If, in the end, the Queen of England decided not to marry him, his pride would be hurt, not his heart.

In the meantime, Victoria's shilly-shallying was making him the laughingstock of European courts, and this was not to be borne any longer. The time had come to take the active role at last and deliver an ultimatum. As he gazed up at mighty Windsor, potent symbol of all he stood to gain or lose, Prince Albert of Saxe-Coburg and Gotha was ready.

※

AT SEVEN-THIRTY, hearing that the Coburg princes had finally been sighted, Victoria walked to the top of the Sovereign's Staircase. She composed herself for their entrance below. In the Queen's childhood, her mother had adjured her to grow tall like her father and his royal brothers, but Victoria had been unable to comply. Her supporters claimed she was five feet one inch; her detractors gave her a bare four ten. In the gutter press, she was known as "Little Vic," which rankled with her. Fortunately, horses, thrones, and sweeping staircases were standard issue for a queen, and Victoria made full use of them. Perched on high, she could look down on her subjects, as a reigning monarch should.

In the covered courtyard below, two young men appeared, both tall and well made, but the younger incomparably the more handsome. Prince Albert, when Victoria had last seen him at sixteen, was a pretty boy. Now he had grown into manhood. His shoulders were broad, his waist slim, his legs thick with muscle. Chestnut hair curled about his face, and he had a thin, elegant mustache. In his stained traveling costume, Albert was remarkable; in full dress uniform at the ball tomorrow, he would be any woman's idea of Prince Charming. Uncle Leopold was quite right: Albert of Saxe-Coburg and Gotha was the handsomest young prince in all Europe.

Prince Albert looked up. The Queen gazed into his large, shining blue eyes; eyes astonishingly like her own. Followed by his brother, Albert ran up the stairs, knelt gracefully to kiss Victoria's hand as queen and then kissed her on the cheek as cousins should. Albert, at five feet eight, seemed very tall to Victoria, and suddenly she found it delightful to look up into a man's eyes, clasp his hand, and feel his whiskers brush her face.

Victoria was a little flustered. The thought of spending the evening without these young visitors was not to be borne. The delays on the journey, the storm at sea, the late hour, the lost baggage—all was at once explained and forgiven. Let her cousins come in after dinner and spend the evening with her and her party. *En famille,* what did it matter if, just this once, they appeared in their traveling dress?

As the Queen recorded in her journal and again in a letter to her uncle Leopold that very evening, "Albert is beautiful!"

Three days later, on October 14, Victoria proposed marriage to her cousin Albert. He accepted. In the first week of February 1840, they were married. With their union, the Victorian age had begun.

OTHER ENGLISH MONARCHS have lent their names to an age or a style— Elizabethan, Jacobean, Carolingian, Georgian—but "Victorian" has a special currency even today. It is an intensely affective word, since it relates to the things closest to all of us, to the way we run our sex lives and organize our families.

By 1914 the term *Victorian* had come to connote all that was stale, respectable, hypocritical, xenophobic, and oppressive for writers such as Lytton Strachey and Virginia Woolf. It became fashionable to argue that the Victorians abroad had been jingoistic tyrants, and smug Philistines at home. A Victorian father was the stern patriarch who cast his daughter out on the street if she took a lover. A Victorian household was a lethal mix of parsimony and show, with a master, a mistress, and servants who knew their place. Victorian religion was a bah-humbug affair, narrow minded, censorious, and sectarian. The ugliness of Victorian art, architecture, and handicrafts was glaringly apparent.

When I was a student at Cambridge University in the 1960s, the received wisdom was still pretty much that the sun had long set over the Victorian empire—and thank goodness! But as the century wound down, the winds of opinion and taste began to shift. A new generation of scholars like Peter Gay and novelists such as A. S. Byatt rediscovered the pulsing vitality of Victorian life, unearthed a fascinating cast of characters, and built bridges between past and present. Young people in England queued up for exhibitions of the Pre-Raphaelites at the Victoria and Albert Museum, gladly voted funds for the renovation of that old monstrosity St. Pancras Station, and redecorated their houses with Liberty prints, lace antimacassars, William

Morris wallpaper, and aspidistras, aka rubber plants. And more fundamentally, by the 1990s, in the United States perhaps even more than in Britain, a lament had arisen over the loss of Victorian values: faith, thrift, discipline, patriotism, responsibility, stability, innovation, entrepreneurship, sexual continence, marital fidelity, parental control, social cohesion.

To tease out the many meanings of Victorian, there is no better way than to reexamine the relationship of the most influential and famous married couple of the nineteenth century. Unique yet representative, inhabiting a bubble of royal privilege yet tuned to the Zeitgeist, Queen Victoria and Prince Albert express many of the complexities and contradictions of the age.

Her marriage had been an idyll and a moral example to the nation, or so at least the Queen claimed after her husband's untimely death. As a giddy, willful girl of eighteen, she, Victoria, had found herself on the throne of Great Britain and completely out of her depth. Then Albert came into her life, a modern Galahad, pure of thought, mighty in deed. As husband and consort, he had solved the problems she faced as queen and made her happier than any other woman before or since. Confronted by Albert's God-given superiority, she had willingly given obeisance as a good wife should.

This was what the widowed Queen told the world, but it was at best a half-truth. To name but a few of the fictions, Victoria had emerged strong and enterprising from a very difficult childhood. Within days of her accession, England's power brokers discovered to their astonishment that this young girl understood the business of monarchy better than any of her male ancestors. Albert, when Victoria married him, was hardly a fount of wisdom, just an overprotected youth fatally confident of his abilities to rule a kingdom. The Queen retreated into domesticity a year or so after her wedding not because she wanted to but because society demanded it, because she had lost her closest allies, because she could not allow her marriage to fail, and because, much against her will, she was pregnant with her second child and saw only more pregnancies in her future. Albert cast Victoria in the role of "kleines Fräuchen," but it was never a good fit for the woman who stood at the very top of Europe's steep social pyramid and always walked several steps ahead of her husband when they emerged each day from their bedroom.

Like so many famous and achieving women of the past, Queen Victoria felt the need to stress frailty, failure, and luck, not strength, competence, and ambition, when writing about herself. However, her fairy-tale account of living happily ever after with Prince Charming was also exceptionally well calculated to serve her most cherished goal: to secure the future of the English monarchy. By playing into the prejudices and desires of her contemporaries, Queen Victoria kept her crown at a time when other kings were losing theirs. Today her great-great-granddaughter Queen Elizabeth II still rides through London every year in a golden coach to open parliament and give the speech from the throne.

The English in the nineteenth century *liked* to hear of female weakness and submission. They had seen Europe shaken to its foundations by a series of revolutions, and male hegemony was one ancient certainty that the vast majority of the population, male and female, was ready to defend at all costs. In 1840, the year that Victoria and Albert were married, no woman in the kingdom of Great Britain and Ireland could vote, be elected to parliament or any other public office, attend the university, or enter a profession. If a woman married, her property, her earnings, her children, and her body legally belonged to her husband, to do with as he willed. The world of business was more hostile to women in 1840 than it had been in 1740 or 1640, and though many women were forced to work, a bare handful could make a living wage.

In its overt misogyny, in its passionate assertion of male superiority in its religious, political, legal, cultural, and religious institutions, Great Britain was typical of its time, but it had one strange constitutional quirk. It was a monarchy, and if an established dynasty failed to produce a legitimate male heir to the throne, England was prepared to allow a woman to reign and inherit the powers and wealth of her royal male predecessors. There was one unwritten but absolute proviso, however. The fabulous promiscuity of a Catherine the Great of Russia was out of the question in England. A man of marked libido such as King Charles II could be accepted, even popular, with the English nation, but, at a minimum, a queen regnant must be a virgin like the great Elizabeth, or a faithful spouse like Mary Tudor, Anne Stuart, and Mary Stuart. Optimally, a queen, if queen there must be, would, unlike her four predecessors, bear sons.

No one in Europe understood the constitutional anomalies and sexual imperatives of the English monarchy better than that inordinately ambitious German family the Saxe-Coburgs. If their plan to marry the heiress of England to one of her Saxe-Coburg cousins were to succeed, not only must the Queen's virginity be unchallenged but her husband must come to the marriage chaste. Any sexual taint acquired in youth might endanger his reproductive success. Thus Albert, not his more mature and manly brother and cousins, was the young man finally designated by his family to win the hand of the Queen of England. Albert was handsome and intelligent and ambitious. He had always done what his elders told him to do, and, above all, he had never shown a flicker of interest in women.

To marry such a youth to a strong-willed, passionate, mature woman was hardly a recipe for conjugal bliss, but dynastic marriages did not aim for happiness, as Lady Diana Spencer would discover in 1981. The long, faithful, loving partnership of Victoria and Albert has come to be a dusty old fact enshrined in the history books, but as a lived reality, it was an extraordinary feat achieved against the odds. A young man and a young woman, one in Germany, one in England, dreamed of finding in marriage things that neither had seen much of as children: love, affection, companionship, trust, intimacy, a private space in which they could be delectably alone—just "we two."

In large part they succeeded, but their marriage was always a work in progress, not a fait accompli, a drama not a pageant. Theirs was a business partnership as well as a marriage, and they engaged in an impassioned, weirdly public contest over who was the senior partner. At different points in the marriage, one spouse would emerge bloodied from battle over dominance, negotiate hard for mere equality, and then fall into the other's arms, intending to fight another day. A careful reading of the letters and diary entries written during Albert's lifetime reveals an Ibsen-esque drama, in which Victoria, that tiny bundle of energy with the core of steel, plays a heroine fighting for survival in a society where women were denied their identity and their pleasure. In counterpoint, we find a modern tragedy, with Albert a romantic hero who quickly metamorphosed into a portly paterfamilias before dying, victim to his own ambition, at the age of forty-two.

At a distance, Queen Victoria and Prince Albert can look like charming tapestry figures, unicorns among flowering meadows, irrelevant to our modern world. But if we listen to their voices up close, we find to our surprise a forerunner of today's power couple—a husband and wife, each with a different personal agenda, but lovers as well as partners in a great enterprise, both leading meticulously scheduled, constantly monitored, minutely recorded, and carefully screened lives. How very twenty-first century!

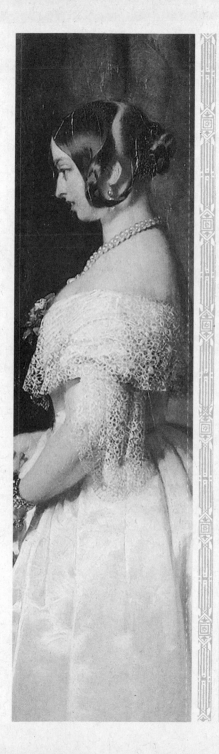

PART ONE

...

$\mathcal{T}$HE
YEARS APART

◆◆◆

VICTORIA

A Fatherless Princess

Charlotte and Leopold

....

HE FOLKTALES OF CHARLES PERRAULT AND THE GRIMM BROTHERS
are surprisingly reliable about the lives of kings and queens in old Europe.
Those tales are full of strange and dangerous royal courtships. Kings and
queens are unable to conceive a normal child. Queens die in childbirth. Or-
phan princesses are sorely beset by uncaring fathers, wicked stepmothers,
and villainous uncles, and only seven dwarfs or a magic donkey's skin can
save them.

The solutions are magical, but the problems were not fantasies. European kings and queens were in fact often neglected or abused in childhood.
As adults they were plagued by the imperative to find a spouse and produce
an heir. They then frequently repeated the cycle of neglect and abuse with
their own children.

Before Princess Victoria of Kent was born, there lived a Princess Charlotte, her first cousin and very like her in character and ability. If Charlotte
had lived and had children, a Saxe-Coburg dynasty would have taken hold
in England in 1817, not 1840, and history books might well chronicle the
joint reign of Charlotte and Leopold. But Charlotte was a princess that no
fairy godmother came to save.

Charlotte's parents, George, Prince of Wales (later prince regent, and
then King George IV), and Princess Caroline of Brunswick, were first
cousins. They had never seen each other before the eve of their wedding.
George loathed Caroline on sight and consummated the marriage in a state
of insulting inebriation. The two separated nine months before the birth of
their only child and thereafter waged an increasingly ugly and public war
on each other. He accused her, not unjustly, of being dirty, uncouth, and

garrulous. She accused him, not unjustly, of promiscuity, malice, and neglect. Unloved and uncared for, Charlotte was a pawn in her parents' acrimonious marital game.

Princess Charlotte emerged from this difficult childhood a woman of considerable abilities, if little education, and possessed of unusual courage and resolution. Wild, headstrong, opinionated, and self-absorbed, Charlotte yet longed for affection and intimacy. At eighteen she had few illusions and fewer friends, and longed to throw off the financial and social straitjacket of her life as an unmarried princess. She was anxious to avoid the fate of her royal aunts, the six talented and beautiful daughters of King George III who as young women were tethered to their dysfunctional parents and barred from marriage. Three in middle age finally escaped into the arms of grotesque bridegrooms, but frustration and boredom gnawed away at the lives of all these princesses.

Like the heroines of so many English novels of the period, Princess Charlotte saw marriage as the answer to her problems. She knew that, as second in line of succession to the English throne after her father, she was the most eligible *partie* in Europe. She also knew that her acceptable marital choices were limited to a handful of unknown foreigners. As two of her spinster aunts had discovered to their cost, tradition and the Royal Marriages Act of 1772 prevented the marriage of an English royal princess with any man, duke or drover, born in the United Kingdom of Great Britain and Ireland. It was common practice for princesses to be married to men they had never met, so Charlotte would be lucky to get a glimpse of her suitors at a ball or state dinner.

Charlotte's father the prince regent also saw marriage as the solution to the problems he had with his daughter. He doted on tiny, cute girls, but Charlotte resembled her large, loud, voluptuous mother, and he had never loved her. Worse, Charlotte was popular with the English people, while he was greeted by catcalls and averted faces when he made a rare public appearance. The regent planned to marry his daughter off to the Prince of Orange, a distant cousin and the heir to the throne of Holland, England's most ancient ally. Orange was, admittedly, a drunken lout, but Charlotte's aunts had been grateful to marry worse.

At first Charlotte agreed to the betrothal. Then, astonishingly, she broke off the engagement and tried to run away from home. Perhaps she had read some novels and believed that young women had a right to choose their husbands. More probably she had made a rational assessment of what a Dutch marriage would mean to her. As Princess of Orange, she would be obliged to spend at least half the year in Holland. While she was abroad, her father might finally obtain the divorce he wanted and then marry a young princess. If a healthy stepbrother were born, Charlotte would no longer be her father's heir. Though she had little love and no respect for her mother, the princess considered it essential to remain in England to support her own and her mother's interests.

Charlotte's unexpected and stubborn refusal of the Dutch prince angered her father, and she found herself a virtual prisoner. Marriage became even more desirable. She was in a hurry to find an eligible European prince properly subservient to her needs and wishes and willing to live in England. Charlotte made a strong play for Prince Frederick of Prussia, whom she found attractive, but he proved unresponsive. Then, as if by magic, at a ball given by her aunt the Duchess of York, another foreign prince appeared before Charlotte. He was charming, and his bloodline was impeccable. He had served valiantly in the recent wars against Napoleon and looked magnificent in his Russian cavalry officer's uniform. If she deigned to marry him, he would owe her everything. His name was Leopold of Saxe-Coburg-Saalfeld.

The seventh child and third son of a bankrupt German princeling, Leopold, ambitious, talented, and handsome, was a youngest son right out of a fairy tale. In 1815 he came to London in the tsar's entourage. Officially he was celebrating the defeat of Napoleon at Waterloo. Unofficially he was wooing the King of England's only granddaughter. It was a bold move, supremely confident and coldly calculated by a man who had nothing to lose by aiming high. With the war over, Leopold was living from hand to mouth, since his private fortune amounted to some two hundred pounds a year. Sponsored by his imperial Russian friends, Leopold had uniforms made on credit, borrowed his brother-in-law Mensdorff's dashing carriage, and set off for London. He was obliged to take rooms over a tradesman's shop and still had trouble paying the rent. But he had an entrée to all the magnificent festivities organized by the prince regent and his brothers to celebrate the peace. Just as he had hoped, Princess Charlotte noticed him.

Now Leopold played a waiting game. He returned to the Continent and corresponded with Charlotte behind her father's back. This correspondence was made possible through the good offices of Charlotte's uncle the Duke of Kent, who was everlastingly at odds with his eldest brother, the regent. There followed a year of negotiations at a distance, during which Leopold aroused the princess's passions by refusing to return to England. At last, wearied by his daughter's intransigence, the prince regent agreed to accept Leopold as a son-in-law. Receiving this fabulous news from Lord Castlereagh, the English foreign secretary, Leopold wrapped himself in a long coat, a feather boa, and a fur muff, and posted full tilt across Europe. In the kind of proof of passion women find hard to resist, he arrived in London from Berlin, exhausted and ill, in the staggering time of three and a half weeks.

The wedding of Charlotte and Leopold was a fairy-tale affair for the whole nation, rather like the marriage of Charles, Prince of Wales, and Lady Diana Spencer in 1981, but with an interesting reversal of gender roles. Charlotte at nineteen, tall, gawky, and inclined to fat, played the part of Prince Charming, heir to the kingdom and untold wealth, while Leopold was a ravishing rags-to-riches Cinderella. The bride's elaborate trousseau was the subject of long, reverent columns in the fashion press, and for her wedding she wore a gown of lace-trimmed silver lama and white satin designed by Mrs. Triaud of Bond Street. But at their wedding, the bride was eclipsed by the glory of the bridegroom. Leopold was reputed to be one of the handsomest men in Europe, and he now wore the scarlet wool uniform of a British general, decorated with his own orders and medals. His belt and sword blazed with diamonds, a gift from his bride's grandmother and namesake, the Queen.

Reportedly the bride giggled when the bridegroom was asked to endow her with all his worldly goods. As everyone knew, Prince Leopold was heir to little and owned less. However, the members of parliament, in rapturous appreciation of their princess and salivating at the prospect of a new, shining line of kings, granted Leopold personally the magnificent annuity of fifty thousand pounds—about two million in today's dollars.

Charlotte was not at all in love with Prince Leopold when she agreed to marry him. As she confided in a letter: "I have perfectly decided & made up my own mind to marry, & the person I have decidedly fixed on is Prince Leopold . . . I know that *worse* off, more unhappy and wretched I cannot be than I *am now,* & after all if I end by marrying Prince L., . . . I marry the best of all those *I have seen,* & that is some satisfaction." Leopold was not in love either. He was already a world-class Lothario and had enjoyed mistresses far more seductive than Charlotte. But if he did not love his bride for her looks and charm, he passionately adored her status as second in line of succession to the English throne. Hence, from the moment he arrived back in England, Leopold set out single-mindedly to win Charlotte's love and become her indispensable counselor and helpmate. Twenty years later, he would train his handsome nephew Albert in the same strategies for the day when Albert would marry Victoria.

Leopold played the part of lover-husband to perfection. During the days of their brief engagement, to her surprise and delight, Charlotte found

Leopold extremely beguiling, as indeed did London society. Within months of their marriage, she was ready to tell the world that he was the perfect husband and that she idolized him. Charlotte also quickly warmed to Leopold's aide-de-camp and general factotum, the young German physician Christian Stockmar. The three were soon inseparable friends. Charlotte and Leopold settled down to married bliss at Claremont, a secluded house in magnificent grounds given to them by the nation at the time of their marriage. As its owners were well aware, Claremont, with its simple furnishings and healthy, happy, modest way of life, could not have posed a stronger contrast to the Royal Pavilion in the heart of the town of Brighton—the prince regent's most expensive and unpopular architectural extravaganza to date.

When, after two miscarriages, Charlotte embarked upon what boded well to be a successful pregnancy, the Claremont idyll seemed complete. As he awaited the birth of his child, Leopold looked eagerly to the future. He was now rich, popular with the English nation, and adored at home, but all this was as nothing to the power, wealth, and status he foresaw for himself in the near future. Only the lives of mad old George III and the disease-

Princess Charlotte and Prince Leopold
at the theater, circa 1816

raddled regent stood between Charlotte and the throne of England. And so passionately did Charlotte now adore him that she was ready to say: "I cannot reign over England except upon the condition that he [Leopold] shall reign over England and myself . . . Yes, he shall be King, or I will never be Queen." Once a healthy child was born, Leopold saw his future assured, if not as king, then at least as prince consort and the sire of a new race of kings. Even were Charlotte to die young, as long as she left children, Leopold would be regent and rule in England.

As soon as the princess went into labor in the early evening of November 3, the Privy Councillors were summoned in haste from London to attend the birth, as protocol demanded. The regent and his mother, apprised of the situation at Claremont, went about their everyday lives quite unconcerned. The old queen, who in her time had given birth to fifteen babies with remarkable efficiency and speed, did not think it necessary to leave Bath, where she was taking a cure.

Prince Leopold sat by his wife's side, holding her hand, murmuring love and encouragement, and Stockmar hovered anxiously in the background. From the beginning of the princess's pregnancy, Stockmar had warned Prince Leopold that the approach taken by doctors attending his wife was ill advised. The English royal doctors subscribed to the doctrine that strong, choleric young women should follow a "lowering" regime when pregnant. Charlotte had been fed a liquid diet low in meat and vegetables, forbidden to exercise, and subjected to regular bloodlettings, which probably led to severe anemia. Stockmar recommended that Prince Leopold intervene in his wife's care, but in the end both the prince and his adviser left Charlotte completely in the hands of English medical men.

The princess's water broke over two weeks after her due date, so she went into labor tired and dispirited, fearing the worst. She continued in heavy labor through the night and the following day, and the baby did not come. Before her marriage, Charlotte had been a strong, athletic young woman, but the miscarriages and now the pregnancy had sapped her strength. Hence, though her cervix dilated, she did not have the strength to push the child out, and her doctors, though they had brought a set of the newly invented obstetrical forceps, did not dare to use them. At last, after some fifty hours of labor, a large and perfectly formed male child was born, dead and resisting all attempts at resuscitation.

The princess received the news of her child's death with resignation. She had still to suffer the agony of having the doctor manually remove the placenta, which had failed to detach. Her abdomen was then wrapped tightly, and she took some light food. Leopold, sad and exhausted but assuming the worst was over, took an opiate and went to bed.

Suddenly the princess complained of terrible pain, went deathly cold, became confused, and had difficulty breathing. She was probably suffering a massive internal hemorrhage, caused by the tearing away of the placenta and concealed by the swaddling of her abdomen. Her doctors administered brandy and hot wine. Warm flannels and hot water bottles were pressed to her stomach. The patient became visibly worse. Horrified by the turn of events, the doctors finally invited Stockmar to examine the princess. He took Charlotte's wrist to feel the pulse, and she murmured, "They have made me drunk, Stocky." He said, quite correctly, that the heat being administered to the patient was counter-indicated. The doctors refused to take Stockmar's advice, but in any case it came too late. Christian Stockmar was holding Charlotte's hand when at two-thirty on the morning of November 6, she died in paroxysms.

It was left to Stockmar to wake Prince Leopold and tell him the news. Overcome with shock and despair, the prince begged Stockmar never to leave him. From this time on, Christian Stockmar became Leopold's indispensable friend, confidant, political adviser, and agent. Their powerful partnership was to arouse the envy and fear of statesmen all over Europe and would be the subject of rumor and gossip for more than forty years. Stockmar was one of the many important things Leopold would pass on to his nephew Albert and his niece Victoria.

The death of Charlotte was a tragedy for the whole nation, not just for her young husband. For the people of Great Britain, the Princess Charlotte had a fairy-tale quality, especially after her marriage. She represented youth, purity, integrity, fidelity, and hope in a royal family that for twenty years had been wallowing in gilded squalor. When the princess died with her baby boy, the whole kingdom, dukes and commoners, stopped to mourn.

Prayers were offered in churches, speeches made in parliament, poems written, and letters and articles printed. The regent had never loved Charlotte, but she was his only child and his claim on the future. Hearing of her death, he was so shocked that he fell ill and almost died. In 1824 an elaborate marble monument to Charlotte was erected in St. George's Chapel at Windsor Castle, paid for by contributions that, the organizers stipulated, could not exceed one shilling. The outpouring of national grief was on a scale not seen in England until 1997 when Diana, Princess of Wales, was killed in Paris.

Wanted, an Heir to the Throne,
Preferably Male

...

*A*T THE BEGINNING OF 1818, ONE ISSUE WAS DISCUSSED END-lessly in Great Britain and all the courts of Europe. Where was the next generation of English kings to come from?

At the time of Charlotte's death, her grandfather George III had long been a demented prisoner at Windsor Castle. George III's thirteen surviving children had given him some twenty grandchildren, but there was only one, Charlotte, who satisfied the requirements of the Royal Marriages Act of 1772. This curious act was drawn up and pushed through parliament by George III, who was determined to prevent his numerous children from marrying anyone he considered unsavory or unsuitable. It forbade any member of the English royal family under twenty-five to marry without the previous consent of the sovereign. No English person even of the highest rank could expect the royal approval. Once over twenty-five, the prince or princess could forego the King's consent by applying to parliament for permission to marry, and then, if parliament consented, wait a year before doing so. But, as Prince Augustus (later Duke of Sussex) discovered to his cost, an adult prince married to a consenting adult Englishwoman according to the rites of the Church of England and in full public view could see his marriage annulled and his children declared illegitimate if his father the King did not approve his choice of spouse.

To understand the royal succession in early nineteenth-century England—or indeed today, since the laws have not changed—several key points must be kept in mind. First, male children always have precedence over female children, regardless of birth order. Second, the eldest son has precedence over the second son, the second over the third, and so on. Third, a royal child inherits its father's position in the line of succession and an English king is succeeded by his eldest son, not by his brother. However, if a king has no child, his heir presumptive is his next oldest brother. If brother number two predeceases brother number one but leaves a son, that son inherits the throne of his uncle.

In its fierce commitment to passing property and titles from father to son and to male primogeniture, England was typical of European countries. Where English law differed from, say, that of Germany and France was in its grudging willingness to accept that, for lack of a son or a brother, a man could pass his estate to his sister or his daughter rather than to a distant male relative. This estate could even be a throne, and the English liked to have the choice of prolonging a dynasty by including women in the line of succession. The Tudor kings Henry VII and Henry VIII had united the kingdom after the long period of civil strife known as the War of the Roses, and they proved competent rulers. Therefore, when Henry VIII's only male child, King Edward VI, died childless, his sister Mary Tudor was allowed to succeed him; and when Mary also died childless, her sister, Elizabeth Tudor, succeeded her. In the twentieth century, when George VI had no sons, the crown passed to the elder of his two daughters, Elizabeth.

Princess Charlotte's death and the stillbirth of her baby son wiped out two complete generations in the English royal family. The succession now went down the list of George III's middle-aged sons by birth order: the prince regent (George, aged fifty-five), the Duke of York (Frederick, fifty-four), the Duke of Clarence (William, fifty-two), the Duke of Kent (Edward, fifty), the Duke of Cumberland (Ernest, forty-six), the Duke of Sussex (Augustus, forty-four), and the Duke of Cambridge (Adolphus, forty-three). The idea of a succession of these gentlemen on the throne cast deep gloom over the whole nation. As the young radical poet Percy Bysshe Shelley put it:

> An old, mad, blind, despised and dying King,
> Princes, the dregs of their dull race, who flow
> Through public scorn—mud from a muddy spring
> Rulers who neither see nor feel nor know,
> But leechlike to their fainting country cling.

A king's children all had to be supported out of the nation's pocket, and the thirteen children of George III imposed a huge financial burden. The King and Queen were famous for their care with money and their preference

THE SUCCESSION TO *King George III*

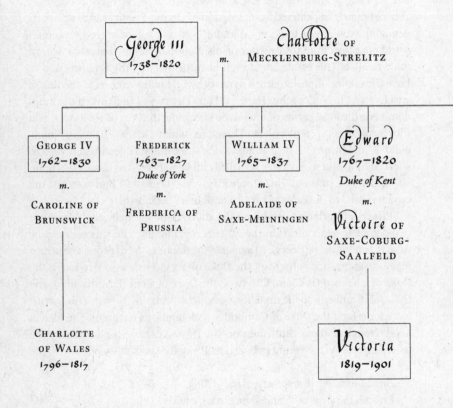

George III 1738–1820 — m. — Charlotte of Mecklenburg-Strelitz

GEORGE IV 1762–1830 — m. — CAROLINE OF BRUNSWICK

FREDERICK 1763–1827 *Duke of York* — m. — FREDERICA OF PRUSSIA

WILLIAM IV 1765–1837 — m. — ADELAIDE OF SAXE-MEININGEN

Edward 1767–1820 *Duke of Kent* — m. — Victoire of SAXE-COBURG-SAALFELD

CHARLOTTE OF WALES 1796–1817

Victoria 1819–1901

NOTE: *Charlotte, Augusta, Elizabeth, Sophia, Amelia, and Mary, the six daughters of George III, were of no relevance to the royal succession, which gives precedence and inheritance rights to males, regardless of birth order.*

ERNEST
1771–1851
Duke of Cumberland
and *King of Hanover*

m.

FREDERICA OF
MECKLENBURG-
STRELITZ

AUGUSTUS
1773–1843
Duke of Sussex

m.

(1) LADY AUGUSTA
MURRAY

(2) LADY CECILIA
BUGGIN

ADOLPHUS
1774–1850
Duke of Cambridge

m.

AUGUSTA OF
HESSE-KASSEL

SIX
DAUGHTERS

GEORGE
1819–1878
King of Hanover

GEORGE
1819–1904
Duke of Cambridge

for a modest, even frugal lifestyle, and their daughters were obliged to follow the parental example. The sons were the real problem. They were, in the Duke of Wellington's famous phrase, "the damnedest millstones about the necks of any government that can be imagined." The seven royal princes resented the fact that so many young English aristocrats had incomes far exceeding their own. No income was ever large enough to satisfy them, and if a royal duke managed to raise a lump sum of, say, 6,000 pounds from parliament or private lenders, he would promptly go out and spend double or more.

The royal dukes' combination of egotism, vulgarity, idleness, promiscuity, and fiscal improvidence bred hatred and resentment on every level of English society. Even today it is staggering to consider the size of the debt they piled up. George, the Prince of Wales, as befitted the eldest son with the largest income, was the most extravagant. At the age of twenty-one, already 30,000 pounds in debt, George was given an annual income of 50,000 pounds to add to his existing 12,000 pounds a year, plus a flat sum of 60,000. In 1786 he was forty-four and now in debt to the tune of 269,878 pounds, 6 shillings, and 7 pence farthing. Between 1787 and 1796, the Prince of Wales ran up debts of 630,000 pounds—approximately 40 million in American dollars. When he agreed to get married, parliament paid off his debts and raised his income, but his spending continued unabated during his regency.

With Princess Charlotte dead, one of the seven royal princes would have to produce a legitimate child who could inherit the throne after the demise of one or more of his or her uncles. Of the seven brothers, three (George, Frederick, and Augustus, numbers one, two, and six, respectively) were extreme long shots in the dynastic steeplechase, since all three were, in one way or another, married but without legitimate offspring as legitimacy was defined by the Royal Marriages Act. Should any of the senior royal princes lose his wife and remarry, the handicapping of the race to an heir would, of course, change overnight.

After his wife Queen Caroline's death in 1821, George IV, at fifty-five, at first was full of plans to find himself a new wife, but, in fact, he did nothing. He was too ill, too immobile, too full of opium and brandy, and too completely under the thumb of his mistress, Lady Conyngham. He died in 1830.

Odds were also against the next brother, Frederick, Duke of York. When Frederick was a young man, his older brother George, then Prince of Wales, asked him to take on the tedious job of supplying heirs to the throne. Happy to oblige his favorite brother and not, incidentally, to ingratiate himself with their father the King and with parliament, Frederick speedily contracted to marry Frederica, second daughter of the King of Prussia, a not unattractive sixteen-year-old he had once seen in Berlin. Unfortunately, the Yorks, Fred and Freda, like the Waleses, George and Caroline, separated within a year of marriage and failed to produce even one child. Given the diplomatic susceptibilities of Prussia, divorce for the Yorks was impossible. In 1820 Frederica, Duchess of York, died, and George once again begged Fred to bite the dynastic bullet and marry for an heir; but Fred, enamored of the Duchess of Rutland, could not be tempted. The Duke of York died, virtually penniless, in 1827.

Augustus, Duke of Sussex, the sixth son of George III, had to be eliminated at the outset, since he too was married (sort of) and had no legitimate offspring (as defined by the Royal Marriages Act).

Thus there were four royal dukes in a position to supply an heir to the throne: Clarence, Kent, Cumberland, and Cambridge, by order of birth and precedence.

William, Duke of Clarence, was third in the fraternal hierarchy, and thus the front-runner with numbers one and two scratched. He was as improvident and fond of luxury as his older brothers, on a much smaller income. Unlike them, he was a proven sire, boasting ten boisterous children by his charming actress mistress, Mrs. Dorothy Jordan. These children were known as the FitzClarences, "Fitz" being a standard marker for illegitimacy in English genealogy. The FitzClarences were accepted at court, though their mother, of course, was not, and all ten would ultimately, by royal patronage or marriage, become members of the English aristocracy. However, Clarence's debts mounted inexorably, and in 1811 he decided, with regret but without warning, to find himself a wealthy and amiable young wife.

For six years his efforts at courtship went for nothing. Miss Tilney Long, Miss Elphinstone, and Lady Berkeley decided they could not afford the Duke of Clarence. Miss Wykeham accepted the Duke's proposal of marriage, but, since she was, like the other four, ineligible under the Royal Marriages Act, the prince regent refused to accept her as a sister-in-law. The tsar's sister found the fat, bumbling, vulgar, pineapple-headed Clarence too ridiculous to even consider as a husband.

But when his niece Charlotte died, Clarence knew what he needed: a German princess of child-bearing age who would satisfy the requirements of the Royal Marriages Act and get him a raise in his parliamentary allowance. With the help of his brother the Duke of Cambridge, viceroy in Hanover, Clarence settled, sight unseen, on Adelaide of Saxe-Meiningen. She was a rather sickly, unattractive young woman of twenty-five, as poor as a church mouse. She was also intelligent, cultured, and pious, but these assets rather counted against her with a fiancé who had gone to sea as a midshipman at fourteen.

The marriage between William and Adelaide proved to be a happy one. Trained by Dorothy Jordan, William was a profoundly uxorious creature, and Adelaide made him feel comfortable. But she was delicate, and though she conceived again and again, only one child, named Elizabeth, lived more than a few days.

The fifth royal brother, Ernest, Duke of Cumberland, was the most energetic, the most intelligent, and the most ambitious of the seven. He was also perhaps the most feared and hated man in England. Cumberland was widely believed to have murdered a valet who had been his homosexual partner and to have sired a bastard with his sister Sophia. These accusations were probably unfounded, but Cumberland was indubitably a violent, rapacious, unfeeling man. He was also head of the ultraconservative wing of the Tory Party and used his influence over his brother George IV to block political and economic reform.

Cumberland, though only brother number five, took an early lead over the other three, since they were bachelors when Charlotte died, and he had providentially thought to acquire a German princess wife in 1815. Cumberland proved his indifference to public opinion and lack of family feeling by choosing to marry Frederica of Mecklenburg-Strelitz. She was once engaged to Cumberland's younger brother the Duke of Cambridge but then eloped with the Prince of Solms, a German nonentity whom she was later suspected of murdering. Queen Charlotte, the wife of George III, also born a princess of Mecklenburg-Strelitz, was Frederica Cumberland's aunt but refused to receive her at court. Nonetheless, the Cumberland marriage satisfied all the provisions of the Royal Marriages Act, and any child born to the couple would be eligible to inherit the English throne. The prospect that the bogeyman Cumberland might eventually come to the throne of England after his brothers—or at least, with his notorious wife, provide the new dynastic line—was viewed with extreme alarm by both statesmen and ordinary citizens in England.

The Duke of Cambridge, the seventh and last brother, was not about to be outdone in the dynastic stakes by his loathed elder brother, Cumberland, and his treacherous ex-fiancée, Frederica of Mecklenburg-Strelitz. Cambridge was comparatively young, he had led a sober life, and, as viceroy in Hanover, he had the list of available German princesses at his fingertips. A mere two weeks after his niece Charlotte's death, Cambridge was standing at the altar with twenty-year-old Princess Augusta of Hesse-Kassel. In

March 1819, in Hanover, the Duchess of Cambridge went into labor with her first child, the first of the post-Charlotte generation.

The Duke of Clarence, Cambridge's older brother, was also living in Hanover at this time, in an effort to save money, since parliament had proved stingy. Clarence's wife, Adelaide, was heavily pregnant with her first child. Hearing that his sister-in-law Cambridge was in labor, Clarence rushed over to the viceregal palace with two friends and sealed off all the doors leading to the birthing room. Just as Privy Councillors were supposed to attend royal accouchements in England, the men watched from an anteroom as the labor proceeded, ensuring that there could be no substitution of babies. As soon as the Duchess of Cambridge delivered her child, Clarence rushed in to "determine its sex by actual inspection." Couriers then rode off to England to announce that George III at last had a legitimate grandson, to be called—what else?—George.

On March 27, in Hanover, a daughter was born to the Duke and Duchess of Clarence, but she died within hours of birth.

Two months later, on May 29, the Duchess of Cumberland in Berlin produced a son, and he too was named George. Since Cumberland was the fifth duke and Cambridge only the seventh, little George Cumberland at birth took a position in the line of succession ahead of little George Cambridge. The paternal aunties, daughters of George III, were overjoyed by the sudden arrival of not one but two healthy male nephews, either one of whom seemed, surely, destined to follow his uncle King George IV as King George V.

But it was not to be. For on May 24, a healthy daughter was born in Kensington Palace to the Duke and Duchess of Kent. Since Kent was the fourth brother, and Cumberland and Cambridge were the fifth and seventh, respectively, the Kent girl was fifth in line of succession to the throne and took precedence over her male cousins. Presuming that her uncles the prince regent, the Duke of York, and the Duke of Clarence produced no child, male or female, and that her own parents did not go on to have a son, this baby girl would one day be queen regnant in England.

The Kent baby would come to be known as Victoria.

*

THE DUKE OF KENT was royal brother number four, and when Princess Charlotte died, he too was an aging bachelor. For twenty-seven years, first in Gibraltar and Canada and then in England after he was forced out of his army command, the duke lived in great content and considerable luxury in the company of his French mistress, known to the world as Madame Saint Laurent. But by 1816, Kent's credit in England had run dry, forcing him to live in Brussels and give over three-quarters of his parliamentary income to trustees in England for scheduled repayment of debt. Kent decided he must give up his mistress. He began looking for a wife who would satisfy the provisions of the Royal Marriages Act, anticipating six thousand extra parliamentary pounds a year as a married man.

At the inception of his quest for a wife, Kent was helped by his niece Charlotte and nephew-in-law, Leopold of Saxe-Coburg-Saalfeld. Kent was a favorite with the young couple, since he had played a small but vital role in their courtship. Prince Leopold had a sister, Victoire, the Princess of Leiningen, who, though a widow and no longer in the flower of youth, fulfilled all the eligibility requirements for marriage with English royalty. Charlotte urged her uncle Kent to go to Leiningen and propose marriage, and so he did.

Unfortunately, although the Princess of Leiningen found the Duke of Kent quite personable, she declined to marry him. She had been married young to the elderly, ugly, gloomy Prince Emich Charles of Leiningen. He was the widower of her maternal aunt, had lost his kingdom and his only son during the Napoleonic wars, and he married Victoire only to beget another son and heir. Except in the bedroom, the relations between the two remained those of uncle and niece. Emich Charles was forced by the great powers after the war to become a "mediatized"—fourth-rank—prince and to exchange his ancestral lands for the small territory of Amorbach near Darmstadt in central Germany. However, he and his children were still ranked as *ebenbürtig,* a matter of primary importance to all German aristocrats. This meant that "they could contract equal marriages with the Royal Houses, and these marriages were recognized as valid for the transmission of inheritances."

Victoire refused the Duke of Kent because she found life a good deal merrier as a widow, even though her income was small and her home modest to the point of decrepitude. She had two children, Charles and Feodora, whose interests would best be served by her remaining in Germany. Furthermore, she was strongly encouraged to refuse the duke's proposal by Herr Schindler, her former husband's master of the household. Schindler was a man of low birth but forceful personality who had become indispensable to her.

So, rebuffed by the Princess of Leiningen, the Duke of Kent returned to Brussels and the loving arms of Madame Saint Laurent until he was catapulted back into action by reading the announcement of his niece Charlotte's death. Kent decided once more to propose marriage to the Princess of Leiningen, this time not in person but through her brother Leopold.

Though still wrapped in a pall of grief and frustration following the deaths of his wife, Charlotte, and their baby, Leopold did all he could to advance the marriage of his sister Victoire to Edward, Duke of Kent. If Victoire married Kent and they produced a child, that child would have a decent shot at ruling England one day. That child would be half Coburg and would owe a lot to Uncle Leopold.

Prince Leopold had no scruples about marrying his favorite sister to the Duke of Kent. He knew that gentleman had a mistress and a mountain of debt, and had committed disciplinary excesses as commander in chief that turned the stomach even of a British army inured to sadism. More troubling was the fact that, in Kent's twenty-plus years of cohabitation with Madame Saint Laurent, he had sired no children. But Leopold's sister Victoire was only thirty-one, she was plump and handsome, and she had already produced two healthy children with a very unpromising spouse. Leopold was ready to bet that the union of Victoire and Kent would be fruitful.

Vigorously lobbied not only by Leopold but by her mother, the formidable dowager Duchess Augusta, Victoire agreed to do her sacred duty by the house of Saxe-Coburg and marry the Duke of Kent. Thus, within six weeks of their niece Charlotte's tragic demise, the dukes of Clarence and Kent were both standing in the chapel at Windsor, listening to their new German brides mangle the words of the Church of England marriage service. Both brothers then repaired to Germany, where their rival brothers Cumberland and Cambridge were already living with *their* German wives, to save money and try to sire an heir to the throne.

Dynastic strategy, not elective affinity, had determined the marriage of Edward, Duke of Kent, and Victoire of Saxe-Coburg-Saalfeld, but all the same they were very happy together. The duke was a considerate lover who enjoyed his wife's company and loved to pamper her—quite unlike the duchess's late, unlamented uncle-husband, the Prince of Leiningen. The Duchess of Kent adored her new husband in return and savored the experience of living in luxury. As a little girl, Victoire had wept in fear of her mother's wrath if she so much as tore her good dress. As wartime wife and then widow, she had a threadbare existence. But everything changed when she married the Duke of Kent. As the new duchess discovered on her first visit to England, even her new spinster sisters-in-law lived on a scale that a king of Bavaria or Saxony might envy. Victoire acquired the clothes, the hats, the jewels, the perfumery, the carriages, the diamond-encrusted miniatures, the thousand charming knickknacks that her new English family took for granted. Where her new husband got the money was not her concern.

When the Kents returned to Amorbach, the duke assumed direction of his new wife's domestic and financial affairs and followed his usual pattern of borrowing and spending money he had no rational expectation of paying back. Finding the house and stables inadequate, Kent launched an elaborate rebuilding project, borrowing two thousand pounds from gullible German bankers. Dingy Schloss Amorbach was besieged by builders.

Within a few months, the duchess was pregnant, and the duke determined they must both return to England. His brothers' wives could give birth in Germany. His child should be born in England, at Kensington Palace, before the eyes of royal relatives and government officials. The legitimacy of his child must be unimpeachable.

Unfortunately, travel required cash in hand, and the duke had exhausted his credit in Germany. His brother the prince regent flatly refused to send him money, noting tartly that crossing Germany and France on rutted roads was hardly recommended for a woman heavy with child. But the Duke of Kent was the most prominent royal liberal, and liberal members of parliament were determined to do anything possible to keep the archconservative Duke of Cumberland or his child from the throne. They raised a lump sum of fifteen thousand pounds to pay the Duke of Kent's way back to England.

Suddenly flush with funds, the duke traveled in style with a party of some twenty-five. His wife brought along from Germany her lady-in-waiting and old friend Baroness Späth; her daughter by her first marriage, Feodora von Leiningen; and Feodora's governess, Fräulein Louise Lehzen. The teenage Charles von Leiningen, the duchess's son, remained in Germany at least for the time being, as rapacious relatives were laying claim to the Amorbach estate. But the key person the duchess brought with her was the German obstetrician-midwife, Madame Charlotte Marianne Heidenreich von Siebold. At a time when women were universally barred from the professions, including medicine, this lady had managed to qualify as a doctor at the University of Göttingen, and, in partnership with her doctor husband, she then made obstetrics a lucrative medical specialty. The German aristocracy swore by Madame Siebold.

An excellent whip, Kent himself, his wife up by his side, took the reins of a well-sprung cane phaeton, a fast, light vehicle precariously perched on two high wheels, but there was also a capacious four-wheel *dormeuse* lumbering in the rear in case the duchess felt the need to lie down. Fortunately, the sun shone steadily, and the party made good time, though accommodations for so many people were hard to find. However, when they finally bowled into London, the Kents were given a cool reception by the royal family. The duke's mother, brothers, and sisters considered him a tedious hypocrite, and the prince regent loathed him. It was with great difficulty that Kent secured the leaky and dilapidated rooms at Kensington Palace he had vacated years before. He then set about procuring furniture and fittings worthy of the new child and its mother.

It was probably not a bad thing that the Duchess of Kent spent most of her pregnancy beyond the reach of the royal English doctors. The weeks she spent jouncing around Europe in an open phaeton and living on innkeeper food seem to have suited her, and she went into labor on schedule. Mindful, perhaps, of the suicide of Sir Richard Croft, the man who presided over the death of Princess Charlotte, Dr. Wilson, the Duke of Kent's personal physician, allowed Siebold to officiate at the birth. Under this lady's care, the duchess had a short labor and a problem-free delivery. Then, to the horror of her own mother and of all her husband's female relatives, the Duchess of Kent refused the services of a wet nurse.

When the duchess went into labor, the Duke of Wellington and other dignitaries were on hand as witnesses, but the prince regent was conspicuous by his absence. As it turned out, the child was only a girl, but she was still fifth in line of succession, and she was strong—plump as a partridge, as her father boasted. When news of the birth reached them, the duchess's family in Coburg cheered. Prince Leopold was delighted to see his pawn advance one more square. But to the truculent regent and his sisters and brothers, this baby girl was unwanted and unnecessary. It would be far better for everyone if the successor of the new generation should be a king, not a queen, especially since girls were exempted from inheriting the family's ancestral domain of Hanover. Wounded in his vanity to learn that his least favorite brother was urging friends to take note of his baby, "for she will be Queen of England," the prince regent took to turning his back on his brother Kent at public events. When Kent turned up at a military review with his baby in his arms, the regent was coldly furious.

The Duke of Kent intended to make his daughter's christening a large, public event. In a letter to his friend the Duc d'Orléans (later King Louis Philippe), Kent said that he and the duchess wished to name their daughter Victoire Georgina Alexandrina Charlotte Augusta. When, as was proper, the Kents asked the prince regent to be godfather to their baby, he agreed without enthusiasm but said he would attend in person. However the regent insisted that the ceremony should be private and advised the Kents in advance by letter that he would not countenance their using the name Georgina. Then, with the small group of family members and the Archbishop of Canterbury gathered about the font, the regent forbade the use of both Charlotte and Augusta. When the duke suggested the name Elizabeth, it too was curtly denied. Finally, with the Duke of Kent fuming in rage and his duchess weeping, the regent grudgingly ordered that the baby be named Alexandrina, after the tsar of Russia, her other male sponsor, and, if a second name was needed, Victoria, after her mother.

The prince regent had aimed to wound his brother Kent and upset his sister-in-law, and he succeeded. He agreed to be the child's godfather and then pettishly refused to allow her to be named after him even though he had allowed his brother Clarence's eldest bastard to be given the name George. He allowed the child only two names even though the most insignificant of princesses received a long string of names when they were baptized. The little girl should have been given names that were traditional in the royal house of Hanover: Mary, Elizabeth, Anne, Augusta, Charlotte, Caroline, or Sophia. Instead she had names so foreign to English history that, when it became virtually assured that the Kent girl would become queen, vain efforts were made on two occasions to persuade her to give up the name Victoria.

The Duchess of Kent never forgave her brother-in-law the regent for his insulting behavior at her child's christening. Henceforward her relations with the members of her husband's family were charged with suspicion and acrimony. But initially at least the baby girl gained more than she lost from the coldness of her royal English relatives. The Duchess of Kent had been allowed to make her own arrangements for her pregnancy and the care of her child, and, in the first, crucial year of her child's life, she made good decisions, not only breast-feeding her baby for six months but insisting she be inoculated against smallpox at the age of six weeks.

The Duchess of Kent had been taught by her brother Leopold and Baron Stockmar to beware of English doctors, but in February 1820, when her husband fell ill with a feverish cold, there was little she could do to protect him. The duke had taken his family to a small rented house in the fishing village of Sidmouth, Devon, purportedly so that they could enjoy the benefits of sea air, but in fact to escape his creditors and save money. Kent's life was important to the Crown, so doctors were dispatched from London and administered the usual enemas, expectorants, stimulants, and purgatives. They drew blood, by lancet, by cupping, by leeches, over and over again, 120 ounces, or 6 pints in all. As the duchess wrote despairingly to her mother in Germany, there was hardly a part of her husband's body that had not been lanced, blistered, or scarified. When the second most senior doctor finally arrived from London, he decreed that if the patient were to recover, more blood must be drawn. The duke wept in agony and despair, the duchess and Baroness Späth tried to intervene, but they spoke little English and had no authority. Within days, the Duke of Kent, who had boasted to the world of his iron constitution, was dead.

Victoria was just one day short of eight months old when her father died. She was too young to mourn, but she suffered a grievous loss. As girl and woman, the Queen was always in search of father surrogates to guide and protect her. She found several good ones: Leopold, Melbourne, Stockmar, her doctor James Clark. But as a child, her high place in the line of succession made Victoria vulnerable to unscrupulous men hungry for power.

The Wife Takes the Child

...

WITH HIS LAST RESERVES OF STRENGTH, EDWARD KENT MANAGED TO scrawl a signature on his will. Contrary to royal tradition and legal precedent, the will named the testator's wife, Marie Luise Victoire, to be the sole guardian of their child, the Princess Victoria. That will had enormous consequences, not just for the child and her mother, but, decades later, for the nation over which the child would reign.

For a mother to receive legal custody and control over her child was not very common in 1821. Until almost the end of the nineteenth century, minor children in England were viewed by the law as belonging not to their parents equally but to their fathers alone. If the father died and made no specific testamentary disposition of his children, the father's nearest male relatives, not their mother, had the right to determine the children's destiny.

For a royal princess to be placed in the custody and under the legal guardianship of her mother was virtually unprecedented. As the Duchess of Kent boasted in 1837, she was "the only parent since the Restoration [the restoration to the throne of Charles II in 1660 following Cromwell's Protectorate] who has had uncontrolled power in bringing up the heir to the throne."

If her father had not made a will, the guardianship and custody of the Princess Victoria would have gone to her eldest male kinsman, the prince regent. As a ward of the Crown, she would have grown up in the household of one of her many female relatives until she was considered an adult and given a household of her own. She would have grown up a Hanoverian, from babyhood an habituée of the English court under the direct influence of her two uncle kings, George IV and his successor, William IV.

A Hanoverian Victoria would have been introduced as a girl to the notorious set that clustered around her uncle George at Carlton House, his opulent London residence. She would have met Lord Melbourne and Lord Palmerston, her future prime ministers, when they were dashing young men about town. She would have matched wits over dinner with some of the great minds of the day. She would have had an education in art, architecture, and design from her uncle George who was in the process of building the Royal Pavilion in Brighton and transforming Windsor Castle into a modern royal residence. She would have grown up with her uncle William's bastards, the FitzClarences, and enjoyed the rough and tumble of a house filled with children. A Hanoverian Victoria would have been a very different woman, a very different queen. History would have been different.

But those who clustered around the deathbed of Edward, Duke of Kent, were quite determined that Victoria should not be given into the care, or negligence, of her paternal relatives. They wanted her to grow up a Coburg, not a Hanoverian. The proud Hanoverian Kent was weak and fearing death, no match for the men at the bedside who shaped the course of events.

The court at Windsor did keep an eye on events in Sidmouth. Kent's brothers York and Sussex both came down to Devon to wish him well and assess the situation for the royal family. When Kent's death seemed imminent, a letter came for him from the prince regent. Expressing deep sorrow and affection, the regent requested the guardianship of Victoria for himself or one of his brothers. But the letter came too late, and the prince regent was not free to go down to Sidmouth for a final reconciliation with his brother Kent. The regent was obliged to remain at Windsor where his father George III was finally dying.

The Duke of Kent's will was probably drafted by none other than Christian Stockmar. This gentleman providentially found himself in Sidmouth with the Kents when the duke fell ill and was in constant communication with his employer, Prince Leopold of Saxe-Coburg. Apprised of the Duke of Kent's serious illness, the prince himself traveled posthaste back from a shooting party in Berkshire and arrived in Devon in time for the signing of the will. The trustee named under the will was the Duke of Kent's chief aide-de-camp, Lieutenant General Frederick Augustus Wetherall. The appointed executors were Wetherall and Captain John Conroy.

·

THE DUKE OF KENT died on January 23, 1820. On January 29, George III died. The new king George IV then fell desperately ill with an inflammation of the lungs, and for a few terrible weeks, it was feared he too would die.

When he regained his strength and replenished the 150 ounces of blood taken by his doctors, George IV became absorbed in two major projects. He would stage the most magnificent coronation England had ever seen, spending the fabulous sum of 243,000 pounds that parliament had voted him and a great deal more. At the same time, he would secure a divorce from his wife, Caroline of Brunswick, the details of whose scandalous conduct and obscene attire in Italy had long been reported to him by spies, German relatives, and traveling Englishmen. The royal divorce proceedings of 1820 brought Queen Caroline to trial in the House of Lords on a charge of "licentious, disgraceful, and adulterous intercourse" with an Italian groom. The trial ended in catastrophic failure for the King and his ministers. No divorce was possible, and George IV's coronation of July 19, 1821, was marred by Caroline, who hammered at the doors of Westminster Abbey in a vain attempt to take her rightful place as queen. The King's only comfort came when, a few weeks later, Caroline fell ill and died.

During this frenzied public activity by the King in London, the Duchess of Kent coped with death and debt. With her husband's embalmed body stretched out in a velvet-shrouded coffin amid ostrich plumes and tall silver candlesticks, the Duchess of Kent discovered that she was virtually destitute. The 15,000 pounds that the duke had received from his liberal political backers just a year earlier was all spent. Even at the exorbitant rates charged to profligate royal dukes, no further credit was available. There was no cash on hand to pay the embalmer's and undertaker's fees, to settle with the landlord, get the duke's body transported to Windsor for burial in St. George's Chapel, or to pay for the duchess and her household to get away from Devon.

From both her husbands, Marie Luise Victoire of Saxe-Coburg-Saalfeld inherited debt rather than revenue, but at least Leiningen left her a home. Amorbach was an estate rather than a realm, but it had been hers, in trust for her son, Charles. The Duke of Kent and Strathearn, Earl of Dublin, by contrast, owned no domain and no town house—only a country estate near London that was mortgaged to the hilt, up for sale, and attracting no buyers. So the dowager Duchess of Kent found herself in England with the clothes she stood up in, the bedstead, and the little dog she had brought from Germany but very little else.

It was true that as a member of the royal family she could not be thrown into debtor's prison. It was also true that she would have the six thousand pounds a year in dower income settled upon her by parliament at the time of her marriage, in addition to her own three hundred pounds a year. To any ordinary widow, such an income amounted to a fabulous fortune.

However, if Edward, Duke of Kent, had taught his wife anything, it was that royal living in England was impossible on six thousand a year.

In her difficulties, the duchess turned to her eldest brother-in-law, the new King of England, expecting assistance on the magnificent English royal scale. It was not forthcoming. In the midst of all his coronation preparations, the irksome divorce proceedings, and the usual chores of governance, King George IV did not merely forget about his widowed sister-in-law the Duchess of Kent and her child. He actively snubbed and spurned them. Other members of the royal family followed the King's lead. Edward Kent's three sisters in England, Mary, Augusta, and Sophia, as well as his sister-in-law Adelaide Clarence, wrote notes, paid visits, and commiserated with the grieving widow in her native German, but paid no bills and offered no loans.

George IV was usually generous toward his female relatives, but he heartily disliked the Kents. From childhood, George IV had found his brother Edward a hypocritical bore, and he never took a fancy to Edward's wife. She was a Coburg, and since the death of his daughter Charlotte, George IV had developed a strong dislike of Coburgs in general and in particular of Prince Leopold, Charlotte's widower and Victoire's youngest brother.

Given the King's own vast mound of debt, the fabulous architectural projects he was intent on, and the eternal demands on his privy purse from extravagant brothers and needy sisters, George IV did not intend to waste precious resources on a sister-in-law he disliked. Let Victoire of Saxe-Coburg-Saalfeld-Leiningen-Dachburg-Hadenburg-Kent return to Germany where she belonged. In Germany one could live like a king on six thousand English parliamentary pounds.

As for the child Victoria, George IV had barely set eyes on her, and he absolutely refused to countenance the possibility that one day Victoria Kent might rule in England. The whole question of the succession to the throne put the King in a rage. George IV had once been the Prince Charming of all Europe, and his failure to sire an heir rankled. As the King saw it, from the moment of Victoria Kent's birth, her father, her pushy mother, and her oleaginous uncle had been crowing that this child would be Queen of England. Edward Kent's will, giving the guardianship of the Princess Victoria to her mother, and thus to her uncle Leopold, was the last straw.

So George IV washed his hands of the whole problem of his niece Victoria. Let the child be a Coburg. Let Leopold, with his fifty thousand from parliament, and the whole pack of German relatives take responsibility for the child and be damned with them. The child would do as well in Germany as in England, and if she didn't, if she died, it would, in the King's view, be no tragedy. Victoria already had two healthy male cousins, George Cumberland and George Cambridge, and a king was worth ten of a queen. Even better, the Duke of Clarence's young wife, Adelaide, was pregnant and set to provide an heir. King George himself, once he had got rid of his wife, Caroline, might marry again and astonish the world by producing a little Prince of Wales.

Just as the King had hoped, in December 1820 the Duchess of Clarence gave birth to a baby girl who became third in line of succession after her uncle York and her father. The King was exultant, the Clarences gloated, and the Kent ménage at Kensington Palace fell into despondency. The King decreed that the new Clarence baby should be christened Elizabeth Georgina Adelaide. This was a further calculated insult to his sister-in-law Kent, since Elizabeth and Georgina were two of the names that the King as prince regent had refused to allow the Kents to give their daughter. But Elizabeth Clarence died of a bowel constriction when she was three months old, and the savage disappointment the King felt when he received the news did nothing to soften his heart toward Victoria Kent.

When in February 1821, Lord Liverpool, the prime minister, begged George IV to make provision for the Princess Victoria, the King refused, saying, "*her* uncle [Leopold] was rich enough to take care of her." It was as if the King refused to acknowledge that Victoria was, in fact, as much his niece as Leopold's. George IV was bent on driving his sister-in-law Kent back to her native Germany.

When Lord Liverpool communicated to the Duchess of Kent and her advisers the unwelcome news that the King absolutely refused to give any financial support to the Princess Victoria, Prince Leopold understood that something significant had occurred. Far from contesting the Duke of Kent's will, the house of Hanover was handing the child who might be queen over to the house of Coburg. Leopold replied that he was happy to take responsibility for his niece and underlined formally what was involved. "Remember that it was not I who grasped at the management of the princess, but that the princess is by the King in this manner confided to me, and H. Maj. [His Majesty] thereby delegates to me a power which belongs to him."

Victoire, dowager Duchess of Kent, had no head for finance, but she understood family politics very well. Each of the King's insults struck home. Enjoying such wealth and power, he had chosen to knock her to the ground when she was already on her knees. She would never forgive him, or his brothers who stood by. Baby Victoria had been rejected by her father's family. From now on, the Duchess of Kent was prepared to believe the worst of the English royal family, to credit any report of their meanness, their hatred, and their plotting against her.

Fortunately, she was not without protectors. There was her brother Leopold. He and she had been close as children. Even though he had turned into a pedantic bore, forever lecturing her on English history and nagging her about money, Leopold's brilliance and acumen were legendary in the family. There was Stockmar, a tiresome hypochondriac and inveterate busybody, but the supreme man of business. Last but not least, there was Captain John Conroy (or Major Conroy, as he now generally preferred to be known), who was so forceful and manly and so devoted to her interests. Leopold and Stockmar were forever going off on some mysterious political errand, but dear John could be relied upon to stay right by her side.

■

WITHIN DAYS OF THE DEATH of the Duke of Kent, Prince Leopold assumed the direction of his widowed sister's affairs. It was clear to him and to Stockmar that the duchess was ill equipped to deal with the problems facing her. It was also clear to them that the chances Leopold's niece Victoria had of becoming Queen of England one day would be jeopardized if she were brought up abroad. English monarchs were peculiarly at risk. The English parliament had already beheaded Charles I, sent James II into permanent exile, and on two occasions chosen a new king. It was xenophobic enough to refuse a German queen and choose one of her male cousins to rule instead.

To ensure that Victoire did not return to their family in Germany, Leopold settled the rent for the Sidmouth cottage, got the duke's body off to Windsor for burial, and paid the travel expenses to London for his sister and her household. He prevailed on Mary, the Duchess of Gloucester, George IV's favorite sister, to intercede with the King and secure for the dowager Duchess of Kent and her household the apartments at Kensington Palace that had been her husband's. In March 1820, Leopold arranged for Victoire formally to give up all claims on her late husband's estate for both herself and her child, leaving the creditors to pick those meager bones.

Leopold then arranged to let his sister have an additional three thousand pounds a year from his personal funds. One thousand was to be earmarked for summer holidays at the sea or in the country, since the duchess had no country residence. He also enabled his sister to take on debt by guaranteeing a loan. In early 1820, the Duchess of Kent, Prince Leopold, and General Wetherall together floated a bond with Coutts the bankers for twelve thousand pounds, which translated into six thousand in cash. The duchess used this money to establish her household at Kensington Palace, buying furniture, linen, plate, a carriage, horses, and so forth. The duchess borrowed a further six thousand pounds in April 1821. This time, since little Princess Elizabeth of Clarence had just died and Princess Victoria was once again third in line of succession after her senior uncles, Victoire was able to find other gentlemen apart from her brother willing to guarantee the loan.

In later years, Leopold often recalled with what tender affection and alacrity he had taken on the role of surrogate father to Queen Victoria. At best this was half the story. During the infancy of his niece Victoria, Prince Leopold was a gloomy hypochondriac known in the British press as His Parsimonious Highness. He lived well but had few outlets for his abilities, energies, and ambitions. Ostracized at the English court, where George IV would barely even acknowledge him, Leopold spent at least half the year traveling in Europe, visiting relatives, taking the waters, cultivating his political connections, and discreetly indulging his sensual appetites. A mistress was essential to Leopold throughout his life, and, whereas he successfully advocated a life of purity and connubial exclusivity to his niece Victoria and his nephew Albert, he did not practice what he preached.

Family pride and personal ambition were Prince Leopold's prime motivators, and the calculations he had made when promoting the Kent marriage in 1819 still held good. The fat little girl baby with the runny nose whom he at last took in his arms in the icy Devon cottage where her father had died stood a reasonable chance of being Queen of England one day, and she was half Coburg. The gratitude of monarchs is a very valuable commodity, so it made sense to Leopold to invest in this niece's future. He certainly had the time and money to play the role of darling uncle for a few weeks a year.

And the financial aid Prince Leopold gave to his widowed sister cost him remarkably little. The prince assumed none of his brother-in-law Kent's debts: Queen Victoria settled these as one of her first orders of business after ascending the throne. As to the not inconsiderable debts that the Duchess of Kent incurred between 1820 and 1837, these too were settled not by her brother Leopold but by her daughter once Victoria became queen.

The fifty thousand pound annuity he was given by parliament when he became Princess Charlotte's husband was almost the whole of Prince Leopold's fortune. Thus the three thousand pounds he allotted his sister for a few years came from the British taxpayer, not the Coburg family. Furthermore, Leopold did not give up his parliamentary stipend when in 1831 he went off to Belgium to be king. Instead his agent Stockmar negotiated a settlement with the English government whereby the new king would repay his debts, maintain his English property, support his English charities, pay his English servants and pensioners, and then generously give the remainder of his appanage back to the British exchequer.

To the outrage of the British government and public, the king's expenses turned out to account for most of the fifty thousand a year for a great many years. Until the end of his life, King Leopold was able to come to England regularly and to offer Claremont to deposed members of European royal families without digging into his own pocket. The debts he claimed to have run up in England between 1818 and 1830 turned out to amount to a whopping eighty-three thousand pounds, and the king declined to give an account of them. So much debt was puzzling for a man known to be extremely careful with expenses and an excellent money manager. The accumulated payments to his sister may well have been bundled into the declared debt. If so, the English taxpayer paid twice for the financial support that King Leopold claimed to have so generously afforded the Kents.

·

IF HIS INITIAL motivation was less than altruistic, Prince Leopold's occasional watchful presence and his brotherly influence on Victoria's mother were undoubtedly important factors in the girl's early childhood. Though she saw her uncle quite rarely, Queen Victoria remembered that her happiest times as a child were spent at Leopold's country estate at Claremont or at the seaside hotel his money paid for. At Claremont she was agreeably spoiled by Louise Louis, her dead cousin Charlotte's old dresser, who greeted her like the Second Coming. She enjoyed the fact that Leopold talked to her seriously, as if she were a grownup, and she used to weep when she had to leave her "Dearest Uncle."

In her London home too, Victoria, until age ten, had a measure of her uncle's protection. Even when abroad, by letter and through Stockmar, Leopold kept in touch with the Duchess of Kent's affairs. When he returned to England, it was in no small part to see his niece Victoria. With each passing year, the odds on her succeeding to the throne of England improved, and Leopold set out to charm the child and command her affection just as he had once charmed and won the affection of his wife, Princess Charlotte. He succeeded. Queen Victoria herself declared in later life that her uncle Leopold was the only father she had ever known and that she adored him. Leopold probably loved Victoria as much as he was capable of loving anyone, and the bond between the two proved strong and lasting.

However, by 1827, when Victoria was eight, Leopold and Stockmar were spending more and more time in Europe, first negotiating the possibility that Leopold would become king of the new kingdom of Greece, and finally settling him on the equally new throne of Belgium. The dream Leopold had long entertained of one day becoming regent in England for his niece Victoria faded before the reality of being king in his own right. From 1831 King Leopold was fully occupied defending Belgium against the furious Dutch, warding off the power of France, keeping the rival Belgian political factions in check, forging dynastic alliances for Coburg family members, and beginning a new Belgian dynasty with a new teenaged wife. There was little time to worry about his niece in England.

Victoria never bore them a grudge, but her uncle Leopold's departure for Brussels and the simultaneous disappearance of Stockmar to Coburg were a disaster for her. She was now left to the tender mercies of her mother's right-hand man, the newly minted baronet of the Guelphic Order of Hanover, Sir John Conroy.

．

JOHN CONROY WAS a career adventurer, expert manipulator, and domestic martinet. An Irishman born in Wales, he had small means, some ability, and mighty ambition. He believed he could trace his ancestry back to the ancient kings of Ireland.

He made his career in the British army during the Napoleonic wars but, to the disdain of fellow officers, steered clear of battles. Conroy moved up the ranks by marrying Elizabeth Fisher, the tall, handsome, vacuous daughter of his superior officer, Major General Fisher, whom he served in various administrative capacities in Ireland and England. When General Fisher died suddenly in 1814, Conroy entered the Duke of Kent's household through the good offices of Bishop Fisher, his wife's uncle, who had been Kent's tutor. This seemed like a step up. Though the duke was not known for paying the members of his household, he promised Conroy advancement in his military career. As it turned out, the Duke of Kent was the last man to get favors out of the army bureaucracy at Whitehall, and when he died, Conroy was still a captain. With a tiny Irish estate and a minor civil servant's sinecure on which to keep a wife, a mother-in-law, and a growing family, Conroy needed to find a new source of revenue fast.

Conroy was with the Kent family in the Devon cottage when the duke died. Named an executor to the duke's will, he at once established himself as a useful man, devoted to the interests of the duchess. Victoire of Saxe-Coburg had always relied on men to run her life for her. When Emich

Charles of Leiningen, her first husband, died, she quickly fell under the control of Leiningen's steward, Herr Schindler. Now she came under Conroy's dominance, leaning on his strong right arm, weeping on his manly shoulder, and allowing him to worry about the money for her.

Conroy was especially valuable in the duchess's German-speaking household in the early days because he was a native speaker of English. Hitherto the duchess had resisted all efforts to teach her the language, but Conroy succeeded where the Duke of Kent and Prince Leopold had failed. Though always happier in German and French, the Duchess of Kent could henceforth pass muster at dinner parties and court ceremonies in her adopted country.

The Duchess of Kent brought Conroy with her to Kensington Palace. There he unearthed a gold mine in the shape of King George IV's aging spinster sister, Princess Sophia. This lady, once beautiful and full of longing, had had a disastrous liaison with one of her father's less prepossessing courtiers, which resulted in the birth of an illegitimate son. This secret shame prevented Sophia from ever marrying, and her son, once he came to adulthood, was a constant thorn in her side. John Conroy charmed Princess Sophia and won her complete confidence. He took over control of her affairs, had no trouble facing down the importunate son, and made Sophia a regular part of the Duchess of Kent's social circle. In return for Conroy's gallant company and filial care, Sophia became Conroy's spy, reporting in detail on what was said and done at Kensington Palace in his absence and at the Court of St. James's, where she had access to the private society of her brother kings, George IV and William IV. She also gave him money and estates that enabled Conroy to live like a rich man.

By the time Leopold was installed in Belgium, Conroy and his family, though maintaining an agreeable suburban London residence, lived to all intents and purposes at nearby Kensington Palace, and traveled with the duchess as part of her household. Conroy served as the duchess's comptroller, but he was also her secretary and interpreter, her public relations officer, her counselor, her confidant, and her political agent in dealings with King, court, and parliament.

Cynical men of the world like the Duke of Wellington were sure that Conroy was the duchess's lover. They were probably wrong, but Conroy had a familiar way of dealing with her that the Court of St. James's observed with shock and distaste, so violently did it flout every rule of royal etiquette. According to Conroy's biographer Katherine Hudson, Conroy lived in a convenient fantasy world in which he and his family were royal too. Against all the evidence, Conroy believed that his wife, Elizabeth Fisher Conroy, was an illegitimate daughter of the Duke of Kent. He was thus Princess Victoria's brother-in-law, and his children were her nieces and nephews. He once mystified Victoria by saying that his daughters were as high as she.

Leopold underestimated Conroy. Busy and blinded by aristocratic disdain, he saw Conroy as his English agent and believed what Conroy told him. He failed to see how effectively Conroy was controlling the flow of information in and out of Kensington Palace, how thoroughly Conroy had taken control of the duchess's affairs. Only gradually was it borne in upon the king of the Belgians that the lowly Conroy had ambitions that paralleled and might frustrate his own.

Both exceptionally ambitious men who saw the child Victoria as a tool in their own advancement, Conroy and Leopold had much in common, but only Conroy understood this. As a result, Sir John was able to exploit the blind spot of a king who prided himself on his astuteness. It was only after Victoria became queen that King Leopold started referring to Conroy as a "Mephistopheles" and comparing his influence over the Duchess of Kent to "witchcraft."

People in England had no trouble figuring out Sir John Conroy. Great men like the Duke of Wellington, Lord Charles Greville, and Lord Melbourne wondered to each other how the Duchess of Kent could be deceived by such an obvious blackguard. But the duchess connived in her own deception. Victoire of Kent was a traditional man's woman: sociable, pliant, not very bright, but convinced of her own importance. When she was put down, when her needs were not met, like a spoiled lapdog she showed her teeth. The more Conroy annoyed her English relatives, the more she liked him.

The duchess had no desire to see her brother Leopold regent in England. She had enjoyed being regent in Germany in her first husband's tiny realm, and she intended to be regent in England in the happy event that her daughter succeeded to the throne as a minor. As the years went by, as the dynastic odds for Victoria improved, as her own social and financial situations rose, the duchess became increasingly imperious. After her brother-in-law William came to the throne, she was livid when Prime Minister Wellington refused her demand for the status (and the income) of a dowager Princess of Wales. As Victoria edged closer to the throne, the duchess also became more and more envious, reminding her daughter that if the Duke of Kent had lived, she, not Victoria, would have been Queen of England after William IV's death.

The duchess liked Conroy, she was comfortable with him, and she viewed business, especially financial business, as a male preserve. Conroy seemed all efficiency to her, and, since he was her man, she assumed that his interests and ambitions dovetailed with her own. She tolerated Conroy's presumption and paid no attention to his financial dealings. She and Conroy were, for at least eight years, an effective team.

It is one of the oddities of history that Victoria Regina et Imperatrix (Queen and Empress), the woman who launched a dozen dynasties and put fear into the hearts of courtiers and children alike, spent her youth in thrall to a man who had no legal authority over her, a man who was neither nobleman nor kinsman—a man she loathed.

That Dismal Existence

*T*HE FIRST YEARS AFTER THE DEATH OF THE DUKE OF KENT WERE VERY difficult for his widow, but his child, Victoria, was happy. Cold, dirty, drafty, vermin-ridden Kensington Palace was the only home she had ever known, and, since she was rarely taken to her uncle's court, she had no sense of being a royal poor relation. The ups and downs in her dynastic status affected her mainly because they made her mother unhappy and Sir John Conroy cross.

Victoria as a little girl did not know that she was likely to inherit the throne of her uncle George IV. She was always addressed as "Princess" and certainly understood that she was part of the royal family of England, but the possibility that she might one day be queen was carefully kept from her. This unawareness shaped her sense of self in crucial ways. Unlike George IV, who became Prince of Wales virtually at birth, Queen Victoria did not move out of the cradle convinced of her own supreme importance. As princesses go, she was not especially vain, self-absorbed, and inconsiderate.

At first baby Victoria was nestled in a cocoon of love and attention spun by her mother, her nurse Mrs. Brock, her mother's lady-in-waiting Baroness Späth, and old Louise Louis at Claremont. For the most part, the child was allowed very little contact with her father's kin. However, two of her uncles, the dukes of York and Sussex, used Kensington Palace as their business address, so they did manage to see something of their Kent niece.

Uncle Sussex, Queen Victoria recalled in some reminiscences she set down in 1872, was a very tall man with a loud voice, a weird toupee, and a room full of clocks. Though he was kind, she found him rather alarming. Uncle York was shy, and he won her affection by buying her a donkey and treating her once to a Punch-and-Judy show. When Uncle York died in early 1827, she was very sad.

Victoria was often naughty and temperamental, but so frank and clearsighted that she disarmed her elders. After one stormy episode, the Duchess of Kent admonished her daughter, "When you are naughty, you make me and yourself very unhappy." "No, Mama," retorted the feisty tot, "not me, not myself, but you."

As Victoria moved out of infancy, her constant companion and best friend was her half sister, Princess Feodora von Leiningen. Twelve years separated the two, but they still had much in common. Like Victoria, Feodora had lost her father when she was very young. Her early years in the small German town of Amorbach had few luxuries, but she and her older brother Charles were the center of their mother's life. Then the widowed Victoire von Leiningen married the Duke of Kent and became pregnant with her third child. When the Duke of Kent decided his baby must be born in England, Feodora was separated from her brother and her home, carried off to a new country, and immersed in a new language. As a teenager, she was forced to adapt as best she could to the bewildering reversals of fortune her mother endured.

Beautiful and talented but poor and unimportant, the big sister watched as her mother, her old friend Baroness Späth, even her governess Lehzen, all became engrossed in the little sister. It is a tribute to both sisters that they became friends and not enemies. Feodora must have often felt envy and resentment, but she had a generous nature as well as a lovely face. She became her little sister's ally and best friend as well as her shadow. Though the two were parted young and were rarely together as adults, their friendship was never broken. One of Victoria's first acts as queen was to send much needed money to her sister in Germany. Over the years, Victoria amply repaid the love, protection, and sympathy that Feodora gave her when she was little.

From Feodora, in a sense, Victoria inherited the most important person in her life as a child: her governess, Fräulein Louise Lehzen. When Victoria turned five, her grumpy but devoted nurse, Mrs. Brock, was dismissed, and Lehzen (as she was always known in the duchess's household) took over the little girl's care. Victoria found it "a sad ordeal" to lose Brock, and at first she feared her new governess, a severe, buttoned-up, intelligent woman who could put the fear of God into little girls as ably as any nun.

A German pastor's daughter, Lehzen came to England in 1817 with the Duchess of Kent as the Princess Feodora's governess. In 1824 she was in her midthirties. Even for a nineteenth-century governess, the terms of

Lehzen's employment were severe. She had no regular time off, and there is no record that she had any friends or interests outside the ducal household. The duchess even forbade the governess to keep a diary, since in the past such documents had proved damaging to royal employers. Lehzen obeyed. In the eighteen years she was with the Duchess of Kent's household in England, Louise Lehzen reportedly never took a day off.

A foreigner of humble origins without personal resources, Lehzen was wholly dependent upon her employer. The Duchess of Kent confidently assumed that she could buy the governess's gratitude and loyalty for a few pounds a year and the privilege of living in a palace. She expected Lehzen to give unselfish devotion to her temperamental child.

What she did not expect was that Lehzen would love Victoria as her own, care for her passionately and intelligently, and thereby win Victoria's love in return. Louise Lehzen became Victoria's mother in all but name, and by the time of the princess's accession, Victoria had taken to calling Lehzen "Mother" in private. Whereas the Duchess of Kent became increasingly greedy for money and power, the governess was both principled and disinterested. Her ambitions were for Victoria, not for herself. Sensing this, the child gave respect, affection, and trust in return.

Lehzen took secret strength and satisfaction from the fact that she was educating a Queen of England. Her idea of what that queen should do and think was very different from her employer's. Where the duchess and Conroy envisaged Victoria as a meek little maiden, obedient to their wishes, Lehzen wanted a strong, informed woman, a second Queen Elizabeth. Beneath her dowdy black clothes, Louise Lehzen was a fiery soul, nourished on the literary masterpieces of the Sturm und Drang movement. At Amorbach Castle, her recent home, Goethe had written *Hermann und Dorothea*, and Schiller had written *Wallenstein*. Lehzen once told a member of Conroy's extended family that she "could pardon wickedness in a queen, but not weakness."

When forced to choose between the interests of her employer and of her tutee, at first secretly, then overtly, and at last defiantly, Lehzen chose the child.

＊

BEGINNING IN 1824, Louise Lehzen set out to curb the child Victoria's temper and improve her manners. More controversially, since society rather prized ignorance in a woman, she tried, with the collaboration of the principal tutor, Dr. Davys, to interest the little princess in learning. She succeeded. Though Queen Victoria had neither the intellect nor the scholarship of her great predecessor Queen Elizabeth I, she was intelligent and disciplined, fluent in three languages, and an impassioned student of history.

Lehzen was severe but, by the standards of her day, an enlightened educator. Even privileged children of Victoria's generation were routinely smacked, shaken, caned, and whipped, locked up in dark closets, or sent to bed without supper. However, in the documentation on Victoria's youth, we do not find the references to corporal punishment that crop up frequently, for example, in the accounts of the youth of the Queen's own children. When the little Princess Victoria was naughty, she was reproved, reasoned with, and sent to stand in the corner, not beaten.

Victoria's early childhood was quite spartan but, unlike a surprising number of royal children before her, she never suffered from want. She was fed small, regular quantities of simple foods like bread soaked in milk, then considered wholesome for children. A cup of tea was a huge treat. She was warmly clothed and firmly corseted. Corsets were considered necessary to support the weak backs of little children, and they became second nature to women well into the twentieth century. However, the rooms the Princess Victoria lived in, even as an infant, were extremely cold by modern standards. The apartments at Kensington Palace occupied by the Duchess of Kent from 1820 to 1836 were, as Victoria later reminded her sister Feodora, "dreadfully dull, dark, and gloomy." Victoria ignored the rats and the black beetles, became impervious to the cold, and developed immunities that served her well in later years.

Though her daily routine was quiet and tedious, her food plain, Victoria had occasional splendid treats and marvelous presents befitting a princess. On May 24, 1826, Prince Leopold arranged a celebration of his niece's seventh birthday. Among her birthday presents was a matched pair of diminutive Shetland ponies and a tiny phaeton—the gift not of her uncle but of the Marchioness of Huntley, a family friend. To her rapturous pleasure, the princess drove Lehzen around the huge park at Claremont in this carriage, with a boy postilion in green and gold livery on one pony and an outrider going before.

Later in the summer of 1826, there came an unexpected overture from King George IV. The Duchess of Kent and her two daughters were invited to come to Windsor for several days. Victoria had met her uncle king on at least one previous occasion, but this was the first time she was his guest. Enormous of girth, heavily powdered and rouged, bewigged and corseted, George IV was a grotesque figure, but little Victoria was unafraid, and the two hit it off at once. When they met, the King said, "Give me your little paw," and Victoria promptly complied, and even kissed his appalling cheek.

She went pink with delight when the King pinned to her dress a diamond-encrusted miniature of himself, an ornament that only the closest members of his family and set were permitted to wear.

At Windsor, John Conroy faded into the background, and Victoria could enjoy herself. Fifty years later, she vividly remembered what fun it had been to see the wapitis, gazelles, and chamois in the royal menagerie at Windsor, and to fish from a barge on Virginia Water. One day she was snatched up and taken for a drive in the royal phaeton, with the King himself at the reins. The King's sister, Aunt Mary Gloucester, held on to her tightly so she did not fall out as the fast, high carriage bowled through the park. Victoria's mother was terrified, but Victoria loved every minute.

Like her uncle George and most of the English royal family, Victoria passionately loved music, and she was enchanted by the band concert that was held at Windsor each evening. The King asked his niece what tune she would like his band to play. Natural courtier that she was, the seven-year-old princess replied, "Oh uncle King, I should like 'God Save the King' better than any other tune." When asked at the end of her visit what she had most enjoyed, she replied, "Driving out with you, uncle King." Victoria also noticed that her uncle King paid a good deal of attention to her beautiful stepsister, Feodora, and she picked up on the thrilling fact that marriage between the two was under discussion at court.

The English royal family was now enamored of the little Victoria Kent. With her fat cheeks, blue saucer eyes, and receding chin, the princess looked every inch a Hanoverian—"l'image du feu roi" (the image of the old King, George III), as her mother boasted to the Countess of Granville. The visit to Windsor seemed to herald a rapprochement between Windsor and Kensington, but, in fact, Victoria saw her uncle George only once again, at a large state occasion.

The visit to Windsor of 1826 raised warning bells in John Conroy's mind. George IV was showing an interest in Princess Victoria, and the child had taken to court life like a duck to water. Conroy's interests depended on the growing power and wealth of the Duchess of Kent, and the duchess's fortunes, in turn, hinged on her retaining control over her daughter Victoria. Under no circumstances must the child be taken into the care of her royal English uncles and given her own household and her own staff, like the eight-year-old Princess Charlotte one generation earlier.

Conroy wasted no time in reminding the Duchess of Kent how extremely damaging it would be if she allowed relationships with the English court to become more friendly and frequent. He flattered the duchess's amour propre by framing the issue in moral and maternal terms. The King,

Conroy told the duchess, was angling to take control of Victoria, and if he succeeded, the princess would be in moral danger. The King's household was a cesspool, and he was hated and despised in England. Even worse, behind George IV loomed the sinister figure of his brother and chief adviser, the Duke of Cumberland. This man harbored the ambition to be king after his childless older brothers and to place his son George on the united throne of England and Hanover. Who knew, whispered Conroy, whether little innocent Victoria would survive if committed to the custody of those wicked uncles.

Victoire of Kent chose to believe Conroy. She went rarely to court, was not a great reader, and still had trouble following English conversation. Conroy and his devoted ally Princess Sophia were her main sources of information. Thanks to Conroy and no thanks at all to her royal in-laws, the duchess now circulated comfortably in English society, held court at Kensington Palace, and dined out with her own coterie of friends and political allies from the Whig Party.

The duchess was ignorant but not naive, and Conroy's interpretation of English society appealed to her prejudices. Her own sister had experienced eight years of orgies and sadistic excesses at the court of the Russian tsar. At Amorbach, Victoire had personally superintended the lying-in of her brother Ernest's mistress, Pauline Panam. Her first husband's Leiningen relatives had done all they could to steal the family estate from her and her son, Charles. Why should the English royals, who had always been so openly hostile to her, be any different?

Foreseeing a threat to his growing authority from Prince Leopold, Conroy also worked to detach the duchess from her own family. Conroy reminded the duchess that Prince Leopold and her eldest brother, Ernest, the present Duke of Saxe-Coburg and Gotha, led the kind of droit du seigneur life that was no longer tolerated by respectable people in England. The duchess herself had fortunately arrived in the nick of time to prevent the little princess from speaking to one of Leopold's mistresses, who was boldly walking the sacred ground at Claremont. Such incidents could not be tolerated. Purity of thought, word, and deed must be the watchword at Kensington Palace, where a tender young girl was being educated to be queen.

The Duchess of Kent saw golden prospects ahead once her hated brothers-in-law were all dead. She therefore accepted that her daughter Victoria should be carefully shielded from the dubious moral atmosphere that prevailed at Coburg and Claremont as well as Windsor. She was willing to sacrifice people she claimed to love on the altar of her own ambition to be regent and rule England in Victoria's name.

■

THE FIRST PERSON sacrificed was her elder daughter. In the Princess Feodora, Conroy saw a danger to himself and his employer. At home Feodora was increasingly discontented and rebellious, and her little sister, Victoria, adored her and tried to be like her. Conroy observed Feodora's personal triumph at Windsor. The girl was now in her late teens, exceptionally beautiful and with perfect manners—no wonder that old roué the King had noticed her. Two rich and powerful elderly men, the Duke of Nassau and the Duke of Schomberg (the Austrian ambassador in London), had shown a willingness to marry Feodora even though she had no personal fortune. Either of these men, however personally distasteful to a young girl, would have been a brilliant match. Feodora would have a home in England and, as a married woman, could be expected to exert some influence over her mother. Conroy decided that the time had come to marry Feodora off to some harmless German and get her out of the country.

"I must unequivocally state to you," Conroy wrote to the duchess, "that it is not only essential to the interest and happiness of the Pss. Feodora that she should marry soon, but it is necessary for your and the Pss. Victoria's interest that it should take place—the influence you ought to have over her [Princess Victoria] will be endangered if she sees her elder sister not so alive to it as she should be—and recollect, once your authority is lost over the Princess V you will never regain it."

For Feodora, too, marriage seemed the only option. She was frustrated and unhappy at Kensington Palace. She felt her mother neglected her. She had no friends. She hated Conroy and deeply resented his tyrannical hold on her mother's household. As Feodora recalled in a private letter to Victoria in 1843: "When I look back upon those years which ought to have been the happiest in my life [her years at Kensington Palace], I cannot help pitying myself. Not to have enjoyed the pleasures of youth is nothing, but to have been deprived of all intercourse and not one cheerful thought in that dismal existence of ours, was very hard. My only happy time was going or driving out with you and Lehzen; then I could speak and look as I liked."

In 1827 Augusta of Saxe-Coburg and Saalfeld, the mother of the Duchess of Kent, came for a visit to Kensington Palace. On her return to Germany, she took her granddaughter Feodora with her, and, at the end of the year, the princess's engagement to Prince Ernest of Hohenlohe-Langenburg was announced. He was a fourth-rank prince with a postage-stamp kingdom. He had no money. But he was only thirty-two and a nice man, so Feodora eagerly agreed to her mother's choice of husband. The couple were married in England in February 1828 and then returned to Germany to take up residence at the notoriously cold, cavelike Schloss Langenburg. For many years, the penurious Hohenlohes lived on the charity of relatives, but their marriage was long and successful.

With Princess Feodora out of the way for good, John Conroy did another piece of house cleaning. He persuaded the Duchess of Kent to dismiss her lady-in-waiting, Baroness Späth, on the specious grounds that the lady was too extravagant in adoration of the Princess Victoria. Späth had been with the duchess for twenty-five years and thought she was her friend as well as her lady-in-waiting. She was without personal resources, and escaped destitution after leaving England only because she was taken into the household of the warm-hearted Princess Feodora.

Späth's sudden dismissal was a sharp shock to Princess Victoria, who had known the baroness all her life, and even more to Louise Lehzen. Späth had been Lehzen's only real friend in England. The dismissal also caused a sensation at the Court of St. James's, eternally starved for information about life at Kensington Palace. The Duke of Wellington hypothesized that the Princess Victoria had observed some "familiarities" between her mother and Conroy, had told Späth, who in turn, remonstrated with her employer and was promptly dismissed. Lehzen, too, it was reported at George IV's court, would soon be shown the door. But Lehzen managed to keep her mouth shut and cling to her position.

In January 1830, Adelaide, Duchess of Clarence, Victoire's sister-in-law and closest friend at court, a woman whom it was hard to dislike, wrote to the Duchess of Kent to express her grave misgivings about Conroy. "He [Conroy] has never lived before in court circles or in society, so naturally he offends against the traditional ways, for he does not know them . . . In the family it is noticed that you are cutting yourself off more and more from them with your child . . . this they attribute to Conroy, whether rightly or wrongly I cannot judge; they believe he tries to remove everything that might obstruct his influence, so that he may exercise his power alone, and alone, too, one day reap the fruits of his influence. He cannot be blamed for cherishing dreams of future greatness and wanting to achieve a brilliant position for his family; no one can take this amiss in him, but everyone recognizes these aspirations, towards which his every action is directed . . . only he must not be allowed to forbid access to you to all but his family, who in any case are not of so high a rank that they alone should be the entourage and companions of the future Queen of England."

Victoire Kent was mortally offended by this attempt to interfere in her affairs. Conroy was thoroughly alarmed by the letter and determined more than ever to prevent the English royal family from having access to Victoria.

·

IN 1830, WHEN WILLIAM, Duke of Clarence, came to the throne as William IV, Conroy felt extremely confident. Through the auspices of his "chère amie" Princess Sophia, he had been created a baronet of the Hanoverian order and so was now Sir John. At Kensington Palace, his hold over the household was undisputed. Of all the loving and loyal people who had clustered around the Princess Victoria and tried to protect her interests—her sister, Feodora; Baroness Späth; her uncle Leopold; Baron Stockmar; her uncle York; Baroness Lehzen—all but her governess Lehzen had died, moved far away, or been dismissed by the duchess at Conroy's behest.

Tall, handsome, confident, and wily, John Conroy was used to getting his way. Throughout his career, he had successfully used women as tools for his own advancement—first his wife, then Princess Sophia, then the Duchess of Kent. But Princess Victoria was a bigger opportunity than Conroy had dared to dream of as an aspiring army officer with no enthusiasm for combat. The child who might one day be queen offered prospects not only of wealth and status but power, especially if she came to the throne as a minor. Conroy viewed Princess Victoria as a puny, insignificant gosling that someday would lay golden eggs.

But the newly minted Sir John made the misogynist's mistake. He saw Victoria as a key to be turned, not a mind to be won. With the duchess's acquiescence, all the power of the father was vested in him. The possibility that the curly-haired little creature growing up before his eyes might one day pose a threat to his ambitions seemed ridiculous. Unlike "Dearest Uncle" Leopold, who, on his rare visits to England, went out of his way to earn Victoria's trust and affection, Conroy worked to break her will. Day in and day out, he snubbed and sneered at her, aiming to destroy her spirit.

From 1830 to 1837, the famous Kensington System for educating the Princess Victoria came into full effect.

The Kensington System

...

*T*HE KENSINGTON SYSTEM, AS IT LATER CAME TO BE KNOWN, WAS DEVISED and implemented by Sir John Conroy with the full cooperation of the Duchess of Kent. It had two interlocking parts: the first, domestic and covert; the second, political and public. Internally the Kensington System was designed to limit the Princess Victoria's freedom and mold her to Conroy's will. Externally it was a public relations campaign that presented the Duchess of Kent as an ideal mother and made it impossible for family members in England or in Europe to challenge the duchess's guardianship and seek custody of the princess.

The Kensington System became more oppressive as Victoria grew older and nearer to the throne. Its effects on her were serious. At four, Vickelchen, as she was then known to her mainly German-speaking family, was a small, fat, curly, voluble bundle of energy who "set all the world at defiance." At seven, Victoria Kent, as her English cousins called her, was a disciplined and mannerly child in shining good health, who held out her hand with royal aplomb to be kissed but could still be bossy when a child was brought in to play with her. At eleven, the Princess Victoria of Kent was like an exotic animal in a circus, going through her paces for an admiring public under the watchful gaze of her trainers, and then returning obediently to her cage. At sixteen, with a dozen royal suitors panting at her heels, she was amenorrheic and suffered from headaches and back pain. At seventeen, as her uncle king tottered on the edge of death, Victoria was virtually a prisoner in her own home.

She suffered not from neglect or physical abuse but from surveillance and stress. She lacked basic freedoms. She was not free to choose her friends and spend time with them. She was prevented from forming close relationships with members of her extended family, especially those who loved and took an interest in her. She was not allowed to gossip with servants or to play with other children without adult supervision. She could not freely express her thoughts and feelings, since her letters and journal were routinely censored, and any private conversation she did have was subject to report and reproof. Above all, she lacked a freedom that most of us take for granted—the freedom to be alone and unobserved.

For the first eighteen years of her life, Queen Victoria was never alone in a room by herself. Someone was with her not only when she ate and did her lessons and took her exercise but when she slept, washed, and used the chamber pot. When Victoria was a small child, her mother, the Duchess of Kent, rarely went away overnight, and if she did, the nurse, Mrs. Brock, was with the child. After 1824, Louise Lehzen never left Victoria's side during the day. She was required always to be within earshot when the princess was in the company of visitors. Victoria had a bevy of servants and teachers, and she lived in a palace, but she had no day nursery to play in or night nursery to sleep in, and hence no private place where she could keep her things.

Until the day of her accession, Victoria slept in her mother's bedroom on a small bed next to her mother's four-poster. Lehzen stayed with her until the duchess came to bed and dismissed the governess for the night. Victoria did her lessons in her mother's sitting room until she was sixteen, when she at last acquired a sitting room of her own. She never went outside unaccompanied, and as she got older, the group accompanying her got larger, so there was no chance of her ever slipping away. Queen Victoria once told her daughters that until the day of her accession, she was forbidden to go down a staircase unless someone held her hand.

Everything Victoria said or did was monitored. If a friend or relative came to call, if a tutor came to give a lesson, if a child came to play, if a footman came in to mend the fire, Victoria's mother, Lehzen, John Conroy himself, or one of his seven family members was always present to supervise the event and overhear the conversation. When Victoria was having her hair done, either she read aloud or Lehzen read aloud to her from some educational book. That way the princess had no chance to chat with the maid. All of Victoria's letters were looked over before they were posted, especially if they were written to her relatives.

At thirteen the princess was given a journal by her mother and instructed to record the events of her day, writing first in pencil, then copying over in ink. The journal was not the child's private possession, a place where she could freely lay out her thoughts and emotions. Both her mother and Lehzen read the diary regularly. Victoria's early journal tells us little about what she was thinking and feeling and makes no mention of the difficulties she faced as a late teenager. Nothing in the journals could be used against the duchess and Conroy.

Conroy built a wall between Victoria and everyone in the world except her mother, himself, and his family, but the wall was made of glass so that the princess could be constantly on view to the world. This combination of isolation and exposure, of constraint and performance, placed enormous stress on Victoria's youthful mind and body.

When resident at Kensington Palace, Victoria was taken out each day for exercise in the gardens, which were open to the public. Londoners spotted the princess on her outings, first pushed by her nurse in a baby carriage; then walking hand in hand with her older sister and escorted by a huge footman; then riding, first a donkey, then a pony, then a horse. In the summer, as a tiny creature, she could be viewed just outside her mother's ground-floor apartments, bowling her hoop or gravely watering her feet along with the flowers. On her seaside holidays, she could be observed playing on the sands. Visitors allowed inside Kensington Palace were enchanted to see the princess at the far end of her mother's sitting room, playing quietly with her large collection of dolls. These were small, plain, inexpensive creatures, 132 in all, for which Victoria and Lehzen created identities, composed dramas, and sewed costumes. The dolls were the friends Victoria was not allowed to have, and she played with them until she was fourteen.

•

WHILE KEEPING AN increasingly tight grip at home, Conroy worked to promote the political and financial interests of the Duchess of Kent in the outside world. The man was a blackguard, as many gentlemen in England asserted in private, but he was a brilliant and resourceful agent with a preternaturally modern understanding of public relations.

Conroy was middle class despite his fanciful family tree. Unlike the aristocratic sycophants who haunted the Court of St. James's, he had a sense of the rapidly growing power of the middle classes in England and of the Protestant evangelical values they espoused. Change was in the air. The excesses of the French Revolution had led to a grassroots rejection of the freethinking, free-loving, atheistic, liberal society of the late eighteenth century. Conroy understood that in England king and government had less unchallenged authority than in any other monarchy and could not risk flouting public opinion. He saw that the English people hated George IV because he was corrupt, promiscuous, and profligate, and that none of George's brothers was capable of raising the reputation of the house of Hanover in England.

So, in preparation for the reign of the virgin Queen Victoria, over which he intended to preside, Conroy built an image of purity, modesty, and decorum around the Duchess of Kent. It had little basis in the lady's Coburg past, but it worked because it was so in tune with the spirit of the age. Victoria as princess was formed in the image dreamed up by Conroy. As queen she patented, registered, and made it her trademark. Victoria hated Conroy, but still she learned from him.

In 1825 Conroy successfully lobbied parliament to increase the Duchess of Kent's allowance by six thousand pounds a year. To Kensington Palace's vast satisfaction, the Princess Victoria was referred to in the House of Commons as the heir presumptive even though her uncles York and Clarence were both alive. One of Conroy's allies, Lord Darnley, complimented the Duchess of Kent upon the "propriety, domestic affection, and moral purity" with which she was rearing her child. Darnley called her "unexampled in prudence, discretion, and every amiable quality that could exalt and dignify the female character."

When the Duke of Clarence came to the throne as William IV in 1830, the childless royal couple tried to take custody of their little Kent niece, for whom they felt great affection. Conroy moved swiftly and effectively to prevent this. He insisted that Victoria could not be subjected to the tainted moral atmosphere at court where the new King's ten bastard children were welcomed. Cleverly throwing a wedge between the new King and parliament, Conroy assured ministers that William IV had not long to live, that Queen Adelaide was barren, and that therefore immediate provision must be made for the minority of Queen Victoria. Unsurprisingly, the King was outraged and Queen Adelaide wounded by this salvo, and the chasm widened between Windsor and Kensington.

Conroy also launched a public relations campaign on behalf of the Duchess of Kent. His goal was, first, to make it impossible to separate Victoria from her mother or indeed to question the propriety of that lady's custody of her child. Second, to establish that the duchess was the right and proper person to be appointed regent in the event of the Queen's minority. Conroy succeeded brilliantly, and he and the duchess began to feel that they held all the trump cards.

In 1831 a panel of clerical dignitaries was invited to Kensington Palace to interview the Princess Victoria and evaluate her scholarly and spiritual progress. In their subsequent report, the bishops professed themselves delighted with the princess. Her Highness's command of Scripture, religious history, geography, French, German, Latin grammar, arithmetic, and the history of England far surpassed that of other young persons of her age, they noted, and she was also very adept at drawing.

The Archbishop of Canterbury was also summoned to Kensington Palace for a private interview with the duchess. His Grace was charmed when Victoria's mother confided in him how much she idolized her daughter and how often she doubted her own worthiness to educate such a precious child. She sent to the archbishop the glowing reports prepared by his ecclesiastical brethren. These were then consigned to the safety of the archives of Lambeth Palace, the archbishop's official residence, as further documentary evidence of the excellence of the Kensington System. In due course, parliament decreed that, in the event of a minority, the Duchess of Kent should be sole regent for her daughter Victoria.

On only one point did his Grace the Archbishop of Canterbury in 1830 question the Duchess of Kent's education of her daughter. Had the Princess Victoria been told of her lofty destiny, the archbishop asked the duchess. With the King, George IV, visibly failing, surely this was now necessary. The duchess replied that the Princess Victoria had hitherto been carefully shielded from knowledge of her position in the line of succession, but that indeed she was now perhaps old enough to be told the truth.

And so, two months before her eleventh birthday, at the end of her usual lesson in English history, the Princess Victoria reopened her book to find inserted in it a newly updated genealogy of the English royal family. It showed that only her dying uncle George IV and her uncle William, Duke of Clarence, stood between her and the throne. The conversation went as follows:

VICTORIA: I never saw that before.
LEHZEN: It was not thought necessary that you should, Princess.
VICTORIA: I see I am nearer to the throne than I thought.
LEHZEN: So it is, Madam.
VICTORIA (after some moments): Now, many a child would boast but
    they don't know the difficulty; there is much splendour, but there
    is more responsibility! (Holding up the forefinger of her right
    hand and then putting her hand in Lehzen's) I will be good!

For generations in England, the image of the young princess, suddenly and solemnly apprised of her illustrious destiny, raising what is always called her tiny finger and saying twice over "I will be good," was a kind of folk legend.

Fighting Back

...

B Y 1831, THE PRINCESS VICTORIA OF KENT WAS HEIR PRESUMPTIVE to her uncle William IV. All attempts by the King and Queen to produce a healthy child had failed, and, though the Queen was still quite young, the King was in declining health. It was now clear to William IV that he must make an effort to reach out to his niece Victoria and bring her back into the fold of the English royal family. He had some small initial successes, but, to his anger and sorrow, proved incapable of breaking Sir John Conroy's hold over the Duchess of Kent and the duchess's hold over her daughter.

Protocol demanded that a lady of the highest nobility should become Victoria's governess, and the King appointed his friend the Duchess of Northumberland. The King also appointed James Clark as Victoria's personal physician, and the earnest young Scottish doctor quickly earned the princess's trust and friendship. Seconded by King Leopold, William IV was able to prevent Sir John Conroy from getting rid of Baroness Lehzen. Sir John now recognized Lehzen as hostile to the duchess's interests.

Despite this change of personnel at the palace, the Kensington System remained intact and became increasingly rigid as Conroy and the duchess felt themselves under attack. The two made sure that the princess was never able to speak privately with her new governess or any of her tutors. When the Duchess of Northumberland attempted to take an active part in Victoria's education, Victoria's mother had the temerity to dismiss her. The King was reduced to fuming impotently.

In 1834, to combat the influence of Lehzen, Conroy brought an ally into Kensington Palace. Lady Flora Hastings, an unmarried lady from an aristocratic Tory family some twelve years older than the princess, became

Victoria's lady-in-waiting. Lady Flora had fallen under Conroy's spell, and she was happy to act as Conroy's spy. Victoria detested her from the outset but was powerless to block the appointment. As she stoically recorded in her diary, Lady Flora or Miss Victoire Conroy, Sir John's oldest daughter, or both were with her every minute of the day, at home or away.

Life at Kensington Palace was not all gloom for the teenaged princess. Riding, music, drawing, and painting watercolors were sanctioned activities, and she enjoyed them all. Victoria loved her horses, extolling the merits of each in her journal, and her equestrian prowess was admired when she rode out with her party in Hyde Park. Her greatest moments of freedom came when she was galloping her horse and outdistanced her escort.

Music was an important part of Victoria's heritage from the Hanoverian as well as the Coburg side, and she was an accomplished amateur pianist and singer. Opera was a passion with her, and in her sixteenth year, she was overjoyed to begin singing lessons with the world-renowned bass Luigi Lablache. He was an exuberant Neapolitan who was funny and treated the princess like a fellow musician. She wished she could have a singing lesson every day. The Duchess of Kent had a fondness for drama, so her daughter was often to be seen at London theaters, leaning eagerly out from her box to follow the action. When she returned home from a play or an opera, Victoria, who had been taught to draw by competent professionals, would try to capture the moments of delight by sketching the performers from memory.

Victoria's mother's most thoughtful birthday present came on May 19, 1835. A private concert was arranged for the princess's sixteenth birthday at which four of the greatest singers of the day—Lablache, Antonio Tamburini, Giulia Grisi, and Maria Malibran—sang selections from various operas. Victoria had learned much of the vocal material and was already a connoisseur of operatic singing. She knew what an immense treat she had been given. Her diary entry for the day ends with the exuberant: "I was *most exceedingly* delighted."

But such moments of delight were rare. The invisible net around the Princess Victoria tightened as she grew older, while relations between her mother and the King and Queen deteriorated. As Queen Victoria recalled in an 1859 letter to her eldest daughter, she was "always on pins and needles, with the whole family hardly on speaking terms. I (a mere child) between two fires—trying to be civil and then scolded at home! Oh! It was dreadful and that has given me such a horror of Windsor which I can't get over."

From the summer of 1831, Victoria was taken by her mother and Conroy on royal progresses through the provinces, exposing her for the first time to the view of large crowds. She visited the country homes of the aristocracy, attended balls and dinner parties, received the keys of cities, and listened to speeches of welcome by municipal worthies. As many remarked, Conroy acted like the princess's prime minister.

These progresses infuriated the King. William IV felt that his sister-in-law Kent was acting as if he were already dead and she was regent of England. Victoria herself hated the trips more with each year. She loved to see new things and meet new people and had boundless energy when she was happy, but Conroy made her feel like a circus attraction.

But Conroy had a genius for public relations, and the new versions of medieval progresses he developed were an important innovation. George IV had been too unpopular to risk much travel within his own realm. William IV was marginally more popular in the nation than his brother, but poor health kept him close to London. Conroy saw that by forming bonds with distinguished people outside London society and making an impression, however fleeting, on ordinary folk, the princess would forge links with the British people that went over the heads of the court and the government and thus secured her position.

Conroy's insistence that the royal family needed to move outside court circles was a lesson Victoria was primed to learn. As queen, she continued to make forays into the provinces, especially Scotland, and these helped shape public opinion. In the nineteenth century, European monarchies came increasingly under attack, but Victoria was secure on her throne. As she understood very well, this was because the people felt that they knew her and gave her their love and loyalty.

In the 1830s, contact with royalty was an exceptionally rare commodity, even for the greatest of England's families, and Victoria was a huge success wherever she went. The princess always seemed delighted to meet people and interested in everything shown to her. With her small frame, red-blond ringlets, and blue saucer eyes, she was not perhaps pretty, but she was courteous and polished, unaffected and modest.

Her voice was her greatest beauty, and people were thrilled by it. It was warm, clear, ringing, and quintessentially English—Dr. Davys had worked hard on her as a child to eliminate every trace of German accent and intonation. During these lengthy tours, the Princess Victoria met a great many people and learned a little about the country she was destined to rule. When she visited the industrial Midlands for the first time, the gloomy mills, flaming smokestacks, and sooty, emaciated citizens shocked her.

Though tiring, the progresses also offered the princess some welcome adventures. On two occasions, she was in real danger and had the chance to show her mettle. Once, she was aboard a sailing yacht that lost its way and crashed into a hulk in the harbor, destroying its mainmast. The princess's mother cowered belowdecks, but Victoria, who loved life at sea, remained up top. As the sailors worked frantically to save the vessel, she calmly looked on, chewing on a mutton chop.

On another occasion, the princess's lead carriage horse caught its leg in the traces, and in the resulting struggle, the carriage turned over. Victoria managed to extract herself, help her mother out, and grab her darling spaniel Dash from the luggage compartment. She then pulled her mother behind a stone wall as the crazed horses, who had regained their feet, stampeded down the road.

·

TRADITIONALLY IN PROTESTANT royal families, a child's confirmation marked his or her coming of age. Though it suited the duchess and Conroy to keep Victoria a child as long as possible, when Victoria turned fifteen, they were unable to delay her confirmation any longer. King William IV announced that he wished to give his niece and heir her own income and her own household, but once again the Duchess of Kent played the motherhood card. She insisted that Victoria's fervent wish was to remain under her mother's care. Since she never let the girl out of her sight or allowed her to speak privately, it was impossible to contradict the duchess. So the princess remained at Kensington Palace.

The duchess did exploit the confirmation to try once again to dismiss Lehzen, arguing that Victoria no longer needed a governess and Lehzen was an improper person to be a member of the heir presumptive's household. Fortunately, both King William and King Leopold were fully aware of how important Lehzen was to Victoria's health and happiness, and on this issue they were able to prevail. Nonetheless, in one of the many hectoring and pious letters she addressed in these years to her increasingly mulish daughter, the Duchess of Kent begged Victoria to remember her position and treat Lehzen as a servant, not a friend.

Now that she had officially "come out," the Princess Victoria was more frequently at court, and her life was enlivened by the steady stream of princely suitors who turned up in London. On the subject of Victoria's prospective husband, as on everything else, the Duchess of Kent and Conroy were at loggerheads with King William and his brothers.

During the summer after her sixteenth birthday, anticipating an even more exacting round of public duties, Victoria lost weight, had trouble sleeping, and suffered from sick headaches and back pain. She pleaded with her mother to be afforded more leisure and privacy. She wished to forego the next royal progress through England that Conroy had mapped out for her and which she knew offended her uncle the King. William IV had found it necessary to stipulate that when she ventured offshore, the Duchess of Kent had no authority to order the twenty-one-gun salute traditionally reserved for the sovereign.

Victoria's request to spend a quiet summer was denied, and she was called a foolish, undutiful girl. She completed the tour, a notable success in all her private visits and public appearances. But her vitality, which had so impressed people when she was a little girl, was now at low ebb, and her menstrual cycle became irregular. Amenorrhea is a common symptom in teenage girls under extreme stress, but it complicated the various schemes afoot to marry Victoria off.

Alarmed by her daughter's increasing intransigence, the Duchess of Kent summoned Baron Stockmar to investigate and give his advice. Stockmar was his usual forthright self, and he advised the duchess, in essence, that it was in her interest to dismiss Conroy and make peace with her daughter. Conroy had no difficulty in persuading the duchess to ignore Stockmar's advice.

But Stockmar rang loud warning bells in Brussels, and King Leopold decided that he himself must now take a hand. In September 1835, Leopold and his wife, Louise, came to meet the Kensington Palace party at Ramsgate, a seaside resort in Kent, not far from Dover, that had long been a favorite with the Coburgs. Victoria was ecstatic, since it was over four years since she had last seen her uncle Leopold, and she knew her aunt Louise only from letters. The queen of the Belgians was only seven years older than Victoria and immensely chic, if frail and retiring, especially in the presence of her husband.

King Leopold was one person whom John Conroy could not prevent from speaking alone and in confidence to the princess. On two separate occasions, her uncle talked to Victoria at length. She underlined in her journal that her uncle had given her "very good and valuable advice," but prudently refrained from specifying what that advice was. Leopold also took a long walk alone on the sands with Sir John Conroy, but made no headway with him at all.

Throughout the visit of the Belgian royal couple, Victoria was, as she liked to write, very merry, but she was struggling against illness and felt extremely unwell. Fever and pain, joined with the sorrow and panic of seeing her most important ally once again sailing across the channel, laid the princess low once King Leopold had left.

Victoria had grown to love and trust her personal physician, Dr. James

Clark, but when the princess took to her bed, Conroy sent Clark back to London with the Belgian minister. When Clark returned, he was permitted to examine the princess only cursorily. Lehzen, nursing Victoria night and day and driven almost frantic with anxiety, tried to describe the princess's condition to Clark but was told by the duchess to shut her mouth. Then Lehzen was not allowed to know what Clark had diagnosed and prescribed.

At this point, the Duchess of Kent and Sir John Conroy were becoming desperate and willing to take risks. King William was a very sick man, and more and more people in government and court circles had begun to suspect that the Princess Victoria was living under duress. The English royal family and the extended Coburg family were now solidly lined up in opposition to Conroy. Some bold and decisive act was needed to protect Sir John's situation and prospects.

So, while the Princess Victoria was weak, feverish, and confined to bed, Conroy and the duchess tried to browbeat her into signing a document appointing Conroy as her personal private secretary in the event of her accession to the throne. Supported by Lehzen, Victoria found the strength to refuse. As she later told Lord Melbourne, "They [Mama and Conroy] attempted (for I was still very ill) to make me promise beforehand, which I resisted in spite of my illness, my beloved Lehzen supporting me alone."

After three days, when the princess was delirious with a very high fever and a racing pulse, it finally occurred to the duchess that Victoria might be in danger of dying. To risk killing the goose that laid the golden eggs was in no one's interests, so a local doctor was called in as discreetly as possible. He pronounced the princess's condition to be very grave, and Dr. Clark was recalled. Under his fatherly care, the princess slowly regained her health, remaining at Ramsgate for over five weeks.

Exactly what was wrong with the Princess Victoria in the fall of 1835 has been much discussed. It is possible that there was an element of youthful neuroticism in the illness, as Sir John and the duchess argued. However, Queen Victoria herself was told that she had typhoid, a life-threatening disease. Whatever the diagnosis, Victoria was clearly very ill, and Sir John Conroy and the Duchess of Kent were unprincipled to try to exploit her illness for political gain.

They had also badly miscalculated. Lehzen and Victoria were now openly united in opposition to the Kensington System, and they had found an ally in Clark. The princess knew that she was supported from afar by King Leopold and that, though increasingly debilitated, her uncle king was looking for ways to help her.

King Leopold and Baroness Lehzen were now in secret correspondence

Fearing for his niece's safety at the hands of the increasingly reckless Conroy, and convinced that his sister Victoire was under some kind of diabolical spell, Leopold had decided that the solution was to get his niece married as soon as possible. He had his candidate picked out: Albert, younger son of his elder brother, the Duke of Saxe-Coburg and Gotha. He wanted Lehzen to urge Victoria to become engaged immediately, even if marriage must wait until both partners were more mature.

"I talk to you at length and through you speak to Victoria," wrote King Leopold to Baroness Lehzen on May 1, 1836. "For years Victoria has unfortunately been treated as a mere matter for speculation . . . her youth as well as her future gave ample opportunities for a thousand avaricious schemes . . . Only two people cared for her for her own sake, that is, you, dear Lehzen and I . . . and because this was so we were systematically persecuted, for it was particularly feared that the child might grow fond of us, and find in us friends apart . . . The chief plan has been, since 1828, to drive you away. Had I not stood firm . . . you would have followed Späth . . . Had I not come to England last year, and had I not had the courage, in Ramsgate, to tear apart the whole web of intrigue, Clark would never have learned the true state of affairs, and God knows what would have become of the Princess . . . The Princess's 17th birthday marks an important stage in her life; only one more year and the possibility of a Regency vanishes like an evil cloud. This is the perfect time for us, who are loyal, to take thought for the future of the dear child."

King Leopold explained to Baroness Lehzen that Prince Albert, though very young, was the best royal marital prospect that Germany had to offer at that moment. Furthermore, he could personally attest that his nephew had the intelligence and education to serve as Victoria's adviser once she became Queen. Furthermore, Albert's "youth was the guarantee for his pure unspoilt nature."

If Leopold had hoped to find an easy tool for his purpose in Baroness Lehzen, he was wrong. Lehzen was no doubt dazzled by becoming suddenly the confidante of a king, but she too had her ambitions and her plans, and they did not coincide with Leopold's. On the issue of Victoria's imminent marriage, Lehzen for once was on the side of the duchess and Conroy. She saw Victoria as a second Queen Elizabeth, virgin and independent of male influence. She had no wish to see her darling princess married to a bossy young Coburg protégé of King Leopold and Baron Stockmar.

In any event, the Princess Victoria was charming to her cousin Albert when he came to England at the time of her seventeenth birthday. She thanked her uncle "for the prospect of great happiness you give me in the

person of Dear Albert." But she offered no immediate prospect of an engagement. Victoria did not believe that she needed a husband to protect her from her mother and Conroy. In a year, she would be eighteen and in a position to protect herself.

The Princess Victoria was still young, but she was not weak. As a small child, she had received a treasure of love and care, and somehow, through ten years of isolation and emotional deprivation, she made the store last. She watched the mother who had loved and protected her as a young child metamorphose into a wicked stepmother, intent on wealth, status, and power, but she did not stop loving and trusting.

At Conroy's hands she suffered, bowing her head and holding her tongue, but she translated the tyrant's lessons into survival tactics. When she heard the man who in private treated her like an imbecile proclaiming his devotion to her before large crowds, she silently but irrevocably condemned him as a hypocrite and a villain. Soon it would be her turn to speak and Conroy's to listen. Soon she would have power.

AFTER HER RETURN from Ramsgate, Victoria found life at Kensington Palace exceptionally dull and lugubrious. At least she occupied new, airy rooms that the duchess had commandeered against the King's strict instructions, and she had been prescribed lots of fresh air and few lessons by the amiable Clark.

Her mother was now in open combat with the King, as their dispute over the new suite of rooms at Kensington Palace indicated. In August the Duchess of Kent went further, refusing to accept the invitation to Queen Adelaide's birthday banquet. The duchess said she would come a few days later if she found it convenient. This act of breathtaking rudeness showed that Victoire Kent believed she could snub the King and Queen of England with impunity, since she herself would soon hold the reins of power.

The duchess did, however, go to Windsor on August 21, 1836, for the feast to celebrate the King's birthday, and she brought her daughter Victoria with her. When William IV rose to acknowledge the toast to his health, he turned to the Duchess of Kent, who was seated next to him, and launched into a furious diatribe that each of the hundred guests could hear.

"I trust in God that my life may be spared for nine months longer," the King roared, "after which period, in the event of my death, no Regency would take place. I should then have the satisfaction of leaving the royal authority to the personal exercise of that Young Lady, the Heiress Presumptive of the Crown, and not in the hands of the person now near me, who is surrounded by evil advisors and who is herself incompetent to act with propriety in the station in which she would be placed! I have no hesitation in saying that I have been insulted—grossly and continually insulted—by that person, but I am determined to endure no longer a course of behavior so disrespectful to me. Amongst many other things, I have particularly to complain of the manner in which that Young Lady has been kept away from my court."

The battle lines were now drawn between Windsor and Kensington, and for the next nine months, Victoria was kept under virtual house arrest. "The Monster and Demon Incarnate," as Victoria later referred to Conroy, still held sway at Kensington Palace, and the princess's life continued to be one of "great misery and oppression." Efforts made by the dying King and his ministers to intervene on her behalf were indignantly repelled by the duchess and Conroy. When a letter carrying the King's sign manual or seal came from William IV with orders that it be placed in the princess's hands alone, the duchess received the messenger with her daughter and took the letter from her. When the King received an answer, refusing his offers of a separate income and household, he declared, "Victoria has not written this." The King was right. The duchess and Conroy were now not only sequestering the princess but corresponding in her name and keeping crucial documents from her.

In the spring of 1837, as her eighteenth birthday approached and the state of the King's health declined, it was clear that Victoria would be queen within months. Consequently, the duchess and Conroy had to change their goals while adopting increasingly severe means. Victoria was subjected to remorseless pressure to agree to accept a regency until she was twenty-one and to appoint Sir John Conroy as her confidential private secretary. That position, which had been created to serve kings who were incapacitated, would allow Conroy to run the new queen's domestic life, control her revenues, and conduct the affairs of state for three years. The Duchess of Kent went about saying that her daughter lacked the intellectual capacity to reign alone. She claimed that Victoria herself was anxious for a regency to be appointed until she was twenty-one.

By this time, Baron Stockmar was in London at the behest of King Leopold and the Coburg family, talking to English ministers and the people surrounding the dying King as well as to the Kensington Palace set, and sending regular reports back to Germany and Belgium. Stockmar was the supreme diplomat and had long conducted the key business transactions of the Coburg family all over Europe. It was Stockmar in no small measure who had secured the kingdom of Belgium for Leopold and the Portuguese queen as a bride for Leopold's nephew, Ferdinand of Coburg-Kohary. Even the Duchess of Kent was not prepared to show this man the door, and so, hoping perhaps that he could resolve the impasse between Conroy and her daughter, she allowed Stockmar to speak to the Princess Victoria alone for the first time.

He was impressed by Victoria's self-possession and her fierce determination to keep the rights and privileges that would be hers as queen in her own hands. "Her feelings seem . . . to have been deeply wounded by what she calls 'his [Conroy's] impudent and insulting conduct' towards her," wrote Stockmar to King Leopold. "Her affection and esteem for her mother seem likewise to have suffered from Mama having tamely allowed Conroy to insult the Princess in her presence . . . O'Hum [Conroy] continues the system of intimidation with the genius of a madman, and the Duchess carries out all that she is instructed to do with admirable docility and perseverance . . . The Princess continues to refuse firmly to give her Mama her promise that she will make O'Hum her confidential advisor. Whether she will hold out, Heaven knows, for they plague her, every hour and every day."

Stockmar was unable to prevail on the duchess to change her course of action, and he and Conroy, who for years had maintained a facade of friendly relations, had a falling out. However, before he too was banished from Kensington Palace, Stockmar had succeeded in procuring Victoria a private interview with Lord Liverpool, a former Tory prime minister. This respected independent witness was able to inform the Melbourne government that the heir to the throne was not an imbecile. Despite everything her mother claimed on her behalf, she neither needed nor wanted a regency.

The duchess summoned from Germany her son, Charles Leiningen, to play the heavy brother and bring Victoria to heel. Charles Leiningen was dependent on his mother for money and status, and for some weeks he was firmly in the Conroy camp. However, Leiningen, who was neither stupid nor mean, balked when he heard Conroy say, "If the Princess Victoria will not listen to reason, she must be coerced." Charles Leiningen told his mother in German to do no such thing.

■

EARLY IN THE MORNING of Tuesday, June 20, 1837, the doorbell rang out repeatedly for admittance to Kensington Palace. When a porter finally appeared, he discovered that the insistent visitors were the Archbishop of

Canterbury and the Lord Chamberlain, who had ridden over as fast as they could from Windsor Castle. They demanded to see the Princess Victoria at once.

There was no doubt why the two men had come. The death of William IV had been expected for some days. All the same, the Duchess of Kent stalled for time, insisting her daughter could not be woken. Probably she wanted to send a messenger for Conroy, whose house was nearby. But the two men persisted, and the duchess was forced to give way. She went upstairs, woke Victoria, and bade her come down at once. The princess put on her dressing gown and, for the last time, held her mother's hand as she came down the staircase. Baroness Lehzen followed behind with smelling salts. At the door to the room where the two men were waiting, both the duchess and Lehzen fell back. Victoria went in and shut the door. Smelling salts would not be needed.

The first day of Queen Victoria's reign set a pattern. Having spent the last weeks locked in her room, taking her meals alone, she was suddenly the center of a whirlwind of activity and conducting business of every kind. She loved every minute of it. After the archbishop and the Lord Chamberlain had left, the Queen had her hair done and put on a black dress. She had breakfast and wrote letters—one to her uncle Leopold; one to her sister, Feodora, signed "your devoted and attached sister VR." At nine the prime minister came for the first meeting. The rapport was immediate. In Lord Melbourne Victoria knew at once that she had found a friend and protector.

At a quarter after eleven there was a meeting of the Privy Council, an advisory body chosen by the sovereign from among the princes of the blood (that is, the senior royal men), court officials, and current and former ministers of state. Then followed another meeting with the prime minister, then more meetings with officials and with relatives. The Queen lunched and wrote another letter, this time to her widowed aunt Adelaide, expressing her deep sorrow at the King's death and assuring the Queen dowager that she could remain at Windsor for as long as was convenient to her.

The Queen had several meetings with Stockmar that first day. Conroy was the subject of numerous discussions, and Victoria, though she refused to see either her mother or Sir John, was besieged by letters and notes from them. Conroy gave Stockmar a list of his demands to pass on to Melbourne: "a pension of 3,000 pounds a year, the Grand Cross of the Bath, a peerage and a seat on the Privy Council." Amazingly, Melbourne acceded to most of the demands. The Coburg family, as represented by Baron Stockmar, and the English government were, it seems, so anxious to avoid any scandal that they were willing to promise almost anything to the duchess's impudent and overbearing majordomo. Conroy would remain a thorn in Queen Victoria's flesh for many years to come.

Happy to leave the horrid task of negotiating with Conroy to Stockmar and Melbourne, Queen Victoria did what she could to form her household to her taste. She dismissed Sir John Conroy, though the man continued to be part of her mother's household. She rewarded her faithful friend James Clark by naming him chief physician in ordinary. She decided to move as soon as possible away from Kensington Palace and into Buckingham Palace, the royal residence in the heart of London that had been under construction for two reigns. In the meantime, she ordered a bedroom to be prepared and her things moved out of her mother's rooms.

She appointed Baroness Lehzen lady attendant on the queen, a new title that the two must have discussed carefully in their few private minutes. "My dear Lehzen will always be with me as my friend, but will take no situation with me, and I think she is right," Victoria wrote in her journal that night. Sadly, the time would come when Baroness Lehzen would regret that she had not taken a "situation" with the Queen, relying instead on love and loyalty.

Late that night, the Queen kissed her mother's cheek, walked upstairs unassisted, and went to bed. For the first time in eighteen years, mother and daughter would sleep apart. Upstairs Victoria completed her journal entry for that tremendous day—orderly, precise, cool except for the extravagant underlinings. Here at last we have the authentic, uncensored prose of the Queen, writing now not for her mother but for herself and for the historical record:

"Tuesday, 20th June.—I was awoke at 6 o'clock by Mamma who told me that the Archbishop of Canterbury and Lord Conyngham were here and wished to see me. I got out of bed and went into my sitting-room (only in my dressing-gown) and alone and saw them. Lord Conyngham (the Lord Chamberlain) then acquainted me that my poor Uncle, the King, was no more, and had expired at 12 minutes p. 2 this morning, and consequently I am Queen . . . At 9 came Lord Melbourne, whom I saw in my room, and OF COURSE quite ALONE as I shall always do all my Ministers."

By alone, Queen Victoria meant without her mother, Conroy, the Conroy family, and all the Conroy hangers-on like Lady Flora Hastings. But she spent no more time by herself after her accession than before. Even when the Queen was at her desk, absorbed in doing her business and writing her journal and her endless letters, there was always a maid of honor hovering in the background, a page in the hall, a dresser darning in a corner. Anxious at night, the Queen slept until her marriage with a maid one door away and Baroness Lehzen next door. At Buckingham Palace, the Queen ordered a hole to be made in one wall to allow her free communication at night with Lehzen in the adjoining room. Until the death of her husband, it is doubtful if ever in her life even for an hour Queen Victoria was alone in a room.

But if "alone" meant unique, one of a kind, Victoria was right to underline the word. To be a queen regnant was to be alone, and solitude would prove to be a heavy burden.

Victoria, Virgin Queen

...

W HEN VICTORIA CAME TO THE THRONE, SHE CAUSED A SENSATION. Many people had seen her, some had been presented to her, but no one knew the new Queen, least of all those who had lived with her all her life. In public Victoria's mother and Sir John Conroy had spoken for her, and in private they shouted at her, disparaged her, and refused to listen. In the final days before Victoria's accession, as part of their campaign to keep the power of the Crown in their own hands, Conroy and the duchess whispered to the world that the heiress presumptive did not have the intelligence to rule alone, and it is possible they actually believed it. After years of abuse, Victoria had learned to keep her thoughts to herself.

Then overnight, without rehearsal, Victoria stepped into the starring role of queen, and amazed everyone by her mastery of script and blocking. The prelates, ministers of the Crown, and court officials who came in the first days to "kiss hands" and swear allegiance were enraptured by the Queen's poise and her modest yet confident assumption of power. They remarked on her marked physical resemblance to her grandfather George III, the last king in memory to earn the people's respect. At last Victoria was permitted to speak for herself, and her glorious, bell-like, feminine voice—"a silver stream flowing over golden stones," in the words of the famous actress Ellen Terry—was accepted immediately as the voice of the nation.

When the Queen drove out in state to open parliament for the first time, ordinary folk lined the streets to catch a glimpse of her. The assembled lords and commons listened reverently as the tiny young woman in her ermine and diamonds, now romantically slender and pale after her long ordeal, gave the speech from the throne without a waver. When the Queen held her first official assemblies for male visitors, called levees, English notables and foreign diplomats attended in droves. In her journal Victoria proudly recorded that in one session three thousand men kissed her hand.

When the Queen announced that she intended to review the Household Cavalry on horseback as the young Queen Elizabeth had done, her mother was appalled, and the Duke of Wellington strongly advised against it. I know horses, pontificated the hero of Talavera and Waterloo, and no horse can be trusted to behave at a military parade with a woman in the saddle. But Victoria was not to be dissuaded. Perched sidesaddle on her great horse Leopold, dressed in a modified version of the Windsor uniform, the Star of the Order of the Garter on her breast, the Queen cantered up the lines and saluted the troops in perfect form. The massed bands played, the pride of England's army fired and skirmished and dashed feverishly to and fro, but the Queen had her horse under complete control. "I felt for the first time like a man, as if I could fight myself at the head of my troops," the Queen confided to her diary.

Victoria's coronation in June 1838 cost only seventy thousand pounds, a fraction of her uncle George IV's, but it was greeted with general rejoicing. The unprecedented crowds of people massed all along her route to and from Westminster Abbey made the Queen feel both proud and humble. When the crown was placed on her head, the Queen looked up into the gallery where her dearest friend, Baroness Lehzen, was sitting, and the two exchanged a smile. Together they had come through, and the victory was theirs. The Queen also found the presence of Lord Melbourne at her shoulder an immense comfort, although she worried that the ordeal of bearing the massive sword of state aloft during the processions would be too much for him. Suffering from an intestinal disorder, Melbourne had taken opium and brandy.

The coronation was a triumph for the young Queen, though not for the old men in charge of the arrangements. Both the Earl Marshall and the Archbishop of Canterbury had forgotten exactly what order the complicated ceremony should follow, didn't bother to look it up, and didn't believe in rehearsals. Rather to the Queen's surprise, wine and sandwiches were laid out on the altar of a side chapel for the principal performers, but apart from that, nothing much got organized. At the Queen's insistence, the massive state crown was made smaller and lighter to fit her head. She still got a headache when wearing it, but at least when peers lurched forward to touch the crown in their ritual sign of allegiance, they did not dislodge it from her head. When one old nobleman toppled backward down the stairs leading to the throne, the Queen charmingly came forward to offer him her hand. When the archbishop insisted on jamming onto her fourth finger the coronation ring that had been made for the pinky, she did not shriek or faint. The weighty orb and scepter were put into her hands far too early, but she managed not to drop them. She processed into and out of the abbey with grace and dignity despite the eight young lady trainbearers who kept getting their feet caught in their own trains.

When night fell, Victoria repaired to the Duchess of Kent's rooms at the far side of Buckingham Palace, not because she wished to talk over the events of that extraordinary day with her mother but to get a better view of the fireworks. The Queen assured Lord Melbourne that she was not at all tired, and she wrote in her diary a long, detailed monarch's-eye view of the coronation that is one of the most delightful documents in Victorian letters.

Charles Greville, the recording secretary to the Privy Council, who saw a good deal of Victoria in the months after her accession, noted in his diary how very much she was enjoying being Queen. "Everything is new and delightful to her. She is surrounded with the most exciting and interesting enjoyments; her occupations, her pleasures, her business, her Court, all present an unceasing round of gratifications. With all her prudence and discretion she has great animal spirits, and enters into the magnificent novelties of her position with the zest and curiosity of a child."

Though assailed by new challenges at every turn, Victoria felt happier and healthier than ever in her life before. To her half sister, Feodora, in Germany, she wrote on October 23, 1837: "I am quite another person since I came to the throne. I look and am so well. I have such a pleasant life, just the sort of life I like. I have a great deal of business to do, and all that does me a world of good." To her uncle King Leopold of the Belgians, she wrote how much she liked and trusted Lord Melbourne, adding: "I have seen almost all of my other Ministers, and do regular, hard, but to me *delightful,* work with them. It is to me the *greatest pleasure* to do my duty for my country and my people, and no fatigue, however great, will be burdensome to me if it is for the welfare of the nation."

Over the years, Leopold and Baron Stockmar had received extravagant expressions of girlish affection from Victoria, and they assumed that she would take her cues from them, especially in foreign policy. They soon learned their mistake. The new Queen was ready to take advice but had no intention of being anyone's puppet. When she smelled condescension or manipulation even from "Dearest Uncle," she said no with gracious aplomb. Once Victoria had been lonely and snubbed, but now, with such seasoned and deferential statesmen as Lord Melbourne and Lord Palmerston constantly at her elbow, she felt more than ready to take on the worlds of domestic politics and international diplomacy. The Queen not only held cabinet meetings with her ministers, she rode out in the afternoons with them on twenty-five-mile adventures that took her out of London, chatted vivaciously with them over dinner, and played her favorite parlor games with them.

•

IN HER PERSONAL finances, Queen Victoria was determined from the beginning not to repeat the mistakes of her uncle George IV. The Queen was not the richest woman in England. That honor belonged to Angela Burdett-Coutts, a multimillionairess who inherited the Coutts banking fortune from her mother. A number of Englishmen—the dukes of Devonshire and Westminster, to name only the most prominent—were many times richer than the Queen. Nonetheless, Victoria was a very wealthy woman, and, having escaped the greedy clutches of Sir John Conroy, she took on the management of her own money.

This was unusual. Law and custom increasingly excluded English women from the world of business. Having no head for figures was considered an asset in the female citizen. But Victoria had inherited some financial

Queen Victoria riding out between
Lord Melbourne and Lord John Russell

acumen from her paternal grandfather, George III, and her maternal grandmother, Duchess Augusta of Coburg. She was good at figures and diligent with paperwork. She had an exceptional memory; she was a shrewd judge of men even as a raw girl; she knew how to delegate; and she had an associate she trusted. Prime Minister Lord Melbourne offered advice to Her Majesty on her personal affairs when he was asked, but Victoria mainly relied on "dearest Daisy"—that is to say her former governess, Baroness Louise Lehzen. The lady in attendance on the Queen served not only as secretary in private correspondence, but also unofficially as the comptroller of Her Majesty's household.

In money matters, as in so much else, Louise Lehzen had an admirable influence on the young Victoria. Forced to work for her living since girlhood, paid a miserable wage by her employer, the Duchess of Kent, Lehzen had always been frugal, but she had her own code of honor. She was honest in her dealings, and she did not prize money and possessions for themselves. Even when Victoria became Queen, the baroness made no demands for status or fortune: for her it was enough to be an acknowledged power behind the throne and to live constantly in her darling's company. Unlike Sir John Conroy and his cronies during Victoria's minority, Lehzen has never been charged with keeping false accounts or misappropriating funds.

Lehzen understood basic economic precepts: live within one's income, keep an eye on the servants but pay their wages, check the tradesmen's bills but settle them quickly, add up the pounds, shillings, and pence every month. These were things Victoria's profligate German mother and debt-ridden English uncles could not teach her. The princess had a fierce love of honesty and truth and she loved and respected her governess; so the lessons fell on fertile soil.

In the days immediately after her accession, Victoria found herself very uncomfortably placed. Her mother had never allowed her any discretionary money, and the new Queen now found herself with vastly increased expenses, and her income from parliament had yet to be voted through. Coutts the banker obligingly loaned the Queen the money she needed to tide her over, and was both surprised and gratified when she paid it back as soon as her income from the civil list began to flow into her pocket.

Victoria than allocated fifty thousand pounds from her first year's privy purse to pay the debts that her father had contracted before her birth, which her mother had left outstanding. When the Duchess of Kent told people that she was responsible for the debt repayment, Victoria was privately furious but publicly silent. She sent some welcome money to poor relatives, notably her half sister, Feodora. She paid her personal servants generous wages and was a sympathetic and considerate mistress. She took time out of a busy life to scrutinize her milliner's bills.

Given their lack of experience in the world of business, and the complexity of the royal financial situation, Victoria and Lehzen together did an honorable and competent job. They had a sense of fiscal responsibility and a horror of debt. This in itself was a revolution in royal affairs.

IN HER SOCIAL LIFE, Queen Victoria kept close to the staid and virtuous model developed by her grandfather George III in his first years on the throne. She found her friends among the high aristocracy, as English kings always had, she took people very much as she found them, and had a strong appetite for fun, but she showed none of George IV's precocious taste for vice.

During the period between Victoria's accession and her marriage, Prime Minister Lord Melbourne was indisputably the person closest to the Queen. Such a close rapport between a monarch and a prime minister was not unprecedented, but it was rare. Melbourne saw the Queen almost every day, often several times a day at her urgent request, and there was a room reserved for him at Windsor Castle. Melbourne saw Victoria far more often and more often alone than did the Duchess of Kent, who, when she wished to speak to her daughter in private, was forced to request an appointment.

Melbourne could not have been more different from Sir John Conroy. He never shouted; he sought the Queen's company, encouraged her to talk, treasured her friendship, and was such a font of droll sayings and racy anecdotes that Victoria could hardly wait to commit them to her diary at the end of the evening. Melbourne slid effortlessly into the role of the doting father Victoria had never known. Within weeks of her accession, he was her dearest friend and indispensable companion as well as her chief adviser. King Leopold had fully expected to control his niece, both directly through his visits and letters, and indirectly by putting Baron Stockmar at the Queen's side. Leopold and Stockmar were great political strategists, but they had failed to appreciate how much influence a handsome, sympathetic man of the world could have over an inexperienced young woman.

Lord Palmerston, the foreign secretary, Melbourne's old friend and contemporary and a most charming man with women, was also a favorite with the Queen. Victoria happily deferred to Palmerston's vast diplomatic experience and allowed him not only to dictate her official communications with other European powers, but also to advise her in her private correspondence with her uncle Leopold.

In the evenings and at weekends when the Queen was, as it were, off duty, Melbourne, Palmerston, Melbourne's sister, Lady Emily Cowper, Lady Cowper's daughters, sons-in-law, and grandchildren, together with various members of the charming and rakish Paget clan, were key members of the Queen's domestic circle. The Pagets were relative newcomers to the English aristocracy and had risen in society in large part because they were handsome, energetic, and fun, and thus invaluable in relieving the tedium of court life, especially for the sovereign.

Virtually all the members of the Queen's inner set belonged to the Whig aristocracy, as Tory aristocrats were not slow to notice. Whigs and Tories were the two political parties who stood on each side of the aisle in parliament and had taken it in turns to rule England since the seventeenth century. As the nineteenth century progressed, the Whigs decided to call themselves Liberals and the Tories became known as Conservatives, but in the first years of Queen Victoria's reign, the difference between the two parties was economic and historical rather than ideological. The Whigs were more urban and cosmopolitan and drew more of their income from commerce and industry. Instrumental in securing the Crown of England for William and Mary in 1688, they had also been supportive of the switch from the Stuart to the Hanoverian dynasty. There was an element in the Whig Party, especially outside of parliament, that was enthusiastic about political and social reforms—expanding the franchise, allowing Catholics, dissenting Protestants, and Jews to take public office and attend the universities, regulating the savage labor practices in the industrial sector, and so on.

The Tories were identified with the interests of the landowners, and they were the party of the political diehards who hated all things foreign, including ideas, and hankered after the good old days when Charles I ruled England by divine right. However, the leaders of both Tory and Whig parties were part of the landed aristocracy, and virtually every member of the House of Commons as well as of the House of Lords was a landowner with a title in his family if not to his name. Together Whigs and Tories formed the small political oligarchy that ruled England, and the policies each government followed when it came to power related more to the exigencies of the moment than to fixed political principles. The parliamentary Whigs and Tories were united by one fundamental conviction: that it was their birthright to rule England.

In the English royal family it was traditional for the King to be a Tory and the Prince of Wales to be a Whig, but the choice of party was a matter of personal antagonism not political ideology. Of the seven sons of George III, five were Tories but two were Whigs, including Queen Victoria's dead father, the Duke of Kent. He had become affiliated with and supported by the Whigs in no small part because his brother Cumberland was affiliated with and supported by the Tories. The circle that had formed around the Duchess of Kent at Kensington Palace between her husband's death in 1819 and her daughter's accession in 1837 was also composed of Whigs, largely because George IV had turned Tory when he became king and William IV and his brother Cumberland had always been Tories, and the duchess hated her brothers-in-law.

The fact that, at the time Victoria came to the throne, the government was Whig under Lord Melbourne was largely a matter of luck. The Tories had ruled England almost continuously during the previous five decades, and Melbourne was a very reluctant prime minister. But luck, rather than her parents' affiliation with the Whig Party, proved definitive. The young Queen became a fervent Whig mostly because Lord Melbourne was a Whig, and Lehzen—who may actually have had some political ideas—was a Whig, and they were her closest and most trusted friends.

WHETHER WHIGS OR TORIES, the people who gathered around Victoria in the first three years of her reign were loyal servants of the English Crown and intensely protective of the young Queen herself. Those who had seen the damage done to English political institutions and English society by the madness of George III, the profligacy of George IV, and the stupidity of William IV knew that the monarchy must start a clean page if it was to survive. Observers at court such as Princess Lieven, wife to the Russian ambassador, and Charles Greville could see that Victoria was a hot-blooded Hanoverian like her father and also a woman who needed a man to lean on, just like her mother. Sensitive to the erotic undercurrents in the Queen's attachment to him, Lord Melbourne knew that his most important duty to the new monarch was to keep her virginal image intact until she married. His own conduct must be beyond reproach.

But Melbourne and the older members of the Whig set that clustered around Queen Victoria before her marriage were in no way prototypic examples of the sexual values we have come to call "Victorian." They had lived through the regency and the reign of George IV. Lord Conyngham, Victoria's first lord Chamberlain, the man who came to tell her that she was queen, was the son of George IV's last and most rapacious mistress. Conyngham installed his mistress as housekeeper at Buckingham Palace, and was observed embracing her. Reform was in the air in the English court, the sins of the past were being swept under the rug, but the new standards of housekeeping were still far from rigorous.

William Lamb, second Viscount Melbourne, had for thirty years led a life as tragic as it was dissolute, and his reform barely preceded Victoria's accession. It was thanks to the talents in salon and boudoir of his mother, Elizabeth Milbanke Lamb, that the Lamb family was raised to an English peerage. As the second Lord Melbourne once remarked, his mother was "a remarkable woman, a devoted mother, an excellent wife—but not chaste, not chaste." Elizabeth Milbanke Lamb's four younger children, including the future prime minister, were all considered far too intelligent and handsome to have been sired by her husband. The resemblance between the adult Lord Melbourne and his mother's intimate friend Lord Egremont was striking, and it was rumored that the Prince of Wales himself could be the father of the younger Lambs.

The young Lambs were brought up in the sexually anarchic set of the fifth Duke of Devonshire, his first wife, Georgiana, and his mistress (later second wife) Lady Elizabeth Foster, and their children and nieces and nephews. William Lamb knew Lady Caroline Ponsonby, Duchess Georgiana's niece, when they were children, fell in love with her, and married her. Both were brilliant, fascinating, neurotic adults who found promiscuity normal. He had a taste for sadomasochism, which she found difficult to satisfy. She liked to dress as a boy and took lovers, most famously Lord Byron. After the poet threw her over, Lady Caroline sent Byron a letter, enclosing a tuft of blood-stained pubic hair she had hacked off with a scissors. She went mad and had to be confined. Throughout his wife's short and tragic life, Melbourne remained kind and loving, but he took several mistresses, including (or so her husband claimed in court) the famous author and women's rights activist Lady Caroline Norton. After he reluctantly agreed to become prime minister, Melbourne was twice named in divorce proceedings, but since nothing could be proved against him in court, he managed to survive the scandal.

Lady Emily Lamb, Melbourne's sister, followed happily in the footsteps of their mother. She too married a rich, dull, complaisant husband, Peter, fifth Earl Cowper, gave him a legitimate heir, and then found her pleasure elsewhere. Lady Emily Cowper was part of the notorious set that surrounded George IV as prince regent. She was rumored to have had a series of lovers, including the prince regent himself (who reportedly had sired one of her brothers), though she was careful to ensure that there were no compromising documents. Her elder daughter, Minnie, was said to be the fruit of a long liaison with Lord Palmerston.

How much Queen Victoria knew of the past lives of her dear friends Lord Melbourne, Lord Palmerston, and Lady Emily Cowper is not known. Probably a highly sanitized version of their lives was told to her, in dribs and drabs, as needed. Lehzen, who was close to Lord Melbourne and had her ear to the ground for court gossip, probably knew a good deal. What she decided to pass on to her royal mistress in the dead of night as they talked through the hole connecting their bedrooms, we shall never know.

·

THE FIRST EIGHTEEN months of her reign were a triumph, but then Victoria began to feel the strain. The novelty of her situation had worn off. The company of men twice her age who were too gouty to dance and snored in concerts was no longer quite so much fun. A line of thousands of men waiting to kiss her hand became an ordeal. She felt exposed at court, the subject of endless gossip and nasty cartoons in the press. Of course, she had Lehzen, her oldest friend, her accomplice, her spy, and her amanuensis. Lehzen was essential. All the same, as a mere Hanoverian baroness with no official position, Lehzen had necessarily to remain in the shadows.

Victoria's mother should have been her daughter's protector and adviser but instead subjected the Queen to an unending stream of annoyance and criticism. The duchess would not dismiss Sir John Conroy from her service. She protected him fiercely, refusing point-blank to allow anyone to audit the financial records over which Sir John had long presided. She expected Victoria to pay her debts, which in the end amounted to some eighty thousand pounds, without any inquiry into their nature, and could see no way to manage on an income that Victoria had increased by eight thousand pounds a year.

It was, as Victoria recorded in her diary, "*torture!*" to be obliged to live with her mother. And yet, as an unmarried woman still legally underage, she could not live alone without causing a scandal. Leopold, Stockmar, and Melbourne were for once unanimous in opining that if Victoria moved her mother out of the palace, the monarchy could fall. So the Queen lodged her mother in apartments as far away from her own as possible and saw her only in public. This studied neglect only fueled the duchess's rage. What can you possibly have against dear Sir John, who is so completely devoted to me? asked the duchess. Take care you do not make Lord Melbourne King of England, warned the duchess. *Oliver Twist* by that vulgar Mr. Dickens is no reading for a young person, much less a queen, opined the duchess. It is quite unbecoming for a woman to take so much wine at dinner, snapped the duchess. If only you would do your duty by your family and the nation and marry your cousin Albert, sighed the duchess.

In 1839 Victoria made some important mistakes that left her tired and disillusioned. She allowed the rumor to circulate that the unmarried Lady Flora Hastings, whose abdomen was suspiciously swollen, was pregnant—perhaps by Sir John Conroy! Lady Flora had been no friend to the Queen in the Kensington Palace days, but medical examination proved that she was a virgin, and within months she died of liver cancer.

As the false pregnancy scandal was coming to a boil, the Queen also caused a constitutional crisis known as the Bedchamber Affair. Victoria took on the whole English political establishment by intransigently citing her royal prerogative to appoint or retain her ladies of the bedchamber, regardless of their political affiliations. She did so in order to keep Melbourne by her side as prime minister, and she succeeded. The leader of the Tory Party, Sir Robert Peel, a cold, silent, scholarly man the Queen could not bear, felt obliged to stay out of office. Melbourne's Whig government limped on. The newspapers were merciless in their critique of "Little Vic." She had grossly insulted Lady Flora, a blameless lady of high birth. She had dared to challenge the balance of power between the two political parties and to assert her right to the same royal power and privilege last enjoyed by George III. People no longer gathered to cheer the Queen in the streets. When she went to the races at Ascot, she was hissed by two ladies of the court, and cries of "Mrs. Melbourne" were heard.

By the summer of 1839, Victoria was confessing to Lord Melbourne that she felt bored and disinclined to work hard. Perhaps she was wrong to enjoy what she called "business." Melbourne agreed: "You lead rather an unnatural life for a young person; it's the life of a man." The arrival in London on a state visit of Grand Duke Alexander, the tall, handsome, attentive heir to the tsar, made it all too plain to the Queen, and indeed to the whole court, what she was missing in her life. But even as she was dancing till dawn and falling a little in love with the grand duke, domestic policy and international diplomacy were still of vital interest to her. As soon as some great issue was being debated in parliament, Victoria's passion for public affairs flared up, and she was awake until the small hours, writing letters and journal entries.

It was four and a half months after Victoria waved a tearful good-bye to her imperial Russian guest when Prince Albert appeared at Windsor Castle. This second time, the youth her whole family was crazy for her to marry turned out to be, *mirabile dictu,* the incarnation of her desire. Albert was so beautiful, and they had so much in common. He was so very tender and loving, and assured her that he had never loved any other woman. They would live happily ever after.

But even when she lost her heart, Victoria did not lose her head. Her happiness now depended on Albert, yet all the same she was determined to have him and everything else as well. She would rule England, manage an independent income of 385,000 pounds, hold sway at Windsor and Buckingham Palace, possess enough diamonds to cover her from head to toe, and enjoy her Prince Charming too. The marriage, as the Queen saw it, was to be on her terms, and Lord Melbourne reassured her it would be. Both, however, were deceiving themselves.

PART ONE

...

$\mathcal{T}$HE

YEARS APART

ALBERT

A Motherless Prince

BIOGRAPHICAL CAVEAT

*U*NTIL DIANA, PRINCESS OF WALES, CAME ALONG, FULL DISCLOSURE
and transparency were not to be expected from royal persons. Almost from
the cradle, princes and princesses realized just how interesting they were to
the world and became intent on controlling their legacy and swathing their
lives in the mystic aura of majesty. Members of royal families zealously built
up a trove of documentation for posterity and regularly purged it of items
they were unwilling to imagine in a memoir or a history book. When
Princess Beatrice, Queen Victoria's youngest daughter, produced a heavily
cut and censored transcript of the handwritten volumes of her dead
mother's journals, and then burned the originals, she was a case study in
this dual royal compulsion to keep and destroy records.

For Queen Victoria the record kept was so large, so detailed, and so frank
that censorship failed even in regard to the Queen's unhappy early years
over which the English royal family sought for two generations to draw a
veil. A clear, comprehensive, and nuanced account of Queen Victoria's
youth has become possible in the last half century and greatly enhances
the Queen's reputation. It humanizes Victoria when we know the challenges she faced as a girl. It adds to her stature when we learn of the abusive
collusion of her mother and Sir John Conroy. Unlike the Wizard of Oz, Victoria had nothing to fear if a little dog pulled the curtain back. Here in the
temple reserved for royalty was a formidable woman whom people idolized
whether she emerged in a diamond tiara or a poke bonnet.

Unfortunately, the same is not true for her husband. The deeper one
plumbs the biographical literature on Albert, prince consort, the more
likely it seems that the standard account of the prince's life before his mar-

riage is a myth that even the nineteenth century found hard to credit. Albert as child and youth remains a puzzle because only timid steps have been taken to move beyond the account left us by his first, best informed, most dedicated, and certainly most influential biographer: his wife, Victoria.

※

AFTER ALBERT'S DEATH, Victoria's mission was to inscribe Albert's name upon the world's consciousness and claim for him a place among the great of history. A full-scale biography of her husband was an obvious priority, and since the Queen liked order and chronology, the first biographical task she set herself was to recapture her husband's German years. She zealously collected every piece of paper relating to the prince consort that she could find at Windsor or could call in from Germany. She lovingly set down for the record little things that Albert himself had told her about his youth. She solicited the recollections of those who had known him then. She collaborated actively with Albert's private secretary, Charles Grey, in compiling and writing a book.

The resulting work, published in 1867, is usually known as *The Early Years of the Prince Consort* and attributed in bibliographies to General Sir Charles Grey. However, it is more useful and accurate to identify it as Queen Victoria's first major foray into print. The book is identified on its spine as Queen Victoria's Memoirs of the Prince Consort: His Early Years. The title page reads: The Early Years of His Royal Highness the Prince Consort compiled under the Direction of Her Majesty the Queen, by Lieut.-General the Hon. C. Grey. Queen Victoria's crest appears on the book's spine, and her 1867 signature, Victoria R, is written in gold on the cover.

Most of the information we have today about the prince consort's youth is derived from *Early Years*. The documentation it presents is invaluable. But, as the biographer of a German boy, Queen Victoria suffered from crippling handicaps.

In the first place, she did not know her husband as a boy and had few firsthand memories of him to share. In their first twenty years, Victoria and Albert saw each other only for a few brief, tense, and closely chaperoned weeks in 1836. The Queen was also singularly ill equipped to tell the story of a boy growing up in Germany. Until she was a grandmother she did not really know any boys, and she did not have an in-depth knowledge of Germany. She visited there for the first time in 1845, four years after her marriage, and, surrounded by German royalty and by some sixty-one of her Coburg relatives, she got a luxury tourist's view of the country.

Victoria assumed that Albert had given her an accurate picture of himself as a boy. In fact, though the prince consort often wept nostalgic tears for his lost German home, he was remarkably reticent about his life before coming to England. Whereas Victoria was committed to putting every detail of her life down on paper so she could relive it later, Albert was not. For a royal person, the autobiographical urge was, in fact, singularly absent in him. As an adult, he wrote volumes and volumes of memoranda as well as thousands of letters, but no memoir, not even an autobiographical sketch. His diary is resolutely impersonal. Even to his wife, Albert imparted only tiny shards of memory.

To supplement and give life to her account of her husband's youth, Queen Victoria turned to those who had known him. Certain people came forward, but more did not. In many ways, the most fascinating thing about *The Early Years of the Prince Consort* is identifying those who either chose not to collaborate with the royal biographer or, conceivably, were not asked. The most deafening silence comes from the prince's brother, Ernest, the man who, Albert once wrote, spent not even one night apart from him in his first nineteen years. *Early Years* contains no reminiscences and only one letter from Duke Ernest—written to Queen Victoria just before her wedding and thus in her possession—and a handful of letters from Albert to Ernest for which the prince had presumably kept copies. The regular correspondence between the two brothers that began in the fall of 1839 and ended only with the prince's death was not made available to the Queen, to Charles Grey, or to Theodore Martin, the man commissioned to write up the prince's years in England.

The male friends from Albert's childhood and youth who contributed to the Queen's volume were those willing to substantiate its author's exalted opinion of her husband. These German men grieved for Albert, their lost friend or kinsman. They had an interest in promoting the fortunes of the Saxe-Coburg family. They understood Queen Victoria's power and knew how fiercely loyal she was to friends. What sense did it make to challenge the preconceptions and shade the sunny vision of the most important woman in Europe?

But the Queen's golden legend of her husband was severely tailored not only to her needs but to Albert's own neuroses, and in the end it served him badly. Behind the gilt and incense, the real Albert Coburg was far more complicated and interesting than the man portrayed in his wife's adoring book.

■

THE KEY TO PRINCE ALBERT's life lay, in fact, in the duchy of Coburg and the history of the Saxe-Coburg family, just as Queen Victoria suspected. But it was the key to a coded text that was intentionally kept hidden. What Duke Ernest II, King Leopold, Baron Stockmar, and the other men who had been close to Albert in youth wanted to conceal, what Albert himself wished to forget, was that in his Coburg years, he hated Coburg and all it stood for. Far from the fairy-tale kingdom the Queen saw on her visits, Coburg-Gotha throughout the prince's lifetime and beyond was a tiny, poor, feudal polity ruled by licentious, frivolous, self-absorbed, debt-ridden dukes: Albert's father and brother. Albert came to England determined to shake off the evils of the past, start from scratch, and realize his own idyll of the King. Hence he boarded up the door to his past.

Only when we have understood the real Coburg and seen how radically Albert reacted against it can we appreciate all that was odd, visionary, and remarkable in the achievements of Albert as prince consort. Only once we have taken into account the unremitting stress that reaction imposed on him can we explain his weaknesses. Only once we have comprehended how far, despite himself, his acts and attitudes were shaped by the family and the society he grew up in can we evaluate his successes and failings as a husband, a father, and a statesman.

8.

The Coburg Legacy

"Ich werde neben unermüdlichem Streben und Arbeiten für das Land, dem ich im Zukunft angehören soll, und wo ich zu einer hoher Stellung berufen bin, nicht aushören, ein treuer Deutscher, Koburger, Gothaner zu sein."

"I shall, while tirelessly striving and working for the country to which I shall henceforth belong and where I am called to a higher station, never cease to be a true German, a true Coburg and Gotha man."

—Prince Albert, writing to his stepgrandmother, November 28, 1839, two months before his wedding

...

ERMANY TO ALBERT WAS THE *VATERLAND*. THIS IS HOW HE REFERS to it consistently in his private letters. But the German fatherland to which Prince Albert of Saxe-Coburg belonged as a child was only a mental construct, a glorious memory or a pious hope, not a geographical and political entity.

Germany had once been the Holy Roman Empire, but by the mid-seventeenth century that empire had become a fraying patchwork of sovereign states ruled by kings, princes, archdukes, dukes, electors, margraves, landgraves, archbishops, bishops, and so forth. Some German nation states were smaller than Liechtenstein (sixty-one square miles) is today, and most were poor, rural, and sparsely populated. Industrialization came late to Germany, and commerce was difficult in a region so fragmented. By 1800, many English factory owners and Dutch merchants enjoyed fabulous wealth, while German rulers held court in moth-eaten velvet, feeding their families on credit.

The German states varied considerably in size, but they had one thing in common. All their rulers were men. According to the ancient Salic law that prevailed in Germany into modern times, no woman, whether single or married, could directly inherit the money, real estate, or titles owned by her family, though her husband or son could, for example, inherit from her father or uncle. As a result of this legal structure, based on the largely mythical code of an ancient German tribe, women had few opportunities to enter the public sphere and show mastery. Queen Victoria, as we have seen, could inherit the kingdom of Great Britain and Ireland from her childless uncles, but not the kingdom of Hanover in Germany. There Salic law was in force, and the kingdom passed from William IV to his next oldest brother, the Duke of Cumberland.

One result of Salic law was that German misogyny was of a deeper dye than its English counterpart. England in the seventeenth century had produced Queen Elizabeth, the greatest ruler in its history, and in the nineteenth it allowed Angela Burdett-Coutts to inherit one of the great banking fortunes from her mother. Part of the contempt for women that we shall find Prince Albert expressing throughout his life was due to the fact that he was a member of the atavistically sexist German aristocracy.

Each German ruler was absolute lord in his own slice of territory and presided with due pomp over his own court. Political rights and civic participation varied from one German state to another, and in the larger German towns there were flourishing commercial and professional families, Jewish as well as Christian. Around the turn of the eighteenth and nineteenth centuries, this class produced many of the geniuses of Germany's golden age: among them, Goethe, Beethoven, and Kant. It would also produce Karl Marx. However, throughout the nineteenth century, political power remained in the hands of hereditary rulers, and government for the most part was the jealously guarded preserve of the landed aristocracy.

German rulers during Albert's youth were feudal in their outlook and repressive in their methods. They viewed their states as private property, personal fiefs. They took their rank and their name from those fiefs, but they were constantly looking to trade up. They showed little of that primal loyalty to the land that right-wing philosophers from Herder to Heidegger have extolled as peculiarly German.

Coburg, the state where Prince Albert was born, offers a case study in these attitudes. At the time of his birth, Coburg was a tiny national entity— two hundred square miles or so, with a population of some forty thousand.

The primary identification of Duke Ernest, Albert's father, was not with Germany, which did not really exist. It was not even with Coburg, though this was where he spent much of his time. It was with the international royal caste. What mattered to him was not the good opinion of the people in his fief but his reputation in the courts of greater monarchs. To hold his own with his fellow princes meant getting as much as possible out of his estates and giving as little as possible back. It meant squeezing the peasantry, not sending them to school. It meant grandiose building projects, so that there should be a palace and an opera house and a magnificent park to impress visiting grandees, even if that meant destroying humbler dwellings. When Coburgers and Gothaners, fired by the ideals of the French Revolution, began to question his corrupt administration and exploitative fiscal policies, Duke Ernest I changed his rhetoric to suit the times but also used tax revenues to purchase personal fiefdoms. There he could continue to rule autocratically, as his personal acquaintance the tsar did in Russia.

Coburg was a top-heavy society with a disproportionately large court and administration surrounding the duke and his family. Rewards even at the top were meager, and graft, bribery, influence peddling, and chicanery were endemic. Middle-class families competed to win the duke's favor only to find, as we shall see in the case of the Stockmars and the Bauers, that the price of favor was very high.

Lower down the social scale, people paid heavy taxes, had few property rights, and no access to an independent judiciary. The Coburg men were expected to provide labor in the homes or on the estates of their lord, and they were also expected to fight his battles. When Duke Ernest II was an enemy of the invading Napoleon, Coburg men fought the French, to no avail. Ten years later, when the duke found it advantageous to be the ally of Napoleon, Coburg men were rounded up, conscripted into the French army, and sent off to fight in Russia, whence few of them returned. Coburg women were still subject to the droit du seigneur, and, as we shall see in the case of Caroline Bauer, for fatherless women becoming the mistress of a duke or prince was the best available career option.

The ancient medieval town of Coburg, with its seven thousand or so inhabitants, was the Duke of Saxe-Coburg and Saalfeld's capital, but he didn't think much of it. Ernest I, Albert's father, tried by every means open to him to persuade the Emperor Napoleon to give him Bayreuth. He planned to transfer his capital, his principal residence, and his court to that marvelous Bavarian city. Only when the mirage of Bayreuth finally faded did Duke Ernest plunge massively into debt in order to renovate the Ehrenburg Palace and update the center of Coburg. After the war, as we shall see, Duke Ernest I gave up Saalfeld for Gotha, happy to change his name accordingly.

The political rhetoric of the Saxe-Coburg family changed markedly once Prince Leopold had established links with Great Britain that his nephew Albert would build upon. In extremely reactionary circles in nineteenth-century Germany and Austria, Coburg became a code adjective for a person seeking democratic reform and constitutional monarchy along the British and Belgian models. It is clear from his memoirs that Duke Ernest II, Albert's older brother, saw himself as a prophet of enlightenment. However, it is far from clear how much changed in Coburg or even in Gotha, where the populace seems to have been more politically motivated and less personally reliant on the ducal family. In his personal administration and style of governance, Duke Ernest II followed the model set down by his father as far as circumstances would allow.

Prince Albert left Germany when he was twenty and cannot be held responsible for his father's and brother's administrations. However, he certainly knew what was going on in Coburg and Gotha. Duke Ernest I and Duke Ernest II were always in debt, constantly pestering their English relatives for financial assistance. Albert, liberal with his advice but grudging with his wife's money, had a negligible influence on affairs back home. There is little indication, at least in his published letters, that he had any more concern for the welfare of Coburgers and Gothaners than did his father and brother. What concerned him were his family's solvency, property rights, and territorial claims. Ideologically committed to the unification of Germany, Prince Albert was still desperate to ensure that the duchies of Saxe-Coburg and Gotha remained sovereign states, since his second son, Alfred, had been designated to succeed his brother as duke.

POOR AND UNIMPORTANT in the eyes of the world, the German royal families in the eighteenth and early nineteenth centuries were at their historical nadir. However, they had one precious asset: their children. Since there were many German rulers, there were many royal German children, and there was a steady market for those children in the courts of the greater nations. The kings of Russia, Austria, France, Spain, England, and Portugal needed wives of a rank equal to their own. Since no lady in those countries, however rich and ancient her family, could be of equal rank to her sovereign, a king needed to find a foreign princess as a bride. After the seventeenth century, an astonishing number of the queen consorts of the great nations were born German princesses.

These immigrant ladies were a source of prestige in their native land, and they sent money home. They invited their German relations to coronations and royal marriages, paid their traveling expenses, and entertained them magnificently. They helped to arrange the marriages of their German menfolk to neglected princesses in their adopted countries. When George IV married his German first cousin, Caroline of Brunswick, his sister Charlotte married the heir to the king of Württemberg. Charlotte took her dowry and her parliamentary annuity to Germany with her and for decades kept the kingdom of Württemberg afloat for her husband and stepson.

Since they counted upon marriage to shore up their finances, German royal houses were obsessed with matters of rank, privilege, etiquette, and genealogy. It is no accident that the *Almanach de Gotha*, listing and ranking the members of the top European royal and noble houses, was compiled and printed in Germany and was heavily slanted toward German families. Entering the marriage market, a princely German father needed to advertise his products and identify the competition.

Germany scored two particularly fabulous dynastic successes in the eighteenth century. First, in 1714, to the envy of his peers, the Elector of Hanover was called over by the English political oligarchy to take the throne. The Hanoverian ruler was chosen to be George I, King of Great Britain and Ireland, because he was a Protestant and because his maternal grandfather had had the foresight to marry Elizabeth Stuart, daughter of King James I. Second, tiny Anhalt-Zerbst married one of its princesses to the heir to the Russian throne. He was mentally deficient, and a coup d'état in 1762 made his wife empress of all the Russias. The Princess of Anhalt-Zerbst is known to history as Catherine the Great.

The Wettin family of Saxony in central Germany was also well placed to produce royal brides. During the Protestant Reformation in the fifteenth century, the Wettins had split into two unequal branches. To its eternal humiliation, the senior, or Ernestine, branch had been forced by fortunes of war to accept the minor territory of Thuringia, while the junior, or Albertine, branch retained the ancestral Saxony, with its capital of Dresden and the title of elector (after 1815, king). In the course of two centuries, little Thuringia split further into five duchies: Saxe-Gotha-Altenburg, Saxe-Meiningen, Saxe-Hildburghausen, Saxe-Weimar-Eisenach, and Saxe-Coburg-Saalfeld. The total population in the Ernestine duchies was about three hundred thousand, and the five ducal families were constantly intermarrying and sparring with one another for territory.

Over several generations, the Wettin dukes of Thuringia married into the English royal family. The Duke of Saxe-Gotha managed to marry his daughter Augusta to Frederick, the eldest son of King George II of England. Frederick died young, but Augusta had at least the satisfaction of seeing her eldest son succeed his grandfather as George III. In 1817 the Duke of Saxe-Meiningen married his eldest daughter Adelaide to the Duke of Clarence, later King William IV.

However, by the late eighteenth century, it was becoming apparent to all the Wettins that the ducal family to beat was the Saxe-Coburgs. Coburg was perhaps the smallest and poorest of the duchies, but, with his second wife, Augusta of Reuss-Ebersdorff, the unremarkable Duke Francis produced seven remarkable children. The four girls, Sophie, Antoinette, Juliana, and Victoire, were attractive, biddable, and, as it proved, fertile. The three boys, Ernest, Ferdinand, and Leopold, were Adonises, and the two younger ones had inherited their mother's brains as well as their father's looks.

The Coburg children grew up in the hard days of the Napoleonic wars. For more than twenty years, Coburg stood in the path of armies from France, Austria, Russia, and Prussia. Coburg men were pressed into service in one army or another, and rural Coburg was ruined by double taxation and the insatiable demands of the military for food, shelter, and forage. Members of the ruling family were forced to flee for their lives on more than one occasion, and survival mattered more than pride. Duke Francis died in 1806, and from this point, the fate of the Coburg family rested in the hands of the formidable dowager Duchess Augusta, the vain and vacillating new Duke Ernest, and Ernest's youngest brother, the brilliant and resourceful Prince Leopold.

War for a poor German peasant has usually meant death and destitution, as Bertolt Brecht shows in his play *Mother Courage and Her Children*. But for a man of the ruling class, war was a time of opportunity. The army was the only career option open to poor young men of the high German Protestant aristocracy, and for centuries Germany had trained Europe's officers and supplied mercenaries to the world. The three Coburg brothers, Ernest, Ferdinand, and Leopold, understood that the Napoleonic conflict could be their chance to find fame, status, and money if they could only gain the ear of those in power. Thanks to their elder sisters, Sophie, Juliana, and Antoinette, they did.

In 1795 Empress Catherine of Russia, formerly Princess of Anhalt-Zerbst, summoned to Saint Petersburg the three elder Saxe-Coburg-Saalfeld daughters and their mother. The empress intended to choose one of the three girls as bride for her sixteen-year-old grandson, Grand Duke Constantine. He was already making a strong bid to become the Caligula of his generation, and, as the owner of many serfs and the commander of a regiment,

THREE GENERATIONS OF THE *Coburg Family*

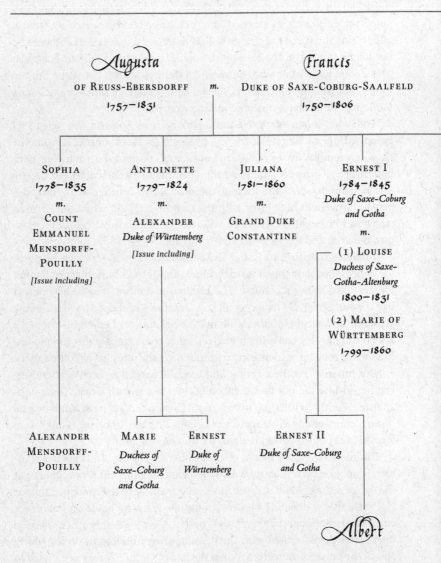

Augusta
OF REUSS-EBERSDORFF
1757–1831

m.

Francis
DUKE OF SAXE-COBURG-SAALFELD
1750–1806

SOPHIA
1778–1835

m.

**COUNT
EMMANUEL
MENSDORFF-
POUILLY**

[Issue including]

ANTOINETTE
1779–1824

m.

ALEXANDER
Duke of Württemberg

[Issue including]

JULIANA
1781–1860

m.

**GRAND DUKE
CONSTANTINE**

ERNEST I
1784–1845
*Duke of Saxe-Coburg
and Gotha*

m.

(1) **LOUISE**
*Duchess of Saxe-
Gotha-Altenburg*
1800–1831

(2) **MARIE OF
WÜRTTEMBERG**
1799–1860

**ALEXANDER
MENSDORFF-
POUILLY**

MARIE
*Duchess of
Saxe-Coburg
and Gotha*

ERNEST
*Duke of
Württemberg*

ERNEST II
*Duke of Saxe-Coburg
and Gotha*

Albert

had opportunities to inflict pain that would have aroused the envy of his contemporary the Marquis de Sade. None of this mattered to the Coburg family, fighting for survival in a war zone.

The Coburg girls were beautiful, but their shabby dresses and pathetic jewelry raised titters at the magnificent Russian court. Constantine dismissed all three girls as apes. But Catherine was determined to get her dissipated young grandson married, and one day she was watching from a window as the three Coburg girls alighted from a coach. Encumbered by her long court train, the eldest girl, Sophie, tripped and fell out headfirst. The second girl, Antoinette, sprawled on the dirt next to her sister, but the third, little Juliana, fourteen, hopped down nimbly. "That's the one," said Catherine, and Constantine and Juliana were married.

Following Juliana's success in Russia, Duchess Augusta was able to secure the Duke of Württemberg as a husband for her daughter Antoinette. He was a repulsively ugly glutton, but he was connected by marriage with both the English and Russian royal families and so a great catch. Antoinette and her family spent the turn of the nineteenth century at the Russian court and were in high favor with the tsar. As a result, when the German states were reorganized in 1815, Württemberg, along with Prussia, Saxony, Bavaria, and Hanover, became a kingdom.

Juliana's marriage to Grand Duke Constantine was short and hellish. Caroline Bauer, who was close to the ducal family in Coburg throughout her life, recorded in her memoirs: "The brutal Constantine treated his consort like a slave. So far did he forget all good manners and decency that, in the presence of his rough officers, he made demands on her, as his property, which will hardly bear being hinted of." After some eight years, Juliana fled Russia and took up residence in Switzerland, on the margins of polite society.

But Juliana's brothers Ernest and Leopold, as well as her Württemberg brother-in-law, did not find it difficult to get along with Grand Duke Constantine. For them Juliana's marriage was a fabulous success. Intimate and lasting connections with members of the Russian imperial family were formed and yielded golden rewards for the Coburg family.

Thanks to the good offices of his brother-in-law Grand Duke Constantine, Leopold of Saxe-Coburg was made a captain in an infantry regiment at the age of six, a colonel at seven, and, after transfer to the more prestigious Horse Guards, a general at twelve. In his late teens he made an important career in the Russian cavalry. Duke Ernest, Juliana's eldest brother, was also intermittently associated with the Russian army and fought on the losing side at the battle of Austerlitz. When the fate of Germany was negotiated in Vienna at the end of the Napoleonic wars, tiny Saxe-Coburg-Saalfeld man-

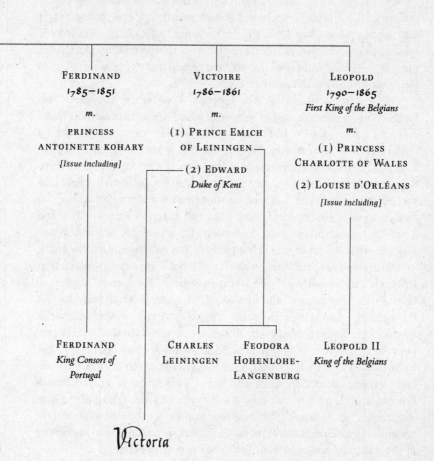

FERDINAND
1785–1851

m.

PRINCESS
ANTOINETTE KOHARY

[Issue including]

VICTOIRE
1786–1861

m.

(1) PRINCE EMICH
OF LEININGEN

(2) EDWARD
Duke of Kent

LEOPOLD
1790–1865
First King of the Belgians

m.

(1) PRINCESS
CHARLOTTE OF WALES

(2) LOUISE D'ORLÉANS

[Issue including]

FERDINAND
*King Consort of
Portugal*

CHARLES
LEININGEN

FEODORA
HOHENLOHE-
LANGENBURG

LEOPOLD II
King of the Belgians

Victoria

aged, thanks to the close ties forged between the ducal family and the imperial family of Russia, to retain its status as one of the thirty-nine sovereign states in the new German federation.

Sophie Coburg, the eldest sister, was instrumental in the rapid rise of Ferdinand, her middle brother. Sophie held off from marriage until her twenties and then married a French émigré soldier, Emmanuel de Pouilly (later Mensdorff-Pouilly). This was apparently a love match, but it too proved to be dynastic magic. Emmanuel de Pouilly was an extraordinary man, a great soldier, and the implacable enemy of Republican France. He placed his sword at the service of the Austrian emperor and proved to be a great war commander. De Pouilly was largely responsible for convincing the Coburg family to finally take a stand on its aristocratic feudal principles and take arms against Napoleon. Prince Ferdinand of Coburg followed his brother-in-law into the Austrian army, where both won military glory. After the war, de Pouilly was raised in rank, and he and his sons became pillars of the Austrian army and diplomatic corps.

Prince Ferdinand and Prince Leopold, if not their braggart older brother, Duke Ernest, proved to be good at war. They were personally brave and good leaders of men. But military success was not enough, since army officers spent far more money than they earned. Marriage to an heiress, not war, was the road to advancement for the sons of a minor duchy. All three Coburg brothers needed to translate their prowess on the battlefield into success in the ballroom. Ladies could not resist a uniform, and, once the battle was won, medals for bravery and royal orders of Emperor This and Saint That were the essential decorations for a perfectly tailored, waist-hugging red jacket worn over skin-tight breeches and shining leather boots.

Having moved to the Russian court and lobbied vigorously, Duke Ernest was for a time betrothed to the youngest sister of his friend Grand Duke Constantine and thus of the new Tsar Alexander I. That marriage fell through, for reasons explored below. Prince Ferdinand was smarter or at least luckier. Well regarded at the Austrian court, he won the hand of perhaps the richest heiress in Hungary, Princess Antoinette Kohary. With her he founded a new dynasty that ruled for generations in Portugal and established numerous close links with the Orléans family of France. Prince Leopold was the most successful of all. As we have seen, as part of the Russian delegation, he brought his medals to London for the Waterloo celebrations, won the hand of the Princess Charlotte, second in line to the throne of Great Britain, and eventually became king of the Belgians.

The Napoleonic armies brought revolution and democratic ideas to Germany, and these had great influence upon the German commercial and professional classes. However, once the wars were over, and the reorganization of the German states had been enforced by the victorious Great Powers, the surviving German rulers were determined above all to set the clock back and regain their grip on power. It was in this reactionary atmosphere that Prince Albert grew up.

FOR GENERATIONS THE Coburg men married for money, status, and power. For lasting dynastic success, they had to be prolific sires, and they were careful of the company their wives kept. However, only in the case of Prince Albert did the Coburg family consider it important for its males to be chaste. Quite the contrary. The tall, handsome Coburg dynasts believed that, when it came to the family business of sex and reproduction, practice makes perfect. They had strong libidos and took full advantage of the droit du seigneur at home and of their sexual opportunities when abroad. Duke Francis of Saxe-Coburg, Albert's paternal grandfather, was a notorious womanizer, and his successors, Duke Ernest I, Albert's father, and Duke Ernest II, Albert's brother, followed closely in his footsteps.

The sexual mores that prevailed in the Saxe-Coburg family during Prince Albert's childhood were vividly described by two discarded mistresses, Pauline Panam and Caroline Bauer. To get a sense of the ducal court in which Prince Albert was raised and how extraordinarily it differed from the court he established in England after his marriage to Queen Victoria, one needs to read the sensational memoirs of Panam and Bauer.

Pauline Panam was a fatherless French girl of Greek mercantile extraction and exotic beauty. By her account, Duke Ernest seduced her in Paris when she was fourteen. In 1808, at her lover's urgent behest, Panam made the journey from Paris to Coburg. She was told that she would be a lady-in-waiting to the duke's mother. Panam's only companion on her long and arduous journey into southern Germany was her little niece. In obedience to instructions given by the duke, who did not want to pay for a male escort, the two young girls were dressed as boys. When Panam's hat fell off en route, loosing her glossy black hair, the male travelers became importunate, and the girls became very anxious to reach their destination. But as Panam finally drove through the dingy, silent streets of Coburg at night, her relief turned to shock and dismay. Schloss Ehrenburg, Duke Ernest's medieval town residence, looked like some grotesque, smoke-blackened stable yard to the young Parisian who had seen Versailles and the Louvre. As the girls stood gazing disconsolately up at the palace's arrow slits, two fat rats came scuttling out of the building and ran between their legs.

Panam was not allowed into the palace but was whisked off to a secluded farm by one of the duke's loutish henchmen. There for some weeks she remained, still disguised as a boy. She cut a gallant figure and, to her amusement and the duke's titillation, attracted the amorous advances of several peasant girls. Even after Panam insisted on putting on women's dress and making herself known in Coburg as the duke's mistress, she was still forced to live in hiding. Panam was never privileged to enter the fabulous Hall of Giants inside the palace or see the fairy-tale glory of Schloss Ehrenburg when it was lit up with thousands of lamps and candles for a ducal celebration. On one occasion, she was summoned for a night rendezvous with her lover at Schloss Rosenau, his favorite retreat. After a long walk in a violent rainstorm that soaked her to the skin, Panam waited outside the house alone for hours. Finally she was obliged to climb up a ladder to the duke's window and, when this proved too short, to scramble onto a chair he lowered for her from his bedroom.

Panam became pregnant by the duke and was sent to Amorbach, the home of her lover's sister Victoire of Leiningen (the future Duchess of Kent and mother to Queen Victoria), to have her baby. After being housed in a cowshed and treated like a scullery maid, Panam fled back to Coburg with her baby son, demanding her rights and threatening to reveal all to anyone who would listen. She and Duke Ernest continued to have sexual relations on and off for a number of years, and he seems to have loved her as well as lusted after her. However, in financial matters, Panam had to deal with the duke's mother, Duchess Augusta, and his brother Leopold. Augusta had probably faced problem women like Panam during the reign of the late unlamented Duke Francis, and, though she made promises to Panam, these were never made good.

Duchess Augusta, as grandmamma to both Queen Victoria and Prince Albert, has received very good press from English royal historians. Her great-grandchild Princess Beatrice loyally translated and published excerpts from Augusta's wartime diary. In her letters to Pauline Panam, however, Duchess Augusta emerges as a cynical intriguer straight out of that late-eighteenth-century fictional sensation *Dangerous Liaisons*. As for Leopold, Panam claims that he tried to rape her one day early in her pregnancy. Grand Duke Constantine, Duke Ernest's brother-in-law, befriended Panam, but also wanted her for his mistress. Panam says the Coburg family tried to have her assassinated on several occasions and to kidnap her son, whom she had stubbornly insisted on naming Ernest.

On one occasion Duke Ernest was furiously angry when Panam threw a small coin to a blind beggar. She took him for a miser, when, in fact, he was just perennially short of cash. As Grand Duke Constantine once sneered to Panam, Duke Ernest was lord over six peasants and two village surgeons. The Saxe-Coburgs had palaces and courtiers and magnificent connections but less disposable income than Panam's dead father.

Despite all her tears and pleading and threats, Panam never received the annuity that Leopold and Duchess Augusta promised. However, she survived, and she got her revenge by publishing her memoirs in Paris. The dramatic story of her liaison with Duke Ernest was substantiated by transcripts of letters that Panam had exchanged with different members of the Coburg family. The book was a bitter wound to Saxe-Coburg pride. The fact that Duke Ernest had seduced a fourteen-year-old girl was of no great consequence—such behavior was commonplace in the aristocracy. But the Coburgs' own letters and Panam's long campaign of revenge against them showed that the family was too weak, too poor, or too mean to get an annoying girl out of the way and silence her. It was probably the furor aroused by Panam's book that destroyed Duke Ernest's chance of marrying the tsar's sister and thus equaling the marital successes of his two brothers.

Caroline Bauer was a native Coburger, and she could have explained to Pauline Panam why in sixteen years she never saw the very modest sums of money Duke Ernest promised her. Even before the Napoleonic campaigns ravaged central Germany in the early 1800s, the Saxe-Coburg family was in bankruptcy. Duke Ernest's grandmother, Sophie Antoinette of Brunswick, had tried to live like her sisters, who married the kings of Prussia and Denmark, and she had quickly run through the Coburg family fortune. Duke Ernest's father, Duke Francis, who reigned for only six years, inherited a total annual income for the duchy of 86,000 talers and debts of over a million.

To eke out the meager allowance of 12,000 talers allotted by his creditors, Duke Francis borrowed from his wealthier subjects, including Caroline Bauer's own maternal grandfather, Ernest Frederick Stockmar. This wealthy merchant and court official in Coburg was ruined as a result of loaning his ducal employer 17,000 talers. The money was never returned, and not a penny was paid in interest. However, the ducal Coburgs acknowledged their debt to the now impoverished Stockmars in devious ways.

Christian Stockmar, a man we have come across again and again in our story so far, was the oldest son of Ernest Frederick Stockmar. After his father was ruined, Christian Stockmar was obliged to begin life as a humble army doctor, but then he had a stroke of luck. He attracted the attention of Prince Leopold, younger brother of Ernest, the new Duke of Saxe-Coburg. He became first Leopold's doctor and then his agent, counselor, and man of business. As we have seen, Stockmar moved to England when Leopold married

Princess Charlotte. He became Charlotte's beloved friend but refused to intervene in her pregnancy even though he believed that her doctors were ruining her health and endangering her unborn child. Christian Stockmar was holding Princess Charlotte's hand as she hemorrhaged to death after childbirth.

After Charlotte's death, Leopold and Stockmar became even closer. Stockmar proved an exceptionally able and devoted servant, and he was careful to make few demands on his notoriously stingy employer. Stockmar understood that it was in his interests to acquire an independent source of income, and in 1821 he married his rich and disagreeable cousin Fanny Sommer and sired three children. Busy with the affairs of his demanding patrons—first Leopold and Ferdinand, and then Queen Victoria and Prince Albert—Christian Stockmar returned to Coburg only for brief visits.

Caroline Bauer was Christian Stockmar's first cousin. Her mother, Christina Stockmar Bauer, was a native Coburger who as a girl played with the ducal daughters Sophie, Antoinette, and Juliana of Saxe-Coburg. When Herr Bauer, a soldier, died young, the Bauer family fell on hard times. Caroline was able to persuade her widowed mother to allow her to go on the stage, and she quickly found success as an actress. One night when Caroline was playing in Dresden, Prince Leopold of Saxe-Coburg happened to be in the royal box. Leopold was visiting his kinsman, the King of Saxony, and was still in deep mourning for his wife, Princess Charlotte. He saw an extraordinary resemblance between Caroline Bauer and his dead wife. After one or two private meetings with the actress, Leopold had his chief counselor Christian Stockmar persuade Caroline to come to England with her mother and become Leopold's morganatic wife.

Unmoved by questions of family honor, Stockmar persuaded his aunt and cousin to accept Prince Leopold's terms, which included a modest annuity. The women came to England, were housed in a secluded villa, and met with an astonishingly cold reception from Leopold. According to Caroline, she went through a form of wedding ceremony with Leopold, at which her cousin Christian was present, but she and Leopold had sexual relations only for a matter of weeks. Otherwise all that the prince required of her on his rare visits was to sing arias and read tedious German books. Leopold listened and "drizzled," picking out silver and gold threads from the trimming on old uniforms, and storing them in a little box so that the precious metals could be reused. Bauer claims that Leopold was such an industrious drizzler that he salvaged enough silver to make a tureen. This, with a characteristic mixture of pomp and parsimony, he presented to his niece, Victoria.

After Leopold moved her to an even more isolated house near Claremont, his English country estate, Caroline and her mother could take no more. They escaped back to Germany, and Caroline returned to the stage. Unlike Pauline Panam, she did get her annuity and probably a pleasant country estate near Coburg. She was apparently even invited to the palace.

However, if Caroline Bauer found it in her interests to keep silent during her lifetime, she never forgave King Leopold for his loveless tyranny or cousin Christian for pandering her to his employer. She wrote a three-volume memoir telling the story of her life and her disastrous liaison, and directed that it be published after her death. Bauer's memoir, even more than Panam's, caused a sensation, since at the time of publication, the Coburg family was cutting a magnificent figure on the European social and political scene.

PRINCE ALBERT WAS the avowed heir and disciple of three native Coburgers: his father, his uncle Leopold, and Christian Stockmar. All three were ambitious and held themselves in very high esteem. All three were cynical and unrepentant misogynists who traded women like merchandise. Purity, conjugal devotion, and fine moral scruples were not things that Ernest, Leopold, and Stockmar took seriously in their own lives.

One of the many long-term schemes hatched by these three men was to produce from the ranks of the younger Saxe-Coburgs a royal consort for England who would promote their interests and realize their grand geopolitical designs. Ernest's younger son, Albert, was eventually their choice. Albert would be their man, a man in their own image—in all things but one. Albert would be virtuous, he would be clean, and he would be monogamous. As a result, he would have healthy children, and he would found a dynasty that would rule Europe. This grand plan actually came to pass.

To realize the family blueprint and also to achieve his personal goals, Prince Albert had to forget the real Coburg and invent a new one, heavily sanitized. Any memory of the Panams and Bauers in his Coburg past must be erased. Father, uncle, and counselor must be reinvented as faithful spouses, loving fathers, and moral men—as hegemonic nineteenth-century England was then challenging the world to define moral.

For Duke Ernest, King Leopold, and Baron Stockmar, this mythomanic exercise by their protégé was noble and gratifying. For Queen Victoria it was an essential tool in guaranteeing the monarchy in England at a time of rising republican activism. On Prince Albert himself, the gap between fiction and reality took a tragic toll.

9.

A Dynastic Marriage

...

DUKE ERNEST I OF SAXE-COBURG-SAALFELD, PRINCE ALBERT'S FATHER, succeeded to his father's duchy in 1806. His goal in life was to raise Coburg out of the third tier of German states. During the Napoleonic wars, his lofty schemes to marry a sister of the tsar, enlarge his domains, and move his capital city to beautiful Bayreuth all came to nothing. Other desirable marriages fell through, and only in 1817, when he was thirty-three years old, was Ernest able to find an heiress willing to marry him.

Ernest's bride was the seventeen-year-old Princess Louise of Saxe-Gotha-Altenburg. Gotha was one of the five little Ernestine duchies of Thuringia but almost three times larger than Saxe-Coburg-Saalfeld. Viewed from the Coburg side, the marriage was especially desirable because the ancient and formerly fertile ducal family of Gotha was faced with extinction. Louise's mother, a princess of Mecklenburg-Schwerin, died giving birth to her, and although Louise's father, Duke Augustus, quickly married Caroline of Hesse-Kassel, he had no children by her. Under Salic law, Louise could not inherit from her father, and so Duke Augustus's heir was his only brother, Prince Frederick, a lifelong bachelor. Frederick had made various attempts to marry but failed, reportedly because of his "moral state."

Negotiations for Louise of Gotha's marriage began as soon as she reached puberty. She was the last descendent of her noble house, and if she could not rule in Gotha, her husband or her son could. Louise's income-bearing property from her mother would also pass from her father to her husband at the time of her marriage.

Though she was not consulted about whom she would marry, or when, Louise was not unhappy at the prospect of becoming a wife. Her father was a difficult, distant man. Absorbed in his music and poetry, he showed her no affection. Louise's stepmother Caroline, on the other hand, was possessive. The Duchess of Gotha had raised Louise from babyhood and resented anyone her stepdaughter befriended. The person Louise cared for most was Augusta von Studnitz, an intelligent, serious girl one year younger than herself. With Augusta, Louise could gossip, tell jokes, discuss love and men, and speak in confidence. Almost everything we know of Duchess Louise we learn from the letters she wrote as a young wife to this dear friend.

Louise of Gotha was a sensitive, naive girl of sixteen when she was betrothed to Duke Ernest of Saxe-Coburg in the summer of 1817. She was not a classic beauty, but her frank and lively manner charmed everyone she met. Both in physique and in temperament she bore a close resemblance to the young Queen Victoria. Louise had been nourished on old tales of courtly love and was ready to fall in love with her husband. When she saw the man that her father intended her to marry, she was happy. Tall, athletic, and dashing, with crisp chestnut curls, Duke Ernest was the image of the perfect knight Louise had dreamed about. Anonymous letters alerted Louise to Duke Ernest's amorous past, but she chose to ignore them. How could a man with such melting brown eyes ever hurt her? And since the Coburg and Gotha families were decided on the match, what choice did she have?

At first all went well. As Pauline Panam had discovered, Duke Ernest liked young, boyish women, and so he was not insensible to his wife's charms. For a year or two he showered Louise with gifts, redecorating all her apartments in his various palaces, arranging elaborate celebrations for her birthday and at Christmas, having her portrait painted over and over again, and taking her with him on visits abroad. Louise's own dowry money was paying for these attentions, but still she was delighted. She called her husband angel and master, and was happy only in his company. When the duke agreed to take his wife to his favorite retreat, Schloss Rosenau, a picturesque pseudomedieval house he had created about four miles from Coburg (and the very house into which Pauline Panam had climbed via the window for a rendezvous), Louise was enchanted. Louise's ecstatic letters in the first year of her marriage read strikingly like those of the newly married Queen Victoria extolling the beauty and virtue of her Albert.

The young duchess's letters intimate that she responded to her husband's experienced lovemaking with ardent enthusiasm, and within three months of marriage, she was pregnant. Two years later she had given birth to two large healthy sons, Ernest Augustus Charles John Leopold Alexander Edward, born in Schloss Ehrenburg on June 21, 1818, and Francis Charles

Augustus Albert Emanuel, born at the Rosenau on August 26, 1819. The two sons were known as Ernest and Albert, the names of the two sixteenth-century brothers who had founded the two branches of the Wettin family.

*

THE TWO LITTLE COBURG princes were imbued from babyhood with a sense of their own importance. Ernest, an engaging and intelligent child with his father's tall, fine body, was by right of birth the more important of the two. He was heir apparent to his father's duchy of Saxe-Coburg and heir presumptive to his maternal grandfather's duchy of Gotha. Yet from Albert's birth, Ernest stood in the shadow of his younger brother, and the older the boys grew, the greater was Albert's ascendancy over Ernest. Or so Queen Victoria was told.

At the outset, looks probably had a great deal to do with this ascendancy. Little Ernest's aunts Juliana, Antoinette, and Victoire, and his uncles Ferdinand and Leopold had all leaped up the European social ladder because their exceptional good looks had attracted exceptional marriage partners. Even those who loved little Ernest recognized early on that his face would not be his fortune. Apparently there was something unattractive about the shape of Ernest's lower jaw. In letters, his mother and grandmother commented matter-of-factly that he was "not pretty." Ernest was probably made to understand from earliest childhood that he had failed to be as handsome as his Coburg father and uncles, and failed to be as clever as his Gotha mother and his uncle Leopold. And he was equally aware that his little brother succeeded triumphantly where he failed.

Albert as a child was ravishingly pretty. On the day of his birth, his grandmother Augusta recorded how captivated she was by his huge "squirrel" eyes. She at once began to nurture dynastic ambitions for the child, which she communicated to her daughter in England, the Duchess of Kent. Louise of Gotha wrote to her friend Augusta: "Ernest is really big for his age, lively and intelligent. His big brown eyes sparkle with wit and vivacity . . . Albert is superb—quite extraordinarily beautiful; has big blue eyes, a sweet little mouth—a pretty nose—dimples in each cheek—he is tall and lively. He has three teeth, and though he is only eight months, he is already beginning to walk." Albert was not just beautiful, he was quick to learn and easy to love. A deeply affectionate tot, he followed his uncle Leopold around like a shadow when that gentleman visited Coburg, kissed his grandmother's hand repeatedly when she took him out for a carriage ride, and was so engaging that even his father found it impossible to take a stick to him when he was naughty.

In an age when many children died in infancy, Albert became the family pet not just because he was beautiful but because he was delicate. As a baby and small child, he was subject to digestive problems and frightening attacks of croup. He learned to submit with precocious resignation to the leeches and blisters that the doctors applied to his skinny little body. Albert tired easily and never seemed to get enough sleep, though he usually went to bed with the sun. Once, when he was three, Albert was observed falling out of his chair without waking up and then lying on the floor dead asleep. When it was time for the princes to go to bed, Albert was happy to be carried upstairs.

Prince Albert as a small boy was also shy. When introduced into a large group of people, he would cover his eyes, refuse to speak, and even run away. Once his mother had him dressed up as cupid for a children's fancy dress party; four-year-old Albert simply stood next to the little girl who was his appointed partner and howled.

As was customary to women of her class, Duchess Louise gave the care of her sons over to servants when they were born, and she and the duke often left Coburg on family visits and state business. However, Louise's letters prove that she was a loving and attentive mother who played with her children when she was at home and took pride and delight in watching both of them grow up.

But Duchess Louise preferred Albert to Ernest and made no secret of it. According to the testimony submitted to Queen Victoria around 1866 by the princes' tutor Christoph Florschütz, among the difficulties he encountered on entering the Duke of Coburg's service "was the partiality shown in the treatment of the children by their mother. Endowed with brilliant qualities, handsome, clever, and witty, possessed of eloquence and of a lively and perfervid imagination, Duchess Louise was wanting in the essential qualifications of a mother. She made no attempt to conceal that Prince Albert was her favorite child. He was handsome and bore a strong resemblance to herself. He was in fact her pride and glory."

Louise preferred Albert because he was beautiful and precocious but also because he seemed to her a Gothaner, not a Coburger. He was her son, whereas Ernest was the duke's. Louise was a woman of intelligence and well educated by the standards of her day. According to King Leopold, her father read Persian poetry with her when she was a child. Duke Ernest, on the other hand, was generally considered the least intelligent and able of the three sons of Duchess Augusta. He spoke haltingly, even stammering when unsure, and when he found himself in the counsels of the great, he was treated like a buffoon. Prince Albert was very verbal, beginning to talk at eight months and expressing himself perfectly by the time he was two.

Albert continued to take after his mother well into his teens. This is the testimony of no less than Baron Christian Stockmar, who knew Duchess Louise very well. When he saw the teenaged Prince Albert for the first time in many years, Stockmar wrote to King Leopold: "The Prince bears a striking resemblance to his mother, and, differences apart, is in many respects both in mind and body cast in her mould. He has the same intellectual quickness and adroitness, the same cleverness, the same desire to appear good-natured and amiable to others, and the same talent for fulfilling this desire, the same love of 'espiègleries' [practical jokes], and of treating things and men from the comical side, the same way of not occupying himself long with the same subject."

When Ernest was four and Albert three, Duke Ernest sent away his sons' nurse, Fräulein Müller, and brought in a tutor not just to give them lessons but to supervise every aspect of their care. The new tutor was a twenty-five-year-old bachelor, Christoph Florschütz, usually referred to in the literature by his surname alone. He had already been tutor to the sons of Duke Ernest's sister, Sophie Mensdorff, and his pupils were required to address and refer to him as "the Counselor" ("der Rath").

Even in royal households, it was rare to appoint a tutor before a prince turned eight. Duchess Louise is not known to have protested the appointment, and in her extant letters, she barely mentions the tutor. Duchess Caroline, however, the boys' stepgrandmother, who was prepared to take their part against their father, protested that they were much too young to be cared for by a young man. Albert in particular, she wrote to Duke Ernest, was frail and needed a woman's care, especially at night. But the duke was adamant.

At the instigation of Prince Leopold, grand strategist of the whole Coburg clan, Stockmar had arrived in Coburg to observe the progress of the princes. He reported that whereas Albert "was aggressive and self-confident with other children in their games, and particularly when playing soldiers, he was strangely quiet and quick to cry at home." For Ernest I of Saxe-Coburg, the mere implication that his three-year-old son was turning into a sissy was a call to arms. And in any case, the duke had his reasons for wishing to weaken his wife's hold over their sons.

Queen Victoria once sympathized with her husband about the early loss of his nurse. She herself remembered what a severe trial it had been for her when Nurse Brock had left, and she was put in the care of the governess, Louise Lehzen. But Prince Albert would have no sympathy. "Even as a child," the Queen recalled in her memorandum, "[the prince] showed a great dislike to being in the charge of women, and rejoiced over the contemplated change." Albert was only three, but he understood that to be the son his father desired, he needed to look down on women and abjure their care.

※

AFTER THE BIRTH of the second child, it was clear to all in Coburg and Gotha that the ducal marriage was going bad. With new sources of income and credit since his marriage, with a healthy male heir and a second male child as insurance, with the annexation of the duchy of Gotha to Coburg now virtually guaranteed, Duke Ernest saw no further reason to curb his appetites. He returned to his bachelor ways, traveling without his wife, and openly pursuing any attractive woman who came along. He hunted most of the day when he was at home and caroused most of the night with men friends. Even his mother complained that she hardly ever saw him. Duchess Louise was bored with her husband's relatives and the Coburg ladies-in-waiting he had chosen for her. Wounded to the quick by her husband's indifference, falsely accused of flirting when she had been faithful, trying perhaps to regain the duke's attention, she began an affair with a nineteen-year-old courtier, Alexander von Hanstein.

The end to the marriage came in 1824. Duchess Louise's father had just died, quite unexpectedly, and her uncle, the new Duke of Gotha, was close to death, so the duchess had no close male protector and adviser. Maximilian von Szymborski, her husband's Polish aide-de-camp and boon companion, came to Duchess Louise with an ultimatum. Szymborski had been spying upon the duchess. He accused her of having an adulterous liaison with Hanstein, and told her it could not continue. Louise would be permitted to leave the duchy as a free woman, retain the income she had inherited from her mother, and might eventually be granted a divorce that would enable her to marry again. But in return for her freedom she must give up all claims to her ancestral realm of Gotha in favor of the Duke of Coburg, and agree never again to see her sons Ernest and Albert. After some negotiation, Duchess Louise agreed to her husband's terms, signed an act of separation, and prepared to leave.

Was Duchess Louise a feckless woman who sacrificed her sons in order to be with her young lover? Queen Victoria, who certainly did not approve of adultery, did not think so. She sympathized with her husband's young mother, understanding that once her husband accused her of adultery Duchess Louise had little choice but to accept his terms, which were relatively lenient. Duke Casimir, a sixteenth-century ancestor of Duke Ernest I, upon whose portrait Duchess Louise as a young bride once gazed in horror, locked up his unfaithful wife for life in a fortress, put her lover in another, and let them both rot.

Even in 1824, women in Europe were still virtually the possessions of their husbands. However misused, they had no legal right to divorce, and, in the event of a separation, they had no rights to their minor children. In some aristocratic circles, an adulterous man might turn a blind eye to his wife's affairs, or even encourage them if it suited his pocket or his political ambitions. But a woman had always to exercise discretion. A hint of scandal could destroy her social position, and proof of misconduct could endanger her life. Louise of Gotha was not discreet, her husband wanted to be rid of her, and she suffered the consequences.

Duke Ernest had planned for his wife to make a quick and quiet exit from Coburg, but in this at least he was thwarted. Duchess Louise was the last descendent of the ancient house of Saxe-Gotha-Altenburg, and even in Coburg she was far more popular than her husband. When the people of Coburg heard that she was being forced into exile, they acted. A crowd of men came to the castle at Rosenau, put the duchess in her carriage, got between the shafts, and pulled her all the way back to Schloss Ehrenburg, just as if she had been a bride. After that, the mob went off to Ketschendorf, the home of the dowager Duchess Augusta on the outskirts of the town, and forced Duke Ernest to drive with his two sons back to the Ehrenburg, where his wife was waiting. Then the crowd demanded that Szymborski, who was widely hated, should be delivered up to them. Szymborski managed to escape with his life, but only by a trick.

The Coburgers' extraordinary demonstration of love and support for his wife did nothing to sway Duke Ernest. Duchess Louise left Coburg on September 4, 1824. In the final letter to her friend Augusta, she writes: "Parting from my children was the worst thing of all. They have whooping cough, and they said, 'Mamma is crying because she has to go away while we are ill.' Poor little mice, may God bless them." Louise never again saw her native Gotha, her friend Augusta, her adoring stepmother, or her sons.

In 1825 Louise's uncle Duke Frederick died, and, after some long and acrimonious negotiations among the five ducal families, Gotha was officially united with Coburg. Duke Ernest and his sons changed their name to Saxe-Coburg and Gotha. In 1826 a divorce was secretly put through, and Louise married Alexander von Hanstein. She and her husband lived comfortably on the income from her estates, and Louise's kinsman, the Duke of Saxe-Hildburghausen, gave Hanstein the title of Count of Pölzig and

Baiersdorf. Pölzig went on to have a distinguished career as an officer in the Prussian army.

Louise found happiness in her second marriage, but she had few years to enjoy it. Already in 1822, two years before her exile, she reported to her friend Augusta that she had severe stomach pains and inflammation of the bowels, and had suffered a hemorrhage. In February 1831, she went to Paris to consult the famous Dr. Antoine Dubois and was told she had inoperable cancer of the womb. After five months of agony, Louise of Saxe-Gotha-Altenburg, Countess Pölzig, was dead, about a month before her thirty-first birthday.

One of the strangest things in the biographical literature on Albert, prince consort, is the recurring allegation that he was not the child of Duke Ernest. The rumor of Albert's bastardy may have been spread by word of mouth in the gossipy courts of nineteenth-century Europe. In the twentieth century, the rumors began to appear in print from the pen of men who, for one reason or another, disliked the prince consort. The allegation was based on the known fact of his mother's adultery with Hanstein and on the observed fact that in his sexual mores and his financial management Albert was remarkably unlike his father and his brother.

Some writers argued that the prince consort's father must have been Jewish. As evidence of this, Jewish writers alleged the prince consort's great intelligence and vast culture. Others, of an anti-Semitic bent, pointed to the large sums of money the prince was able to amass and the large properties he was able to purchase during his two decades in England.

Veteran royal biographer David Duff was also convinced that Prince Albert was not the son of the Duke of Coburg and advanced an even more audacious hypothesis: that Albert was the illegitimate son of his uncle Leopold. Albert's life paralleled and extended his uncle's in extraordinary ways, Duff pointed out. The two were very alike. Albert became virtually Leopold's adopted son in his late teens, and all his life he was closer to Leopold than were Leopold's Belgian sons and daughters. Using the evidence of Leopold's own letters, Duff placed Leopold in Coburg around the time of Albert's conception. He accused royal historian Theodore Martin of a cover-up, since, in his official five-volume biography of the prince consort, Martin denies that Leopold was there at that time.

But the idea that Albert was not his father's son is nonsense, a tissue of innuendo and prejudice floating free of fact. The evidence of Duchess Louise's extant letters is that she was deeply in love with and faithful to her husband until at least 1822. (Albert was born in 1819.) It is a canard that

Prince Albert was a bastard, but how fascinating that so many upstanding biographers and historians of royalty have found it irresistible!

Family likenesses are funny things. Sometimes sons are like their grandfathers or their uncles. Sometimes, though male historians have trouble with this, sons are like their mothers and grandmothers and aunts. All the evidence suggests that Prince Albert inherited his tall, handsome body from his father; his brilliant mind, his love of learning, and his sensitivity to social wrongs from his mother.

THE COBURG PRINCES, aged five and six, were eyewitnesses to the extraordinary events of 1824. Intelligent little boys, they surely had some intimations that their father and mother had for some time not been in agreement. They were watching when a crowd of angry citizens forced their father to drive back to the Ehrenburg Palace. They were in the palace when the mob outside howled for Szymborski's head. Soon after, when they were both ill with whooping cough, their mother came and wept to tell them she was going away. They never saw their mother again and apparently were never given any news of her during her life. Even news of her death probably came to them in the extraordinary form of the announcement of their father's wedding. According to Queen Victoria, it was not until after his own marriage that Prince Albert was told how much his mother had suffered in her last year, and he wept for her.

Within days of their mother's departure, the princes' father went away too. For five months the two little boys were left in the care of "der Rath." What the duke instructed the tutor Florschütz to tell his sons about their mother, when it dawned upon them that she was not coming back, is not known.

The idea that his small sons might need him after all the distressing events they had experienced seems not to have occurred to the Duke of Coburg. Children, for men like him, existed for the benefit of their parents, not vice versa. Having got rid of his wife, the duke had to mend his bridges with relatives abroad, and he was in need of pleasure. He had provided his sons with a capable young tutor. After a year's trial, the duke felt confident that Florschütz understood his duty. Duchess Louise had babied Albert and hurt Ernest, who was a real chip off the old Coburg block. What the boys needed was a firm male hand.

Duke Ernest's sense of responsibility for his sons extended to a request that they write to him regularly and keep a diary of their daily activities that he could read on his return. Letters to absent parents and diaries were a common educational exercise for upper-class schoolchildren in this period, to be carefully supervised and scrutinized by tutors and governesses. All the same, for a sensitive, articulate child like Albert, they were a precious link and a needed outlet for emotion.

Albert's letters and diary are full of sadness and loss. He makes no reference to his mother, but he is free to say how much he misses his father. The five-year-old prince artlessly records how often he cried. He cried because the Rath pinched him to explain that *pinch* was a verb. He cried because his cough was so very bad and worrisome, because he was punished for not putting his books away, because he wrote a letter so full of mistakes that the Rath tore it up. Albert ends each letter to his father: "Think of me with love, your Albert." Once he begs the duke to bring him a doll that nods its head.

Is it any wonder that Albert cried? Both his parents were gone in bizarre circumstances, and he did not know when they would be back. For a five-year-old, this was already tragic. If, as is all too likely given his intelligence, Albert gathered from adult conversations that his mother had been sent away in disgrace, and he feared that she would not be returning, this would have been traumatic. Duchess Louise was young, pretty, witty, capricious, and fun. Everyone except her husband and his henchmen loved her. Albert was like his mother—everyone said so—and that had been a source of deep happiness to the boy. She made no secret of the fact that she loved him more than his big brother, that he was her "pride and glory."

What happens to a sensitive, precocious boy when such a mother suddenly disappears? Surely the bottom drops out of his world. Did Albert blame himself for his mother's disappearance? Did he hate her for abandoning him? These would be normal reactions for a small child hit by inexplicable loss. Did Albert identify with his mother, so small and childlike? Did he remember that she had dared to quarrel with his father before she suddenly disappeared? Did he begin to fear his father?

None of these questions has an answer. Neither Albert nor his brother, Ernest, in all their yards of letters, memoirs, and memoranda, ever recorded memories of the time when they lost their mother. If they confided them to anyone, their secrets were faithfully kept.

According to the 1866 testimony of Florschütz, testimony solicited by Queen Victoria and sanctioned by Albert's brother (by this time Duke Ernest II of Coburg), the princes did not miss their mother. In fact, the duchess's departure was more a cause of relief than sorrow to the boys, since she was not a good mother. "Duchess Louise was wanting in the essential qualifications of a mother," wrote Florschütz. "She made no attempt to conceal that Prince Albert was her favorite child . . . The influence of this partiality might have been most injurious."

If Florschütz is to be believed, the Coburg princes swiftly got over the "difficulties" caused by their parents' dispute in 1824 because they received far better care from him than they had from their mother. "It is a satisfaction to me to reflect that these sad events did not interfere permanently with the happiness of my beloved pupils, and that, with the cheerfulness and innocence of childhood, they retained their respectful and obedient love for their parents. Thus deprived of a mother's love and care, the children necessarily depended more entirely on that shown by their tutor; and he is conscious of . . . having given himself up with unceasing solicitude . . . to the good of his pupils. And he was rewarded by their . . . love and confidence, their liking to be with him, and the entire unreserve with which they showed their inmost thoughts and feelings in his presence."

Today mothers are expected to raise their small children of both sexes. Biologists, psychologists, and therapists as well as parents all agree that a young child's mother, however imperfect, is the center of its world and the object of its passionate adoration. There is also a consensus in the social sciences that the early mother-child relationship forms a template for adult relationships. If the course of a child's love for its mother is interrupted in some way by death, separation, or betrayal, the effects on the child's development are deep and permanent.

Who can believe that Prince Albert was unaffected by his mother's disappearance? On the contrary, the prince's development as a sexual being and all his subsequent relationships with women were shaped by the fact that at the vulnerable age of five he was abandoned by the person he loved most.

The Paradise of Our Childhood

ERNEST PROBABLY SUFFERED LESS THAN ALBERT WHEN THEIR MOTHER went off. Her preference for his younger brother must have hurt. Now he was the heir to both Coburg and Gotha, after his father he was the most important person at both courts and in both duchies, and the path in life laid out for him was congenial. He adored his brother, Albert, and was ready to protect him. With their mother gone, he would be the most important person in Albert's life. Together, with the Rath's help, they would negotiate life with their alarming father.

For his part, Albert concentrated on doing everything asked of him as well as he could. Handsome and brilliant, he would be the perfect boy and win the love and admiration of all who knew him.

For some six years after their mother's disappearance, Prince Ernest and Prince Albert settled into a routine, traveling only once beyond the eight hundred or so square miles of Coburg-Gotha to visit their Mensdorff cousins in Mainz in the Rhineland. The Duke of Coburg himself was away for many months every year, and the Ehrenburg Palace, which was undergoing extensive renovations and extensions, was often closed up. Although Duke Ernest kept his mother and stepmother-in-law at arm's length when he was at home, during his absences he allowed his sons to pay longish visits to Duchess Augusta at her villa at Ketschendorf, just outside Coburg city, and to Duchess Caroline in Gotha, a day's journey away. However, the Coburg princes spent most of their time at the Rosenau. All of these arrangements indicate a father of limited means, intent upon his building projects, his opera stars, and his visits to the courts of more important relatives.

The grandmothers' houses were more relaxed than the Ehrenburg and less spartan than the Rosenau. The older ladies would provide small treats for the boys when they were young—a picnic expedition to a local beauty spot, a new pet goat, a visit to a fair with pocket money to buy "a Turkish crescent, a whip, an eagle, and a crossbow." Later there were outings to the theater and opera, which the boys enjoyed very much. All the same, there is no real evidence that the two grandmothers were able to fill the gap left by the boys' lost mother, as some of Albert's biographers have suggested. Grandmother Augusta was a sharp, imperious old woman who suffered neither fools nor naughty boys gladly. Duchess Caroline adored her grandsons—Albert was the image of her beloved lost stepdaughter—but she was a worrier and terribly deaf. Neither grandmother had much influence over Duke Ernest's treatment of his sons, though Duchess Caroline is on record as trying to protect them. The boys soon learned from their father to take the love of the old women for granted and spend as little time with them as possible.

Apart from their father, Florschütz was the most important person in the princes' lives, and the closeness between tutor and tutees grew apace. Florschütz was an enlightened educator. Though he was himself a fine example of the educated, hard-working, and ambitious bourgeois Protestant, he acted on the presumption that all work and no play made the princely Jack a dull boy. He gave his charges ample time to get outside and to develop their personal interests. As a result, in comparison to the daughters, much less the sons, of the Anglo-Saxon Protestant meritocracy of their generation, the Coburg princes were not remarkably advanced when they were children. But this liberal educational policy reaped rich results in the end. Both princes grew into well-informed, intellectually curious, highly cultured adults. One of the puzzles in this family history is why, when it came to educating his own sons, especially the eldest, Prince Albert did not take more leaves out of Florschütz's book of pedagogy.

Florschütz himself did much of the teaching when the princes were young, and he stressed natural science, modern languages, modern history, and, most radically, philosophy, with which the German universities of the day, though not the ducal courts, were on fire. Prince Albert learned some Latin but no Greek. Though he was taught English and French from an early age, and could read and write both languages well by his teenage years, Albert was not a natural linguist like Queen Victoria and was not taught by native speakers. He always retained a heavy German accent in both languages. In general, Albert as a boy excelled in European history, German literature and composition, natural history, art, and music, and all his life, his interests continued to be in science, technology, and art. None of this prepared him very well for life at the Court of St. James's. The highborn Englishmen among whom Albert was fated to spend his adult life were soaked in the classics as boys, to the neglect of the sciences, and as adults considered French and Italian the languages of civilized men.

Music was something that Prince Albert breathed like the air in his native Germany. Most of the great composers before the 1820s started their careers as court musicians in little German kingdoms like Prince Albert's own Coburg. His mother's father, Duke Augustus of Saxe-Gotha-Altenburg, was for a time the patron of Carl Maria von Weber. Music making was the commonest form of entertainment among all classes in Germany, and amateur musicians were often highly proficient. Tiny Gotha had its own theater, orchestra, and singing groups, touring companies brought the latest operas each year, and music was an integral part of life at the Saxe-Coburg court. Uncle Leopold, among his many attributes, sang as well as many professional singers, and when members of the ducal family got together, they made music.

Albert started piano early and then progressed to the organ. As late teenagers, both he and his brother turned to composition, and either probably could have earned his living as a musician. Ernest in later life wrote a couple of successful operas, which were performed in Gotha or in his brandnew opera house in Coburg. Albert as a youth completed at least two pieces of religious music for organ and choir and twenty-six *Lieder und Romanzen* (songs and romances). After he took up life in England, Prince Albert's compositions were performed at royal events like the christenings or weddings of his children, but as a musician he had a charming modesty. As he once explained, he and his wife both loved music and dedicated time to performance in order to better appreciate the genius of others. When Felix Mendelssohn came to the English court, the Queen and prince begged him for a lesson, and he found them apt and appreciative pupils. When the sheet music blew away, the Queen herself picked it up, a royal tribute to genius.

Albert's interest in natural history was bound up with his love of the Thuringian countryside. Coburg and Gotha in his lifetime were no bigger than villages by our modern standards, and the landscape surrounding them remained virtually untouched by industry throughout the nineteenth century. Albert's father owned a number of small country residences, each offering beautiful views, walks, and rides, but Albert loved his birthplace, Schloss Rosenau, more than any other house. From the little attic bedroom he shared with his brother and tutor at the Rosenau, the young prince had a spectacular panorama of wooded hills and a beguiling river. In the afternoons, tutor and pupils, with an enthusiastic dog or two at their heels, would roam far and wide, scrambling up rocky hillsides to find a falcon's nest, tracking deer, and collecting birds eggs, plants, insects, and rock specimens. These they made into a little natural history collection that grew into the Ernest-Albert Museum at Coburg. His native landscapes were etched into Prince Albert's memory, and it was these, and the clean, scented air, that he missed above all when he moved to smoky London.

The princes, if not poor Florschütz, who had no free time or holidays, were encouraged by Duke Ernest to form friendships with males their own age. They were especially close to their Mensdorff cousins, the sons of their aunt Sophie, who had once been Florschütz's tutees themselves. Also, from 1825 until 1833, each Sunday afternoon from two to seven, a dozen well-born boys were invited to the castle to play with the princes. When possible, the boys played outside, and one of their favorite games was to reenact the chivalric adventures of their Saxon ancestors. They went hunting for birds in summer and skated and sledded in winter. When confined indoors, they played contentious games of chess, put on concerts, and wrote small plays that they staged for the pleasure of the ducal court.

Albert and his brother were also guests of honor at the annual celebrations their father arranged for local schoolchildren. On these feudal occasions, the ducal party looked on approvingly as the children played games with carefully restrained exuberance. Cake and wine were served in the afternoon and roasted sausages in the evening, to the delight, we are told, of the young guests.

Class hierarchy was rigidly observed in Coburg. The boys summoned to play at the castle on Sundays were the sons of court officials and expected one day to take over their fathers' jobs. The distinction in rank between the princes and their playmates was never forgotten, and Ernest and Albert were not subjected to the brutal challenges other boys faced in the woods, the classroom, and on the playground. All the same, Albert was allowed to enjoy some of the rough and tumble of a normal boy's life, and he was not cut off from the world by an invisible wall of privilege and surveillance like the young Victoria at Kensington Palace. The Ehrenburg Palace was in the heart of the city of Coburg, and a busy local inn operated only a stone's throw away from the Rosenau. Prince Albert as a boy was occasionally permitted to sit down for bread and cheese and beer at a table in that inn's courtyard, just like any other local lad.

Albert had a slightly malicious streak, and as a boy he loved to play practical jokes and make fun of people. He was an excellent mimic and had his friends in stitches with his imitations of older folk. He had a gift for drawing cartoons and caricatures—a little book of cartoons was one of his engagement gifts to Queen Victoria—and he specialized in inventive practical jokes. On one occasion, young Albert filled some pea-size glass vials with a noxious chemical and tossed them onto the floor and into the boxes of the theater in Coburg. Another time, his cousin Princess Caroline of Reuss was infuriated to discover that Albert had filled the pockets of her cloak with soft cheese. Not to be outdone, Caroline collected all the frogs she could find and put them in Cousin Albert's bed. This was excellent revenge since, Queen Victoria solemnly informs us, Prince Albert had a horror of frogs and toads all his life. Perhaps he was afraid of turning into one, like the prince in the Grimms' fairy tale.

The Coburg princes' peaceful routine of lessons and nature walks applied only in their father's absence. When at home, Duke Ernest demanded his sons' company, always at breakfast, often for dinner, and, as they grew older, at the daily hunts and evening parties. In the duchy of Coburg, Duke Ernest progressed from one residence to another like a renaissance prince. After 1826 when he acquired his ex-wife's domain of Gotha, these peregrinations could, to the Duke's manifest satisfaction, be extended to the palace in Gotha and the country house of Reinhardsbrunn. Duke Ernest liked to live outdoors and to eat in public. Whenever possible, his breakfast was served in a different place each day on the grounds of his current residence, or at a local beauty spot. With so much traipsing to and fro, the meal often lasted for several hours and was an ordeal for the servants. Thirty years later, as master of chilly Balmoral Castle, Prince Albert too loved to eat alfresco.

Since the duke tended to be abroad during the summer, the regular progresses from one residence to the next in the dark months were hard on the whole court. Winters in central Germany were severe, and people forced out on the roads fell off their horses, got stuck in snowdrifts, or tumbled into freezing rivers. Duke Ernest enjoyed the challenge of bad weather and thought his sons should too, but Duchess Caroline worried constantly about her grandsons' catching their death of cold. "Is it not too long a day's journey from Coburg to Ichtershausen for the dear children," wrote Albert's stepgrandmother to Duke Ernest on November 26, 1826, "and in this horrible weather? Would it not be better to make this stage in two days? Excuse this advice, but I am afraid the children will arrive unwell."

Such grandmotherly protests were in vain. On the longer journeys, in rain, sleet, or snow, the duke and his sons always traveled in an open carriage or sled, an exercise in machismo that raised eyebrows even at the time. Albert, like his uncle Leopold, felt the cold intensely, but there were no fur-lined robes and feather boas for him as a boy. In his memoir, Duke Ernest II recalled how as boys he and his brother were "hardened in every way. I remember that we once rode in the depth of winter over the mountain road from Coburg to Gotha, and suffered fearfully from the intense cold. On such an occásion, our father expected us to show the self-command of grown men." Florschütz, who also had to endure the hardships the duke imposed, describes the boy Prince Albert as "rather delicate than robust, though already remarkable for his powers of perseverance and endurance."

To Florschütz's regret, all the travel and social activity when their father was at home left almost no time for the princes to attend to their studies. Ernest, who closely resembled his father, was probably happy enough with court life. He and Albert were both keen shots, eager to kill a gross of birds sent up by the beaters or put some iron into a corral of deer at a battue. But at the end of a long day outside, Albert, unlike his father and brother, craved privacy, quiet, and sleep. Evening parties were an ordeal. He had no small talk, despised gossip, avoided wine, and found rich foods indigestible. But only by taking part in court life and following the duke in his incessant wanderings, hunts, and parties could Prince Albert be near his father, and, to judge from his boyhood letters, he longed for his father's attention and approval.

Was Prince Albert happy as a child? This question has been often debated in the biographical literature, and it is impossible to resolve. The letters and journals from the period that have been published since the prince's death are carefully selected and probably censored. As adults, neither brother cared to find the Proustian madeleine that would unlock the felt experience of the past.

In the few general comments about his childhood that we have on record, Albert contradicted himself. Not long before his death, the prince told the Queen that his childhood had been the happiest time of his life, which cannot have been much comfort to his wife of twenty-one years. In sympathetic response to her mother's distress after the prince consort's death, Vicky, the Princess Royal, wrote to Queen Victoria that her father had told her privately "that he could not bear to think about his childhood, he had been so unhappy and miserable, and had many a time wished himself out of this world."

To Vicky, the child so loved and so like himself, who faced the grim reality of life at a German court, Albert probably told the truth. In youth, he suffered a good deal, the victim of his father's selfish and autocratic ways, the unwilling witness to the corruption at his father's court, and never free to express his feelings. "From our earliest years," wrote Albert's brother somewhat cryptically to Queen Victoria in December 1839, "we [Albert and I] have been surrounded by difficult circumstances, of which we were perfectly conscious, and perhaps more than most people, we have been accustomed to see men in the most opposite positions that human life can offer." In a May 1840 private letter to his brother, Prince Albert could be more direct, almost accusing: "You well knew the events and scandals that had always happened in Coburg Castle and the town, and just this knowledge has made you indifferent to morality."

But apart from such scattered and discreet statements, Ernest and Albert, as boys and adults, kept their thoughts about their father and his court to themselves. Ambitious and proud men, united in their commitment to the Coburg dynasty, they saw no advantage in leaving for posterity a trove of revealing private documents.

In 1857 Albert (by then prince consort) wrote to his brother that he had wished to be in Coburg for the recent visit of his second son, Alfred. "I longed to be with you and to have experienced all the dear memories Alfred's presence awakened in your soul, when you walked in our beloved quiet, Rosenau park, and when you showed him the paradise of our childhood." As this quotation makes clear, by "paradise" the prince meant the natural beauty that surrounded him in childhood and gave him so much comfort. Also part of that paradise was the loving and loyal companionship of his constant companions: his brother and his tutor.

·

THE YEAR 1831 BROUGHT significant changes in the little world of Coburg-Gotha. To the immense excitement of the whole Wettin clan, Prince Leopold was selected by the Great Powers (England, France, Russia, and Austria) as first king of the Belgians. In short order, the new king set about founding a dynasty with Louise of Bourbon, daughter of the French king, Louis Philippe. In August, the boys' mother, Louise of Saxe-Gotha, Countess Pölzig, former Duchess of Saxe-Coburg-Saalfeld, died in Paris, unbeknownst to her two sons in Coburg. In November the lives of Albert and Ernest were touched directly when their paternal grandmother died in Coburg. Dowager Duchess Augusta of Saxe-Coburg was the acknowledged architect of the family's early successes and officially an object of adoration among her children and grandchildren. Her passing marked the end of an era.

In July 1831, Duke Ernest traveled across to England to visit his youngest sister, Victoire, at Kensington Palace. The Duchess of Kent had received an increase in her parliamentary stipend and could entertain her German relatives in style. As usual, Duke Ernest traveled without his sons. "I wish I was with you, to see all the sights that you will have seen," wrote

Prince Albert to his father with precocious pedantry. "Though I should like to be with you, yet we like being here also, and are very happy at the Rosenau. The quiet of the place, too, is very agreeable, for our time is well regulated and divided." At five, Prince Albert had dared to write to his father of his unhappiness and to ask for a doll that nodded its head. By eleven he had learned to ask for nothing and express only obedience and contentment.

As soon as he learned of the death of his wife, Duchess Louise, Duke Ernest went a-courting again, fantasizing perhaps of a rich and nubile bride like brother Leopold's. But the Duke of Coburg's eligibility had only declined with age, and the best wife he could find was Princess Marie of Württemberg. She was a notable connection, since Württemberg (along with Prussia, Bavaria, Saxony, and Hanover) was in the first rank of German states, allied by marriage with the royal families of England and Russia. On the other hand, Princess Marie was already thirty-three years old, and she was also her husband's niece, the daughter of his sister Antoinette. Even among European aristocracy, marriage between uncle and niece was increasingly discouraged, and in England it was against the law. It says something of the unhappy condition of unmarried German princesses that Marie was prepared to marry her dissolute and debt-ridden old uncle.

Duke Ernest's second marriage was an extreme case of the Coburg tendency to practice endogamy and keep money in the family. It was a qualified success at best and, given the clout wielded by the Württembergs, getting first the money and then a divorce was not an option for the duke this time. A severe and melancholy lady, Duchess Marie was tempted by invalidism, not adultery, and, if she put up with her husband's infidelities, she gave him as little as possible in return. She bore him no children and led an increasingly separate life over which, it seems, the duke had no control. With her stepsons Ernest and Albert, first cousins she had known all her life, she remained on friendly terms until her death.

What the princes thought of their father's choice of a bride we do not know, but on the surface, as usual all was filial obedience. From this point on, when Prince Albert went traveling, he wrote to his "dear mamma," describing his activities with rather more than his usual animation. History has been grateful for this. Only when he had become semi-independent in his nineteenth year did Prince Albert venture a comment on the peculiarities in the relationship between his father and stepmother. Duke Ernest and Duchess Marie were invited to attend the coronation of Queen Victoria. The duke accepted the invitation, but his wife declined to accompany him. "So you go to England to the coronation," Albert wrote to his father in May 1838. "It is really a pity that mamma should not be going also; it would have been more natural, and I am sure the Queen will be very sorry not to see her. At the same time, I must say that I never thought dear mamma would make up her mind to accept such an invitation."

IN APRIL 1835, by special arrangement and at their urgent request, both Prince Ernest, aged seventeen, and Prince Albert, aged sixteen, were confirmed at the same time. The lengthy and solemn Lutheran confirmation ceremony, which included a public doctrinal examination, was held in the Hall of Giants at the Ehrenburg before a host of relatives and local dignitaries. Queen Victoria's half brother and half sister, the Prince of Leiningen and the Princess of Hohenlohe-Langenburg (Feodora) were present to hear the princes give their affirmation of faith. Duchess Marie, their stepmother, was conspicuous by her absence. The confirmation marked the end of childhood for both princes, and the time had now come for Duke Ernest to take his sons abroad for the first time.

On this introductory tour, the princes still traveled very much on the cheap. They went first to Mecklenburg to attend the celebrations of the fiftieth anniversary of the accession of the Grand Duke of Mecklenburg-Strelitz, their dead mother's grandfather. They then stayed briefly in Berlin, where they were presented at the Prussian court, and went on to visit family members in Dresden, Prague, and Vienna. The two princes were well received, but travel and court life proved not to Albert's taste. To his stepmother/cousin Duchess Marie he wrote stiffly: "I can assure you, dear Mamma, that we are quite well and that we have enjoyed ourselves in Mecklenburg as well as in Berlin. It requires, however, a giant's strength to bear all the fatigues we have had to undergo. Visits, parades, rides, déjeuners, dinners, suppers, balls, and concerts follow each other in rapid succession, and we have not been allowed to miss any of the festivities." Albert was still very much the little boy who crawled into a corner to sleep at evening parties and who cried when forced to attend a dance.

Now that both Ernest and Albert were officially "out," it was time for the family to decide on their futures. Ernest was heir to a duchy increasingly troubled by democratic protests and possessed of more pretensions than revenues. Albert had a title and a small legacy from his mother, if his father could be persuaded to give up the money. The single career option open to a German prince was the army, but Europe was at peace, and the promotion possibilities for the aristocratic officer caste were correspondingly poor. Duke Ernest could afford for only one of his sons to go into the army, and since Prince Ernest was well disposed to the military life, he was the obvious choice.

Both princes would eventually have to marry for money, the Coburg clan's favorite road to riches. They were intent on keeping the newly acquired wealth and prestige in the family. If an attractive young Coburg could not marry up the social hierarchy, he or she must at least marry a rich cousin. Each new Coburg child who reached adulthood, whether male or female, was scrutinized carefully for marital and reproductive potential. Nothing was left to chance, or inclination.

By the standards of his caste, Albert's key asset in life was not his intellect, integrity, or love of study but his striking good looks. He was a promising stud horse with good bloodlines, expected to sire a set of young colts that would take the racing world by storm. Any personal ambitions and youthful dreams the prince might have must wait until the reproductive duties had been attended to. As his adult life would prove, Albert could have succeeded as a professor, geologist, botanist, statistician, musician, engineer, or bureaucrat, and probably found satisfaction in his work. But the one thing that the younger son of a German prince could not do in the early nineteenth century was train, take up a profession, and earn money.

Traditionally, aristocratic young blades were encouraged to get lots of reproductive practice in before marriage, but here Prince Albert's position was anomalous. From early childhood, his name was linked to his cousin Victoria, and by the time both were young adolescents, their families were dead set on the marriage. Victoria, as heir presumptive to the throne of England, was uniquely empowered to dictate the terms of her marriage, and her mother, under Conroy's influence, had trained her to prize moral purity. Victoria dreamed of a partner as chaste as herself, a man who had never loved a woman, and who would be hers alone. Given the sexual mores of early nineteenth-century royalty, finding such a man was about as easy as finding a unicorn. Fortunately Victoria's uncle Leopold and Baron Stockmar anticipated her wishes and were busy breeding the mythical creature in their own paddock.

Leopold and Stockmar had seen the ravages wrought by venereal disease on the noble houses of Europe. They saw the value of a virgin and therefore untainted prince in the next round of the fabulous dynastic game they had been playing in England for decades. In his pretty, fragile, precocious, docile nephew Albert, Leopold saw possibilities from an early age. Stockmar was much less sure.

Training for the Big Race

THE PRINCESS VICTORIA OF KENT WAS THE GREATEST HEIRESS IN EUROPE. She was also half-Coburg, so the whole Coburg clan was focused on finding her a Coburg husband with whom she could found an English dynasty that would be three-quarters Coburg.

Albert Coburg was the sentimental favorite. Dowager Duchess Augusta, the family matriarch, had picked him out in his cradle as the ideal mate for her granddaughter, the little English mayflower, as she referred to Victoria in an early letter. However, by 1835, Albert faced some rivals in the family. His older brother, Ernest, as well as Duke Ernest of Württemberg (Duchess Marie's brother and thus the Coburg princes' first cousin/stepuncle) were pushed by different factions in the Coburg family.

In some ways Ernest Coburg, stronger, taller, and more mature, was more suitable than Albert, and Duke Ernest of Coburg pressed his elder son's candidacy with vigor. Feodora of Hohenlohe-Langenburg, Victoria's half sister, who lived in Germany, also warmly recommended their cousin Ernest to Victoria in a letter. Prince Ernest himself was eager to try for Victoria's hand. However, he and his father were unable to make any headway against King Leopold and Stockmar. Those two gentlemen refused to countenance a marriage between Victoria Kent and Ernest Coburg. Ernest had not inherited the fabled Coburg looks, but he had inherited the notorious Coburg libido.

In May 1836, much to the wrath of King William IV, who was busy fielding his own contenders for Victoria's hand, Duke Ernest brought his sons to Kensington Palace for their first visit to England. The real purpose of the visit was to arrange a secret engagement between Victoria and Albert, but Stockmar had insisted that the young people should be kept in the dark about their elders' plans. Victoria was an experienced player of the courting game and did not need to be told what was afoot. Albert, it seems possible, did not understand what his mission in England was. Certainly he failed to play the part expected of him, and there was no engagement.

The elders who carefully observed the two young people together were in no doubt as to what had gone wrong. There was nothing of Cherubino in the makeup of Prince Albert at sixteen. The art of sweeping a damsel off her feet had not been part of the curriculum at the Rosenau. Rather the contrary. In the family circle, allowed to express himself in his native language, encouraged to play the piano and sing duets, permitted to shine, Albert could be interesting and "merry"—a key attribute for Victoria. But he showed not a flicker of interest in the opposite sex, and in his letters home, the best thing he could say about Victoria was that she was "agreeable."

Duke Ernest and his sons traveled directly from England to Belgium to report back to Uncle Leopold. Their colt had been entered in a race before he was ready to run, but he still had excellent potential. Neither the Princess Victoria nor her mother seemed inclined to accept any of the suitors proposed by the ailing King of England. The Coburg family still had a few years to train Albert and bring him to physical maturity. King Leopold, who saw a lot of his own looks and intellect in Albert, now resolved to get his nephew away from his father's court and small-town life in Coburg-Gotha. Leopold would organize his nephew's education and invest in his future. Since kings are very busy men, especially when their thrones are new and tottery, Leopold instructed Stockmar to take Albert in hand. More remarkably, given his reputation for parsimony, he opened the royal checkbook.

Stockmar was persona much more grata at the Court of St. James's than at the court of Coburg. Thus he knew Princess Victoria quite well but Prince Albert hardly at all. When he did have a chance to study Albert, he wondered whether the boy could succeed as Victoria's husband and consort. Victoria was smaller and looked meeker than her ill-fated cousin Charlotte, but she had as much will and as much pride, and her husband would have no easy time of mastering her. Did Albert have any sense of what he was taking on, wrote Stockmar to Leopold, not only with Victoria but with England, which had no love of foreign princes, especially German ones called Coburg? Was Albert ready of his own accord "to sacrifice mere pleasure to real usefulness?" Was he just filled with boyish pride and naive ambition? "If simply to fill one of the most influential positions in Europe does not satisfy him," Stockmar went on, "how often will he feel tempted to regret what he has undertaken. If he does not, right from the start, regard it as a serious and responsible task upon the fulfillment of which his honour and happiness depend, he is not likely to succeed." Poor Albert, just seventeen!

Despite his doubts, Stockmar accepted the assignment of facilitating the marriage of Victoria and Albert. He was bored at home in Coburg with his disagreeable wife. He enjoyed living in England, which he saw as the greatest nation on earth. For decades, long before the Crown of Belgium was won, Leopold and Stockmar had conceived a grand geopolitical plan in which enlightened European monarchs would lead their peoples toward economic and social progress through carefully controlled and limited democracies. England was the kingpin in this system, and the approaching accession of a new, presumably malleable, half-Coburg queen regnant offered all kinds of possibilities. If Stockmar indoctrinated Albert and Victoria, each in turn, if they then married and founded a new dynasty, they might change the future of Europe and realize the Leopold-Stockmar vision.

Therefore Stockmar emerged from retirement and, despite his notoriously frail health, started shuttling across the English Channel. He had been Princess Charlotte's dear friend. Now he was Victoria's. In the difficult weeks just before Victoria's accession and for months afterward, Stockmar was at the Queen's shoulder, vying with Prime Minister Melbourne for influence. At the same time, at first through correspondence and finally in person, Stockmar masterminded Prince Albert's education—his *Bildung*, as the Germans say. From the fall of 1836, Duke Ernest of Saxe-Coburg and Gotha grudgingly yielded to his brother Leopold the control of his younger son, Albert. Prince Ernest too yielded to his brother. For the next few years, Ernest was content to play second fiddle, offering support, encouragement, and social cover as Albert was trained to win Victoria's hand.

First King Leopold dispatched the two Coburg brothers to his royal French in-laws for a short visit. Albert and Ernest were given a gratifying reception at Louis Philippe's brilliant court, but Albert took no pleasure in Paris. The city, he found, was noisy and crowded, his hotel shabby and cramped. Then the Coburg princes returned to Brussels for eight months to stay in a quiet and comfortable house paid for by their uncle. Florschütz was still with the princes, but Baron von Wiechmann was also appointed as governor to supervise their lives. Wiechmann was a tedious old soldier, and Ernest quarreled with him a lot, but the high-ranking Wiechmann was a key indicator of Albert's rising status and the expectations of his handlers.

In Brussels Albert's political education began in earnest at the hands of some of the most eminent men in Belgium, and he gave proof of exceptional intellectual mettle. A Belgian government minister gave him and his brother lessons in contemporary politics. The princes improved their French in the classroom and in the salons. The Reverend Mr. Drury, who had once had the honor of corresponding with Lord Byron, was retained to teach them English literature. The mathematician Adolphe Quetelet, often called the father of modern statistics, shaped Prince Albert's thinking on economic issues in crucial ways. But almost more important to both young men than the lectures and tutorials was the experience of living in Brussels, the capital city of one of the richest and most modern nations in the world. Coburg-Gotha was still an oppressive semifeudal state. Now in Brussels Albert got a taste of the democratic ideas and social patterns he might expect to meet in England.

Ernest and Albert enjoyed Belgium. When Duke Ernest wrote that he would expect to see them at home in Coburg for the Christmas holidays, Prince Albert wrote back with extreme politeness and equal firmness that it was impossible for them to leave Brussels. "Such an expedition would require five or six weeks, and our course of study would be quite disturbed by such an interruption. We told dear uncle the purport of your letter, and he said he would write to you on the subject." And that was that. The dreamy, passive boy of the Rosenau was emerging from his father's shadow—into his uncle's.

The next stage in Stockmar's grand plan was for the princes to move on to a university. There, in Prince Albert's phrase, they would "get more wisdom." The Wettin elders in Saxony and Thuringia were apoplectic just thinking of the incendiary notions the Coburg princes would pick up at a university. Even Stockmar found it difficult to find the right academic environment for his two prize pupils. Berlin, Stockmar informed King Leopold, was inadvisable mainly because "a certain dissoluteness is as epidemic in Berlin as the influenza." Conservative, autocratic Vienna was equally out of the question. In the end, Stockmar chose the University of Bonn, though it too was conservative by Belgian standards. The princes Ernest and Albert, together with the faithful Florschütz and the increasingly irritating Wiechmann, took up modest lodgings in April 1837 and began studying law.

Prince Albert did only two semesters at Bonn, but his eighteen months as a student prince were probably the most congenial of his life. He was not radicalized in either his political or religious views, but he loved the work, attended lectures conscientiously, and experienced a "rage for reading." He and Ernest became friends with several other young aristocrats from families close to their own: the Grand Duke of Weimar, Prince William of Löwenstein-Wertheim, Count Erbach, and the new, young Duke of Mecklenburg-Strelitz. As Prince Albert wrote to his friend Prince William in October 1838, some months after leaving Bonn, "I believe that the pleasant days which we spent together [at the university], partly in useful occupations, partly in cheerful intercourse, will ever appear to me as the happiest of my life. In spite of our unrestrained intimacy [*Ungenirheit*] and our many practical jokes, the utmost harmony always existed between us. How pleasant were our winter concerts—our theatrical attempts—our walks to the Venusberg—the swimming-school—the fencing ground-! I dare not think back upon all those things."

Albert still lived under the careful eye of his tutor and governor, who sent regular reports on him to King Leopold, Baron Stockmar, and Duke Ernest. The reports were laudatory and reassuring. Unlike the typical student, Prince Albert had a profound distaste for drinking, whoring, and fighting. When not studying, he played the organ in the local cathedral, composed music, took long walks in the company of friends, played with his beautiful greyhound Eos, swam in the river, fenced in competitions (careful not to scar his handsome face), sang lieder, and engaged in long discussions of philosophy and law. Thanks to Uncle Leopold, he also had a little money to spend at last and bought his first pieces of art: sketches by Dürer and Van Dyck, the beginning of a notable collection. Singing drinking songs with his aristocratic friends, doing wickedly accurate imitations of Wiechmann and his professors, and drawing lively caricatures were the full extent of the wild oats Albert is known to have sowed in these eighteen months of (comparative) freedom.

·

THIS IS THE CANONIC portrait of Albert the Chaste drawn by Queen Victoria in her account of her husband's early years. Faced with the mass of evidence the Queen presents, with her certainty that she was the only woman with whom Prince Albert ever had sexual relations, and his well-documented scorn for the female sex and discomfort in mixed society, a number of historians over the years have hinted that the prince was homosexual.

They insinuate that, given wholly into the care of a lonely, frustrated young man when he was very young, Albert developed an "unnatural attachment" to the tutor with whom he and his sexually precocious brother shared a tiny attic bedroom. As a student, his homosexual tendencies could flower. Bonn in the early nineteenth century was not notorious for its male prostitutes like Berlin, but intense male friendships were as common at the university there as at Oxford and Cambridge. While his brother followed in their father's brothel-hopping footsteps, Albert led a blissful social life with young men who, like himself, did not need female society to have a good time.

In mid-nineteenth-century Europe, both men and women of all classes moved effortlessly and without censure across a range of emotions and practices that today would be categorized as either homosexual or heterosexual. Boys and girls, men and women, habitually shared their beds with friends, relatives, and even complete strangers of their own sex. Males and females openly kissed, embraced, walked arm in arm or arm around waist, and expressed passionate love for members of their own sex without attracting adverse notice. Among aristocrats, who had the money and the leisure for advanced erotic exploration, homosexual acts were common and celebrated in a flourishing pornography industry. It is not incidental that Donatien de Sade was a marquis.

Throughout Europe, upper-class boys in exclusive schools and regiments were routinely exposed to homosexual advances. Some unfortunates were raped by masters or older boys. Some had youthful affairs without feeling guilt or anxiety. Many men who had shown a pronounced preference for sex with other men eventually married and sired children. Very, very occasionally men were hideously punished for "unnatural acts," but overall society's preference was to respect the privacy of the bedroom and ask no questions. As the writer and critic J. M. Coetzee has put it, people in the nineteenth century by and large "did not feel they needed to ask themselves what the amative content of intimacy [between men] might be . . . because their notion of intimacy did not boil down to what the men in question did with their sexual organs."

Nonetheless, even if it is easy to document that after the age of five Albert's intimate relationships were all with men (except for his love of his wife, the Queen), even if it is possible to argue that the young Albert could have experienced homosexual love, there is not one scrap of hard evidence that he did. This is not surprising. He was a man of great renown, major achievement, and small popularity who died tragically young and had a loyal band of friends and relatives. In the years following his death, the person who assiduously collected and lovingly savored the records of Prince Albert's boyhood was his wife. Queen Victoria was the last person likely to uncover evidence that her husband had not slept with women because he preferred to sleep with men.

NEWS FROM ENGLAND intruded on Prince Albert's idyllic time in Bonn. In June 1837, William IV died and Victoria became Queen. Albert wrote her a dutiful letter of congratulations in English, to which she dutifully replied. But for the next eighteen months, Victoria gave only a cursory thought to her cousin Albert. She complained to Uncle Leopold that when Albert wrote to her, neither his English nor his French was up to par. Leopold felt it wiser not to mention Albert anymore.

Nonetheless, all Europe buzzed with reports that the Queen of England planned to marry Albert of Saxe-Coburg and Gotha. For a young man, it was demeaning to have to wait for a woman to give him the nod. Therefore, on the advice of his uncle Leopold and with the consent of Queen Victoria, who was kept abreast of every stage in her cousin's Bildung, Albert did not go back for his summer vacation to Coburg or to Brussels. Instead, with his faithful brother, tutor, and valet in tow, he disappeared into the Alps for a long walking tour through Switzerland and then continued on for a visit to Northern Italy.

Long, strenuous walks in beautiful mountains were infinitely more to Albert's taste than hobnobbing at the court of the French king. With his favorite companions since childhood, Albert was very happy during that summer. Even when the weather turned bad, Albert insisted on doing each stage of the journey through the mountains on foot. But he did not completely forget his duties as a Coburg prince. He compiled a scrapbook of his travels that he sent to his cousin Victoria at her request. It contained an edelweiss he had picked and a scrap of paper in Voltaire's handwriting for his royal cousin's increasingly famous collection of autographs.

After months away, the princes Albert and Ernest paid a cursory visit to their relatives in Coburg and Gotha. Their grandmother Caroline noticed appreciatively that dear Albert was now in superb physical shape. All the same, the grandsons spent a total of nine and one quarter hours in her house, most of them asleep in bed. Back at Bonn by the beginning of November, the princes planned to spend Christmas in Brussels but had to defer the visit until January. Prince Albert had seriously injured his knee and was unable to travel. No doubt under orders to bring his equestrian skills up to Queen Victoria's high standards, Albert missed a jump when riding in an indoor arena and banged his leg against a wall.

By late January, however, he was once again able to take long walks, and he and his brother spent the whole of February in Brussels. As Albert explained to his grandmother, who he knew would be upset not to see him in Coburg for the holidays, going to Brussels was important for his future. The visit would give him and Ernest "the opportunity of learning more distinctly what uncle [Leopold] thinks of the coming separation, next spring, of our [his and Ernest's] hitherto united lives, and also of giving him, at the same time, our own views of it. That moment [of separating] is, in its saddest form, ever before me. We would, therefore, as long as time allows us, do all we can to soften its pain and to gild the pill."

In fact, Leopold was especially anxious to explain viva voce to Prince Albert where he stood with his royal English cousin. Stockmar at the English court was reporting that Victoria was a confident and conscientious monarch. She loved her work and was deeply absorbed in her relationship with her prime minister, Lord Melbourne. She saw Melbourne every day, often several times a day, and corresponded with him constantly. She was in no hurry at all to see Albert. "The chief question," wrote Prince Albert to his father from Brussels in February 1838, "is now as to my mode of life in the meantime [until Victoria finally made her mind up, one way or the other]. For the first half year it is settled that I should remain at Bonn. We have now got through the most difficult of our studies, and intend to turn the summer to account in learning modern languages, and reading political works. After that I am to travel in accordance with your wishes and those of my uncle, in order to learn to depend more upon myself. This plan is also most agreeable to myself, and uncle is trying to get for me as traveling companion a well-informed young Englishman—a Mr. Seymour."

The phrase "in order to learn to depend more upon myself" is significant. Finally it seems to have dawned on Duke Ernest, King Leopold, and Baron Stockmar, all men who formed their closest relationships with men and vastly preferred male company, that Prince Albert's "pure" life with his brother, his tutor, and bosom friends like Prince William of Löwenstein came to him a little too easily. His patterns of behavior to date were indeed an excellent preparation for monogamous married life in puritanical England. In a world where venereal disease was endemic, they boded well for his reproductive success. But they were not good training for courtship. Queen Victoria had more power and autonomy than any other woman in the world. She could not be led obediently to the altar by her family like an ordinary princess.

But Albert was far less preoccupied with Queen Victoria than with the impending separation from his brother. He was faced with the dissolution of the familiar and deeply comforting intimacy with Ernest and Florschütz that he had known since he was five years old. The prospect almost broke his heart. Only Cart would remain with him, and Cart was only his valet. As soon as the academic semester was over, Florschütz would retire after fifteen years of selfless service. In November Prince Ernest of Coburg would move out of his brother's shadow and begin an independent life, taking up his commission in the army of their kinsman, the king of Saxony. As Albert wrote to his friend Prince William of Löwenstein: "The separation will be frightfully painful for us. Up to this moment we have never, as long as we can recollect, been a single day away from each other. I cannot bear to think of that moment."

As they had as boys, Prince Ernest and Prince Albert spent the late summer and fall of 1838 together in Coburg, mainly at the Rosenau. Ernest was unwell, causing his family great anxiety. Both young men were sadly conscious that things would never be the same again. As Albert wrote to Ernest on August 29, 1839: "Whatever may be in store for us, let us remain one in our feelings. We have, as you correctly say, found what others seek in vain, during all their lives: the soul of another that is able to understand one, that will suffer with one, be glad with one: one that finds the same pleasure in the same aspirations."

In fact, they almost died together. When staying overnight at the ancient and largely unoccupied Ehrenburg Palace, Prince Albert was awakened by a strange smell. A servant had left some papers on top of a stove in a room some four doors away from the one where he, his brother, and Isaac Cart were sleeping. The old timbers and easily flammable paintings and draperies were already burning when Prince Albert got to the room. Instead of leaving as quickly as possible, he and Cart recklessly closed the windows and doors and fought the flames with jugs of water, bedding, and clothes while Ernest ran downstairs to get help. It was probably thanks to the rapid reaction of Prince Albert and Cart that the Ehrenburg Palace suffered only minor damage. On this occasion, as on many others subsequently, Prince Albert showed bravery, leadership, and presence of mind.

At last November came, and Duke Ernest and Prince Albert with due pomp accompanied Prince Ernest some way on his road to Dresden. The parting was wrenching—Albert wrote that he could barely hold back his tears before the assembled princes and princesses—and on his return home, Albert wrote to his stepgrandmother Duchess Caroline:

> Now I am quite alone. Ernest is off over the mountains, and I am left
> behind, still surrounded by so many things which allow me to pretend
> that he is in the next room . . . We accompanied Ernest as far as
> Lobenstein, where we spent the evening and the following morning at the
> home of our dear great-aunt . . . The next morning brought the pain of
> parting . . . We . . . then drove home, this time without Ernest, arriving

*at ten o'clock at night, almost frozen to death. We traveled, as usual, in
an open Droshky, and had to endure 16 degrees of cold while crossing the
lovely Frankenwald. Now Ernest has slept through his first night at
Dresden. Today he will be feeling slightly empty. Now I really have got to
get out of the habit of saying we and use the egotistic, cold-sounding
pronoun I. With we every thing sounded much softer, for we expresses
the harmony between two souls and I expresses the individual man's
resistance to external forces, and also, admittedly, his trust in his own
strength. I am afraid of tiring you as I rattle on like this, but in the
present silence it is a comfort to be able to talk freely.*

＊

ALBERT WAS NOT ALLOWED to stay at the Rosenau and mope. Within days
of Ernest's departure, he began a three-month tour that would take him all
through Italy and then back into Switzerland to meet up with his father and
some of his Mensdorff relatives. Albert had a new and unexpected traveling
companion: Baron Stockmar. Though he dreaded cold and fatigue, Stockmar was dispatched from England to undertake this lengthy tour in the
depths of winter at the joint behest of King Leopold and of Victoria herself.
The final stages in Albert's Bildung were now at hand. No one better than
Stockmar himself could prepare him for the complex and difficult new life
that seemed likely to open before him.

Six months earlier, Prince Albert had loved walking through the Alps,
even when it snowed. He had enjoyed his ten months in Brussels and his
two semesters at Bonn. But he did not much like Italy, probably because he
was unhappy and could not even say it. He felt the cold at least as sharply as
Stockmar. Rome was a disappointment, and, though he appreciated Italian
art, architecture, and music, he hated Italian society and the Catholic religion. "In many, many respects the country is far behind what one had expected. In the climate, in the scenery, in the study of the arts, one feels most
disagreeably disappointed," he wrote pompously to his friend Löwenstein.

He was still the same Albert, indifferent to ladies, eager for solid instruc-
tion, and with a slightly mean sense of humor. In Florence at a ball, the
Duke of Tuscany remarked of Albert to the wife of the British ambassador,
"Here is a prince we may be proud of. The beautiful young lady waits for him
to dance, while he is busy listening to the man of letters." Granted a private
audience with Pope Gregory XVI, Prince Albert found it necessary to correct His Holiness on the Greeks' cultural debt to the Etruscans. When the official who had brought the Coburg party to the Vatican grabbed the pope's

foot to kiss and was kicked in the mouth, Albert had a mad fit of the giggles and was shooed out of the room.

In February Albert and Stockmar were joined by a young English nobleman, Lieutenant Francis Seymour. This gentleman's job was to speak English with the prince, offer some youthful (but not dissipated) companionship, and report back to Queen Victoria. Seymour, who went on to a successful career in the English army and at Victoria's court as General Sir Francis Seymour, later wrote a description of the prince in Florence. Seymour claimed that Albert led an exemplary life, ate simply, drank only water, toured ruins and art galleries, took long country walks, enjoyed discussions over tea with Baron Stockmar, when that gentleman was well enough to come down, and was asleep by nine. "[Prince Albert] had been accustomed to such early hours in his own country that he had great difficulty in keeping himself awake when obliged to sit up late," wrote Seymour.

Albert himself paints a rather different picture in a letter he wrote at the time to his friend Löwenstein. "I have lately thrown myself into the whirl of society. I have danced, dined, supped, paid compliments, have been introduced to people, and had people introduced to me; I have spoken French and English—exhausted all remarks about the weather—have played the amiable—and, in short, have made 'bonne mine à mauvais jeu' [pretended to look pleased when dealt a bad hand]. You know my *passion* for such things, and must therefore admire my strength of character that I have never excused myself—never returned home till five in the morning—that I have emptied the carnival cup to the dregs." In the same bitter vein, Prince Albert wrote to Florschütz that he was under orders to "go into society, learn the ways of the world and vitiate my culture with fashionable accomplishments. And I will do it."

Stockmar, meanwhile, was supplying the Queen, King Leopold, and Duke Ernest with his acerbic reports on the prince's progress. Stockmar praised the prince's talents, enjoyed his company, but bemoaned his lack of interest in politics and his poor stamina. He reported that the prince was not "empressé" (enthusiastic and attentive) in his dealings with women and lacked "les belles manières." Stockmar attributed this fault to Albert's motherless childhood and the lack of cultured, intelligent women in his life. He opined that the prince would "always have more success with men," damning with faint praise.

In the summer, Albert returned to Coburg and, as he lamented to his friend Löwenstein, was obliged to dawdle around exchanging compliments before he could get away for a fortnight with his brother in Dresden. "Then

I must go to a place that I hate mortally," he wrote, "that charming Carlsbad, where papa is taking the waters, and much wishes me to be with him. I hope this campaign will be over by the middle of August." Carlsbad was a spa, one of the holiday resorts notorious for sexual dalliance. The visit may have been Duke Ernest's own contribution to the "campaign" to win Victoria's hand, a final attempt to prepare his son Albert for the reproductive duties that lay before him, and he may even have succeeded. More probably Albert, following the dictates of his uncle and of Stockmar as well as his own inclinations, managed to resist to the bitter end the "corrupt moral atmosphere" his father generated.

WITHIN THE YEAR, Albert would marry—Ernest was his best man—and take up life in England. At the time of the wedding, Ernest disgraced himself by his sexual exploits in London, causing his brother much embarrassment at the English court. Even worse, Ernest in early 1840 was infected with venereal disease and was causing grave anxiety in the family. This fact is established conclusively by a passage from a letter Albert wrote to Ernest from Windsor Castle on January 1, 1841:

> I am deeply distressed and grieved by the news of your severe illness. I have to infer that it is a new outbreak of the same disease which you had here [at Windsor in February 1840, at the time of Albert's wedding]. If I should be wrong I should thank God; but should I be right, I must advise you as a loving brother, to give up all ideas of marriage for the next two years and to work earnestly for the restoration and consolidation of your health . . . to marry would be as immoral as dangerous . . . for you. If the worst should happen, you would deprive your wife of her health and honour, and should you have a family you would give your children a life full of suffering . . . and your country a sick heir. At best your wife could not respect you and her love would thus not have any value for you; should you not have the strength to make her contented in married life (which demands its sacrifices), this would lead to domestic discord and unhappiness . . . For God's sake do not trifle with matters which are so sacred.

Albert's solemn strictures made no impression on Ernest. Perhaps they never had. Ernest was determined to marry and, like his father before him, deludedly thought his marital prospects were brilliant. Duke Ernest I, Prince Ernest's father, tried to marry him to a Russian grand duchess, but this plan came to nothing. While Ernest was at Windsor at the time of his brother's engagement, Queen Victoria floated the beguiling idea that he should marry her first cousin, Princess Augusta of Cambridge. This glittering prospect also came to nothing. Perhaps Augusta, an opinionated young woman, was not interested in Ernest Coburg. Perhaps Albert decided that having Ernest reside in England with an English wife would not be good for his own marriage or for the precious Coburg family reputation.

Obliged to fall back on a second-tier German princess, Ernest married Alexandrine, daughter of the Grand Duke of Baden on May 3, 1842. Prince Albert did not travel to Coburg for his brother's wedding. He had already forbidden his brother to come to England during his wife's second pregnancy in 1841, as Victoria had been seriously upset by her brother-in-law's conduct at the time of her wedding. Prince Ernest was not invited to Windsor to attend the christening of his first nephew, the Prince of Wales.

Prince Albert's gloomy premonitions about his brother's marital prospects proved right on the mark. Alexandrine of Baden was not yet twenty-two, in excellent health, and certainly a virgin when she married, but she never had children and seems to have feared infertility early in her marriage. That she was infected by her husband's disease and made sterile seems all too likely. In 1844 Alexandrine officially adopted her husband's nephew Alfred, acknowledging him thereby as the heir presumptive to the duchy of Coburg. Ernest himself was not sterile, and throughout his life he apparently pursued women with the kind of zeal he devoted to shooting animals and birds. He had a succession of *maitresses en titre* at the court of Coburg, whom Alexandrine humbly countenanced, and he managed to sire at least three illegitimate children.

Royal biographers have not been anxious to establish exactly when and where Ernest Coburg was infected with venereal disease. This was especially true for Queen Victoria even though early in her marriage she discovered her brother-in-law was a cruel and licentious man. However, the question of Ernest Coburg's venereal disease has an important bearing on our understanding of the young Albert. In the family correspondence of 1838 through 1840 and the Queen's diary, there is a series of casual references to Ernest being seriously ill and causing concern—in Brussels, in Coburg, at Windsor when he famously had "jaundice" during the period of his brother's engagement. The venereal disease could have been contracted as early as 1837 when, to the merriment of Albert, Ernest was incurring the wrath of General Wiechmann in Brussels and Bonn. But if Ernest contracted venereal disease when he and Albert were students, Albert must have known, since according to Albert's own letters and diaries from the period, he and Ernest were more like identical twins than brothers, sharing lessons, lectures, activities, and friends.

One part of Albert's golden legend, as narrated and carefully documented by his widow, is that he had an ascendancy over his older brother from an early age. Men who knew the brothers in youth, like King Leopold, testified for the Queen that by force of will, character, and intellect, Albert took the lead in all the brothers' affairs. Putting together Queen Victoria's account of her husband's early years and the facts now known about her brother-in-law's adult life, can we really believe that as soon as Ernest got to Dresden on December 1, 1838, he stopped being a replica of his exemplary younger brother and metamorphosed into a carbon copy of their vain, philandering, egotistic, improvident father? Either Albert's purity or his authority must suffer if it were proved that Ernest, his alter ego, the Jonathan to his David, the Damon to his Pythias, fell into vice as early as Brussels or Bonn, while he looked on in impotent acquiescence.

The relationship between Albert and Ernest before 1840 is a historical enigma. It suited both to have it so. We shall probably never know the truth.

$\mathcal{T}$OGETHER

12.

Victoria Plans Her Marriage

...

VICTORIA AND ALBERT'S ENGAGEMENT AT WINDSOR IN OCTOBER 1839 was followed by a few weeks of bliss. Only the prince's father and stepgrandmother, King Leopold, Baron Stockmar, and Lord Melbourne were told, and Victoria was especially insistent that her mother should not know. Albert's brother, Ernest, the official chaperone, conveniently went down with "jaundice," allowing the young couple to spend quite a lot of time alone. They did all the things the Queen liked best. They rode out together, sang and played duets, looked at albums of etchings side by side, and played with their dogs. Victoria adored Albert's greyhound Eos, who followed them everywhere and was so perfectly tame. She was overjoyed to find that Albert had become a superb dancer. In private, in her fiancé's arms and with Ernest at the piano, she at last tasted the delights of waltzing.

Victoria drew Albert's picture. Albert corrected the mistakes in Victoria's letters. Seated on a little blue sofa, Victoria nestled in Albert's bosom, and, when he sat at the piano, she dropped kisses on his head as she passed. He responded eagerly, embracing her passionately, telling her over and over again how much he loved her, and covering her hand with kisses—how small it was in comparison with Ernest's! He called her *Vortrefflichste*, most splendid of women. Savoring an intimacy that she had craved since childhood and that he had not expected to enjoy, they were deliriously happy. Never would they be quite so happy again.

■

AS WORD OF THEIR Queen's impending marriage seeped out, Victoria's subjects were titillated by the peculiar, one could say unique, problems facing the royal couple. Who would wear the breeches, saucily demanded English commentators. Humor of this kind was supremely distasteful to Prince Albert, in no small measure because he was, in fact, obsessed by the very same question, framed more delicately. Who would have the upper hand in the marriage, he or Victoria?

For every other married couple in Great Britain, the answer was preordained and crystal clear, if not undisputed. The vast majority of both men and women in the nineteenth century agreed that by nature, religion, law, and immemorial custom men were superior to women. Biological science and social theory buttressed men's claims to supremacy not only in politics, administration, and business, but also in the home. According to the legal doctrine of "feme covert," a British woman who married lost all her independent legal and civil status. She and her husband were viewed by the law as one entity, and that entity was he. A married woman's property, unless controlled by her natal family through a prenuptial agreement, was her husband's. Anything she earned was legally his to do with as he willed. She could not buy or sell property or enter into any legal transaction without his leave.

A husband could legally enforce sexual congress on his terms. He could physically chastise his wife, sequester her in the home, or commit her to a madhouse without much fear of the law. The children of the marriage were, in effect, the property of the husband, and through his last will and testament he could dispose of them as he chose even after death. Divorce for a husband was possible, if unpleasant and expensive. For a wife it was prohibitively difficult. The message to a woman in mid-nineteenth-century Great Britain was clear: Like a child, a felon, or a madman, she had no role to play in the public sphere. In the marketplace she was at most a consumer. Her place was in the home. Her duty and her pleasure must be to obey her menfolk, and dedicate her life to her family.

But Victoria was not just a woman. She was a woman who reigned, a queen regnant, and this changed her relationship to every man and woman. The anomalousness of her situation was keenly apparent to her contemporaries at the time of her accession. As the radical politician Lord Brougham plaintively explained in an anonymous pamphlet: "An experienced man, well stricken in years, I hold myself before *you*, a girl of eighteen, who, in my own or any other family in Europe, would be treated as a child, ordered to do as was most agreeable or convenient to others—whose inclinations would never be consulted—whose opinion would never be thought of—whose consent would never be asked upon any one thing appertaining to any other human being but yourself, beyond the choice of gown or cap, nor always upon that: yet before you I humble myself."

When Victoria decided to marry, the anomaly of her legal and civil status became even more pronounced. In certain respects, she seemed the traditional bride. She was small and very feminine. She came to marriage as a guaranteed virgin, since she had been watched night and day since her birth. She was likely to bear children, since she was healthy, sexually mature, and came from a line of fertile women. All of this was eminently pleasing to the patriarch in Prince Albert. But as a social and legal entity, Victoria was far more man than woman.

As Queen of England, Victoria was at the apex of national power and international status. Far from being a purely domestic creature, sheltered from the world, she had an exceptionally busy and demanding full-time job, and her whole life was lived in the public eye. England was very rich, and Victoria occupied the top of the governmental pyramid. She had a huge salary and enjoyed a luxurious lifestyle at state expense. She was also wealthy in her own right.

None of this would change when the Queen married. Governed by the British constitution, not British civil law, Victoria was the only woman in Great Britain and Ireland to whom the law gave full, independent legal control over her income and possessions whether or not she was married. Most of what Victoria had she could not sell, bequeath, or otherwise alienate. For her lifetime she held what she had in trust for her successor in a unique kind of entail. Her chief source of income, her parliamentary allowance under the civil list, was hers by virtue of her position as head of state.

These were the facts of Victoria's life. She knew them well, and, with some important provisos, they were very much to her taste. She took her duties and responsibilities as queen seriously, and enjoyed the work of monarchy. She was aware that she showed more talent for the job than most of her male predecessors. She reveled in her power and her independence.

Albert's situation was very different. He was a very young man of great integrity and ability with very little experience of life outside the home and the classroom. He was a proud youth, confident of being the equal of any man and better than most. At the same time, he was conscious that most European princes were richer and more powerful than he. He was a misogynist, confident of being superior to all women without exception, who was yet obliged to make marriage his career. Victoria, Queen of England, was the most magnificent mate to whom he could possibly aspire. Becoming her

husband was, pun intended, his crowning achievement. What he brought
to his marriage were the traditional gifts of a princess bride: beauty, pedi-
gree, chastity, and the promise of royal children. Prince Albert was a man of
reason who prided himself on his self-control and cool temperament. But
the discrepancy between his self-image and the world's opinion gnawed at
the roots of his peace.

As Victoria and Albert spooned on the little blue sofa, each had a secret
agenda. Victoria was determined to change as little as possible in her delightful life as queen. She intended to have her Albert and her own way. She
would continue to see her ministers *alone!* She would remain independent
by retaining control over her property, her 385,000 pounds from the civil
list, and her private income.

Albert, for his part, was determined to institute the traditional balance
of power between husband and wife by becoming the master in his wife's
house. He would manage her worldly goods even if he could not own them.
Educated in statecraft by King Leopold and Baron Stockmar, Albert planned
to take the reins of power from Victoria once they were married. He would
leave her queen only in name.

BETWEEN OCTOBER 1839, when Prince Albert arrived at Windsor Castle,
and the wedding in February 1840, Victoria held all the trump cards. Like a
princess in a fairy story, she imposed upon Albert a series of tests and or-
deals. The prince had to beg through family intermediaries for an invitation

to come to England to see the Queen. When the invitation came, it was grudging and issued on the strict proviso that Her Majesty committed herself to nothing. After Victoria had looked Albert over and decided that, indeed, he was the husband she was looking for, her first impulse was not to clasp her beloved in her arms but to go into delicious conclave with her prime minister over how exactly she should propose and what arrangements would have to be made for the wedding.

Only then did Victoria summon Albert to her boudoir in her ancestral castle for a private interview. She proposed marriage, never doubting, for all her maidenly protestations, that he would accept. She magnanimously conducted the proposal interview in German, since she knew Albert was at a disadvantage in English. Victoria cooed her adoration and shed tears over the sacrifice Albert was making in marrying her, but the very structure of the proposal spoke volumes. Victoria, Queen of Great Britain and Ireland, of her free choice, was condescending to marry a mere prince of Coburg because she found him agreeable. Very much the great lady, she was also very careful to save his feelings.

Now that she had made her decision, Victoria was eager to have Albert by her side. She set the marriage date for February 10, and on November 14, Albert left Windsor for Coburg, stopping for a few days en route at Wiesbaden, where his uncle and Baron Stockmar were both waiting for him. There, according to Stockmar's memoirs, "All the circumstances and difficulties connected with Prince Albert's position in England were submitted to a detailed and exhaustive discussion." The Coburgs had no trust in the security of the regular mails, knowing government officials all over Europe routinely opened letters, so a special system of couriers was set up between London, Coburg, Wiesbaden, and Brussels. As soon as Albert left for Coburg, Stockmar traveled to London, charged with negotiating the marriage settlement.

One thing that was certainly part of the discussion between Albert, his uncle, and Baron Stockmar was Lord Melbourne and the prime minister's relationship with the Queen. Stockmar and Leopold had known Melbourne, Palmerston, Wellington, and all the other key players on the English political stage for twenty years. They had grown old with them. While Melbourne was enduring the Byron scandal and Palmerston (reportedly) was bedding three of the five most powerful women in British society, Leopold was conducting clandestine affairs with women in England and abroad, seconded by his invaluable agent, Stockmar.

From the day of Victoria's accession, King Leopold had been dismayed to hear from Baron Stockmar, his agent at the Court of St. James's, how completely the Queen fell under her prime minister's spell. Lord Melbourne for two and a half years had been both surrogate father and political mentor to the young Queen of England. Victoria adored Melbourne, laughed with him, relied on him, quoted him, adopted his friends and relatives as her own best friends and intimate companions. Cynical people such as the Duke of Wellington, Charles Greville, and Princess Lieven, the wife of the Russian ambassador, were saying that Victoria was in love with Melbourne though quite unaware of it. Such gossip could not fail to be distasteful to Victoria's idealistic young fiancé.

The Coburg party, which comprised Victoria's bitterly aggrieved mother as well as King Leopold and Duke Ernest, blamed Melbourne for the public relations debacle over the Lady Flora Hastings case and for the bedchamber crisis that had brought the Queen's reputation so low in 1838. They were well aware that the prime minister at the outset had been, at best, lukewarm about Prince Albert as a husband for Queen Victoria. While at Windsor, Albert had met nothing but exquisite politeness and warm approval from Lord Melbourne, who was anxious to establish good relations with his beloved queen's husband-to-be. But all the same, the prince from the outset was primed to see Melbourne as his chief rival for the Queen's attention and regard, a secret adversary. The events in England over the next three months did nothing to change the prince's mind on this point.

Once back in Coburg, if left to himself, the prince would have probably wallowed in the melancholy task of saying farewell to friends and family while packing his green student lamp and other prized possessions into one or two trunks. But Albert had little time for tears. Filled with pride and happiness, the Coburgers and Gothaners put on a giddy succession of celebratory breakfasts, shooting parties, dinners, balls, and galas well calculated to upset a young man who hated rich food, drank no wine, and liked to get to bed early. A distinguished party of English peers came to the Hall of Giants at Coburg bearing the insignia of the Order of the Garter, Britain's highest honor—a gift from Queen Victoria—which Prince Albert received at the hands of his father. In another solemn ceremony, the weeping Albert renounced his German nationality and became British.

Throughout all this frenzied round of activities, Victoria could not be neglected for a moment. Though far away, the Queen received constant reports on the prince's doings, wrote to him at least once every day, and went into hysteria if a fat love letter did not land on her plate each morning. The prince sat for a portrait that his beloved could gaze upon in his absence. He set to music a poem in honor of Victoria that his brother, Ernest, had composed. And he wrote every day at length, responding to the crescendo of insults from England, where, it seemed, no one was happy that the Queen had engaged to marry her cousin of Coburg.

The opposition Tory leaders in parliament, headed by the Duke of Wellington, suggested that Prince Albert of Saxe-Coburg and Gotha might be a closet Catholic, and thus constitutionally barred from marrying an English sovereign. The Tories cited the fact that both Albert's uncle Leopold and his cousin Ferdinand had converted to Catholicism when they became the kings of Belgium and Portugal, respectively. All of Coburg saw it as a slap in the face when the English parliament demanded to see Prince Albert's Protestant credentials. It was a point of honor in Prince Albert's family, and a well-established historical fact, that a Coburg ancestor had been one of the first supporters of Martin Luther and the Reformation. However, Duke Ernest swallowed his pride and commissioned Stockmar to compose the necessary memorandum on Prince Albert's lifelong and ineradicable devotion to the Protestant religion.

King Leopold had been one of the first to hear of the engagement of his niece and nephew, and he argued strenuously that Albert must receive an English dukedom when he married. As the king saw it, the prince's success in his difficult new role depended on sealing his identity as an Englishman by making him an official part of the establishment, independent from his wife. Subsequent events proved that Leopold was right, but in 1839 he could not prevail. Melbourne insisted that it would not do for Prince Albert to be a member of the House of Lords, and thus involved in politics, and the Queen preferred Melbourne's advice to her uncle's. For his part, Albert declared that he would never stoop to an English dukedom, since a son of the royal house of Coburg outranked any English peer. In England, where many lords had genealogies as long and estates much larger and richer than Coburg-Gotha, this came off as a piece of pathetic rodomontade from a youth of twenty.

The issue of the prince's precedence had also to be addressed before the marriage, and on this Victoria, Albert, and Uncle Leopold were of one mind. Precedence was a matter of burning importance among members of European royal families. At court, immense resources of scholarship and ingenuity were devoted to deciding who should lead whom into dinner, who should sit where at table, and who should "give the step" (*donner le pas*)—in other words, walk behind whom when the time came to move in or out of a room or residence. Queen Victoria was determined that her husband should take precedence over everyone in Great Britain except herself, but on this issue she met with determined opposition not only from parliament but from members of her own family.

Her uncle Ernest, the much-loathed Duke of Cumberland, now king of Hanover, refused point-blank ever to yield precedence to Albert. Her uncle Cambridge was almost as recalcitrant. Her uncle Sussex agreed to give way to Albert, but only on the condition that the Queen make a duchess of his morganatic wife, Lady Cecilia Buggin, and receive the lady at court. The Tories in parliament also wished English royal dukes to have precedence over the Queen's German husband. They pointed out that if as they fervently hoped, a Prince of Wales was born, that young man on his majority must have precedence immediately after his royal mother. Frustrated in parliament, Victoria was advised by Charles Greville, secretary to the Privy Council and an expert on English constitutional law, that she had the power to give her husband precedence after herself within Great Britain. She duly issued letters patent to that effect.

As a loyal wife-to-be, Victoria raised the issue with her ministers of making Albert her king consort. A sharing of royal power, in which the male spouse would in fact have executive authority and carry out the Crown's business, was what Queen Mary Stuart had demanded for her husband, William of Orange, before they came to the throne in 1688. It was what Princess Charlotte, just before her tragic death, had said she wanted for her husband, (then) Prince Leopold of Saxe-Coburg. It was what Ferdinand of Saxe-Coburg-Kohary, first cousin to both Victoria and Albert, enjoyed once his 1838 marriage to the Queen of Portugal was buttressed by the arrival of a male heir.

But Prime Minister Melbourne refused to take the Queen's request before parliament. "For God's sake, say no more about it, Ma'am," he exclaimed, "for those who can make Kings can unmake them!" Her Majesty, at whatever personal cost, must bear the constitutional burden of monarchy alone, said Melbourne. Sad but resigned, Her Majesty gave way.

The unkindest cut of all to Albert's pride at the time of his engagement was financial. He fully expected to receive on his marriage a parliamentary allowance of fifty thousand pounds a year for life. This was what fat, useless Prince George of Denmark, husband of Queen Anne, had enjoyed in the seventeenth century. It was what Uncle Leopold, even after he became king of a sovereign nation, had been paid ever since 1815 when he married Princess Charlotte. It was what Queen Adelaide was granted on the accession of her husband William IV and that she continued to receive until her death. Melbourne and the Whig cabinet assured the Queen that there would be no difficulty in securing for her husband the traditional appanage of a royal spouse.

But Melbourne was lazy, his government weak, and parliament sulky.

The Tories unearthed their social conscience and joined with the radical faction of the Whigs in insisting that, since the economy was in decline and the working poor were in dire distress throughout the nation, the time had come to cut government expenses, including the civil list. To a very young, virtually penniless German gentleman who was marrying a very rich woman, thirty thousand a year, at a time when decent middle-class families managed on a few hundred, was surely enough. Thirty thousand pounds was, in fact, approximately the total annual revenue of the duchy of Coburg-Gotha, but the Coburgs would never cease to mourn the twenty thousand a year that should by rights have been Albert's. They laid the blame squarely upon Lord Melbourne's shoulders.

In fact, the Tories could afford to snub Prince Albert, since hostility to the royal marriage cut right across party lines. The nation was solicitous of the Queen's happiness, keen to see her married, and anxious for the birth of a Prince of Wales, but few people in England had much enthusiasm for Prince Albert of Saxe-Coburg and Gotha. Royal bloodlines were of fierce importance in Germany, but they meant less and less in nineteenth-century England. Birth privilege and political power had long been firmly yoked to wealth in Great Britain, and Albert had no money. As a member of a royal caste, Prince Albert felt destined to rule the world, but even most conservative Englishmen had ceased to believe in the divine right of kings. Ever since Magna Carta, English aristocrats had seen themselves as kingmakers, and the homage they gave to the sovereign was always conditional on his (or her) good behavior.

Albert was also foreign and in English eyes ipso facto inferior. Tories and Whigs alike were fiercely xenophobic, and even British radicals had an ingrained sense of national superiority. Prime minister and plowman all pretty much saw Prince Albert as an imported royal stud with no assets but his handsome face. As a contemporary broadsheet rhyme put it:

He comes the bridegroom of Victoria's choice,
The nominee of Lehzen's vulgar voice;
He comes to take 'for better or for worse'
England's fat Queen and England's fatter purse.

And if the British parliament was proving intransigent and the British press was taking pot shots, Victoria, at a distance of several hundred miles, was not at all the sweet, confiding little creature of the blue sofa. When Albert begged his betrothed to take two weeks away for a honeymoon, she refused. A honeymoon was quite impossible for the Queen of England,

Victoria wrote. Perhaps her dearest Albert did not understand that she was quite indispensable to the business of government and liked to be close to parliament when it was in session and to her ministers at all times. Albert had crossed a line and was sharply reminded about the no-trespassing sign.

Then there was the issue of the prince's household. Albert assumed that when he came to England, he would be free to bring his own team of aides with him from Germany. His cousin Ferdinand had been accompanied to Lisbon by his tutor Dietz, and the two of them took over the Portuguese affairs of state, with, it must be admitted, very bad results. At the very least, Albert counted upon having a German who was fully in his trust to serve as his private secretary and treasurer. In this way, Albert himself would control his financial affairs and be independent.

It was thus a terrible shock when the prince learned that, on the contrary, his fiancée intended to name Englishmen from her private circle to fill all the positions in his household. Lord Melbourne's personal secretary, George Anson, a member of a noted Whig family, was to be the prince's personal secretary. Albert begged Victoria repeatedly and in the mildest and most plaintive of terms, to allow him to have some Germans about him. Victoria informed him that he must be content to bring with him from Coburg his librarian, his valet, and his greyhound.

This matter of the private secretary was still unresolved when Prince Albert arrived in England for his wedding. In the end, faced with an ultimatum, he was forced to give way, and, in fact, he and Anson soon became close friends and allies. But the prince indulged in one small gesture of defiance. On reaching his majority, Albert had inherited an income of 2,400 pounds a year out of his mother's estate. Determined that this money at least was his to do with as he willed, before leaving Germany, Albert assigned his brother, Ernest, to act as his trustee and manager. German money should stay in Germany, where no Englishman could touch it.

When parliament created difficulties for her dearest Albert, Queen Victoria was a veritable dragon, breathing flames of anger and defiance. As far as lay in her power, she bestowed honors on Albert, granting him precedence next to her own, giving him the Garter, and making him a field marshal in the British army, to the fierce indignation of the senior officer class. But all these things were in her power, and there was the rub. Power, not protection, was what Albert sought from his wife-to-be.

Victoria could play the loyal little woman to her heart's content. Parliament and the cabinet, especially the cabinet presided over by Lord Melbourne, would ensure that Her Majesty gave away nothing that was hers.

Charles Greville, a cynical man who observed the Queen closely, was sure that, in her heart of hearts, Victoria was not sorry that her husband would remain so financially and socially dependent upon her.

*

THE ROYAL WEDDING was scheduled for early February, always a dark and dreary month in Britain but especially so in nineteenth-century London, where the air was clogged with soot. Traditionally royal weddings were private affairs, held in the evening, but the Whig government insisted that Queen Victoria's wedding should be celebrated in daylight at the Chapel Royal at St. James's Palace. Thousands of people could see the Queen and her husband go by and, as it were, get some entertainment for their tax money. Reluctantly, Victoria yielded to her ministers, but in all other matters relating to the wedding arrangements, she had her way, careless of gossip and censure.

The bridegroom and his party, she decreed, should lodge with her at Buckingham Palace. If her mother and other narrow-minded people thought it improper for bride and groom to be under the same roof, that was just too bad. Albert always preferred to err on the side of propriety, but he was in no position to question his fiancée's arrangements. She was footing the bill not only for the wedding but for the travel expenses and "outfits" (clothing and all other personal items found necessary) of the whole Coburg party. Albert did write begging Victoria to choose as her bridesmaids only young ladies whose mothers had led irreproachable lives. Prime Minister Lord Melbourne, who was in a position to know, delicately intimated that ten such paragons of womanly virtue were not to be found among England's great families, so the Queen ignored this request too.

Victoria dictated the guest list for her wedding, and she invited only five Tories. One of the favored five was Lord Ashley, who hardly counted, since he was married to Lord Melbourne's niece. No Tories, not even the Duke of Wellington, were invited to the wedding breakfast. Albert wrote that he thought it a mistake for the Queen to identify so passionately with the Whigs, arguing that the monarchy should be above political party. Again the Queen took no notice. As Victoria saw it, the Tories needed to be punished, since they had proved to be her enemies in the parliamentary debates over her marriage.

While Albert was finding the three-month separation before his marriage an ordeal, Victoria too was troubled by doubts and worries. How exactly would she square the solemn oaths she had taken at her coronation with the equally solemn oaths she would take at her wedding? What did it mean for a queen to endow her husband with all her worldly goods? Could she find it in her heart to promise to love, honor, and obey when she had found so much pleasure in doing as she liked? To be a good wife, must she cease to be queen in all but name? It made her ill even to think of such things, and for a while it was feared at court that the Queen had measles and the wedding would be postponed.

On the way to London for his wedding, Prince Albert arrived in Brussels tired and peevish, as King Leopold duly reported to his niece Victoria. The Coburg party was then subjected to an unusually long and stormy Channel crossing and emerged at Dover, as the prince wrote to his fiancée, as pale as wax candles. However, the prince received a rousing welcome as he journeyed to London from the coast. When Albert arrived at Buckingham Palace, Victoria was waiting for him at the door and threw herself into his arms, an extraordinary lapse of protocol.

On the day of the wedding, the bride woke to pouring rain and mist, and at once penned an affectionate little note, inquiring if her beloved had slept well and assuring him that the weather must break. When the bride was dressed, she invited her husband-to-be to come see her in her wedding dress. This was another breach of decorum, but on this day it was Albert's admiration that Victoria craved, not the cheers of the masses. Instead of the heavily jewel-encrusted gold and silver cloth of traditional royal bridal gowns, the bride had chosen a white satin dress trimmed with a deep yoke of English lace. On her bosom she wore the modest sapphire brooch that Albert had given her, and a crown of orange blossoms, not diamonds, on her head.

For his part, the groom looked ravishingly handsome. For the first time, he was wearing the scarlet coat of a British field marshal, decorated with the blue sash, star, and chain of the Order of the Garter. The uniform jacket was cropped to the waist in front, swallow-tailed behind, and the prince had made sure that it fitted him like a glove. Skintight buff pantaloons, flat black court slippers, and a large white satin bow on one shoulder completed the prince's costume. To the modern eye, this paragon of masculine modesty seems to have chosen to wear ballet tights for his wedding, but such was the military fashion of the day.

The groom's party set off first from Buckingham Palace and was cheered on its route despite the rain. Arriving punctually at the chapel, flanked by his father and brother, also tall and fine in their German uniforms, Prince Albert looked pale. He was visibly disconcerted by the aggrieved remarks that the Duchess of Kent, just behind him, addressed to her sister-in-law, Queen Adelaide. Victoria's mother felt that she had not been given her proper prominence in the chapel.

The bride was prompt, and though the ten gawky maidens carrying her train made for a bumpy progress down the aisle, Victoria was too ecstatic to mind. The marriage ceremony was underrehearsed, and Albert, still uncomfortable in English, struggled at times. Victoria, blushing yet radiant, played her part to perfection. Remembering the problems she had encountered at her coronation, she had made sure that Albert's ring slid easily onto her fourth finger. When the Queen vowed to love, honor, and obey, her gloriously limpid voice electrified the guests who had been crammed into the little chapel. When the prince read his vows, the Queen was observed to turn directly toward him and gaze raptly up into his face. After the ceremony, people noticed the way the Queen warmly embraced her aunt-in-law, Queen Adelaide, and shook hands with her mother. In the vestry, bride and groom waited patiently as Earl Marshall, the Duke of Norfolk, who insisted that it was his right to sign the register first, searched through all his pockets for his spectacles.

Back at Buckingham Palace for the wedding breakfast, Victoria spent ten minutes alone with Lord Melbourne. Throughout the ceremony he had hovered close by the Queen's side, his eyes dim with tears and wearing a new coat that he had joked to her would be the toast of the event. The special relationship the prime minister had enjoyed with his sovereign was winding down, and Melbourne at least knew it. Victoria also spent a half hour alone with Albert. She presented him with a ring, and he urged that there should never be any secrets between them. His campaign for political power could not begin too early.

There were seven simultaneous and duly hierarchical wedding breakfasts featuring two hundred of the thickly iced and marzipaned fruitcakes traditional in English weddings. The main cake, bearing effigies of bride and groom, was nine feet in circumference and had to be carried in by four men. Breaking away early from the festivities, Victoria changed into a white satin morning gown trimmed with swan's down and a deep-brimmed bonnet that shielded her face from the inquiring gaze of the public. Thereupon, as she recorded later that day, "Dearest Albert came up and fetched me downstairs, where we took leave of Mamma and drove off at near 4, Albert and I alone which was *so delightful.*"

The bride had decided against buying a new carriage for her wedding and went off in an ancient barouche. Charles Greville found the equipage astonishingly shabby, but it was escorted all along the route to Windsor by a troop of carriages and cheering outriders. Arriving at the castle, the bride and groom first toured the private apartments that Victoria had had refurbished, and the prince discovered that, as at Buckingham Palace, Baroness Lehzen slept next door.

Both Queen and prince then separated to change their dress for a third time that day. Albert donned the dark blue Windsor uniform that was reserved for men dedicated to the Queen's private service, and then sat down at the piano to calm himself with music. On this first night, the Queen and prince had reduced their retinue to a minimum: just two gentlemen and two ladies. Dinner was served for the party of six, but for once Victoria had no appetite and after dinner had to lie on the couch with a sick headache. Albert sat on a stool by her side, holding her hand and whispering endearments. The bridal pair retired early to bed and were spared the taxing rituals and coarse jests whereby royal couples of the past on their wedding night were put into bed by the ladies and gentlemen of the bedchamber. Bride and groom did not get much sleep, and when she awoke next morning, Victoria gazed with delight on her sleeping husband's beautiful white neck, revealed by the loose nightshirt he wore.

Many couples have foundered on the reefs of their wedding night, and Queen Victoria in later life tended to regard brides as lambs for the slaughter, poor innocent young things surrendered to the criminal passions of men. But for her and Albert at Windsor in 1840, it was all moonlight and roses and a fair wind. It seems clear from the Queen's journal that not only did she and her husband consummate their marriage at the first opportunity but that Albert was able to initiate her into the pleasures of sex. This immediate success was of crucial importance in determining the course of the marriage. Victoria was a sensual, self-willed woman with warm Coburg and Hanoverian blood in her veins. The experienced men of her court saw her as ripe for the plucking. To secure his wife's affections, and to make himself indispensable to her, Albert needed to satisfy her physically.

In the light of history, Albert's success has seemed a given. He sired two children in his first twenty-two months of marriage, and then seven more. All the same, it is puzzling that conjugal felicity came to the royal couple so easily. According to the testimony of those who knew him, Albert had never slept with a woman before his marriage. He assured his wife that he never felt a flicker of desire for any woman but her. None of this bodes well for marital success, as the wife of poor virginal John Ruskin could testify. Albert was a healthy twenty-year-old who came from a long line of libidinous men, but he was very tired and tense when he and Victoria finally found themselves alone. Both he and his handlers—his father, his uncle Leopold, and Baron Stockmar—must have felt some twinges of anxiety.

It helped that the bride was both passionate and innocent. It helped that the first woman the prince took into his arms had long been his destiny. Albert was above all a dutiful man, and duty dictated that he finally give rein to his own sensuality and make love. It helped that the prince's wife was not a stranger but his first cousin. In the European aristocracy where first cousins married routinely, and uncle-niece marriages were not unknown, a touch of incest was a kind of aphrodisiac.

It helped that Victoria was so like Albert's mother, the only woman he had ever loved and whom he had tried hard to erase from his memory. Until he was five years old, Albert was adored and petted by a tiny, plump, vivacious young mother who made no secret of how much she preferred him to his brother and his father. Now, as if by a miracle, another woman of the same physical type and temperament had come into his life, adored him even more extravagantly, and was his for life.

Sexual compatibility was to be the bedrock of the marriage of Victoria and Albert. However, from the beginning, erotic passion was divided unequally between them. She was madly in love; he was pleased to be adored. This was what the courtiers who kept watch over the two recorded in their letters and diaries. It is what we today can deduce from the couple's extant private papers.

But sex is only one part of intimacy, and physical intimacy was crucial to both husband and wife. The success of Victoria and Albert's marriage came out of the happiness and peace they both found in bed together. Victoria before her wedding never spent a night alone, and for the twenty-one years of their marriage, she required her husband to come to bed with her. This was one issue on which she laid down the law as woman and as queen. Albert too was accustomed from birth to sharing a room or even a bed with his brother or tutor, and found it hard to be alone, especially at night. Albert yearned to be a "we," not an "I," though on his own terms. Even at the height of his political and charitable activities, the prince returned to his wife by nightfall, whatever it cost him in fatigue and inefficiency.

Queen Victoria and Prince Albert lived in a fishbowl, set apart yet under constant observation. In bed they were alone, unseen, and delectably together, free to speak their minds as well as act out their passions, united against the whole world. It was just "we two." As Victoria wrote in heartbroken fragments after Albert's death: "I who felt, when in those blessed Arms clasped and held tight in the sacred hours at night, when the world seemed only to be ourselves, that nothing could part us. I felt so v[ery] secure."

Bearing the Fruits of Desire

...

THE DAY AFTER THEIR WEDDING, QUEEN VICTORIA AND PRINCE ALBERT took breakfast at about nine, and early in the afternoon were on view to the general public, walking arm in arm on the terrace at Windsor Castle. Later that day it was Albert's turn to plead a sick headache and lie on the sofa while Victoria held his hand. Cynical men of the world like Wellington and Greville were convinced that the prince had failed to meet the challenge of his first wedding night. It would be only months before they realized how wrong they had been.

The Queen had agreed to a three-day honeymoon at Windsor, but the privacy and quiet that Albert craved were not to be had even for that brief time. Dozens of court officials arrived at the castle within hours of the bridal pair, Prime Minister Melbourne was in constant attendance, Baroness Lehzen hovered in the wings, and every eye was on the Queen and the prince. Albert looked weary and ill at ease. Victoria was in roaring high spirits. She had an intimate dinner party for ten on the second night and on the third a dance for a large and exuberant party. Albert retired to bed early, but the Queen danced until midnight.

Though the first months of the marriage were delightful for Victoria, they left Albert deeply dispirited. The prince arrived in his new wife's country prepared to find fault, and he did not have to look far. Court life was as little to his taste as ever, the polluted air around Buckingham Palace gave him constant sore throats, and English food turned his stomach. Winters in England were much less extreme than in Germany, and his father had trained Albert to endure cold without complaint, but the dank winter chill that prevailed inside his wife's palaces seeped into the prince's bones. Why on earth did the English prefer fireplaces to stoves when most of the fireplace heat went up the chimney?

The frost on the inside windowpanes equaled the frosty welcome Albert received at court. He came to England convinced that Englishmen in general were inferior to Germans because they cared only about money and were indifferent to art, music, and philosophy. As he saw it, the English of the higher classes were either stupid and superficial—their heads crammed full of silly jokes, hunting anecdotes, and remarks on the weather—or else cynical and immoral. Either way, they were unworthy of his regard. Unsurprisingly, sensing the contempt and disapproval that lay beneath the prince's glacial politeness, the great men of England did not warm to the Queen's new husband.

Germany for Albert was already taking on a misty glow. When not actually in their company or answering their eternal begging letters, the prince was able to forget that his own father and brother were at least as promiscuous as certain English dukes, and spent a great deal of their time thinking about money, or, in their case, the lack of it.

As for the women who were introduced to the prince, very willing to be charmed by such a handsome young man, they too soon turned cold and censorious. A hint of flirtatiousness, a shadow of immorality were anathema to the prince, and he had nothing to say even to the virtuous and intelligent ladies of his wife's household. Queen Victoria was conscious of her own plainness, was surrounded by beautiful women, and had been warned by her friend Lord Melbourne that all husbands had a roving eye, yet she never felt the need to be jealous. Albert's fidelity to her was adamantine. No other woman made any impression on him.

Isolated, homesick, a fish out of water, Albert was very unhappy. His wife, while professing to idolize him, treated him more like a gigolo than a husband. He was allowed to blot her signature on state documents, and that was all. In a letter to his university friend Löwenstein, Albert complained that he was not "master in the house." Fears he had entertained in Germany about Victoria's stubborn nature and small mind revived. Albert confided in Stockmar that he found Victoria "naturally a fine character, but warped by wrong upbringing."

Albert showed his discontent. He retired to bed early and sometimes fell asleep after dinner parties or even at the theater. When his wife chatted and joked with her former friends, he looked sour. When she accepted an invitation to some great man's house, he made it clear that neither the company nor the entertainment provided was to his taste. Music was one of the passions that Victoria and Albert shared, and the Queen made much of her husband's superb musical talents. Yet when she asked the famous singers Giovanni Battista Rubini and Luigi Lablache to come give a private concert, Albert snoozed. As one of Queen Victoria's ladies reported maliciously on this occasion: "Cousin Albert looked beautiful, and slept as quietly as usual, sitting by Lady Normanby"—incidentally one of the most celebrated beauties at court.

For months after his move to England, Albert remained as pale and ailing as on his first days. Parting with his father after the wedding caused him an agony of tears, even though Duke Ernest had made unpleasant advances to Victoria's ladies and was already being a thorough nuisance about money. Brother Ernest's sexual exploits and need for cash if anything outpaced his ducal father's, but when he also left England, the Queen found her husband weeping in the corridor and deaf to her comfort. How could she understand his feelings, he said, when her own childhood had been so unhappy? The myth of Albert's idyllic childhood and the close relationship he had enjoyed with his father was being born.

BUT ALBERT'S UNHAPPINESS did not last long. Change was in the offing, and the balance of power between husband and wife was about to shift dramatically. Queen Victoria missed her second period after the wedding. When it became clear that she was pregnant, she was distraught. She had long understood that it would someday be her duty to give an heir to England, but she felt no desire to advance that day. The prospect of bearing a child was a nightmare all the more dreadful since the physical facts of pregnancy and labor had been scrupulously hidden from her.

Victoria was aware that labor was an ordeal and that women not infrequently died as a result of giving birth. This was bad enough, but she also observed that even a healthy and uneventful pregnancy was an immense bore. In the mid-nineteenth century, pregnant women of the leisure classes were enjoined to curtail their physical activities, to disappear discreetly from society once their condition could no longer be concealed by corsetry, and to spend the last weeks before delivery under virtual house arrest. Victoria's favorite daytime pastimes since her teenage years had been galloping across country and dancing until dawn. These activities would not be countenanced for a queen bearing the hope of the nation.

Victoria made no secret of the fact that she was unhappy to be pregnant. She said so even to German relatives she knew would be overjoyed by the news. She wrote forthrightly to Albert's stepgrandmother, Duchess Caroline of Gotha: "I must say that I could not be more unhappy. I am really upset about it and it is spoiling my happiness. I have always hated the idea and I prayed God night and day to be left free for at least six months, but my prayers have not been answered and I am really most unhappy. I cannot understand how anyone can wish for such a thing, especially at the beginning of a marriage." To Uncle Leopold she was even more brutally frank: "*The thing* is odious and if all one's plagues are rewarded only by a nasty girl, I shall drown it, I think. I *will* know nothing else but a boy. I never will have a girl."

Albert's reaction to the pregnancy could not have been more different. His hopes and ambitions in England hinged on his siring at least one heir to the throne, and he fancied himself as father to a large brood of adoring children, stamped with his own image. Encouraged to take the long view by Leopold and Stockmar, he already envisaged an English Saxe-Coburg dynasty that, with all Great Britain's power and wealth behind it, could spread over Europe and change the course of history.

Until the late summer, Victoria persisted in living as much as possible as she had done before her marriage. Lord Melbourne continued to see almost as much of her during the day as her husband did. The Queen gave the prince no access to state papers and saw her ministers alone. In the evenings she preferred to play parlor games rather than discuss the issues of the day. She feared, she said, to open up subjects that might provoke disagreement with her dearest husband. What she meant was that the affairs of state were her business alone.

By the third trimester of Victoria's first pregnancy, things took a decided upswing for Albert. Stockmar was back in England, to the prince's delight and relief, and the two began to plan political and marital strategy in detail. Stockmar was able to negotiate with parliament that, should Victoria die after giving birth to an heir, Prince Albert would become sole regent, without a council. Victoria's uncles were furious at being passed over, but for the first time Albert had his way.

In June when Victoria was to give the speech from the throne opening parliament, Albert rode by her side to the House and took a throne next to her own in the chamber. By August the prince was permitted to help his wife get through the paperwork that landed on her desk every day. Impressed by her husband's talent for bureaucracy, Victoria ordered that he be given his own key to her dispatch box and made him a Privy Councillor. Albert wrote to Stockmar, who had returned to his own family in Coburg for a time: "I have come to be extremely pleased with Victoria during the last few months. She has only twice had the sulks . . . altogether she puts more confidence in me daily." When Victoria was no longer able to appear in public, the prince began to represent her at official events, and he gave his first speech in English, to the Society for the Abolition of Slavery.

As the Queen's confinement approached, the death of Princess Charlotte one generation earlier was on the minds of everyone at the palace and indeed in the nation at large. Stockmar, who had observed that tragedy so closely, was in a good position to advise Albert. Clear on his strategies, happy in his duties, and filled with new energy, the prince made it a priority to monitor his wife's physical condition and plan the lying-in. This birth was too important to be left in the hands of the women or of Sir James Clark, the Queen's personal physician. Victoria adored Clark, but he had played a disastrous part in the Lady Flora Hastings affair. Albert selected Dr. Charles Locock, a Scottish obstetrician of excellent reputation, to supervise the delivery.

Throughout the pregnancy, Albert danced attendance on Victoria, appearing at her side whenever she required him, at the sacrifice of his own leisure and sport. When Victoria went into labor around one in the morning several weeks before her due date, Albert was by her side, together with the Duchess of Kent, and one maid. Baroness Lehzen was not present during the labor. The duchess's attendance on her daughter was the first clear sign that Albert was successfully negotiating a rapprochement between his wife and her mother, his aunt. Locock was in charge of the delivery, but three other doctors sat in the next room with the door open. One further room away, Prime Minister Lord Melbourne, Foreign Secretary Lord Palmerston, the Archbishop of Canterbury, and other dignitaries waited and listened. Albert stayed with his wife until she vigorously pushed out a large, perfectly formed baby girl at two in the afternoon of November 21.

Locock, who thereafter became jocularly known in Britain as "the Great Deliverer," had some very uncomplimentary things to say in private about the Queen's fat, barrel-shaped body and her unembarrassed references to her condition. But Locock was competent and lucky enough to have a strong, healthy parturient, so all was well for mother, baby, and doctor. What Locock thought of the prince's attendance at the bedside is not known. It was extremely rare for a nineteenth-century man of any class to be present at the birth of his children. Albert was not just present but actively involved. By putting aside social convention and taking on the modern role of childbirth coach, Prince Albert won his wife's gratitude.

It was an immense relief that Queen Victoria had negotiated the treacherous shoals of pregnancy and childbirth so successfully. All the same, the royal couple was very disappointed that their child was only a girl. When Locock informed the Queen that she had given birth to a princess, Victoria stalwartly answered, "Never mind, the next will be a prince." Albert wrote enigmatically to his brother, Ernest, "Albert, father of a daughter, you will laugh at me." Lord Clarendon, writing to Lord Granville in Paris, was more pragmatic: "Both the Queen and Prince were much disappointed at not having a son. I believe because they thought it would be a disappointment to the country, but what the country cares about is to have one life more, whether male or female, interposed between the succession and the King of Hanover [Victoria's senior uncle, Ernest of Cumberland]."

King Leopold wrote to congratulate his niece on the birth of little Victoria Adelaide Mary Louisa and to wish that this should be the first of many such happy events. The Queen was sharply taken aback: "I think you will see with me the great inconvenience a large family would be to us all, and particularly to the country, independent of the hardness and inconvenience to myself; men never think, at least seldom think, what a hard task it is for us women to go through this *very often*." But within two months of arising from her weeks of enforced bed rest and being carried to and from her sofa by her devoted husband, Victoria was pregnant again, and on November 9, 1841, she gave birth to a healthy son.

The second pregnancy was more resented than the first, the labor longer and more painful. "My sufferings were really very severe," wrote the Queen, "and I don't know what I should have done but for the great comfort and support my beloved Albert was to me." While the nation rapturously celebrated the birth of a Prince of Wales, the first since the birth of George IV in 1762, Victoria sank into postpartum depression. She felt trapped. The world's congratulations, her family's joy, her husband's obvious delight, and the close bond of affection and care that had grown up between them over the past twenty-one months could not make up for her loss of the pleasures, energy, and freedom that pregnancy drained out of her life. For the first two years of her reign, she had been free, galloping her horse across Windsor Great Park, ready to take on the world. Now she seemed doomed to be hideous, swollen, and aching, chained to a sofa, hidden from the public view like a thing of shame, wheeled out every day for exercise like a dog. And since Albert delighted in his new role as father, hours that she and Albert had spent alone together now had to be devoted to their growing family.

That the Queen wished to ensure that her children did not come between her and her husband is disarmingly clear in a famous painting of 1841 by Landseer. Prince Albert, looking extremely handsome, is the picture's focus of attention. The prince's dress is casual, yet the star of the Order of the Garter pinned to his coat establishes his exalted status. He wears hunting dress, and the loosely knotted collar reveals a few inches of the white throat his wife so admired. He has on a pair of long, red suede boots that the Queen found particularly dashing, and one magnificent leg clad in skintight breeches is thrust forward at the center of the picture. The prince has his right hand clasped on the top of his thigh while the other hand caresses the head of the greyhound Eos, who is looking adoringly up into her master's face. Queen Victoria stands at her husband's shoulder, and they are looking into each other's eyes. The Queen is shown in a low-cut white satin dress not dissimilar in style to her wedding dress. Though plump and bosomy, she gives no indication of being in the advanced stages of her second pregnancy. It would be more than a hundred years before any public image of a pregnant English queen was permitted to appear.

On the other side of the room and of the painting, separated from her parents by Eos, a small bench, and two other dogs, is little Vicky, recently given the title of Princess Royal. A sturdy toddler, who, given the absence in the picture of her brother Bertie, could not have been a year old, she stands, her bonnet thrown back, incongruously fondling one of the array of dead creatures that her father has brought back from the hunt.

For Queen Victoria, Albert was at the center of life. What mattered was the relationship between the two of them. The children, charming and decorative no doubt in their own way, lived on the margins of their parents' happiness, more tolerated than welcomed by their mother. This would be true for the next seventeen years.

QUEEN VICTORIA BORE seven more children. The nine came in groups, at a slowly diminishing rate: a girl, Victoria (Vicky), in November 1840; a boy, Albert Edward (Bertie), in November 1841; a girl, Alice, in April 1843; and a boy, Alfred (Affie), in August 1844. Two girls then, Helena in May 1846 and Louise in March 1848; followed by two boys, Arthur in May 1850 and Leopold in April 1853, and, finally, Beatrice in April 1857.

For a woman of the Queen's generation, a family of nine was not uncommon. Rich and poor, profligate and virtuous, the Victorians had a lot of children. Women were, overall, better nourished, came to puberty younger, and were hence more fertile than in previous generations. The deleterious effects of multiple pregnancies on a woman's body were of little concern to the Victorian medical profession, though many women and babies died in childbirth. The main difference between the royal couple and most contemporaries was that the Queen is not known to have suffered any miscarriages and that she emerged vigorous and healthy after her nine complete pregnancies. Given her fertility, she was a lucky woman to be alive at forty, as she was well aware. The queen of Portugal, Maria da Glória, who was almost exactly Victoria's age and as a teenager married Ferdinand, another Saxe-Coburg first cousin, bore eleven children, and died when she was thirty-five.

Another huge piece of good luck was that all nine of Queen Victoria's children grew into adulthood. Unlike many women of her generation, Victoria never had to watch a son or daughter die in childhood. Her luck becomes clear when we compare her not only with a royal peer like Queen Maria of Portugal, several of whose children died young, but with her own daughters and granddaughters. Between 1860 and 1914, a surprisingly large number of babies born to members of the English Saxe-Coburg dynasty, most of them boys, died in childbirth or from childhood diseases.

But even if Queen Victoria turned out to be, in her own words, "good at" childbirth, her pregnancies continued to be a terrible burden. Indeed, as Albert's sexual prudery took hold of her, she became more and more embarrassed by her condition. When she was carrying Leopold and Beatrice, the Queen found the ignorant yet inquiring eyes of her two oldest children, the teenaged Vicky and Bertie, especially hard to bear.

Victoria's attitude toward pregnancy and childbirth was most clearly expressed in a letter to her daughter Vicky in March 1858, soon after Vicky was married and only a year after the Queen had borne her ninth child.

> *"Now to reply to your observation that you find a married woman has much more liberty than an unmarried one; in one sense of the word she has,—but what I meant was—in a physical point of view—and if you have hereafter (as I had constantly for the first 2 years of my marriage)—aches—and sufferings and miseries and plagues—which you must struggle against—and enjoyments, etc. to give up—constant precautions to take, you will feel the yoke of a married woman! I had 9 times for 8 months to bear with those above-named enemies and real misery (besides many duties) and I own it tried me sorely; one feels so pinned down—one's wings clipped—in fact, at the best (and few were or are better than I was) only half oneself—particularly the first and second time. This I call the 'shadow side' . . . And therefore—I think our sex a most unenviable one."*

As a young married woman, Queen Victoria could not be sure how long her obstetrical luck would hold. It was certainly not her ambition to compete with her paternal grandmother, Queen Charlotte, mother of fifteen children. If Queen Victoria had had a choice, her childbearing might well have ended with the birth of Alfred when she was twenty-five. An heir and a spare was all England needed, and since the Queen inconveniently gave birth to girls before boys, that meant four children. Victoria understood very well that more children were a threat to her life when they were in utero, a drain on her time and energy when they were young, and a financial burden for the country when they were adults.

But like most women of her nation and generation, Queen Victoria did not have a choice. Her wishes and preferences did not determine the size of her family. She had nine children because she was fertile, because she loved to go to bed with a husband who found the role of paterfamilias deeply satisfying, and because she knew nothing about nonreproductive sex.

Some primitive birth control measures, such as caustic douches and crude physical barriers to conception, were available to mid-Victorians, but they were nasty and ineffective and practiced mainly by prostitutes. Most married couples who wanted to limit their family size had only two options, abstinence and abortion. Virtuous husbands like Albert, who came chaste to their weddings, felt they had every right to find sexual satisfaction with their wives. As for abortion, it was no longer a legal option in a modern Christian nation that prided itself on its high moral standards.

Prince Albert could have nothing to do with abortion and birth control. In a gossip-ridden atmosphere like the Court of St. James's, such things could not be kept secret from the press, and even suspicion would damage the monarchy. But Albert's repugnance for all things sexual, which only grew as he aged, also cut the royal couple off from the practical and private information on nonreproductive erotic practices that had been available in aristocratic circles twenty years earlier.

An older man of the world like Lord Melbourne could have explained to Prince Albert how to make love without getting his wife pregnant, but such a conversation between the two men is unthinkable. An older woman of the world like Lady Emily Cowper, Melbourne's sister and the daughter of that famous aristocratic courtesan, the first Lady Melbourne, could no doubt have offered Victoria a hint or two on nonphallic pleasure, and one can imagine the Queen listening and even taking notes. But Lady Cowper, after she married the notorious old roué Lord Palmerston in late 1839, ceased to be part of the Queen's intimate circle.

Once Albert took control of his wife's affairs in 1841, he made absolutely sure that Victoria's ladies-in-waiting and maids of honor were women of absolute discretion as well as irreproachable morality. Everything the young Victoria knew about sex and reproduction she learned from her husband, and these were two areas in which the prince's thirst for information ran dry.

Whigs and Tories

...

FOLLOWING THE BIRTH OF HIS FIRST CHILD IN NOVEMBER 1840, PRINCE Albert was in a far stronger position. Surely now his ambitions to take on a meaningful, independent role in matters of state and in the household would be realized. But two people close to the Queen blocked the mastery he sought in both the political and domestic spheres. Those two were Prime Minister Lord Melbourne and Victoria's former governess, Baroness Louise Lehzen.

The prime minister was far too urbane and devoted to the Queen's interests to allow any open rift with the Queen's husband. He was also a man of power in English politics and thus a redoubtable foe. But if Victoria had believed that Albert would take Melbourne as his surrogate father and political mentor just as she had, she was deluding herself. The two men could not have been more different. The silent struggle between them could not be resolved by negotiation.

William Lamb, Viscount Melbourne, was an English aristocrat in the eighteenth-century mold: rich, handsome, worldly, cynical. Although his family was only two generations removed from the professional middle class, the prime minister was very much the grand seigneur, winning the allegiance of peers, the admiration of inferiors, and the friendship of accomplished women by his ease, wit, and charm. He was not ambitious, yet the highest political power in England had been thrust upon him.

Victoria's prime minister was quite as intelligent and well informed as her husband, but in different fields and in a very different style. Albert was an excellent musician and music critic. Melbourne blithely admitted that he had a tin ear. Albert had been taught good schoolboy English and French, plus a little Latin, but his mind was formed by his native German. Melbourne was an excellent classicist, had superb French and good Italian but little if any German. Melbourne was a connoisseur of art and a walking compendium of information about English history and politics, but he wore his erudition lightly. One of the great stylists of his day, Melbourne rarely said or wrote anything that was not funny, piquant, incisive, and memorable. Albert had a heavier, more systematic mind, and his interests ran to science, technology, and metaphysics. He liked to lecture, to philosophize, and to derive practical policy from abstract principles. His specialty was the lengthy memorandum, in German or ponderous English. To the Court of St. James's, he seemed more like a tutor or a music master than a prince.

In English domestic politics, the two men were poles apart, and here the comparison was distinctly in the prince's favor. Melbourne was a die-hard conservative who did not believe in progress. His main commitment was to preserve the privileges of the Whig-Tory oligarchy, and he was deaf to the cries of the poor and oppressed. Both feudal and progressive in his social philosophy, Albert was a spirited defender of the working class. He favored social and political reforms as the intelligent way to defuse public discontent, quell rebellion, and keep kings on their thrones.

Melbourne was an Englishman, convinced of the superiority of all things English, a courtier to the English monarch by birth and training, a native of the ingrown world of British politics. Albert was proudly a German and therefore an alien in xenophobic England. He was also an internationalist and a rationalist who saw Britain as part of Europe and was reluctant to say "my country right or wrong."

And whereas Albert, a married man at twenty, was conscious of having led a blameless life, Melbourne was a very recently reformed old roué. The erotic subtext that for a time had made Victoria's relationship with her prime minister so delightful to both disgusted Albert. For him Melbourne was a tainted old man, representative of the corrupt order in British society and politics left over from George IV, a pernicious and dangerous influence on the Queen.

■

LORD MELBOURNE WAS too powerful a man for Albert to tackle head on, and the prince's political advisers abroad urged him to do nothing hasty. Time, and paternity, were on his side. Melbourne himself had told Stockmar as early as 1838 that his ministry was hanging on to power by a thread, and in the summer of 1841, the Whig government was defeated in parliament by a vote of no confidence. The prime minister was forced to call a general election, and Queen Victoria campaigned vigorously and openly for the Whigs. She dragged her reluctant spouse to Brocket Hall, Broadlands, and Panshanger, the country homes of Melbourne, Foreign Secretary Lord Palmerston, and Palmerston's wife. Behind her husband's back, and with the connivance of Baroness Lehzen, Victoria contributed money to the Whig Party from her private purse. But to the Queen's chagrin, the Tories were returned with a large majority, and Lord Melbourne ceased to be prime minister.

Prince Albert had foreseen this turn of events, and he knew that only two years before his wife had damaged the monarchy by refusing to accept Sir Robert Peel, the leader of the Tories, as her prime minister. A tall, reserved, awkward man of few words, Peel had none of Melbourne's polished ease with royalty, and the Queen could not bear him. In May the prince opened secret negotiations with Peel on how the transfer of power could be managed, and the two men hit it off immediately. When the time came for a change of ministry, Albert had enough influence over his wife to persuade her to accept the new prime minister with good grace.

When Sir Robert Peel became prime minister of England in August 1841, Lord Melbourne was heartbroken—not to lose power but to lose his place next to the Queen. In bidding farewell to Her Majesty, he remarked with characteristic grace and fatherly directness, "For four years I have seen you daily and liked it better every day." Victoria missed Melbourne very much at first, and the two continued to correspond, mainly on personal matters. This correspondence aroused Albert's suspicions. He dispatched his secretary George Anson to Lord Melbourne's London residence with a long memorandum penned by Baron Stockmar. Melbourne was charged with acting unconstitutionally and endangering the Crown by writing to the Queen behind the new prime minister's back. Melbourne exploded with anger—"God eternally damn it, flesh and blood cannot stand this!" he said to Anson, who had once been his own private secretary and friend—but there was nothing he could do. The prince and Stockmar now called the shots. In November 1842 Lord Melbourne suffered a devastating stroke, and he died, a broken man, in 1848.

Victoria never lost touch with her old friend and mourned him when he died. But under Albert's influence, she came to doubt the value of her past emotions and the validity of her memories. Albert had become her oracle. He judged Melbourne severely and viewed his wife's relationship with her first prime minister as an unfortunate aberration. The Queen castigated herself bitterly for the mistakes made in the second year of her reign when she was under Melbourne's influence. "A worse school for a young girl or one more detrimental to all natural feelings and affections cannot well be imagined," she wrote, "than the position of a Queen at eighteen without experience, without a husband to guide and support her."

WITH MELBOURNE GONE and Victoria increasingly absorbed in domestic cares and dependent upon him, Albert rejoiced to find that the balance of power had swung decisively his way. For the next twelve years, the prince served as his wife's private secretary, saw all the documents submitted to her, was present at all her meetings with ministers, communicated with the ministers and court officials directly, dictated many of his wife's official responses, composed endless memoranda, and engaged in a vast private correspondence with powerful men in England and abroad.

For many years Albert's access to power was not known to the public or even to many people at court. When the Whigs returned to power in 1846, Lord Charles Greville was flabbergasted to discover how completely Victoria was ruled by her husband. Albert had become so identified with the Queen, Greville noted in his diary, that they "are one person, and as he likes and she dislikes business, it is obvious that while she has the title, he is really discharging the functions of the Sovereign. He is King to all intents and purposes." By 1842, in letters and conversation Victoria habitually used the first person pronoun "we" in reference to her own thoughts and actions. That pronoun was not the lordly plural of her ancestor kings but useful shorthand for her oneness with Albert.

The Coburg party rejoiced in the prince's transition to power behind the throne, seeing it as the inevitable result of his superior abilities. In fact, however, the fortuitous change in English government that brought Peel and the Tories into office, plus the Queen's absorption in her pregnancies, were probably the decisive factors. When Melbourne and his Whigs were defeated, Queen Victoria was in the final stages of a very unwelcome second pregnancy and full of anxiety about her approaching confinement. For the time, at least, the fight had gone out of her, and she longed above all to feel at one with the husband upon whose support she now relied. Albert, on the other hand, was personally and philosophically aligned with Peel's moderate Tories. He forged an alliance with the two most important Tory politicians, Peel and the Duke of Wellington. This initial alliance provided a template for his successful relationships with successive governments between 1841 and 1853.

The Iron Duke, as Wellington was called, occupied a unique place in English social and political life. He was the supreme hero of the Napoleonic wars, having successfully defeated the army commanded by the Emperor Napoleon's brother in Spain and then the army commanded by Napoleon himself at the battle of Waterloo in 1814. After the war, he became the leader of the Tory Party and served several times as prime minister. At the outset, Prince Albert's relationship with the Duke of Wellington was a tactical move, not a personal friendship. Wellington had spearheaded the opposition to Albert in parliament before the royal wedding. He had shown a marked distaste for the Saxe-Coburg connection and had raised the issue of Prince Albert's Protestant credentials. He had played a key part in the parliamentary debates that cut Prince Albert's income and denied him precedence. Furthermore, Wellington too was a man formed during the regency of George IV, and he always had an ongoing relationship with a woman who was not his wife. When the Iron Duke was almost eighty, his current inamorata came within a hair of suing him for breach of promise.

But Wellington, unlike Melbourne, was not just a political figure who went in and out of office. He was a national hero, a symbol of British might, and so Prince Albert found it politic to close his eyes to Wellington's personal life and forget the slights of the past. The rapprochement with Wellington was highly productive. The two men formed a mutual admiration society, and in 1851 Wellington sought to persuade the prince to take over from him as commander-in-chief of the British army. The prince refused, but he was nonetheless gratified. In token of his regard for the duke, and as a shrewd publicity move, Albert named his third son Arthur—the Duke's given name—and chose Wellington as the child's chief sponsor.

In an exceptionally revealing letter to Wellington in 1851, Prince Albert explained his conception of the "peculiar and delicate" role he played as Victoria's husband. The consort to the Queen of England, wrote Albert, should

> entirely sink his own individual existence in that of his wife, aim at no power by himself or for himself—should shun all contention—assume no separate responsibility before the public, but make his position entirely a part of hers—fill up every gap which, as a woman, she would naturally leave in the exercise of her regal functions—continually and anxiously watch every part of the public business, in order to be able to advise and assist her at any moment in any of the multifarious and difficult questions or duties brought before her, sometimes international, sometimes political, or social, or personal. As the natural head of her family, superintendent of her household, manager of her private affairs, sole confidential adviser in politics, and only assistant in her communications with the officers of the Government, he is, besides, the husband of the Queen, the

tutor of the royal children, the private secretary of the sovereign, and her permanent minister.

Prince Albert was even closer to Sir Robert Peel than to Wellington. Peel was a man of extraordinary brilliance. After taking a double first at Cambridge in classics and mathematics, he entered parliament at the age of twenty-one, made a maiden speech that at once marked him as a coming man, and became home secretary at the age of thirty-four. Here at last was an Englishman whom the prince could look up to and learn from, an Englishman whose German was almost as good as his Greek, Latin, and French. Soon, Albert was loaning Peel his personal copy of the ancient German epic *The Nibelungenlied.*

As a minister of state, Sir Robert Peel proved exceptionally able, but he was never a popular favorite or a beloved cabinet colleague. Unpopularity was one of the things he shared with Prince Albert. Peel was what we would call a technocrat, a moderate conservative, intent upon gradual social and political reform. The ultraconservative faction in his party known as the High Tories distrusted him for his progressive views as much as they looked down upon him for his low origins. The son of an extremely wealthy and socially responsible Lancashire textile magnate, Peel was sensitive to the misfortunes of the industrial working class and stressed the responsibilities of factory owners to their employees. As prime minister he pushed through legislation designed to limit working hours and improve the conditions in factories and mines. This alienated M.P.s in both parties who represented the interests of the industrial north.

Dislike of Peel within his own Tory Party turned into implacable hatred in 1846, the time of the great potato famine in Ireland. The Corn Laws were an old protectionist measure that forbade the importation of cheap foreign wheat, thus keeping the price of bread high and increasing the profits of the landed gentry at the expense of the poor. The High Tories regarded the benefits they received from the Corn Laws as sacrosanct. A firm believer in free trade and an advocate for social justice, Peel forced the repeal of the Corn Laws through parliament with the support of the Whigs and into the teeth of the opposition from the right of his own party, led by Benjamin Disraeli. Peel knew that the repeal was political suicide for him, but he chose duty over ambition. Within months, the High Tories found a pretext to defeat Peel's government, preferring a weak Whig government to an effective Tory one.

Prince Albert had wholeheartedly supported Peel in his reform measures, and when the repeal of the Corn Laws was debated in the Commons, the prince was in the balcony to hear Peel's historic speech. The High Tories, who had never taken to the prince, bitterly resented this open gesture of support from the Crown. For their part, the radical faction of the Whig Party in parliament grumbled that the prince was acting against the constitution by attempting to influence English politics. Realizing his mistake, the prince never again attended a debate in the Commons, but the damage was done.

■

EVER SINCE THEIR engagement, Prince Albert had preached to Queen Victoria that the Crown must be above party and above all must not be swayed by personal preference in relations to ministers. But finding a prime minister and a set of policies he wholeheartedly believed in, Albert became quite as much a Peelite Tory in 1841 as Victoria had been a Melbournite Whig in 1838. Both Peel and Prince Albert confidently anticipated that Peel would return to power sooner or later, so the two continued to correspond and meet regularly after Peel left office. Albert did not see this correspondence to be unconstitutional or a betrayal of the prime ministers who succeeded Peel, as he had alleged in the case of Victoria's correspondence with Melbourne.

History has decreed that Prince Albert was right to ally with Peel, one of nineteenth-century England's great statesmen. It has commended the prince, a very young man, newly arrived in England, for changing his political tactics and shading his political principles as he gained experience. All the same, in the lessons that Albert preached to his wife, in the guilt he laid upon her for her ardent support of Lord Melbourne and the Whigs, there was a double standard of which the prince appears to have been unconscious.

When Victoria came to the throne, she was inexperienced, isolated, and vulnerable. That she succeeded so brilliantly at first was to her credit. That she made some mistakes was to be expected. There is little sign that Albert understood Victoria's difficulties or appreciated her achievements before their marriage. To put himself in the shoes of an eighteen-year-old girl thrust into the highest and most conspicuous position in the country was beyond him. He judged his wife more than he sympathized with her. The glare of publicity was not an issue for a prince of Coburg, and far from lacking support, Albert had been micromanaged at the later stages of his teenage Bildung by his uncle and Stockmar. As he saw it, Victoria was a woman, she made mistakes, and she needed a man to show her the way. He was a man, and a superior one, and men learned from experience. It was as simple as that.

Complacency was the shadow side of Albert's righteousness. It would be increasingly characteristic of an age that has been labeled Victorian but was, in its origins, Albertian.

15.

Dearest Daisy

$\cdots$

Wɪᴛʜ ᴍᴇʟʙᴏᴜʀɴᴇ ɢᴏɴᴇ, ᴀʟʙᴇʀᴛ ᴄᴏᴜʟᴅ ᴛᴜʀɴ ʜɪꜱ ᴀᴛᴛᴇɴᴛɪᴏɴ ᴛᴏ ʜɪꜱ bête noire, Baroness Louise Lehzen.

Ever since Queen Victoria's accession in 1837, her former governess had been delightfully busy. The baroness served as amanuensis to the Queen for much of her private correspondence and looked after her private accounts. She was the Queen's chief liaison with the government bureaucrats who ran the royal residences, and she carried keys as a sign of her authority in the household. Unlike the aristocratic ladies in waiting, Lehzen was happy to do humble things like putting the Queen's correspondence through the letterpress and keeping an eye on the laundry. With her love of caraway seeds and notepaper decorated with little steam engines, the baroness was a figure of fun at court. Despite this, she got on well with most people. She was heart and soul a Whig, it was true, but she never used her influence with the Queen for personal gain.

Before Victoria's accession, the Coburg party (excluding the Duchess of Kent) had been careful to form an alliance with Lehzen, whom they saw as a key player in the struggle against Conroy. At different times, both King Leopold and Baron Stockmar corresponded with the baroness. But once Prince Albert came to England, he and the baroness became rivals for the love of the Queen. The Coburg party, which now included Victoria's mother, decided that if the royal marriage was to work as planned, Lehzen had to go.

Prince Albert found Baroness Lehzen personally repugnant and politically dangerous. The baroness continued to hover close to the Queen, silent and watchful in the background, just as she had during the first twenty years of Victoria's life. The prince felt the baroness's presence as an intrusion, especially since, unlike most of the courtiers, she understood German, the language the Queen and prince used for their private conversations. When the Queen retired to her rooms to dress and have her hair done or prepare for the night, Lehzen was with her, and the two women gossiped and laughed. This was hardly surprising, but something about Lehzen's passionate devotion to Victoria offended Albert. In his eyes, Lehzen was a narrow, gossiping, middle-class spinster, quite unfit to be the friend of a queen.

Albert also contested the authority Lehzen exercised in his wife's household, which he felt should be his as the Queen's husband. The baroness made him feel like a dependent in his own home. When he ventured to protest or make suggestions as to how things might be done more efficiently, she resisted with vehemence.

The prince also took the side of the Duchess of Kent in Queen Victoria's ongoing dispute with her mother. In his first unhappy months in England, Albert found a sympathetic ear in his aunt the duchess. He and she were natural allies against the Melbourne-Lehzen axis. Albert considered it a child's duty to love his or her parents, whatever their faults, and he found it shocking that Victoria had little good to say about her mother. Rather than sympathize with his wife for the miseries of her childhood, the prince blamed her governess for bringing her up badly. It suited the prince to cast his aunt in the role of Lehzen's victim rather than as an ambitious egotist who had made her daughter's life wretched.

Albert realized that Victoria's mother was a silly woman and that her relationship to Conroy had been a great mistake. He certainly had no wish to live with her. When he took over the domestic reins, he always made sure that the Duchess of Kent maintained a separate residence. However, Albert found most women silly and annoying, and he considered it natural and proper that his aunt had always turned to strong men for advice and support. He simply didn't like Conroy. Albert himself intended from now on to supply the strong male arm his aunt required. Under his guidance she proved happy to take on the new role of doting mother and grandmother.

In his dealings with Prime Minister Melbourne, Prince Albert had maintained a cool politeness. But he felt safe enough to quarrel openly with Baroness Lehzen. In his letters home to Germany, the prince became vituperative, referring to the baroness as "the hag" ("die Blaste") and calling her "a crazy stupid intriguer." He convinced himself that Victoria feared

Lehzen more than she loved her and would, in the end, be grateful to him for getting rid of her. He accused his wife of being "infatuated" with Lehzen and treating her as "an oracle." The Queen declared this to be nonsense.

Victoria was sadly torn between her new husband and her old friend. She accepted that her husband had legitimate grievances, and she knew that Lehzen irritated Albert. All the same, she owed her former governess a great deal, and trusted her. When Albert challenged her about her closeness to the baroness, Victoria was angry. It was as if she was once more a helpless child cooped up in Kensington Palace with no friends of her own. If she and Lehzen had the occasional chat, what harm could that do?

As to the accusation that Lehzen was a political influence, the Queen hotly denied it. She vowed that she had never consulted Lehzen on matters of policy or shown her any state documents. Albert refused to believe her. He saw Lehzen as an enthusiastic ally of Lord Melbourne, as was indeed the case. He was sure that the baroness encouraged the Queen to maintain her personal hold over state business and royal affairs. She probably did.

After the departure of Lord Melbourne in the late summer of 1841 and the birth of the Prince of Wales in November, the antagonism between Prince Albert and Baroness Lehzen came to a boil over the superintendency of the royal nursery.

Nursery arrangements were normally in the purview of a married woman, and when her first child, Vicky, was born, Queen Victoria duly hired a wet nurse, Mrs. Roberts, and a governess, Mrs. Southey, plus various nursery maids. She also allowed Lehzen to extend her domestic responsibilities to the nursery. This would have seemed normal to both women, since in great families at that time a young mother often asked her own governess to supervise the early education of her children. Both of Lehzen's pupils, Princess Feodora and Queen Victoria, were eloquent testimony to Lehzen's credentials as an enlightened educator. However, Prince Albert and his trusted confidant and adviser, Baron Stockmar, found the Queen's nursery arrangements unacceptable.

Stockmar had strong views on the education of royal children, especially of the heir to the throne. In a long memorandum of 1841 that the Queen and the prince studied with rapt attention, Stockmar surveyed the sorry educational history of the Hanoverian kings and the bitter enmity between kings and their sons. George III and Charlotte, his queen, had been a prudent and respectable couple, Stockmar observed, but somehow the education of their sons had been sadly deficient. All seven of George III's adult sons had rebelled and fallen into evil ways in one way or another. George IV and William IV, the two eldest, were, in the baron's view, such very bad kings that it was a marvel the English monarchy had survived.

The moral of the story, opined Stockmar, was that a monarch must pay particular and sustained attention to the upbringing of his or her children and establish the closest relationship possible with them, especially with the Prince of Wales. From the cradle, Stockmar admonished his royal tutees, it was essential to establish a step-by-step educational program for the princes and princesses. This process would shape the young natures to conform to their parents' ideas and values, inspire the young minds, and lead the young bodies in the paths of virtue. The Prince of Wales could do no better than aspire to emulate the virtues and match the intellect of his illustrious father.

Queen Victoria rapturously agreed that Bertie must be shaped into a second Albert, and, as one might guess, the prince was fully persuaded by Stockmar's ideas. They confirmed his sense of self and conformed to his exalted ideas of the paternal role. They encouraged him to forget that if he himself was a pattern of virtue, his father was not, and that he and his brother, Ernest, had been brought up like twins but were now, to put it mildly, very different men. The prince had no use for Lord Melbourne's gentle observation to the Queen that education could certainly "mould and direct" but could not "alter a child's character."

Visiting the nursery frequently and without warning, the prince found the Queen's nursery employees to be neither reliable nor efficient. Vicky was a very colicky baby, and her wet nurse was observed drinking a good deal of beer and eating a lot of cheese. The prince was horrified by the lack of security at the palace and installed a complex system of locks to which he kept the keys and which the staff found very wearisome. When Prince Albert came into the nursery one day and found all the windows shut and the nurse, wrapped in shawls, sitting in front of a blazing fire, he was horrified. He, Victoria, and a consensus of doctors believed that the health of children depended on their getting as much fresh air and cold water, and as little food, as possible.

Far more fatefully, the prince also arrived unannounced in the nursery one day and discovered Baroness Lehzen seated with the royal baby in her lap. This was the kind of lèse-majesté that Prince Albert would not countenance in anyone and found unforgivable in Lehzen. Even the wet nurses were instructed always to breast-feed standing up, as a sign of respect to their august charges. According to the prince's rules, servants did not rock the royal babies in their arms or cuddle them. Nursery personnel carried the little princes and princesses around or held their hands only until they were capable of walking alone.

Queen Victoria was slow to regain her health and spirits after the birth of her second child, so after Christmas Prince Albert took her to their uncle's house at Claremont for rest and privacy. On their return, the royal couple were horrified to discover that little Vicky, fourteen months old, was pale, gaunt, and feverish. Vicky had been unwell since the fall. She resisted weaning, found it difficult to digest solid food, and was dosed by the Queen's doctor, Sir James Clark, with such toxic medications as calomel, a product loaded with mercury, and laudanum, a liquid opiate. Alarmed when the child went thin and listless, Clark fed her cream, butter, and mutton broth, which she promptly threw up.

Any pediatrician today would have connected Vicky's illness with the advent of a little brother. The child's decline coincided with the final months of her mother's pregnancy, when the Queen was unwell and anxious about the childbirth ordeal ahead and Prince Albert was busy and worried. Vicky, as all observed, was an exceptionally sensitive and precocious infant, and she sensed something important and dangerous in the air. When she was first taken to see her newborn brother, sleeping in the crib that had only recently been her own, she howled in distress. The Christmas festivities were dominated by celebrations for the birth of the new heir to the throne, and Vicky found that she was no longer the center of attention and everyone's pet. When both parents went away to Claremont without her, Vicky was far too little and far too upset to understand, and she expressed her feelings in the only ways open to her. Not eating was a sure way to attract attention and care, and her health plummeted.

But instead of understanding their tiny daughter's distress and giving her the attention she craved, the Queen and the prince had a series of blazing rows over who was responsible for the child's illness. Prince Albert was quite clear that he bore none of the blame. When Vicky was born, the prince was disappointed that she was not a boy, but he soon came to adore her. She was unusually pretty, lively, precocious, and affectionate, the very image of Albert himself as an infant. Like called to like, and there sprang up a special rapport between father and eldest child. Thus when Albert saw little Vicky so ill, he was heart-stricken. The deaths of the baby princesses born to Queen Adelaide and King William IV were much on Prince Albert's mind, and he feared his darling Pussy was dying of consumption. Furious with indignation and fear, Prince Albert blamed his wife, Baroness Lehzen, and the nursery personnel they had hired for killing his child.

When Albert attacked her for what her chosen staff had done to their

*Prince Albert
with Vicky,
his eldest child*

child, Victoria was extremely hurt and defended herself with passion. She too found baby Vicky delightful and, though she refused to breast-feed her, gave her as much love and attention as the busy royal schedule permitted. She too was extremely distressed to see the child so sick. She did not believe that she or Lehzen had neglected Vicky. Victoria raged that Albert had a distorted view of her relationship with Lehzen. She accused the prince of envy and ambition. After two attempts to explain her feelings, the Queen became so angry that she told Albert she wished she had never married.

Albert walked away, certain of being in the right and furious at being treated like a schoolboy. He holed up in his private apartments and for several days refused even to speak to his wife. Both husband and wife appealed by letter to Baron Stockmar for support and advice. Victoria, full of contrition, begged the baron to use his influence with Albert. Certain of Stockmar's sympathy and understanding, Albert narrated the scenes he had had with Victoria in detail, which is how we come to know about them. As his coup de grâce, the prince sent Stockmar a note that he had written for his wife and which he authorized Stockmar to give to Victoria when she seemed ready to surrender. The note read: "Dr. Clark has mismanaged the child and poisoned her with calomel and you have starved her. I shall have nothing more to do with it; take the child away and do as you like and if she dies you will have it on your conscience."

The effect of this missive was decisive. Victoria burst into tears, capitulated, and repented her sins. Albert had been unhappy and was now mortally offended. She could no longer imagine a life without him. It was up to her to do whatever was necessary to regain his love and make him happy.

As in most violent quarrels between people who love and need each other, there was fault on both sides on this occasion. Albert was a devoted father, quite right to keep a close eye on Dr. Clark. He was right to argue that calomel is a terrible thing to give a sick child. Victoria's choice of nursery staff had not been inspired. She was a busy woman, unenthusiastic about bearing children, and she spent less time in the nursery than her husband did.

But Victoria was also right to be upset when her husband criticized her management of the nursery and accused her of killing their child from neglect. She was right to accuse her husband of being ambitious and irrationally jealous of Baroness Lehzen. The prince was using Vicky's illness to assert his control over the nursery and thus over the lives of his children from babyhood. Having increasingly surrendered the business of state to her husband, Victoria was now being asked to give up even her authority in the nursery. In fact, from this date the Queen distanced herself emotionally from the nursery and never gave her younger children the love and admiration she had given to Vicky.

The letters exchanged among Victoria, Albert, and Stockmar about the illness of the Princess Royal in early 1842 are precious evidence of the way Albert and Victoria struggled for dominance. According to Albert's brother, this was not the only occasion when the Queen pursued her husband along the corridors and hammered at his door, begging him to come talk things through. On one occasion, Victoria reportedly stalked out of her husband's room in rage, returned penitent some time later to find the door locked, and knocked at the door. "Who is there?" asked the prince. "The Queen of England." No response. Another knock. "Who is there?" "Your wife, Albert." The door was unlocked. In the end, Victoria was always the one to give in, beg pardon, and swear to be a better little wife in the future. Albert's cool temperament, logical arguments, and fixed resolve proved far more effective in their battles than her fits of passion.

In the spring of 1842, husband and wife were once more in each other's arms, happily reconciled. An intelligent and responsible new governess, Lady Sarah Lyttelton, was hired to the satisfaction of both parents, and the little Princess Royal thrived once more. The Queen still did not abandon her old friend Baroness Lehzen without a struggle. She begged her husband to see Lehzen as she actually was, a perhaps limited but capable woman who was selflessly devoted to the royal mistress she had helped through very difficult days and who deserved to live out her life near her darling. But Albert was adamant. The mere sight of Lehzen in a corridor was anathema to him. He prided himself on being a fair master, but he had no scruples about securing Lehzen's dismissal. She was a servant who had dared to rise above her place. She was personally abhorrent to him. She had to go.

In September 1842 Baroness Lehzen set off for Germany in a new carriage presented to her by the Queen, valiantly claiming that she was no longer needed and so preferred to return to her native land. Victoria could not face saying good-bye in person, but she gave her former governess a handsome pension of eight hundred pounds a year. Over the next years, the two women kept up a regular correspondence and had two private meetings when the Queen was on visits to Germany. The last time Queen Victoria saw her "dearest Daisy," Louise Lehzen was standing on a station platform near her German home watching the train bearing the Queen and the prince go by, and waving her handkerchief. The train did not stop. Louise Lehzen continued to write to Queen Victoria, but at some point her letters became unintelligible, and in 1870 she died.

THE EXILE OF LEHZEN confirmed the ascendancy of Baron Stockmar over the royal couple. It also showed the Machiavellian side of Stockmar's nature.

Baron Christian Stockmar had been influential in the life of Queen Victoria ever since she was eight months old. He attended the deathbed of her father, the Duke of Kent, and ensured that the duke's will supported the interests of his master, (the then) Prince Leopold, and the Coburg family. After 1838 Stockmar also played a key role in Prince Albert's life, and when the prince became engaged to Victoria, he insisted that Stockmar come with him to England. From 1840 until 1857, the baron served as the prince's political mentor and occasional agent. When apart, the two men corresponded regularly. It is not too much to say that, after the deaths in 1850 of George Anson, Prince Albert's first private secretary, and of Sir Robert Peel, Christian Stockmar was the prince's only friend.

Stockmar was in England for at least six months of almost every year, and he enjoyed a unique and privileged position in the royal household. The baron had his own rooms reserved for him at Buckingham Palace and Windsor Castle. Prince Albert dashed in to see his old friend almost every day for long conversations, and, as the royal children got older, they dropped in on Stockmar too, treating him like a surrogate grandfather. Stockmar came and went as he pleased, and without warning. When he left England, he was always followed by urgent letters from his royal English patrons begging to know when he would return. Renowned for his ferocious dyspepsia and delicate state of health, Stockmar was the only man seated at the Queen's dinner table who was permitted to wear long trousers instead of the knee breeches of court evening dress. He alone got up from table and ambled off to his own rooms before the Queen arose and released her guests. Stockmar's position attracted a great deal of attention, and by the 1850s he had become a legendary figure in England and on the Continent.

Christian Friedrich Stockmar prided himself, not unjustly, on speaking his mind to the powerful. His extant letters to Prince Albert show clearly that he never hesitated to criticize and reprimand his royal masters. Even his enemies agreed that he was a man who could not be bribed, who kept to the shadows in all his dealings with royalty, and who asked for few material rewards. His expenses, it is true, were paid out of the civil list, either by King Leopold or by Queen Victoria, but when he finally retired to Coburg, he was not a rich man. The German title of baron accorded to him first in 1821 was the minimal qualification for attendance at court.

In their private letters and in their public statements, both Queen Victoria and Prince Albert are effusive in their expressions of gratitude for all Baron Stockmar did for them and for their children, and this praise is not undeserved. His memoirs reveal him to be wise and humane, a dedicated public servant. This passage from one of his last letters gives the flavor of the man:

> Were a youth just entering on life to ask me now, what is the highest blessing which a man should strive for, I should answer him, love and friendship. Were he to ask me, what is the most valuable possession which a man can attain to, I should answer him, the consciousness of having loved and sought after truth, and having willed what is good for its own sake. Everything else is empty vanity and a feeble dream.

But for all his philosophical memoranda, retiring manners, and caustic tongue, Stockmar was a man of fierce ambition. He was aware of having unusual ability, he took risks, and he enjoyed early success. He wanted his place in history and consciously took on the role of éminence grise, first to King Leopold and then to Prince Albert. Like the famous royal counselors of seventeenth-century France, the Cardinals Mazarin and Richelieu, he had his share of ruthlessness and guile.

By 1841 Stockmar had been an international diplomat and agent to kings for more than twenty years, and he had come to believe in his own myth of omniscience. However, when he took over the roles of marriage counselor and educational guru to Queen Victoria and Prince Albert, his limitations and prejudices became glaringly evident. Stepping outside one's areas of expertise and laying down the law is always dangerous, and Stockmar knew less than most men about women and children. His own marriage was hardly a model. He had married his cousin Fanny Sommer because he needed money and she had some. He sired three children, but, as his own son admits, when his children were young "now and then it happened that several years passed by without his seeing wife or child." Unsurprisingly, his long and habitual absences from home made his wife bitter and resentful.

And though Stockmar befriended women, he had no regard for them. All his close relationships were with men. When in 1815 he saw clearly that the doctors of his new friend Princess Charlotte were mishandling her pregnancy and delivery, Stockmar did not intervene. When in 1826 his then employer Prince Leopold offered morganatic marriage to his first cousin, Caroline Bauer, and carried her off to a life of neglect and seclusion in England, Stockmar assisted the seduction. When in 1842 Queen Victoria fought with Prince Albert to retain the love and support of her oldest and must trusted friend, Baroness Lehzen, Stockmar was instrumental in getting rid of Lehzen.

Stockmar's delusions of omnipotence and his overt misogyny can be seen clearly in the following account he gave in the 1850s of the role he played in England at the time of Queen Victoria's accession in 1837. As Stockmar remembered it, Prime Minister Lord Melbourne, Foreign Secretary Lord Palmerston, the cabinet, the Privy Council, parliament, and the court, to say nothing of Queen Victoria herself, had been mere puppets in his hands.

"[The Queen] was quite a girl and knew nothing of the business, and was surrounded by women such as the Baroness Lehzen, who knew as little or less, and wished to lead her. I saw nothing was to be done till they were removed. So I looked around, and saw who there was to guide her. I induced her to put herself under Melbourne. He was not a fit person to be the guide of a girl . . . put around her some persons he should not—would not try to make the court moral—because he said it was no good trying—Courts always had been immoral, and would always be. But he was still the best person we could get, and we got rid of the influence of the women."

Stockmar loved and was, in his way, loyal to Queen Victoria. However, he was German enough to be convinced that the English Constitution was an unfortunate aberration in that it allowed women to rule. Stockmar was

Prince Albert's man, heart and soul. In Albert he saw the perfect instrument of his own geopolitical strategies. A remark by Stockmar after Victoria had angrily and painfully given birth to her second child in a year exposes the disjunct between Victoria's wishes and interests and those of the Albert-Stockmar-Leopold axis. "I expressed [to Peel, the new Prime Minister]," wrote Stockmar to the departed Melbourne, "my delight to see the Queen so happy and added a hope that more and more she would seek and find her real happiness in her domestic relations *only* [my italics]."

Christian Stockmar had personal reasons for helping Prince Albert to get rid of Baroness Lehzen. Stockmar and Lehzen had more in common than either the baron or the prince were willing to acknowledge. Both began life as talented but impoverished Germans of the professional class, obliged to seek their fortunes in the employ of royalty. The relationship that Lehzen had with Queen Victoria uncomfortably aped Stockmar's own with Prince Albert. Lehzen wished Queen Victoria to be like that great female autocrat Queen Elizabeth, just as Stockmar wished Albert to be a second King William of Orange, who ruled for his wife Queen Mary. Lehzen encouraged Victoria to keep her power and maintain her private independence of her husband. The Queen trusted her and listened to her. Stockmar urged Albert to assert himself as a husband and take over the government. Albert was all ears.

The alliance of Victoria and Lehzen was a threat to the alliance of Albert and Stockmar. When Albert was able to send Lehzen into exile, the balanced square became a triangle with Stockmar in the pivot position, and Albert's influence over his wife was decisively enhanced.

Stockmar once remarked that if Baroness Lehzen had only been a little quieter and more sensible, she could have lived out her life at the palace, but this was the baron at his most hypocritical. Stockmar knew Albert's hatred of Lehzen to be obsessive, and he stoked those fires. He knew that exile to her sister's home in Germany meant misery for Lehzen just as it would be misery for him to retire to Coburg to live with his wife. But he had no pity.

As it turned out, both Stockmar and Lehzen had similarly unhappy endings. Both found themselves exiled to German backwaters, and both took cold comfort in their memories and their correspondence with royalty. According to the memoirs of Stockmar's cousin Caroline Bauer, Fanny Stockmar took her revenge when her husband finally retired from the international scene and put himself at her mercy.

AFTER THREE YEARS of marriage, the balance of power had swung decisively toward the husband. As Greville noted in surprise, the prince was now privy to all the affairs of state and dictated royal policy, king in all but name. With the departure of Baroness Lehzen, the prince assumed control of his wife's finances, both her income under the civil list and that from her private estates. He was master of his own household, having wrested even the management of the nursery and the education of the children from his wife's hands. Albert, it seemed, had won the struggle for dominance.

Both husband and wife professed their satisfaction at this turn of events. The Queen claimed that she was the happiest and most fortunate woman in the world because she had married Albert, and he was perfection. True and lasting happiness was now hers, she wrote in her letters and journal, because she acknowledged Albert as her master and embraced the traditional role of a married woman. Confirmed in his masculinity, confident in his superior ability, the prince was pleased that his conception of marital relations was finally being realized. Though foreseeing squalls ahead—women were such fickle jades!—he commended his wife for seeing sense. Victoria was the most delightful companion a man could wish for, he told his brother.

After the fiery independence and delight in business that she displayed in the years before her marriage, Victoria's enthusiastic acquiescence to Albert's dominance is disconcerting to a twenty-first-century reader. But the Queen was a realist with few good options. She was pregnant with her third child in three years and fearing that it would not be her last. She had lost her closest female friend, and she felt vulnerable. She was now dependent on her husband as friend and confidant as well as lover. With new family commitments added to the old ceremonial duties, she had more than enough to occupy her. By bending, not breaking, hunkering down and conserving her energies, Victoria was maximizing her chances of survival at a time when a woman compounded her loss of strength and risk of death with each additional pregnancy.

Since she had opted to marry and had chosen Albert of her free will, since custom decreed that a woman must look up to her husband, and since a queen regnant of England could not look up to an ordinary man, then Albert must, ipso facto, be extraordinary. The perfection of the Queen's husband was an article of faith on which both she and Albert could build a marriage.

The new feminine deference, the decision that business was man's work, was both reality and pretense for Victoria. She had the luxury of appearing to wish to give up her power and prerogatives to her husband, confident that the English Constitution would never allow her to do so irrevocably. Melbourne and Peel, Whig and Tory, were agreed that if the public learned that Albert functioned as king, the monarchy would be at risk. Victoria might meekly savor Albert calling her "kleines Fräuchen" (little wifey) when they were alone, but when the two emerged from the bedroom each morning, he fell into step behind her.

Victoria had not forgotten the oaths she had taken at her coronation, and she still aspired to be a great queen. Deeply in tune with the nation, Victoria now sensed that marriage and motherhood held the key to her dynastic success. The people over whom she was titular ruler loved her in no small part because she appeared to correspond to their feminine ideal. They did not love her husband because he was *her* ideal man, not theirs. This was a fact she might decry out of wifely duty, but it was an unspoken source of power. Furthermore, Victoria was a shrewd judge of men, and she recognized real ability in her husband. She and Albert had the same financial and political goals. In a man's world, the prince could realize those goals better than she could alone. By her admiration and trust, she could empower and energize him. They would be a formidable team.

And the sacrifices would not all be on her side. In return for giving up so much, Victoria, a charming egotist with no tolerance for boredom, expected a great deal from her husband: total fidelity and constant companionship, comfort and security, and an unending succession of new pleasures and sensations. The Queen was like a fat tiger, content with the cage, answering to the whip, but lashing out from time to time, and daring her tamer to get careless. Albert would have his work cut out to keep his wife happy.

Albert Takes Charge

...

MAKING HIS WIFE COMFORTABLE AND SAFE WAS ONE OF THE FIRST tasks Albert set himself in 1842 when he could at last call himself "master in the house." Already in the early months of his marriage, while the Queen was closeted with her ministers, the prince was poking around in the domestic arrangements and taking notes. Albert was not used to comfort. His beloved little country house the Rosenau had been less than cozy. His family's ancestral palace at Coburg had been an antiquated firetrap. All the same, the prince proceeded to be appalled by the waste, dirt, and disorder he found at Windsor Castle and Buckingham Palace.

The servants were slovenly and disobedient. Below stairs at Buckingham Palace, the corridors were lined with refuse and infested by rats and roaches. At times whole suites had to be closed off when the stench from the drains became intolerable. Treasures were everywhere but sadly neglected. The Windsor Castle library was crammed with rare books and manuscripts, but there was no good catalog. Open a cupboard and out fell some dusty drawings by Leonardo da Vinci or a pile of George III's correspondence.

Security at Buckingham Palace was so lax that the curious and the mad had little trouble getting in. A youth who became known to the press as "the Boy Jones" was found in the palace on three separate occasions, once by Baroness Lehzen under the sofa in the Queen's sitting room. Jones boasted of the nights he had spent sitting on the throne, eating the Queen's food, and peeping at the baby princess in her crib. He said he "was desirous of knowing the habits of the people, and thought a description would look very well in a book," a singularly modern remark.

Queen Victoria took all this domestic anarchy in stride. From birth she had been subjected to dirt, cold, and discomfort, and emerged the stronger for it. She apologized to her guests, swallowed what was put in front of her as quickly as possible, dressed warmly, and got outside as much as possible. But entropy ate at the prince's soul. On an income of hundreds of thousands of pounds a year, Her English Majesty should be better served. To buttress his personal observations, Albert commissioned Baron Stockmar to do an exhaustive analysis of the Queen's domestic situation. The result was a lengthy and fascinating memorandum entitled "Observations of the present state of the Royal Household; written with a view to amend the present scheme, and to unite the greater security and comfort of the Sovereign with the greater regularity and better discipline of the Royal Household."

Kings of England had long bemoaned the Byzantine ways of the Royal Household and tried to exercise more control over their income from the civil list. George III as a young man had struggled mightily to keep within his budget. His reward at court was the reputation of being a killjoy. George IV rejected the penny-pinching ways of his father but was careful to let sleeping bureaucrats lie. This king's solution to the royal budget problem was to fall shamelessly into debt and wait until parliament bailed him out. Victoria, on her accession, was scrupulously honest with her privy purse and private income, but if she had tried to reform the royal household, she would surely have failed.

However, when her husband presented the annoyances of everyday palace living as problems that he could solve, and when he furthermore insisted that by sound management he could greatly increase her personal wealth, Victoria made no objections to his proposed reforms. In fact, she overflowed with admiration. Such energy. Such attention to detail. Such determination. Such plans. Dearest Albert was truly amazing and deserved to be given carte blanche.

WHEN THEY BEGAN their financial partnership, Victoria and Albert suffered from an extreme case of what sociologists call "relative deprivation." They felt poor and needy, even though Victoria was one of the wealthiest women in the world. In many ways, their domestic situation was closer to that of tenants than landlords, and they had surprisingly little authority over many of the people who served them.

The Queen was the highest paid public official in the kingdom, receiving an annual grant of 385,000 pounds from parliament. She used three large state properties in prime locations as her private residences—Buckingham

Palace, Windsor Castle, and the Royal Pavilion at Brighton—and she was also titular lord over the palaces of St. James's, Hampton Court, and Kensington Palace in London, plus Holyrood House in Scotland. She had a great art collection, dating back to the Middle Ages but vastly expanded by her uncle, George IV. On her way into her private chapel at Windsor, the Queen passed through a tiny room full of Holbeins. On the walls of her homes, masterpieces by Rubens, Van Dyck, and Canaletto jostled for space with holiday sketches by royal amateurs.

The Queen had her own stable and took to the sea on her private yacht. Since she found coal dirty and gas smelly, all her homes—even Windsor Castle, with its vast underground furnaces—were heated by beech logs, already a rare and expensive commodity in industrial Britain. Victoria was also independently wealthy. At the time of her accession, she derived an income of about 120,000 pounds a year from her residential, farming, industrial, and mining properties in the duchies of Lancaster and Cornwall. And the Queen had a small army of servants and a mountain of household goods. She never opened a door, carried a parcel, did up a button, or slit an envelope for herself. She ate breakfast and tea modestly off Sèvres porcelain but lunched off solid silver. She could entertain 150 guests at state dinners with plates, cutlery, serving dishes, saltcellars, and epergnes all made of gold.

But parliament had seen fit to allot her less money a year than her two predecessors, apparently because they had been men and were thus expected to spend more. This second-class budget seemed very unfair to Victoria. The elderly George IV and William IV had no legitimate children when they acceded, but Victoria was young and hoped to have at the minimum two sons to secure the dynasty. Royal children, until they came of age and were voted a separate income from the civil list, were a severe drain on their parents' resources. The Queen's personal fortune was also smaller than it seemed. The 60,000 pounds from the duchy of Cornwall constituted a large part of her income, but this belonged to the Prince of Wales and would actually become his to spend when he turned twenty-one.

For his part, Prince Albert could never forget that his appanage was 20,000 pounds a year less than that enjoyed by Queen Adelaide, William IV's widow. The allotments the Queen and prince received under the civil list were also very unlikely to increase. Due to the fabulous extravagance of George IV, members of parliament had taken to debating whether the royal family gave value for money.

And then there was the vexed question of the Guelph treasure and who owned it. Amassed in the reigns of the first three Georges, this treasure included a solid gold dinner service and Queen Charlotte's jewels, valued in 1750 at 70,000 pounds. Victoria was quite sure that the Guelph treasure was hers—and that she needed it, since, in comparison even with other European monarchs, her collection of jewelry and plate was meager.

Great Britain started off as a poor offshore island and much of the treasure of the English Crown was melted down under Oliver Cromwell's Puritan Protectorate in the early seventeenth century. The greatest collection of Tudor and Jacobean plate is in the Kremlin, not the Tower of London. George IV, that great dandy, wastrel, and art connoisseur, did his best to build up the royal collections, buying jewels and plate among other valuable things. All the same, when Victoria acceded to the throne, she found that her jewelry was hardly commensurate with the wealth and power of the nation she represented to the world.

As a child, Victoria had been kept away from the courts of her uncle kings and, even when she became heir apparent, she was given relatively few valuable presents. New royal husbands could usually be counted on for a set of necklace and earrings in emeralds or rubies, at a minimum, but the best that Albert Coburg could do was a sapphire brooch. One of Victoria's bridesmaids, Lady Sarah Villiers, when she married Prince Esterhazy, was given jewelry far more valuable than the Queen's.

Victoria did have a crown, the one that had been specially reconfigured for her coronation and that featured two historic gems, King Edward the Confessor's sapphire and the Black Prince's ruby. The new state crown was lighter than the old one but still disproportionate to Queen Victoria's small frame. It gave her a headache, especially since it had to be secured to her small, smooth head by long jewel-headed hatpins. On state occasions, a lady-in-waiting had the nerve-racking job of pinning on Her Majesty's crown, and once Lady Sarah Lyttelton jabbed a pin in at the wrong angle. The gallant Victoria allowed herself a wince of pain, and the jab became a joke between the two women. However, by the early 1850s, Queen Victoria had taken to replacing her crown with an exquisite diamond-and-pearl coronet that had been made for George IV. But for the first twenty years of her reign, when she dressed up for the season, Victoria wore her grandmother Charlotte's jewels almost every day. She was especially fond of a rope of pearls, supposedly the finest in Europe.

The problem with the Guelph treasure was that Victoria's uncle Ernest, the king of Hanover, claimed that it was his under the will of his mother, Queen Charlotte. The British government fiercely resisted the Hanoverian claim, but after a lawsuit that lasted for twenty years, the decision was made in favor of Hanover. The British government decided to give back the

Guelph treasure, which was a bitter disappointment not only to Queen Victoria but also to the Hanoverians who had expected a large cash payment in lieu.

·

WHEN PRINCE ALBERT took on the task of reforming the royal household, he found that he had very little control over the income his wife received under the civil list. The Queen's fixed expenses were enormous. She had big, aging properties to maintain with over one thousand people on the active payroll and the pension list. The 385,000 pounds a year Victoria received from parliament divided up as follows: 131,250 pounds for the salaries of the royal household, 172,500 for the expenses of the royal household, 13,200 for the royal bounty (pensions and charitable giving), 60,000 for the privy purse (the Queen's personal expenses), and 8,040 "unappropriated."

The royal household was as much an abstract concept as a practical entity. It referred to all the functions, activities, and facilities of the monarch every day of the year and in every place of residence. It was made up of all the staff involved in that life, from the Lord Chamberlain to the mistress of the robes to the head gardener to the under scullery maid. The royal household was a division of government, administered by four separate and autonomous governmental entities: the Lord Chamberlain's Department, the Lord Steward's Office, the Commission of Woods and Forests, and the Master of the Horse. Queen Victoria referred to them once as the "charming departments which really are the plague of one's life."

The four departments were administered by well-bred young men who needed an income but usually had better things to do than work. All four were inefficient, reserving their active energies for turf wars all the more ferocious because the turf had never, over the centuries, been fenced. They answered in theory to parliament, which exercised weak and intermittent control, and, in fact, to the Treasury Department. The Lords of the Treasury had the power of the purse and were the supreme guardians of turf. They made it their business to question bills, require exhaustive lists of expenditures, cut staff, and withhold payments, and generally make lesser bureaucrats know who was boss. On the other hand, when complaints came in, the Lord Chamberlain and his colleagues could always blame Treasury.

The employees who composed the royal household were paid out of the Queen's civil list, but they were *not* her employees. Though their job was to serve her, they were not obliged to obey her. Only the specific governmental department that hired a worker could sack him. As a result, standards of service in the royal palace were lower than in middle-class homes where a cook who burned the roast could be dismissed on the spot.

Among the four rival departments, the Commission of Woods and Forests excelled in procrastination and inefficiency. It was responsible for maintenance and repairs at the royal residences, all of which posed special problems that the commission ignored to the best of its very considerable ability. Persuading the commission to send in a man to put a door back on its hinges, mend a windowpane, or plane down the wooden table of the pastry chef took diplomatic talents of the highest order. If another department or individual fixed the broken window, the commissioners arose in protest, ready now to remove the offending new pane.

Jurisdictional problems arose constantly. As Baron Stockmar noted in his 1842 memorandum, the Queen at times shivered from cold because "the Lord Steward lays the fire, but the Lord Chamberlain lights it." Why were the palace windows so dirty that at times the Queen could not tell if it was raining? Answer: because the Lord Chamberlain's men cleaned them inside and the commissioners' men cleaned them outside, but never at the same time.

When a job needed to be done, a requisition in due form would need to be submitted to the proper department, as the Duchess of Sutherland, Queen Victoria's first mistress of robes, soon discovered. Two rooms at St. James's Palace were allocated to the duchess for the official use of herself and her staff and to house the Queen's state robes. But when the Duchess of Sutherland was shown her two rooms, she found them completely empty. Politely, the duchess wrote to the Lord Chamberlain, requesting chairs, tables, rugs, fire irons, a clothespress, a clotheshorse, a chest of drawers, a mirror, and locks on the doors. The request was surely modest, and the duchess was not only an important state officer but a lady of ancient birth, vast wealth, and great beauty with long experience at court, but she got nowhere at first. The Lord Chamberlain replied within two days with equal politeness that the matters addressed by Her Grace in her most recent communication lay outside his jurisdiction. No wonder the official name for an application to a governmental department was a "craving"!

Internal reform of such an entrenched bureaucracy was incremental and ineffective at best. The royal household constituted a system of state patronage of particular value at a time when people of all classes perpetually tottered on the edge of ruin. It was not just the lower servants who worked the system to their advantage. A maid of honor as well as a scullery maid might slip a silver spoon in her pocket, and was more likely to get away with it. Each Lord Chamberlain got two thousand pounds a year, which was significant even to a nineteenth-century English peer. After the coronation, a decorous tussle occurred between the lord chancellor and the Archdeacon of Windsor over who should get the new solid silver inkstand that had been ordered to facilitate the Queen's sign manual during the ceremony.

Why would a Lord Steward or a Commissioner of Woods and Forests seek to reform an institution from which they personally benefited and through which they obtained the undivided loyalty of thousands of their fellow citizens?

A VERITABLE BUREAUCRATIC Hercules, Prince Albert was determined to cleanse the Augean stables he found at Windsor and Buckingham Palace. His campaign for domestic reform was the toughest he ever faced, a wearisome "infinitude of tiny minutiae," as he himself confessed. But he was determined to prevail, and, rather to the surprise of Stockmar, who often criticized the prince for his lethargy, he proved to be a master of bureaucracy. Dreamy, cultured Albert metamorphosed into the consummate committeeman and negotiator, a devotee of meetings, a master of memoranda, and an indefatigable supervisor. Both the cabinet ministers and the gentlemen of the Treasury warmed to the prince, finding him a reasonable man who was prepared to make a deal and never went over budget.

Thanks to the excellent relations he developed with successive British governments after the premiership of Sir Robert Peel, the prince was able to persuade the Treasury to pay for things without depleting the Queen's privy purse. Buckingham Palace was impossibly small for a modern royal family, argued the prince. His children were stacked up in the attics, and, while one of the Queen's levees or drawing rooms could attract two thousand people, the largest room in the palace accommodated only five hundred. Parliament heeded the prince's complaints, and after 1845, Buckingham Palace was significantly reconfigured, enlarged, and modernized at the taxpayers' expense. The royal yacht was powered by sail and made the Queen seasick, reported the prince. Parliament promptly ordered a new, steam-powered royal yacht. The Queen was enchanted by the speed and safety of rail travel, parliament learned. A royal train was procured for the use of Her Majesty's family and household.

The prince's most important internal reform was probably to persuade the departments to appoint a master of the household in each of the royal residences. This permanent official lived in and took responsibility for coordinating the work that needed to be done to keep the place clean, well run, and in good repair. Once the prince took control, when foreign royalty came to stay or a major public event took place, such as the funeral of the Duke of Wellington, the men and women of the Lord Chamberlain and the Lord Steward could be counted upon to rise magnificently to the occasion.

In his relationship with the royal servants, Albert established himself as a strictly fair but attentive and tenacious master. Under his management, guests no longer wandered the corridors at Windsor for hours at night, trying to find their bedroom. Foreign diplomats did not blunder in on the Queen while she was dressing. The royal children were safely locked away in their nursery, to which their father kept the key. Such fires as the Queen would permit were lit on command. Items like candles, biscuits, and paper for the water closets were doled out carefully. The butler was under notice to keep the liquor bill low, especially since the Queen's husband drank water or, perhaps, in memory of his native Germany, beer.

The prince made least headway with the Commission of Woods and Forests. When a new water closet was being installed at Buckingham Palace, the commission rose up in fury, not because the plans had the disadvantage of emptying the sewage directly onto the little roof under the Queen's dressing room, but because they originated in the Lord Chamberlain's department. The most intractable problem, however, was with the drains, which came under the commission's rubric. Experts came in every few years to investigate and look grim, but even Prince Albert failed to get a modern drainage system installed in London or Windsor. This meant that for all their wealth, members of the royal family were subject to the ravages of infectious disease like ordinary folk. Medical care was freely available for all palace residents, but even Harley Street doctors at that time had few weapons to combat the regular outbreaks of cholera and typhoid that occurred when the cesspools overflowed into the drinking water.

Thanks to the prince's energetic domestic campaign, within a few years, the comfort enjoyed by the English royal family was the envy of their foreign relatives. As Vicky discovered when she moved to Prussia in 1857, the Prussian royal household drew all its water from a single pump in the courtyard, and water closets were unknown in German castles. And the Germans found the Russians abhorrently dirty!

Having bearded the beast of bureaucracy in its lair, the prince was able to turn with relief to those parts of his wife's estate where government officials had little or no sway. In managing the family money, Albert was outstandingly successful. He proved to have a combination of drive, vision, and administrative compulsiveness that would have made him a great captain of industry. These were bourgeois skills, unremarkable in mercantile families, habitually despised by aristocrats, and revolutionary for royals.

Deeply interested in agriculture, the prince introduced the latest in modern farming methods to the royal farms. He improved the breeding strains of the royal cattle and sheep. He designed and built in Windsor Great Park a superb new dairy, conforming to the most exacting standards of hygiene. He installed a central laundry for the royal household at Kew in London that saved hundreds a year in lost or pilfered clothes and in salaries for washerwomen. He masterminded, supervised, and, along with the Queen, collaborated actively in the first exhaustive catalog of the royal collections. He had the royal pianos tuned regularly. He hired responsible men to manage his wife's and son's real estate and mining interests, kept an eye on the men he had chosen, and invested the profits wisely. The income from the royal estates soared under the prince's management.

By 1845, Albert had wrapped his wife and family in a protective cocoon of comfort and privacy that no previous English sovereign had ever known. He earned the gratitude of parliament by his prudence and thrift. He earned the rapturous admiration of his wife. He created an idyll of family life that his children sought to re-create as adults. He won the approval of the English middle classes by espousing their values. Through the prince's efforts, the English monarchy entered into a period of unparalleled prosperity, and when he died his wife was many times richer than at her accession.

Yet Albert's assertion of control won him few friends in his own household. Victoria, as generous and appreciative as she was demanding, was adored by her servants. Albert was publicly obeyed and secretly resented. When the prince cut the wages of a housemaid from forty-five to thirty-five pounds a year, when he abolished the ancient perquisite of serving wine every night to a nonexistent official, when he pocketed the prize money for a champion ram at a county fair, dukes sneered and drovers grumbled.

The discontent was voiced by a newsman called, appropriately, Jasper Judge. This gentleman wrote for the Windsor local paper and was a stringer for the London press. Judge published a stream of articles and books excoriating the Queen and the prince for the public money spent on them. There was the new stable at Windsor that cost the Treasury forty thousand pounds. There was the fact that the royals were the major Windsor landlords and yet paid no local property taxes. There was the human waste from the castle and barracks that overflowed into the Windsor streets whenever it rained hard.

Jasper Judge accused the Queen and the prince of being hard-hearted landlords who thought only of their own pleasure, especially when it came to hunting. In his columns, Judge told the story of the poor woman gathering sticks who was set on and viciously bitten by the dog of one of the prince's gamekeepers. He reported the case of a poor man brought to court for poaching four pheasants and six pheasants' eggs from the royal estates. The poacher was tried *in camera* and ordered to pay a fine of ten pounds and eleven shillings or spend four months in Reading gaol.

Jasper Judge's press campaign infuriated Prince Albert. How could such a man be allowed to attack the monarchy with impunity? When his father and brother needed more space for their castle or their new opera house, they had no difficulty securing it. In Coburg, a political troublemaker like Judge would have been horsewhipped by one of the duke's henchmen and forced out of his home. In England this was not possible, but Albert refused to let Judge get the better of him.

At first Prince Albert tried bribery, only to discover that Judge could not be bought. He then brought legal action not only against Judge but also against Judge's son and his publishing associate, who were bankrupted and forced into exile abroad. Judge hung on in grim determination, but when he naively advertised an exhibition of etchings by the Queen and the prince, Albert saw his chance. Judge had purchased the etchings quite legally from the Windsor man who had printed them, but the prince took him to court for stealing the copies of the etchings and displaying them without their owners' permission. The prince prevailed in court. Judge was convicted, jailed, and ruined.

None of these legal proceedings made Albert popular with the English people.

The Court of St. Albert's

...

$\mathcal{2}$N THE MIDDLE AGES, A ROYAL COURT AND A ROYAL HOUSEHOLD WERE much the same thing—the informal group of nobles chosen by the king and queen as their constant companions as they journeyed about the country. By the seventeenth century, royal courts were more selective and more centralized, following the model of Louis XIV's Palace of Versailles, and there was a clear distinction between the court and the household.

To the end of the eighteenth century, the royal household remained the exclusive domain of members of the aristocracy, while the royal court was relatively inclusive, consisting of a variety of people useful to the monarch. Ministers, officials, and mistresses were not infrequently of low birth but still took their place at court. In France under Louis XIV, any man with a hat and sword had the right to enter the Palace of Versailles and see the king. Until the French Revolution, on the "Fete de Saint Louis," French nationals and even foreign tourists were permitted to gawk at Louis XVI and Marie Antoinette as they ate "the great repast"—"le grand couvert." However, by the mid-nineteenth century in Great Britain, court functions were by invitation, and only a few thousand people at most ever gained entrance to a royal palace or saw the Queen close up. When at the time of the Crimean War Queen Victoria personally pinned Victoria Crosses, the new medals for valor, on the chests of returning veterans and touched the hands of men of all classes, she was conscious of doing something new and radical.

There could be no king or queen without a court, and a regular part of a monarch's time must be devoted to court functions. This the Queen and Prince Albert were quite clear about. The essential function of courtiers was to confirm by their own lofty social status the supreme status of their master or mistress. The essential satisfaction of courtiers was to shine in the sovereign's reflected glory. Each year the calendar of events at the Court of St. James's, as the court of the ruling British monarch is called in the language of diplomats and royal officials, was fixed in advance. To levees, where the only woman present was the Queen, ambassadors, foreign dignitaries, dukes, country squires, and government officials were ceremonially admitted. At the so-called "drawing-rooms" at the palace, debutantes were escorted by their female sponsors to curtsy to the Queen or her representative and thus enter society officially. State banquets were given for visiting dignitaries.

People came to these stiflingly formal events to be seen, to see friends, perhaps to do official business, but above all to come close to the Queen. If Her Majesty addressed a remark to them, they were gratified. If she was not there, they grumbled. If they knew her husband would be representing her, most were dissatisfied and one or two stayed away, declining to kiss the hand of a mere Prince of Coburg. Such abstentions never went unnoticed. Court events were reported in careful detail in the court circular, since the people who mattered wanted to know who attended.

A small group of courtiers composed the household, and their duty and privilege was to be close to the Queen and her family. This group was selected by Her Majesty and paid by the Lord Chamberlain's office to attend the Queen and the prince from the moment they came down to breakfast to the moment they retired to their private suites at night, every day of the year. Even on their wedding night, court etiquette did not permit Queen Victoria and Prince Albert to be alone.

The traditional qualifications to become a member of the household were high birth and superb connections, but in so powerful and rich a country as England, the household by the nineteenth century attracted mainly a genteelly impoverished subset of the nobility. Younger sons like Lieutenant Seymour, widows in distress like Lady Lyttelton, and girls with more ambition than opportunity like Mary Bulteel went into the family business of waiting at court, rather as other Britons might go into plumbing or haberdashery. Though it was considered indelicate for them to say so, they needed a royal salary and free accommodation to keep up with their kin and educate their children.

Both Queen Victoria and Prince Albert saw the court as a fact of life, the price of royal privilege. The young Victoria had not been brought up at court, and in the first three years of her reign, she was thrilled to be always the center of attention and free to pick the members of her household. The young Queen assumed that, like all her royal predecessors, she would choose her friends and companions from the ranks of England's high aristocracy. She enjoyed paying country house visits and surrounding herself with young and beautiful people. But from the outset, Victoria was wary of the aristocratic attendants who surrounded her all day. She knew that their interests and her own only partly coincided, and she was always careful to keep her own counsel.

Court gossip, the young Queen quickly discovered, was a perennially irksome problem. Everything the royal family did was monitored, parsed, and, all too often, reported. Royal gossip was a rare commodity that courtiers peddled at London dinners and country house weekends, and that the popular press was increasingly eager to pick up. Lord Frederick Paget, for example, whose family had enjoyed great favor and privilege in the first years of Victoria's reign, was deputed by the Queen to go to Germany as part of Prince Albert's escort from Coburg. When scurrilous (and accurate) reports appeared in the English press about the prince's paltry outfit and his fear of the sea, Lord Frederick was identified as the anonymous source and ceased to be welcome at court. Learning her lesson, Queen Victoria kept the great aristocratic families at arm's length. Never in fifty-three years of reign did she have a male favorite like Queen Elizabeth I's Earl of Essex. Never did she allow a wellborn woman to have power over her as Sarah, first Duchess of Marlborough, did over Queen Anne. After Albert's death, she chose male favorites of humble birth who owed everything to her: the Scot John Brown and the Indian Abdul Karim.

If Victoria was wary of courtiers as a group but was fond of selected ladies and gentlemen in attendance, Albert regarded the English court as a whole with black distrust. As a boy at his father's small provincial court, Albert was already a square peg in a round hole, a quiet, bookish prig in an aristocratic society dedicated to protocol, political intrigue, financial misappropriation, adultery, and gossip. As a teenager, the prince was quickly worn down by the social whirl at the French and German courts he visited. At the same time, simply because, as the son of a duke, he received such lavish praise at home and had privileged access to court life all over Europe, Albert came to feel a great sense of superiority. In Brussels and at the University of Bonn, he was encouraged to see himself as the cream of the German intelligentsia as well as the German aristocracy. Winning the hand of the Queen of England more than confirmed Albert's high idea of his own worth. As his brother, Ernest, would later remark, Albert "was contemptuous of mankind in general."

The prince, not without reason, viewed Germany as the cultural center of the world. Like most other Germans, he had little admiration, if great envy, of the mercantile might of Great Britain. Furthermore, Albert had been primed by his uncle and Stockmar to regard his future wife's court as a larger, richer, more powerful version of the court of Coburg—in other words, a pack of jackals in heat. Hence, even before his marriage, the prince envisaged a sweeping reform of the Court of St. James's and of the royal household. For a man destined to spend his adult life in a foreign country, he had a toxic combination of arrogance and xenophobia.

ON HIS ARRIVAL in England, Prince Albert was received warmly and courteously by courtiers and commoners alike, but his egotism received a painful reality check once the wedding was over. He had expected to attack England's manifest defects from a position of strength but found himself at once on the defensive. The English were at least as chauvinist as the Germans, and they had international power to back their sense of national superiority. As the painful negotiations over the royal marriage proved, almost no one in England except its queen found the younger son of the Duke of Saxe-Coburg and Gotha to be remarkable.

In his first year in England, Albert met noblemen at court and in the country whose amiable politeness masked a boundless scorn. What kind of man was beholden to his wife for his status and his fortune, they seemed to ask? Women at court were inclined to like the prince at first because he was handsome, but they soon turned hostile when he proved insensible to their charms. The prince's skills and talents all too often told against him. A superior musician, talented painter, art connoisseur, and botanist, a man with a boundless appetite for facts and figures, Albert was met with barely concealed yawns and sneers in English society. To the average milord, the prince's philosophical approach to problems was futile, his love of nature sentimental, his interest in science and technology incomprehensible, and his command of information pedantic.

Faced with this painful initiation into English social life, the twenty-year-old Prince Albert proved unequal to the task of smiling at the bad hand fate had dealt him, to use his own expression. He found Englishmen to be dissipated in town, and stupid, boring, and uncultured in the country. That so many of them had incomes far exceeding his measly thirty thousand from the civil list, and lived in homes that made Buckingham Palace look like a modern maisonette only made matters worse.

The prince could not hide the fact that the country house weekends he attended with the Queen were purgatory for him. Sensing his displeasure, the people who were presented to him on these occasions in their turn found the Queen's new husband less than charming. Not only did the prince have a German accent, he also had no small talk. His handshake was stiff and curt, his coat oddly cut, and he was obsessive about protocol even at times when it was customary for royal gentlemen to relax with members of their entourage. Unlike most men his age, in Germany as in Britain, Albert did not care to get drunk or eat large meals, and he did not smoke. He was good at billiards and cards, but he refused to partake in the high-stakes gambling that had been the chief diversion at court in the previous two reigns. It was obvious to all that the prince was ready to bolt when an amateur soprano of noble birth sat down at the piano.

*

NEITHER PRINCE ALBERT nor the English aristocracy had any interest in letting the general public know how strained relations were between them. Unexpectedly, hunting was where the animosity became most apparent. On the foxhunting field, the English aristocrat's passions ran too high for loyal silence, and the prince's reluctance to run with the hounds was news. Odd reports appeared in the press questioning the prince's sportsmanship and thus the English identity he had ceremonially assumed in 1839. His love of the European battue, where animals were rounded up for mass slaughter, was considered a sign of his secret allegiance to England's enemies.

The furor over hunting was far from inevitable. When he arrived in England, Prince Albert was a superb all-around athlete. He hiked, he fenced, he swam, he skated, he played ice hockey. Above all, he was a fearless rider and a superb shot, capable of taking out a hundred grouse or hare in a single day. He surely anticipated that these skills would make him friends among the English sporting set. In fact, in December 1843, staying at Belvoir, home to one of England's most famous packs, the prince won the admiration of the foxhunting fraternity by keeping up with the hounds while experienced riders were taking falls all around him.

This well-publicized exploit could have been the beginning of Albert's rapprochement with the English country set, but it was an isolated experiment. For this the Queen was partly to blame. Riding to hounds was considered too dangerous for Victoria, even before she began to have children, and she turned sulky when Albert went off after the fox without her. To placate his wife, the prince agreed to go out only occasionally, on his home territory with the Windsor pack.

Albert could certainly have got around his wife's objections if, to his methodical mind, chasing a pack of hounds across country at the risk of life and limb had made any sense. But it did not. So much time spent, so much damage to the crops, for one fox, if the hounds managed to catch him! And foxhunters scorned the creature comforts. A hot lunch was crucial to the prince's well-being, but English sportsmen never stopped for more than a cold buffet under a tent. Thus it was easy for Albert to indulge Victoria and hunt only on his own turf and his own terms.

Unfortunately, the prince failed to grasp the symbolic importance of fox-hunting to the English. For him, as for most European aristocrats, the number of animals killed was the key to a good day's hunting. When a French count or an Austrian baron went out with his guns and his loader, he expected that at the end of the day, regardless of his level of skill, he would have a pile of corpses to display to his admiring retainers and womenfolk. To a remarkable extent, a highborn man's reputation and self-esteem hinged on how many deer, boar, rabbits, ducks, geese, quail, partridge, pheasants, sparrows, or whatever he killed in a day. To ensure that the numbers were impressive, the European upper classes perfected the battue.

At first, the creatures on a lord's estate were treated with tender, loving care. Nests were protected, chicks were hand raised, pregnant does were cherished like favorite daughters; stags could feed to their hearts' delight on a farmer's crops. Then the hunting season arrived, and in a meadow below the forest, a large canvas enclosure was set up by the lord's servants. At the center of the enclosure was a sturdy chest-high barrier behind which the hunters and their loaders would stand in safety. In a shady area, chairs were placed so that ladies could watch the sport at ease. Then beaters drove the game down to the meadow and into the enclosure. There the hunters waited, ready to shoot at point-blank range as the terrified animals ran to and fro, trying in vain to escape. For a more moderate day's sport, hundreds of birds were caught, crammed into baskets, and then released in a dazed flurry.

Given these feudal methods, a nobleman could rack up astonishing statistics, all carefully noted in his game book to impress peers and posterity. Prince Albert's father, who died at the age of forty-eight, claimed in his lifetime to have killed 75,186 birds and beasts. Albert's brother, who traveled as far as Ethiopia in his search for wild game and had better guns, could not quite match their father's statistics. He claimed in his fifty-six years of sport to have killed 3,764 red deer, 2,792 wild boar, 44,916 hares, and 13,202 pheasants.

In England, things were different, since England had an empire but few large, wild animals at home. Africa and India offered a range of big game that made the European sportsman salivate, and safaris were cheap and reasonably safe and comfortable. An English peer who wished to impress his neighbors needed an Indian tiger skin on his hearth or an African wildebeest on the walls of his game room as well as a fat game book. But within the British Isles, the difficulty, discomfort, and danger of the hunt came to matter as much as the count.

The English national sport was foxhunting, in which men spent passionate hours on horseback, often drenched to the skin, jumping gates and hedges. Foxhunting was not a sport for sissies, but it was not exclusively a male sport. A few women hunted, seated sidesaddle in very long and tight habits that increased the difficulty and danger. In Scotland, the prey was different, but the principal was the same. Forsaking their beloved pink coats for tweeds, lairds, assisted by gillies, stalked deer over bare, rough terrain that, before telephoto lenses, set the odds in favor of the deer.

The prince's hunting reputation took a severe blow in 1845 when he took his wife to Coburg and Gotha for the first time, and his brother, Ernest, organized a battue in his honor. When the reports of this event appeared in the English press, it was a public relations debacle for the Queen and the prince. Some doggerel from the pages of the satirical magazine *Punch* captures the scene of the battue and the English response:

> *Sing a song of Gotha, a pocket full of rye*
> *Eight-and-forty timid deer driven in to die;*
> *When the sport was over, all bleeding they were seen*
> *Wasn't that a dainty dish to set before the Queen.*
> *The Queen sat in her easy chair, and looked as sweet as honey.*
> *The Prince was shooting at the deer in weather bright and sunny;*
> *The bands were playing polkas, dress'd in green and golden clothes*
> *The nobles cut the poor deers' throats, and that was all Punch knows.*

Albert learned that battues were taboo in Great Britain, and he never indulged in one again.

■

MOCKED BY THE London smart set, sneered at by the country squires, spied on by the press, caricatured in humorous magazines and penny dreadful broadsheets, Prince Albert took action. Once the cynical Lord Melbourne was out of the way and his new friend and political soul mate Sir Robert Peel was prime minister, Albert determined to be master of the court and the household. He carefully monitored the invitations to levees and drawing rooms sent out by the Lord Chamberlain's office to ensure that no unworthy persons appeared at the Court of St. James's. He urged Victoria to do the same, and she obeyed.

The prince's iron rule was that no persons could be admitted into the presence of the Queen if they had even the slightest blot on their characters. A girl suspected of an illicit liaison, a woman whose brutal husband divorced her, a youth falsely accused of cheating at cards, an unlucky man who fell into bankruptcy, could protest to the Lord Chamberlain or send pitiful letters to the Queen, but they were still barred from court. By 1844, the prince had set the pattern for court life that would prevail more or less unchanged until his wife's death in 1901.

To their intense indignation, members of the English royal family were subject to Prince Albert's new regime. The result was that, as a wife, Victoria was as alienated from her English uncles, aunts, and cousins as she had been as a girl. Partly this was the result of the uncles' pride and intransigence. Ernest Cumberland, King of Hanover, Victoria's eldest uncle, viewed the Saxe-Coburgs as a third-rank German dynasty, and flatly refused to walk behind Prince Albert. The king urged his brothers in England not to yield precedence. However, Prince Albert, convinced that Uncle Ernest had incited the Tory Party to heap insults on him before his marriage, was also out for revenge. On one of Ernest Cumberland's rare visits to England for a family wedding, the king and the prince jostled for precedence, and Albert pushed the old man down some stairs. This incident appealed to Albert's rather cruel sense of humor, and he and his wife accounted it a personal victory.

The family of Adolphus, Duke of Cambridge, was also rude to the newly married Albert on various public occasions. Cambridge, like his brothers Cumberland and Sussex, was outraged when Prince Albert was appointed sole regent in the event that Queen Victoria died having left an heir to the throne. Tit for tat, the prince decided that Mary and Augusta Cambridge—large, loud, boisterous young women, admittedly, but first cousins whom the Queen had known since childhood—were quite unfit to be her friends. As for their brother George, he was not only an unprincipled rake with a string of acknowledged bastards but had also once been Victoria's most touted and most reluctant suitor. Albert would have none of him.

Things came to a head between the two branches of the English royal family when Prince Albert learned that the Duchess of Cambridge had presented her lady-in-waiting Lady Augusta Somerset, daughter of the Duke of Beaufort, to Queen Victoria at a drawing room. The duchess had done so specifically to clear the young lady of the charge of having borne an illegitimate child to her son, George Cambridge. The prince professed to be scandalized that such a young lady should be at court. He persuaded the Queen to turn her back on Augusta Somerset in public and refuse to speak to her. The Cambridges were furious at this slight, the whole court took the part of Lady Augusta, and the prince was obliged to back down. However, from this point on, the Cambridges came to the palace only to pay their court or for large family parties where their absence would have caused comment.

■

OBLIGED TO LIVE constantly in the company of persons who represented an aristocratic elite he viewed with suspicion and hostility, Albert was especially vigilant toward the members of the household. He viewed his wife's ladies-in-waiting and his own equerries as potential spies and traitors, not friends and confidants, and he enjoined Victoria to do the same. Even members of the Queen's personal household were scrutinized and then minutely monitored by the prince.

Albert made it clear to equerries and maids of honor that he would regard it as treachery if, even in their private letters, they gave information to anyone about the domestic lives of their royal master and mistress. He forbade the members of the household to keep diaries during their years in waiting. Today these rules seem to be clear infringements on personal freedom, but they were apparently obeyed throughout the lifetimes of Prince Albert and Queen Victoria and, indeed, well into the twentieth century. A sense of noblesse oblige, sharpened by a fear of royal wrath, explains this loyal obedience, but a delight in exclusivity also came into play. Anything a courtier reported about the royal family in private conversations was all the more delicious and prized because it was forbidden.

Impeccable behavior was enforced even more fiercely on members of the household than on members of the court in general. The senior ladies-in-waiting were enjoined to chaperone the junior ones. Any hint of improper behavior that reached the prince's ears would result in immediate dismissal and permanent disgrace. To ensure that there was no amorous dalliance at the court of Queen Victoria, individual members of the royal household were no longer allowed to walk the grounds of Buckingham Palace in their rare hours off duty. The young equerry Henry Ponsonby and the young maid of honor Mary Bulteel did manage to fall in love while in waiting, but they kept their relationship a close secret until they were ready to announce an engagement. They then took the Queen's evident vexation in good part—Victoria hated to lose people she enjoyed and were useful to her—got married very fast, and moved to Canada until Her Majesty forgave them.

As a result of the prince's strict control, life at Queen Victoria's court became tedious in the extreme. Imagine a regular evening party in which only a handful of those present, and those not the wittiest, are allowed to initiate conversation. The members of the household who were on duty spent hours leaning against a wall and hoping that the Queen or the prince would deign to address some comment to them. Henry Ponsonby, who lived most of his adult life at Queen Victoria's court, admitted that royal dinners were "awful." At his first dinner with the royal family as an equerry, he waited until the fish course before daring to address the young lady seated next to him, since he suspected she was related to the Queen. Can one wonder that Queen Victoria ate very fast and Prince Albert retired to bed early?

The first month in waiting was a thrilling ordeal for a young woman who dreamed of becoming the Queen's friend, but under the regime of Prince Albert, the thrill quickly wore off. The new maid of honor found that she was merely an extra on the royal stage, perfectly interchangeable with twenty-three other ladies. Little was required of her, the pay was excellent, the accommodation elegant, the sheets silk, the hot water for baths unlimited, but her work was wearisome. Since it was strictly forbidden ever to turn one's back upon a member of the royal family, the key skill required of women at court was to walk gracefully backward, even when wearing a train and a headdress trimmed with ostrich feathers eighteen inches high. Since it was strictly forbidden to sit down in the presence of royalty unless expressly invited to do so, stamina was vital for the long evenings spent standing in tight corsets and high heels.

A new maid of honor was greeted with kindness by the royal family and carefully inducted by the senior ladies into the complex rituals of court life. Thereafter she barely registered on the royal consciousness unless she made a faux pas. Bored in the evening, the Queen might ask a lady for news of her family and seem fascinated by accounts of life outside the palace. Her Majesty gave excellent presents but no confidences. As for the prince, he might notice when one of his wife's ladies played a wrong note or used the wrong case for a German preposition, but he had no interest in what she might say.

EVEN AS THEY obeyed, the English social elite chafed at Albert's rules and at the moral censure it implied. The High Tories, when they briefly came into office in 1852, had a much harder time than the Whigs or the centrist Peelite Tories in coming up with lists of prospective household officials that would satisfy the prince. When presented with Prime Minister Lord Derby's list—which included his close relative Lord Wilton, a gentleman with a checkered past—the prince was aghast. "For the Household appointments Lord Derby had submitted a list of young gentlemen of which the greater part were the Dandies and Roués of London and the Turf. I prepared a counter list of some twenty respectable Peers of property." Nonplussed, the Earl of Derby, who firmly believed that he and his ultra-Tory supporters were the backbone of the nation, said it would be very difficult to follow the prince's directives, it might even bring his embryonic ministry to an abrupt end, but he would try. He then referred with oblique humor to the famous remark made by Lord Melbourne twelve years earlier that the prince's "damned morality" would ruin everything.

Lord Derby was not the only man to be unsettled by the prince's intransigent moral code. Old courtiers looked back with a certain nostalgia to the days of George IV when life at court was sleazy and dangerous and fun. They watched in silent indignation as the Prince of Coburg withdrew his wife and family behind closed doors as far as possible and even established an invisible wall to keep out the members of the household. The Queen and the prince now rarely made country house visits in England and rarely dined out in town. Unlike his wife's uncles, the prince never became a member of one of the exclusive London men's clubs like White's. He did not offer epicurean stag dinners to friends, in part because he was careful with his money, in part because in England he had so few friends. Ceremonial dinners were obviously torture for him.

Mary Bulteel Ponsonby was the rare courtier who expressed the low opinion of Prince Albert held by many of her class, and even she kept her opinions off the record throughout her long life; her reminiscences were published only in 1927. Mary Ponsonby spent eight years in waiting, loved and admired her mistress the Queen, and observed the prince closely, pityingly, and without affection. She felt that he was not happy, though he smiled a great deal. She acknowledged that he was an "unselfish, kindhearted, truthful, and just man," who treated his servants with exemplary fairness. She says that some members of Albert's household—she names no names—liked him and mourned when he died. However, she also alleges that the prince treated his gentlemen as servants, delivering orders and reproofs with no respect for their feelings or their rank. The prince's policy, Mary Ponsonby says, was to make "no single great friend among the ministers or even among the household," and members of his staff found this "unpleasant." Here she is surely reporting what her more circumspect husband, Henry Ponsonby, equerry to the prince for several years, told her in confidence.

A woman of strong intellect and broad culture who had traveled a good deal in Europe, Mary Ponsonby came to some cutting conclusions in her secret memoir. The prince "was in ability on the level of a very intellectual German of the second line . . . He was without a spark of frankness. His manner was the least pleasant thing about him unless he was perfectly at his ease, and this rarely happened. [His] self-consciousness completely prevented one's recognition of being in the presence of a 'Grand Seigneur.' He gave one much more the impression of being an excellent tutor."

Mary Ponsonby is surely speaking for many of her class, and her derogatory comments go a long way toward explaining why Prince Albert became so alienated from his natural allies among the English aristocracy. Members of the household might abjure diary writing and censor their correspondence, but an eloquent silence, a grimace, or a few words in strict confidence were all that were needed to make Prince Albert almost as unpopular as the sinister and ultra-conservative Duke of Cumberland had been one generation earlier, though for very different reasons.

When Albert kept his wife's uncles and cousins at a disapproving distance but invited his debauched brother to come for Christmas at Windsor, without his wife; when he, the second son of a Duke of Coburg, insisted that the fabulously wealthy heir to an ancient English duchy should personally hand him his coffee; when he obliged a heavily pregnant English duchess to stand in the shadows of the royal box all through an opera; when he refused to hunt at other men's places, or smoke and drink port with the men after dinner; the word went out. The political and social establishment of England concluded that Prince Albert was an unappealing and ungrateful German who condescended to all things English. He had turned his merry, nonjudgmental wife into a censorious prude just like himself. In his pride and his ambition, he was a danger to the Crown and to the nation.

■

THE STERN CODE of morality championed by Albert and embraced by Victoria was not, in its inception, killjoy bigotry. It was an ethical, rational, and necessary reaction against the excesses of the past. It was also a code they practiced as well as preached. The Queen and the prince were chaste, faithful, and devoted in no small part because members of their parental generation had been dissolute, treacherous, and cruel. They were prudent managers of money because their parents had struggled in a sea of debt.

There were also sound political reasons for undertaking the reform of the English court. As Leopold and Stockmar had amply memorialized for Albert's benefit, the English monarchy had come close to foundering during the reigns of the profligate sons of George III. English society as a whole in the mid-nineteenth century was becoming more puritan in its beliefs and practices. Especially for a female monarch, a chaste and prudent lifestyle was essential.

The news that their Queen's court was now so respectable was met with enthusiasm in the country at large and in the press. Queen Victoria's hold on the affections of her people greatly strengthened, as she herself was already boasting in a letter to her uncle Leopold in 1844. "It was a fine and gratifying sight to see the myriads of people assembled, more than at the Coronation even, and all in such good humour, and so loyal; the articles in the papers, too, are most kind and gratifying; they say no Sovereign was more loved than I am (I am bold enough to say) and that, from our happy domestic home—which gives such a good example." When other kings were being toppled from their thrones, the English monarchy stood firm. Albert deserves credit for this.

However, when it came to morality, there was a real difference between husband and wife. As Queen Victoria was prepared to admit, Albert was much stricter than she. From the first days of her reign, she had shown herself to be both respectable and responsible, and yet not straitlaced or judgmental. Her husband was all four, and became more so each year. The war on sin at the Court of St. James's that the prince waged so zealously for two decades was not wholly rational. Strategically it met certain goals for the Queen and the English monarchy, but tactically for the prince himself it spelled disaster.

As Lord Melbourne foresaw at the outset, the Prince of Coburg's obsession with morality, however attractive to Methodists and evangelical Anglicans, won him few friends among England's ruling families. He was rash to set himself up at the age of twenty as moral arbiter to his adopted nation and to lead a reform campaign at court. He risked appearing to be a real-life Pecksniff—Dickens's sanctimonious, condescending hypocrite—and thereby alienating the power brokers of England, both Whig and Tory. For a man who sought not only to rule his wife's kingdom but to take the lead in European politics, this was singularly ill considered.

Finding Friends

...

HROUGHOUT THEIR MARRIED LIFE, VICTORIA AND ALBERT LIVED A strange kind of crowded solitude, especially when they were in London and Windsor during the season when parliament was in session. All day, every day, people could be seen milling around the Queen and the prince— children, family members, visiting guests, ministers, secretaries, comptrollers, gentlemen- and ladies-in-waiting, pages, and the hundreds of servants. Yet all too often, each day the only vital human contact was between the two of them—a half smile exchanged across the room, her hand tucked into his elbow as they went into dinner, a whispered comment in German, their private language, during a levee. For most of their day, like two extremely rare fish, the Queen and the prince swam circles together in a magnificent glass bowl, under the watchful eye of their custodians and visitors until, mercifully, the lights went out.

Theirs was an immensely stressful life, always on guard, always observed. No public appearances, however routine and scripted, could be taken for granted. The royal couple usually met with rapt applause, but boos could never be ruled out, and assassins might lurk in the crowd. The prince had schooled himself to endure court life, but the strain always showed. As for Victoria, she was the *prima donna assoluta* in the touring royal company, and the demands of her public and ceremonial roles sapped even her immense reserves of energy.

Victoria was peculiarly alone. She had been cast as a girl into the starring role of queen regnant on a binding lifelong contract, and all the other principals were men. As the Queen later wrote to her newly married daughter Vicky, who had suddenly been thrust into the hostile environment of the

Prussian court: "That you should feel shy sometimes I can easily understand. I do so very often to this hour . . . Think however of what it was to me, a girl of eighteen, not brought up at court as you were—but very humbly at Kensington Palace—with trials and difficulties, to receive and to be everywhere the first." Anyone who has found herself the token woman in a crowd of important men will understand why, as Queen Victoria grew older, she suffered a combination of stage fright and ennui. Even though she was always charming and rarely made a mistake at her public appearances, she increasingly limited them even during the life of her husband.

For Victoria, the perfect way to relax was to be alone with her husband, but in the royal residences this was possible only in their bedroom at night. Albert was happiest in the company of one or two beloved male friends like Prince William of Löwenstein, but, again, this was something that he almost never enjoyed once he moved to England. Evening parties at Windsor or Buckingham Palace always included women as well as men, and though Albert habitually spoke to his wife and other female relatives, he usually dallied over the port and cigars with the other men for barely fifteen minutes before rejoining the ladies. He not infrequently attended large all-male dinners with municipal worthies or army officers but found the food unpalatable, the speeches interminable, and the company dull. It was all too apparent that the prince could not wait to get home to his wife and his dispatch box. The prince loved sport and regularly played billiards or ice hockey and went hunting with the gentlemen of his household. However, his habitual reserve and insistence on protocol made even these lively occasions more an opportunity to demonstrate superiority than to build friendship.

One of Albert's most compelling visions when he came to England was that he and his wife would create a happy, united, loving family. As the children were born, this vision became a reality in which the prince took enormous pride and pleasure. Family, the prince believed, should be the essential focus of life for himself and the Queen. Around the warm, compelling nucleus formed by himself, Victoria, and their sons and daughters, the numerous members of their extended family would group. There would be no need for other friends.

Victoria rapturously endorsed Albert's vision. She was willing to admit, as he was not, that hitherto she had never known happy family life. With her passionate nature and boundless need for affection, Victoria felt safer and happier than ever before in the tight cocoon her husband wove around her. Whereas as a young woman the Queen had delighted in balls, elegant soirees, and dinner parties for dozens, she now liked family picnics, cozy tea parties, and intimate dinners en famille, though, sadly, these latter were only possible when the court went into deep mourning.

Enjoined by her husband to make no close friendships with her ladies-in-waiting, Victoria increasingly turned to her mother for everyday companionship and understanding. After Sir John Conroy's death, the Duchess of Kent was finally prevailed upon to open her financial records and acknowledge that huge sums were unaccounted for. At last she admitted that Sir John, while claiming devotion to her interests, had not only swindled her but driven a wedge between her and her daughter for his own ends. For her part, Victoria admitted that she had been too influenced by Lehzen. It suited both mother and daughter to give up the bitterness of the past, and Victoria's growing family proved a natural bond between the two. The duchess was a loving, generous, and indulgent grandmother who was careful, it seems, not to offend her son-in-law by questioning the way he was bringing up his children.

Prince Albert played an important part in the rapprochement between the Queen and the Duchess of Kent. He was fond of his aunt, and he was happy to serve as her chief counselor and financial adviser. Thanks to him and Sir George Couper, the excellent gentleman Albert appointed as her comptroller, the duchess cleared her debts, paid her bills on time, and put the financial scandals of the past behind her. With her status and reputation now secure, the duchess enthusiastically embraced her new role as, in effect, Queen Mother. Remembering that both his wife and her mother had quick tempers, Prince Albert prudently insisted that his mother-in-law always maintain separate residences, paid for out of her own civil list income. However, even if she did not precisely live with her daughter, the Duchess of Kent was a constant and beloved figure in royal family life.

Apart from Dear Mama, Dearest Uncle Leopold and his family were frequent and welcome guests, either staying with their royal English relatives or paying calls from their own home at Claremont. In fact, the king of the Belgians spent more time in England than his nephew Albert thought quite prudent in a head of state. The Queen's Leiningen half brother and half sister, whose financial situation was not easy, also came frequently to England with their families as Victoria's guests.

Duke Ernest I of Saxe-Coburg ceased to visit his son Albert and daughter-in-law Victoria within a year of their wedding, insulted that they declined to send the sums of money he requested. When the duke died in 1844, Prince Albert wept inconsolably and the Queen shed tears of sympathy, but the death was in many ways a solution to a festering problem. As for Albert's brother, Ernest, he came to England as often as possible and, unlike the Leiningens, was not very welcome. Once she realized his true character, Queen Victoria never took any pleasure in her brother-in-law's company, but she found it impossible to keep him away. When Ernest married, she liked and pitied his wife, Alexandrine, specifically invited her to come for visits, and was furious when Ernest persisted in coming alone.

Quite apart from these close relatives, Prince Albert liked to surround himself with members of German royal houses, most of whom could claim some distant kinship with him and the Queen. The language and cultural background of these people matched his own, and they appeared appropriately awed by his hospitality. Anytime in diary or letters that Albert happens to mention his current house party, we drown in a hyphenated deluge of Saxes, Mecklenburg-Strelitzes, Württembergs, Hesses, Hohenlohes, Coburg-Koharys, Hohenzollern-Sigmaringens, and Schleswig-Holsteins.

Although generous with their hospitality, the royal couple saw their guests mainly in the evening in large groups. They appreciated guests like the king of Saxony who could be trusted to amuse themselves and not get in the way of their busy hosts. Victoria had an iron-clad routine. Albert was out much of the day, either escorting his wife to public events or on business of his own, and he hated gossip and small talk even when he was at home. The chasm in status and wealth that yawned between the English royal family and their German relatives made relationships touchy. Neither the Queen nor the prince spent much time tête-à-tête even with visitors they dearly loved.

In many ways the English Saxe-Coburgs found relations easier and more relaxed with the family of Louis Philippe d'Orléans. The king and queen of the French were not only related by marriage but were fully the peers of the Queen and the prince. In the late summer of 1843, Victoria and Albert for the first time crossed the English Channel in the royal yacht to pay a private visit to Uncle Louis Philippe at the Chateau d'Eu on the coast of Normandy. The weather was fine, the countryside glorious; Louis Philippe, his Sicilian queen, and their numerous children proved to be charming hosts; and for six days the English royal couple felt deliciously at home in France. There were elaborate fêtes champêtres, intimate family dinners, and sea bathing for Albert. The prince enjoyed himself, as he was given precedence as if in England, and found the French king apparently willing to negotiate man to man such thorny international affairs as the marriages of the Spanish queen and her sister-heir. Victoria, meanwhile, had the kind of free-ranging, confidential chats with Queen Amélie and her delightful daughters and daughters-in-law that she rarely permitted herself at home.

The Queen and the prince returned from Normandy confident that they had not only made real friends but had managed to persuade Louis Philippe not to marry his younger son to the Spanish infanta and thus disturb the balance of power in the Iberian Peninsula. When the king of the French broke his promise about Spain within months, they felt deceived, but the friendship was too precious to be allowed to die. Queen Victoria kept her promise to invite Louis Philippe to come to England for a state visit, the first by a reigning French monarch in centuries, and to invest the king with the Order of the Garter, England's highest honor. The visit was a much-needed boost to the aging Louis Philippe's prestige and pride. It was also a very family affair, with Queen Amélie writing to Queen Victoria in advance of the visit, begging her not to allow the king to eat too much or endanger his life on horseback.

Unfortunately the 1844 state visit to England was the zenith of Louis Philippe's reign. However delightful *entre amis*, the king of the French was a lackluster ruler, blind to the political realities of his native country. In 1848 he was violently deposed, and the whole Orléans clan was forced to make a run for safety. Like so many notable political exiles, from Giuseppe Mazzini to Karl Marx, they headed for England and arrived with nothing but the disguises on their backs. Queen Victoria welcomed them warmly even though she was within days of giving birth to her sixth child and had not irrational fears for her own throne in that year of revolution. Prince Albert made a collection of his children's discarded clothing, which, one suspects, was received with less enthusiasm than it was given. King Leopold of the Belgians allowed his Orléans relatives to move into Claremont.

Victoria was a notably loyal friend. Until their political fortunes in France changed and they were able to reclaim some of their property and assets, the Orléans family was supported out of the Queen's privy purse and formed part of her intimate social circle. All the same, it was clear that, however much kings and queens might like to see themselves as part of a caste that moved easily across borders, the friendships among them were subject to the vicissitudes of international politics.

∎

FRIENDSHIP IS SOMETHING that most of us take for granted and know we cannot do without. We find it in offices and sports clubs and reading groups, in letters and online, over tea and over the telephone. But friendship, companionship, and collegiality are exceedingly rare and precious commodities for members of royal families. Both Victoria and Albert felt the lack of congenial friends acutely in their daily lives, and the intimate friendship they had for each other could not quite suffice.

Kings and queens had much in common but could very rarely spend time together even in an age of steam yachts and trains. Extended family members were either taboo, like the Cambridges; or disagreeable, like Duke Ernest; or at odds, like the Hohenzollern-Sigmaringens and the Schleswig-Holsteins. Even Vicky and Bertie, the royal couple's eldest children, were still too young to be good company, at least in their mother's eyes. At the end of each long day, the royal couple could at last dismiss the members of the household and turn with relief to each other, but being partners in business as well as bedfellows did not always make it easy to relax.

For the simple companionship and reliable affection that make the stresses of living bearable to busy people, the royal couple had to look somewhere hidden and unexpected. They found it not with royal peers or noble retainers but with persons at the very bottom of the social pyramid. Deep in the wings, out of the spotlight, were the largely anonymous men and women whom the royal couple counted on, relaxed with, and, perhaps, loved more than any others—their maids and valets.

In the daily drama of royal life, costume played a crucial role in bolstering the confidence of the two star actors and ensuring that their performances were well received. Any slip in presentation—the prince's hat that courtiers giggled at, the Queen's bonnet that protected her face from the sun but also from the curious gaze of reporters—could result in an unfavorable review. By their midtwenties both Victoria and Albert were impatient with fashion and yet fanatically concerned with appearance. They spent all too many hours of the day dressing, and their reliance on the skills and attention of their dressers increased each year. Every day, like a small child or an actor faced with a quick change of costume, the Queen stood while someone helped her into dresses. A maid did the Queen's hair, fastened the laces, buttons, and rows of tiny hooks and eyes, carefully positioned the various necklaces and brooches and earrings with which the Queen liked to festoon herself, tied her shoes, handed her a reticule and a tiny, exquisitely laundered handkerchief embroidered *VR*, and opened the door as she swept out.

Victoria employed a squad of seven or eight maids, classified as either dressers or wardrobe maids. They were the Queen's personal servants, not employees of one of the pestilential government departments. She was free to hire, fire, or reward them as she chose, recruited them with great care, and tried them out for several months before offering them a permanent position. Some of the dressers were foreign, mainly German. All came recommended by the Queen's relatives. Most had parents or siblings or cousins who also had served a member of the royal family.

The range of the dressers' duties was wide, and their expertise considerable. The dressers made many of the Queen's garments from scratch and were also at times asked to make garments for royal daughters or other relatives. If a garment needed to be altered—and with a constantly pregnant mistress, this happened regularly—the dresser took the dress apart and put it back together again. Since the sewing machine had yet to be invented, all this was done by hand, with invisible stitches. At least one of the dressers was a skilled milliner who trimmed not only the Queen's hats but hats sent over from Germany by the Queen's half sister.

If a pet dog tore the Queen's dress, if she got mud on her skirts, if her felt hat with its delicate grebe feathers got wet, if her muslin bodice caught a drop of turtle soup, each stain had to be removed and each rip repaired before the garment was put away. White cotton and linen items like shifts, petticoats, nightgowns, and handkerchiefs were carefully tagged and listed by the dressers, dispatched to the central laundry at Kew, and carefully counted and checked off when the garments returned, duly bleached, washed, starched, and ironed with consummate art. When a dress was brought out from the closet, it had to be fluffed out and any creases pressed before it was presented to the Queen.

The dressers were also in charge of maintaining the Queen's private rooms. Cleanliness and order were a passion with Queen Victoria, and every item in her suite had to be set out exactly as she liked it, from the solid gold set on her toilet table to the crowd of ornaments and piles of correspondence on her desk. The Queen's jewelry collection was a major responsibility for the dressers, as was the Queen's journal. Every day the dresser on duty locked the journal away from the curious eyes even of family members. Victoria liked to use different writing paper in different locations—at Balmoral, paper headed with a sketch of the castle, and so on. When she went into mourning, her paper was heavily edged in black. It fell to the dresser to ensure that the appropriate paper was ready on Her Majesty's desk.

Unlike the Queen's aristocratic ladies of the bedchamber, who had little to do and took it in turns to come into waiting for three-month periods, the working-class dressers all put in sixteen-hour days, seven days a week, most weeks of the year. Everything had to be ready for when the Queen awoke, usually around seven-thirty, and putting her clothes away after a ball or a grand dinner could take hours. When the Queen was at home, the dresser on duty would help her to dress and then spend the rest of the day in the dressing room, mending and sewing, ready to respond immediately to Her Majesty's bell. The other dressers would be engaged with needlework and cleaning, but one came up to the dressing room at mealtimes so that the woman on duty could go down for her food.

The dressers were subject to all of Prince Albert's moral strictures, but in any case they had too little free time to stray far. An afternoon off was a rare treat, possible only if the Queen was sure to be away and gave her explicit permission. The wardrobe maids were on duty even at night. One of them was required to sleep on the makeshift bed in the dressing room next to the Queen's bedroom. As Victoria interestingly remarked once to her daughter Vicky, she was so nervous at night that she always had a maid on call next door, "even when Papa is with me."

The dresser on duty's worst headache was probably not the endless dressmaking and mending and folding but the planning. She had to have the details of the Queen's schedule well in advance in order to ensure that every item of apparel was ready to be put on in a hurry. Royal birthdays had to be carefully noted. If one fell while the Queen was in mourning, colored clothing would be laid out in place of the black for that one day. When the Queen went out of town, as she came to do more and more, everything she could possibly need had to be thought through in advance, checked with Her Majesty in person, collected, organized, packed, and then on arrival unpacked, pressed, and so on. Never one to waste time, Victoria became a whirlwind of activity when she was abroad, and her dressers were on their feet for most of the day and night.

Unsurprisingly, Victoria's dressers were, for the most part, strong, young women, and they left her service after only a few years to marry or return to their native country. One exception was Marianne Skerrett, who entered the Queen's service in 1837 when she was about forty and stayed until 1854, rising to be her head dresser. When Baroness Lehzen left England in 1843, Marianne Skerrett seems to have taken over many of her duties with the Queen and in some measure at least replaced her in the Queen's heart. Skerrett, as she was known in the royal household, was a woman of humble birth and modest education, but, like her royal mistress, she could read and write fluently in French and German as well as English. As head dresser, Skerrett dealt with tradesmen, paid bills, answered begging letters, wrote for recommendations of other dressers and maids, and sometimes acted as the Queen's amanuensis in corresponding with her family. Queen Victoria described Skerrett as "a person of immense literary knowledge and sound understanding, of the greatest discretion and straightforwardness." Skerrett spoke her mind, and her power was respected.

Queen Victoria was a demanding employer, but people were eager to work for her. Domestic servants in the nineteenth century, especially women, were generally overworked and underpaid, and the Queen paid good wages: 200 pounds a year for the first dresser, 120 for the second, 100 for the third, and 80 for each of the wardrobe maids. In 1843 Charlotte Brontë was happy to get 16 pounds a year, plus room and board, as a teacher in Brussels, and her hours were also long and her holidays few. On the other hand, a senior lady-in-waiting got 500 pounds for her three months in the household.

Unlike many employers, the Queen could be counted upon to pay the wages every quarter, and the perquisites enjoyed by her personal servants were substantial. Food and lodging were free, and the dressers had decent rooms and ate very well. Within the whole household of servants in the royal palaces, a rigid hierarchy prevailed, and below stairs the Queen's private servants were high in the order of precedence. At Christmas and on their birthdays, the dressers received thoughtful and substantial gifts from their royal employers such as a piece of clothing, a bolt of fabric, an elaborate etui, or a gold pin with a small pearl. The royal children, who treated the dressers like aunties, made them little things or bought trinkets out of their pocket money. If a dresser fell ill, she was given the best care that a royal doctor could provide and allowed ample time to convalesce. On leaving the royal service, a dresser received a decent pension, which, again, the Queen could be counted on to pay each quarter.

The publication in 1994 of a set of letters written by Frieda Arnold, one of Queen Victoria's dressers, for the first time allowed a glimpse of life behind the scenes at the palace. Arnold was born into a middle-class German family, but after her father died, she was obliged to train as a seamstress and to enter service. Arnold was intelligent and well read despite her limited formal education, and she devoted her few hours of leisure to drawing and painting. Like Prince Albert, the dresser was desperately homesick for Germany and appalled by the dark, sooty atmosphere of London. However, she was interested in everything she saw in her new life and paints vivid word pictures of Windsor, Osborne, and Balmoral.

Even in these wholly private communications that the Arnold family kept to itself for over a century, Frieda scrupulously obeyed Prince Albert's rules and maintained a vigilant silence about the lives of her royal employers. Though she and her fellow maids lived closer to the Queen and the prince than anyone else, though the wardrobe maids actually spent the night in the room next to the one where the Queen and the prince slept, Arnold is discretion personified. She recounts one innocuous little remark

Queen Victoria addressed to her in Paris. She says how delighted she was when, one Christmas, the Queen gave her "a circular box of colours . . . a roll-up case of pencils . . . and a block book." But she describes no scenes between the Queen and her husband and other members of the royal family even though their intimate conversations were generally conducted in German, her native language. Arnold does not even say much about her work, except that it took all of her energy and intelligence.

Mary Ponsonby hated the fact that the Queen and the prince were distant toward members of the household like herself but close to their personal staff. "You felt that they [the Queen and the prince] were pretty nearly indifferent as to which maid of honour, lady-in-waiting, or equerry did the work, they were on more natural terms with the servants," wrote Ponsonby. "One result was that their standard of taste ran the risk of being vulgarized." Mary Ponsonby prided herself on her enlightened social views, but she was still a tremendous snob. As the documented examples of Marianne Skerrett and Frieda Arnold prove, the Queen's dressers were cleverer and better educated than many of the maids of honor.

The Queen enjoyed the company of her dressers because they were like her—intelligent, good at their jobs, easy to talk to, unpretentious. They were cultured but not intellectual. She could relax with them. She could talk family problems with them. And she could trust them.

Perhaps the most famous diarist of the mid-Victorian era was Lord Charles Greville. He is said to have known many important people, witnessed many important events, and listened at many important keyholes. Historians still quote the racy anecdotes he recorded about the royal family. Frieda Arnold did not need to listen at keyholes. She helped the Queen of England out of her evening bath and into her thin silk nightdress. She heard the morning dialogue of the Queen and the prince and brought their children in to see them. She had the key to the drawer where the Queen's journal was locked up every day. But unlike Lord Charles, Arnold, even posthumously, would not stoop to betray the Queen's trust. She had nobility of soul, not blood, and she kept silent. This too is what is meant by Victorian.

■

VICTORIA'S MAIDS WERE important to her but not even Skerrett mattered to her as much as the valet Isaac Cart did to Albert. When the prince came to England, the Queen allowed him to bring with him from Germany only his greyhound Eos, his librarian Dr. Schenk, and his valet, Cart. Eos died, much mourned, of old age. Schenk soon returned to Germany. Cart remained in the prince's service until August 1858, when he died. The Queen and the prince were in Europe at the time. "While I was dressing," wrote the Queen in her journal, "Albert came in, quite pale, with a telegram saying 'My poor Cart is dead, he died quite suddenly' . . . I turn quite sick now writing it . . . I burst into tears. All day long the tears would rush every moment to my eyes . . . Cart was invaluable, well educated, thoroughly trustworthy, devoted to the Prince . . . He was the only link my loved one had about him which connected him with his childhood . . . I cannot think of my dear husband without Cart . . . we had to choke our grief down all day."

Reportedly, Isaac Cart was a Swiss who in April 1829 became valet to both Coburg princes. Albert's tutor Florshütz calls him "a faithful, attentive, and obedient servant" who "deserved the confidence reposed in him." In October 1838, when Albert and his brother, Ernest, were threatened by a fire in a nearby room in the Ehrenburg Palace, Cart, according to Albert's report, "lifted a marble table with incredible strength and threw it against the bookcase enveloped in flames, causing it to fall down," thus helping to subdue the fire. In August 1840, Albert's first year in England, the prince wrote to his brother: "My birthday passed by, but how different from what it used to be. Cart, with his embarrassed congratulations in the morning, when he always begins to laugh, and good old Eos, were the only well known faces." In old age, Cart supervised the work of the prince's staff of valets, many of them German. Frieda Arnold mentions in her letters that Cart was very kind and helpful to her as she adjusted to her new life in England.

This is about all the published information available about Isaac Cart. Unlike Arnold, he is not known to have left any letters or reminiscences. The valet is an almost invisible figure in Albert's life, yet no one knew the prince so well; not his father or his brother, not even his wife. Was Cart a surrogate father? Surely. Was he a friend? Hardly. But he was indispensable, even though other men could be trained to do his work. For the prince, Cart's death was like a small coronary infarct, soon overcome but leaving a small area of the heart dead.

A Home of Our Own

...

QUEEN VICTORIA AND PRINCE ALBERT WERE OBLIGED TO SPEND MONTHS of every year at their official London residence, Buckingham Palace, and at Windsor Castle, some thirty miles away. However, from the moment he arrived, Prince Albert literally could not stomach London. The city's morals seemed to him as filthy as its air. The prince was a forward-thinking man, dedicated to promoting technology, commerce, and industry, but he had grown up among the green hills of Thuringia. The fertile, smoky monster that was London brought the costs of industrialization too close to him for comfort. As he wrote to his stepgrandmother in Gotha early in his marriage: "I felt as if in paradise in this fine fresh air [at Windsor], instead of the dense smoke of London. The thick heavy atmosphere there quite weighs me down. The town is also so large that without a long ride or walk you have no chance of getting out of it. Besides this, wherever I show myself, I am still followed by hundreds of people."

Windsor Castle generally suited Albert much better than Buckingham Palace. Not only did its age and magnificence make it the proper setting for a great dynasty, but its huge estate afforded excellent sporting opportunities. But the castle had one important drawback in the prince's eyes. It was situated in the heart of the busy little town to which the castle owed its name. Ancient public footpaths crossed the royal estates, and when members of the royal family walked out on the castle terrace to take the air, total strangers could stare at them.

Once he took charge, Albert managed to close off the terrace and limit public access. Encouraged, he visualized razing much of the town of Windsor, leaving the castle in splendid isolation. He had plans and estimates drawn up and submitted them to the appropriate government ministry. However, the notion of pulling down the town of Windsor was too much even for the prince's friends in government, so the plans had to be shelved. Albert was forced to accept that Windsor Castle could never be his perfect retreat.

In contrast to her husband, Victoria initially had nothing against London. She had been born and bred in Kensington, and she moved into Buckingham Palace in the heart of the city as soon as she could. Though she had fond memories of her childhood visits to the seaside and to Claremont, her uncle Leopold's country home, the young Queen's idea of getting away was a three-day honeymoon at Windsor, and she did not like living at the castle much. It brought back traumatic childhood memories of her mother and her uncles quarreling. Above all, Windsor was, as the Queen once plaintively remarked, *a castle*, and no one expected to be comfortable in a castle.

It took barely two years of marriage for Victoria to accept that in London her husband could be neither healthy nor happy. Overnight, or so it seemed, she changed from town mouse to country mouse. The Queen now craved seclusion and clean air and preferred a pony cart on a country lane to a smart horse in Rotten Row, the exclusive circuit for riders in Hyde Park.

Calm, beauty, and unpolluted skies could, of course, be found on the large country estates of dozens of English noblemen who would have been delighted to entertain the royal couple. Sadly, the prince did not care to visit, and the Queen no longer went anywhere without him. One solution to the prince's dilemma was to borrow a castle, and in 1842 he did just that. The Duke of Wellington, now in high favor, obligingly offered to move into an inn for a few weeks and allow the royal family to use Walmer Castle, the residence near Dover he used in his capacity of warden of the Cinque Ports. In late November, the Queen and the prince set off for the Kentish coast, bringing with them their two infants, a large staff, and a set of household goods worthy of a renaissance monarch on a progress through the Loire valley.

November is hardly a propitious month for a seaside holiday on the south coast of Great Britain, and even with all their things on hand, Victoria and her family were not entirely comfortable. Walmer was old, and even the Queen found it drafty. All the same, she and Albert enjoyed the intimacy of life away from London, and came back feeling closer to each other and more relaxed. They'd had a family holiday and were keen to do it again.

The family holiday was a Victorian social institution, made possible for queen and costermonger alike by the swift development of the railway system. It was no accident that, returning from Walmer Castle, the royal party embarked on the brand-new line between Dover and London's Charing

Cross. Around 1840, British private companies pushed out spurs of train track at a pace that matched the growing speed of the trains themselves. In 1830 a man who could afford to change horses every hour might travel perhaps fifteen miles an hour by post chaise. This was a lot faster than had been possible fifty years earlier and followed improvements in road engineering and coach design. But by the mid-1840s, the new express trains were able to cover a dizzying hundred miles in two hours, and they did not get tired or fear the dark. Suddenly London and Manchester, Birmingham and Bristol, even Glasgow and Dover, became hours instead of days apart.

The railways were a revolution that cut across class boundaries. The rich, who had always traveled, took quickly to trains, which offered both speed and privacy, and they found railway stock an excellent investment. But with three classes of carriage and the odd holiday special, even modest families could afford railway tickets. London barrow boys could have a day by the sea at Southend. Colliers from the Yorkshire pits could fill their lungs with the bracing air of Blackpool. Shopkeepers could pray for sun during their precious week of bed and breakfast in Margate. Artistic types could take a rundown cottage in the Cotswolds and paint hay wains like Constable. At Great Uncle Charles's vicarage in the Lake District, the London literati could breathe the heady air of Wordsworth and Coleridge. For a long, leisured summer, Auntie Ethel on the Norfolk Broads would have her hands full with wind-burned young sailor nephews and nieces tracking mud through the house.

Before Victoria, monarchs did not take family holidays. A royal progress was certainly not a vacation. George III retired to the coast a few times to try to regain his health, and George IV liked Brighton, but both kings spent most of their lives in or near London. Government depended on constant and rapid communication between monarch and ministers, and from Roman times, the English government was centered exclusively in the capital city. Wherever they were, the kings held court every day and were on view to the public as soon as they walked out the door.

But the railways, together with the telegraph, made it possible for Queen Victoria to conduct her royal business far from the capital. This was a bureaucratic revolution upon which Prince Albert, in his constant search for privacy and fresh air, was swift to capitalize. The Queen was suddenly free to travel abroad when parliament was not in session. She and her husband could buy a private estate where it suited them, a place where their family could withdraw, protected by broad acres and high walls. They could invite whom they chose and needed no permissions from Woods and Forests to mend a pane of glass. The ministers of the Crown would come as visitors, not masters. Above all, what Prince Albert called "the inquisitive and often impudent people" would have no right of access.

Their new preference for private family holidays further alienated the royal couple from the landed aristocracy, one of whose functions in the past had been to offer regular splendid entertainments to royalty. However, it brought them closer to the hearts of the 99.9 percent of the population whom the Duke of Devonshire would never have invited to meet the Queen at Chatsworth. By reaching over the heads of the elite, Victoria and Albert connected with the middle and lower classes, whose social and political power, though still small, was growing. Nothing advanced the cause of monarchy in the British Isles better than snapshots of the royal family on holiday, as Victoria and Albert soon came to realize.

The German painter Franz Winterhalter in his oil portraits made both the Queen and the prince majestic in ermine and diamonds, tailcoat and silk breeches. The *Illustrated London News* produced fairy-tale drawings that enhanced the royal faces and elongated their figures. Such adroit flattery was startlingly absent from the new photographic images that were eventually reproduced and distributed to the general public. Here was Victoria, tiny and plain in shawl and sunbonnet, presiding over a picture-perfect family that would eventually include four little Alberts in kilts and five miniature Victorias in lampshade hats. Here was the prince, chubby and balding, in tweeds and boots ready for healthy outdoor fun or a planning session with the estate manager. The photos were amateurish, but their message was simple and powerful: Look, they are just like us!

THE ROYAL HOLIDAY idyll was many years in the making. It began with a state visit to southern Scotland in 1842, followed by two private Scottish holidays. It continued with the Queen's purchase of Osborne House on the Isle of Wight off the coast of Kent in 1844. It reached its culmination with the prince's acquisition of Balmoral in the Scottish Highlands in the late 1840s. For Victoria, Osborne was paradise, and the times she spent there with Albert were bathed in a golden glow. At Balmoral Albert became the laird, a feudal dream come true. It was the only place he felt fully alive.

Victoria and Albert first went to Scotland in 1842. After bearing two children within twelve months, the Queen was up for an adventure, and the poetry and fiction of Sir Walter Scott she had read since girlhood convinced her that Scotland was romantic. The prince too liked the idea of Scotland, but Her Majesty's ministers thought she was slightly mad to want to go.

Apart from a brief visit by George IV in 1822, no British monarch had been north of the border since the mid-seventeenth century.

Scotland, in the opinion of Sir Robert Peel and his colleagues, was far too dangerous for the Queen. For centuries, the country had been identified with the house of Stuart and had fiercely resisted the establishment of Victoria's great-great-great-grandfather George I on the throne of Great Britain. Etched with blood into the Scottish psyche was the brutal defeat at Culloden in 1746 of "Bonnie" Prince Charlie and his mainly Scottish army by the British under the Duke of Cumberland, Victoria's great-uncle. Worse yet, the terrible economic downturn of the 1840s was hitting Scotland hard, and there had been a good deal of civil unrest in the big towns and the industrial areas. What if the Scots proved to be better shots than the English and the Queen was assassinated as she drove through the steep and narrow streets of Edinburgh? Victoria laughed off all these fears and insisted on going.

The royal party proceeded by sea, sailing up the east coast of Britain to Grafton, the port of Edinburgh, on the yacht *Royal George*, accompanied by several other vessels loaded with servants and baggage. Victoria imagined a romantic excursion, "alone" on her yacht, sitting on deck sketching picturesque seascapes, but things did not turn out quite like that. The *Royal George* was a clumsy old tub that had to be towed much of the way, and all her passengers were violently ill. Victoria was normally a good sailor, but on this trip she was nauseous and spent much of the time belowdecks. She was, it turned out, in the first weeks of a third pregnancy. She had little privacy. A flotilla of boats put out from each of the various ports along the way, and telescopes were trained eagerly on the decks of the royal yacht for a glimpse of the Queen. Victoria could not wait to get off the yacht and gave no warning of her imminent arrival at Grafton, to the annoyance of her Scottish welcoming committee. However, once on dry land, the Queen recovered her spirits, and Edinburgh gave her and her husband a rapturous welcome. People were charmed by Victoria's plain dress and friendly, unassuming ways.

This first excursion north of the border followed the medieval pattern of the royal progress. The Queen and the prince moved almost every day from one great nobleman's house to another and were constantly in society. Even when they drove across barren hills, they were accompanied by gentlemen riding next to the carriage, and in each village a crowd gathered. All of this was familiar to Victoria. Her routes in town and out were always lined with people anxious to see her.

For Prince Albert, the crowds and constant social demands, however gratifying to his pride, were onerous. But once Edinburgh was left behind and he could walk and hunt, he too cheered up. Scotland reminded him of his native Thuringia—mountainous, sparsely populated, untouched by the industrial revolution—and he found much in common with the Scots.

After that first trip in 1842, Queen Victoria was happy to get home to Windsor and consign the *Royal George* to the scrap heap. However, Scotland had a clear attraction for the royal couple, and they returned with their older children for private vacations in 1844 and 1847. Now they ventured farther north, touring the Highlands by carriage and boat, kept much more to themselves, and enjoyed solitude. Even days of torrential rain could not dampen their enthusiasm for Scottish holidays.

Albert took at once to the lowland Scots he met on his first visit. Like the Coburgers and Gothaners, they were strong in their Lutheran-Calvinist Protestant tradition, but they were also rich in the philosophical, economic, scientific, and legal achievements of the Scottish enlightenment. But it was in the Highlands that Albert felt truly at home. In his dealings with both lairds and gillies, Albert found that mixture of deference and intimacy that he remembered with nostalgia from his native Coburg. The rural Highland Scots, gallant in defeat, proud in their threadbare gentility, had an undying tradition of loyalty to their liege lord. They were willing, it proved, to honor the Stuart in Queen Victoria and forget that she was the butcher of Culloden's great-niece. With these Scots Prince Albert found common cause in a scorn of England, where money, not blood and brains and bravery, made the man. He had a romantic vision of the Highlander as virile and independent, virtuous yet passionate, just like himself.

The lonely spaces of Scotland fed Albert's soul. The hunting was hard but exhilarating, and he came home happy, hungry, and ready for bed. Though regularly wet to the skin, he had few colds. A contented man, Albert was more easy and natural with the people he met than he had ever been at the great English country houses. To his Scottish hosts, he felt able to unveil his talent for mimicry and invite their laughter with his comic imitations of Bonn university professors.

Victoria was equally enchanted. Her darling Sir Walter Scott had not lied. The Scottish countryside was astonishingly beautiful and the people picturesque. Barefoot children shyly waved. Beautiful girls in plaid shawls, their red hair streaming down their backs, gazed at the Queen in wonder. Tall, muscular men begged to know when Her Majesty might come again. How different it all was from the squalid indifference of the Pimlico slums that flanked Buckingham Palace.

With Albert delightfully invigorated, Scotland fed a royal love affair now entering its second decade. It also, as we see in the Queen's journal entry for

Wednesday, September 18, 1844, unconsciously opened a tiny window onto other romantic possibilities that Victoria would explore, only much later.

The Queen and the prince set off at nine in the morning on two ponies, "attended only by Lord Glenlyon's excellent servant, Sandy McAra, in his Highland dress." This Sandy led his royal charges straight uphill to give them a panoramic view of "the Falls of the Bruar, Ben-y-Chat, Ben Vrackie, Ben-y-Glo, the Killiecrankie Pass, and a whole range of distant hills." It was a glorious day and, in her own words, "the most delightful, most romantic ride" the Queen had ever had. "Here we were with only this Highlander behind us holding the ponies (for we got off twice and walked about)—not a house, not a creature near us, but the pretty Highland sheep, with their horns and black faces,—up at the top of Tulloch, surrounded by beautiful mountains."

In Scotland, better than anywhere else, the Queen of England found the realization of her concept of "aloneness." It consisted of her and Albert happy together in a beautiful place far from prying eyes—with a silent, trusted servant on hand to ensure their security and minister to their needs. In Sandy McAra we find an early avatar of John Brown, the passionately devoted gillie whom Albert hired and promoted and then bequeathed to his wife as perhaps his most precious gift.

The idea of buying property in the Highlands was born probably as early as the royal visit of 1842. Land there was cheap, and, as the Queen's journal shows, the main features in her mental map of Scotland were property boundaries, not mountains and lochs. As she traveled about, Victoria automatically noted who owned what. But the railway was slow in coming to Edinburgh and Glasgow, and it took days to reach Inverness or Oban by sea. Governing from the Highlands was not yet possible. While nursing their Gaelic fantasies, the royal couple turned to the south coast to satisfy their immediate need for a private place outside of London.

※

IN THE SPRING of 1843, Queen Victoria was successfully brought to bed with her third child. Though the baby was only a girl, a grateful nation presented Her Majesty with a new royal steam yacht, named—what else?—the *Victoria and Albert*. In the late summer of 1843, as we have seen, the Queen and the prince set out on their new toy for a cruise of the English south coast, followed by a private visit to Louis Philippe and his family at their private estate at Eu on the coast of Normandy.

On their return to England, Victoria and Albert had a moment of revelation. The king of the French had the Tuileries, the Louvre, Saint-Cloud, Versailles, Fontainebleau, and who knew what else, but he regarded these properties as business addresses. For rest and relaxation, Louis Philippe and his family repaired to Normandy. What the English Saxe-Coburgs needed was an English Chateau d'Eu. The big question was: Could they (by which they meant she) afford one?

Economy-minded radicals might cavil that the Queen of England already had a home by the sea, since she had inherited the Royal Pavilion in Brighton. But, like Windsor and Buckingham Palace, the Royal Pavilion was a Crown property, ruled by the various government departments, and, in any case, neither the Queen nor her husband liked the place. The extraordinary mix of Mogul minarets and Chinese dragons at Brighton made Prince Albert queasy. As for Victoria, it would be many years before she styled herself Empress of India and developed a passionate interest in the subcontinent.

Brighton was also no longer the secret fishing port playground of the very rich that it had been around 1810. By the 1840s, the town had grown up all around the Royal Pavilion and was increasingly frequented by low-class persons who mobbed the royal family when they ventured out on the front. Worst of all, the ghost of George IV wandered the Royal Pavilion. For Prince Albert the building was synonymous with promiscuity and excess.

The Lords of the Treasury were far from distressed to learn that the royal couple had no use for the Royal Pavilion. It had always been a drain on the exchequer. The decision was made to get rid of it, and between 1846 and 1848 the Pavilion was stripped down to the studs. The most precious furnishings and artworks were stored for use in other royal palaces, the rest were sold at auction, and the external structure was scheduled for demolition. The prince's favorite builder, Thomas Cubitt, famed for his upscale town houses in Belgravia and Bloomsbury, was poised to develop the site, but then the local people of Brighton stepped in. They decided their city would not be the same without its Royal Pavilion, however raped and despoiled, and in 1850 the Brighton Corporation managed to borrow sixty thousand pounds from the Bank of England to buy the property. One of the jewels of Regency architecture was saved, despite its royal proprietors.

The speed with which the Royal Pavilion was sacked was due in part to the fact that in 1844 the Queen and the prince found the perfect location for their private pied-à-terre. It was the Osborne House estate on the Isle of Wight, just across the Solent from Southampton and Portsmouth, and thus very handy for future trips to the Continent. The house was an undistinguished Georgian structure, but it stood on some thousand wooded acres sloping down to a private beach and had a magnificent view. Prince Albert planned for his wife to buy and take title to the property just like any private citizen. This would place the estate entirely under his control. His two closest confidants, his secretary George Anson and Prime Minister Sir Robert Peel, were far from sure that the Queen should incur such a major expense and were nervous about the administrative problems of running the government on an island. However, once it became apparent that the prince could not be dissuaded from his plan, Peel acquiesced and Anson was dispatched to negotiate the sale.

Osborne's owner, Lady Isabella Blatchford, was a shrewd woman who counted on getting 28,000 or even 30,000 pounds for her estate, but she was no match for the prince and his agent. A one-year rental on the property for 1,000 pounds was agreed upon, and the prince moved his wife and family in during the summer. Faced with evicting her sovereign lady the Queen, Lady Isabella agreed to accept 26,000, and still had to haggle over the estimated value of her furniture.

The Queen thoroughly enjoyed her first holiday at Osborne House in October 1844. For her, Lady Isabella's small rooms and middle-class appurtenances had the charm of novelty. But the ministers of the Crown shoehorned into the attics grumbled, and the servants were sullen, so Albert had no difficulty persuading his wife that a much larger building was needed. In June 1845, the Queen laid the foundation stone for the new Osborne House, which, to her rapt admiration, Albert was designing himself with the help of Thomas Cubitt. This gentleman was an experienced builder but not a trained architect, and he was more than willing to defer to his royal client. The work went on apace, and by the summer of 1846, the royal family was able to move into its private wing of the house. The larger section for guests, servants, and offices was completed by 1851.

With the increasingly fast train service from London and a private steamer at their disposal, the royal pair soon found that Osborne was feasible even for three-day weekends. By 1850, the Queen could leave Buckingham Palace at seven in the morning and be wheeled out in her bathing machine for a quick dip by ten-thirty. But for everyone except the members of the royal family, Osborne involved a good deal of work and inconvenience.

On a good day, ordinary mortals took at least twice as long to get from London or Windsor to Osborne, and on many days the sea crossing was hard on the weak of stomach. The ministers and household officers deputed to attend on the Queen were not enthusiastic about Osborne even in fine weather. For days on end, they had to abandon the office and the social whirl of London for evenings spent playing Fox and Geese or listening to Her Majesty taking a crack at bel canto. A week by the sea was no holiday for Victoria's personal staff, since the two large coaches full of baggage with which she invariably traveled took several hectic days to pack. Separated from their families and crammed into tiny bedrooms, Victoria's servants swore that the soft sea air on the Isle of Wight was murder on their constitutions.

But, in the eyes of the Queen and the prince, all this inconvenience and extra work was a small price to pay. For a few precious weeks and the odd weekend every year, the English Saxe-Coburgs could breathe in clean salt air, take healthful exercise, and pretend that they were any ordinary family with a private train, two private stations (one on and one off the island), a private boat slip on the mainland, a private yacht they hadn't had to buy, a flock of servants, and a rapidly growing private income to buy little luxuries like paintings and statues and rare shrubs. Marie Antoinette had had the Petit Trianon. Victoria would have Osborne.

The house that Prince Albert built was an Italianate villa divided into two separate pavilions. The two sections were connected on the first floor by a gallery festooned with pictures and statues, and in the basement by a dark, narrow corridor along which the servants scuttled with food from the distant kitchens. The house featured two mock campaniles of different sizes (a water tower and a clock tower), a loggia, and terraces going down to the sea. As time went on, the Queen and the prince were able to acquire another thousand acres or so of surrounding land to further insulate them from Cowes, the nearby town. The building and landscaping of the new Osborne cost the Queen some 200,000 pounds, a large sum given her declared income, but the prince had no problem finding the money. Whether some of the profits realized by the sale of the Royal Pavilion and its effects were diverted into the financing of Osborne was a secret between Prince Albert and the Lords of the Treasury.

Osborne was the height of modernity, designed to give its owners the maximum comfort, privacy, and security. Its vaguely Renaissance shell was supported by cast-iron girders and designed to withstand fire. It had modern drains and water closets, plus bathrooms with hot and cold running water. With the technical assistance of the renowned chemist and inventor Dr. Lyon Playfair, the prince devised a system whereby the human sewage could be used for fertilizer on the estate. For the Queen, with her long, wide skirts and yards of petticoats, the water closets were a revelation, and within a few years she was refusing to go anywhere that did not have one for her private use.

Osborne also had special recessed windows and double insulation to protect against the sea winds. Some of the doors were of glass to extend the sea view through the house. However, there was no central heating even though the Queen and the prince were usually by the sea in May, often a chilly month, and on weekends during the fall and winter. Victoria had found the under-floor central heating at the Royal Pavilion oppressively warm, so Osborne made do with fireplaces.

For Queen Victoria, Osborne had a delicious coziness. The bedrooms, dressing rooms, living rooms, and nurseries on the upper floors of the family pavilion were pretty but unpretentious, and the private reception rooms in the royal wing were intimate by the standards of Windsor or Versailles. The dining room, drawing room, and billiard room were arranged *en enfilade* around the central staircase, and this design allowed members of the royal family to descend into the dining room unseen by members of the household. Evenings were more relaxed, since the room design allowed the royals to entertain guests in one section while behind some large pillars the ladies and gentlemen in attendance could sit down and even converse among themselves.

As a visitor to Osborne House can still see today, the young Victoria and Albert were people with big checkbooks who were eclectic and exuberant in their tastes. In this, their first real home, the royal couple put together stuff of all kinds: old masters and works by up-and-coming artists, ceramics, tesserae, and tiles, statues and busts, family portraits and sketches by family members, a superb billiard table, folksy bedroom furniture, eight-foot-tall china torchères, garden seats cut out of hunks of coal, and white marble sculptures of the four eldest royal children dressed as the seasons.

For his children, who spent more time each year at Osborne than could their parents, the prince ordered a fully furnished Swiss chalet. It was charmingly miniature by palace standards yet big enough for two servants to live in and for the royal daughters to play cook and housekeeper. Outside the chalet was a shed in which the princes and princesses kept their sets of garden tools for their imposingly large individual garden plots. Somehow the royal children were expected not only to keep up a regular schedule of lessons and make a natural history collection to rival their father's in Coburg, but also to learn to bake a loaf of bread, grow a potato, and make a chair.

The royal couple were enthusiastic collectors of paintings by contemporary artists. In the public rooms and in the shared rooms of the private wing, they gave pride of place to large expensive canvases by fashionable painters like Winterhalter and Landseer. There were also a number of landscapes by

German artists—Koekoek, Achenbach, Lindemann-Frommel—more famous then than now. But in his bedroom-dressing-room-bathroom suite, Albert hung his growing collection of paintings and drawings by early Italian and Flemish artists. He had developed a taste for the quattrocento during his Italian visit of 1838–39 and was able to pick up unfashionable pieces by Duccio, Fra Angelico, Gozzoli, Memling, Cranach, Giorgione, Mantegna, and Bellini for next to nothing. Today the prince's bedroom Bellinis are the pride of the national collections, while his Winterhalters and Landseers are historic wallpaper for the royal residences.

Perhaps the most surprising thing about Osborne is the royal couple's predilection for sumptuous nudes, both male and female. A fresco by William Dyce, commissioned by Prince Albert for the head of the main staircase, shows *Neptune Entrusting the Command of the Sea to Britannia*. A chastely dressed Britannia salutes a naked Neptune, whose private parts are considerably hidden by a horse's wind-tossed mane. Accompanying Neptune is an attractive set of naked young mermen and mermaids whose fish tails begin around their knees, allowing a plentiful display of buttock and bosom. Britannia is flanked by a young gentleman clad only in a hat who turns his beautiful back to the viewer. Under one arm the youth holds an arrow, identifying him as Mercury, while he wraps the other arm affectionately around the shoulders of a bearded man in a classical version of the sarong. Plato would have liked the picture, and so did Prince Albert.

Even more astonishing is the painting of Hercules and Omphale by Josef Anton von Gegenbaur that was Queen Victoria's wedding gift and today graces the wall of the prince's bathroom. It shows a magnificently muscled, half-dressed man, seated by the fire with a spindle in his hand, being embraced by a beautiful naked woman. The picture is indisputably erotic, and becomes more so once one knows the story behind the painting. According to Apollodorus, the mighty hero Hercules killed his male companion Iphitus in a fit of madness. To expiate this crime, Hercules agreed to live for three years as a slave to the Lydian queen, Omphale, who took him as her lover and, finally, her husband. Hercules expressed the terrible shame he felt as Omphale's slave by donning women's clothing and spinning thread by the hearth like a woman.

Even for a Greek myth, this is provocative material. The artists of classical Greece would have none of it, but the perverse eroticism of the mighty hero Hercules reduced to a feminized slave spoke to the Hellenistic and Baroque periods. Why the conventional Gegenbaur took up the subject in the mid-nineteenth century is unclear, but the appeal of his canvas to Victoria and Albert is not. Dumpy little Victoria, wreathed in yards of checked gingham, liked to imagine herself as the voluptuous Omphale. Albert knew himself to be a mighty hero in disguise, even though obliged in daily life to walk several steps behind his wife and get her to sign the checks. The erotic side of the royal marriage is expressed far more clearly in their art collection than in their letters and journals.

Today architectural experts tend to sneer at Osborne, opining that while the site is, of course, glorious, the house itself is ugly. The received wisdom is that the articulation of the two wings is awkward, the plaster work in the main reception rooms undistinguished, and the exterior a timid mishmash of styles that falls far short of that fabulous anachronism the Royal Pavilion at Brighton. The prince consort, critics contend, had a way with ornamental shrubs but should have left architecture to the professionals.

Even when it was new, Osborne was controversial. To the young middle-class German girl Frieda Arnold, Victoria's dresser, it was a triumph. To the aristocratic Englishman Charles Greville, it was a monstrosity. To a grand seigneur like the Duke of Devonshire, busy in the 1840s refurbishing the glories of Chatsworth, Osborne was even more nouveau riche than Buckingham Palace. To a plutocrat like the Duke of Westminster, willing to spend 600,000 pounds on a single residence, Osborne, with its folksy tiles, fake statues, and faux marble columns, was cheap. However, to the majority of Englishmen in the nineteenth century, Osborne was an ideal home for a gentleman's family. It inspired enormous public interest and was often copied.

For Queen Victoria, Osborne was perfect because Albert created it and she first lived there in her twenties, when she and he were full of joy and perfect companions. At Osborne Victoria could be within sight of Albert almost every minute of the day. The two as always sat down side by side to get through the business of state, and even business had its charms when it was conducted together. Both spent several hours each day in their private apartments working on their correspondence and their journals. They took it in turns to do the piano practice that both thoroughly enjoyed and took very seriously. "Dear Madam, you really must do that passage again; it is so impertinent to Mozart to libel it so," Lady Mount Edgcumbe, the senior lady-in-waiting, remarked to the Queen one day at Osborne. And once their duties were done for the day, the royal couple could have fun.

When Albert went out on the estate, the Queen rode with him when her condition permitted, and the only escort they needed was a boy to open the gates. When the Queen was pregnant, she pottered around in a little pony cart, getting out to sketch, admire the view, or proudly watch her husband consulting with the workmen. She liked to sail, and she found it refreshing to immerse herself in the sea in the sanctuary of her bathing machine. In the evenings, when Albert played billiards, the Queen could watch or make music with her ladies-in-waiting and her guests. There were also parlor games, perhaps an experiment with table tapping, or a game of whist, though the prince did not think highly of his wife's card play. Then, husband and wife would wish the company good night quite early. After taking her bath or her shower in her beautiful new bathroom, the Queen could stand with her husband on the balcony facing the sea and listen as Albert's whistle coaxed the nightingales to sing. Then the two could retire to the new bedroom with the special lock Albert had designed that could be operated without getting out of bed.

■

PRINCE ALBERT ENJOYED life at Osborne, especially perhaps the hours he spent there with his children, but the real pleasure of the house for him came in the designing, the building, the decorating, and the landscaping. Once the place was complete, he lost interest, but fortunately by this time the railway had reached Edinburgh and Aberdeen, and the prince himself felt rich enough, in one way or another, to purchase a second estate, much farther away and much more isolated, in the Highlands of Scotland.

In May 1848, Prince Albert, sight unseen, took over the twenty-seven-year lease on Balmoral, a 17,400-acre estate on the bank of the river Dee owned by the trustees of the Earl of Fife. It was high up between Ballater and Braemar, in an area renowned in Scotland for its low rainfall. The royal family's first visit to its new rental was such a success that the prince quickly determined not only to buy Balmoral but to twist the arms of neighboring landowners to sell him the abutting properties of Birkhall, Abergeldie, and Ballochbuie so that he could really feel lord of all he surveyed.

Balmoral was wild, and its abundant game was a major incentive for the prince. In the early years, red deer and roe deer were so common that they came right up to the house, begging to be shot. Albert was happy to oblige, and he spent many of his days in Scotland deerstalking, sometimes allowing his wife to accompany him. Delighted, Victoria was careful to keep her distance and stay very quiet, even for hours on end. The local people were enjoined to stay away from any area where the prince was hunting, but if someone strayed in by mistake and scared away the deer, the Queen was quite irate that dear Albert's day should be spoiled.

In one painting of the royal family at Balmoral, the German painter Carl Haag showed the prince on his return from a successful deer-hunting excursion. Albert is attired in the newfangled Highland outfit that he promoted and that showcased his superbly muscled legs. The tartan of the kilt is the one he personally designed, and the sash and star of the Garter are on his jacket. The prince is standing at the main door to the castle, proudly displaying to his wife, her mother, and her ladies the magnificent stags he has shot that day.

Haag shows Victoria, elegant in evening dress, smiling fondly at the dead creatures spread before her, and this was not wholly a fiction. It is true that the Queen had little taste for blood sports, did not like guns, and was wary of the stupidity of huntsmen. When, on the occasion of Bertie's christening, her uncle Ferdinand peppered the beloved greyhound Eos with buckshot, she was hysterical. Happily the dog recovered. When Lord Canning almost shot the infant Prince of Wales, she was furious. But as a woman and a landowner of her generation, she knew that Albert and his male guests could not be happy unless they were shooting things.

The negotiations with the Fife trustees over the acquisition of Balmoral were protracted, and for seven years the royal couple spent some six weeks in September and October in the "old" castle. The accommodation for a growing family, officials, attendant ministers, and servants was extremely cramped. Report has it that the billiard room was so small that the Queen and her ladies had to move around the room to enable the gentlemen to take their shots. Small or not, Balmoral suited Queen Victoria, who liked pretending to be an ordinary middle-class wife and mother. However, once again the ministers and the ladies grumbled, and as soon as Prince Albert took title, he launched an ambitious plan to erect a new, much larger structure and to raze the old one.

As at Osborne, the prince served as his own architect, finding in William Smith of Aberdeen an experienced builder who could be counted upon to put his employer's ideas into stone without any argument. In Scotland Albert the architect played things safer. He built a castle in the medieval style, with asymmetrical windows and rooms on correspondingly different levels. He used a pale gray local stone, Glen Gelder granite. Men were recruited from far and wide to build the castle, and Scottish stonemasons completed the restrained but charming external decoration.

Several small strikes by the workmen for better work conditions took the prince by surprise. A Highlander like Sandy McAra might be happy in the role of feudal servant to his laird, but a Scottish workman from the south had a strong sense of his rights and was ready for industrial action. The prince gave way, as he could not afford adverse press coverage, and the house went up smartly. In 1855 Queen Victoria was able to occupy the family's private quarters, and on August 30, 1856, she recorded in her journal arriving at Balmoral to find "the tower finished as well as the offices, and the poor old house gone."

Frieda Arnold, Queen Victoria's dresser, visited the brand-new castle in 1855. On her six-hour carriage journey from Perth to Balmoral over the Pass of Glenshee, Arnold was swept away by the desolate beauty of the countryside, its "sublime stillness and endless peace." A visitor today will feel the same. Arnold, like Prince Albert, was deeply nostalgic for her native country, and she saw at once how much the new Balmoral resembled a German hunting lodge. On a grander scale, and with the modern bathroom conveniences that he and his family now found essential, the prince had recreated his father's Schloss Rosenau. Surrounded by wild and mountainous country, with the pleasant sound of a river ever in the background, Albert could relax.

Queen Victoria was delighted with Balmoral. She felt that a Canaletto or a Rubens was superfluous there, since every window was a frame for sublimity. When in Scotland, the Queen spent as much of the day as possible outside. She rode her pony uphill on paths newly blazed for her use. With her faithful kilt-clad gillie leading her horse, she forded rushing streams, her long skirts trailing in the icy water. Covered with waterproofs and rugs, she took long drives in a high open carriage to local beauty spots for family picnics and sketching parties.

In the Highlands, Victoria was an attentive neighbor to her fellow landowners, and an eager patron of the Highland games at nearby Braemar, but her instinct was to get away from people, not seek them out. The local crofters learned to keep their distance from the Queen when she was out on one of her jaunts. On the other hand, if she happened upon someone by accident, she stopped and chatted, rapturous if, at first, she was not recognized. She took to dropping in on women in the primitive cottages known as bothies, bringing food and warm clothing, pleased to be welcomed, amused when an old woman criticized a sock she had knitted.

For even more solitude, the Queen took to retiring for a few nights each year to Alt-na-Guithasach, a barely accessible spot reached by boat across Loch Muick. She improved the route, had a path along one side of the lake chipped out of the granite, and extended the lodge or shiel to accommodate herself, a couple of family members, a lady-in-waiting and a gentleman-in-waiting, a lady's maid, and a crew of boatmen and gillies. For Queen Victoria this was simplicity and seclusion. Frieda Arnold found Loch Muick desolate and marveled at the lives of the wife and daughter of the Queen's keeper there. This woman and her little girl regularly spent weeks alone in their tiny home, far from human contact and aid, while her husband was at Balmoral, helping with the shooting parties. Victoria was always generous in paying for her pleasures in money, but, as Arnold delicately suggests, she did not always see the price in human suffering. The lonely little child, the gillie in his "Highland dress," wading through freezing mountain streams, the piper playing in the pouring rain—all this was for Victoria a backdrop like Loch na Gar, the peak that towered over Balmoral Castle.

The picturesqueness of Scotland seems never to have palled for Victoria. Though most of her food was imported from Edinburgh or Windsor, she relished such typically Scottish foods as finnan haddie (smoked haddock), oatmeal porridge, oatcakes, and shortbread biscuits. She liked scotch better than wine and even ate haggis. To judge from her journal entries, the bagpipers at Balmoral serenaded her endlessly, and by night and day men could be seen outside her castle dancing reels. One innovation at the new Balmoral was a ballroom built for the so-called gillies balls. People came from miles around to dance into the small hours, liberally wetting their whistles with the local brew. Queen Victoria adored these occasions and insisted that her family and her visitors attend. She mastered all the Scottish dances, and for hours on end could whirl like a top to the skirl of the pipe and the whoop of the sweating, inebriated men.

Needless to say, Balmoral was a taste that most of the court ladies and gentlemen, the royal officials, and the ministers of state refused to acquire. It took a day of nonstop travel—two days with a layover—to get to the castle, and once you got there, there was nothing to do. Deeside may have been statistically the sunniest part of Scotland, but it could still see rain for days on end. During the Queen's fall visits, the cold was often frightful once the sun went down, with ice on the lawn, snow on the hills, and a howling gale in the uncarpeted halls. As for the decor, it looked like middle-class kitsch to anyone used to the splendors of Woburn Abbey and Blenheim Palace. All those giant thistles, as witty Lord Clarendon remarked, would kill the appetite of a donkey.

Not everyone found it delightful to go on a jaunt to a local waterfall, even with the piles of waterproofs and woolen blankets and provisions the Queen laid on for her guests. The Highland men that the Queen and the prince found so charming were surly with lesser mortals. Visiting hunters got tired of stag shooting after a while, since it often involved hours of fruitless walking in treacherous terrain. Prince Albert himself got fed up with watching the deer run away and concocted a plan to connect the high bare plain where his prey liked to congregate with a series of tunnels from which he could shoot undetected. This highly rational project did not meet Scottish standards of sportsmanship and was dropped.

But despite small gaffes like this, Prince Albert was popular in Scotland. The Highlanders took it as a compliment when he built his German version of a Scottish castle, festooned his house in Royal Stuart tartan, and added a silver-encrusted sporran and jeweled dagger to his Garter star in the evenings. Ever since the Great Enclosures, when the lairds evicted their tenant farmers to make sheep farms, Deeside had had more lambs than children, and the coming of the Saxe-Coburg family brought some modest affluence. Albert was a good landlord who understood farming. He improved the dwellings of people on his estate, established schools, paid good wages, and patronized local tradesmen. In six weeks the Queen's household got through 13,225 pounds of red meat alone. Some of this, as well as some of the game shot by the prince and his friends, reached the protein-starved women and bairns in the bothies.

The roads into the Highlands continued to be lonely, but with the Queen's messengers traveling them constantly every fall, some improvements were inevitable. Hiking and riding trails opened up, and tourists began to trickle in. Plaid was fashionable, and kilts became all the rage for small boys all over Europe when the royal princes wore them at public events. It is no wonder that when Victoria first drove out to Balmoral from Aberdeen, a bewildering succession of victory arches was constructed along the road to welcome her. With the Queen and her family in the Highlands, Scotland felt a little less like a conquered nation or an abandoned colony.

And the Queen was never safer than when she wandered the roads near Crathie, riding her pony or driving her trap with a single companion by her side, a tiny woman in a giant bonnet, a plaid shawl, and a muddy tweed skirt, startlingly, deliciously, daringly "alone."

The Greatest Show on Earth

...

*T*HE QUEEN AND THE PRINCE DID NOT SPEND THEIR WHOLE YEAR ON their private estates, and they had far less leisure than most of England's upper crust. The prince especially dedicated himself to the business of government, and he was increasingly active in charitable organizations and arts groups.

On the spectrum of mid-nineteenth-century British politics, Prince Albert was a moderate Tory, even a Liberal on some issues, but never a radical. In his capacity as the Queen's chief adviser and personal secretary, he worked smoothly with government ministers of both parties, and in domestic affairs his was consistently a voice of enlightenment and a force for good.

He was intelligent and exceptionally well informed on the issues of the day, from the design of small-bore rifles for the army to reform of the church schools in Ireland. When he agreed to chair or sponsor an organization, be it the Society for the Abolition of Slavery, the Royal Horticultural Society, Trinity House (an organization devoted to saving lives at sea), or the Committee to Erect the New Houses of Parliament, he was an inspiration. He did his homework, was an exemplary correspondent, delivered thoughtful speeches, and always tried to think the issues through without prejudice.

He was in favor of social reform far more than his wife, who found it difficult to sympathize with the problems of people she did not know. Albert saw poverty as an ethical issue that, as the public voice of the Crown, it was his duty to address. He did all he could to investigate labor conditions in person, and the industrialists and engineers who took him round a system of locks here or a woolen mill there were always impressed by the depth of his knowledge. In his public speeches as well as in his committee work, he sought to convince the nation that its greatness depended on finding solutions to the problems of the poor. Reading the official reports that unveiled the horrendous conditions prevailing in British mills and mines, he contacted Lord Shaftesbury, who was leading the campaign for industrial reform, and offered to preside over the Society for Improving the Condition of the Working Classes.

Albert was a scholar at heart, and he brought a valuable European perspective to the question of university education. He was a rare bird in England's establishment in the mid-nineteenth century because he was as passionately interested in science and technology as he was in music and the arts. Keen to put his ideas into practice, he allowed his name to be put forward for election to the chancellorship of the University of Cambridge. Dyed-in the-wool conservatives among Cambridge graduates did their utmost to block the prince's election, but, happily, they failed. Far from content to be a figurehead, Albert placed himself at the head of the Cambridge dons who were convinced that the university could regain its status as an intellectual powerhouse only if it encouraged scientific and technological research and stressed mathematics and the sciences for its undergraduates. Albert and his supporters managed to push through a substantial program of curricular and administrative reform in the face of ferocious opposition from classicists and theologians. It was in no small part thanks to Prince Albert that Cambridge University was dragged, kicking and screaming, into the modern world.

The culmination of the prince's work as a committee chairman was the Great Exhibition of the Works of Industry of All Nations of 1851. This proved to be the cultural sensation of the mid-nineteenth century, and it was generally agreed by the prince's contemporaries that it never would have come off without him. The opening of the exhibition on May 1 was Albert's finest hour.

AN INTERNATIONAL INDUSTRIAL exhibition could obviously not be the work of one man, but Prince Albert worked as chief fund-raiser, lobbyist, and organizer, intelligently exploiting the power of the Crown. Neither he nor Queen Victoria contributed much financially. Even the seed money for the exhibition came from public subscriptions not from the prince's pockets, though these were no longer as empty as he liked people to believe. But the Queen's name was invaluable in getting the project off the ground, and the prince contributed at every stage. As chair of a committee notable for its diligence and efficiency, he worked harder than anyone else.

The infant Victoria
with her mother,
the Duchess of Kent

Princess Feodora
of Leiningen,
Queen Victoria's
beloved half sister

A sketch by the teenaged Victoria of her chief ally, Baroness Louise Lehzen

Prince Albert's father, Ernest I, Duke of Saxe-Coburg and Gotha, circa 1816

Sir John Conroy, the man Victoria loathed and her mother trusted

Prince Albert's mother,
Duchess Louise of Saxe-Gotha-
Altenburg, circa 1820

Leopold of
Saxe-Coburg-Saalfeld,
Victoria and Albert's favorite
uncle, circa 1816

Prince Albert's brother
Duke Ernest II of
Saxe-Coburg and Gotha,
1840

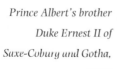

Lord Melbourne, Queen Victoria's adored first prime minister

Lord Palmerston, with whom Prince Albert wrestled for control of foreign affairs

In the 1841 painting by Sir Edwin Landseer Windsor Castle in Modern Times, *the young husband and wife are shown gazing into each other's eyes and paying no attention to their eldest child, Vicky, who incongruously fondles an array of dead creatures her father has brought back from the hunt.*

Baron Stockmar, confidential adviser to three generations in the Saxe-Coburg family

Emperor Napoleon III, whom Queen Victoria found unexpectedly delightful

Neptune Resigning to Britannia the Empire of the Sea,
the fresco over the main staircase at Osborne House

Queen Victoria hated blood sports, but in Carl Haag's 1854 painting Evening at Balmoral, *she appears to gaze with delight at the deer her husband has killed that day.*

Interior view of the Great Exhibition of 1851 showing The Amazon, *a controversial sculpture by John Absolon that pleased Queen Victoria*

*The marriage of the Princess Royal and
Prince Frederick William of Prussia, January 1858*

*The royal family at Osborne House in 1857. From left to right: Alice, Arthur,
Albert, Bertie with Leopold in front of him, Louise, Victoria with Beatrice on
her knee, Alfred, Vicky, and Helena*

The idea of the Great Exhibition was not the prince's. It probably came from Henry Cole, one of the many hyperactive, multitalented, pragmatic visionaries that Victorian Britain was producing. Cole (1808–1882) did not come from England's ten thousand ruling families, and he was not an Oxford man. At fifteen he entered the Public Record Office as an assistant keeper and, through a combination of clear vision and administrative efficiency, rose rapidly through the bureaucracy. Cole is credited with designing the legendary Penny Black postage stamp, wrote children's books and music criticism, designed a prize-winning tea service, and, in old age (as Sir Henry Cole, director of the Victoria and Albert Museum), commissioned the first commercial Christmas card.

An artist as well as a technocrat, Cole was dismayed by the low standard of industrial design in Great Britain, and he became an active member of the Royal Society for the Encouragement of Arts, Manufactures and Commerce. This body drew largely on the commercial and industrial middle classes, and it included such eminent men as the engineers Isambard Kingdom Brunel and Robert Stephenson, the architect and builder Thomas Cubitt, the ironmaster Charles Fox, and the chemist Lyon Playfair. Prince Albert was the society's president.

The energetic Cole put on two small national exhibits in London, visited several more abroad—notably the ambitious Quinquennial Paris Exhibition of 1849—and began to think big. What if London were to stage an industrial exhibition so wide ranging that the whole world would sit up and take notice? The artistic, technological, and manufacturing products of Great Britain and its empire would be given pride of place, but an invitation would be extended to all the nations, from China to the United States to Egypt, to send samples of their products. The British people would see the wealth and beauty of nations spread before them. Manufacturers and inventors would submit their work to the scrutiny of expert panels in hundreds of categories and receive prizes that would translate into orders and sales. And the exhibition would attract so many visitors that it would be self-funding.

Prince Albert quickly grasped Cole's vision and added his own. Albert was instinctively an internationalist. He liked to see himself as a world statesman, and for him peace and prosperity were moral imperatives as well as practical goals. The prince envisaged the Great Exhibition as a forum where the nations would come together in both celebration and competition, where swords would be beaten into steam engines, barometers, and piano rolls. As host to the exhibition, Great Britain would showcase its economic power, its enlightened political system, and, not incidentally, its beloved royal family.

Swept away by her husband's enthusiasm, Queen Victoria appointed a Royal Commission for the Exhibition of 1851 under Prince Albert's chairmanship and including three senior politicians from both sides of the aisle: the Duke of Wellington, Sir Robert Peel, and Lord John Russell. A date was settled and also a site: Hyde Park, a short drive from Buckingham Palace. Plans were made, subscriptions were canvassed, invitations to exhibit were extended, a catalog was put out to tender. The prince and his fellow commissioners fanned out across England to enlist support and undertook a vast correspondence. The building subcommittee ran an international competition to design the exhibition hall, hated the 245 designs that came in, and hatched a design of its own—which everyone else hated.

The idea of a giant international exhibition in the very heart of London caught the imagination of people in the industrial North and Midlands, but opposition mushroomed in southern circles of power. The High Tories, who were strongly protectionist in their commercial policies and viewed all international projects with suspicion, were opposed to the prince's exhibition on principle. The wealthy people who lived around Hyde Park and rode out when in town in the section of the park known as Rotten Row foresaw thousands of visitors trampling their sacred turf, seducing their maids, and making off with their silver.

Hostile editorials appeared in the *Times*. Questions were raised in parliament. Who would bear the cost if the exhibition proved a failure? How many of Hyde Park's ancient trees would be felled to erect this monstrous building? What scar would be left upon the land? The commission was planning for hundreds of thousands of visitors, many of them foreigners. This surely meant that traffic and business in central London would be at a standstill and crime would rocket. Colonel Sibley, a reactionary Tory member of parliament, denounced the prince's Exhibition as a new Tower of Babel, and summoned hail and thunder down upon it. In the end, parliament voted in favor of holding the exhibition in Hyde Park only because one of the exhibition's most stalwart supporters, Sir Robert Peel, who had been expected to lead the debate in the Commons, was thrown by his horse and died.

Having secured its site, the commission's next big headache was the vast structure that would house the exhibits. The members had a design for a solid, conventional brick building, but the estimated cost of just the raw materials exceeded their budget, and the construction was unlikely to be completed by the proposed opening date. Then one of the commissioners had the good luck to run into Joseph Paxton, who was in London for a meeting of the board of the Eastern and Midlands Railway Company. Paxton, like Henry Cole, was a self-made man and an even greater success story. He started as a gardener's boy, attracted the attention of the Duke of Devonshire, became his head gardener, designed and built the famous new conservatory at Chatsworth, and, under the duke's patronage, became one of Britain's foremost horticulturalists, landscape architects, and, finally, architects. Along the way, Paxton invested his savings in railway stock and became a rich man.

Hearing of the commission's building problems, Paxton admitted that he had an idea of his own. Never one to let the grass grow under his feet, Paxton at his board meeting doodled a design on the blotting paper, and within nine days he had drawn up complete plans. When the commission failed to adopt his design at once, Paxton did an end run around the bureaucrats. He published a sketch of the proposed building in the *Illustrated London News,* and his design was chosen by public acclaim. People at once took to calling the building the Crystal Palace.

Paxton envisaged a much larger version of the Chatsworth conservatory. It would be a vast, multistoried pavilion, built of prefabricated units of iron and glass, 1,848 feet long by 454 feet wide, tall enough to enclose the great elms in the park, and covering some nineteen acres. Cutting-edge iron production made the Crystal Palace technologically viable. The recent abolition of the tax on glass made it financially sound, though it would take one-third of Great Britain's total annual production. The structure of each of the units was based on a vast lily pad from the Amazon that Paxton had managed to grow in a heated pool at Chatsworth and christened the Victoria Regia. Amazingly, its fan of intersecting ribs enabled this rare plant to support the weight of a human being.

Construction of Paxton's glass house proceeded apace, but even intelligent people like the Astronomer Royal feared that it would be unable to withstand vibration. It was at moments like this that the importance of having the Queen's husband as the chair of the committee became apparent. When the building was up, but before the public had been admitted, Prince Albert arranged for a detachment of soldiers to march up and down the galleries, first in broken cadence, then in lockstep. The glass panes remained intact. Another worry was that with the giant trees of the park roofed into the building, the sparrows would soil both visitors and exhibits. Different solutions for getting rid of the sparrows were touted. Finally the prince consulted his friend the Duke of Wellington. "Sparrow hawks," His Grace is reputed to have retorted.

PRINCE ALBERT QUITE enjoyed snubbing the High Tories who had proved so hostile not only to himself but to his beloved dead friend Peel. Nonetheless, envisaging his exhibition as a giant demonstration of peace and democracy in action, he ardently wished for the approbation of his peers—members of the royal families of Europe. He urged other monarchs to come to London, share his vision, and offer their congratulations. When all but King Leopold refused to come, Victoria was furious, and Albert took refuge from depression in work.

Whether envious of Britain's industry or scornful of its prince's energy, the crowned heads in Vienna, Moscow, Madrid, Lisbon, The Hague, Hanover, Munich, and so on would not come to London. They saw armed maniacs at every street corner and feared assassination. The memory of the great revolutions of 1848 was still fresh in royal minds, and London was notoriously the haven for radicals and anarchists of every nation. As the prince wrote to his stepmother: "Just at present I am more dead than alive from overwork. The opponents of the Exhibition work with might and main to throw all the old women into a panic and to drive myself crazy. The strangers, they give out, are certain to commence a thorough revolution here, to murder Victoria and myself, to proclaim the Red Republic in England."

To the tsar of Russia, in particular, the whole concept of the exhibition was distasteful and dangerous. In his view, ancient dynasties like his own ruled by divine right, and the creeping democratization preached by Prince Albert and his uncle Leopold had to be stopped at all costs. And so, when Queen Victoria asked the London *corps diplomatique* to designate a representative to make a speech at the exhibition's opening ceremony, the Russian ambassador persuaded his fellow ambassadors and ministers to refuse Her Majesty's offer. Word of this discourtesy inevitably hit the English press, and the English people were incensed against the tsar, whom they regarded, not unreasonably, as a sadistic tyrant. Three years after the end of the Great Exhibition, fierce anti-Russian sentiment in the British people, fostered by the popular press, would catapult Britain into war with Russia in Crimea, against the best judgment of her political leaders.

Queen Victoria and Prince Albert particularly counted on the presence at the exhibition's opening day of their dear friends Prince William, heir to the throne of his brother King Frederick William of Prussia, his wife, Princess Augusta, and their two children. Ever since the birth of the Prince of Wales, for whom he chose the king of Prussia as chief sponsor, Albert had been painstakingly establishing warm relations with the Prussian royal family. In 1848, when Prince William was forced by a revolutionary mob to flee Berlin, he was greeted like a long-lost brother by the English royal family. Victoria and Albert were stunned when, at the eleventh hour, the king of Prussia had second thoughts and forbade his brother to come to England for the exhibition.

Once more Prince Albert put pen to paper and tried to shake His Prussian Majesty out of his fears for his relatives. "Mathematicians have calculated that the Crystal Palace will blow down in the first gale," wrote the prince in high sarcasm to King Frederick William IV on April 14. "Engineers—that the galleries would crash in and destroy the visitors; political economists have prophesied a scarcity of food in London owing to the vast concourse of people; doctors—that owing to so many races coming in contact with each other, the Black Death of the Middle Ages would make its appearance, as it did after the Crusades; moralists—that England would be infected by all the scourges of the civilised and uncivilised world; theologians—that this second Tower of Babel would draw upon it the vengeance of an offended God. I can give no guarantee against all these perils . . . but I can promise that the protection from which Victoria and I benefit will be extended to their persons." Unwilling, perhaps, to be thought a coward by a woman and a mere junior Prince of Coburg, King Frederick William finally allowed his relatives to cross the channel.

The fears voiced by the crowned heads of Europe that they would be assassinated if they came to London were far from fanciful. In 1850 a madman fired a pistol at Queen Victoria as she drove out from the palace, and soon after, another madman hit her on the head with the knob of his cane as she emerged from her uncle Cambridge's house. Despite these attempts on her life, when it came time to open the Great Exhibition, Queen Victoria refused to show fear.

When she stepped into her open carriage for the drive to the ceremony, she was wearing full court dress of pink and white satin as if for a prorogation of parliament or a levee. Her head, neck, arms, and hands glittered with jewels, she wore ostrich feathers in her hair, and on her bosom was pinned the Koh-i-Noor, then the largest diamond in the world, all 191 carats of it. A better target could hardly be imagined, especially when the sun came out just as the Queen drove up to the Crystal Palace, her diamonds echoing the brilliant flash of the glass. Some seven hundred thousand people had gathered to see the royal party drive by, but not a shot was fired. Those vast crowds of ordinary citizens whom foreign kings regarded with such suspicion proved to be Victoria's best bodyguard.

In the vast central transept of the Crystal Palace, twenty-five thousand invited guests were waiting. The Queen stood silent under a huge canopy close to the central fountain, smiling in evident pleasure, and allowing her husband to do the talking. As she recorded in her diary a few hours later, she felt even more proud and humble than on the day of her coronation. Everything was perfect, just as Albert had planned it. The exhibition was sure to be a huge success. How pleasant to see the discomfort of those nasty ambassadors who had refused to take part in the ceremony.

After the exhibition was declared officially open in the Queen's name, a Chinese gentleman in his native costume suddenly walked forward and prostrated himself in front of Victoria. Since there was a small Chinese exhibit but no official Chinese representative, the man was allowed to bring up the end of the procession of foreign notables. Only later was it established that he was a mere commercial agent, not some visiting dignitary. The unrehearsed juxtaposition of this unknown foreigner and the English Queen was a perfect symbol of the cultural phenomenon that would be the Great Exhibition of 1851.

At the end of the opening ceremony, Handel's "Hallelujah" chorus was sung by a choir of six hundred, accompanied by the biggest organ in the world and an orchestra of two hundred. The sound was almost lost in the huge structure. The Queen returned home in a kind of ecstasy. "The tremendous cheers, the joy expressed in every face, the immensity of the building, the mixture of palms, flowers, trees, statues, fountains . . . and my beloved husband the author of this 'Peace Festival,' which united the industry of all nations of the earth,—all this was moving indeed . . . God bless my dearest Albert, God bless my dearest country, which has shown itself so great today."

■

QUEEN VICTORIA DID not visit the Crystal Palace only on opening day in full regalia. She had already visited it twice before the opening, and she went repeatedly thereafter, bringing her children and her guests. She was sure that no one enjoyed the Great Exhibition as much as she did, but a great many people came close. Prince Albert and his commission had conceived of the exhibit as a boost to industry and commerce and as a tool for educating the masses. In the end, their exhibition proved to be a fabulous success because it was fun for all kinds of people. The eighty-three-year-old Duke of Wellington, tiny, stone deaf, and tottery on his pins, was mesmerized by the exhibits, which included a larger-than-life statue of himself. Equally delighted was Mary Kerlynack, an elderly Cornish woman who walked seven hundred miles to buy her ticket and got to tell her story to the Queen and the press. As Victoria herself noted: "The immense crowd of manufacturers with whom we have spoken have gone away delighted. The thousands who are in the Crystal Palace, when we are leaving, are all so loyal, and so grateful, never having seen us before. All of this will be of use not to be described. It identifies us with the people."

Word of the wonders of the exhibition spread like wildfire, and the new railways made London accessible as never before. Newspapers all over the world had pictures and articles and firsthand reports. Friends wrote to friends, either urging them to come or begging for a bed. William Makepeace Thackeray published a long and sentimental poem. It ended:

> March, Queen and Royal pageant, march
> By splendid aisle and springing arch
>   Of this fair Hall!
> And see! Above the fabric vast
> God's boundless heaven is bending blue,
>   God's peaceful sun is beaming through
>   And shining over all.

The cartoonists for the magazine *Punch* had five months of superb material, foreign and homegrown. London theaters closed for want of clients, and the streets of Manchester and other great industrial towns were reported, with patriotic hyperbole, to be empty.

The exhibition had something for everyone, and everyone was invited. One of the organizing committee's strokes of genius was to institute a price system that differed from day to day. For wealthy families there were season tickets for three guineas and a pound. Some days a day ticket cost five shillings, some days, one shilling. On a few days, entry was free. If you could not afford the price of admission, it was fun just to go to Hyde Park, which had become the people's park. For free you could walk around the magnificent new gardens, make fun of the foreigners, admire the flags of the nations fluttering atop the great pavilion, ooh and aah when suddenly the 12,000 fountains sprang into the air circulating 120,000 gallons of water, scrutinize the prince's model working-class home (improbably complete with piped water, water closet, kitchenette, and separate rooms for the children), and watch the fireworks at night.

Inside the Crystal Palace, there was far too much to see in a single day. A young toff who had never worked in his life could tour a suspiciously clean, quiet, and spacious working cotton mill or a replica lead mine, minus the toxic dust. Art lovers who had never ventured across the seas saw replicas of some of the world's greatest statues as well as original works commissioned for the event, such as the controversial statue of a bare-breasted Amazon on horseback. (Queen Victoria really liked it.) Men of business could see what their competitors in France and the United States had to offer. Housewives could examine silks from India and China, printed cottons from Egypt and France, carpets, wallpapers, furniture, pianos, indoor plants, pump organs, doorknobs, and a delirious array of knickknacks. There were inventions of all kinds: electric telegraphs, coffee roasters, clocks, musical instruments, fire engines, locomotives, a steam-powered sugar cane crushing machine, and the handgun with a revolving cylinder recently perfected by Samuel Colt. There were geological samples and botanical specimens, a stuffed dodo, a stuffed elephant complete with howdah, the ivory throne of the Rajah of Travancore, and dinosaur models reconstructed from fossil remains. At times the vast central transept became an arena, variously featuring a circus, a military band, or an orchestra.

As the *Punch* cartoonists pointed out, the exhibition brought together illiterate farm workers in smocks, smart young men about town, and neatly starched bank clerks. The sheer size of the building and the number of visitors encouraged a certain degree of social license. Young ladies happily lost sight of their mamas in the crowd and met up with young gentlemen in Messrs. Schweppes's refreshment rooms. Wives abandoned their husbands to the tender mercies of the Irish help and met friends for lunch at the exhibition. Middle-class parents from the provinces turned up at the Crystal Palace with all the children and a bag of sandwiches. Working-class families on a spree tasted ice cream and Jell-O for the first time and were not sure they liked them. Tradesmen abandoned their normal line of work and turned to catering for the tourists.

During its five and a half months, 6.2 million tickets were sold to the Great Exhibition, an unprecedented number given that the entire population of Great Britain at the time was about 20 million. On a single day in July, 72,000 people poured through the doors, all seeking entertainment and illumination, all needing bathroom facilities and transportation. The vast catalog was a best seller. Between the ticket booths, the shop, and the cafes, over a half million pounds changed hands. At the end, when all the bills had been paid, the organizing committee found itself with a profit of 186,000 pounds and decided to use it for the purchase of seventy acres in Kensington. On this site in due time would rise the Science Museum, the Natural History Museum, and the Victoria and Albert Museum. Victorians called it Albertopolis.

The political classes throughout Europe in 1851 were amazed by the

Great Exhibition in London. Here was liberal democracy in action. The massive crowds were calm, orderly, and patient, though only fifty policemen, armed with wooden clubs, stood by to keep the peace. It seemed that no one made a scene, no one got trampled, no one was arrested, no one was assassinated, no one threw stones. Thunder and lightning did not smash the great glass house into smithereens. Sparrow droppings did not land on the buttered buns. The Koh-i-Noor diamond, which the Queen put on show in the British section, was returned to her without incident. And the building was pulled down as swiftly as it was put up, carted off to the then outer London suburb of Sydenham, reassembled, and made even bigger. How extraordinary!

The exhibition did not draw everyone's praise. The political theorists Karl Marx and Thomas Carlyle, who agreed on very little else, were among the few middle-class men who turned their noses up at this capitalist extravaganza. English cabinet ministers and many members of parliament visited the exhibition, as did courtiers who needed the royal favor, but by and large the aristocracy and landed gentry held off. People who habitually traveled abroad did not need to see copies of Greek sculptures or stuffed elephants. Great landowners had no use for pipe organs and no interest in baroque telegraph machines or barometers made of leeches. For the Tories in parliament, the Great Exhibition was one more reason to dislike the prince consort.

By definition, the Crystal Palace was not an exclusive venue. Even on a five-shilling day, the exhibition was the most atrocious crush, and one could never be certain whom one might bump into. If beer was not served in the refreshment rooms, neither was wine, and warm lemonade and stale ham sandwiches were not everyone's treat. If the Queen cared to look like a little middle-class frump and hobnob with the unwashed, that was entirely her own affair. If the prince cared to spend his life working on committees with ill-bred upstarts like Henry Cole and Thomas Cubitt, let him. Even as the ties binding the ordinary British man and woman to the royal family were strengthened, the isolation of the Queen and the prince and their family from the English aristocracy also deepened.

WHEN THE GREAT Exhibition closed, Prince Albert was intensely relieved but too tired and sad to feel triumphant. He had recently and unexpectedly lost his two closest English friends: his private secretary George Anson, only thirty-nine, and Sir Robert Peel. Anson, Albert told Victoria, was "almost like a brother," Peel "a second father." The frantic months of activity that preceded the opening of the exhibition left Albert so "weak and fagged" that he could barely eat or sleep. He was never the same man again.

His work for the exhibition brought Prince Albert into daily communication with some of the most brilliant and entrepreneurial Englishmen of his day, men he could respect, compete with, and learn from—men like himself. He was never happier than in the society of scientists, artists, musicians, and intellectuals. But these were men called plain Mr. X or Professor Y. Most were middle class, some were common, and they did not own homes in Mayfair or country estates in Hampshire. They did not appear at levees, and the Queen could never invite their wives to tea. When the prince met such men, they backed out of his presence and stood while he sat. Albert could preside over such men and make speeches to them, he could consult them, he could tour factories and gardens and bridges with them, he could persuade his wife to give them knighthoods or even peerages. But he could not make them his friends, or so he believed, because at heart he was a conventional man who never wholly shook off the provincial attitudes of his father's small, impoverished German court.

William Hartington Cavendish, the sixth Duke of Devonshire, could have taught the prince some lessons in English upper-class social mores, had the prince cared to know the duke. The bachelor duke was the immensely rich scion of one of England's greatest families, a man of great culture, few words, and shy charm. Careless of gossip, he could take the gardener's boy Joseph Paxton as his lifelong friend and companion, help Paxton to fame and fortune, and still be welcome in every home in England, except Osborne. Devonshire was rare but not unique. In English clubs, on English hunting fields, in English committees, it was slowly becoming possible for a nobleman like Lord Palmerston and a middle-class gentleman like William Nightingale to establish companionable relationships. Their wives and sisters and daughters might even be allowed to exchange visits.

But in Germany such relationships continued to be social apostasy, and Albert was a royalist conservative with liberal tendencies, never a radical. Protocol and etiquette were the scaffolding that supported the Prince of Coburg's ego.

Lord Palmerston Says No

...

NEVER DID PRINCE ALBERT ENJOY AS MUCH POPULARITY WITH ORDINARY British citizens as on October 15, 1851, when the Great Exhibition of the Works of Industry of All Nations closed. But the mob is ever inconstant, as Albert and his friend Stockmar liked to remind each other at sententious in- tervals, and the prince's fall from grace was rapid. By November 1853, he was the most distrusted man in England, and the rumor around London was that he and the Queen would soon be committed to the Tower. England was eager to go to war with Russia, and the Queen's husband was widely consid- ered to be the tsar's friend or even his agent. Prince Albert's German birth and odd accent, his foreign friends, his internationalism, all of which had been handsomely showcased at the Great Exhibition, were now viewed by press and public alike as prima facie evidence of treason.

The nation had suddenly woken up to the power the prince was wielding behind the scenes. Could it be, editors asked rhetorically, that Queen Victo- ria was a mere puppet, manipulated by her husband to serve the interests of foreign powers? Radicals and reactionaries alike took to pontificating in parliament on the dangers that "King Albert" posed to the nation.

To accuse the Queen's husband of treason was a vicious libel, yet the critics had seized upon a fact that needed to be brought to public attention. Queen Victoria had withdrawn into domesticity and was becoming more and more depressed and self-absorbed with each successive pregnancy. She was trying hard to conform to the role of "kleines Fräuchen" her husband allotted her, and took a backseat in state affairs. She frankly admitted this to her uncle Leopold in an 1852 letter: "Albert grows daily fonder and fonder

of politics and business, and is so wonderfully *fit* for both—such perspicac-
ity and such *courage*—and I grow daily to dislike both more and more. We
women are not *made* for governing—and if we are good women, we must
dislike these masculine occupations; but there are times which force one to
take *interest* in them *mal gré bon gré* [whether one likes it or not] and *I* do of
course, *intensely.*" It is distressing to the modern ear to find the great Queen
Victoria dutifully parroting her husband's patriarchal platitudes, but King
Leopold was no doubt delighted.

In the face of the vitriolic press attacks of 1853 and 1854, both Victoria
and Albert saw the prince as an innocent victim, and many of his critics
were indeed rash, prejudiced, and ill informed. Nonetheless, a strong case
can be made that Albert's hubris had opened him up to justified criticism
and that he and the British government had very different notions of patriotism. Since 1846, the prince had made a determined attempt to take over
Britain's European affairs. He was convinced that he had a combination of
talent and status that made him uniquely fitted to mastermind English foreign policy and conduct the nation's diplomacy. Not content with asserting
jurisdiction over the foreign office in his wife's name, the prince secretly
conducted diplomatic negotiations with foreign monarchs over the heads of
British ministers of state.

This lunge for power eloquently revealed how little the prince subscribed to English political values and how much he underestimated the
power of the English political establishment. All the same, Great Britain was
nothing if not pragmatic, and if Albert's foreign policy had been successful,
it might well have been applauded. Unfortunately the prince's confidence in
foreign affairs was equaled by his inexperience, his verbosity, his Germano-
mania, and his bad luck. He was, as he presented himself, a man of vision,
principle, and intelligence. He worked very hard and sincerely believed his
motives and actions to be beyond reproach. Unfortunately, when put to the
test of events, the Albertian vision turned into nightmare, principle shaded
dangerously into Coburg self-interest, and intelligence foundered in rhetoric.

Luckily for Britain and especially for Queen Victoria, who ran no small
risk of losing her throne, Prince Albert ran up against a formidable political
opponent ready to challenge him on key constitutional issues. That opponent was the longtime English foreign secretary Henry John Temple, third-
Viscount Palmerston. If any one man was responsible for waking the prince
from his dream of becoming a great European statesman, it was Lord
Palmerston.

BOTH PRINCE ALBERT and Queen Victoria were earnest students of British history and the British constitution, but they read them rather differently from other people. They knew as well as anyone that parliament under Oliver Cromwell had executed King Charles I, and that aristocratic cabals had sent King James II into permanent exile and, subsequently, when the Stuart dynasty died out, invited the Elector of Hanover to rule in England. They agreed that the extensive political power and executive oversight enjoyed by the first three Hanoverian kings during the eighteenth century had been eroded by the decline into madness of George III, the immorality of George IV, and the inadequacy of William IV. But rather than seeing this loss of royal power as progress toward a more equitable and productive society, they fiercely condemned it. Their mission in life was to turn the clock back to the glory years of the young George III.

In the hearts of both the Queen and the prince, the seeds of the doctrine of the divine right of kings lay ready to sprout. Far from seeing the Queen as a figurehead, they believed that supreme authority in the nation was vested in her. They envied the personal power wielded by the rulers of Russia, Austria, and Prussia even as they affected to deplore the cruelty and injustice underpinning that power. They envisioned themselves as enlightened autocrats and were convinced that the British nation would be happier and more prosperous if they, not parliament, dictated national policy. They fought any measure likely to convert constitutional monarchy into parliamentary democracy, which they saw as a way station on the road to a republic.

The assertion of royal prerogatives and powers came into play in the close, daily relationship between the Crown and the fifteen or so members of parliament who formed the cabinet or executive arm of the British government. The phrase "Her Majesty's Government" was, for Queen Victoria, not a form of words but a statement of fact. The constitution made the Queen responsible for initiating and leading the negotiations to form a new government, and ministers were said to serve at the Queen's pleasure. Victoria and Albert deduced from these formalities that she had the right, after due consultation, to dismiss any minister she found inadequate or retain one she found satisfactory even if parliament rejected him. Her assertion of that right had been at the heart of a constitutional confrontation with Sir Robert Peel in 1839 that had caused the Queen's popularity to plummet. Albert criticized the timing, tactics, and tone his wife had used at that time, but far from questioning her understanding of her rights and prerogatives, he reinforced them. Now that he was at the helm of royal policy, he was sure that things would be handled better.

In domestic affairs, the modus operandi of the Crown, as it is now useful to refer to the Victoria-and-Albert political team, was both rational and moderate. Between 1842 and 1846, the prince had a seamless entente with the Tory prime minister Sir Robert Peel and felt he had mastered the English executive and legislative systems. The famine in Ireland and the repeal of the Corn Laws were the defining problems facing Peel and his cabinet, and the prince was enthusiastically in favor of the moderately reformist solutions they proposed. In gratitude for the support he received from the Crown, Peel seconded the prince in his efforts to purge the court of immoral elements and to reform the management of the royal household. Unfortunately for Peel, his close association with the prince did nothing to ingratiate him with the right wing of his Tory Party, which had nourished a profound dislike of Albert from the moment his engagement was announced.

Peel was duly defeated by his own party in 1846, but discreet cooperation continued between the Crown and successive ministries. The Queen and the prince demanded to be fully informed on cabinet discussions, gave advice to ministers in regular meetings, made written corrections and edits on government documents, contributed memoranda, mostly in the prince's hand, but refrained from appearing to dictate government policy. A gracious smile from the Queen to a new cabinet member worked wonders in the policy sphere. The vast majority of ministers at this period, Whig and Tory, came from the aristocracy, and all were devoted monarchists. It was their pleasure to obey their sovereign lady as long as she made sense and did not encroach on their own prerogatives. The less the *Times* newspaper heard about the actual negotiations between a complaisant cabinet and an assertive Crown, the better for both parties.

But if in domestic affairs the Queen and the prince were ready to give way, in foreign affairs they were determined to take the upper hand. By 1847, the attention of British statesmen was being urgently directed to the political unrest throughout Europe. The prince felt it was time he asserted control and exercised day-to-day management of the foreign office. As Victoria and Albert saw it, diplomacy was the prince's special field of expertise and his special area of accreditation. Europe was ruled by a small group of monarchs. Who better to deal with the tsar of Russia and the emperor of Austria than Prince Albert of Saxe-Coburg in the name of his wife and cousin, the Queen of England?

The pretensions of the royal couple to foreign policy expertise were aided by the strange jargon used in nineteenth-century European diplomatic communication. Ambassadors and envoys referred to themselves in the third person and used each person's full official title. Their accreditation was always to the country's monarch. In all her correspondence with officials, Queen Victoria always referred to herself in the third person: "the Queen wishes to point out that she . . . " and so forth. But in the letters to foreign rulers that Queen Victoria wrote, or that were drafted for her, she was addressing her peers. Therefore she saluted the king or emperor as "Dear Brother," the queen as "Dear Sister," and used the habitual first person pronouns I or we.

In most of Europe, these diplomatic expressions reflected the political reality. The emperor of Austria had agents whom he had chosen to carry out his policies. However, if he chose to go over the heads of those agents and deal directly with, say, his fellow sovereign the tsar of Russia, he was free to do so. In England the forms had ceased to reflect the political reality, but Queen Victoria preferred to deny this.

Queen Victoria saw foreign affairs as an extension of family affairs. She was related in some degree to virtually every royal house in Europe, and in genealogical lore even her husband could not compete with her. Foreign policy for Victoria consisted in no small measure of her writing careful missives in beautiful French (the international language of diplomacy) to her kinfolk. One day she might advise her first cousin's wife the queen of Portugal to be more careful in choosing her intimate associates. The next she might beg her distant Austrian relation for his own good to be kinder to the Italians and Poles even if they did show a foolishly rebellious spirit; or her Dutch cousin to stop bothering dearest Uncle Leopold in Belgium; or her French uncle Louis Philippe to drop the idea of marrying one of his sons to the Spanish infanta. When war threatened to break out in any part of Europe, the Queen was stricken with angst. If Uncle France started fighting Uncle Austria over Italy, whose side should she be on?

In her husband the Queen saw the means to translate her inchoate ideas of royal powers and prerogatives into solid policies. A down-to-earth woman of limited education and no intellectual pretensions, Victoria was bowled over by Albert's display of theoretical brilliance. He was at once a philosopher and a historian of political tactics and prided himself on deriving policy from first principles, unlike the old muddlers down at the foreign office. Albert digested policy papers as other men ate dinners, and he could handwrite a ten-page memorandum in English or German before another man finished shaving.

In 1848, when Germany was shaken by revolution and the Prussian royal family was ousted by a mob, the prince went so far as to write a constitution for a new Germany of which he sent copies to "Berlin, Vienna, Dresden, Munich, etc." He also sent a copy to his brother in Coburg, imperiously instructing Ernest to do all he could to get the constitution adopted by the newly created assembly of German states. Prince Albert's constitution went nowhere, to the surprise of no one but his wife and himself.

The Queen and the prince agreed that with due diligence they had the means to achieve dominance in European diplomacy. Custom dictated that every document relating to foreign affairs—the official diplomatic correspondence of the foreign office, the unofficial reports sent back to London from ambassadors, ministers, and envoys abroad; even the minutes of the British cabinet's discussions of foreign policy—come before the Queen and the prince every day in the dispatch boxes. To this avalanche of documents Prince Albert and Queen Victoria applied themselves with special zeal. Obviously they did not have enough hours in the day to read it all, but they were insistent that it all come through their hands. Both the prime minister and the foreign secretary met with the Queen and the prince regularly to discuss British foreign policy, and of these meetings the prince himself made and circulated lengthy memoranda.

The Crown's new assertion of control over foreign affairs was from the start a practical nightmare for the men at the foreign office. Foreign affairs had grown immensely more complex since the days of George III—a monarch in any case whose diplomacy led to the loss of the American colonies. With the invention of the telegraph and improvements in the postal system, the quantity of information available about other countries increased massively. On the other hand, even with the telegraph and an expensive system of personal couriers, if a rebellion against Austria broke out in northern Italy or a coup d'état was staged in Paris, quick response from Great Britain became impossible if the Queen and the prince were holed up at their country lodge on Loch Muick.

But far more important than the practical difficulties were the political questions. Who set international policy for Great Britain—the Crown or the cabinet? Who was more capable of representing the nation to the world and protecting its interests, the Queen's husband or the foreign secretary? And what if those two eminent gentlemen failed to agree on what policies should be pursued? There was one man in England who was quite sure that he knew the answer to these questions, and in 1847, the year that Prince Albert began to throw his foreign policy weight around, that man was once more England's foreign secretary. Lord Palmerston believed he was the right man to conduct England's foreign affairs, and, unlike Prince Albert, he had thirty years of experience in government and international diplomacy to back up his confidence.

※

HENRY JOHN TEMPLE, third Viscount Palmerston, was one of the most fascinating men of his time. Born in 1784, Palmerston inherited his father's modest Irish peerage and a heap of debt when he was only seventeen. A brilliant and ambitious youth, he looked to make a career in politics, and the one advantage of being a mere Irish peer was that he could take a seat in the Commons, the more powerful of the two houses of parliament. All the same, Palmerston knew from the outset that, lacking wealth and high rank, he would need to be smarter than the other fellows to get to the top.

Unlike most of his aristocratic friends, Palmerston took advantage of the educational opportunities available at the universities of Edinburgh and Cambridge, and then traveled widely, picking up excellent French and Italian and some German. These languages would stand him in good stead in his career. After several attempts, Palmerston managed to get elected as a Tory member for the pocket borough of Newport in the Isle of Wight. His maiden speeches in the Commons so impressed the party elders that they offered him a seat in the cabinet as chancellor of the exchequer when he was only twenty-five.

Palmerston certainly needed the income high government office would bring, but, to everyone's surprise, he turned down the exchequer. He did not feel that his talents lay in oratory and knew he would be constantly on his feet in the combative House of Commons, defending the government's economic policy. Instead he accepted the noncabinet post of secretary for war, and for almost twenty years, he labored in obscurity at the War Office. It seemed that the Palmerston rocket had fizzled, but ambition still burned in Palmerston's heart. In the words of novelist Anthony Trollope, "he took it all as it came, resolving to be useful after his kind, and resolving also to be powerful," and his social and sexual talents kept him afloat in the highest levels of British society. Tall, handsome, and witty, the young Palmerston was a member of George IV's debauched set and a good friend to Lord Melbourne before that gentleman became a model of propriety.

While competing actively on the hunting field and in the bedroom, Palmerston was emphatically not the average aristocratic ministerial drone. He had strength and vitality as well as intelligence, and he more than earned his salary at the War Office. He mastered the minutiae of budgets, was tough on his staff, learned the ways of bureaucracy, and became comfortable making speeches in the House. Powerful English men welcomed Palmerston into their gun rooms and their councils. Powerful women opened their salons and their boudoirs to him because he was amusing and discreet. When finally the political gods brought the Whigs back to office, Palmerston had turned Whig without changing any of his political ideas, and he was the obvious choice for foreign secretary. In the first years of Victoria's reign, he played the part of wise old uncle to perfection, and the Queen was enchanted by the nonchalant ease with which her foreign secretary handled foreign rulers, including her uncle Leopold.

But then the Queen decided to marry, and Palmerston's luck turned. Aging roués with more debt than income were precisely the kind of men Prince Albert made it clear at the outset he intended to banish from his wife's society. Palmerston's chances of surviving the new Albertian regime hit bottom around the time of the royal engagement in October 1839. Late one night, screams echoed through the notoriously disorienting corridors of Windsor Castle. They came from the room currently occupied by Mrs. Brand (later Lady Dacre), one of the Queen's ladies-in-waiting. Expecting, apparently, to renew acquaintance with an old flame, Lord Palmerston had blundered into Mrs. Brand's room. Even when apprised of his mistake, he persisted in his amorous pursuit. Mrs. Brand resisted, managed to summon help in time, and Lord Palmerston wandered back to his own room.

An attempted rape hardly redounded to the credit of England's foreign secretary, especially since it occurred just before Lord Palmerston's long-awaited marriage to the widowed Lady Emily Cowper in December 1839. The new Lady Palmerston cannot have been pleased by her husband's exploit, but she apparently took it in stride. Emily was a woman of the world, the daughter of one of the eighteenth century's great aristocratic courtesans. Back in 1810, when Emily was young and close to the prince regent in more ways than one, Lord Palmerston's attempt to renew some old Windsor liaison would have made no stir, and the virtuous Mrs. Brands of the world knew better than to take a position at court. Now, of course, things were different, and morality was the watchword at Windsor. Lady Palmerston would need to take her husband firmly in hand and explain to him that if he wanted a future in politics, he had to keep his legendary libido in check.

When the newly married Prince Albert got word of the Brand affair, he was furious. It confirmed all his views on the immorality of the English ruling class, and he declared himself shocked that the sanctity of his own marriage had been defiled. Albert then pragmatically filed away the report of the incident as possible ammunition against Palmerston in the future, and in the meantime kept up a semblance of courtesy with the popular and powerful foreign secretary. The house of Coburg owed Palmerston a debt, since he had been instrumental in securing the throne of the new kingdom of Belgium for Uncle Leopold. Palmerston was also amusing and well informed, and in the long, tedious palace evenings in the year after his marriage, the prince enjoyed discussing European affairs with the foreign secretary. Albert was gratified when his line of argument seemed to win, failing to realize that Palmerston had lived at court for far too long to fall out with Her Majesty's husband over the port. But when Palmerston was swept out of office in late 1841 with the rest of the Melbourne government, the prince breathed a sigh of relief. That pigheaded old man and his disreputable wife would now wander in the political desert and could safely be barred from court.

But the Palmerstons were experienced fighters and were far from ready to surrender the field. Whereas Emily's elder brother Lord Melbourne faded into invalidism and irrelevancy once he left office in 1841, Palmerston remained a powerful and active force in opposition. Queen Victoria and Prince Albert as bride and groom had found it unseemly that people in their fifties like Lady Cowper and Lord Palmerston should marry, especially since their wedding tended to confirm the old gossip about their long-term liaison. What they in their youthful arrogance failed to understand was that the Cowper-Palmerston marriage was an inspired political alliance as well as a stab at personal happiness. Harry and Emily were supremely well matched. As the husband of a beautiful, charming, intelligent, rich woman whose friends were the best people in society, Palmerston at last had the money, the social setting, and the personal security he needed to get to the very top of British politics. Lady Palmerston made her husband happy, as he did her, and she was a political power in her own right. In the last and most successful decades of Palmerston's life, she was his best adviser and most trusted amanuensis. Theirs was one of the great marriages of the century.

Confident that, sooner or later, the political dice would roll again, Palmerston had fun during his years in the political wilderness from 1841 to 1846. With Emily's money he could at last afford to sit back and relax, indulge his passion for hunting, launch some much-needed improvements to his Irish estates, entertain his friends at Broadlands, and grow into the new role of stepfather and grandfather to the enchanting Cowper clan. With ample spare time, he could think long term, read eclectically, travel through his beloved France, keep up his vast correspondence at home and abroad, write for the newspapers, speak out in the Commons, and consolidate his position in the party. When the protectionist wing of the Tory Party colluded with the radicals to bring down the Peel government, and the Whigs under Lord John Russell were returned to office, Lord Palmerston went back to the foreign office. He quickly came under sniper fire from the newly confident and assertive Prince Albert.

*

IF THE PRINCE and the foreign secretary differed fundamentally in their personal values, they clashed in cabinet and memorandum over political ideology and diplomatic strategy. The foreign policy that Lord Palmerston developed during his terms as foreign secretary (1830–1834, 1835–1841, and 1846–1851) was sly but neither complex nor mysterious. What mattered to England was all that mattered to Palmerston, since he had no doubt that England was the greatest nation in the world and deserved to be. His job as foreign secretary was to promote the interests of the country and protect individual British citizens abroad. If this meant an alliance with France against Russia today, and with Russia against France tomorrow, so be it.

Palmerston was loyal to the Crown and personally devoted to Queen Victoria, but he had little use for foreign monarchs. Whether tyrants or weaklings, he saw them as corrupt and inadequate, and he did not care if they hated him. Palmerston was keen to spread English values and institutions to the world, and, as long as there was no risk of harming England's interests, he was ready to tweak the tails of foreign autocrats. He sent money and guns in secret to the Risorgimento (the Italian liberation movement), offered encouragement to democratic elements in Spain and Portugal, welcomed the exiled Hungarian patriot Lajos Kossuth to his house, and condoned the attack launched by outraged British brewery workers on a notoriously brutal Austrian general. England under Palmerston became the chosen place of refuge for revolutionaries and political extremists from all over Europe, including an obscure German political theorist named Karl Marx.

If Palmerston had a bête noire, it was Russia. In his very first foreign policy speech in the Commons in 1828, Palmerston fulminated about the threat Russia posed to Britain's safety and British values. He evolved the theory that Russia and Great Britain were engaged in a "Great Game" for control of the Balkans, the Levant, and the trade routes to India. He was personally repelled by Tsar Nicholas II. He considered him a tyrant who for personal gain kept his nation in the dark ages and prevented it from enjoying the rights and opportunities of a free society. As foreign secretary in the 1830s, Palmerston adopted a fiercely anti-Russian policy and wrote or commissioned articles in the popular press that inflamed British opinion against Russia. The tsar, who took an even more personal view of foreign affairs than Queen Victoria, knew that he had an implacable enemy in Lord Palmerston.

The one movement for national unification and democratic reform in Europe that Palmerston seemed to have no time for was in Germany. The neglect was more apparent than real and obeyed both the first and second rules of Palmerstonian diplomacy: defend British interests, spread English values. Certainly his lordship agreed that the German people, like any other, had the right to choose its own political future, that the fragmentation of Germany was a barrier to economic progress, and that Austrian hegemony was inimical to German prosperity. But Palmerston feared that a new, unified Germany at the heart of Europe would alter the balance of power and threaten English interests as a free Hungary or a republican Spain could not. The Kingdom of Prussia was aiming to be the kernel around which the new Germany would form, and Prussia was openly hostile to Britain and its constitutional form of government. Prussia was a repressive, militaristic society ruled by a medievally minded king and a tiny, ultraconservative camarilla. The Prussians saw Russia as their governmental ideal and chief ally. Palmerston did not like the Prussians.

And so the foreign secretary acted vague whenever the topic of German unification came up in cabinet, as it did not infrequently, given the Crown's pronounced pro-German sympathies. In general, Palmerston was hostile to autocratic Austria, but he tacitly supported its efforts to keep Germany a weak and divided Austrian satellite. In view of the consistently violent aggression of the German Empire between 1860 and 1918, Palmerston's prescience is remarkable. Palmerston could be stubborn and impulsive. Given that he often was dealing with China and Greece on the same day, he made mistakes. But on certain key issues, like Germany, he saw things clearly, as the prince did not.

Lord Palmerston's liberal interventionism and contempt for diplomatic niceties made him a hated man in the courts of Europe but raised his profile at home. Reports that the tsar of Russia went into apoplexy at the mere mention of Lord Palmerston's name; that Palmerston had no use for the French, as they were always up to something sneaky; that he routinely kept foreign ambassadors kicking their heels in his waiting room—all this did Palmerston no harm in English political circles. A tall, heavily built, balding sexagenarian who could still stand for hours at his lectern-desk, reading dispatches late into the night after a long day out with the guns in the pouring rain, Palmerston, like Winston Churchill in the mid-twentieth century, seemed the incarnation of John Bull, the English equivalent to Uncle Sam.

Prince Albert, and Queen Victoria under her husband's tutelage, hated

Lord Palmerston. They referred to him derisively in their private German correspondence as "Pilgerstein." The Queen and the prince cared deeply when their royal foreign brothers and sisters wrote to complain about the British foreign secretary. With her plain speaking and her devotion to country, Victoria in many ways resembled Palmerston, but she reflexively identified British national interest with her own as queen. She sympathized with the problems of other sovereigns and liked to give them the benefit of the doubt, especially perhaps when they were manifestly out of their depth. When Palmerston badgered the queens of Spain and Portugal, Victoria flared up.

Prince Albert had a more complicated response to what he regarded as the foreign secretary's lack of principle and sins of protocol. If Sir Robert Peel came close to making an English statesman out of Prince Albert, Lord Palmerston brought out the "true German, Coburger, and Gothaner" in him. On the one hand, the prince assumed a lofty and philosophic view. High principle and clearly enunciated goals were, Albert believed, essential in diplomacy. Hence he condemned Palmerston's foreign policy as unclear, wavering, and immoral. But fundamentally Prince Albert's response to the foreign secretary was visceral, just as it had been with Baroness Lehzen. Palmerston was distasteful to the prince, and he also blocked the prince's path. He was ipso facto an obstinate and disrespectful servant to the Crown and deserved to be dismissed. Such servants did not last a week in Berlin or even Lisbon.

Albert was convinced that the survival of the Saxe-Coburg dynasty in Britain depended on other kings and queens abroad retaining their thrones. That most of those monarchs—like Victoria herself—were of German origin was to the point, since Prince Albert was as ardent a Germanophile as Palmerston was an Anglophile. Albert had been fed from infancy on the Coburg legend and on the glorious history of the German Holy Roman Empire. Thus when Lord Palmerston seemed to favor the republican factions in Portugal, Albert ignored the manifold tribulations of the oppressed Portuguese people and leaped to the defense of his first cousin King Ferdinand. When Austria brutally crushed the forces of the king of Sardinia, setting back the cause of Italian unification by decades, Prince Albert was jubilant and sent a letter of personal congratulation to the Austrian emperor. While giving lip service to constitutional restraints and political reform, he found reasons to explain why the Austrian emperor reneged on all his promises of internal democratic reform once he had the army at his back again. That the Mensdorffs, Albert's favorite uncle and cousins, were high officials in the Austrian army and diplomatic service reinforced Prince Albert's pro-

Austria tendencies and facilitated his seductively intimate communication with the Austrian imperial family.

Prince Albert claimed to have political principles, but, in fact, he veiled monarchical self-interest and Coburg dynastic ambition in lofty rhetoric. In principle, Albert was the champion of the small, independent kingdom, especially if the ruler of that kingdom was his distant cousin Otto in Greece. But Albert's overriding international mission was the reunification of Germany under Prussia, so he did not come to the defense of little Denmark when Prussia made moves to swallow up the Danish duchies of Schleswig and Holstein. And when the Germans met in an ill-fated parliament to debate how best to unify the country, the dynastic Albert was horrified at the suggestion that smaller states like Coburg and Gotha might lose their independence in a new Germany. That would mean that he himself would lose his revenues and privileges as Prince of Coburg and that his son Alfred would lose the succession to his brother Ernest's throne. Albert was ready to fight with old Stockmar as well as with his wife's brother Charles Leiningen, who had surprisingly changed into a radical democrat, to maintain the independent sovereignty of tiny Coburg.

*

IF THE FIGHT FOR foreign policy supremacy between the foreign office and the Crown was rooted in ideology, it was waged mainly on procedural grounds. Her Majesty complained over and again to Lord Palmerston about his failure to observe the established protocol in his diplomatic correspondence. The following note is typical. "Osborne, 20th August 1848. The Queen has received an *autograph* letter from the Archduke John (in answer to the private letter she had written to him through Lord Cowley) which had been cut open at the Foreign Office. The Queen wishes Lord Palmerston to take care that this does not happen again. The opening of official letters even, addressed to the Queen, which she has *of late* observed, is really not becoming, and ought to be discontinued, as it used never to be the case formerly."

When Lord Palmerston failed to comply with Her Majesty's requests, the Queen and the prince took the prime minister, Lord John Russell, to task for his failure to assert his own statutory right to direct foreign affairs and keep his foreign secretary in line. Lord John was intelligent, principled, and ambitious, but he was also a ditherer who deferred to his wife at home and to his foreign secretary in cabinet. The prime minister was well aware that Palmerston had strong support in parliament and was the most popular politician in England. Russell had important measures that he wanted to get through parliament, notably a new Reform Bill to widen the franchise. Without Palmerston, the Russell ministry was doomed, and so for several years Lord John bobbed and weaved in a vain attempt to keep his Queen and his colleagues happy.

Dissatisfied by the prime minister's evasions, the royal couple summoned Lord John for grueling personal interviews as if he were an errant schoolboy. The Queen and the prince pointed out, quite accurately, that Lord Palmerston was conducting key aspects of foreign policy without consulting the Crown, and they repeatedly asked for his dismissal. The Crown's displeasure with Lord Palmerston and efforts to get rid of him are well captured by the long memorandum signed "Victoria R" of September 19, 1848, that records the Queen's conversation with her prime minister at Balmoral. It begins: "I said to Lord John Russell, that I must mention to him a subject, which is a serious one . . . namely about Lord Palmerston; that I really felt I could hardly go on with him, that I had no confidence in him, and that it made me seriously anxious and uneasy for the welfare of the country and for the peace of Europe in general."

In an all-out attempt to get Palmerston dismissed, in July 1850 the prince dug up the old issue of Palmerston's attempted rape of Mrs. Brand ten years earlier. According to the memorandum Prince Albert composed after his private meeting with Russell: "How could the Queen consent to take a man as her chief advisor and confidential counsellor in all matters of state, religion, Society, Court, etc. who as her Secretary of State and while a guest under her roof at Windsor Castle had committed a brutal attack upon one of her Ladies? had at night by stealth introduced himself into her apartment, barricaded afterwards the door and would have consummated his fiendish scheme by violence had not the miraculous efforts of his victim and assistance attracted by her screams saved her?" Russell, taken aback, agreed that this was all very bad, and that he had heard other similar stories.

The purple prose of the memorandum in Albert's own hand reveals how important a part sexual morality played in determining the prince's attitude toward the British foreign secretary. The Palmerstons in their youth had not played by the rules of premarital chastity and conjugal fidelity that Albert lived by. The prince was sure that his higher standards of morality entitled him to lead the nation. Lord John Russell showed his weakness as a statesman and as a friend when he failed to tell the prince that Palmerston's behavior ten years earlier, however reprehensible, had no bearing on his current competence as foreign secretary. That Russell kept Palmerston in the cabinet indicates that this was what he thought but dared not say.

Exasperated by Palmerston's obduracy and Lord John's shilly-shallying, the royal couple took another tack and sat down at their adjoining writing desks to compose a letter. In August 1850, the Queen specified to Lord John exactly what she wanted from Lord Palmerston *"in order to prevent any mistake in the future"* [QV's underlining]. She required "(1) that he will distinctly state what he proposes in a given case so that the Queen may know as distinctly to *what* she has given her Royal sanction; (2) Having *once given* her sanction to a measure, that it be not arbitrarily altered or modified by the Minister; such an act she must consider as failing in sincerity towards the Crown, and justly to be visited by the exercise of her Constitutional right of dismissing that Minister. She expects to be kept informed of what passes between him and Foreign Ministers before important decisions are taken . . . to receive the Foreign Despatches in good time . . . The Queen thinks it best that Lord Russell should show this letter to Lord Palmerston."

Cornered, and never happy to be out of favor with the Queen of whom he was paternally fond, Palmerston agreed to abide by the terms of the letter. In so doing, he conceded the Crown's constitutional right to dismiss a minister. This concession infuriated Palmerston's allies and weakened him in the cabinet, where, in fact if not in theory, ministers no longer considered that they served at the Queen's pleasure.

In late 1850, the Don Pacifico affair hit the headlines, and the Crown was sure that at last Lord Palmerston had overplayed his hand. The house in Athens of the merchant David Pacifico was burned down by a mob, and the Greek government of King Otto scornfully refused to consider his rather exorbitant claims for restitution. Pacifico was of Portuguese Jewish origins, but he had been born in the British possession of Gibraltar, and he appealed to the British government to defend his interests. Lord Palmerston, without consulting Lord John Russell or his cabinet colleagues, ordered a British naval squadron to sail to the Mediterranean, where it captured Greek vessels and blockaded the port of Piraeus. After two months, the Greek government capitulated and settled Pacifico's claims.

France and Russia, Britain's treaty allies in support of the fragile new monarchy of Greece, howled in protest at this bullying. The foreign secretary was formally censured in the House of Lords. But when Palmerston stood up before the Commons to defend his actions, his five-hour speech carried the day, and the motion of censure against the government was defeated. In words that have been quoted by British historians ever since, the foreign secretary declared: "As the Roman in days of old held himself free from indignity when he could say *Civis Romanus sum* [I am a Roman citizen], so also a British subject, in whatever land he may be, shall feel confident that the watchful eye and strong arm of England will protect him from injustice and wrong." To the horror of the Queen and the prince, Lord Palmerston stayed on at the foreign office.

But then the foreign secretary got careless. When in December 1851 Louis-Napoleon Bonaparte, the president of the French republic, staged the famous coup d'état of the 18th Brumaire and declared himself emperor of the French, the British government was taken aback, and the Queen and the prince were appalled. The name Bonaparte was anathema to every European monarch, and in 1848 Louis-Napoleon Bonaparte himself had helped to topple the Orléans dynasty with whom the Coburgs were closely linked. With characteristic impulsiveness, Palmerston telegraphed off a letter of congratulations to the new French head of state, without any prior consultation with his prime minister or his sovereign. It was not that Palmerston personally approved of Napoleon III—or, indeed, any other French head of state—but rather that he was sure that Britain would be dealing with the new emperor for the foreseeable future, whether or not they liked him.

As events would prove, Palmerston was perfectly right, but his congratulatory note was a blatant contravention of the terms he had agreed to abide by in his relations with the Crown. Queen Victoria rose up in holy wrath. Injured in his amour propre, Lord John Russell lost his temper, and the rest of the cabinet was now fed up with Lord Palmerston. The foreign secretary was asked to return the seals of his office and retired crestfallen to the backbenches. The Queen and the prince were jubilant. Victoria wrote to her uncle Leopold: "My Dearest Uncle,—I have the greatest pleasure in announcing to you a piece of news which I know will give you as much satisfaction and relief as it does to us, and will to the *whole* of the world. *Lord Palmerston is no longer Foreign Secretary.*"

But no one was better at playing the underdog than Palmerston, and, unlike Prince Albert, he knew how to manage the press and manipulate public opinion. The word got out that Prince Albert, after years of trying, had at last managed to sack good old "Pam," which was pretty much the truth. At court and in government circles, it had long been known that the prince habitually carried on the business of state in his wife's name, but it suited all the power sharers to keep that news to themselves. But once a respected statesman like Palmerston was sent off like a whipped schoolboy just because he would not let the prince dictate to the foreign office, then the gloves were off as far as the English political establishment, Tory and Whig, was concerned. The whispering campaign against the prince as a foreign traitor began, and British politics entered a period of dangerous weakness.

■

AS LORD JOHN RUSSELL had feared, his government soon collapsed once Palmerston left the cabinet. Lord Derby and the High Tories, whom the Queen felt obliged to call upon next, were soon defeated in the Commons. Then a coalition of Whigs and Peelite (moderate) Tories was cobbled together under Lord Aberdeen, with Lord Clarendon at the foreign office. The Aberdeen ministry was, overall, personally agreeable to the Queen and the prince, and showed a delightful willingness to cooperate with the Crown. But 1853 was a very bad time for the nation to be in the hands of a cabinet that was incapable of reaching agreement on any issue of substance and of a Crown that was under withering attack. Russia was making a determined move to topple the Ottoman Empire and assert control over the territories around the Black Sea. Napoleon III, counting on a victorious campaign against Russia to shore up his shaky hold on power, loudly proclaimed his intention to support Turkey against Russian aggression, and called on Great Britain to honor its treaty obligations to do the same. England was stumbling into a war that its leaders knew all too well did not serve its interests.

Queen Victoria and Prince Albert were not warmongers. They fully supported the Aberdeen government's attempts to placate the tsar and keep the French emperor from engaging in a mad pursuit of Napoleonic *gloire.* The Queen had nightmares when she thought of the soldiers who would die and the families that would be ruined. The prince, who had long campaigned in vain for more money for the army, feared the worst. Lord Aberdeen, who had lived in Russia as a young man and was personally known to the tsar, was a pacifist who believed in diplomacy, not war. He had a beloved brother in the army who was sure to see combat.

But the English people wanted to go to war. Patriotic fervor stirred the nation, and members of parliament pontificated that Britain had grown soft, too ruled by "Calico and Cant," as *The Spectator* put it. The death of the Duke of Wellington in 1852 roused the nation to reconsider its past glories on the battlefield and to bemoan the loss of the martial spirit that the Iron Duke had personified. British popular opinion had long been deeply antagonistic toward Russia, a vast empire that openly opposed the liberal democratic institutions that Britain held dear: an elected parliament with full control over the public purse, the subordination of the army to civilian control, trial by jury, judicial independence from the executive, and a free press.

So when Russia defeated the Turkish navy at Sinope, and the Crown and its pet government proved unwilling to declare war, the British people were enraged. Their quarrel was not especially with Aberdeen, a decent man doing his best in a tough situation. It was not with Queen Victoria, a wife and mother who properly delegated the business of the nation to her ministers. It was with Prince Albert, a foreigner who had dared to intervene between the sovereign and the nation's elected representatives. The popular press treated its readers to lurid stories of the prince as a lackey in the service of England's continental enemies, specifically Russia. At one point, a crowd gathered outside the Tower of London, persuaded that the Queen's husband would soon be brought there to face a charge of treason.

When vicious attacks on her husband began to appear in the press, the "*intense*" interest in state business that Victoria had felt before her marriage revived. Albert needed her, and she felt fully justified in asserting her authority as sovereign and flying to his rescue. Blazing with anger, the Queen demanded that the government organize the prince's defense. In a special Commons debate, the prince's long, unselfish, and meritorious service to his adopted country was extolled from both sides of the aisle, and the right honorable members were adjured to wipe every smear from His Royal Highness's good name. But the prince had received a severe reprimand from the public, and his political ambitions were deeply impaired.

Albert put the best face on things he could, but his pride and self-confidence had received a heavy blow. He had aimed to take his wife's place at the helm of the ship of state, and now he was once again forced to bow to her power and rely on her support. It was humiliating. In thirteen years, nothing had changed. More tolerated than loved at court, receiving at best token loyalty from the British aristocracy whom he despised, Albert had reached over the heads of the establishment. He had made a play for the support and even the love of the increasingly influential British professional and mercantile classes by championing their social values. Now suddenly these very people had turned on him. Victoria was adored by the English people; he was hated.

Lord Palmerston had set his attack dogs loose on the prince, but he quickly called them off. The prince had questioned his competence, undermined values he held sacred, and put the nation at risk, and so he had fought to win. But he was not an aggressive or vindictive man, and once he saw Albert bloodied, Palmerston joined the chorus of support for the prince in the Commons. The important thing now was to concentrate on affairs in the Black Sea, where war now seemed inevitable.

Palmerston believed that had he been in control of foreign office policy in 1852 and 1853, the Great Powers of Russia, Austria, France, and Great Britain would have patched together a settlement in the Balkans. He was probably right. Foreign courts hated Palmerston, but they knew where they stood with him. Napoleon III could bully Aberdeen but not Palmerston. The tsar grew bold in part because he knew that his declared enemy Lord Palmerston was in disgrace, and he believed that his good friend Lord Aberdeen would never go to war with Russia.

But in 1854 Lord Aberdeen did declare war in support of Britain's allies France and Turkey, and with a sinking heart sent a British expeditionary force to destroy the Russian fortress at Sebastopol in the Crimean Peninsula. It was an ill-conceived campaign, and from the outset it ran into the intractable problems of weak supply routes and rampant infectious disease. Lord Palmerston now had occasion to regret that, in the matter of Russia, he had deserted his usual pragmatism in favor of political theorizing and demagoguery. He was the man most responsible for the anti-Russian fervor sweeping the country, and he saw that the country would pay for his mistakes. Like the Crown and the Aberdeen ministry, Palmerston saw no reason for England to go to war with Russia in defense of Turkey in 1854. The Ottoman Empire was the most reactionary, corrupt, and dysfunctional of all European autocracies. Britain had no outstanding national interests at stake in the Balkans, and, if its navy was strong, its army was not.

If popular opinion pushed the Aberdeen government into war with Russia against its will, the British nation quickly discovered that patriotic zeal alone did not win wars, especially a war fought half a world away. Once the Crimean campaign began, the *Times* reporters were able to telegraph back reports of how gallant British soldiers had to fight not only the armies of the tsar but the criminal inadequacy of their senior officers. Men deprived of boots and greatcoats, eating shreds of raw meat in the snow, dug into the frozen mud below Sebastopol and met the combined onslaught of the Russian winter and cholera, dysentery, and typhoid. Called to account in the House of Commons for its abominably lax conduct of the war, the Aberdeen government fell, and Lord Palmerston was swept into office as prime minister by collegial enthusiasm and public acclaim. In the teeth of resistance from the entrenched army bureaucracy at Whitehall and from the medical corps in the Crimea, he and his cabinet colleagues got the men through a second winter, coordinated with the French army the combined assault that led to the surrender of Sebastopol, and in the spring of 1856 negotiated a peace treaty with the new tsar, Alexander II. Thus ended a short, bloody, expensive, and pointless war.

*

WHEN WAR WITH Russia was declared, Queen Victoria put her doubts and fears aside and concentrated all her energies on victory. She had always taken her official title of commander in chief of the armed forces with the utmost seriousness, and she now threw herself into the war effort. Understanding at last that Palmerston represented a force in English politics that they could not withstand, and perceiving the need for national unity, Queen Victoria and Prince Albert fully cooperated with the new head of government. As a result, the British government worked with outstanding efficiency and focus. In cabinet there was now no strife between the prime minister and the Crown, just serious and informed discussion of what had to be done next.

One crucial source of information came from the eyewitness reports written from the main army hospital at Scutari by Lord Palmerston's neighbor and sanitarian ally, Florence Nightingale. Unlike army officials bound by a code of silence, this lady was prepared to say how the military procurement system had broken down and to list exactly what the soldiers needed to survive not just in the field but in the hospital: shirts, sheets, socks, beds, soap, toweling, mops, basins, brooms, plates, trays, knives, forks, spoons, shoe brushes, coconut matting. Queen Victoria wrote: "We are much struck by her [Nightingale] . . . wonderful, clear, and comprehensive head. I wish we had her at the War Office!" When the Queen asked specifically what she could send to the men as personal gifts, and suggested Eau de Cologne, a light toilet water, Nightingale replied: "The Queen ought to give something which the man will feel as a daily extra comfort which he could not have had without her. Would some woolen material do, cut up into comforters for the neck when the man began to get out of bed? . . . Or a brush and comb for each man? or a Razor for each man. As to the Eau de Cologne, a little gin & water would do better."

Her Majesty was not at all put out by Nightingale's asperity. It was the result of stress and overwork, and she rightly saw it as a mark of respect from one woman warrior to another. In addition to knitting socks and comforters with her daughters, Victoria sent all kinds of gifts for the ordinary soldiers, including magazines and books and etchings of the portrait of her son Arthur with his godfather the Duke of Wellington. These gifts were extraordinarily prized and, to Nightingale's impotent fury, were confiscated by the officers as too good for common men.

Since her marriage, Queen Victoria had moved further and further out of the public eye, but during the Crimean War she was once again a presence in the nation. She toured barracks and hospitals, awarded medals, and publicly rejoiced with her people when news came of great victories against fearsome odds at the Alma, Balaklava, and Inkerman. Filled with new energy and confidence, the Queen seized the opportunity to ride out to review

Queen Victoria reviewing the troops during the Crimean War

her troops, on horseback and in uniform, just as she had as a girl, and her popularity soared to new heights.

In a welcome change from the grim news from the front, the *Illustrated London News* was lyrical in its praise of Her Majesty's excursion at Aldershot on her "superbly caparisoned charger." The magazine offered its women readers a detailed description of the beautifully tailored new uniform tunic the Queen had come up with. It was scarlet, just like a real officer's, and decorated not only with the blue ribbon and cross of the Order of the Garter but also a crimson and gold sash with "gold bullion tassels." Two more such tassels decorated the Queen's black felt hat, together with "a plume of red and white feathers." In 1857, two months after the birth of her ninth child, the Queen reprised her role as Hippolyta, queen of the Amazons, distributing the new Victoria Crosses for valor in Hyde Park, sitting sidesaddle on her horse, wearing her magnificent tunic and hat. The Queen was emerging at last from the shadow side of life, as she called childbearing, unaware that darker shadows awaited her.

IN APRIL 1856, THE QUEEN wrote to Lord Palmerston: "Now that the moment for the ratification of the Treaty of Peace is near at hand, the Queen wishes to delay no longer the expression of her satisfaction as to the manner in which both the War has been brought to a conclusion, and the honour and interests of this country have been maintained by the Treaty of

Peace, under the zealous and able guidance of Lord Palmerston. She wishes as a public token of her approval to bestow the Order of the Garter upon him." This was the highest honor in the Queen's gift, and few prime ministers received it.

Queen Victoria and Lord Palmerston emerged from the Crimean War as winners both in their own eyes and in the eyes of the world. Victoria felt reinvigorated and knew that she was beloved. Palmerston became prime minister in February 1855 and remained so almost continuously until his death in 1865. The judgment of history as well as of his contemporaries is that Palmerston was a great statesman, and along with Gladstone and Disraeli one of the three greatest British statesmen of the nineteenth century. His statue rightfully stands in Parliament Square. His struggle with Prince Albert is a mere footnote.

Prince Albert did not fare as well. While Palmerston established a firm grasp on executive power and the prince's wife received the plaudits of the public, Albert labored unselfishly and intelligently behind the scenes. The Palmerston cabinet and the parliament recognized his contributions to the war effort, but the press and public were kept largely in the dark on the prince's work, for fear that the old accusations of treasonous intervention should be sounded. The record shows that Prince Albert worked as hard as anyone to ensure a British victory over Russia and to strengthen the country after the war. As Britain began to move hesitatingly toward a reform of the army, the cabinet came to rely on the expertise in matters of arms and military equipment that the prince had acquired through his extensive correspondence with the technologically and strategically advanced German states. Britain owes him a debt for his wartime service.

The fight with Lord Palmerston occurred when Prince Albert was only in his early to midthirties, but it left him far more depleted than his elderly opponent. That the "Pilgerstein" he had so often denigrated to his German correspondents as an ass and a rascal was now a proven war leader and the country's idol was a blow to Albert's intellectual vanity. That the new prime minister proved to be as gracious and forgiving in victory as he had been implacable and vigorous in combat somehow rubbed salt in the prince's wounds.

The Crimean War also went a long way to redress the balance of power between Victoria and Albert. However eager the Queen might have claimed to be for her husband to govern in her stead, it was now clear to both that parliament, the cabinet, and the public would not allow him to do so. She as sovereign was the official source of power, but she could exercise that power only through, or with the consent of, her ministers. The British constitution, as Albert repeatedly complained, made no previsions for the status and functions of the consort to a queen regnant. He could advise her and serve as her private secretary, but even that was her choice, not his right. Any attempt a consort made to overstep the bounds of his subordinate role would be resisted by the British political establishment and could endanger the monarchy.

The war allowed Victoria to display once again the star quality that had made her accession in 1837 such an exciting political moment. At least until the Prince of Wales grew up, no one in the family could fill the symbolic function of the monarchy better than the Queen. She was still the marquee attraction, Prince Albert merely her understudy whose occasional appearances emptied the stalls. These were the basic facts, though neither the Queen nor the prince liked to look them in the face.

When late one night in September 1855 the news came of the fall of Sebastopol, the royal family was at Balmoral. The Queen recorded in her journal: "In a few minutes, Albert and all the gentlemen, in every species of attire, sallied forth, followed by all the servants, and gradually by all the population of the village—keepers, gillies, workmen—up to the top of the cairn [where a victory bonfire had been laid a year earlier]. We waited, and saw them light it accompanied by general cheering. The bonfire blazed forth brilliantly, and we could see the numerous figures surrounding it—some dancing, all shouting . . . About three-quarters of an hour after, Albert came down, and said the scene had been wild and exciting beyond everything. The people had been drinking healths in whisky, and were in great ecstasy."

In Victoria's hurried account, Prince Albert suddenly comes alive for us. We see him aroused from sleep, grabbing the first clothes to hand, and dashing headlong uphill to drink whisky, and dance and shout in ecstasy around the bonfire with all the local men. This is the friendly, athletic, impulsive Albert that his wife and his children, especially his daughters, adored. This was the Albert the English people might have loved but were never permitted to see.

Blue Blood and Red

...

*T*HE YEAR 1853 WAS DIFFICULT FOR THE ENGLISH ROYAL FAMILY. Even as tensions arose in the Balkans and Russia went on the warpath against Turkey, cracks were appearing in the high varnish of the royal marriage. The Queen was due to give birth to her eighth child in April 1853, and she was prey to what the prince called "great and foolish nervousness." Relations between husband and wife were tense, and there were times when conversations ended with her screaming in frustration and his stalking off. They then communicated for a while by letter, for which biographers have been grateful.

Victoria blamed her husband for the physical discomfort and social limitations she endured when pregnant. She claimed that, like most men, he had no understanding of all that women sacrificed to bring children into the world. The raw animality of motherhood was increasingly hard for her to bear. Pregnant, Victoria felt less like a queen than a cow, and while she was still willing to pay the price of intimacy, the price went up with each child.

Albert felt that Victoria exaggerated. He had felt generally less healthy since his move to England, especially when in London, and his work for the Great Exhibition had taken a huge toll. What were a few contractions in comparison to the constant pain and debility he suffered and which he never allowed to interrupt his work or to ruffle his temper? His wife's complaints reinforced his view that women were weak, irrational, selfish creatures, and his cool disapproval added fuel to the fire of his wife's discontent. He protested that he did everything in his power to alleviate sufferings for which he was "the occasion" but not the cause. His duty, he said, was to remain calm and work toward reconciliation with his wife, but he could not be expected to forgive the unjustified imprecations she heaped upon him.

There was blame on both sides in these marital squabbles, and the couple could have used a friend more impartial than Baron Stockmar. There is no doubt that Queen Victoria was spoiled, hot tempered, and demanding and often made life difficult for her husband, and yet it is Victoria who wins our sympathy. After a cooling-off period, she was always the one ready to admit she was wrong and to promise to try to do better in the future. Albert was both more rational and less gracious. In the end, the doctrine of Albert's infallibility, to which both husband and wife subscribed, served neither of them well. It turned the prince into a sanctimonious monster and the Queen into a hysterical nag.

It was not silly for Queen Victoria to fear pregnancy and labor as a threat to her life. Many women in her time died in childbirth, and delivering seven healthy babies without serious complications was no guarantee that a woman would have as much luck with the eighth. Most mothers can attest that the pain of labor is not a figment of a nervous imagination, as Albert seemed to believe, and understand why Victoria became more anxious as her due date approached. Twentieth-century medicine has documented how repeated pregnancies drain a woman's vitality and hormonal swings play havoc with her emotions. This is what Victoria felt in her body and tried in vain to make her husband understand.

To modern eyes, Victoria was a kind of heroine not just because she averaged a healthy child every two years but because she endured labor while an eager crowd of elderly statesmen and clerics peered through the door. In such circumstances, some complaint is surely in order. And despite the nervous anxiety that her husband reproved her for, she was quite capable of making rational choices. When her dear old friend and physician Sir James Clark told her that some doctors were experimenting with chloroform to dull the pain of labor, the Queen insisted on trying it.

Three weeks before the due date in the fall of 1853, when the royal family was at Windsor, a raging fire broke out in the dining room of the castle only two rooms away from where the Queen was sitting. Victoria stayed calm while Albert supervised the work of the firemen, getting soaked to the skin in the process. As usual in a crisis, both husband and wife reacted well, but the fire ratcheted up their anxiety. Getting so wet was not at all what Albert needed, given his susceptibility to colds, but the main worry was for the Queen. Both the Princess Royal and the Prince of Wales had been several weeks premature at birth, so the prince called the Queen's familiar old delivery nurse in early to be on the safe side.

In fact, the pregnancy proceeded normally, and Dr. John Snow, a pioneer in the use of anesthetics, was on hand for the birth. Every ten minutes or so during the third stage of labor, Snow poured half teaspoons of chloroform onto a handkerchief, folded it into a kind of filter, and held it to the Queen's nose. Her fourth son, Leopold George Duncan Albert, was delivered safely, and Victoria was delighted with Snow's ministrations. In 1857, for the delivery of her ninth child, Beatrice, she again had recourse to chloroform.

The birth of Prince Leopold was a milestone in the history of obstetrics. The use of the new anesthetic drugs for women during labor was extremely controversial. Clergymen denounced the practice as a sin, claiming that the pain women experienced in childbirth was God's will, the punishment for the original sin of Eve in Eden. Eminent doctors warned that they had seen chloroform and ether transform respectable matrons into libidinous monsters who made improper advances to their physicians. But once Victoria, beloved monarch and epitome of respectability, announced how grateful she was to be spared delivery pain, the criticism died down in England. By her example, the Queen authorized other parturient women to request anesthesia without guilt.

But even the wonderful Dr. Snow could not stop Victoria from sinking once again into postpartum depression. She would fly into a passion for no reason at all, or so it seemed to Albert, and blame him for all her woes. In May 1854, after a violent scene over some inconsequential problem with the royal catalog, the prince was unable to calm his wife down. He went off to his own rooms and composed a memorandum, explaining his predicament, and adjuring Victoria to be reasonable and control her temper. Remembering the recent fire, he advised her to stop "imprudently heaping up a large store of combustibles," by which he presumably meant the long list of grievances she held against him.

*

ONE OF THE MAIN reasons why Victoria could at times be so difficult was that she saw less and less of her husband, missed him, and minded that he did not miss her. From the beginning, she had been the lover and he the beloved. As time went on, her love and need for him only grew, while he seemed to feel her love almost as a burden.

The growing friction between husband and wife is hinted at in two of the letters the prince wrote to his wife in 1851 and 1853. They had a binding covenant between them that he would write to her at least once every day he was away from home. Thus when Albert went to Ipswich to attend a scientific meeting of the British Association for the Advancement of Science in July 1851, he wrote Victoria a long and newsy letter, ending on a note of teasing affection: "You will be feeling somewhat lonely and forsaken among the two and a half millions of human beings in London, and I too feel the want of only one person to give a world of life to everything around me." But in June 1853, a brief note signed "your devoted A" ends with a plaintive little German poem. The repetition of the pronoun *du,* which is used in German between lovers, stresses intimacy, but the poem ends in reproach. "Du, du liegst mir im Herzen / Du, du liegst mir im Sinn, / Du, du machst mir viel Schmerzen, / Weisst nicht wie gut ich dir bin." (Thou, thou liest in my heart / Thou, thou liest in my soul / Thou, thou causest me great pain / knowest not how good I am to thee.)

Part of their unwritten contract had been that, in exchange for his becoming master of all aspects of their joint life, he would guarantee her comfort and her amusement. In her mind, this meant that he and she would be together as much as possible. As Victoria once told her friend Princess Augusta of Prussia: "I only feel properly à mon aise [at ease] and quite happy when Albert is with me." To her daughter Vicky, Queen Victoria explained that Prince Albert "meant everything to me. I had led a very unhappy life as a child—had no scope for my violent feelings of affection, had no brothers and sisters to live with—never had a father—was . . . not . . . on an at all intimate, confidential footing with my mother . . . and did not know what a happy domestic life was!" All this changed thanks to her husband. "Papa's position towards me is therefore of a very peculiar character, and when he is away I feel paralysed."

After thirteen years of marriage, the Queen and the prince still breakfasted, usually dined, and habitually slept together. They worked on documents and correspondence side by side under identical green lamps copied from Albert's beloved old student lamp. He still prepared elaborate presents for her, planned tours and vacations for her, and arranged for special treats. He hovered over her when she was pregnant. But as the years went by, like most married men, the prince became absorbed in his business.

As his responsibilities expanded, Albert found less and less time for the shared activities Victoria looked forward to: sketching, singing, playing piano, riding out, looking at albums, playing parlor games. Traditionally in royal courts, such minor social duties would fall to a married queen's gallant male attendants, not her husband. They fell to Albert, since he was loath to allow any man to strike up a personal relationship with his wife.

Deprived of Albert, her ideal companion, Victoria was left feeling strangely lonely and neglected in the midst of her large and busy household, especially during the months she spent in London and Windsor. At her husband's insistence, she had a guarded relationship with the women in attendance on her, and, in any case, she was not fond of all-female society. The light went out of her life when the prince left the palace for the day.

For Albert the social isolation his wife felt so acutely did not register. He was very busy with his books and documents. He found the serious discussion of committee meetings and the manly conversation of hunting parties far more interesting than parlor chitchat in mixed society. Dreamy and indolent as a boy, Albert had turned into a workaholic, and even when purportedly vacationing at Osborne or Balmoral, he was consumed by politics and business. Though the royal couple had no public and ceremonial duties to cope with when living on their private estates, the flow of documentation continued unabated, and there was always at least one minister in attendance. The prince spent hours catching up on his reading and his personal correspondence, and he engaged in long discussions of domestic and foreign policy issues with his male guests. Hours of his day were devoted to estate management, building projects, and local development schemes. All this left little time for his wife. No wonder Victoria was delighted if Albert agreed to let her accompany him out deerstalking.

In letters to close kinfolk like Uncle Leopold or Sister Feodora, Victoria rhapsodized over Albert's aptitude for business, but this exaggerated praise hid resentment. She remembered a time when she had been doing the business and liking it. She remembered a time when he had been less busy and more fun. To convey just how busy the prince was during the season, she wrote:

> "It will give some idea of the multifarious nature of the Prince's pursuits, if we mention briefly a few of the subjects that engaged his attention within a few days of his return to Windsor Castle on the 14th of October [1852]. The next day he distributed the prizes of the Windsor Royal Association. On the 16th he meets Lord Derby [the Prime Minister], Lord Hardinge, Lord John Manners, the Duke of Norfolk, the Dean of St Paul's, the Garter King at Arms, and the Secretary of the Office of Works, to settle the complicated arrangements for the funeral of the Duke of Wellington. On the 19th he is busy with negotiations for the purchase by the Exhibition Commissioners of land at Kensington. Next day finds him engaged with Mr. Edgar Bowring in making the final corrections in the Report of the Committee of Commissioners, as to the disposal of the Exhibition Surplus, a very elaborate and masterly document. The same day he had to master the general results of the Cambridge University Commission's report and to communicate them in his capacity of

*Chancellor to the authorities of the University. On the 22ⁿᵈ he settles
with Mr. Henry Cole and Mr. Redgrave the design of the Duke of
Wellington's funeral car. Two days afterwards, in a personal interview
with Lord Derby, he goes into the details of the Government measures,
which are to consist of an acknowledgement of Free Trade, Lightening of
the burdens of Manufacture and Agriculture, Reduction of the Malt Tax,
of the Duty on Tea . . ."*

And so on for another half page. As this list makes clear, for at least the
half year when parliament was in session and the royal family was in London, the Queen and the prince had very little time together. She was unhappy about this.

Their children constituted another point of friction. The Queen's enduring need for the prince's love was eloquently expressed by the babies she
continued to produce, but she had no strong maternal feelings. "Abstractedly, I have no tender for them [babies] till they have become a little human,"
Victoria wrote in 1859 to her daughter Vicky, who was in ecstasies over her
own first-born son. "An ugly baby is a very nasty object—and the prettiest is
frightful when undressed—till about four months; in short as long as they
have their big head and little limbs and that terrible frog-like action."

Even as they got older, her children bored Victoria. She told Princess Augusta of Prussia in 1856 that once her eldest daughter Vicky was married,
she did not expect to miss her as Augusta missed her married daughter:
"With me the circumstances are quite different. I see the children much less
and even here [London], where Albert is often away all day long, I find no
especial pleasure or compensation in the company of the elder children.
You will remember I told you this at Osborne. Usually they go out with me
in the afternoon . . . and only exceptionally do I find the rather informal intercourse with them either agreeable or easy . . . I am used to carrying on
my many affairs quite alone; and then I have grown up all alone, accustomed to the society of adult (and never with younger) people."

Albert, to the contrary, reveled in the company of his children, at least
once they had learned to walk and talk. With the birth of the Prince of
Wales in 1841, Albert became king of the nursery, and he was a far more
active and engaged parent than his wife. He enjoyed swinging a baby in his
huge dinner napkin, teaching a three-year-old to turn somersaults or an
eight-year-old to skate. He loved to lead an excited group of tots on shell-
collecting expeditions or to take teenaged sons out on the moors. It was usually the prince who read the daily reports from governesses and tutors,
corrected the smaller children's table manners, and grilled the older ones

about what they had learned that week. Victoria generously acknowledged Albert's talents as a father in her journal and letters. She made their father's perfection an article of faith for her children. But the subordinate role allotted to her in home life was irksome at times. As the older children entered their teens, she wanted to have a bigger say in their upbringing.

She rather resented the hours that Albert devoted to the children when they were all on vacation. Athletic and high spirited, the children brought out the boy in Albert, and he seemed unusually carefree and happy with them. At times Victoria joined in the fun. But "romping" with the children was not easy in the bell skirts and heavy layers of petticoat that women wore at that time, and when she was pregnant the Queen was forbidden to engage in vigorous exercise. Watching her growing family at play with their father, Victoria was more than a little envious, especially of Vicky, who was her father's special pet.

LITTLE LEOPOLD QUICKLY proved to be a new strain on his mother's nerves and his father's resilience. He was skinny and failed to thrive as an infant despite a change of wet nurse. When he began to move around, it became clear that there was something seriously wrong. When Leopold fell and bumped himself, he was horribly bruised, his joints swelled up, and he had to be put to bed, howling. The royal doctors had no difficulty in making their diagnosis. The disease the prince suffered from, though rare, had long been described in the medical literature. Leopold suffered from hemophilia.

A full understanding of hemophilia was reached only after the First World War when the ideas of Gregor Mendel had finally been accepted and developed into the modern science of genetics. However, even in 1854, certain key facts were well established, notably that the bleeding disease tended to run in families and that it affected only boys.

In 1803 John Conrad Otto, a Philadelphia doctor, made a major conceptual breakthrough. Otto published a paper entitled "An Account of a Hemorrhagic Disposition Existing in Certain Families." Otto traced a single hemophiliac family back to 1720, when the first woman to be identified as what we would now call a carrier arrived in New Hampshire. He identified three key facts: (1) The sufferers, whom he called "bleeders," were boys. (2) They inherited the disease from their mothers, who did not manifest any bleeding problems. (3) Some of the bleeders' sisters had sons who were bleeders in their turn. Thus the disease was carried through the generations from healthy mother to healthy daughter. Otto was not the first medical observer to suggest that hemophilia was a disease that boys inherited from their mothers, but his report was the most careful longitudinal study to date. In an 1828 paper called "Uber die Hämophilie oder die erbliche Anlage zu todlichen Blutungen" ("On Hemophilia or the Hereditary Tendency to Fatal Bleedings"), Friedrich Hopff of the University of Zurich went over the same ground as Otto. Hopff called the disease hemophilia, the name subsequently adopted by medical science.

Medical knowledge filtered into general practice very slowly in the early part of the nineteenth century, and, though Otto and Hopff are now famous in medical history, in their day they were not prominent physicians. However, their specific observations and conclusions may have been particularly slow to gain general acceptance because they posed a new and daunting challenge to the medical profession.

A diagnosis of hemophilia was simple for a doctor to make and terrible for a parent to receive. It meant that their baby son's blood was failing to clot normally, filling his internal cavities and joints and causing excruciating pain. The disease was incurable and treatment at best inefficacious. Most afflicted boys died when very young. A hemophiliac baby who fell out of the crib or merely banged his head on a chair when he started to crawl suffered abnormally severe damage and could easily die. Case studies in the medical literature showed that even if a child survived infancy, his large joints gradually became deformed by arthritis as a result of internal bleeding. The few hemophiliacs who lived into their teenage years suffered chronic pain interspersed with periods of agony and were severely restricted in their activities. The extremely rare adult sufferer was haunted by the knowledge that he could kill himself with a careless slip of the razor, a stumble on the stairs, or a neglected hemorrhoid.

Otto's new information on the ancient bleeding disease offered no ideas for better treatment and would only increase the anguish of affected families. A woman who was coping with a son afflicted with episodes of unstanchable bleeding would learn that, mysteriously, the fault for the child's problems lay with her, adding guilt to her sorrow. She was advised that if she had other sons, they too could face a short life full of pain. A girl who held the hand of her hemophiliac brother as he writhed in agony might hesitate to marry if she understood that her sons and grandsons might suffer like her brother. Was it useful to such families to understand how the disease worked and look to the future with dread? Surely the best course for a responsible physician was to keep silent, advise the parents to watch their child with an eagle eye, and accept the will of God.

There is no indication that the royal doctors who attended the infant Prince Leopold had read the papers by Otto and Hopff. To the contrary, the likelihood is that Prince Albert was never introduced to the term *hemophilia*. However, even if Sir James Clark or one of the other doctors at Buckingham Palace had got word from an American or Swiss correspondent about the newly named hemophilia and its transmission, he would not have rushed off to tell the Queen and the prince.

Hemophilia was a disease of the blood and a disease of boys. Given that inheritance was preferentially carried through the male line in all families, hemophilia was likely to have dire consequences for anyone. But for royal families, obsessed with genealogy and pure breeding, blood had an almost mystic significance. Even a suggestion that certain members of the international caste of royalty had developed a "hereditary tendency to fatal bleedings" would be catastrophic. If Otto and Hopff were right—and medical science over the course of the nineteenth century would amply confirm their observations—the fact that Prince Leopold of England suffered from hemophilia meant that he had inherited the disease from his mother. What doctor, or indeed what husband, would have the courage to tell Queen Victoria that she had a "hemorrhagic disposition" and that some of her five daughters were likely to have it too and cause "fatal bleedings" in their male children?

For several generations the Saxe-Coburg family had been famous for its fertility and its beauty. It married its children to kings and queens where possible or, failing that, to first cousins, keeping power and wealth within the family. This policy had been spectacularly successful, and the English branch of the family sired by Prince Albert was now poised to reach even greater dynastic glory. Prince Leopold's unfortunate joint problems could not be allowed to jeopardize the family's advance. Given the state of medical care and the catastrophic and incalculable risks involved in the bleeding disease, the course of action was intuitively obvious. The nature of Prince Leopold's illness must be kept secret, and the best way to keep a secret is not to know it. Willed ignorance, especially in the extended family itself, was essential. The Queen, whose state of mind was considered so delicate and whose frankness was renowned, must not be given the facts about hemophilia and its transmission.

As the first parent confronted with the problem of hemophilia, as the parent who believed it his duty to assume complete responsibility for his family, as the most intelligent, well-informed, and powerful male in his family for several generations, Prince Albert is the person most likely to have decided on the course of action to be taken in regard to Leopold's illness. Whether or not an actual policy was formulated at any one stage or by any one person is not known, and in some ways it does not matter. What we know is that both Prince Albert and Queen Victoria during their lifetimes and their descendents for two generations thereafter faced the family's problem of a "hereditary tendency to fatal bleedings" in male children with silence, denial, and calculated ignorance.

The Buckingham Palace doctors, sensitive to their patrons' concerns— and eager to remain at court—probably made no inquiries and gave as little information about Prince Leopold's medical problems as possible. Prince Albert was a calm and rational man, forever boning up on the technicalities of mill machines, small-bore rifles, or cattle breeding, but it does not seem that he asked questions of his doctors or launched inquiries into the medical literature. In their five-volume biography, the Queen and Theodore Martin never mention any memoranda the prince wrote on hemophilia. Baron Stockmar was a physician as well as the prince's best friend and chief counselor. Surely the two men must have discussed Prince Leopold, but no letters or journal entries have been published to indicate what was said between them.

What we know is that Prince Albert handled Prince Leopold's hemophilia as if it was asthma or arthritis or some other distressing, possibly life-threatening and yet garden-variety ailment. He expressed the hope that the boy would grow out of his difficulties and insisted that comparable cases had never occurred in either his own or the Queen's family, which was true. He tailored a system of care to address his son's weaknesses and supervised the caregivers diligently. He clearly understood, and made his wife understand, that Leopold must be wrapped in cotton wool if he was to survive.

Though he definitely did not see it that way, Prince Leopold was lucky. Before the advent of safe blood infusions, a hemophiliac born in a palace had a far better chance of survival than a hemophiliac born in a cottage or a tenement. While under his parents' supervision, Leopold was watched night and day. This was not as difficult as it might seem, since, according to Prince Albert's strict instructions, no royal child could be left alone. Even two of the older children—Vicky and Bertie, or even Bertie and Affie— could never be left alone together: The presence of a tutor or governess or servant was always required.

Leopold was a plucky, willful child who longed to lead a normal life and kept putting himself at risk, but, remarkably, he got through the crises of bleeding. Presumably the many servants his mother was able to employ were devoted and highly competent, and her doctors opted not to take any "heroic" measures. Amazingly some nineteenth-century physicians tried to treat their hemophiliac patients by bleeding them, an expeditious form of homicide.

Neither Queen Victoria nor Prince Albert was involved in the daily care given to their son Leopold, and he probably saw less of them even than his siblings did. He was confined more to the nursery quarters, both parents had heavy workloads, and, of course, Leopold was only one of nine. Queen Victoria was critical of Leopold as a boy. She liked pretty, obedient, healthy children, and he was ugly, ungainly, and regularly at death's door. However, the Queen became frantically anxious when Leopold had what she called a "bruising." She hovered over his bedside, and this was probably unhelpful to both the boy and his caregivers. As Grigory Rasputin would prove in his care of Victoria's hemophiliac great-grandson Alexei, calm authority and hypnotic assurance can stop internal bleeding as if by magic. Prince Albert was kinder and more sympathetic to Leopold. He himself had often been ill as a child, and he saw in the boy his own quick intelligence and love of learning. However, Leopold was a drain on his father's time and energies, and he caused friction between his parents at a time when they were beginning to have serious marital issues.

Had Leopold died in one of his serious bleeding episodes, his parents would have mourned him most sincerely. But parents in the nineteenth century were obliged to accept that children often died, and Leopold, from the dynastic point of view, did not seem to be an important child. He had three handsome and healthy older brothers. Between them, Bertie, Affie, and Arthur could ensure the future of the Saxe-Coburg dynasty both in Great Britain, where Bertie would succeed his mother, and in Coburg, where Affie would succeed his uncle Ernest. Perhaps a kingdom would be found for Arthur too sometime in the future.

Prince Albert and Queen Victoria gave exemplary care to their son Leopold. He not only survived childhood but married and produced a son and a daughter before he died at the age of thirty-one. This was something of a landmark in the annals of hemophilia. But just as important as giving Leopold the best chance of life possible was keeping his disease secret. Extreme discretion was the watchword. In family letters, that were so often copied and sent on, Leopold's health problems could be alluded to in general terms, but no details would be given of what was wrong with him, and no name would be put on his condition. The impression given to friends and even the extended family was that Prince Leopold was ill from time to time and suffered from physical handicaps. This was sad for the boy and difficult for the family, but it was not important.

For two generations, the dynastic policy followed by Prince Albert and Queen Victoria was a fabulous success. By 1914 the royal families of Russia, Prussia, Spain, Greece, Sweden, Norway, and Romania, as well as Great

Britain, were all directly descended from Queen Victoria and Prince Albert. Following the example of the illustrious founders of the dynasty, first cousins were encouraged to marry first cousins when no kings and queens were available. Since all these cousins shared a small pool of names, notably Victoria, Albert, Ernest, William, and Frederick, it became necessary to use nicknames to distinguish one from another. Thus Queen Victoria wanted to marry her granddaughter Alix of Hesse to her grandson Albert Victor ("Eddy"), third in line to the throne, but Alix refused. Eddy's brother, the future George V, was extremely anxious to marry his first cousin Marie of Edinburgh, but her Russian mother did not like him, so Marie was quickly sent off to Romania to marry the crown prince of that country. William (Willy), the heir to the throne of Prussia, wanted to marry his first cousin Ella of Hesse, but she refused him. However, Ella's sister Irene did marry Willy's brother Heinrich (Henry), and her brother Ernst (Ernie) did marry Marie's sister Victoria Melita ("Ducky").

But the laws of genetics apply even if you refuse to learn them, and, since the Saxe-Coburgs continued to marry and procreate with such enthusiasm, they got their education the hard way. So much endogamy joined to so much privilege seems to have had dire results on the all-important males of the family. The men of the far-flung Saxe-Coburg and Gotha-Windsor dynasty up to World War II were a generally lackluster set of drones, profligates, and stuffed shirts. Porphyria, the terrible disease of the blood that caused the madness of George III, cropped up again in Queen Victoria's Prussian descendents. Worse yet, each generation in the family produced more bleeding sons who suffered and died young and more guilt-racked mothers who helplessly watched and wept.

In 1894 a Saxe-Coburg princess named Alix of Hesse-Darmstadt achieved the most magnificent Coburg marital coup of all. To the delight of her grandmother Queen Victoria, who had largely brought her up, Alix married Tsar Nicholas II of Russia, where she was known as Tsaritsa Alexandra Feodorovna. Alix and Nicky were passionately in love and children came quickly, but, to Alix's growing distress, the first four children were all girls: Olga, Maria, Tatiana, and Anastasia. Now we know that it is the father who determines the sex of a child by passing on his Y or X chromosome, but at the time, a mother felt responsible if she produced only girls. Finally a son, Alexei, was born in 1904, but the rejoicing lasted barely a day.

Like his mother's brother Frederick ("Frittie"), her uncle Leopold, and her nephews Waldemar and Henry, Alexei was a hemophiliac. His case was so serious that doctors found it difficult to stanch the bleeding when the

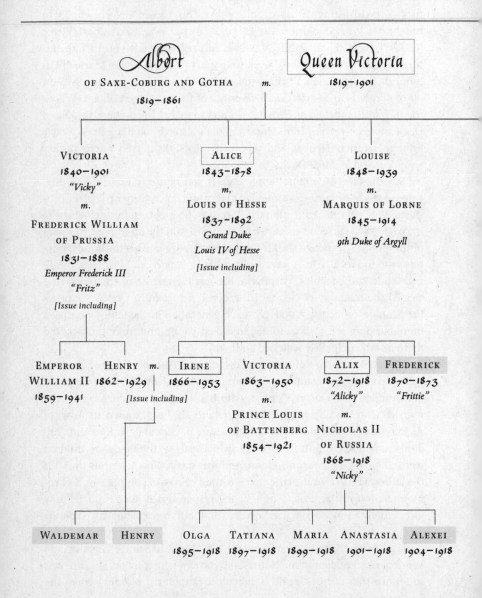

Albert
OF SAXE-COBURG AND GOTHA   *m.*   *Queen Victoria*
1819–1861   1819–1901

VICTORIA
1840–1901
"Vicky"
m.
FREDERICK WILLIAM
OF PRUSSIA
1831–1888
Emperor Frederick III
"Fritz"
[Issue including]

ALICE
1843–1878
m.
LOUIS OF HESSE
1837–1892
Grand Duke
Louis IV of Hesse
[Issue including]

LOUISE
1848–1939
m.
MARQUIS OF LORNE
1845–1914
9th Duke of Argyll

EMPEROR   HENRY   *m.*   IRENE
WILLIAM II   1862–1929   1866–1953
1859–1941   *[Issue including]*

VICTORIA
1863–1950
m.
PRINCE LOUIS
OF BATTENBERG
1854–1921

ALIX
1872–1918
"Alicky"
m.
NICHOLAS II
OF RUSSIA
1868–1918
"Nicky"

FREDERICK
1870–1873
"Frittie"

WALDEMAR   HENRY   OLGA   TATIANA   MARIA   ANASTASIA   ALEXEI
                      1895–1918   1897–1918   1899–1918   1901–1918   1904–1918

Queen Victoria's Family

KEY TO SYMBOLS: ▓ *Indicates known hemophiliacs*

☐ *Indicates known carriers*

ALBERT EDWARD
1841–1910
Prince of Wales
Edward VII, "Bertie"

m.

**PRINCESS
ALEXANDRA OF
DENMARK**
1844–1925
"Alix"

ALBERT VICTOR	**GEORGE V**	**LOUISE**	**VICTORIA**	**MAUD**
1864–1892	1865–1936	1867–1931	1868–1935	1869–1938
Duke of Clarence	*"Georgie"*	*m.*		*m.*
"Eddy"	*m.*	**ALEXANDER**		**HAAKON VII**
	PRINCESS MARY	**DUFF**		**OF NORWAY**
	OF TECK	1849–1912		1872–1957
	1867–1952	*Earl of Fife*		
	"May"			

[Issue including]

EDWARD VIII
1894–1972
Duke of Windsor
"David"

ALBERT
1895–1952
George VI
"Bertie"

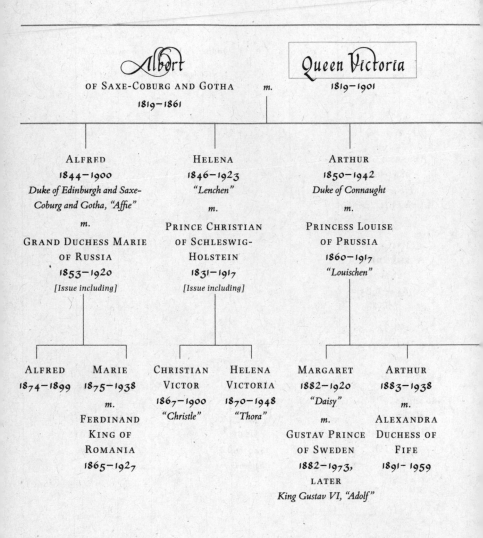

Albert

OF SAXE-COBURG AND GOTHA   m.

1819–1861

Queen Victoria

1819–1901

ALFRED

1844–1900

Duke of Edinburgh and Saxe-Coburg and Gotha, "Affie"

m.

GRAND DUCHESS MARIE
OF RUSSIA

1853–1920

[Issue including]

HELENA

1846–1923

"Lenchen"

m.

PRINCE CHRISTIAN
OF SCHLESWIG-
HOLSTEIN

1831–1917

[Issue including]

ARTHUR

1850–1942

Duke of Connaught

m.

PRINCESS LOUISE
OF PRUSSIA

1860–1917

"Louischen"

ALFRED

1874–1899

MARIE

1875–1938

m.

FERDINAND
KING OF
ROMANIA

1865–1927

CHRISTIAN
VICTOR

1867–1900

"Christle"

HELENA
VICTORIA

1870–1948

"Thora"

MARGARET

1882–1920

"Daisy"

m.

GUSTAV PRINCE
OF SWEDEN

1882–1973,

LATER

King Gustav VI, "Adolf"

ARTHUR

1883–1938

m.

ALEXANDRA
DUCHESS OF
FIFE

1891–1959

Queen Victoria's Family

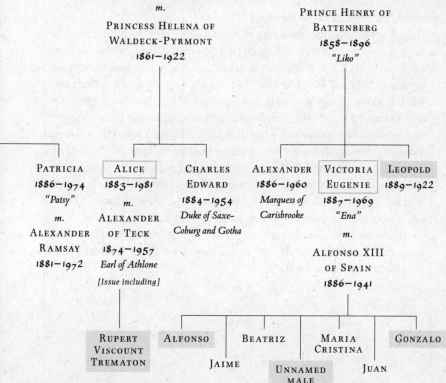

LEOPOLD
1853–1884
Duke of Albany

m.

PRINCESS HELENA OF
WALDECK-PYRMONT
1861–1922

BEATRICE
1857–1944

m.

PRINCE HENRY OF
BATTENBERG
1858–1896
"Liko"

PATRICIA
1886–1974
"Patsy"

m.

ALEXANDER
RAMSAY
1881–1972

ALICE
1883–1981

m.

ALEXANDER
OF TECK
1874–1957
Earl of Athlone

[Issue including]

CHARLES
EDWARD
1884–1954
*Duke of Saxe-
Coburg and Gotha*

ALEXANDER
1886–1960
*Marquess of
Carisbrooke*

**VICTORIA
EUGENIE**
1887–1969
"Ena"

m.

ALFONSO XIII
OF SPAIN
1886–1941

LEOPOLD
1889–1922

**RUPERT
VISCOUNT
TREMATON**

ALFONSO

JAIME

BEATRIZ

**UNNAMED
MALE**

MARIA
CRISTINA

JUAN

GONZALO

umbilical cord was detached. For this his mother *was* responsible. She had passed to her son the defective X chromosome that had come down to her from her mother and her grandmother. Finally the Saxe-Coburg luck ran out. A hemophiliac prince had been born whose disease mattered because he was the only male child and the heir to a great empire. Tsarevitch Alexei's hemophilia led quite directly to the success of the Bolshevik Revolution and to the cellar at Ekaterinberg where he, his parents, and his four sisters were shot to death at point-blank range in 1918.

Nicholas and Alix went into marriage wholly ignorant of the "hereditary tendency to fatal bleedings" in her family. Young and in love, they might have married even had they known, willing to take risks that still had not been calculated. As the medical historians D. M. and W.T.W. Potts note: "The failure of the tsar's family to appreciate the genetic risks was not due to ignorance in Russian scientific circles. More likely it was due to the isolation of the royal family from the intellectual life of the country and the scientific ignorance of the narrow circle of aristocrats and politicians with whom they associated." The Saxe-Coburg policy of secrecy and willed ignorance had been all too successful.

A few years after the wedding of Alix and Nicholas, medical authorities in Spain did point out to their king that Ena of Battenburg, the beautiful, healthy, young English princess he wished to marry had two hemophiliac brothers. Alfonso XIII trusted his eyes, not his doctors, and married Ena— with dynastic results that only just fell short of the Russian tragedy. One wishes that Alix and Ena, both favorite granddaughters of Queen Victoria, had been given some idea of what they were taking on when they married kings of tottering dynasties desperate for healthy male heirs. As their first cousin Marie, Queen of Romania, explained in her memoirs, Queen Victoria's daughters and granddaughters were "kept in glorious . . . but dangerous, and almost cruel, ignorance of realities." Their upbringing was based on "illusions and a completely false conception of life."

By the early twentieth century, the Saxe-Coburg family was the most famous case study of hemophilia in the history of medicine. Hemophilia had become known as the royal disease.

French Interlude

···

F LEOPOLD'S BIRTH IN 1853 WAS A SEVERE SETBACK TO QUEEN VICTORIA'S health and morale, by 1854 she had bounced back. This was as well, as the nation was at war with Russia, her workload was heavier, and she was again on the public stage. Her zest for life was on full display in 1855, when the royal family of Great Britain and the imperial family of France exchanged visits and, rather improbably, became bosom friends.

Great Britain and France were allies during the Crimean War, with their armies fighting on the plains below Sebastopol. The new ruler of France, Napoleon III, was anxious to profit personally from the English alliance. Shunned as an interloper by continental monarchs, the emperor saw Queen Victoria as his best hope for sponsorship in the royal club. Every court in Europe now knew that Prince Albert held the key to Buckingham Palace and that the only way to get close to the Queen was through him. Therefore, as an opening move, the emperor invited Prince Albert to come to Boulogne in August 1854 to spend some days reviewing the French troops and conferring with military leaders.

Napoleon III was not the kind of man Prince Albert habitually cared to cultivate. He was a nephew of the great Napoleon Bonaparte, whose ravaging armies were still recalled with horror in little German states like Albert's Coburg. He was a supreme political opportunist and had touches of the mountebank, the roué, even the opium eater. In smooth charm he was not unlike Benjamin Disraeli, a rising political star in Great Britain whom Prince Albert could not abide. However, flattered to be treated as an expert in military matters, Prince Albert agreed to come to Boulogne. As a lengthy memorandum by the prince himself testifies, he and Napoleon III had hours of weighty conversation on political issues and personalities. When Napoleon III asked for a state visit to England, Prince Albert said he would ask his wife, which the emperor correctly interpreted to mean yes.

Prime Minister Lord Palmerston and Foreign Secretary Lord Clarendon were rather surprised when the Queen agreed to receive the French emperor and empress at Windsor. Only ten years earlier, King Louis Philippe had enjoyed a magnificent state visit during which he received the Order of the Garter and was welcomed into the bosom of the English royal family as a beloved uncle. To the dismay of Queen Victoria and Prince Albert, the 1848 revolution, in which the then Prince Louis Bonaparte had played a principal role, toppled Louis Philippe from his throne, and the whole Orléans clan went into exile in Great Britain. By 1855 Louis Philippe was dead, but his children let out a furious cry of lèse-majesté when they learned of an impending state visit to London from their mortal enemies, the usurping Bonapartes.

Even Victoria was a little surprised to find herself preparing for the imperial couple's visit. She had the state guest apartment at Windsor redecorated in the violet satin and gold eagles she favored, ordered her own gold toilet set to be put out for the empress, and tactfully requested that the Waterloo Room should be referred to for this occasion as the Picture Gallery. She felt virtuous to be putting aside personal feelings for the national good, and for once was deaf to the views of her extended family. Full of martial zeal and policy initiatives, Victoria was bent on using her personal influence to consolidate the entente with France, smooth over the often contentious negotiations between the allies on the battlefield, and restrain the emperor's impetuous instincts.

She also had a nervous curiosity to meet the man in person. She was now accustomed to receiving guests from abroad and could rely on the smooth precision of Albert's domestic management, but most of her houseguests were German family members. Louis Bonaparte and his Spanish wife, in contrast, were an unknown quantity. They were exotic, even louche, the kind of people Albert made sure she never met. The prospect of spending days in their company made Victoria's heart pound.

Charles Louis-Napoleon Bonaparte (1808–1873) was one of the most fascinating men of his generation and a politician of the first rank. During the reign of his emperor uncle, he lived for part of his youth in Augsburg, retaining traces of a German accent in French. After the final defeat of the Emperor Napoleon I's army at the battle of Waterloo in 1815, Louis led the life of an outlaw, a prisoner, and an exile, returning periodically to France to try to incite a revolt against the restored Bourbon monarchy. For a number of years, he lived on his wits in England, where he learned excellent if accented English. Force of will and an invincible sense of destiny brought him back into French politics in 1848, when he became the president of the new French republic. Three years later, he suspended the constitution, organized a plebiscite, and declared himself Napoleon III, emperor of the French.

The new emperor was a small, skinny man with a large head, an extraordinary mustache, and a libido to match. He had great charisma and was irresistible to women. In 1853, having failed in his quest for a royal bride, Napoleon sent shock waves through Parisian high society by choosing to marry a Spanish woman at his court, Eugenie de Montijo, who, remarkably, had resisted his advances. Eugenie was acknowledged to be one of the most beautiful women in Europe, but she was in her late twenties and her name had been linked to several men. She was the kind of woman a petty German ruler like Albert's brother might take as a mistress or marry morganatically but certainly not choose as the mother of a new dynasty.

During the week that the Bonapartes spent with the Saxe-Coburgs at Windsor, the emperor flirted expertly with the Queen, and Victoria fell under his spell. At the very first dinner, Louis enchanted his hostess by recounting how he had once stood in the crowd in Green Park to watch her drive by on her way to her first prorogation of parliament. In 1840 he had paid forty pounds he could ill afford for a box at the opera from which he could gaze at her and her new husband. At the grand ball in the "Picture Gallery," the Queen and the emperor, both excellent dancers and well matched in height, danced a quadrille to the admiration of all. "How strange to think," Victoria confided in her diary, "that I, the granddaughter of George III, should dance with the Emperor Napoleon, nephew of England's greatest enemy, now my nearest and most intimate ally in the *Waterloo Room*, and this ally only six years ago living in this country, an exile, poor and unthought of." As Foreign Secretary Lord Clarendon remarked, after observing the pair on a number of occasions, Napoleon's "lovemaking was of a character to flatter [the Queen's] vanity without alarming her virtue."

One day of the imperial visit was perforce spent at Albert's Crystal Palace. On the way to and from Buckingham Palace and especially walking down the main nave of the exhibition hall, the royal party was mobbed by enthusiastic, cheering crowds. This was a security nightmare, as Napoleon III had political enemies of many persuasions and was under constant threat of assassination. Acutely aware of the danger, Victoria took her guest's arm and pressed close. "I felt that I was possibly a protection for him," she confided to her journal. "All thoughts of nervousness for myself were past. I thought only of him: and so it is, Albert says, when one forgets oneself, one loses this great and foolish nervousness." Victoria herself survived seven assassination attempts, but she reserved her "nervousness" for childbirth.

Two councils of war were held during the imperial visit to England, the first composed exclusively of men. Prince Albert joined in the discussions and was delighted to be chosen to take notes and draw up the memoranda. Eugenie and Victoria waited outside, and finally, at Eugenie's prompting, Victoria dared to go in to ask the men if they intended to eat lunch. The answer was a polite yes, but they did not, in fact, emerge until it was time for the emperor to dress for the Garter ceremony. Victoria and Eugenie lunched alone. However, at the final council of war, "the presence of the Queen was, of course, indispensable," as Victoria notes with some pride in her biography of her husband. Her signature was needed on the documents her husband was busily drafting.

While the men talked, Victoria and Eugenie were thrown into each other's company, and they hit it off tremendously. Victoria looked with pleasure on Eugenie's beauty, sympathized with her nervousness on state occasions, and appreciated the warmth of her nature. The two women would be friends for the rest of their long lives. Albert too melted before the empress's charm and praised the elegance of her toilettes. "Altogether I am delighted," Victoria confided to her diary, "to see how much Albert likes and admires her, as it is so seldom I see him do so with any woman."

Napoleon III was more than satisfied by the warm relations he and his wife had managed to develop with the English royal family, and he pressed his advantage by issuing an invitation to Queen Victoria to come to Paris in late August. Victoria was pleased, especially since her delightful new French friend assured her that Prince Albert would be given the same precedence on French soil as in England. With rather less enthusiasm, the cabinet, which had a war to manage, agreed to sanction the visit. A large diplomatic party, headed by Foreign Secretary Lord Clarendon himself, was deputed to accompany the Queen and ensure that she and the prince made no unilateral policy moves.

In the eyes of all Europe, Queen Victoria's state visit to Paris in 1855 was very big news. England and France had been rivals since the Middle Ages and enemies on several continents during the eighteenth century, with wars that culminated in the great Napoleonic campaigns. The last time an English monarch had officially set foot on French soil was in 1520, when Henry VIII met Francis I at the Field of the Cloth of Gold. The visit was also a personal challenge for the Queen. The French were known to be making the most elaborate preparations, and the eyes of the world's press would be trained on the English royal couple. Paris was the fashion capital of the world, and Victoria would need to look her best. Even Albert was of the opinion that economy was not in order on so solemn and important an occasion. By good luck, the Queen was not pregnant, and for two weeks at Osborne she devoted unusual time and thought to her wardrobe.

At the outset, things did not bode well for Queen Victoria as England's fashion ambassadress. General Canrobert, the emperor's cousin who had recently resigned as commander in chief of the French army in the Crimea, watched Victoria make her triumphal entry into Paris and was appalled. "In spite of the great heat," he wrote, the Queen " had on a massive bonnet of white silk with streamers behind and a tuft of marabou feathers on top . . . Her dress was white and flounced, but she had a mantle and a sunshade of crude green which did not go with the rest of her costume. When she put her foot on the steps she lifted her skirt, which was very short (in the English fashion, I was told) and I saw she had on small slippers tied with black ribbons which were crossed around her ankles. My attention was chiefly attracted by a voluminous object which she carried on her arm; it was an enormous reticule—like those of our grandmothers,—made of white satin or silk, on which was embroidered a fat poodle in gold." If Prince Albert, in his capacity of fashion adviser, was consulted about the tossing stork feathers or the gold poodle (apparently the work of a royal daughter), we might wonder if he was trying to make his wife look ridiculous.

Fortunately, both the French and the English press were anxious to promote good relations, and the Queen of England's dubious taste in clothes did not make the front pages. Flattered outrageously by the emperor, showered with delicate attentions and gifts by the empress, gloriously sure that she had never looked so attractive, Queen Victoria enjoyed every second of her visit to Paris.

She was indefatigable, refusing to allow even the intense heat to get the better of her. She wore out her French hosts, her English ministers, her ladies-in-waiting, her servants, and her husband. Apart from the many social events and tourist opportunities scheduled by her French hosts, Victoria dragged Albert and maid of honor Mary Bulteel along for an incognito sortie in an open carriage to the Jardin des Plantes and the Grands Magasins du Louvre. How odd it was, she chirped, that in Paris people ate outside on the street, that knives in French cutlery shop windows were arranged in a circle, and that no one saw through her incognito and shouted "Vive la Reine." On a visit to the Hôtel des Invalides, the Queen made her son the Prince of Wales kneel in homage at Napoleon I's tomb, which pleased Napoleon III immensely and made old French soldiers weep.

When the imperial party arrived at the emperor's box at the opera house for a command performance, the national anthems boomed and hundreds of curious faces turned upward in anticipation. The Empress Eugenie, a picture of beauty and elegance despite her pregnancy, held back timidly for a moment. Queen Victoria, who had been doing this kind of thing since she was eighteen and two months, swept forward, greeted the crowd with a broad smile and a practiced wave, and then sat down without a backward look. The crowd was impressed. Experts on protocol emerged to note in the French press that only a real queen never looks to see if her chair is in place. Effervescing with amusement, Queen Victoria won the hearts of the French and got rave reviews in newspapers all over the world.

THE EXCHANGE OF STATE visits between the French and British rulers in the summer of 1855 was royal diplomacy at its best. A political and military alliance between Great Britain and France represented a shift in the balance of power and was watched with rapt attention in all European capitals. Given all that was at stake for France and Great Britain in the ongoing struggle with Russia in both the Crimea and the Baltic, it was important for both governments to have the chance to coordinate strategy at the highest levels of command, find common ground, and begin to trust each other. But the new relationship with the imperial couple was also the catalyst for important changes in the private lives of Queen Victoria and her family.

For several days after her return to England, the Queen could talk and write of little else but France. How exciting it had been to dance in the Galerie des Glaces at Versailles and go out to see a fireworks display that ended with the outline of Windsor Castle sparkling in the sky. Victoria was determined to return to France when she could, if possible incognito so she could meet more interesting people and have more fun.

The hours spent with the emperor had reminded the Queen pleasurably of the time before her marriage when she had ridden out with her attractive German cousin Alexander Mensdorff and danced the mazurka with the tsarevitch. Victoria was very much a man's woman, delighting in male society, and in Napoleon III she found the first man since Lord Melbourne who both liked her as a woman and valued her as a monarch. On her last night in Paris, she remarked to Lord Clarendon: "It is very odd; but the Emperor knows everything I have done and where I have been since I was twelve years old; he even recollects how I was dressed, and a thousand little details it is extraordinary he should be acquainted with." Clearly, Queen Victoria was not accustomed to getting this degree of personal appreciation. To her diary she confided, "I should not fear saying anything to him [Napoleon III]. I felt—I do not know how to express it—safe with him." The word *safe* is very significant here: It is the word Victoria often uses to describe her relationship with her husband.

Unlike his wife, Albert was not unhappy to be back in England. The prince's appetite for late nights and other men's magnificence had never been large, and the rich French cuisine played havoc with his digestive system. He felt well and happy only when he was on his own estate, and even there less and less. State visits reopened the chasm in status between a British queen regnant and a Coburg second son, and even on private occasions Albert found himself eclipsed by his wife. The prince cut a distinguished figure in his uniforms and dress clothes, but he had none of the Queen's infectious charm and ready enthusiasm. His heavily accented French was stilted, while his wife could chat as idiomatically in French as she could in English and German.

As for royal diplomacy, in the public events and even in counsel, the Queen had held the limelight even though her voice was rarely heard. Just to have a woman's presence in a counsel of war was a statement. The emperor gallantly allowed it to be known that it was the Queen herself who had persuaded him not to go to the Crimea to lead his troops in battle personally. Albert was far less sure that he had achieved any real influence over the French ruler. In Albert's early private conversations with Napoleon III in Boulogne, the emperor had listened attentively to all that the prince had to say, but it was far from clear that he had changed his policies. The state visits had offered no opportunities for manly tête-à-têtes. Victoria was the focus of the emperor's attention. She was the one who counted.

If Napoleon III effected a tiny breach in the united front of the royal English marriage, he also gave a significant nudge to the relationship evolving between Victoria and Albert and their eldest children. At Windsor, Emperor Napoleon and Empress Eugenie went out of their way to make friends with Vicky and Bertie, and they urged the Queen and the prince to allow both children to come to Paris for the state visit.

For the Prince of Wales, almost fourteen, Paris was a revelation. Bertie had little in common with his father. He cared for sensations, not ideas and facts; for pleasures, not principles and morals; for suits and boots and uniforms, not books and memoranda and protocols. In France he found what he wanted, what had hitherto been systematically denied him. Leaving his loathsome tutor Gibbs in England and supervised by the urbane Lord Clarendon, the Prince of Wales saw enough of Paris to conceive a lifelong love. Here the women were chic and flirtatious, the men elegant and debonair, the cuisine incomparable, the wine superb, the atmosphere deliciously decadent. What a contrast to the dyspeptic, straitlaced court his father had created in England!

Permitted, in a daring move, to drive out alone with the Emperor Napoleon, Bertie expressed the naive wish that he could be the emperor's son. He and his sister begged Empress Eugenie to allow them to stay on a few more days. When she politely said this was impossible, as their parents could not do without them, the Prince of Wales blurted out: "Not do without us! Don't fancy that, for there are six more of us at home, and they don't want us." Like his mother, the Prince of Wales was depressed to get home. He too determined to return to France as soon as possible for new pleasures and new discoveries. In 1855 the seed was sown of the chubby, elegant, bon viveur boulevardier Prince of Wales who makes cameo appearances as an acquaintance of Swann, the Jewish financier and aesthete, in Marcel Proust's great novel.

For Vicky too the visit to Paris was a door opening onto an enticing world. For her, unlike her brother, that door immediately clanged shut. When Emperor Napoleon III and Empress Eugenie came to Windsor, the Princess Royal was allowed for the first time to attend dinners with the grown-ups. She developed a huge crush on the tall, slender, elegant empress, and Eugenie, sincerely grateful for the girl's admiration, was very nice to her.

As the queen of chic in the world's capital of fashion, Eugenie could see that her new friend the Queen of England chose the wrong clothes, not only for herself but for the teenage daughter who looked so much like her. There was nothing to be done for Victoria, so completely in thrall to her husband's idea of fashion, and obliged to have clothes made by British dressmakers from British fabrics. But the empress devised a plan to help young Vicky realize her dream of coming out in style. Before leaving England, she took the measurements for a life-size doll of Vicky, and she then sent a set of exquisite Paris outfits as a gift "for the doll." Here was diplomatic tact and womanly sympathy of the first order, and Queen Victoria understood it as such. Vicky, with her mother's approval, rapturously wore the doll's wardrobe in Paris.

Eugenie made other thoughtful preparations for Vicky's visit. At home Vicky and her younger sister Alice always shared a bedroom, and the two girls were usually confined to a small room at the top of the house. In Paris, Vicky found that a whole suite had been prepared for her, on the reception floor at the Palace of Saint-Cloud with a glorious view. Again at the request of her hosts, the Princess Royal was allowed to attend the great final ball in the Hall of Mirrors at Versailles. There she danced with the emperor himself and had an eager crowd of young men waiting to claim her hand. It was every young girl's dream.

Victoria, Princess Royal, was still three months short of her fifteenth birthday, but it was now apparent that she had become a woman. She was physically mature (her first period came in the spring of 1855), prettier than her mother had been at the same age, a little taller, her features better, her complexion clearer, her smile less gummy, her bosom fuller. Her formidable intellect, restless curiosity, and strong will were hidden behind the mask of blushing maiden modesty.

None of this was lost on her parents. They knew that Vicky had always been precocious and that she liked to have her own way. Ever since her infancy, it had been a struggle to discipline her and plane down her square edges to fit the round female hole. Now, almost overnight, she had entered the danger zone for young princesses, and it was obvious that she liked male company. Her father saw that the time had come to settle Vicky's future before sexual desire could lead her astray. Luckily he had a husband already picked out for her: twenty-four-year-old Prince Frederick (Fritz) Hohenzollern, son to the heir of the King of Prussia.

Within weeks of returning to England from Paris, the royal family was welcoming dear Fritz to Balmoral for a lengthy private visit. The purpose of the visit was clearly understood by the young man, his parents, and his royal English hosts. Fritz had come to take a long, second look at Vicky and decide whether or not he wished to marry her. Only Vicky herself was, quite deliberately, kept in the dark as to the purpose of the visit.

The Prussian Alliance

...

*T*HE IDEA THAT VICTORIA, PRINCESS ROYAL, SHOULD MARRY THE HEIR presumptive to the king of Prussia was apparently hatched by Prince Albert, King Leopold, and Baron Stockmar when the prospective bridegroom, Prince Frederick William of Hohenzollern (Fritz), was a sad, gangly, silent schoolboy of eleven and the prospective bride was a vivacious toddler, already babbling in three languages. A new Germany, united under Prussia, the strongest of the German states, was Prince Albert's great dream. His personal mission as a diplomat was to convert the ferociously conservative, obsessively militaristic, and fanatically Anglophobic Prussian ruling class into the kind of enlightened autocracy that Great Britain and Belgium had pioneered. The Prussian alliance was to be the capstone of his European foreign policy.

Prince Albert's intention to cozy up to the Prussians became apparent as early as January 1842. To the rage of his father the Duke of Coburg, of his wife's uncle the king of Hanover, and of his uncle the king of the Belgians, Albert chose King Frederick William IV of Prussia to be the first baptismal sponsor to the newborn Prince of Wales. Prince Albert wrote, begging His Prussian Majesty to attend the christening in person. The king of Prussia rarely got farther from Berlin than Potsdam, but on this occasion he traveled to London, bearing a magnificent present for his godson, and prepared to be gracious.

For Albert, this visit was a dream come true. As a youth, he had spent a few days at the Prussian court in Berlin, but such was the force of hierarchy in Germany that a king of Prussia could not be expected to converse with a second son of a duke of Saxe-Coburg. Now Prince Albert was playing host to the king in the magnificent medieval English castle over which he presided. He and His Majesty looked each other in the eye, chatted over breakfast, and rode out side by side in the afternoons. The prince's adviser, Baron Stockmar, was granted personal audiences with the king of Prussia, and, to His Majesty's obvious amazement, ventured to disagree with him.

After the christening of his first son, Albert felt empowered to start a regular correspondence with the king of Prussia. He also welcomed the Prussian minister (ambassador) in London, Chevalier Bunsen, into his exclusive family circle. All was plain sailing until the Queen and the prince paid a visit to Prussia and had a chance to see the Prussian court firsthand. By the 1840s, with the immense improvement in the speed and reliability of communications, the English political establishment was willing for Queen Victoria to travel abroad, and she was eager to visit Germany. For his part, Albert longed to show his wife Coburg and Gotha, where both he and her mother had lived as children, and Bonn, where he had been so happy as a student.

Thus in 1845 the Queen and the prince crossed to Antwerp in the royal yacht. There they were greeted by King Leopold, toured Belgium, carefully skirted the Queen's ancestral Hanover (still ruled by awful Uncle Ernest), and crossed into Prussia. They spent several days on the Rhine and touring various Prussian cities, accompanied by their royal hosts. King Frederick William put on a glittering array of dinners, balls, and concerts, including one featuring Franz Liszt and the new Swedish soprano sensation Jenny Lind. The English royal party then proceeded to Coburg and Gotha, where cheering crowds turned out everywhere for the English Queen with flowers and songs and folk dances. The German relatives, including the Duchess of Kent and King Leopold and Queen Louise, descended en masse. It was hardly a vacation for Victoria, but she glowed with happiness and pride. How she would love to spend her life in a little German hunting lodge like Albert's beloved Rosenau, she confided to her diary.

The one blot on the royal couple's pleasure came at the Prussian king's castle of Stolzenfels. There King Frederick William IV refused to give Prince Albert precedence over an Austrian archduke, the younger son of an uncle of the Austrian emperor. Victoria was separated from her husband, and her discontent was writ large on her face. The Prussian court took notice, and, to Victoria's dismay, critical accounts of the Queen of England's ungracious ways appeared in the press. Albert, whose nostalgia for his beloved Germany had received a reality check, affected stoicism and advised his wife to do the same. In a telling little scene witnessed by the royal governess Lady Lyttelton, Prince Albert put on a Cheshire cat smile and did a neat entrechat, demonstrating to his wife how she should feign pleasure and thus avert adverse criticism in the future. If only for him it had really been that easy!

At last permitted to spend days in the company of the rulers of Prussia, Prince Albert was not impressed. He saw that they were ill educated and deeply prejudiced men, hypnotized by their own greatness and terrified of change. They were also twice his age and seemed stuck in the past. Frederick William himself, the eldest of the four royal Hohenzollern brothers, once admitted: "If we had been born as sons of a petty official, I should have been an architect, William an NCO, Charles would have gone to prison, and Albrecht would have become a drunkard."

Frederick William, the brightest and most cultured of the four brothers, had long been wrapped in a mist of romantic feudalism. He was lapsing into dementia by the time Prince Albert first met him. William, next in line to the throne, was stupider and less educated, deeply neurotic, and at daggers drawn with his wife, Augusta. The army was William's passion and his only area of expertise. The king and his brother heir were at once stubborn and indecisive, an unfortunate combination in an autocrat.

Prince Albert was confident that he could achieve ascendancy over these pitiful specimens. By force of personality, logic, and fact, leveraging his wife's status and England's power, he would convince the kings of Prussia to adopt his theory of monarchy and govern as he thought they should. It would be no easy task. Prussian kings ate flattery with their daily bread and drank obsequiousness with their beer. They did not listen, they pronounced. Albert would need to play the courtier and the hypocrite. For the sake of Germany and the world, he was ready to do it.

In 1848 Prince Albert had his chance to proselytize. Revolution came to Prussia, the mob ruled the streets of Berlin, and the king was forced to accept a program of democratic reform, at least for the time being. Prince William, who had advised shooting down the demonstrators, had to get out of Germany in a hurry. He left his wife, Augusta, and two children at his Potsdam castle to protect his interests and begged to be received in England. Against the advice of Palmerston at the foreign office, who sympathized with the forces of democratic reform, Prince Albert insisted on welcoming Prince William at Windsor. During the months that the Prussian prince was dependent on his hospitality, Prince Albert offered an extended seminar in constitutional monarchy. William appeared responsive and was encouraged to believe that Albert held the reins of England's foreign policy.

When William returned to Prussia, Albert geared up the private Prussian correspondence. He and Victoria wrote not only to William and his older brother, the king of Prussia, but to William's wife, Augusta. She had been born a princess of Saxe-Weimar and was thus a distant kinswoman of Albert and Victoria. Weimar at the end of the eighteenth century had been the center of the German enlightenment. The Prussian court considered the princess to be a liberal and an intellectual and hence saw her as a threat. Prince Albert hoped that Princess Augusta might begin to wield more influence at the Prussian court, and he strongly encouraged a friendship between her and his wife. Letters flew between England and Prussia, carried mainly by private courier, since in Prussia all important mail was routinely opened by the state police.

A tiny fraction of Prince Albert's vast Prussian correspondence has been published in English, and it makes for uncomfortable reading. His own letters prove that even as the prince was advising the Queen to insist that every foreign office document should be presented for his perusal and approval, he regularly divulged cabinet secrets to his royal Prussian friends. He believed, and convinced his wife, that in doing so he was acting out of principle and morality. All means, as he saw it, were noble to achieve the great cause—the reunification of Germany. At the same time, Albert begged his Prussian correspondents not to let anyone know the source of their privileged information. In the labyrinth of the Prussian court bureaucracy, where everything and nothing was secret, these requests were no doubt good for a laugh.

The flavor of Prince Albert's style when writing in his native German to his royal correspondents in Prussia can be felt even in translation. Here are the opening paragraphs of a six-page effusion that he penned in April 1847:

Your Majesty, I must begin my letter by expressing my deep gratitude for the great, unrestricted and gracious confidence you have shown me in your two letters. Indeed I scarcely had a right to expect any reply to my latest lengthy epistle . . . I have decided to reply to Your Majesty without delay, and it imitates the brilliant qualities displayed in your letter—or at least one of them—namely, by replying . . . with absolute frankness and truthfulness. There is no need to assure Your Majesty that, in all our views and opinions on English policy, as well as on European and world policy connected with England, Victoria and I are one, as beseems two faithful married people . . . If however in my communications to Your Majesty there appears, side by side with considerations concerning general world questions, a certain excess, as in my last letter, of purely British feeling, you will, (knowing as I do your truly German sentiments) see in it, I am sure, in future nothing unseemly, but will freely admit, that, though I am incidentally the Queen of England's husband, I am also one German prince speaking to another. It goes without saying that all such out-pourings, whether they come from Your Majesty or are addressed to you, are to be treated by us both with the strictest secrecy, and to be withheld from everyone, including our Governments.

Only days after Prince Albert wrote this letter, King Frederick William gave an impromptu speech to the Prussian assembly. This was 1847, democratic fervor was coming to the boil, and Europe once again faced bloody revolution. The king stated plainly to the elected members that his government consisted of ministers appointed by and answerable to him alone, the divinely anointed king. No elected body, he affirmed, could ever possess a legitimacy comparable to his own. These were the principles that the king sincerely held throughout his life. In 1848 he would give lip service to democratic reform only because his dynasty seemed likely to face the fate of the deposed Bourbons in France.

Learning of the speech, Prince Albert wrote in dismay and amazement to Stockmar: "I have today read with alarm the King of Prussia's speech . . . Those who know and love the King recognize him and his views and feelings in every word and will be grateful to him for the frankness . . . but if one puts oneself in the position of a cool, critical public, one's heart sinks. What confusion of ideas, and what boldness in a king to speak ex tempore; and at such a moment and at such length not only to touch on topics so terrible and difficult, to dispose of them in that slap-dash way." So much for Prince Albert's "absolutely frank and truthful" paean to the "brilliant qualities" of the king of Prussia.

The gap between what Prince Albert expected Prussia to do and what it actually did widened to a chasm in 1854. England and France went to war with Russia. Austria repulsed Russian advances into the Balkans and stood ready to defend the integrity of its empire. Piedmont, a small nation seeking to shake off the Austrian yoke and to become the nucleus for a new, united Italy, demonstrated its commitment to democracy and constitutional government by sending a contingent to fight in the Crimea. But Prussia, the sixth Great Power, whose well-financed army was being honed to a peak of readiness, adamantly remained neutral. The English government and the English nation were outraged by Prussia's refusal to honor its treaty obligations to Turkey, send troops to the Crimea, and reinforce the English blockade of the Russian ports in the Baltic.

Prince William was now regent in Prussia, following the definitive lapse into dementia of his brother King Frederick William IV. The regent refused all Prince Albert's impassioned pleas for his nation to join the Franco-British alliance. When the chips were down, William, like his brother the king, preferred to side, tacitly, with Russia, not with their new friend Prince Albert. In this decision, both dynastic and national interests played a part. The tsar of Russia was married to the favorite sister of the king and the regent of Prussia. The Russian state observed the autocratic principles that the kings of Prussia cherished. As Palmerston's man in Berlin accurately reported to the foreign office, the Prussian government was convinced that it was in Prussia's best interests to keep its army intact and waste no money on the defense of the Turks. Prussia planned to exploit the weakness of the Crimean combatants once they had tired of battle to begin its campaign of territorial expansion.

Prince Albert was angry and distraught at what he regarded as a personal betrayal as well as a cynical flouting of international law. "That every good German desires the consolidation, perhaps the aggrandisement, of Prussia, is intelligible," he wrote to Stockmar, "but physical expansion is, or ought to be, the result of moral strength and struggle, and people ought to see that the war with Russia [that is, Prussia's joining with Britain and France in the war against Russia] would offer many chances to attain the desired object in a way which Europe would regard as consonant with her own interests and those of civilisation. On the other hand, the policy of seeking to embarrass Europe now, in order to fish in troubled waters later on, cannot fail to produce the opposite effects."

Prince Albert could not have been more tragically wrong. Within a few years of the end of the Crimean War, Prussia was moving to incorporate the Danish provinces of Schleswig and Holstein to the north by force of arms, not argument. By 1862, Bismarck had dissolved the troublesome Prussian assembly and was ruling in the name of his aging sovereign. However "uncivilized," Bismarck would prove brutally effective. By 1871, Prussia had metamorphosed into the German Empire, having annihilated Austria and France on the battlefield, swallowed up the small German states, and acquired the French provinces of Alsace and Lorraine as a fabulous bonus.

Vanity was Albert's Achilles' heel, and his wife's adoration left him vulnerable to men like the kings of Prussia. Seeing himself so superior in mind and morals to the Hohenzollern princes, he underestimated them. That they might define the goal of German unity quite differently, that they were far more ruthless in their subordination of means to ends, and saw him as an instrument of policies of their own seems not to have occurred to him.

Prince Albert died before Bismarck came to power and flaunted his policy of "blood and iron." But the prince's misreading of Prussian policy, the Prussian court, and the Prussian royal family was to have tragic consequences for the person he probably loved most in the world: his eldest daughter.

■

CONSISTENTLY DISAPPOINTED in his attempts to influence King Frederick William IV and Prince William, Prince Albert still believed he had a trump card: dynastic alliance. Frederick William was childless. William had only one son, also named Frederick William in the confusing Prussian royal tradition, and known in the family as Fritz. Both brothers were old. If Fritz were to marry an English Saxe-Coburg princess and have heirs by her, the next generations of the Prussian royal family would move in the English Saxe-Coburg orbit and have the power to put Prince Albert's philosophy of government into practice. In his eldest daughter Vicky, Prince Albert saw the perfect instrument for his Prussian policy.

The first big step toward the Prussian alliance was taken in 1851. William, then crown prince of Prussia, his wife, Augusta, his son, Fritz, almost twenty, and his thirteen-year-old daughter, Louise, were warmly invited to come to England to attend the opening to the Great Exhibition. They came and stayed on as Queen Victoria's guests for some four weeks. Both families were on their very best behavior. The two mothers declared a bosom friendship. The two fathers continued their political and philosophical dialogue.

Fritz was enraptured by this introduction to the English royal family. His life at the Prussian court was grim, since his parents quarreled constantly and used their children as weapons against each other. Prince William and Princess Augusta had been forced into marriage. She failed to win his love and trust, and they soon had nothing but contempt for each other. Although Fritz was the essential male child, destined to rule in Prussia, his father favored Louise, seven years younger. Fritz was an obsessively obedient and conscientious child, but he gained no love or praise by being good. His father thought him a weakling. His mother thought he was stupid. Even as a teenager, he was subject to periods of black depression.

In comparison with the Prussian court, Windsor and especially Osborne seemed warm and spontaneous. Queen Victoria and Prince Albert were young and happy in each other's company. They already had seven small sons and daughters and appeared to love them very much. Both the young Prussians were astonished by the free and easy way the English royal children addressed their parents. Fritz flowered before the warm interest of his English hostess. At six foot two, the young Prussian towered over Victoria, but he was so gentle and insecure that he seemed even younger than Vicky and Bertie. A strong bond of affection and esteem was forged between the Queen and the prince. Fritz also felt privileged to hold long conversations with Prince Albert, who treated him like a man, not a backward child.

Most remarkable of all to Fritz was the eldest child, the Princess Royal. Unlike the repressed and awkward Princess Louise, Vicky, only ten, was charmingly outgoing and had opinions of her own. For once encouraged by her parents to show off, Vicky guided the young Prussian visitors around the exhibition, displaying a mastery of technical details as well as flawless German. Since she was so young, Vicky did not need to be closely chaperoned and could chatter away to the Prussian youth to her heart's content. The mothers noted how raptly Fritz watched the little girl. Everything was going as planned. As Queen Victoria wrote to King Leopold: "Might this, one day, lead to a union! God knows it would make us *very happy.*"

Princess Augusta was almost as keen on the prospect of marriage between Vicky and Fritz as Prince Albert. She was locked in a loveless marriage to a man seventeen years her senior, scorned by her female in-laws, and a virtual pariah in her brother-in-law's court. Her family's liberalism linked Augusta ineluctably to England and the Saxe-Coburg school of politics, but ideas meant much less to Augusta than power. She needed a female ally at court and was eager to secure an English bride for her son in no small part because the rest of the Prussian royal family was so fiercely Anglophobic.

Prince William would have preferred a Russian or a German bride for his son. This was the marital policy traditional to Hohenzollern royal princes, and he was a traditionalist to the bone. However, swimming out of his element in liberal, democratic England and agreeably flattered by his English hosts, William was for once prepared to be ruled by his wife. It was unfortunate, in the prince's view, that Vicky looked so much like her mother and was likely to be dwarfish by Prussian standards. But, on the plus side, Queen Victoria was certainly a devoted wife and not at all a cold fish like his Augusta. Above all, she was one of the legendarily fertile Saxe-Coburg women, a key dynastic consideration. Prince William of Prussia was anxious for grandsons.

Queen Victoria had no love for Prussia. When she was a teenager, she and her mother had quickly repulsed the idea of her making a Prussian marriage. All the same, the Queen did everything she could to marry her oldest daughter into the Prussian royal family largely because she knew how important the alliance was to her husband. The Queen was also pragmatic. Though Vicky was only ten, one day she must marry. Prussia was one of the great powers, so a Prussian crown prince would be a suitably great match for an English Princess Royal.

But personal sympathy counted more with Queen Victoria even than dynastic politics or pleasing her husband. For all her isolation, she was in tune with the Zeitgeist, and in Northern Europe arranged marriages were going out of style. Love was all the rage, and young people were increasingly free to choose their mates. In her own marriage, the Queen had come under severe pressure to choose her cousin Albert, but all the same she believed that she had made a choice based on compatibility. Her marriage had worked out because she and Albert loved each other. Victoria quickly took Fritz to her heart. He reminded her of the young Albert. He seemed untouched by the notorious promiscuity of the Prussian royal men. She was sure that, unlike his father, he had the makings of a good husband.

Prince Albert too was agreeably impressed by Fritz. The Prussian prince showed a pleasing readiness to listen and learn. Here was the Prussian disciple that Albert had always dreamed of finding, a young mind he could form, and in this way, shape Prussian politics in years to come. Following the example of his uncle Leopold, Prince Albert looked to the future and assessed the dynastic odds. King Frederick William was mad and in very bad health. The current regent, Prince William, Fritz's father, would probably come to the throne in his early sixties. Fritz was likely to become king while still a young man. It was true that, like his uncle and father, Fritz was weak and indecisive and not especially bright; a soldier, not a scholar. But Albert saw this weakness as a possible asset. Vicky had strength and brains enough for two, and she would be guided by her father. Together, Prince Albert believed, King Frederick and Queen Victoria of Prussia would change the destiny of Europe.

When in the spring of 1855 his wife intimated that their eldest daughter had reached puberty, Albert was ready to act. He invited the young heir to the Hohenzollern dynasty to come to Balmoral to join the English royal family during their annual Scottish retreat. Given the hatred with which Prussia was viewed in wartime Britain, the British cabinet had to be apprised of the Prussian prince's coming so that his safe passage could be assured. Palmerston and his cabinet strongly advised against the visit. They could smell a Prussian dynastic alliance in the air, and they were deeply opposed to it. However, they had no power to forbid the Queen to receive a visitor on her private estate.

Fritz had been eager for an invitation to England to press his suit. Once at Balmoral, he was somewhat frustrated to find how much time he was expected to spend out deerstalking and talking constitutional theory with Prince Albert. He would much have preferred staying close to the royal English ladies, but Vicky was no longer a child and hence was subject to close chaperoning. The young suitor was obliged to watch the girl from across the room and exchange odd snatches of conversation with her at lunch and in the evenings. But it was enough.

Now twenty-four, Fritz had had ample opportunities for sexual exploration both as an army officer and as a university student. His uncles wanted nothing better than to introduce him to their mistresses and favorite houses of pleasure. His aunts wanted nothing better than to find him a German or Russian wife. But Fritz stubbornly remained a romantic: It was his one form of rebellion. For four years, the image of little Vicky burned in his heart. He had found her perfection when she was only ten. Now he saw that she had become the woman of his dreams, and her close resemblance to her mother was delightful in Fritz's eyes. His destiny had long been intertwined with Vicky's, and he was glad.

Full of earnest resolve, Prince Frederick requested a private audience with the Queen and the prince. He declared his love and admiration for them, and expressed a strong desire to become part of their family. He asked for their eldest daughter's hand. Victoria and Albert consented at once, embracing the young suitor. All three wept for joy. The Queen and the prince stipulated that the engagement must be kept secret and unofficial until Vicky was confirmed at sixteen, and thus came of age. The Queen insisted that the marriage could not be celebrated for more than two years, after the bride had turned seventeen. The Queen, the prince, and Fritz then ran off to write letters to family members, key cabinet ministers, and Baron Stockmar, informing them of the secret engagement.

"It is *not* politics, it is *not* ambition, it was my heart," wrote Fritz of his marriage proposal. "[Fritz] is a dear, excellent, charming young man, whom we shall give our dear child to with perfect confidence," wrote the Queen in a letter to her uncle King Leopold. "What pleases us greatly is to see that he is really delighted with Vicky." Queen Victoria had been terribly afraid that her daughter would not be pretty enough to please the tall, handsome young German.

The Queen and the prince's idea was that Vicky should not be told of Fritz's proposal for months or even years. As Albert expressed it to his confidant Stockmar: "The event you are interested in reached an active stage this morning after breakfast. The young man laid his proposal before us with the permission of his parents and of the King; we accepted it for ourselves, but requested him to hold it in suspense as regards the other party till after her Confirmation. Till then all the simple unconstraint of girlhood is to continue undisturbed." But perhaps unsurprisingly, the young man was rather anxious to disturb Vicky's girlish unconstraint and to know if she could return his love. Finally the royal parents agreed that, after all, something needed to be said to Vicky and that Fritz was probably the best person to say it.

On a pony trek up a mountain near the castle, the Queen and the prince allowed the young couple to fall behind unattended. Fritz told Vicky that he would like her to come to Prussia. In fact, he would like her to come to Prussia for good. Vicky blushingly admitted that she would like this too. The two exchanged sprigs of white heather for good luck. As soon as the party got home, Fritz rushed in to tell the Queen and the prince what had occurred.

Then Vicky went into her mother's sitting room, where her parents were anxiously awaiting her. The Queen recorded the scene in her journal that night. "Her Papa asked her if she had nothing more to say. 'Oh, yes, a great deal.' We urged her to speak and she said: 'Oh, it is that I am very fond of the Prince.' We kissed and pressed the poor dear child in our arms then Albert told her how the Prince . . . on the 20th had spoken to us . . . [how he wished] to see more and more of her. I asked her if she wished the same? 'Oh, yes, everyday,' looking up joyously and happily in my face—she was kneeling. Had she always loved him? 'Oh, always!' Albert came in to say that Fritz was there, and I took her in. She was nervous but did not falter in giving her very decided answer . . . He kissed her hand twice. I kissed him and when he kissed her hand again . . . she threw herself into his arms, and kissed him with a warmth which was responded to again and again . . . It is his first love! Vicky's great youth makes it even more striking, but she behaved as a girl of 18 would, so naturally, so quietly and modestly and yet showing how very strong her feelings are."

GIVEN THE NUMBER of persons apprised of the secret engagement, it was inevitable that the news would be leaked. The *Times* newspaper wrote a series of scathing editorials in which it described Prussia as "a paltry German dynasty dependent on the major tyrannies of Austria and Russia" and excoriated the very idea of dynastic alliance between Great Britain and Prussia. "What sympathy can exist between a Court supported like ours on a solid basis of popular freedom, and a camarilla . . . engaged . . . in trampling on the last embers of popular government?" The *Times* expressed doubts that the Princess Royal, already an engaging presence on the national landscape, could find happiness in Berlin. "For our part we wish for the daughter of our Royal House some better fate than union with a dynasty which knows neither what is due . . . to the rights of the people over which it presides, nor the place it occupies in the great European confederacy."

If the *Times* had hoped to influence the Princess Royal's parents, it failed. Prince Albert had no love for the British press in general. He was convinced that the *Times* in particular, commonly and incorrectly seen abroad as the organ of the British government, was a danger to national security. No insult in the *Times* of London went unremarked in Berlin, and the prince saw his Prussian project constantly driven off course by the English press. That a newspaper should attempt to intervene in royal family matters over which he alone had jurisdiction was offensive. As Albert saw it, in affecting to protect the Princess Royal, the *Times* was raising difficulties for her in the new life her loving father had planned out for her.

Fortunately, there was now no turning back, and Prince Albert had no regrets. Though by English law his daughter was too young to commit herself to marriage, the prince regarded the engagement as binding. He knew that the Prussians saw it so. While he was certainly anxious for the happiness of his favorite child, Prince Albert became firmly committed to the prospect of the Prussian alliance in 1851 and never thereafter considered any other suitor for his eldest daughter. He hurried the match in 1855 because there was a nine-year gap in the ages of the prospective bride and groom, and Fritz was obviously ripe to fall into the hands of a wife or a mistress. The attraction between Vicky and Fritz only confirmed his view that this was a marriage made in heaven.

The *Times* campaign against a marriage with Prussia upset Queen Victoria. As the months went on, the romantic mist that Balmoral had cast over Fritz's marriage proposal cleared. The Queen received a disturbing letter from Lady Bloomfield, wife to the British minister (ambassador) in Berlin: "I fear Her Royal Highness's position here will be more difficult than perhaps Your Majesty is fully aware of . . . the real fact is, without living here and seeing the curious anomalous state of this country and the violence and bitterness of political party spirits it is almost impossible to value the true state of affairs at this Court . . . the unhappy divisions and jealousies which exist in the Royal family itself."

Once Vicky was confirmed at sixteen, Berlin demanded that the engagement should be officially announced in the Prussian court circular. This required that an official announcement be issued in England also. When the lord chancellor learned of the engagement, he commented that people would feel it was not right to commit a barely sixteen-year-old girl to a marriage that was to be delayed at least a year. Cut to the quick, Queen Victoria wrote to Prime Minister Lord Palmerston: "The Princess's choice altho' made with the sanction and approval of her Parents has been one *entirely* of her *own heart*, and she is as *solemnly* engaged by *her own free will & wish* to Prince Frederick William of Prussia as anyone *can be* and that *before God*, she has pledged her word . . . The Princess is Confirmed and *old* enough to *know* her own feelings & wishes, tho' she may *not* yet be old enough to consummate the marriage and leave her parents' roof."

Queen Victoria had begun to see that love might not be all her daughter needed in life. She was all too aware that in Berlin her German-born friend Princess Augusta had become a bitter, loveless, paranoid woman. Could the same fate be Vicky's, especially since the Prussians had such hatred for the English?

Baron Stockmar also began to have cold feet. He was now settled in Coburg. However, apprised of the secret engagement, the wizened old diplomat traveled to Berlin at Prince Albert's behest to report on the reception of the English alliance. Stockmar had known Vicky from birth, and he loved her like a granddaughter. She was also the rare female being Stockmar could admire. "From her youth onwards, I have been fond of her," he wrote, "have always expected great things of her, and taken all pains to be of service to her. I think her to be exceptionally gifted in some things, even to the point of genius." Deeply invested in Prince Albert's dream of a united and constitutional Germany, Stockmar from Berlin gloomily prognosticated that though the princess "has the qualities of feeling and mind required . . . that will not be enough . . . For I foresee that she would have to suffer her whole life from mistakes and faults which are to be feared at the very beginning." Like the *Times*, Stockmar was eerily prescient.

If Prince Albert had dispatched Stockmar to report from Berlin before young Fritz arrived at Balmoral ready to propose, the visit might have been of some use, but probably not. The prince's mind was made up, and he was not a man to second-guess himself. All the same, now officially apprised of the difficulties that Vicky would encounter in her married life, Prince Albert took on the duty of preparing her himself. Each day he tried to dedicate an hour exclusively to Vicky, acting as her professor and her political mentor. Vicky was an outstanding student, able to match her father in intellect and in diligence. She was ready for what amounted to a graduate course in international politics, history, and law. She read his vast memoranda with passionate interest, and wrote essays and reports and historical digests of her own. Vicky adored her father and was desperate to earn his approval.

As she later wrote to her mother, she saw him as inerrant, the oracle, the fount of wisdom. Nothing made her happier than to sit at her father's knee, gazing up as he discoursed in his beloved German on the English constitution, German political movements, and European diplomacy. For two years, fierce and focused, proud and principled, Albert and his daughter plotted the future of Germany, confident that their vision must prevail because it was right.

The intensified bond between the prince and his eldest daughter inevitably sent ripples through the royal family. To spend an hour taking lessons one-on-one from his father was Bertie's idea of torture. All the same, the eldest son found it galling to see his big sister shine in the glow of their father's approbation. Unsurprisingly, the Prince of Wales's tutor, in his daily reports to Prince Albert, could report no improvement in his young charge's conduct.

In her journal, Queen Victoria described the day when Fritz asked Vicky to marry him as one of the happiest days of her life, but she found the two years between the proposal and the marriage unexpectedly difficult. When Fritz came over to England, which he did as often as his military responsibilities allowed, the Queen was pushed into the role of chaperone and found it irksome. The physical attraction between Fritz and Vicky was almost shocking to observe. How, Victoria wondered, could her teenaged daughter inspire such passion in a man?

The Queen resented the increasingly close relationship between her husband and her eldest daughter. It was part of the family dogma that Vicky was the image of her father, while Bertie was a caricature of his mother. In Albert's eyes, his daughter Vicky could do no wrong, and it was plain that his greatest pleasure in life was to nurture her young mind. His wife, Victoria, by contrast, was a mass of Hanoverian faults, which it was the prince's sad duty to correct.

Once Vicky was confirmed and officially "out," she was allowed to have dinner with her parents. Albert enjoyed this, Victoria did not. By the end of 1856, the Queen was pregnant with her ninth child. She wanted more time alone with her husband, not less, and found the intelligent scrutiny of her affianced daughter unnerving. If she and Albert agreed about anything, it was that Vicky must be given no sense of what awaited her once she was married. But how was Victoria to account for her swelling body and constricted lifestyle? "We dined with Vicky, who generally leaves us at 10," wrote the Queen in her journal, "and then I have the rare happiness of being alone with my beloved Albert." The prince, exhausted by his wife's litany of complaints and upset by her apparent hostility to their daughter, offered to send Vicky back to the nursery for her meals. The Queen could only capitulate and beg pardon.

Now that she saw so much more of her parents, Vicky grasped how the land lay between them and was as ready as any teenager to capitalize on their differences. The Princess Royal had always had what her mother called "a proud, high spirit," and she resisted the vigorous efforts her parents had made to subdue her will. Her engagement gave Vicky the prominence she felt she deserved, and, though she dreaded losing her father, she looked forward to marriage. As a wife, she would be able to enjoy Fritz's embraces undisturbed. Confident in the adoration of her fiancé, conscious of being cleverer and stronger willed than he, she imagined she would be able to do as she liked in Berlin. She would take charge, just as her father had done.

Vicky began to criticize her mother and refuse to obey her. The Queen, in turn, complained bitterly about her disrespectful behavior. As Queen Victoria remembered this period, Vicky had such an "uneven temper" and was "so unpleasant and unamiable" toward those she lived with and to whom she owed respect, obedience. Caught between the two women, Prince Albert's domestic life was even more fraught.

*

AS THE TIME for the wedding approached, the Prussian government wrote stating that crown princes of Prussia were always married in Berlin. Her daughter's wedding was an area over which Queen Victoria claimed jurisdiction, and she wrote an official letter back that brooked no debate. "Whatever may be the usual practice of Prussian Princes, it is not every day that one marries the eldest daughter of the Queen of England. The question therefore must be considered settled and closed." Vicky would be married in England. Victoria, in her communications with Prussia, was indeed "absolutely frank and truthful," so very different from her husband. One can imagine Lord Palmerston applauding his sovereign's letter.

But in retaliation, negotiations with the Prussian royal family became acrimonious over the financial settlements for the young couple and the composition of the princess's household. Remembering his own friendlessness when first coming to England, Prince Albert wanted his daughter to have a few English women around her in her new country, but the Prussian court refused point blank. Vicky's household would be chosen for her from members of the Prussian aristocracy. As a concession, the group included two young married women her own age.

To Prince Albert's dismay and Queen Victoria's fury, the crazy old king, at the behest of his childless German wife who hated the English, barely increased his nephew's meager allowance. He refused to confer a "morning gift" on the Princess Royal—the rich settlement traditionally made on a Prussian royal bride the day after the consummation of her marriage. This meant that although the Prussian state would pay for all living expenses, the new ménage would have very little discretionary income. As the royal Hohenzollern brothers saw it, in Berlin and Potsdam the English princess would find a luxury that put Windsor Castle to shame. However, she must find the money for such things as clothes, furnishings, books, and travel. How could this be a hardship, since she came from a rich nation and had a rich mother known for her generosity? "I resent bitterly the conduct of the Prussian Court and Government," Queen Victoria wrote in her journal, "and do not like the idea of our child going to Berlin, more or less the enemy's den."

Parliament gave the Princess Royal a dowry of forty thousand pounds and an annual income for life of eight thousand pounds. This was less than her mother had hoped for but still a generous provision and a much-appreciated expression of affection. Throughout her marriage, Vicky and her husband relied on her English parliamentary stipend over which she exercised independent control. Against strong Prussian resistance, Prince Albert insisted that his daughter should have a private secretary of her choice to administer her personal fortune and conduct her private affairs. When Baron Stockmar's son Ernest, known as "the young baron," was chosen for the post, even Fritz protested, claiming (quite correctly) that Ernest Stockmar would be regarded in Berlin as a "secret political agent." Prince Albert wrote back reprovingly to his future son-in-law: "It is not in either of your interests . . . to placate enemies who desire both the political and social failure of the marriage. It is rather your duty to fight for its success in spite of them."

The wedding, to be held at the Chapel Royal in London, was scheduled for January 25, 1858. As the day approached, Queen Victoria was increasingly filled with foreboding. She had taken to referring to her daughter as "poor, dear Vicky." She understood the weight of political hopes that Prince Albert placed on their daughter's young shoulders and feared they would be too much. The Queen could easily imagine the problems that would face a foreign teenage girl at the Prussian court. She knew that her daughter was marrying into a family that was even more hostile and divided than the one she herself had known as a child.

Vicky's youth and innocence had begun to trouble her mother. The Queen saw Fritz's passion and her daughter's ardent response and foresaw the consequences. Politics and history had been explained to the girl, but not how kisses translated into babies. Victoria herself had enjoyed three years of freedom before marriage and had felt rage and regret when she became pregnant for the first time at twenty. Vicky would go to the altar at the age of seventeen and two months, and if she had her father's brain, she had her mother's body. After seventeen years as a wife, Queen Victoria was beginning to see marriage as a lottery that only a handful of women could win.

The night before her daughter's wedding, Victoria broke down in tears. "It is like taking a poor lamb to be sacrificed," she told her husband. Albert refused to yield to his wife's emotion. "Vicky is very reasonable," he declared. "She will go well prepared into the labyrinth of Berlin." When Vicky came to her mother's rooms the next morning to have her hair done and put on her wedding dress, emotion ran very high. In a famous daguerreotype of the Queen, the prince, and their daughter Vicky on the day of her wedding, the bride and her father look serious but composed, but Queen Victoria is a blur. She was too upset to stay still for the photographer.

The wedding was a magnificent affair. Royal persons were stuffed into every corner at Windsor, and the display of gifts to the bride evoked great admiration. They included diamond, sapphire, emerald, and ruby sets from her parents, siblings, and the king and queen of Prussia, a fabulous rope of thirty-six pearls from Prince William and Princess Augusta, and some Brussels lace from her great-uncle Leopold. The Prussian royal family was anxious to impress the world with the opulence of its gifts, even as it planned to keep the young couple very short of money. King Leopold, who, with her father, was to walk the bride down the aisle, was willing to look stingy. Vicky gave her husband-to-be an emerald ring exactly like the one her mother had given her father when they were married and which he always wore on his little finger.

For two days at Windsor, the newlyweds were allowed to be alone and found ecstasy in each other's arms. On the morning after the wedding, they were observed skating on the pond like two carefree children. Then their combined families arrived for more celebrations, and Queen Victoria tried to get accustomed to the sight of her daughter happily taking her husband's arm and walking up to bed with him every night. When the time came for the couple to leave on February 1, the English royal family dissolved in a flood of tears. Vicky presented her mother with a brooch containing a lock of her hair. On her knees, she thanked her parents for their love and care and swore to be a worthy daughter.

Escorting his daughter to her stateroom on the royal yacht at Gravesend, Prince Albert was able to maintain a semblance of calm to the end. But the next day, he wrote to his daughter: "My heart was very full when yesterday you leaned your forehead on my breast to give free vent to your tears. I am not of a demonstrative nature and therefore you can hardly know how dear you have always been to me, and what a void you have left in my heart; yet not in my heart, for there assuredly you will abide henceforth, as till now you have done, but in my daily life, which is evermore reminding my heart of your absence."

Father and Son

I
N MAY 1856, QUEEN VICTORIA DECIDED THAT THE VEXING ISSUE OF
her husband's rank and title must be addressed. After fifteen years of marriage, Albert still had no English title. At the time of their wedding, much to
the fury of her English uncles, the Queen had issued letters patent giving
her husband precedence after her own in Great Britain and Ireland. However, once Albert stepped ashore in Europe, he was again a mere prince of
Coburg, forced to bring up the rear at private and public events and to sit
humiliatingly far away from his wife at dinner unless the ruler of the country took pity on him.

Victoria drew up a memorandum of intent and submitted it to Prime Minister Lord Palmerston. Her words were plain and heartfelt. "It is a strange
omission in our Constitution that while the wife of a King has the highest rank
and dignity in the realm after her husband assigned to her by law, the husband
of a Queen regnant is entirely ignored by the law. This is the more extraordinary, as a husband has in this country such particular rights and such great
power over his wife, and as the Queen is married just as any other woman is,
and swears to obey her lord and master . . . Therefore . . . I have come to the
conclusion that the title which is now by universal consent given him of
'Prince Consort,' with the highest rank in and out of Parliament immediately
after the Queen, and before every other Prince of the Royal Family, should be
assigned to the husband of the Queen regnant once and for all. This ought to
be done before our children grow up, and it seems peculiarly easy to do so now
that none of the old branches of the Royal family are still alive."

In June 1856, the Queen asked Lord Palmerston to discuss her memorandum with his ministerial colleagues, and a "Prince Consort Bill" was

drafted in cabinet. However, in March 1857, Palmerston was obliged to tell Her Majesty that, acting on legal advice, he could not bring the bill forward. The Queen was making claims based on her particular circumstances for an act of parliament that would permanently define the constitutional status of consort to a queen regnant. Ministers declined to do this.

Reminded of the protests by the Queen's uncles fifteen years earlier, Palmerston and his cabinet colleagues were reluctant to grant Prince Albert higher precedence than the royal English princes who were his four sons. What if the Queen should die? For the rest of his life, Albert as prince consort could claim precedence over all his children and their wives, except for the new king and queen. If Albert remarried, he would confer his own precedence upon his second wife. This could not be.

Undeterred, Queen Victoria took legal counsel of her own and learned that she was again authorized to issue letters patent conferring the title of prince consort on her husband. In a letter he sent by special courier, Albert felt obliged to explain the decision to his brother, the head of the Coburg family. "Today I will write upon a topic which I never liked to let you know through the post. It is the title Victoria gave me and which has been announced. I am to have the title 'Prince Consort of the United Kingdom of Great Britain and Ireland.' This ought to have been done, as you thought yourself, at our wedding . . . What pressed the question is the fact that our children, who are all princes of the country and of the house, are growing up. If their father is not a prince of the country, wicked people might later on succeed in bringing up the Prince of Wales against his father, and tell him he should not allow a foreign prince to take a place before him." Protectively Albert asserted that Victoria's position, especially when she went abroad, would be "precarious" as long as her husband "with his lower German title, pretended to have the right of a high English one, one which the Queen could not give him in Germany and which the German courts would not acknowledge. An English Prince has rights as such, and nobody can refuse to acknowledge them; nowhere in Europe."

Why had it become imperative in 1856 for the royal couple to resolve the issue of Albert's title both at home and abroad? One reason was quite obvious. Vicky's marriage to Prince Frederick William of Prussia was already scheduled for early 1858, and a regular exchange of visits with the Prussian royal family would surely ensue. Victoria and Albert had learned in 1845 that a king of Prussia—unlike a friendly emperor of France or an avuncular king of the Belgians—could not be counted on to give Prince Albert precedence in Prussia as a sign of courtesy to the visiting Queen of England.

The other reason was more murky and contentious. If Queen Victoria died in 1856, her husband would become regent for their son. But once the Prince of Wales turned eighteen on November 8, 1859, he would be of age to succeed his mother in the event of her death or of becoming regent if she were found incompetent to rule. Even if the Queen lived on, in 1862 the Prince of Wales would come of age and be entitled to demand precedence immediately after his mother—not only for himself but for his wife, his three brothers, even his five sisters. The idea of Prince Albert crowded out on state occasions, trailing into meals behind his sons and daughters and their spouses, and snubbed by the Prussians was not to be borne. Queen Victoria could do nothing about the succession, but she could at least "give" her husband the highest rank next to the reigning monarch for his lifetime.

For a proud man like Albert, it had always been humiliating to receive such gifts from his wife. But he saw no alternative. Bertie was an affectionate boy, but he could not be trusted to do the right thing by his father. It was all too possible, as the prince admitted to his brother, that "wicked people might . . . succeed in bringing up the Prince of Wales against his father."

It was no secret in the family or at court that neither Queen Victoria nor Prince Albert liked their eldest son very much. They loved him of course— that was a parent's duty—but they could not approve of him. They had no confidence in him. The thought of him on the throne gave them nightmares.

■

HISTORY RECORDS THAT KINGS and their heirs apparent are often bitterly at odds. Shakespeare in *Henry IV* makes sowing wild oats seem an excellent way for young Prince Hal to prepare for kingship, but Hal's father, King Henry IV, clearly did not see it that way. The first three Hanoverian kings were notoriously unable to stand the company of their eldest sons. Queen Victoria followed in the sad old pattern, since, according to her own account, her problems with her son and heir Bertie began at his birth. The prince consort's relations with Bertie began to go seriously wrong when the Prince of Wales was ten.

Part of the problem was Vicky, Bertie's older sister by a single year. The birth of Victoria, Princess Royal, was initially a disappointment to her parents, but even as a very small baby Vicky was remarkable. Before she was one, she had managed to secure her father's interest and affection. His eldest child, the prince felt, was like himself. She was precocious, she did the wonderful things that, reportedly, he himself had done as a little child.

Within months of her first confinement, the Queen was again pregnant

and extremely unhappy about it. The second confinement was far more difficult and painful, but at least the child was male. The Queen later remembered the doctors telling her that things could easily have taken a very bad
turn when Bertie was born, and it took her many weeks to recover. Separated from birth, mother and son failed to bond, but the mother had all too
much time to think and plan. A few weeks after the Prince of Wales's birth,
Victoria wrote to her uncle Leopold: "I have been suffering so from lowness
that it made me quite miserable, and I know how hard it is to fight against
it. I wonder very much who our little boy will be like. You will understand
how fervent my prayers and I am [sure] everybody's must be, to see him re-
semble his angelic dearest Father in every, every, respect. Both in body and
mind." Two years later, even more ominously, the Queen wrote: "I wish that
[the Prince of Wales] should grow up entirely under *his Father's eye* and
every step be guided by him, that when he has attained the age of sixteen or
seventeen he may be a real companion to his father."

Victoria had wanted and needed a son, and the pain and depression the
birth of the Prince of Wales caused her would have been forgiven if he had
proved to be as remarkable as his elder sister. But he was not. He was merely
a normal boy. He walked and talked later than his sister, and he had a
speech impediment. Before his second birthday, he was already being described as slow and stupid. Vicky could run rings around him. As he got
older, it became plain even to those who loved him that the Prince of Wales
was unable or unwilling to become what his father and mother had set their
hearts on: a youthful replica of his father and thus an angel.

Instead Bertie turned out to be what Stockmar ungraciously called an
"exaggerated copy" of his mother. By this the baron meant that Bertie was
a Guelph, not a Coburg, cast in the idle, sybaritic, profligate mold of the sons
of George III. That Queen Victoria was as much a Coburg as Prince Albert,
that the Prince of Wales's Saxe-Coburg uncle, grandfather, and great-
grandfather were also idle, sybaritic, and profligate was something Stockmar chose to forget.

Bertie was a large, fat, beautiful baby, but it soon became plain that he
was physically much more like his mother than his father. His receding chin
and blue saucer eyes were seen as Hanoverian, but the Hanoverian males
were at least tall and imposing. Bertie was unusually small and delicately
made. He matured late. Even as a late teenager, it would have been easy for
him to pass as a girl. Bertie's appearance alone predisposed his mother
against him. Queen Victoria placed extreme importance on the beauty and
height she herself lacked, and she took ugliness in her children as a personal insult. Legs, the Queen felt, were the great physical defect in Coburg

males (with the exception of Albert, of course!), and as a little boy, Bertie had legs that satisfied her. But by the time he was ten, the Queen was lamenting how horridly knock-kneed he looked in court breeches. When Bertie was seventeen, Queen Victoria confessed to her daughter Vicky: "Handsome I cannot think him with that painfully small and narrow head, those immense features, and total want of a chin." In 1861 she found him somewhat improved: In a colonel's uniform at a military parade, the Prince of Wales did not look "at all so very small." Damning her children with faint praise was one of Queen Victoria's specialties in letters to family.

Both Vicky and Bertie were as little children willful and temperamental, hard to discipline. Both were subjected to physical punishment almost as soon as they could walk. Vicky, before she turned five, was largely cured of her temper tantrums when Miss Sarah Hildyard was hired to start the princess's formal education. Vicky, who taught herself to read at age four, had been bored in the nursery, her parents concluded. Miss Hildyard was a remarkable woman who managed to satisfy two exceptionally exigent parents and to win the confidence of her precocious charge. She made her job her life and was a reliable and beloved influence on the oldest princesses until their marriages.

Bertie, by contrast, got more difficult when the lessons started. Food and nice clothes, not the alphabet and sums, interested the little prince. Fed, according to his father's instructions, on meager rations of bread and milk with almost no meat, he was always hungry. The cold baths and open bedroom windows his mother thought salutary did not suit him. Told of the poor little children who lived on crusts in ice-cold tenements, he was unmollified.

Bertie was often a bad boy, but he loved Lady Lyttelton, the superintendent of the royal nurseries, affectionately known by her charges as Laddle. She in turn adored the Prince of Wales, finding him unusually affectionate, loyal, and truthful. Of all the royal children, he was her favorite. As far as possible, Lady Lyttelton downplayed Bertie's naughtiness in her daily reports to the Queen and the prince. When Vicky raged that Bertie had spoiled her game or Alice cried because Bertie pulled her hair, they got little sympathy from their governess. Such was life for most sisters in Victorian nurseries. But even indulgent Lady Lyttelton had to admit failure when it came to teaching the four-year-old Bertie his letters. By the time Bertie was five, his little sister Alice was taller and more advanced than he.

Miss Hildyard taught the Prince of Wales to read and write at a perfectly normal age, and the little boy, for all his pronunciation problems, spoke three languages fluently. But Prince Albert was not satisfied with his son's academic progress or his behavior. Albert had no confidence in women. He wrote to his own old tutor Christoph Florschütz: "The education of six such different children . . . is a difficult task. They are a great deal with their parents and are very fond of them. I don't interfere in the details of their upbringing, but only superintend the principles, which are difficult to uphold in the face of so many women and I give the final judgment. From my verdict there is no appeal." This last statement at least was quite true.

By the age of seven, Bertie was a disruptive influence in the schoolroom, resistant to learning, and responding to mild reproof and punishment by lashing out at his sisters or even his teachers. Watching the Prince of Wales in one of these "fits," the astonished Baron Stockmar decreed that the boy should never be left alone with one of his siblings.

A firm male hand and a serious program of study were clearly needed, and Prince Albert hired Henry Birch as preceptor to head up a team of tutors. Both he and Baron Stockmar intended to monitor the Prince of Wales's progress minutely. Vicky loved the baron. Bertie did not.

Birch was a young gentleman of exemplary reputation who had enjoyed brilliant academic success at King's College, Cambridge, and gone on to become a junior master at Eton. He was heir to a fortune and had taken Holy Orders, since a rich family living was being held for him. Birch did not especially need the eight hundred pounds in salary Prince Albert offered, and he was taken by surprise to discover that the prince and the Queen expected him to give all his time unreservedly to his young charge. They, in turn, were surprised by his protests: Lehzen and Florschütz a generation before had never found it necessary to take a holiday or have friends outside the palace. Birch protested his lack of freedom in vain to Baron Stockmar, but he had contracted with Prince Albert to stay until January 1852 and was a man of his word.

At first Bertie was extremely resistant to the new educational regime. He had disobeyed dear Laddle, given Miss Hildyard a hard time, and made his sisters cry, but now he missed them all. Suddenly he found himself doing five or six hours of study every day, six days a week—even when at Osborne and Balmoral—one-on-one with Mr. Birch or another master. Prince Albert insisted that his son should be so tired at the end of every day that he would fall asleep immediately. Therefore when the lessons were over, Bertie was sent off for hours of physical exercise: riding, nature walks, calisthenics, again on his own. In his leisure time, he was expected to keep a diary detailing the events of his day for his parents and his tutor to read.

Such a schedule was a stiff challenge to the preceptor as well as the boy, but little by little Birch made it work. Despite his name, he was a gifted, caring teacher and an attractive, interesting young man. He saw that his young pupil was extremely sensitive to criticism and could not bear to be "chaffed." He saw that the boy was lonely, so he suggested to Prince Albert that the younger son, Alfred, a more obedient and studious child, should be included in the lessons. After a year or so, Bertie decided that he could trust Birch and opened up. "I seem," Birch told Baron Stockmar, "to have found the key to his heart." Though Bertie was considered too backward to start Latin until he was ten, he began to be more tractable, make progress with his lessons, and to receive praise.

Given the exceptionally close and long-term affection he supposedly enjoyed with his own tutor as a boy, Prince Albert might have been expected to rejoice at the warm relationship developing between his ten-year-old son and Mr. Birch. But he was not. Bertie, though deeply affectionate, was, in his father's eyes, still distressingly idle, superficial, sensual, and rebellious. The boy had developed a crush—what the Germans called a *Schwarm*—for the tutor, and Birch was beginning to express his opinions as if he were in charge of the boy's education. Though Birch offered to extend his contract beyond the January 1852 deadline, Prince Albert refused. He had already found a new tutor far more to his taste.

Birch was not unhappy to shake the dust of Windsor Castle off his feet, but in his final report he did his best for his pupil. He was realistic about the Prince of Wales's faults of conduct and academic limitations, but he insisted that the boy's principal problem was that he was always with adults and "deprived of all normal society with other boys." Eton, Birch opined, would do Bertie good. Other men charged with teaching the Prince of Wales dared to observe in their reports to the prince that the boy was under unremitting pressure to perform in the classroom and frequently so exhausted that he could not think straight. Perhaps, just perhaps, what he needed was less pressure?

Prince Albert thanked the gentlemen for their contributions, but he knew they were wrong. He had no faith at all in the English public schools, where masters, not parents, held sway, and young boys often came under the evil influence of older boys. He was sure that the Prince of Wales needed to remain safe within his family circle if he were to fulfill his royal destiny. Bertie's persistent academic slowness and continuing discipline problems could be solved by more structure and longer hours.

Prince Albert found the man willing to carry out his educational precepts to the letter in Frederick Weymouth Gibbs. Gibbs came of humble, dissenter (non–Church of England) stock. Orphaned as a child, he had been brought up by Sir James Stephens, regius professor of history at Cambridge

University. Gibbs read law at Cambridge, did very well, and was made a fellow of Trinity College. He was then called to the bar but did not succeed in his new profession. Sir James warmly recommended his adopted son to Prince Albert. Gibbs, he wrote, was "exempt from reproach," a model of "Truth, Honour, Sobriety, and Chastity who . . . never quailed before the face of any human being." Stephens admitted that his protégé was "self-confident and has a strength of will which occasionally degenerates into obstinacy."

Austere, scholarly, self-righteous, devoid of charm, Gibbs was almost a caricature of his employer. He was also a poor man with his way to make in life. To be head preceptor to the Prince of Wales was a golden opportunity, especially since the salary had been raised to one thousand pounds a year. Gibbs had no intention of being dismissed after two years like Birch. He aspired be the second Florschütz, companion to a prince until he left the university, and winning his lifelong devotion and gratitude.

Gibbs handled the royal parents and Baron Stockmar far more astutely than Birch had. He was not a man of the cloth and, unlike Birch, could not be suspected of the high church sympathies that the Queen disliked. He enlisted Stockmar's unconditional support. The baron's historical anecdotes and words of wisdom were reverently entered in Gibbs's diary. With his employer and supervisor, Prince Albert, Gibbs claimed to see eye to eye on all points. Bertie must be made to attend and learn out of respect and duty, not boyish admiration. The Prince of Wales's hours of schooling must be increased from six to seven every day. The treadmill must be set to run faster and longer.

Gibbs had every incentive to produce some striking results in the classroom. He was not a cruel or stupid man, and he did his best. But the relationship between teacher and student was doomed from the start. Gibbs—unlike Lehzen and Birch—gave his allegiance to the father, not to the son. For a handsome salary and future expectations, Gibbs undertook to implement an educational regimen that his pupil found overwhelming and humiliating. Gibbs was confident that, in a battle of wills with a ten-year-old boy, he would win. He was proved wrong.

Bertie had showed from the outset that he had no taste for book learning and would learn only from those he loved, on his own terms. He was deeply affected by the departure of Mr. Birch. It seemed that every adult he liked and trusted was taken away from him. He did not like Gibbs at the start, and he soon learned to hate him. As he would amply prove in adult life, the Prince of Wales was far from stupid or incompetent, and he had prodigious energy for things he liked. But as a child, refusing to compete with his sisters, unable to express any of his resentments to his distant mother or his sainted father, he alternated between apathy and rage.

The preeminent fact for Bertie from birth was that he was the Prince of Wales, heir apparent. This had not been true for his mother. He was also male in a culture where mere maleness counted. Humility and consideration for others were virtues preached to the Prince of Wales every day, but they did not take. Protocol ruled even in the palace nursery. Every governess, tutor, servant, and courtier the Prince of Wales met made it clear that he, not his smarty-pants sister Vicky or goody-two-shoes little brother Affie, was the child who counted. On the rare occasions that Bertie appeared in public, walking by his mother's side, holding her hand as if he did so every day, he was almost mobbed. He loved London, the court, parties, excitement, people, being the center of attention.

Back in the classroom, he was the dunce. The loneliness, sensual deprivation, and constant grind of his life were incomprehensible to him. He hated to feel stupid, he hated to be told what to do. He missed his sisters. He wanted friends. All the fury and frustration that Bertie felt about his treatment at the hands of his "angelic dearest Father" and could not express were directed toward the new preceptor.

When asked to do something he did not like, which was most days, the Prince of Wales dug in his heels. When coerced, he erupted in frightening rages and became mildly psychopathic, screaming, biting, spitting, kicking, and tearing up his books. It sometimes took two people to restrain him. He developed a passion for sticks and riding crops, swinging them alarmingly at his siblings and attendants. Knives and scissors had to be carefully kept away from him. He would deliberately get dirt on the servants' uniforms, and once he spilled ink on a dress that a maid had laid out on her bed in preparation for her wedding.

Life for the young Prince of Wales was not all lessons and lectures. His lot was, in fact, easy by the standards of the day. Life at an English public school was far from a lark, and occasionally boys of England's oldest families died of neglect at public school. Tens of thousands of boys working in the mines and brickworks and chimneys of England died before they were eighteen. Royal family life could be warm and affectionate, especially at Christmas and birthdays, and there was far more active intergenerational play than in most families at the time. Prince Albert taught his sons to swim, skate, and shoot, all sports at which he excelled and which they enjoyed. The boys played ice hockey in winter and sailed in summer. They were put on the back of a pony as soon as they could waddle and became expert and enthusiastic riders. There were excursions along the seashore at Osborne, expeditions straight uphill at Balmoral, and hunts at Windsor.

But for Bertie, family life and the company of his brothers and sisters—with whom he was never permitted to be alone—were not enough. The lectures and fact-finding tours that his father specialized in bored him. When he had nothing to say about them in his diary, he was condemned for being dull and stupid. He longed for friends, but even when boys were sent up to Windsor Castle from nearby Eton to play with him and Affie, their father always hovered, watching for who knew what, ready to intervene. The reaction of both princes to such obsessive supervision was to behave like louts, confident that the other boys would not dare resist or fight back. When Affie started to behave as badly as Bertie, the two boys were again separated, and Affie was given his own establishment at Royal Lodge on the grounds of Windsor Castle. The Prince of Wales was bereft.

In comparison with his own father, Prince Albert was a loving and caring parent. He tried always to be there for his children, and he listened to them more carefully and indulgently than their mother. Child abuse by servants was endemic in great Victorian nurseries, but there is no report that any servant abused the prince's children. Lady Lyttelton, who adored the prince consort, found him unusually affectionate and understanding. What other father would rock a baby in his arms, demonstrate to a toddler how to turn somersaults, or stoop down to tie up a small daughter's shoe? Albert's eldest daughters, Vicky and Alice, who, like their brothers, were taught to swim, skate, and ride by their father and received an unusually good education, adored him unconditionally to the end of their lives.

Albert, like many parents, made the mistake of giving his children what he liked, or remembered liking, as a child, and then censuring them if they were unhappy and ungrateful. And he had one obsession not shared by many fathers: He was determined that his sons, especially his oldest son, should be great men, and in his view, sexual purity was the prerequisite for true greatness. This was the code that the prince consort lived by, and it made his relationship with the Prince of Wales increasingly difficult as the boy reached adolescence.

*

WHEN BERTIE TURNED sixteen, he was confirmed and, though not yet of age, officially ceased to be a child. The prince consort was now on high alert. Since Bertie, unlike his "angelic dearest Father," was observably open to the temptations of the flesh, he had to be kept out of the company not just of women but of unworthy young men. It was only when Bertie approached his seventeenth birthday and pronounced himself puzzled by certain things that Gibbs was authorized to explain to him "the purpose and abuse of the union of the sexes."

Bertie was allowed to undertake some walking trips with four carefully selected Etonians his own age. Despite Gibbs, who never left them alone, the youths managed to have fun. Heavily supervised, Bertie visited his sister in Berlin and his uncle in Coburg. He went to Italy, where he saw the new Pope, and Austria, where he met the legendary Austrian statesman Count Clemens Metternich. People abroad found Bertie charming.

Prince Albert gave his son a rather meager allowance and his own residence at Windsor. He handpicked a few young aristocratic men of exemplary morals to be the members of the Prince of Wales's household. Lord Valletort was chosen not only because he was moral and accomplished but because "he never was at public school, but passed his youth in attendance on an invalid father."

The prince consort wrote a memorandum detailing the manner of life he expected to see followed at his son's house: no silly humor, no gambling, no billiards, no lolling in chairs or on sofas, no practical jokes. In his leisure, the Prince of Wales should devote himself to "music, to the fine arts, either drawing, or looking over drawings, engravings, etc., to hearing poetry . . . or good plays read aloud." The Queen and her beloved doctor Sir James Clark, perhaps finding the Prince of Wales to be gaining in weight, devised a diet low in red meat and red wine, strong on seltzer water.

The young men of the household were expected to report on the Prince of Wales to his father, but they rallied to his side against Gibbs. Apparently, instead of bullying his peers as he had as a boy, Bertie was now using his charm and status to win them over. Colonel Lindsay, one of the equerries, wrote to the prince consort: "Mr. Gibbs has *no* influence. He and the Prince are so much out of sympathy with one another that a wish expressed by Mr. Gibbs is sure to meet with opposition on the part of the Prince . . . I confess I quite understand the Prince's feelings towards Mr. Gibbs, for tho' I respect his uprightness and devotion, I could not give him sympathy, confidence or friendship." Gibbs was dismissed when the Prince of Wales turned seventeen.

Queen Victoria reported to Vicky on November 10, 1858: "Bertie vexes us much. There is not a particle of reflection, or even attention to anything but dress! Not the slightest desire to learn, on the contrary, il se bouche les oreilles [he stops up his ears], the moment anything of interest is talked of . . . Poor Mr. Gibbs certainly failed during the last 2 years entirely, incredibly." Colonel Bruce, a stern, straitlaced military man, took over the supervision of the Prince of Wales's life. The Queen and the prince promoted the colonel to general and hoped that he would prove more successful than his predecessor.

Bertie's great wish was to pursue an army career, but his parents dismissed this idea offhand. They conceded that as a kind of reward, he would be made an officer and allowed to do some military training, but that was all. His father intended him to complete an intensive course of studies at the great universities that would properly prepare him for his life as king. Science and technology, the prince consort decreed, were to form an important part of the prince's studies. In his spare time, the Prince of Wales was instructed to tour mines and factories. When he could find time in his increasingly busy schedule, the prince consort himself would instruct his eldest son in European history and political theory.

First the Prince of Wales was sent to Edinburgh to cram under the great chemist (then) Sir Lyon Playfair, who reported that the prince showed interest and ability. Next Bertie was sent to Oxford. The prince consort was forced by university regulations to enroll his son in a college, but he refused to allow him to live in college or to attend lectures with other young men. He installed the Prince of Wales and his large entourage in a house in town. In the evenings, when not hitting the books, Bertie was instructed to entertain elderly academics at dinner. Hearing that Bertie was still managing to make some disreputable friends among the Oxford fast set, the prince consort was indignant. "The only use for Oxford is that it is a place for study, a refuge from the world and its claims," he wrote memorably to his son. Queen Victoria, who found Oxford a horrid, boring place, was inclined to see Bertie's point of view.

Once the Prince of Wales began to make solo public appearances, the ugly duckling was discovered to be a swan. Charming and engaged, a deft conversationalist, Bertie remembered everyone's name and seemed fascinated by everyone he met. He loved to dance, which pleased the ladies, and he was a keen and skilled shot, which pleased the men. His large appetite for food and wine coincided very well with the mores of the English upper classes in that supremely gastronomic era. Society people noticed approvingly that, except for the way he pronounced his r's, he was not at all like his father. The Prince of Wales's incomplete grasp of classical languages and engineering was not held against him.

Bertie, like his mother as a teenager, proved perfectly at ease on ceremonial occasions, and in the summer of 1860 his parents sent him on a state visit to Canada. This was followed by a private visit to the United States at the invitation of President James Buchanan. The Prince of Wales was a sensation in North America, on one occasion volunteering to be wheeled across the Niagara Falls on a tight rope in a wheelbarrow. He shook hands with democratic abandon, and danced every dance at balls—to the despair of his elderly handlers, who were keen to get to bed. His marked attentions to Miss B. of Natchez and Miss G. of Cincinnati did not go unreported. "His Royal Highness looks as if he might have a very susceptible nature, and has already yielded to several twinges in the region of his midriff," reported the *New York Herald* enigmatically. Apart from his successes at the dinners and balls, the Prince of Wales was also given the highest marks for diplomatic tact and presence of mind by foreign secretary the Duke of Newcastle, who was a member of the prince's party.

Queen Victoria was delighted with her son's success, noting to Vicky that he deserved plaudits, since he was so often criticized. Prince Albert, who rarely got mobbed by enthusiastic admirers or received rave reviews in the foreign press, wrote sternly to his son that he should not take his success in the New World as a testament to his own merit. All the adulation had been laid upon him as the representative of his august mother.

Bertie's susceptibility to the charms of pretty girls had not gone unnoticed by his family. One of the first things that the Princess Royal was asked by her mother to do when she moved to Germany in February 1858 was to find a suitable princess for Bertie to marry. Bertie was then sixteen, but both his parents were convinced that he must marry young, perhaps even younger than his father. The prospective bride must, for reasons of politics and family tradition, be a Protestant German princess. She must be very well brought up, very sensible, and very self-possessed to please her future in-laws. She must be very attractive to win and, it was hoped, keep the affections of her husband.

But, though poor busy, harassed, pregnant Vicky pored over the *Almanach de Gotha* and even visited freezing castles to interview teenage girls, she could find no eligible German princess. The only known beauties in the right age group were Alexandra and Dagmar, the older daughters of Prince Christian of Schleswig-Holstein-Sonderburg-Glücksburg—the heir presumptive to the failing king of Denmark—and of his wife, Princess Louise, originally of Hesse-Kassel.

For some time, Victoria and Albert were convinced that a match between the Prince of Wales and a Danish princess was out of the question. Prussia and Denmark were on the brink of war over the duchies of Schleswig and Holstein, Prince Christian's ancestral estates. For the heir to the British throne to marry this prince's daughter would be perceived as a massive insult by Prussia. Vicky's position at the Prussian court, already so difficult, would be severely compromised if she were even rumored to be seeking a Danish sister-in-law. Queen Victoria had also heard unpleasant rumors that Princess Louise, a sister of her aunt-in-law the Duchess of Cambridge, was not at all comme il faut. Queen Victoria, it may be recalled, was seriously on the outs with the women of the Cambridge family.

But the young German princesses did not improve with age and, while he seemed happy to obey his parents and marry, Bertie declared that he would marry only for love. Since this was the family tradition established by Victoria and Albert and continued by Vicky and Fritz, Bertie was on solid ground here. The reports from Copenhagen were increasingly glowing. On behalf of her parents, Vicky met with Alexandra and wasted no time in sending a rave review to her mother. "It is very difficult to be impartial when one is captivated, and I own I never was more so—I never set eyes on a sweeter creature than Princess Alix. She is lovely! . . . She is a good deal taller than I am, has a lovely figure but very thin, a complexion as beautiful as possible . . . Her voice, her walk, carriage and manners are perfect . . ." And so on for three pages.

When Prince Albert was shown a portrait of Princess Alexandra, he remarked, rather unexpectedly, that if he were a young man, he would fall in love with her. When reports came in that the Russian court had also sent for Princess Alexandra's portrait as a possible bride for the tsarevitch, the prince consort decided that there was not a moment to lose.

Bertie was now informed about Princess Alexandra, given her picture, and told by his father that all political reservations about her had been set aside. Would he consent to go to Germany to meet the young lady with a view to marriage? Bertie agreed, but without much enthusiasm. He no longer seemed keen on an early marriage. Nonetheless, in September 1861, the Prince of Wales set out for Germany, supposedly on military matters. He had spent his summer in Ireland at a military camp, learning to conduct drills, and he was now a colonel. Vicky, disregarding the implacable hatred of all things Danish that prevailed at the court of her parents-in-law, arranged a supposedly secret meeting between her brother and the Princess Alexandra at the cathedral at Speyer. This was close to Rumpenheim, the private estate of the Hesse-Kassel family near Frankfurt, where Alexandra and her parents spent their summers. No court in Europe was deceived.

The Prince of Wales's response to meeting Princess Alix for the first time, while courteous, was far less ecstatic than his sister's had been. He did, however, repair immediately to Balmoral to give his parents an account of the meeting, whence Queen Victoria reported to her daughter in Prussia.

"Bertie is certainly much pleased with her [Alexandra]," wrote the Queen, "but as for being in love I don't think he can be, or that he is capable of enthusiasm about anything in the world." This depressed the Princess Royal. Usually a loyal defender of her oldest brother, Vicky wrote to their mother: "I own it gives me a feeling of great sadness when I think that sweet lovely flower—young and beautiful—that makes my heart beat when I look at her—which would make most men fire and flames—not even producing an impression enough to last from Baden to England."

Despite the Prince of Wales's lukewarm response to Princess Alix's charms, the marriage was assumed to be on. Both sets of parents were in agreement. An actual proposal was being planned. Prince Albert, who would maintain control of his son's private income and his revenues under the civil list until November 9, had managed to find time to locate a country property for the newlyweds. He had 600,000 pounds of his son's money in hand and planned to spend it on the acquisition of Sandringham, a large estate in a windswept, isolated part of Norfolk. It would, in his view, suit Bertie and Alix admirably.

Neither the Queen and the prince in England nor their eldest daughter in Germany had heard the gossip that was making the rounds in the courts of Europe. The Prince of Wales had picked up a mistress in Ireland and had brought her back to England.

Problems in a Marriage

...

No SOONER HAD VICKY DRIVEN OFF WITH HER NEW HUSBAND TO take the boat from Gravesend than her mother discovered that she missed her extravagantly. This was something of a surprise to the Queen, the prince, and their daughter. Victoria had once cheerfully admitted to her friend the then Princess Augusta, Vicky's new Prussian mother-in-law, that she did not much enjoy her daughter's company and did not expect to miss her much once she married and moved away.

Victoria began to write to her daughter in Berlin every day, sometimes several times a day, and once the relationship between mother and daughter became largely epistolary, it blossomed. Ever since childhood, the Queen had been obliged to conduct many important relationships by letter. She had a deep and faithful love for members of her extended family—notably her half sister Feodora von Hohenlohe, her half brother Charles Leiningen, and her uncle Leopold—and she saw them whenever possible. But these people all settled abroad when the Queen was still a little girl, so their relationship was kept alive by the written word. As a girl, Victoria's letters had been subject to censorship. One of the great pleasures of her accession to the throne had been that she was at last free to write what she wanted to whom she pleased and to receive and keep all the letters written to her.

As queen, Victoria came to understand that even in her private correspondence, she needed to keep up a certain vigilance. On the continent of Europe, it was customary for the letters of important persons to be intercepted and opened before they were delivered. This meant that expensive private couriers were necessary if a member of the family had something confidential to impart. Even when exhausted and scribbling away late at night, Victoria always had to be aware that, in the short term, anything she wrote could get into the wrong hands, and, in the long term, might be quoted in the history books. Despite these constraints, she spent hours of every day on her private correspondence. Her style was plain and seemed artless, but she was a highly sophisticated and effective correspondent. She knew how to stamp her personality on the page and keep the flame of friendship burning.

The epistolary relationship between mother and daughter took a year or so to settle down. At first the Queen was bossy and annoying. She demanded to know every tiny detail of her daughter's new life, and she got cross when the details were not forthcoming. "I wish you for the future to adopt a plan of beginning your letters with the following sort of headings," wrote Victoria three weeks after her daughter had sailed from England. "Yesterday—or the day before, we did so and so; dined here or there and then where you spent the evening. If once you omit for days what you do— I shall be quite at sea—and it makes me sad, and feel the separation painfully. You must promise me, my dearest . . . This won't give you any trouble."

There was a week in April of the first year in which the Queen wrote some very personal letters to her daughter and heard nothing in reply. She became frantic and reproached Vicky harshly. She reported that rumors were going around the European capitals that both she and her daughter were pregnant, and begged Vicky to deny the rumors as she did. Queen Victoria was being selfish, and a male rebuke was not long in coming—not from Vicky's husband but her own. Prince Albert earnestly chastised his wife for asking Vicky to spend so much time writing to her and for criticizing Vicky so unjustly. At once, the Queen was all contrition. "Never, pray, fatigue yourself writing to me—pray don't. I dare not tell papa that I did scold you, for he always fears you exhaust yourself writing to me."

It turned out that the princess had replied to her mother but that her letters had been delayed. Vicky had discovered that all her English correspondence was being opened by the spies her new Prussian in-laws had appointed to her household, so she was forced to arrange for letters to be routed via the network of couriers run by the Rothschild banking house. All the same, Queen Victoria had been right to suspect something important was up in Berlin. The rumor that Vicky was pregnant was true. The princess was anxious to hide her condition from her mother until it was absolutely confirmed, knowing that the Queen would be terribly upset.

When Prince Frederick William, Vicky's husband, wrote to inform his mother-in-law officially of the pregnancy, Queen Victoria replied instantly on May 26, declaring it "horrid news." She had wanted her daughter to have at least a year of happiness before entering what she called the shadow side of marriage. But Vicky's pregnancy was now a fact that had to be dealt with, and Victoria soon took a new approach. She wrote to Vicky in June: "I delight in the idea of being a grandmamma; to be that at 39 (DV) [deo volente, God willing] and to look and feel young is great fun, only I wish I could go through it for you, dear, and save you all the annoyance."

Gradually, as the correspondence continued, Victoria's letters revealed a woman Vicky as a girl had not known. The distant, disapproving mother whose hand must be ritually kissed and whose temper was uncertain metamorphosed into a down-to-earth, sentimental, limited, sharp-tongued but lovable mama who, by a trick of fate, found herself on a throne and was desperately in need of a good friend.

For her part, Vicky had realized within months of moving to Germany that her mother had not been wrong to weep at her wedding and call her a lamb for the slaughter. In her husband, Fritz, Vicky had indeed found the ideal lover and life companion. Theirs was to be one of the great tragic love affairs of the nineteenth century. But love was not enough for happiness, and Vicky's girlish confidence in having her way in Berlin was soon dispelled. Realizing her father's political blueprint was far harder than either of them had ever imagined in their delightful tutorials, surrounded by spies, disliked and distrusted by the members of her husband's family, finding an implacable enemy in Otto von Bismarck, Vicky too needed a friend who could fully enter into her situation and be trusted absolutely. She found that friend in her mother.

The turning point in the relationship between Victoria and her eldest daughter was the birth of Vicky's first child, Friedrich Wilhelm Viktor Albrecht von Hohenzollern, known to his family as Willy and to Englishmen in the First World War as Kaiser Bill. As the Queen told her daughter soon after the birth, "There is no longer anything between us I cannot touch with you, and a married daughter be she ever so young is at once on a par with her mother." When Vicky visited her family at Osborne in the summer of 1859, she was delighted to find that her mother now treated her like a sister and approved of everything she did. Queen Victoria openly admitted how "delightful, soothing, and satisfactory" she now found the "intercourse" with Vicky. "My heart requires sympathy," she wrote, and "the possibility of pouring out its feelings quite openly to one who will feel for & understand me." On her return to Berlin, Vicky wrote to her mother: "I never had a correspondence that I enjoyed so much because it is so natural and like thinking aloud." The Queen and her daughter became friends and allies for life.

As this relationship took hold in the first years of Vicky's marriage, both women saw it as complementary to the relationship that the princess had with her father. Both Victoria and Vicky saw themselves as chief worshippers at the shrine of Saint Albert. "I maintain Papa is unlike anyone who lives or ever lived or will live," wrote Victoria to her daughter. "Dear Papa has always been my oracle," Vicky replied. But the prince consort had not expected to compete with his wife for his favorite daughter's time and sympathy, and it was unnerving to see that now Victoria was pouring out the details of her private life not just in her journal but in letters to their daughter. For Albert, the growing closeness between his wife and his daughter was a threat not just to his own relationship with Vicky but to his dominance in the family.

Prince Albert had experienced his wife's powerful talent for putting herself on paper when they were engaged to be married, but he had not reckoned on its effect on their daughter. He knew that he himself lacked the same talent. In person, in the close family circle at Balmoral or Osborne, he could be funny and lighthearted and charming, the man his wife and daughters so loved. But he used the written word to instruct and inform, not beguile or confide. In the letters to his daughter that have been published, the prince all too often sounds boring and trite, more like a retired professor than a concerned young dad.

When Vicky moved to Berlin, Albert discovered just how essential she had been to his comfort. The prince's emotional need in adulthood was to re-create the symbiotic relationship he had enjoyed with his brother in their Coburg days. As boys, he and Ernest had been one soul in two bodies, or so he remembered. His relationship with his wife was not of this kind. He loved Victoria and was dedicated to her care. Her adoration was as necessary to him as the air he breathed. Together they had built a successful marriage. But Victoria was not like him. Albert did not think much of women in general, and even as a woman, Victoria did not meet his standards.

Thus, as his eldest daughter came into adulthood, the prince was overjoyed to find in her a soul mate and an ideal companion. Vicky was serious, brilliant, industrious, and submissive to his leadership, and, unlike Ernest, she was chaste as well as passionate. From the cradle, she had been peculiarly responsive to her father's mind. Vicky was his complement, formed in his image.

But now Vicky was gone forever. He himself had prepared, even hurried, her departure, thrusting her into the arms of a loving man who rightly expected to be first in her life. His daughter was dedicated to fulfilling his wishes and carrying out his policies in her new life. The Prussian alliance had proceeded exactly according to plan. But, ironically, he was now left with a gaping hole in his everyday existence that none of his sons, especially the eldest, seemed capable of filling. He was bereft, and there was no one to blame, no one even to mourn with now that Stockmar was gone. And life with Victoria was not getting any easier as she and Albert entered their forties.

WITHIN MONTHS OF the Princess Royal's departure for Berlin in February 1858, the Queen and the prince were quarreling over their ongoing correspondence with her and the visits to Germany that they planned. Albert got wind of Vicky's pregnancy before his wife, presumably via the Stockmars. Unlike Victoria, he could be counted on to welcome the news that a grandchild was expected. The prince consort at once planned a quick solo incognito trip to Germany in May to see his daughter. Victoria told Vicky that she had agreed to let her husband go "though you know how miserable and, from my isolated position, lost I am without my master." After Albert's return, the Queen told her daughter that during her husband's absence, she had kept so busy and was so determined not to "give way" that she did not miss him nearly as much as she had in 1844 or 1854. "I assure you dear that in Town and at Windsor I see very little of dear Papa very often, and often much less than you do Fritz—from the children, etc."

By July of the same year, Queen Victoria and Prince Albert were planning a joint visit to their daughter in Germany and quarrelling over who should go with them. Victoria wanted to take Alice and Helena along, but Albert categorically refused. He insisted that the younger girls would prevent them from giving Vicky their full attention. More probably, Prince Albert did not wish German princes to come flocking around his second daughter, who, with his permission, was already being courted by Prince Louis of Hesse-Darmstadt. Alice was beginning to express some hesitation about marriage, so the prince may also have decided against letting her see her older sister in the miseries of the first trimester. Writing of the disappointment that Vicky's younger sisters were feeling at being left behind, Queen Victoria commented that her husband was "very hard-hearted and a great tyrant on all such occasions."

Queen Victoria liked Louis of Hesse, a tall, blond, tongue-tied, and, reportedly, chaste young German who conformed to her ideas of male beauty and seemed to be good husband material. All the same, she was in two minds about Alice getting married. The Queen now regretted allowing Vicky to be married so young and blamed Prince Albert for hurrying the match. She was determined that Alice would be at least eighteen at her wedding and would not be sent into exile in Germany far away from her parents' protection. Timidly, and with little success, Victoria was starting to challenge her husband's absolute authority over the family and even his judgment. The question now became: Whose side would Vicky take, her mother's or her father's?

The prince continued to express disapproval of his wife's constant flow of letters to Berlin. "Papa says you write to me too much," Victoria wrote to Vicky. "He is sure you make yourself ill by it, and constantly declares (which I own offends me very much) that your writing to me at such length is the cause of *your often not writing fully to him* [my italics]." The Queen was at Balmoral, and, for once, bored and unhappy. Despite her express wishes, Prince Albert had insisted that their fifteen-year-old son Alfred (Affie) must go to sea and begin his career as a naval officer. "Papa is most cruel upon the subject," wrote Victoria to Vicky.

Vicky's personal secretary, "the young" Baron Ernest Stockmar, complained to his father that the princess was driven to desperation by her mother's constant complaints and requests for information. Ever the busybody, old Stockmar, of course, passed this news on to Prince Albert and asked him to intervene. On October 4, 1858, Queen Victoria wrote to her daughter: "If you knew how Papa scolds me for (as he says) making you write! And he goes further, he says that I write far too often to you, and that it would be much better if I wrote only once a week! . . . I think however that Papa is wrong and you do like to hear from home often. When you do write to Papa again just tell him what you feel and wish on that subject for I do assure you—Papa has snubbed me several times very sharply on the subject and when one writes in spite of fatigue and trouble to be told it bores the person to whom you write—it is rather too much."

Vicky, placed in the invidious position of adjudicating between her parents, assured her mother that she loved her letters, and, as the collection of her letters shows, she wrote back almost as frequently. As often as she could, the Princess Royal also engaged with her father in the weighty political and philosophical dialogue they both enjoyed. In the winter of 1860, she sent her father a full treatise on the Prussian constitution. "Papa is much pleased with your memorandum—which I shall certainly read," wrote Queen Victoria on December 16. "Papa paid you the compliment by quietly telling me (which I am sure is quite true) that I could not have written such a thing. What do you say to this?"

On the general subject of marriage and motherhood, Victoria in the letters to her daughter became increasingly cynical with the years. She recalled how miserable she had been having four babies in the first four years of her marriage. "One becomes so worn out and one's nerves so miserable." She refused Vicky's suggestion that pregnancy was a spiritual experience: "I really think those ladies who are always enceinte quite disgusting; it is more like a rabbit or guinea pig." She insisted that no man could really understand what women suffer and sacrifice when they bear children. "No father, no man can feel this! Papa never would enter into it at all. As in fact he seldom can in my very violent feelings."

After Vicky wrote in disgust that the Prussian men thought women mattered only if they were beautiful and produced heirs, the Queen replied: "That despising of our poor degraded sex . . . is a little in all clever men's natures; dear Papa even is not quite exempt though he would not admit it— but he laughs and sneers constantly at many of them and at their inevitable inconveniences, etc. Though he hates the want of affection, of due attention to and protection of them, says that all men who leave all home affairs—and the education of their children—to their wives, forget their first duties."

Weary of congratulating young ladies on their approaching nuptials, Victoria remarked: "The poor woman is bodily and morally the husband's slave. That always sticks in my throat. When I think of a merry happy free young girl—and look at the ailing, aching state a young wife is generally doomed to, which you can't deny is the penalty of marriage."

In the past, the Queen had often been very vocal about her discontents, but there is something different about her complaints after 1858. They could no longer be explained in terms of her pregnancies and postpartum depression. Victoria is not known to have conceived a child after the birth of Beatrice in April 1857, and the way she and the prince doted on Beatrice indicates they were pretty certain that she was their last child.

There were good reasons why the royal couple might have decided that nine was enough. The management of four princes and five princesses was increasingly onerous. Already expensive, the royal children would, when they came of age, pose a heavy financial burden on the family as well as the state. Even more important than money was the matter of Victoria's health and longevity. What if the next labor went wrong, and the Queen died? This fear haunted both the Queen and the prince. In November 1857, they gazed in horror at the beautiful corpse of their beloved first cousin Victoire de Nemours, who had suddenly collapsed and died after an apparently uneventful confinement. In January 1859, their daughter Vicky and her child almost died in childbirth. Here were eloquent reminders that every pregnancy was a risk to the mother's life. Furthermore, the Queen's violent mood swings and dramatic scenes when pregnant had set off warning bells at court. What if she were to fall into madness like her grandfather George III?

The English government was anxious for Victoria to remain on the throne for the foreseeable future. The Queen was immensely popular. Compared with most other ruling monarchs, she and her husband made an outstandingly effective team. As of November 9, 1859, the Prince of Wales would be of age to succeed, but he was clearly young for his age. Very young kings made mistakes and were often expensive to the nation.

The prince consort was also anxious for his wife to reign happy, glorious, and long, as the national anthem went. She was his access to power in England. As soon as she died, he would have to give up his key to the dispatch box. No longer would he draft the memoranda and make Crown policy, see every cabinet document, and huddle with ministers. As a young man, the prince consort had wished to have a large family for both personal and dynastic reasons. In this regard, he had achieved everything he had wanted, and more. Now it made sense to take precautions with Victoria's life and ensure his son did not come to the throne any time soon.

There is a famous anecdote that appears in many of the secondary books about Queen Victoria. Following the birth of her ninth child, the royal doctors were alarmed about the Queen's health, especially her mental health. They advised the prince that there should be no more royal babies. The prince quickly agreed. Given the same advice, Victoria was upset and said: "Oh, Doctor, can I have no more fun in bed?" Though the anecdote is probably apocryphal, it rings true. At the age of forty, husband and wife were likely to react in different ways to the necessity of limiting their family to nine.

Sexual restraint had not been hard for Albert as a teenager. As he once confided to his close friend and secretary George Anson, "he did not fear temptation with women because that species of vice disgusted him." Now, with so much business to attend to and a wife who had lost her youthful prettiness, abstinence would be easier. Unlike his first cousin Ferdinand, a notorious womanizer who, at about Albert's age, abdicated from the throne of Portugal after his wife the queen died, and went off to live in Paris with an opera singer, Albert desired power and influence, not women. A white marriage would suit him very well.

But Victoria, as her husband often remarked, was not like Albert. She was not a pure spirit. She still felt young. She still found men attractive. She remembered the precious few weeks of pleasure that she and Albert had enjoyed as newlyweds, before the pregnancies began. She was ready to feel them again. She had found it hard to observe the sparks of passion passing between Vicky and Fritz during their engagement. If pregnancy was the price of love, she was still prepared to pay it. Queen Victoria always loved her husband more than any other being. Her feelings for him were, in her own words, "strong and warm," her love "ardent." She longed for him and was faithful in word and deed. But, from the evidence of her letters to her daughter, after 1858 the Queen was beginning to shed the blinkers of passion and take stock of what the rest of life had to offer.

One small indication of the growing coolness between the royal husband and wife can be found in the Queen's day-by-day accounts of her stay at Balmoral in the fall of 1858. At the beginning, for the very first time, she was less than excited to be in Scotland. "I enjoy the scenery and being out very much but I hate the life here," she reported to Vicky. But by October 18, she had quite changed her mind. "I and the girls lunched while Papa was after the stag—and good J. Brown was so attentive to us and so careful," she wrote to Vicky. "He is now my special servant, and there can't be a nicer, better or handier one . . . Brown has had everything to do for me indeed had charge of me on all, on all these expeditions, and therefore I settled that he should be specially appointed to attend on me (without any other title) and have a full dress suit . . . Altogether I feel so sad—at the bitter thought of going from this blessed place—leaving these hills—this enchanting life of liberty—these dear people—and returning to tame, dull, formal England and the prison life at Windsor." It is clear that the prince consort was happy to see his wife personally attended by the handsome gillie. The J. Browns of the world were very useful, and he could make sure that they posed no threat to his marriage or to the monarchy.

"I Do Not Cling to Life as You Do"

...

IN THE FALL OF 1860, THE QUEEN AND THE PRINCE SET OUT FOR COBURG
again. They were hoping this time to steer clear of Vicky's Prussian in-laws
with their protocol, endless military parades, formal concerts, and family
feuds. They looked forward to having a quiet two weeks with their daughter
and son-in-law, getting to know their grandson, Willy, now almost two, and
discussing the ways of the world with dear old Stockmar.

One day, as the Queen and Vicky, armed with their sketchbooks, were
happily chatting to local people in the castle park, Colonel Ponsonby rode
up with news. The prince consort had been involved in an accident but was
unharmed. Concerned but unafraid, Victoria rushed to her husband's side
and found him lying on his valet's bed with a cold compress over his bleeding nose. He had been driving out in an open carriage when the driver lost
control of the horses. The carriage was heading straight for the railway
line, where a cart had stopped to allow a train to pass. The prince jumped
out of the speeding vehicle, incurring cuts and bruises but no broken limbs.
He picked himself up and rushed over to see to the driver, who had been seriously hurt. When Colonel Ponsonby, hearing of the accident, rode up, the
prince consort directed him to the Queen to allay any unnecessary fears.

By presence of mind and physical agility, Albert had escaped a life-
threatening incident, but he was profoundly unnerved. The accident had
been a memento mori. Other men he had known had not been as lucky as
he. In 1842 the young Duc d'Orléans had similarly leaped out of a runaway
carriage, but he had died in the fall. Albert had not been particularly close
to the young duke, but all the same his death plunged Albert into what he
described as consternation and deep distress. "To my imagination it appears

as a mysterious enigmatic lesson full of deep significance, and will long exercise my mind and spirit," Albert wrote about the duke's death. Nine years later, Albert's dear friend and mentor Sir Robert Peel was thrown by his horse and died a lingering and horrible death. Once again, Albert found it hard to recover from the shock and the sorrow of the sudden loss.

In 1860 his unexpected brush with death came at a time when the prince consort was extremely tired and overworked, close to what we would now call a nervous breakdown. He felt as if he was careering down the road to death but could not find the nerve to jump off. That Albert was both depressed and overwrought was quite apparent to those around him in Coburg that fall. "God have mercy on us!" Stockmar said to Duke Ernest. "If anything serious should happen to him, he will die." On his final day in Coburg, Albert and his brother took a walk. "At one of the most beautiful spots, Albert stood still and suddenly felt for his pocket handkerchief," Duke Ernest of Saxe-Coburg remembered. "I went up to him and saw that the tears were trickling down his cheeks . . . he persisted in declaring that he was well aware that he had been here for the last time in his life." The scene Duke Ernest paints is dramatic. We can imagine Albert weeping, saying he was sure he was going to die; Ernest, taken aback, sputtering the kind of banalities we still use for severely depressed people. Don't be absurd. You are only forty years old. You have everything to live for. For pity's sake, get a grip on yourself, brother.

To his wife too, Albert sometimes talked about death. He often told her "Ich hänge gar nicht am Leben; du hängst sehr daran [I really do not cling to life; you cling to it very hard] . . . I feel that I should make no struggle if I were ill—that I should give up at once." Such remarks would make the Queen shudder, and then the prince would pull himself together.

The prince consort's steep decline into ill health and depression can be charted from hundreds of extant paintings, drawings, and photographic images of him. The man aged astonishingly fast. It is as if youth and beauty were a costume he wore for ambition and then put away with relief once the Queen was won and the Saxe-Coburg dynasty in England was secured. The slim romantic hero of the early portraits, with his light mustache and intricately curled hair, soon gave way to the portly, balding, bristle-whiskered stockbroker of the daguerreotypes. Red leather hunting boots were retired in favor of stout shoes. Trousers and long frock coats replaced the body-hugging jackets and breeches. In the first known photographic image of the prince alone, a daguerreotype taken when he was twenty-two or twenty-three, he is already losing his hair, putting on weight, and looking melancholy. An 1855 photograph of Prince Albert at Osborne in his holiday clothes—short, cutaway coat, loud tweed trousers, checked waist-coat, and broad-brimmed hat—shows him strangely somber and preoccu-pied. At thirty-six years old, the man looks fifty.

Two astute female observers who were close to the royal couple peered behind the mask and suspected that all was not well with Prince Albert. Lady Lyttelton, the royal children's governess, was startled to see the ex-pression of melancholy that appeared on the prince's face when he thought no one was watching him. Mary Bulteel Ponsonby, Queen Victoria's maid of honor and friend, was sure that Prince Albert was not a happy man.

Prince Albert aged so fast because he worked too hard and put far too much pressure on himself. His wife saw this but protested in vain. The prince's labors at his desk were prodigious by any standards. During the Crimean War alone, his personal files amounted to forty bound volumes. Apart from the tiring state events he attended with his wife, the prince, as colonel to several regiments and chairman of a large number of charitable and arts organizations, also did a great deal of solo travel. Even for a man with a private train who could order a railway track cleared for his passage on any given day, these out-of-town engagements were an increasing drain. The ceremonial dinners, when the prince was obliged to respond to a string of long speeches and toasts, were both boring and stressful. Committed to reforming the English armed forces, Albert not infrequently found himself standing for hours in pouring rain on a parade ground or an artillery field. Chilled to the bone, he would develop a feverish cold, feel wretched for days, but continue with his crowded schedule. Albert was forever hurrying back to his wife late at night in foul weather, exhausted. His main relaxation was chasing stags.

By 1860, the demands on his time had ratcheted up so far that the prince consort had ceased to take pleasure in work. Insomnia troubled him more and more, and he found it impossible to relax. In May of that year, the royal family was as usual at Osborne, "in the enjoyment of the most glori-ous air, the most fragrant odours, the merriest choirs of birds, and the most luxuriant verdure," as the prince reported to his daughter in Berlin. Os-borne was the earthly paradise that Albert had created for his family, but he couldn't just admit how desperately he needed to rest, soak up the sun, breathe in the scents from his beloved shrubs, and listen to the birds he could identify by call. "Were there not so many things that reminded one of the so-called world (that is to say, of miserable men) one might give oneself up wholly to the enjoyment of the real world," he continued to Vicky. "There is no such good fortune, however, for poor me; and this being so, one's feelings remain under the influence of the treadmill of never-ending business. The donkey at Carisbrook [harnessed to a treadmill], which you will remember, is my true counterpart. He, too, would rather munch thistles in the Castle Well; and small are the thanks he gets for his labour."

Yet no one bound Albert to a life of unending toil. Unlike the Carisbrook donkey, he could have unstrapped himself from the treadmill and munched daisies to his heart's content. Other kings and princes had no problem getting away and relaxing. Even Uncle Leopold took time for himself and felt no guilt over his pleasures. England benefited from the prince consort's dedication and intelligence, but it did not need his hand perpetually on the wheel. There were ministers and a parliament to steer the ship of state, and, by and large, they did a decent job of it. Even Palmerston and Gladstone, men of legendary strength, energy, and efficiency, did not work all the time. They knew a great deal but did not find it necessary to be expert on everything from Schleswig-Holstein to *sfumato.*

But to stop work for more than a few days, to refuse more responsibilities, to delegate, above all to ask his wife to take on more of the duties that were in fact hers constitutionally, would have destroyed the prince's sense of self. He was Atlas, bearing the weight of the world on his shoulders.

The prince spent much of his day writing down the ideas and facts that teemed in his brain, but he was not prone to self-analysis or self-doubt. He considered his wife slightly mad because she dwelled so much on her feelings and needed to "have things out." He graded Victoria in written memoranda on what he saw as her advances in sociability and self-control, sure he was doing her a service. But, once Stockmar retired to Coburg for good, no one performed the same service for him. Albert loved his brother, Ernest, but could neither trust nor respect him. After the deaths of Anson and Peel, there was no friend in England to suggest to the prince that he might be destroying his health, happiness, and long-term usefulness in the pursuit of the chimera of indispensability. Albert certainly felt able to confide in his wife, but she mirrored his exalted opinion of himself and was usually ignored when she ventured to disagree or demur.

Albert criticized Victoria for being vain, self-absorbed, antisocial, neurotic, and weak, yet, ironically, these were more his faults than hers. The Queen, as Lady Lyttelton once observed, had a vein of iron. She was small, but she was strong, producing nine children without, apparently, a miscarriage. She was healthy even when she was pregnant, and she recovered quickly from colds and attacks of what she called rheumatism as well as from the mumps, measles, and scarlet fever she caught from her children. Above all, Victoria's sense of self was strongly grounded in reality despite the isolation she complained of so often. She was spoiled and headstrong, but she could listen, she could reach out, she could at times at least see herself as others saw her. She admitted her passionate nature and gave vent to her emotions. She knew she was not perfect and was quick to apologize and atone. She knew how to relax and delegate, rest and recover.

Convinced of his own perfections, injured by the world's failure to recognize them, Prince Albert maintained a steely composure and was always unwell. He hid his hurt feelings under a smile that deceived no one and alienated many. He took refuge from emotion in an ever-accelerating workload. He had to feel master of his world. For a man whose health had always been precarious, this was double jeopardy.

·

AS AN ADULT, Albert was a tall and strong man, a dedicated and accomplished sportsman famous for dashing full tilt along the endless corridors at Windsor. To attract the young Queen Victoria, he had needed to be in superb physical shape. But the prince's strength and vigor in 1839 had been acquired by a massive effort of will. As a child, he had often been ill with colics, coughs, and fevers, and therefore subjected to the debilitating medical procedures and pharmaceuticals of his time. He needed an unusual amount of sleep. Even as a late teenager, Albert was so easily tired that Stockmar wondered if he was up to the destiny his family planned for him.

Gastric problems troubled Albert all his life. Once he arrived in England, these were exacerbated by the local cuisine, though he soon began to gain weight. In England he also suffered chronically from what he called "catarrh," "fever," and "rheumatism." The polluted air of London probably accounted for the chronic catarrh, or runny nose. The constant fevers and chills may have been due to a contaminated water supply, since the waste-disposal systems at both Windsor and Buckingham Palace were recognized by sanitation experts to be quite inadequate. Only in his personally designed new homes at Osborne and Balmoral, where the air was clean and the water pure, did the prince feel perfectly fit. As for the "rheumatism," it also plagued Queen Victoria and their daughter Vicky at a very young age. Spending so many hours every day reading handwritten documents in poor light and writing with a quill pen was calculated to produce stiff joints and sore tendons.

After ten years of marriage, Prince Albert's health got worse. By his own and his wife's account, the prince's labors over the Great Exhibition of 1851 left him close to collapse. From the end of 1854, when he was assailed in the press as a traitor, Albert remarked more and more often, especially in his letters to Stockmar, how very "fagged" and unwell he was feeling. He suffered appallingly from toothache and gum abscesses. At one point, he apologized to Prince William for not writing, saying that his arm and shoulder were so sore he could not hold a pen.

That his "kleines Fräuchen" was so much more resilient was a constant spur to the prince and an irritation. Victoria was both worried and annoyed by her husband's unending stream of complaints about his health. Her diagnosis was that, like most men, he was a hypochondriac. The Queen had her own health fetishes, and they did not fit well with her husband's ailments. Victoria insisted that her husband, and indeed all her family, open the windows and keep the rooms nice and cold. Fresh, cold air was her sovereign recipe for keeping well, and it certainly worked for her.

Albert never accustomed himself to the icy indoor conditions in the English royal homes. It is true that he had been trained as a child to suffer extreme cold without complaint, since riding for hours through a blizzard in a short jacket was Duke Ernest's idea of manliness. But stoves kept the temperatures cozy inside German palaces. Eighteen years into his marriage, Prince Albert was rising at seven, donning a wig and a padded dressing gown, and shivering over the day's documents. If he dared to have a small fire lit in his rooms, it had to be hastily extinguished as soon as his wife was up.

This matter of lighting fires was one of the silly knots that married people can get entangled in. Albert controlled all aspects of the royal household, and he was not slow to contradict his wife or give her orders. He could certainly have insisted on having a fire in his room. Instead he more or less obeyed his wife but felt free to complain to their daughter about her.

IF ALBERT HAD BEEN deeply depressed in October 1860, at Christmas that year he pulled himself together. The prince had wonderful memories of Christmases in his childhood, which his own father had stage-managed. For his wife, his children, and the entire household, he made Christmas into a fairy-tale event at Windsor Castle, with a huge tree glowing with candles, separate tables heaped up with presents for everyone, dancing, games, carols, and splendid feasts. The prince was the life and soul of the party as always, but the release in pressure lasted for days at most. In the New Year, as usual, one political crisis followed another, either at home or abroad, all requiring his constant attention, or so it seemed.

Family affairs also demanded more of the prince's time than ever. Alice was now engaged to Prince Louis of Hesse-Darmstadt, and, to prepare her for her life in Germany, her father was trying to give her an hour of his time every night. Alice, like her older sister, was a talented and willing student, quite unlike her brother Bertie, and both father and daughter looked forward to their sessions. Unfortunately, the prince was often so busy that he had to cancel.

Leopold's chronic ill health entered a critical phase. On one of his visits to London, Louis of Hesse came down with what the doctors diagnosed as measles. The illness was passed to the Queen and to eight-year-old Prince Leopold, who was ill for several weeks. Then, late in the fall, Leopold had a bad accident and a serious bleed. The Queen wrote to the Princess Royal in Germany how cross she was that the prince consort had insisted she attend a horticultural meeting with him, since Leopold had suffered one of his "bruises" and was very ill. "You say no one is perfect but Papa," wrote Queen Victoria on October 1, 1861, "but he has his faults too. He is often very trying—in his hastiness and over-love of business." On the advice of the doctors, the prince consort sent his ailing son off to the south of France for the winter, entrusting Leopold to an aging courtier, General Bowater. Within a day of arriving in Cannes, Bowater, aged seventy-four, was dead, leaving the child stranded in the care of servants and foreigners.

The problem with Leopold could not have come at a worse time, as Prince Albert was already coping with a full-scale domestic crisis. In March 1861, the Duchess of Kent, Queen Victoria's mother, died. Her health had been poor for some years, but her death was nonetheless a shock. During her mother's final illness, Victoria hovered by the bedside night and day, listening to the tick of her dead father's watch. The duchess had always kept the watch by her, and it was the sound that had punctuated Victoria's every night until her accession. The Queen was holding her mother's hand when the duchess died. This was the first time Victoria had seen death at firsthand, and she was traumatized as well as bereft. Her husband led her gently away, in an agony of weeping.

Over the years of her marriage, the Queen had become increasingly fond of her mother. The duchess was always there in the background of her life, and she came to depend upon her more and more. With her mother as with no one else at court, the Queen could chat in confidence about her husband's latest cold, problems with the children, scandals abroad. The duchess was very game for an old lady, and she still had fashion sense. For her May birthdays, the Queen could count on her mother to give her an especially becoming summer dress.

Victoria suffered a nervous breakdown after her mother died. As the prince consort reported grimly to his brother, the rumor that the Queen of England was going mad was circulating in the courts of Europe. Everywhere the Queen went, she missed the duchess's familiar face and wept inconsolably. For some time, she would not come out of her rooms even for meals. She refused to engage in the business of state and found her children too irritating to bear. She was happiest making detailed plans for her mother's tomb and going through her mother's affairs. She read for the first time the letters her parents had exchanged in their brief marriage and discovered just how much she herself had been loved as a small child. She passionately regretted the ten years or so when she and her mother had been estranged.

The Queen's twentieth-century English biographers found her grief weird and excessive, a prime example of the outdated sentimentality of the Victorian era. Today we are more inclined to believe that mothers and fathers must be mourned, since they cannot be replaced. We see that the death of even an unloving parent can occasion an emotional crisis and a deep reevaluation of life. Today the Queen's wrenching sorrow seems natural and right, since she and her mother had been so close for so long. Victoria was perhaps self-indulgent and extreme in her weeping, but her loss was great, and, in the end, she healed herself with tears.

The prince consort had also been very fond of the mother-in-law, who was also his aunt. The two had been friends and allies. She was one more lost link to his Coburg past. It was the first time he too had seen death at firsthand. But, unlike his wife, he had no time to dwell on his emotions. He had to comfort his shattered wife and try to get her back on her feet. He had to take up the administrative slack caused by Victoria's breakdown. He had to settle his mother-in-law's estate, since only two weeks before the duchess's death, her old and trusted man of affairs Sir George Couper had died. People began to remark on how ill the prince consort looked. In his diary he wrote in June: "Am feverish, with pains in my limbs, and feel very miserable." He kept going, but such bouts of illness recurred throughout the summer.

In August the Queen and the prince made a visit to Ireland, largely to visit their eldest son. By this point in his life, the Prince of Wales had been moved by his father from Oxford to Cambridge. Learning from his Oxford mistakes, the prince consort installed his son and entourage of governor, equerries, private tutors, and servants at Madingley Hall, some distance from the town. Albert went down to Cambridge as often as he could to check on his son and make sure that his instructions were being carried out.

But the Prince of Wales was fast approaching his twentieth birthday, and in a year he would have control over his personal fortune and his income under the civil list. Then he would be free to lead his life as he chose.

To keep him in such tight leading strings seemed ill advised even to stern General Bruce, Bertie's governor. An old military man who believed exposure to army life would be beneficial to the young man, Bruce persuaded Prince Albert to allow Bertie to spend the long vacation at the Curragh, a military camp in Killarney. The price Albert had exacted for this indulgence was high. Bertie would have to show real good will in his studies and pass his exams. In Ireland, where he would be brevetted colonel without a regiment, he would be expected in ten weeks to acquire information and skills that career officers took years to master. He would once again have a separate household, not live with the other officers.

Leaping so many high hurdles would be a remarkable feat for anyone, and the Prince of Wales was an ordinary young man. He had been set up for failure, and, given his parents' visit, the failure was horribly public. For a young man of great pride who had always hated even to be "chaffed" about his faults, the summer in Ireland was a cruel disappointment. Bertie saw himself as a soldier. As a boy, he had idolized the Duke of Wellington and read about the Napoleonic campaigns with passionate interest. Now he found it impossible even to get the men through a drill competently. The Queen commended the superior officers who in their reports on Bertie's progress had refused to show preference to the heir to the throne. It was not a happy trip for parents or child.

In the fall, minus Vicky, Bertie, and Leopold—but plus Louis, now officially engaged to Alice—the royal family was again at Balmoral. The Queen began to revive. Remembering how their first "Great Expedition" in the Highlands had delighted his wife, the prince organized three more. These expeditions were challenging pony treks in the mountains, and two of them again involved incognito overnight stays at country inns. The Queen loved being outside all day on her darling Inchrory or some other pony, with Brown leading her over all the difficult places. She was cheerful when the rain came down and scrambled quickly up when she took a tumble walking on slick rock. She gloried in the scenery and tried to memorize the Gaelic name of every peak spread before her. She loved meeting strange innkeepers who were at first deceived by her assumed identity. Inevitably, to the Queen's great hilarity, someone in the party would slip up and say "Your Majesty," and the next morning a hurriedly assembled pipe band would salute their sovereign lady at breakfast. Victoria had the most fun ever, she wrote, and was ready at last to put aside her mourning.

Back at Windsor, the royal family celebrated the Prince of Wales's twentieth birthday on November 9, but their joy was short lived. News came from Lisbon that King Pedro V of Portugal, twenty-five, and his brother and heir, Prince Ferdinand, had died of typhoid. The Court of St. James's always went into deep mourning for a dead monarch, but this time the royal family's mood matched the black of their dress. The two young men were the eldest sons of Victoria and Albert's first cousin, Ferdinand Coburg-Kohary. On his occasional meetings with his English relatives, Pedro managed to impress the prince consort as a golden young man. To Albert, Pedro seemed to be all that he wanted in a son and heir, all that Bertie was not. "The death of poor, good Pedro . . . has shaken me in an extraordinary way," Albert wrote to King William of Prussia, "for I loved and valued him greatly, and had great hopes that his influence might contribute towards setting on its legs a State and a nation which has fallen low." Queen Victoria confided to her diary: "My Albert loved [Pedro] like a son." The prince consort was unable to sleep, felt horribly cold, and was racked with pain.

ONLY ONE DAY after the tragic news came from Lisbon, Prince Albert learned what others had known for some time: His son the Prince of Wales had become involved with an actress while in Ireland. A letter from Stockmar broke the news, and for two days Albert gathered confirmatory details and brooded. On November 13, reluctantly, without giving her any of the "disgusting details," Albert informed his wife of what he had learned. She was suitably horrified, exclaiming that she would hardly be able to look at her son without a shudder in future. Apparently, on the Prince of Wales's last night at the Curragh camp, there was a great party, and some of his fellow officers, as a kind of joke, smuggled a young actress named Nellie Clifden into his quarters. When the prince returned to England, Nellie came to his Windsor residence.

His son Bertie had yielded to his lower nature. This was what the prince had long feared and struggled to prevent, and it shook him to the core. Must virtuous youths like Pedro die while sinful youths like Bertie lived on? If this was the lesson of life, it challenged everything Albert had lived for. Barely able to control his pen much less his thoughts, the prince consort wrote his son a long, intensely emotional letter. The news of the Clifden affair had caused him, he said, "the greatest pain I have yet felt in this life."

Albert wrote that Bertie had not only lost his innocence but put the monarchy at risk. Prince Albert had heard that Miss Clifden was already known in the music halls of London as the Princess of Wales, and he conjured up a nightmare scenario in which the actress would drag the royal family through the mud. She would produce a child and claim it belonged to the Prince of Wales. "If you were to try and deny it, she can drag you into a

Court of Law to force you to own it & there with you (the Prince of Wales) in the witness box, she will be able to give before a greedy Multitude disgusting details of your profligacy for the sake of convincing the Jury, yourself cross-examined by a railing indecent attorney and hooted and yelled at by a Lawless Mob!! Oh horrible prospect, which this person has in her power, any day to realize, and to break your poor parents' hearts." The prince consort was sure that once the Clifden affair was known in Copenhagen, the marriage to Princess Alexandra would be off. He told his son, falsely, that he had not told the Queen what he knew.

The prince consort was casting his son Bertie as his wife's aunt Queen Caroline, obliged to defend herself before the House of Lords on a charge of adultery and gross misconduct, and Nellie Clifden as Pauline Panam, who blackmailed his father, the Duke of Coburg, by publishing the story of her seduction at age fourteen and the illegitimate son she had borne. In fact, the amiable Miss Clifden, after giving the Prince of Wales some pleasure and comfort he was in great need of, went back to her music hall and her other gentlemen, one hopes a little richer.

As for Copenhagen, the prince consort's fears were exaggerated. The dying king of Denmark was the most notorious old royal reprobate in Europe. His heir Prince Christian, Alexandra's father, though personally decent, had certainly heard worse than the Clifden story. The odd dalliance with an experienced woman was generally seen by the European upper crust as a good apprenticeship for marriage. Prince Christian and his large family, waiting for the king to die, led an almost middle-class existence on an officer's pay. Pure or not, the Prince of Wales was, with the possible exception of the tsarevitch, the greatest catch in Europe.

Bertie, as his parents admitted when they were not angry or disappointed with him, was an extremely affectionate young man. His father's letter drove him to tears of remorse, and he wrote swearing never to sin again. He begged to be allowed to marry as soon as possible. He was deeply grateful that dearest Mama had been told nothing.

Albert could find no comfort or reassurance in his son's letter. On November 22 he felt horribly ill but was determined to go down to Cambridge to talk to Bertie and have things out. First, however, he was scheduled to inspect the buildings at the new Staff College and Military Academy at Sandhurst, a project that he had nurtured from its inception. It was a cold day with drenching rain, and the prince consort returned to Windsor wet to the skin. All the same, the next day he ordered a special train and set out for Madingley Hall, on the outskirts of Cambridge. Intent on a wholly private conversation, the prince and his son walked for some hours. It was pouring rain, and at one point Bertie lost his way. Returning to the house, the prince consort refused a bed for the night and set out at once for Windsor to tell his anxious wife what had occurred. Victoria declared that since Bertie was so very sorry and promised to be better in the future, she would forget all she had been told.

The prince consort had returned to Windsor much easier in his mind. But his insomnia continued, and he lost all appetite. Feeling desperately unwell, he continued to do his work and attend mealtimes as usual. On November 29, at the Queen's review of the Eton Volunteers, it was noticed that the prince consort looked frozen, though he was wearing a fur-lined coat. He was suffering from typhoid fever, probably contracted soon after his return to Windsor from Balmoral at the end of October.

In the developed world today, typhoid is happily not part of most people's experience. To understand what the prince consort went through in November and December 1861, we need to understand the disease and what it does to people. Typhoid develops over several weeks, slower than cholera, though faster than tuberculosis. One contracts typhoid by ingesting food or water contaminated by the feces of an infected person. A person with active *Salmonella typhi* in his or her system can have immunity and be symptom free. This was the case with the famous Typhoid Mary of New York in the 1880s. However, as Albert himself would prove, even a person sick with typhoid can spend some weeks walking around feeling terrible but doing his job. If that job involves food preparation, the consequences can be serious for others.

Salmonella typhi enters the gut, moves into the lymph nodes, the liver, and the spleen, where it multiplies and then disseminates into the bloodstream. Typhoid has been called the nervous fever, and early symptoms may include irritability, headache, cough, gastroenteritis, sweating, restlessness, constipation, diarrhea, insomnia, and extreme malaise. The prince consort reported many of these symptoms well before his visit to Cambridge on November 22. If the body's immune system fails to meet the challenge of the infection, bacteria flood the body, increasing the pain and distress, causing hallucinations and delirium. Death occurs when the abdominal wall is breached, causing peritonitis, or when the bacteria penetrate the brain or the heart.

Albert once told his wife that if he fell ill, he would put up no struggle. He sold himself short. Given the facts of the disease as we know them today, it is a tribute to Albert's stamina and strength of will that on November 29 he was still walking around a parade ground in late fall.

More remarkably, before yielding ground to his illness, the prince consort did one more service to his adopted country. He kept Great Britain out of the American Civil War.

When the War Between the States broke out in the spring of 1861, cotton, not slavery, was on the minds of British politicians and merchants. Official British sympathies were with the South. Southern cotton kept the Lancashire mills working and was a major prop of the British economy. The British government also nourished an old resentment against the Northern states who had initiated the American War of Independence against Britain in the late eighteenth century. When an American warship intercepted the *Trent*, a British transatlantic mail vessel, and abducted two envoys of the Confederacy and their wives, the Palmerston government, which had been apprised that the attack was to take place, erupted in fury. A note was drafted to be sent to the government of President Abraham Lincoln, threatening war if an abject apology were not forthcoming immediately and the captured persons released.

The prince consort read the Palmerston note and saw that the nation was about to go to war with a distant and friendly power over a minor diplomatic incident. Shivering with fever, barely able to hold a pen, he redrafted the note, softening the terms, giving the Lincoln administration a way to back down without losing face. Palmerston, admitting his own haste and poor judgment, sent off the prince's version. The American government in the North, far from anxious to be waging war on two fronts, agreed to the fiction that the captain of the Northern warship had acted without instructions from Washington. An apology was proffered, the Southerners were released.

This was the prince consort's greatest diplomatic act and his last.

◼

EVEN UNTREATED, TYPHOID is fatal in only 10 percent to 30 percent of cases. Before the discovery of antibiotics, three to four weeks would pass between the initial infection and death, and a strong immune system had time to rally. In the 1860s, when Prince Albert fell ill, many people, in far worse circumstances and with far worse care, pulled through fevers like typhoid every day. Queen Victoria believed that she had survived typhoid when she was sixteen. Since in 1861 she was eating and drinking much the same as her husband, her immunity to the disease indicates that she was right. The Prince of Wales would also survive typhoid, in 1872. Unfortunately, when the typhoid bacillus entered the prince consort's bloodstream, his immune system was already severely weakened.

Albert had the misfortune to live in Great Britain when infectious diseases were at historical highs. Though he was a fervent advocate for clean water and good drainage as the birthright of all British citizens, he did not live to see the great public works programs that radically lowered the death rate. He lived decades before Louis Pasteur and Robert Koch identified various disease-causing microorganisms. Only in the twentieth century would drugs be developed to cure certain infectious diseases, including typhoid. That the prince was fastidiously clean as well as a committed sanitarian, that he took fresh air and exercise whenever he could, ate and drank abstemiously, and installed state-of-the-art drains, water closets, baths, and showers in the private residences he designed at Osborne and Balmoral, was one of the ironies of his life.

By December 1, the prince consort was in great distress. His temperature was erratic, he sweated profusely but was terribly cold, he had no appetite, could keep no food down, and had not slept in weeks. No longer able to concentrate on work, he still insisted on getting dressed and wandered aimlessly about the palace. The prince's wife, daughters, and staff read books to him, but he took little pleasure. On December 2, envoys from Portugal came and gave the prince a wrenching account of the deaths of his young cousins and the outbreak of typhoid in the royal palace in Lisbon. Albert told his equerries that it was as well he had no fever, he would certainly not recover.

What he meant by having no fever was that his doctors had not yet made a diagnosis of fever. One of the doctors in attendance was William Jenner, reputed to be the greatest expert in England on what we would now call infectious diseases. Jenner had seen many cases of typhoid and surely guessed what was wrong with the prince. But, aware of the intense anxiety both the Queen and the prince felt at the mere mention of the word *typhoid*, the doctors still talked in terms of influenza or a bad feverish chill. These possible diagnoses were not wholly implausible. Among the first presenting symptoms for typhoid are chills, joint aches, digestive problems, and insomnia. As Clark and Jenner knew very well, the prince had been complaining of one or more of these symptoms increasingly for years and chronically throughout 1861. Already feeling horribly ill, the prince had exacerbated his problems by insisting on going out and getting chilled to the bone on two successive days.

Sir James Clark, who was still the senior royal doctor, knew the Queen and the prince very well. He decided that it was crucial that the patient's fears about "low fevers" should not be encouraged. Clark had no clinical information on the effects of depression on the immune system, but he had seen enough patients to know that some people turned their faces to the wall from sheer sorrow, while others, gravely ill, managed to cling to life. To encourage the patient, and to keep up the spirits of the patient's wife who was constantly with him, Clark held back from making any premature diagnosis.

Repeatedly reassured by the physicians she trusted, the Queen, while reporting her husband's symptoms with her customary clarity and detail, assured her correspondents, notably her daughter in Berlin, her uncle in Brussels, and Stockmar in Coburg, that the prince consort would soon be back on his feet. At first she was dismissive about her husband's health problems and inclined to blame the patient, as we see from her letters to King Leopold. November 26: "Albert is a little rheumatic [sic], which is a plague, but . . . he is much better this winter than he was the preceding years." December 4: Albert's rheumatism "has become an influenza . . . he has difficulty eating and sleeping, and is confined to his room . . . but today a lot better." The situation is "very disagreeable, as you know he is always *so* depressed when anything is the matter with him." December 9: "Every day . . . is bringing us nearer the end of this tiresome illness, which is much what I had at Ramsgate [in 1835] only that I was much worse, and not at first well attended to."

On December 6, Dr. Jenner decided that Clark's psychological strategy must be abandoned. Jenner had, reportedly, observed on the prince's torso the rash of flat, pink spots that is often an early symptom of typhoid. He told the Queen that her husband was suffering from a fever but assured her that there was still every hope. At this point, the doctors insisted that the prince should not dress but should keep in bed. They advised the Queen, who had also gotten no sleep for many nights and was obviously exhausted, to move into a separate bedroom. On December 8, the prince consort became delirious and failed to recognize his wife. His irritability increased, but he also showed moments of deep tenderness toward members of his family. He continued to move restlessly between bed and couch, and from room to room. At his request, the Blue Room at the castle was set up as a sickroom, and the Queen had a cot next door. Both George IV and William IV had died in the Blue Room.

The prince consort's doctors had the full confidence of the Queen but not of the prime minister. Through a secret correspondence with Sir Charles Phipps, the prince's private secretary, Lord Palmerston was kept constantly up to date on events in the sickroom. From the first, he feared the worst and was desolate. Palmerston and the prince had long jousted for power, but Palmerston was above all a patriot. He knew how much the country owed to the prince's intelligence, information, and selfless commitment to public service. Palmerston had also known the Queen since she was a girl of eighteen. He loved her very much, and he knew how deeply her husband's death would affect her.

Acting on strong emotion, Palmerston wrote on December 11, begging the Queen to get some new medical opinions. Victoria was dreadfully upset. It was being suggested not only that the prince was in danger but that he was receiving inadequate care. She replied that the prince consort was extremely irritated by the constant attentions even of doctors he had long known. This was true. The only doctor Albert really trusted was Stockmar, and in his delirium he asked for his old friend. But, determined to show that she was not refusing advice, merely protecting the beloved patient, Victoria permitted two doctors to come but not to stay or be a worry. Sir Henry Holland, an aged society doctor, came but had nothing new to offer. Dr. Thomas Watson, an excellent young clinician, on the other hand, soon won the Queen's approval.

On December 11, the doctors felt that the public needed to know something, so daily bulletins on the prince's state of health were begun. They were short and vague and unalarming. No one outside the government and the court understood the gravity of the situation. But the Queen rightly saw that the bulletins were another sign that things were not going well, and she began to despair and to reach out for the comfort and support of friends. She sent for her former lady-in-waiting Lady Augusta Bruce and for Dr. Gerald Wellesley, the dean of Windsor, her favorite man of the cloth. On December 12, Victoria failed for the first time to record the events of the day in her diary. As for the prince, he knew what was coming. Asked by her father if she had written to her older sister in Berlin, Princess Alice replied that she had told Vicky that he was very ill. "You did wrong," he commented. "You should have told her I am dying. Yes. I am dying."

The prince consort's doctors watched over him night and day, spared no thought or effort, and, given the medical limitations of the day, gave him exemplary care. This was especially true of old Sir James Clark. The unfortunate prime minister of Piedmont-Sardinia, Camille Cavour, who also contracted typhoid in 1861, was allegedly bled to death by his doctors, but the prince consort's doctors did not resort to "heroic" medicine. Palliative care was the best the medical profession of the time had to offer, and this was the approach taken by Clark's team. The prince was given opium and ether to ease his pain and allow him some hours of sleep. He was encouraged, uselessly but harmlessly, to eat simple foods like soup and brown bread. When he seemed close to slipping away, he was revived with brandy. Albert's doctors spoke of allowing the disease to take its course and of having seen many patients recover. This was all accurate and sound.

Perhaps it would have helped if the prince had collapsed and taken to his bed in mid-November, instead of keeping up the hollow ritual of normal life. Perhaps it would have helped if he had been nursed in a warm, quiet, controlled environment instead of wandering from room to room and bed to bed, while his wife spread Eau de Cologne on his sheets and a gaggle of family members, equerries, doctors, and servants looked on. But probably not. Restlessness is a classic symptom of typhoid, and to be tied to a bed would have been cruel. The prince consort had never been alone in a room by himself. The solitude of a modern hospital room would have been torture for him.

Unlike poor typhoid patients in the fever hospitals of his time, the prince was kept warm, well nourished, and scrupulously clean. His shirts and bed linen were changed often. Above all, he was surrounded by love and care and consideration. The visits of his little daughter Beatrice may have cheered him up, even in delirium. Hearing Alice play his favorite chorale in the next room at his request could not stop the torment, but it was a memory of happiness, and an expression of love.

The dying prince's lack of privacy has troubled some biographers. At the time of his death, the onlookers in the Blue Room included his wife, his daughters Alice, Helena, and Louise, his son Bertie, the Queen's nephew Charles Leiningen and his wife, Albert's private secretary Sir Charles Phipps, his German valet Rudolph Löhlein (the successor to Isaac Cart), the dean of Windsor, and presumably one or more doctors. The princesses' governess Miss Hildyard, Lady Augusta Bruce, and her brother General Bruce, the Prince of Wales's governor, huddled in the doorway. But surely it is better to die at home, in the room you have chosen, with people you love all around you.

Alice, the prince's oldest daughter at home, was his best nurse. Her strength and courage never failed. One report has it that she was ready to do things for her father that were considered improper in a woman and a princess—presumably she helped change his linen after diarrhea or vomiting. It was to Alice that the prince confided that he knew he was dying. It was Alice who had the foresight to telegraph her brother Bertie at Cambridge to come, their father was very ill. It was Alice, kneeling at the head of the bed after all the weary days of waiting, who recognized the death rattle; Alice who instantly ran out to get her mother, who had briefly moved next door to give vent to her grief.

Queen Victoria had clung to the belief that her husband was suffering only from influenza. She had refused to summon the Prince of Wales, angry with her son but also fearful that his arrival would set the patient back. She felt impatient at times. She had survived typhoid. Why could Albert not do the same? Could it be true what he said, that he did not cling to life? What could that mean when she and the nation needed him so desperately? What did it say about their marriage?

But for the last two weeks, she hardly left his side, and, though she knew she was no nurse, she did what she could. She was, she thought, courageous. Albert had so often blamed her for her lack of emotional control and her selfishness, but now, when it mattered, she did not weep or show despair. She tried to anticipate his wishes and do just what he wanted. She spoke to him in his native German and translated his words for others. She was courteous and considerate to the doctors. She saw all that Alice did and was impressed and grateful.

When the prince slapped her hand in irritation, she made excuses for him. When he complained that she was refusing to stay with him, she did not say that the doctors had ordered her to leave so that he could rest. When he walked unannounced into her dressing room one evening like a ghost, she was terrified, then took his hand and led him back to bed. When he became alarmed by his reflection in the big mirror and hallucinated that he was in a room at the old palace of Holyrood, she had the mirror lowered and the cot moved. When he was in delirium and failed to recognize her, she did not break down. Coming in to see him in the dawn glow on December 14, she was once again overwhelmed by his beauty. How terribly she loved him. What could life mean without him? When he looked on her with love that awful morning, she begged him for a kiss.

Exhausted by sleepless nights, weary of moving around the palace after her poor wandering tortured love, going through the dispatch boxes by day to do the essential business because she knew he would have wanted her to, Queen Victoria did not give up hope for a long time. But at last, on the night of December 14, she gave way. She fled into the next room and sat down on the floor for a moment in "mute despair." Then, at Alice's urgent summons, she ran back in and took the beloved hand. Already it was cold as stone. Albert took a few calm breaths. Then there was silence. "Oh, this is death!" Victoria cried, "I know it. I have seen it before."

Mourning a Prince

...

*T*HE DEATH OF THE PRINCE CONSORT CAME AS A SHOCK TO THE NATION. When the bells of St. Paul's Cathedral rang ominously out over nighttime London, and the telegraph wires began to sing, everyone outside Windsor Castle and the cabinet was taken unawares, if not exactly surprised.

Sudden death was a frequent visitor to Victorian families, and not just the underfed and overworked poor. The new sanitarians like Edwin Chadwick documented how all classes suffered from air black with soot and water brown with sewage. The new statisticians like William Farr graphically recorded the spikes in mortality that occurred when epidemic cholera was added to endemic tuberculosis. The new serial novelists like Charles Dickens developed a wide palate of colorful death scenes.

The combination of high mortality and rising prosperity created a culture of death and an innovative funerary industry. Keen businessmen were quickly at the elbow of the weeping widow or the guilty heir, ready to lay on a funeral that would impress the neighbors. They could rapidly conjure up a huge, shining black hearse drawn by jet-black horses, their tall black plumes dancing, slowly trotting through the streets, escorted by hired mourners in black suits, black top hats, and black ribbons. A tiny, blond, black-clad boy, quite unrelated to the deceased, was the funeral parlor's coup de grâce.

Thus when the nation heard of the death of the prince consort, it was primed to throw itself into an orgy of mourning. No expense was spared, no effort was enough. On the days immediately following the death, the streets of London were empty, with shops boarded up. All over the country, people and buildings were wreathed in black, shops sold out of black fabrics, and textile mills were mobbed with orders. For weeks and months, clergymen gratified their sobbing congregations with sermons on the classic themes of memento mori: dust to dust; vanity, vanity, all is vanity; death the great leveler; and so on and so forth. Eulogies to the lost prince gushed forth from cabinet ministers and members of parliament, from bishops in the pulpit, from newspaper men in black-bordered editorials, from poets eager to capitalize on the publishing successes of Edward Young's "Night Thoughts" and Alfred Lord Tennyson's book-length *In Memoriam*.

Dissatisfied by such ephemeral tributes to its Queen's dead consort, cities and towns and civic institutions rushed to inscribe them in stone for the long-term edification of the populace. Major cities like Edinburgh, Glasgow, Dublin, Aberdeen, and Liverpool launched vigorous subscription campaigns and then vied with one another in the Gothic extravagance of their Albert Memorials. Little towns like Tenby, Denham, and Abingdon were not to be outdone in their commemorative zeal. Artists cheerfully set to the task of chiseling iconic Albert statues—standing in Perth, sitting in Aberdeen, on horseback in Wolverhampton, in Garter robes at Framingham College, in chancellor's robes at Cambridge, in frock coat at Oxford, on top of a pillar in Abingdon, under a canopy in Manchester, exposed to the pigeons in Dublin, or nestled in a museum in Bombay. Albert libraries, infirmaries, clock towers, and drinking fountains sprang up like mushrooms. Even today it is hard to find a town in England without an Albert Street or—rather ironically, given the prince's dislike of hard liquor—an Albert pub.

These ubiquitous public tributes continued for more than a decade, but they were an expression of guilt rather than sorrow. With the prince consort safely out of the way, the British nation was ready at last to celebrate his superior abilities, pure morals, and hard work. He was a pattern of the virtues that nineteenth-century English society professed to cherish, and to the end of the century, erring youths (his eldest son notable among them) were urged to model themselves after him.

But during his lifetime, Prince Albert had not been loved or even much admired by people outside his family, as those close to the Crown sadly acknowledged. The prince had only one close friend in the royal household, his secretary George Anson, and Anson died in 1851. In his frequent public appearances, Albert was received with more politeness than warmth, and he cut no ice with the English aristocracy. According to royal biographer David Duff, the Earl of Oxford exclaimed, on hearing of the prince's death: "That at least is one foreigner safely out of the way." Lady Dorothy Nevill's husband put on a pair of light-check trousers, which he had been keeping specially for the occasion. Duff goes on: "As Lord Lennox remarked to Sir Henry Cole in October 1862, 'Truth to tell, the "Swells," as a class, did not much care for the P.' " Queen Victoria herself summed it all up when she took her old friend the Duchess of Sutherland into the Blue Room for a last look at the dead prince and murmured, "Will they do him justice now?"

It was unfair of the British to refuse to take the prince consort to their hearts, especially since his wife enjoyed such immense popularity. Logically, the Queen's husband deserved much of the credit for his wife's success. But if the nation was willing to praise Victoria's female submission, it steadfastly refused to take the female role and worship him as she did. To see their Queen in the arms of a German never sat well with the English. England liked the fact that the prince had given the Queen four healthy sons, solving the succession problem. It liked the cozy domesticity that now prevailed at Windsor and Osborne. It liked a court where sexual promiscuity, financial impropriety, gambling, heavy drinking, and coarse language were not permitted. But in their Queen's consort, they were looking for a grand seigneur, not a professor; a stud, not a statesman; a sportsman, not a saint.

And the very idea that the Queen, in her official capacity, was a mere tool in the hands of her German husband, that he, not cabinet ministers, dictated state policy and conducted state business, was political dynamite. A king consort might be acceptable to the Portuguese, but it was anathema to the English.

The English political and social establishment—that tiny minority of the population that saw the royal family regularly—nursed a more nuanced and discrete form of the general animosity toward the prince, which, of course, it helped to shape. Over two decades, top politicians like Lord Palmerston, Lord John Russell, Lord Clarendon, Lord Derby, Lord Granville, Mr. Gladstone, and Mr. Disraeli had been impressed by the prince. Given that even recent kings had found it necessary to rely on the services of trusted private secretaries, it was good to have an intelligent, able, and diligent man at the Queen's shoulder. That the business of the Crown should be run by a man was, in the eyes of Victorian misogyny, self-evidently necessary.

But cabinet ministers and members of parliament, whether Tory or Whig, were aware that the prince had political goals that did not coincide with their own. It was no secret that the prince was aiming to rule in fact as well as name, to rule as William of Orange had ruled in mid-seventeenth-century England and William Hohenstollern still did in nineteenth-century Prussia. Prince Albert was not just a superior private secretary and a dedicated bureaucrat. He was a wily politician, an ambitious statesman, and a power-hungry diplomat. In the Queen's name, acting on her behalf, the prince was systematically undermining the sacred if unwritten constitutional principle of a cabinet of ministers invested by parliament with the responsibility for executive government. For the tiny political establishment of Great Britain, the prince consort's combination of ambition and energy represented a grave threat—to the nation, to the monarchy as they had defined it, to the Queen they loved, and to themselves.

When they had gotten over the shock and sadness, when the mourning had been properly stage-managed, Prime Minister Palmerston and his brethren on both sides of the aisle in parliament breathed a secret sigh of relief. Providence had intervened. An intractable problem was solved deus ex machina. The beauty of British government was that no man, least of all a prince consort, was indispensable. Ministers knew that managing the Queen would be tricky, but they would cope.

For Benjamin Disraeli, the rising power in the Tory Party, the prince consort's death was an opportunity to be seized with both hands. In his published work and parliamentary speeches, Disraeli advanced mystic ideas on monarchy, but he knew that his ministerial advancement was threatened because of the deep antipathy the prince consort felt for him. Thus, when Albert died, Disraeli treated the House of Commons to a brilliant funerary oration well calculated to win the Queen's attention. In a private conversation with the Prussian minister in London, Disraeli was characteristically effusive and double-edged in his praise of the prince: "With Prince Albert we have buried our sovereign. This German Prince has governed England for twenty-one years with a wisdom and energy such as none of our kings has ever shown . . . If he had outlived some of our 'old stagers' [here Disraeli surely had the elderly Palmerston in mind], he would have given us the blessings of absolute government."

It may be doubted how far the ambitious middle-class intellectual Disraeli actually endorsed absolutist government on the Prussian model. But he assumed that his remarks would be reported straight back to Berlin and were likely to find favor with Albert's favorite and adoring daughter, now Crown Princess of Prussia, and thus with the Queen. Benjamin Disraeli subsequently rose to be Earl of Beaconsfield and one of the greatest prime ministers in English history. Though he gave up none of the powers that had accrued to his office, he also reprised Lord Melbourne's role and became one of the Queen's closest friends. Had Albert lived, England would not have had its first and only prime minister of Jewish origins.

If statesmen and politicians saw the death of the prince consort as something of a divine favor to a worthy country, even courtiers close to Victoria felt in their hearts that, perhaps, their beloved Queen, however bereft, was safer on her throne with her husband dead. This was the view expressed privately and late in life by the liberal Mary Ponsonby, who was not loath to imagine Great Britain as a republic. Jane Ely and Jane Churchill, ladies-in-waiting to the Queen for many years, were both Tories, but they were of the same opinion as Mary Ponsonby. All three ladies noticed that the prince consort, for all his manifest virtues, had driven the Crown on a collision course with English political leaders who happened to be their own close relatives and friends. Though of course this could never be said to Her Majesty, the prince's notion of England's good was not, in the end, England's own.

And so, across the nation, in all classes, when Albert died, the mourning was as superficial as it was long, loud, and lavish. The nation wept *for* its Queen but not *with* her.

⁕

ONLY A SMALL handful of people were deeply affected by the prince consort's death. Baron Christian Stockmar in Coburg fell into black despair. He had staked so much on this young princely protégé. Now with Albert dead and the star of Bismarck already rising in the Prussian sky, Stockmar saw his liberal dreams turning to ashes. "I feel right well," Stockmar wrote in March 1862, "that I cannot judge this matter [the death of the prince consort] as one in full possession of his senses; for the thought of the malignity of my personal fate, which has allowed me to live so long that I should endure this cruel blow, drives me at times half mad. An edifice, which, for a great and noble cause, had been reared, with a devout sense of duty . . . has been shattered to its very foundations." Baron Christian Stockmar died the following year.

King Leopold of the Belgians was almost as heart-stricken as his old friend and confederate Baron Stockmar. He received the news of his nephew Albert's death from the Queen herself. Albert had been dearer to him than his own children, the old king confided to Victoria in return. Though he was in poor health, Leopold rushed immediately across to England to support his niece and take charge at Windsor, since the Prince of Wales was obviously not up to the task. It was King Leopold, overruling Princess Alice, who insisted that the Queen should be moved immediately to the privacy of Osborne, on the Isle of Wight, a decision that many of Victoria's ministers later regretted. In 1865 King Leopold died, a hard, sad, bitter man more lamented by his English niece than by his children and his court.

Within hours of the bereaved Queen's arrival on the Isle of Wight on December 19, Duke Ernest II of Saxe-Coburg and Gotha, Albert's brother, arrived, soaking wet from the winter crossing. He took his sister-in-law in his arms in an agony of tears and, during the remainder of his visit, was as usual more trouble than comfort to her and his nieces and nephews. Ernest was a brilliant and complicated man, and his grief for his brother was intense. Since he and Albert had chosen for dynastic reasons to keep silent on their childhood and mythologize their youth, with Albert gone, Ernest lost two decades of intimately shared experience. On the other hand, Ernest had never enjoyed trailing in Albert's wake, and there was comfort in the knowledge that he had the vitality and endurance that Albert lacked. Over the twenty-two years of Albert's life in England, the two brothers had often been at odds over family and financial matters.

Albert's premature death mattered above all for Ernest because it posed a threat to his own international status. The two brothers had always been political allies, constantly exchanging information and devising strategy. The brothers shared the contradictory goal of uniting Germany without losing the independent sovereignty of their duchy. Thus, even as he wept with his widowed sister-in-law, Ernest blamed her and England for killing his brother. For the rest of his life, Ernest sedulously kept up his relations with the English Saxe-Coburgs, exploited his sister-in-law's status, relied on her generosity, and launched vicious attacks in the German press on her and his niece Vicky. Ernest II, Duke of Saxe-Coburg and Gotha, died, unlamented, in 1893.

All nine of Albert's children were deeply marked by his early death, but in different ways. The prince had been a loving, attentive, involved parent from the moment each child took its first breath. For his family, Prince Albert had been fun, the clever mimic and cartoonist, the expert marksman, the gifted singer and accompanist, the master of the revels. He had made a palace into a home, and when he died, the fire went out and the lights dimmed. In their own marriages, his children would strive to re-create what could be called the Osborne experience.

When the prince consort died, four of his nine children were clustered around him: his eldest son, the Prince of Wales, and the princesses Alice, Helena, and Louise. The two youngest children at home, Princess Beatrice and Prince Arthur, were spared the death scene. The eldest child, the Princess Royal, was in Berlin. The second son, Prince Alfred, was away at sea. Prince Leopold, the youngest boy, was still marooned in the south of France, following the sudden death of the elderly courtier sent out to look after him. It must have been terrible for the sick and lonely boy to receive the news of his father's death, yet Leopold was less haunted by his father's legend than his elder brothers.

The prince consort's death cast a very long shadow over relations between the Queen and the heir to the throne. For months after her husband's death, Queen Victoria could hardly bear to be in the same room as the Prince of Wales. "Oh! That boy—much as I pity I never can or shall look at him without a shudder," she confided to Vicky in Berlin. To the end of her life, the Queen had little affection or regard for Bertie, refused to allow him any independent position of consequence, and conducted the business of the Crown with the help of his sisters and his brother Leopold.

Grave, intelligent, withdrawn, responsible, dutiful, humorless Princess Alice, not her brilliant elder sister Vicky, was probably the child most like their father. Alice worshipped the prince consort just as Vicky did, longed for his attention, strove to win his regard, and treasured his every word. After her sister married and moved to Berlin, Alice was overjoyed to take her sister's place in her father's life and, increasingly, in his heart. Her father's death traumatized Princess Alice, although people were too preoccupied with the Queen and with Bertie's engagement to the beautiful Alexandra of Denmark to take much notice. In July 1862, less because she was in love with her fiancé than because her father had wished it, Alice married Prince Louis of Hesse and set out for Germany. Alice's trousseau was black, and her mother made sure the private ceremony was more like a funeral than a wedding. After a life of trouble and tragedy, Alice of Hesse yielded to diphtheria, dying at age thirty-five on December 14, 1878, seventeen years to the day after her father, with the words "dear Papa" on her lips.

The person who regretted most passionately that she had not been with her father in his last illness was his eldest and most beloved child, Victoria (Vicky), the Princess Royal. Her lot was to experience the dying and the mourning from afar. In December 1861, Vicky had just turned twenty-one and was Crown Princess of Prussia, following the recent death of her husband Fritz's uncle king. Her father-in-law William was now King of Prussia. Vicky was also in the first trimester of her third pregnancy, and very restricted in her movements even within the palace. Given the severe physical problems of her son, William, and the fact that her healthy second child was a girl, and thus barred from the Prussian royal succession, her unborn child was a matter of the gravest political and dynastic significance. Though she received almost daily bulletins on her father's health, was apprised by her sister Alice that their father was very ill, and had certainly become very anxious, Vicky was still wholly unprepared for her father to die. When the news came, her first impulse was to set off for England at once, to comfort and be comforted by her family. But her father-in-law the king of Prussia absolutely forbade her to leave Berlin. Her husband went to England alone for the prince consort's funeral. For three months, Vicky and her mother were forced to put their anguish on paper.

After the prince's death, the Queen turned to her daughter in Prussia for advice and support, convinced that Vicky was the person closest to the prince consort left on earth. Bertie, Alfred, Alice, and above all Vicky herself suffered from this official passing of the torch from father to eldest daughter. To the end of her life, Vicky considered herself the prince consort's intellectual and political heir. Her mission in life, and that of her husband, was to realize her father's and Stockmar's vision for Prussia and for Prussian-English entente. When the prince consort died, both Vicky and her husband felt that they had lost their most precious support and inspiration, but they determined to fight on. Convinced that she spoke with her father's voice, Vicky was empowered to embrace her role as her husband's chief adviser. She was only a woman, she felt, but she was her father's daughter, and she would be to Fritz as Albert had been to Victoria.

This choice of role was peculiarly unfortunate and ill advised, as her crafty uncle Ernest probably told her. Prince Albert in England was disliked as a German and distrusted in Germany as an Englishman, and the same was true in reverse for his daughter. Vicky, brilliant, capable, and pure, could not hide her distaste for the Prussian court and the Prussian government and her desire to reform them in the English image. Both Fritz's father William I of Prussia, and his chancellor, Prince Otto von Bismarck, quickly decided that the English-born Crown Princess was their greatest enemy. They believed, falsely, that her loyalty was to her mother, not her husband, and that she was an English spy scheming to betray Prussian interests. All notions of chivalry were abandoned in the attacks upon "the English Woman," at court, in the government, and in the press. Within a year of her father's death, Vicky and Fritz had already been forced out of all part in national governance and were pariahs in Prussia, reviled by the left wing for failing to stand up for democratic values, and by the right wing for their private opposition to the king and his ministers.

Most fatefully, King William and Bismarck passed their hatred and distrust on to Prince William, Vicky and Fritz's eldest son, the future kaiser of World War I. Under their tutelage, this damaged boy became a deranged man all too willing to blame his English mother for all his problems, personal and political. To her death in 1901, Vicky, then dowager empress, was the most unpopular, slandered, and reviled figure in Germany.

It is unlikely that the prince consort's personal influence could have prevented King William I from falling under the sway of Otto von Bismarck.

But there was one key moment when Albert's influence might have been crucial. In 1862, when the legislature dared to oppose his plans for the army, the king of Prussia furiously prepared a statement of abdication that his son had only to sign to become king. Despite his wife's frantic entreaties, Fritz persuaded his elderly father to keep his crown since the coronation oath committed a king to rule until his death. As a result, King William I of Prussia not only lived to be crowned Emperor William I of Germany at Versailles in 1871, but ruled for seventeen more years. Fritz finally acceded to the throne as Emperor Frederick I in 1888 and died of throat cancer three months later. Had the prince consort been alive in 1862, he might have been able to persuade Fritz that his higher duty was to the nation, not his father, and that he must seize the reins of power.

No one ever doubted that if Crown Prince Frederick came to the throne of Prussia, Bismarck and the far-right party would be dismissed, and his wife, Victoria, would be the power behind the throne. As king and queen of Prussia in 1862, Fritz and Vicky would probably have had decades to try to realize her father's political vision. The forces of liberal democracy would have had a better chance of prevailing over militarism and absolutism. It is not absurd to argue that, had the prince consort lived even one more year, had his daughter Vicky had a chance to dictate Crown policy and shape society in Prussia, there might not have been a First World War.

*

WHEN THE PRINCE CONSORT died, everyone had the same question: How will the Queen survive this blow? Will she too lose her hold on life and quickly follow him to the grave? Or will she go mad and perhaps, in a moment of despair, take her own life? Even those who were not unhappy that the prince had gone to his Maker understood that his wife would feel his loss to the core of her being. "Albertolatry" was the religion at Windsor, and the Queen was its high priestess. Would she, like a Brahman widow, throw herself, metaphorically, on her husband's pyre?

In the first moments after Albert's death, Queen Victoria pulled herself together and played her role of grieving widow, loving mother, and dutiful monarch to perfection. Carried out of the Blue Room by her nephew Ernest Leiningen and by Charles Phipps, the prince consort's private secretary, she lay on a sofa, addressing a special word to each member of the household as they filed by in tears to kiss her hand. "You will not desert me? You will all help me?" she repeated heartbreakingly. She gathered her children around her and was even gracious to Bertie when he sobbed that he would try to be all that she wanted him to be.

But the true enormity of her situation hit the Queen when she moved into her bedroom and faced the empty bed. For the first time in her life, she would sleep all alone. In vain attempts to assuage those feelings, on the first night, she went to the nursery, picked up the sleeping Princess Beatrice and took her into her bed. Then she took to sleeping with the prince's dressing gown over her bed, with his nightshirt in her arms, and a plaster cast of his hand in hers. Referring to her husband's death, "I never dreamt of the physical possibility of such a calamity," she wrote to Vicky from Windsor on December 18. "What is to become of us all? Of the unhappy country, of Europe, of all? . . . But how [shall] I, who leant on him for all and everything—without whom I did nothing, moved not a finger, arranged not a print or photograph, didn't put on a gown or bonnet if he didn't approve it—be able to go on . . . ? Oh! It is too, too weary! The day—the night (above all the night) is too sad and weary."

It was worse when she got to Osborne, her favorite place, the place where she and Albert had been a young married couple, happy to be in their own home at last, wandering the estate on their ponies, playing duets, listening to the nightingales, retiring to bed early alone, just the two of them. Albert had brought her security and contentment as well as passion and pleasure, and the bleakness of the future without him appalled her. "I am alas! not old—and my feelings are strong and warm; my love is ardent," she wrote pathetically to her daughter.

The intensity with which Victoria missed Albert dulled with the years, but his death was a wound that never really healed. As a woman, she was inconsolable, and her misery was as egotistic as it was epic. During her reign, Windsor Castle became more dungeon than palace, Buckingham Palace was more or less boarded up, Osborne had the air of a mausoleum, and Balmoral was as bleak as the surrounding moors.

The extremity of desolation that Victoria expressed over and over does not endear her. When, in the early years of her widowhood, we find her declaring that she longed to die and be happy again with Albert in heaven, we take it all with a grain or five of salt. When she says that she and Albert had decided that hell did not exist and that the virtuous could count on being reunited with their loved ones in the hereafter, it seems a little too theologically convenient. The experience of losing a loved partner is hardly rare, and all too often Victoria's emotion was selfish and over the top. Little Arthur laughing over lunch, Vicky writing of a wonderful trip she had taken, a failure by any member of her family and household to commemorate the anniversary of her engagement, would earn a stinging reproof or a fit of weeping from the Queen. Even in her first letter to her uncle Leopold after Albert's death, the multiple underlinings and heightened vocabulary smack of melodrama: "My *own* DEAREST, KINDEST *Father,*—For as such have I *ever* loved you! The poor fatherless babe of eight months is now the utterly broken-hearted and crushed widow of forty-two!" she wrote to her uncle.

The loneliness and longing, the feeling of uncertainty and abandonment that Victoria expressed were genuine. It is not hard to believe that once she was close to suicide. But all the same, the expression she found for her feelings was histrionic. The role of tragic heroine, preparing to follow her loved one into the grave, was one the Queen had wept to see enacted on the stage hundreds of times in her beloved operas. Now that the role was hers in real life, she had a libretto and a score to follow, and they made life a little more bearable, at least for her. The fear of madness had long been used as a weapon against the Queen, but now she found it useful. To press her hands to her temples like Gaetano Donizetti's mad heroine Lucia di Lammermoor and piteously murmur that she must withdraw, as she was losing her mind, was a convenient way of getting out of doing anything she did not feel like.

And if Victoria talked a great deal in the early years about heartbreak and going mad under the burden of state business, she never seems for a moment to have considered the more mundane solutions to her problems: remarriage and abdication. In truth, remarriage was a very difficult and rare option for any Victorian widow in her forties. Passionlessness was what decent men required in their wives. A woman in her thirties was already considered to be old for marriage, and widows who remarried were greeted by hostility and prurient jocularity. For Queen Victoria, remarriage was virtually impossible. At twenty, she had been able to count the number of eligible suitors on the fingers of one hand. Now there was not one that would please both her and the English nation. German royal families no doubt could muster a few impoverished old bachelor roués willing to take on a widow in her forties, if she was rich enough. But Victoria had no wish to marry a man like her brother-in-law Ernest or the debauched misogynists Vicky had found at the court of Berlin. Among her fellow countrymen, Victoria could probably have found a man to her liking, but the ancient political barriers against a monarch marrying a subject remained.

And to remarry, Victoria would almost certainly have had to abdicate, and, even as she lay long nights in her bed, aching for Albert, she never considered it. In seeking to comfort and support her mother in the days following her father's death, Vicky knew exactly what line to take. "I can so well understand that you wish to die dearest Mama, to be with him again," she wrote in January 1862, "but who then would carry out his wishes, would work out all he has begun with so much trouble and so much love? You know, beloved Mama, what would most likely be the fate of the nation if God were to remove you now. In twenty years all that causes us such alarm with Bertie may be changed and softened. But heaven forbid beloved Papa's work of 20 years should be in vain. God requires immense sacrifices of you and has imposed such difficult duties on you but He has given you adored Papa for a guide . . . Your children and your people have need of you—you would not have them doubly bereaved when this blow is already as much as they can bear."

And so, in the spirit of sublime self-sacrifice, Victoria determined to live for her country and her children. The unworthy Bertie must wait for the throne. Her mission was clear: to represent the sainted Albert on earth, voice his views, realize his vision. Pleasure must be put aside. The stony path of duty must be trodden with bleeding feet.

And having Albert in eternal bliss, impatiently awaiting her, instead of on earth, busy running her kingdom for her, had its advantages. From early in their marriage, both she and Albert had used the pronoun we for their joint life, their joint enterprise, and their joint policy, but more and more with the years "we" had meant "I, Albert, in Victoria's name and taking her consent for granted." Now speaking as Albert and Victoria, male and female, she could reclaim the ancient royal "we" and speak with as much authority as her male predecessors. As an unmarried queen, Victoria had delighted in having her way. Yielding to Albert's will and taking him as her lord and master had gone against the grain. Now, as the dead man's disciple, citing his example, preaching his gospel, she would again be master in her own household, head of the family, the sacred embodiment of the Crown. "I am also anxious to repeat one thing," wrote Victoria to her uncle Leopold ten days after Albert's death, "and that one is my firm resolve, my irrevocable decision, viz that his wishes—his plans—above everything his views about everything are to be my law! And no human power will make me swerve from what he decided . . . I am also determined that no one person, may he be ever so good, ever so devoted among my servants—is to lead or guide or dictate to me."

The Latin word order of the inscription placed on the coffin of the dead prince—"Augustissimae et potentissimae Victoria Reginae conjugis percarissimus"—makes the point very well. Her Most Puissant and August Majesty, Queen Victoria, asserts ownership of a most beloved, dead husband.

FOR AT LEAST three years, Queen Victoria was very, very unhappy, but she coped, and she had compensations—first and foremost the process and ritual of mourning, which had always held a peculiar fascination for her. The Queen's dressers always had her mourning clothes ready in case a distant relative or dim European duke should die. Now the Queen had the satisfaction of seeing every person she met, from the youngest princess to the scullery maid, wreathed in dull black from head to toe. In 1864, court ladies were at last permitted to wear gray, white, and purple, but mauve was still considered too frisky.

For the rest of her life, Queen Victoria's wardrobe was uniformly black and unadorned. Plain, high-necked gowns replaced the low-cut, elaborately embroidered pink and blue creations of the Queen's married years. On her head, ugly caps with the widow's peak replaced the flowers and wheat ears, the ropes of pearls and diamond tiaras. The fabulous display of jewelry ceased, and the Queen agreed to wear a tiny new crown around her bun only on rare state occasions. The message was clear. The Queen had never cared for fashion, only for her husband's compliment. Why bare her shoulders, put diamonds on her breast, and dress her hair when there was no one to comment on her beauty?

The newly widowed Queen with her children

To reinforce and publicize the message, the newly widowed Queen sat for a remarkable number of oil paintings and photographs. The painted portraits were copied and distributed to close family and friends. The photographs were for the public as much as the family album. Seated next to a bust of the prince consort, the Queen appears young and comely in a painting by Albert Graefle. She wears a severe black dress and white widow's cap, but an ermine robe stretched fancifully over the back of her chair marks the fact that she is queen as well as widow. A photograph of her in a big black hood and fur-trimmed dress shows her looking down somberly at a little miniature of the prince. Several photos show her surrounded by ashen-faced children, her face turned in adoration to the bust of the prince or gazing at his portrait in her lap. Years later, in the portraits of the Queen surrounded by her children and their spouses and their children, some representation of the dead prince consort would always be included.

A vital task facing the Queen within hours of her husband's death was to create her own clean and sanitary version of what the Germans called a *sterbe-zimmer*—a death chamber. Photographers were called in at once to capture the appearance of the Blue Room as the prince left it at 10:50 p.m., December 14, 1861. Repainted, kept meticulously clean, with fresh flowers strewn on the bed daily, the room was kept for the Queen's lifetime as if Albert might at any moment walk back into it and take up his life again. The towels were changed, and hot water was brought in for shaving each day. The glass with the last dose of medicine lay on the bedside table, and the blotting book lay open next to the pen on the writing table.

Such death chambers were not uncommon—there were several, shrouded in cobwebs, in the vast royal warrens of Berlin. But Victoria had no intention of stopping there. Her pleasure was to create sacred spaces where she could commune with the dear departed. Her duty was to ensure dearest Albert's place in history and keep his example before the ungrateful world.

And so, whatever the desolation that overwhelmed her at night, that kept her for years from the public's view, and made the lives of her family and her court miserable, the Queen was all activity and business during the day. Within days of the death, she was begging the crown princess in Berlin "to help me in all my great plans for a mausoleum (which I have chosen the place for at Frogmore) for statues, monuments, etc." The Italian sculptor Marochetti, the German painters Winterhalter and Grüner, who had enjoyed the prince's patronage, were admitted to see the widowed Queen even before the 1861 Christmas holiday began. Over the next year, architects, sculptors, painters, and artists in glass and ceramic were busily planning for the transformation of St. George's Chapel at Windsor to accommodate the Albert Memorial Chapel and the construction and decoration of the Royal Mausoleum at Frogmore on the grounds of Windsor Castle.

The Queen at the outset keenly studied all the proposed memorials across the nation. She contributed her own money but was also an efficient fund-raiser with parliament and private groups. She was anxious to show Albert as she remembered him: young, handsome, athletic, virile. A rare moment of disagreement between the Queen and her daughter in Prussia occurred when Vicky attempted a bust of her father and made the nose, in her mother's opinion, too thick. For several years, the only occasions when the Queen could be persuaded to appear in public was for the unveiling of a statue of her husband—in Windsor Great Park, at Balmoral, in Aberdeen, in Coburg.

For the Queen, the Royal Mausoleum at Frogmore was the most important monument. Here, barely a year after his death, Albert's coffin was transported, to lie in a massive sarcophagus surmounted by a statue by Carlo Marochetti. Here, accompanied by her daughters and her ladies, Victoria came to weep in the early days of her widowhood. Here she came with members of her family each year on sacred anniversaries until the end of her life. Here Victoria herself would be buried by Albert's side, under a statue that Marochetti also made in the 1860s, capturing the Queen in eternal, and idealized, youth. Even today the mausoleum at Frogmore is open to the public for only a few hours a year and is known almost exclusively from pictures.

The most important monument from the nation's point of view was the National Albert Memorial in Kensington Gardens, just a stone's throw from the Royal Albert Hall, itself fronted by a huge statue of the prince in a Shakespearian doublet. The Victoria and Albert Museum, whose seed money came from the Great Exhibition of 1851, is close by. The first planning meeting for the memorial occurred within a month of the prince's death, and the London municipal worthies decided that even though the project was to be publicly funded, the Queen should be allowed to choose the design. Her choice, a monument by George Gilbert Scott, the most famous and most pompous of Victorian architects, was slowly completed over the next fourteen years. Perhaps because people had been able to watch the huge thing go up stage by stage, or because the nation and the royal family had by 1876 finally tired of unveiling statues to a dead prince, there was no inauguration ceremony.

The Albert Memorial, as it came to be known, features a seated prince, dressed in Garter robes, court breeches, and pumps, the catalog of the Great

Exhibition of 1851 in his hand. Over the giant bronze statue rears an immense, gilded, Gothic-style canopy, making the monument into a shrine. Surrounding and beneath the main figure is a complex of statuary by various British artists. On the four corners are figures representing the continents of Europe, Asia, Africa, and America. Australia had certainly been "discovered" by the 1860s, but presumably it upset the symmetry and so failed to make the cut.

BY 1864, QUEEN VICTORIA was still almost invisible to the public, but her household noticed that she was beginning to recover her zest for life. This was due in part to the simple passage of time but also to the presence by her side of a Scotsman named John Brown.

Albert had filled many key functions in Victoria's life and, as the years went by, she found that many of those functions could be filled quite effectively by ministers, secretaries, comptrollers, and the like. But Victoria still had two unmet affective needs that servants of the Crown such as Benjamin Disraeli, Henry Ponsonby, and Charles Grey could not fill. She wanted to feel safe and protected, and she wanted to be number one in the life of at least one person. John Brown emerged to meet those needs, and from about 1864, when he became a year-round member of her household, to 1883 when he died, Brown was essential to her. Heart and soul, he was her liege man, and he devoted his life to her at no small cost.

John Brown was a Highlander, a tall, strong, handsome man, seven years younger than the Queen, who was first employed on the Balmoral estate as a gillie, working with the horses and dogs, managing the game, working as a beater and loader, leading the ponies on royal excursions. Brown won the commendation of the prince consort for his good sense and loyalty, and he then became a favorite with the Queen. When the widowed Victoria returned to Balmoral, Brown not only led her pony on the steep trails but drove out with her on her excursions in a pony chaise. His courage and resourcefulness were credited with saving her life on several occasions. In 1864 she decided that Brown was too important to her comfort to be left behind in Scotland, and so he was promoted, given the title of the Queen's Highland Servant, allotted a new set of suits, and brought to Osborne and Windsor. Brown quickly graduated from cleaning the Queen's boots and washing her dogs to serving as her personal attendant, messenger, and intermediary, to becoming her favorite companion.

Brown soon won notoriety in the royal household for his familiar ways with the Queen, whom he sometimes was heard addressing in his deep brogue as "wummin." He lifted her down from her pony and wrapped her shawl around her. Once he was heard ordering her to keep her chin up, for heaven's sake! On another occasion he chided her for her ratty old dress. Brown was capable of denying the Prince of Wales access to his mother, since she was taking her nap. At Balmoral, Brown and the Queen would go off on excursions in the pony chaise, fortified against the cold by wraps, shortbread cookies, and flasks of whisky, which, Brown declared, Her Majesty vastly preferred to tea. At the annual Gillies Ball, Victoria shocked her family by trimming her dress and hair with plaid and whirling happily on Brown's sinewy arm, looking shockingly young and happy again. That Brown had a taste for whisky and was often too inebriated to perform his duties did not improve his stock with the royal family.

Between 1865 and 1870, rumormongers and scandal sheets in Europe spread the word that the Queen of England was secretly married to Mr.

"A Brown Study,"
1867

Brown. Perhaps she had even had a child by him. In Great Britain, the Queen's officers were able to protect Her Majesty's reputation in the mainstream press. However, the public was fascinated by Brown, and anyone with access to the court watched him and the Queen attentively. One cartoonist in a short-lived radical periodical called the *Tomahawk* dared to show the British lion lunging at a kilted gentleman smoking a pipe, his back to the throne. However, the decision made by the Queen's advisers was to simply keep a lid as far as possible on the rumors and make sure that nothing substantive came out. Brown, for all his faults, kept the Queen happy, and he had no political agenda and no political base. He depended on the Queen's good favor, his loyalty was exclusively to her, and though he became arrogant and difficult, he posed no real threat. When, following Brown's death, Queen Victoria formed a not dissimilarly close attachment to her Indian servant Abdul Karim, even the Prince of Wales, who had loathed the Highland Servant, looked back on the Brown era with nostalgia.

Were Victoria and John Brown lovers? A number of people in the nineteenth century thought so, but the eyewitness reports are all at third- or fourth-hand. The excellent 1997 movie, starring Judi Dench and Billy Connolly, is provocatively titled *Mrs. Brown* and establishes how much affection bound Victoria to John, how he protected her, and what fun they had together, but it refrains from showing the two in bed. The most authoritative twentieth-century biographies of the Queen—Elizabeth Longford's in 1964 and Christopher Hibbert's in 2000—deny the possibility of physical intimacy. Hibbert, a scrupulous scholar, devotes a long footnote to the sources that claim to have evidence that the Queen had allowed John Brown "every conjugal privilege," but his text comes to the orthodox conclusion that the Queen was "innocent." Longford declared: "That the Queen was neither John Brown's mistress nor his morganatic wife should be clear from a study of her character."

What Longford and Hibbert meant was that Queen Victoria would be lessened in their eyes had she slept with John Brown and that they are relieved to report that there is absolutely no hard evidence that she did. However, writers with no loyalty to the monarchy such as Dorothy Thompson assert that the lack of hard evidence is in itself a proof of intimacy. If the memorial that the Queen prepared for the dead Brown, and wished to publish, was so "innocent," why did her staff burn it, along with Brown's own diary? Hibbert drily confirms Thompson's sensational claim that, at the Queen's express wish and deliberately without the knowledge of her family members, Victoria's doctor, Sir James Reid, placed a picture of John Brown in her coffin, and put a lock of his hair in her dead hand. This indicates that Prince Albert and John Brown had a certain equivalency to Victoria as a woman.

ANOTHER KEY ELEMENT in Victoria's successful new life as a widow was her career as an author. Writing was almost as vital to the Queen as eating, and the most important monument she constructed to the dead Albert was not in stone but in text—the six tightly spaced volumes of biography she commissioned, supervised closely, and partly wrote. Within months of Albert's death, she began her collaboration with Sir Charles Grey, and they completed the one-volume *The Early Years of the Prince Consort* by 1867. Victoria then went on to guide Professor (later Sir) Theodore Martin through the arduous five-volume *The Life of His Royal Highness the Prince Consort*. Emboldened, and encouraged by her staff, Victoria then published two volumes of extracts from her Highland diaries in her own name, a paean to the dead prince that became an international best seller.

Victoria's authorized biography of her husband is rarely read today, even by nineteenth-century experts, but it still offers more hard information on the prince consort than any other. It also has a massive bias. Martin states explicitly in his introduction that his job was to present Queen Victoria's view of the prince consort, not his own. The great strength of the work is that Martin is a kind of ventriloquist's dummy through which Victoria, the person closest to Albert for twenty-one of his forty-two years, speaks to us.

The great weakness of the biography, especially of the first volume, with which the Queen was most intimately associated, is that it paints the portrait of a man who is very difficult to like or sympathize with. As a young wife, Queen Victoria chose to worship her husband as the perfect man. As an insecure young husband, Albert found it both natural and pleasant that his wife should constantly descant on his perfections. Both husband and wife constructed a narrative whereby Albert from infancy was without stain, impervious to carnal temptation, a modern Galahad.

But once these private fictions were committed to print, they looked suspiciously like hagiography masquerading as biography, and hagiography had a waning hold over the public even in the nineteenth century. The stated intent of Victoria's biographical project was to set her husband among the great of history, but in this she failed. The Queen made strenuous claims for her husband and praised him to the skies, but simply by taking possession of his life and placing her stamp upon it, she set the prince consort in her shadow. He emerged from her account as a passive creature, cast in the image of a powerful woman's desire.

Furthermore, by portraying her husband as Albert the Chaste, Queen Victoria feminized the prince, the last thing he would have wanted. Across cultures, lifelong sexual continence has been a virtue required of women, not men. The great male saints—Paul, Augustine, Jerome, Francis, Dominic—were not virgins or monogamous married men but reformed libertines. They constructed their own narratives and commanded the respect of their peers and posterity by showing how hard won had been their battles for purity. Albert and Victoria collaborated in constructing a myth that fatally denied all evidence of struggle and thus all dramatic interest.

The kindest interpretation Victoria placed on her husband's death for the public was that he was an angel, too good for a wicked world, and now happy in heaven. Her harshest judgment in private was that he had lacked "pluck" and given in to death, instead of fighting. In their married lives, they had been partners as well as lovers, and the rhetoric of her submission always hid a subtext of competition and rebellion. By 1855, at the height of the Crimean War, the marriage had begun to fray as Victoria reveled in her new prominence with the public as a wartime queen. This encouraged her to assert her will in family affairs. How things would have gone between the two had Albert lived is impossible to imagine, but it is clear that by 1859 Victoria was already chipping away at Albert's pedestal.

If the marriage of Victoria and Albert was as much a power struggle as a love story, then Victoria proved to be the stronger. If their partnership was also a contest, then she was the winner. She took possession of the prince in death as he had taken possession of her in life. In her black dress and widow's cap, she lived to play the tragedy queen, Victoria, Regina et Imperatrix, for forty more years. Albert had staked his life on becoming *the* Eminent Victorian, and yet he would find no place in Lytton Strachey's famous book. His was the tragic role. The power and the glory were hers.

Acknowledgments

TOURING BEAUTY SPOTS ASSOCIATED WITH BRITISH ROYALTY IN EN-
gland, Scotland, and Germany was one of the perks of writing this book,
and I usually had a friend to share the experience. My first visit to Windsor
stands out in memory because my sister Rose came along. My experience
of the Scottish Highlands carpeted in bluebells and yellow gorse was blissful in no small part because Judith Weltman was with me. Similarly, the
Isle of Wight and Osborne House were fun because Margot Gill was by my
side. Margot has been a great resource on British royal lore throughout this
project.

For a long time I put off a visit to Prince Albert's beloved Coburg and
Gotha as I had no German contacts and my German was rusty. I need not
have feared. All the officials I met in those charming towns went out of
their way to be helpful, and my German visit proved far more rewarding
than I had ever dreamed possible. Schloss Friedenstein in Gotha offered a
mine of information, and my discussion there with Sandra Gerlach was instrumental in my formulation of the relationship between Prince Albert
and his ancestral domains. Things went even better in Coburg where the
central tourist office is a model of efficiency. They presented me with a superb poster of Queen Victoria and her family gathered in Coburg for a wedding and immediately put me in the capable hands of Gerhard Harten.
Once convinced that I knew my Coburg history and could keep pace with
him even uphill, Herr Harten volunteered to be my chauffeur as well as my
guide and whisked me around every castle and monument connected to
the Saxe-Coburg family in the area. I am greatly indebted to his erudition
and friendliness.

From the beginning, everyone I knew seemed fascinated by my tales of
Queen Victoria's marriage. My gratitude goes out to all the members of my
reading, Russian, tennis, and bridge groups whose enthusiasm sustained

me when it seemed *We Two* would never get finished. Thanks especially to two members of the Russian group, Tanya Kaye and Rita Bykhovsky. Tanya made insightful comments on early portions of the manuscript, and Rita and I had a number of detailed and ardent discussions about the Russian royal family. To my psychiatrist friend Francesca von Broembsen I always turn for expert advice on how family relationships play out and are put into words. My son Christopher Gill, a specialist in infectious disease, is my medical guru. My discussions of hemophilia and typhoid owe so much to Chris's expert advice and help with literature searches. My fellow grandparent/child-care-giver Ken McElheny read inchoate versions of many chapters and put his editorial zeal and historical expertise at my disposal. I inflicted multiple versions of later chapters on Maggie Byer, who has that mix of sharp criticism and effervescent praise every writer dreams of. Maggie hacks through the jungle of my prose, and the shape of the sentences in this book owes much to her. Thanks, Ken and Maggie, for devoting so many hours to my book. Thanks also to my beloved sister-in-law Linda Crosskey for the photograph of me that appears on the book jacket.

Once the manuscript was finalized, it was exciting for me to work with the team at Ballantine Books. Philip Bashe, the copy editor, and Nancy Delia, the production editor, were models of zeal and accuracy. Barbara Bachman's design for the book surpassed all my expectations. Lisa Barnes took on the job of my publicist with contagious enthusiasm. I can rely on Lisa to get back to me within the half hour whenever I hit even the smallest glitch. Jillian Quint has coordinated relations between me and the editorial and production staff, and her calm efficiency, lightened by flashes of humor, has earned my admiration. I wish her well in her new editorial career. But my special thanks go to Random House executive editor Susanna Porter, a dedicated and meticulous reader. In Susanna the great tradition of American editing lives on in difficult times. Reading my manuscript time after time, she homed in on errant details. She picked up on thematic patterns. She was generous with her praise. And then, when the close reading was done, she grasped what was new and interesting about the whole project and pushed me to take the final step into interpretation. How lucky I am to have had Susanna as my editor.

Jill Kneerim and her colleagues at Kneerim and Williams have now seen me through two books, and I can no longer imagine doing without them. Leslie Kaufman in the New York office took time out of a busy to schedule to read the tricky first part of the manuscript and reassure me I was on the right track. As for Jill Kneerim herself, she is my cheerleader, adviser, and therapist as well as my agent. She is my friend. When she goes on vacation and turns off the BlackBerry I feel abandoned. Jill's special contribution to the manuscript was to urge me to tell a story, not just collect materials and write pretty sentences, a tough lesson for ex-academics like me.

Writing is a lonely slog much of the time, and it is thanks to the unfailing love and support of my family that I sit glued to my word processor year after year. My husband, Stuart, not only makes sure that I never lose a line to computer malfunction (or user stupidity!) but also uncomplainingly accepts that some nights we will not meet for dinner as I am engaged in a ten-hour bout with a tough chapter. My children, Catherine and Chris, and their terrific spouses are the center of my world. And every week I have the joy of watching my six grandchildren grow up—Bronwyn fourteen, Fiona eleven, Delia seven, Kalkidan three, James three, and Susanna one. My claims to being a family historian rest on regular practice of what George Sand called "the art of being a grandmother."

Notes

PRELUDE TO A MARRIAGE

3   **All afternoon Queen Victoria had been** We are fortunate to know in great detail what Queen Victoria was doing, saying, and thinking in the year of her engagement and marriage. There are numerous contemporary letters and memoirs, but above all there is the Queen's journal. When she first began her journal, at the age of thirteen, the then Princess Victoria wrote a dutiful and dull account of her engagements, the people she met, the operas she saw, and so forth. The entries for the early years offer limited insight into her thoughts and feelings, since the princess wrote in the certainty that both her mother and her governess, Louise Lehzen, read everything she wrote. However, by the time she came to the throne, Queen Victoria had acquired the habit of diary writing, and so she wrote freely and often at length, almost every day, from 1837 to her death in 1901. In 1912, soon after the death of Victoria's eldest son and heir, Edward VII, and with the full support of the new King George V and Queen Mary, Viscount Esher transcribed the diaries up to the year of the Queen's marriage. Esher subsequently published a judiciously selective, extensively annotated two-volume work entitled *The Girlhood of Queen Victoria: A Selection from Her Majesty's Diaries Between the Years 1832 and 1840* (London: Longmans, Green & Co.; New York: John Murray, 1912). Every transcription involves some amount of editing, and Esher was a man of the English courtier class, anxious to promote the interests of the royal family. But he was also a man of intelligence and finesse, committed to preserving the historical record. Esher was aware that Queen Victoria's journals were one of the most precious documents in the history of the British monarchy and, even if they could not respectfully be published as written, must be kept in the archives for posterity. Sadly, however, Queen Victoria in her final years had read through her journals, marked the passages she wished to be preserved, and then committed the volumes to the care and discretion of her youngest daughter, Beatrice (Princess Henry of Battenberg). Beatrice was a Victorian in the worst sense of the word, and in the last years of her life, she took it upon herself to preserve her mother's legend by censoring her mother's work. She read through all the diaries, transcribed a text in her own hand, and then burned the original volume. The few sections of the Queen's journals that were published in her lifetime prove how much precious information was lost when Princess Beatrice bowdlerized and abridged. Thus Queen Victoria's journals exist only in the form of transcriptions and fragments.

4   **Nemours made a rapid exit** Nemours subsequently married another Victoria, or Victoire,

as the name often became, the Queen of England's first cousin Victoria of Coburg-Kohary, the eldest daughter of her uncle Ferdinand.

4 **Given her druthers** This was the opinion of Lord Palmerston, then foreign secretary, who wrote to Lord Granville: "After being used to agreeable and well-informed Englishmen, I fear [the Queen] will not find a foreign prince to her liking" (Anthony Trollope, *Lord Palmerston*, London: Isbister, 1882, p. 66).

4 **But unfortunately, not one** By the late eighteenth century, it was already an article of faith in English political circles that the delicate balance between Whigs and Tories that made England a great nation would be destroyed if the monarch married into one of the main aristocratic families, most of which were firmly allied with one party or the other. The monarch, it was believed, must be above political party. As a result, no English monarch or heir to the English throne married a British commoner between 1660, when the future James II married Anne Hyde, until Charles, Prince of Wales, married Lady Diana Spencer in 1981. Charles's grandfather George VI also married a commoner, Lady Elizabeth Bowes Lyon, but their marriage occurred before anyone imagined that George would become king.

5 **She herself had been officially entered** To take one example, by the age of seventeen, Maria da Glória, the queen of Portugal, had been married twice, and she was exactly Queen Victoria's age. Queen Maria was first married to her stepmother's brother, but he died within months of the marriage, thus further weakening her tenuous hold on the throne. In January 1836, Queen Maria was married by proxy to Ferdinand of Coburg-Kohary, Queen Victoria's cousin.

5 **If her maternal and paternal relations** The eldest son of a reigning English monarch is known as the heir apparent. Victoria was heir presumptive to her uncle William IV, the presumption being that King William and his wife, Queen Adelaide, would not produce an heir apparent.

5 **He distrusted the ambitions** The dynasty composed of Georges I, II, III, and IV, and William IV is usually referred to as the house of Hanover, or, in earlier times, the house of Brunswick. However, as the future king William IV remarked to his fellow midshipmen when he was a fourteen-year-old boy sent to sea, the family name was Guelph.

5 **William's preferred candidate** Officially, members of royal families have no surname, even, apparently, on their passports. However, given that nineteenth-century royal persons tended to use the same Christian names over and over, in private correspondence they had various ways to distinguish between one family member and another, chiefly nicknames (Vicky, Bertie, Affie) and first name plus title (George Cambridge, Victoria Kent). When entering into the relationships between different members of the royal family, I found it useful at times to adopt the royal shorthand.

5 **The Duke of Cumberland was heir** Salic law in Germany precluded women from inheriting lands and titles, so Victoria could not be Queen of Hanover.

5 **Given the risk of hereditary blindness** George Cumberland eventually succeeded his father as King of Hanover. The Blind King, as he was known, did a creditable job until his kingdom was swallowed up by Prussia.

5 **He was a tall, strong young man** The Cambridge branch of the British royal family did in fact rejoin the main trunk when Princess Mary of Teck, George, Duke of Cambridge's niece, became the queen consort of George V. Queen Mary was Queen Elizabeth II's grandmother. Queen Mary was a redoubtable lady, far more intelligent and energetic than her husband.

5 **He, or his mother, was assiduous** Queen Victoria's early diary features meticulous lists of the numerous presents she received for Christmas and her birthday from relatives, friends, and attendants.

6 **He did not fancy his cousin** As a youth, George Cambridge emulated his uncle Clarence (William IV) by taking up with an actress and producing several illegitimate children, who were known as the FitzGeorges.

6 **Their answer was a diplomatically expressed** This refusal to entertain the idea of a Prus-

sian marriage is somewhat ironic. In the next generation, alliance with the Hohenzollerns became a cornerstone of Prince Albert's foreign policy. See chapter 24.

6   **"I am really *astonished*** Esher, vol. 1, pp. 47–48, King Leopold's original emphases.

8   **The Queen faithfully recorded** For these conversations on the subject of marriage, see Esher, vol. 2, pp. 207, 215, and 225–226.

10   **In the meantime, Victoria's shilly-shallying** Ibid, p. 139.

10   **His shoulders were broad** There seems no doubt that at the time of his engagement and marriage, Prince Albert was at the peak of physical perfection. Even his enemies agreed that he was extremely handsome, though they criticized his legs as too heavy.

12   **Albert cast Victoria in the role** "Es ist kleines Fräuchen" ("It is little wifey), Victoria said to Albert when he was close to death and failed to recognize her. Apparently this was one of the affectionate diminutives he used for her.

12   **Like so many famous** I attribute to Jill Ker Conway the important observation that famous women find it necessary in their memoirs to downplay their talents and attribute their achievement to luck and the support of others.

PART ONE: THE YEARS APART | *Victoria: A Fatherless Princess*

Chapter 1: CHARLOTTE AND LEOPOLD

18   **She accused him, not unjustly** Charlotte once remarked to Stockmar: "My mother was bad, but she would not have become as bad as she was if my father had not been infinitely worse." *Memoirs of Baron Stockmar* cited by Christopher Hibbert, *George IV*, Penguin Books, 1973, p. 484.

18   **Three in middle age finally escaped** For the most complete and carefully documented account of the six, see *Princesses: The Six Daughters of George III* by Flora Fraser, New York: Knopf, 2005.

18   **Orange was, admittedly, a drunken lout** In *Princesses*, Flora Fraser offers evidence that the king of Württemberg, husband to the Princess Royal, eldest daughter of George III, was a brutal homosexual who actively abused his wife.

19   **Charlotte's unexpected and stubborn refusal** Prince Leopold wrote that he was able to communicate with Princess Charlotte only with the help of her uncle the Duke of Kent, since "she was treated as a kind of prisoner." Cecil Woodham-Smith, *Queen Victoria*, New York: Knopf, 1972, p. 13.

19   **He had served valiantly** The portrait by Sir Thomas Lawrence of Prince Leopold in his youthful military glory can be seen in the Waterloo Room at Windsor Castle, above one of the doors, on the same wall as the three kings of England George III, George IV, and William IV. The standard work in English on King Leopold of the Belgians centered on his relations with Queen Victoria is *My Dearest Uncle: A Life of Leopold, First King of the Belgians* by Joanna Richardson (London: Jonathan Cape, 1961). The key book on Leopold's early life is *Die Coburger Jahren des Prinzen Leopold bis zu seiner Englischen Heirat 1816* by Harald Bachmann, Sonderdruck aus des Jahrbuch der Coburger Landesstiftung (The Coburg Years of Prince Leopold, Up to His English Marriage in 1816), a special issue of the *Journal of the Coburg State Foundation* in 2005 to commemorate the 175th anniversary of Leopold's accession to the throne of Belgium on July 21, 1831. Based on the extensive correspondence of the Saxe-Coburg family and their representatives in the Coburg archives, this book, unavailable in English, contains detailed new information.

19   **Officially he was celebrating** The letters Leopold wrote to his family show that even before he set out for London, he intended to make a play for Charlotte. He wrote to his brother the Duke of Coburg in June 1815: "The Emperor [of Russia] has given me permission to stay here [England] as long as it suits me. I only decided to do so after much hesitation, and after certain very singular events made me glimpse the possibility, even the probability, of

realizing the project we spoke of in Paris. My chances are, alas, very poor, because of the father's opposition" (*My Dearest Uncle*, p. 26). Leopold's mistress Caroline Bauer claims in her memoirs that Leopold was promoted as a husband for Princess Charlotte by the Grand Duchess Catherine of Russia. The Russian government was anxious to prevent the strengthening in the alliance of England and Holland that would occur if Charlotte married the Prince of Orange, as her father wished. See *Caroline Bauer and the Coburgs* (London: Vizetelly), translated and edited by Charles Nisbet.

20 **His belt and sword blazed** For the details of Charlotte's wedding, see Joanna Richardson, *My Dearest Uncle*, pp. 39–42. Richardson quotes several admiring appraisals of Prince Leopold's looks as a young man.

20 **"I have perfectly decided** Richardson, p. 28.

20 **He was already a world-class Lothario** Richardson (p. 19) says that Prince Leopold at the age of seventeen was seduced by Hortense de Beauharnais, the daughter of Napoleon and Josephine, and the mother to the future Napoleon III.

20 **But if he did not love** Biographers of Leopold have liked to say that Princess Charlotte was the great love of his life and that after her tragic death he could never love another woman. One of the revelations of Bachmann's book is that as a late teenager the then Prince Leopold had a passionate love affair with Pauline von Tubeuf but was not allowed to marry her, as she was not of royal rank. From this point, Leopold seems to have seen women as tools. Immersed in self-love and devoted to his own interests, Leopold did become fond of Charlotte, since she not only put him at the top of the social pyramid but quickly came to offer the adoration he demanded and to respond to his will. Leopold used his tragic love of Charlotte as a weapon against his second wife, the unhappy and ill-fated Louise d'Orléans.

22 **"I cannot reign over England"** Charlotte, in conversation with Madame de Boigne. (Richardson, p. 51). Here Charlotte is echoing the sentiments of Queen Mary Stuart, who in the seventeenth century insisted that her husband William of Orange should be coruler and, in fact, take over all the political power and administrative functions of the monarch. See *The History of England* by Thomas Babbington Macaulay, Everyman's Library, Dent, vol. 2, p. 15.

22 **As soon as the princess went** Charlotte's labor was a very public affair. Apart from her husband, Stockmar, various female attendants, and a growing number of doctors who clustered around her bed, the following state officials were stationed in the anteroom: Lord Bathurst, Viscount Sidmouth, the Archbishop of Canterbury, the Bishop of London, the chancellor of the exchequer, and the lord chancellor (Richardson, p. 54).

22 **Stockmar recommended** Stockmar's reason for not intervening was, as he later explained in his memoirs, that if something went wrong with the birth, he would be the perfect scapegoat.

22 **The princess's water broke** Soon before she went into labor, Charlotte wrote a heartrending letter to her mother, wishing she had a woman she loved by her side, and almost desiring death. See Monica Charlot, *Victoria the Young Queen*, London: Blackwell, 1991, p. 7.

23 **Christian Stockmar was holding Charlotte's hand** The consensus in 1817 was that the doctors had bungled the delivery. Napoleon, learning the news while in exile on St. Helena, demanded to know why the English did not stone their accoucheurs. The lowering regime for pregnant women came under attack, and within a year, Sir Richard Croft, Charlotte's chief doctor, committed suicide when it seemed that another woman under his care would die in labor. As Stockmar later summed things up, "It therefore appears that, weakened by the preceding long-continued and depressing treatment, the princess died of exhaustion from the fifty hours' labour. Probably she would have been saved if mechanical help had been employed soon enough. The English physicians refused to give it, as it was their principle never to use artificial means when nature alone could effect the delivery . . . It is impossible to resist the conviction that the princess was sacrificed to professional theories" (*Memoirs of Baron Stockmar*, ed. Ernest Stockmar, London: Longman's, Green & Co., 1873, vol. 1, p. 65). Stockmar discussed the death of Princess Charlotte with

his cousin Caroline Bauer, who at one point was Prince Leopold's mistress. Stockmar told Bauer that he could have saved the princess if he had been in charge of the case. Bauer blamed her cousin Christian for not even trying to intervene to save his friend. Both Leopold and Stockmar certainly erred on the side of pusillanimity and self-preservation. Leopold never blamed Stockmar.

Chapter 2: WANTED, AN HEIR TO THE THRONE, PREFERABLY MALE

24 **At the time of Charlotte's death** For more on this unfortunate king, see *King George III* by John Brooke (New York: McGraw Hill, 1972), one of the great books on the British royal family. The King did manage to recover from the first critical onset of his disease (probably porphyria), as we see in Alan Bennett's wonderful play (later a film) *The Madness of George III*. However, the recovery was only temporary. Several of George III's sons, including George IV, seem to have suffered from less debilitating forms of the same ailment, and those surrounding Queen Victoria, including her husband, were constantly afraid that she was showing signs of the disease.

24 **George III's thirteen surviving children** Charlotte herself was legitimate only by the peculiar legal standards of English royal marriages. In 1785 George, then Prince of Wales, entered into an act of marriage with Maria Fitzherbert, a rich double widow who was a practicing Roman Catholic. The Act of Settlement of 1701 laid down that no prince who married a Catholic could become King of Great Britain and Ireland. The prince's wedding ceremony was therefore conducted in great secrecy. However, an ordained Anglican priest presided, and the marriage was duly witnessed by the bride's uncle and brother, and attested in a certificate drawn up in the bridegroom's own hand and given to the bride, who managed to keep possession of it until her death. The document is now in the Royal Archives at Windsor. After this event, any other person in England but a royal prince would have been legally barred from marrying again, but, though the marriage was rumored at the time, no proof of it was brought forward, thanks to the loving forbearance of Maria Fitzherbert. And so in 1795, the prince was able to "marry" his first cousin Caroline of Brunswick and beget Charlotte. Caroline of Brunswick famously remarked: "Well, I have committed adultery with only one man, Mrs. Fitzherbert's husband." Had Mrs. Fitzherbert come forward with her marriage certificate in 1820, the new King George IV might have been forced to abdicate, his daughter Charlotte would have been declared illegitimate, and his brother the Duke of York would have succeeded him as, presumably, Frederick I.

The Royal Marriages Act has never been repealed, and it explains some of the marital arcana of the British royal family even of late. In the 1950s, the present Queen's sister, Princess Margaret, renounced her engagement to the commoner and divorcé Group Captain Peter Townsend, since her father, King George VI, opposed the marriage. The marriage of Charles, Prince of Wales, to Mrs. Camilla Parker-Bowles was delayed for similar reasons.

25 **In the twentieth century** Today Japan faces a constitutional crisis since the heir to the imperial throne has a daughter and no sons, and it is currently impossible for a woman to be emperor.

25 **The succession now went down the list** The daughters were irrelevant, since there were so many brothers. The daughters of kings matter only when brothers and nephews die, in which case a son or grandson may inherit a throne. This was the case with George I, who owed his claim to the English throne to his grandmother, a daughter of King James I, who married the elector of Hanover. George III, while in sound mind, prevented his daughters from marrying while of reproductive age, in part to simplify the issues of the succession, and in part because he felt he could not afford grandchildren from his daughters. One daughter, Sophia, did have an illegitimate child. Late in life, Charlotte married Frederick I, king of Württemberg. Elizabeth married Frederick, Landgrave of Hesse-Hamburg. Mary married her first cousin the Duke of Gloucester. All three married princesses were childless.

25 **As the young radical poet** P. B. Shelley, "Sonnet: England in 1819," *Poetical Works*, Oxford University Press, 1970, pp. 574–575.

28 **The seven royal princes** The Duke of Devonshire, the richest of all English peers at this time, had an annual income of 150,000 pounds a year, immense country estates, numerous town and country homes, and owned some 119 acres of real estate in central London.

28 **Between 1787 and 1796** I use the multiple for British 1796 pounds to American 2004 dollars suggested by Toby Faber in *Stradivari's Genius*, New York: Random House, 2004, p. 85.

28 **Odds were also against** On the Duke of York, see Roger Fulford, *The Wicked Uncles* (New York: Loring and Mussey, 1933), and Morris Marples, *Wicked Uncles in Love* (London: Michael Joseph, 1972). Frederica, Princess of Prussia and Duchess of York, is a very interesting character. She and the duke had no children and probably did not continue marital relations after the first year, but they remained good friends and companions until the duchess's death. She was eccentric but much loved and respected by her rural neighbors and servants. A fierce opponent of blood sports and supporter of animal rights, the duchess kept dozens of dogs as well as cats, monkeys, parrots, kangaroos, and other animals. The great love of her life was her lady-in-waiting and constant companion, Mrs. Bunbury, next to whom she is buried in Weybridge Church. Frederica would merit a full, modern biography, but a lesbian animal rights activist has so far had no appeal with today's English historians, whose special scholarly interest seems to be royal heterosexual promiscuity.

29 **Augustus, Duke of Sussex** As a young man, the then Prince Augustus married Lady Augusta Murray. In fact, he married her not once but twice, the second time quite publicly in St. George's Hanover Square, where all the best people got married. Augustus and Augusta produced two children whom they named (what else?) Augustus and Augusta. But the prince's father, George III, when he finally heard of the marriage, had it declared null and void by the ecclesiastical Court of Arches. The prince's children by Lady Augusta were thus made illegitimate and out of the line of succession to the throne. Prince Augustus did his best by his children, but he soon found it financially necessary to reconcile with his father by separating from Lady Augusta, and was created Duke of Sussex as a reward. Subsequently, Sussex took up a happy and stable relationship with the widowed Lady Cecilia Buggin, with whom he intended to contract a morganatic marriage as soon as his "wife" died. In 1830 the former Lady Augusta, Countess d'Amerlund, died, and the Duke of Sussex again repaired to St. George's Hanover Square to marry his darling Lady Cecilia. She never received the title of Duchess of Sussex, but the royal family liked her, and she was received in private by King William and Queen Adelaide. In 1840 Queen Victoria recognized her uncle Sussex's wife officially and gave her the title of Duchess of Inverness. This permitted Cecilia to be seated on state occasions—if not next to her husband, at least at the far end of the table of duchesses. On Augustus, Duke of Sussex, see Roger Fulford, *The Wicked Uncles*, pp. 253–284, and Morris Marples, *Wicked Uncles in Love*, pp. 199–226.

29 **However, Clarence's debts mounted** Mrs. Jordan, who also had three children by earlier relationships, did her best to keep the whole family afloat by continuing to earn money in theatrical touring companies. Wags wrote humorous verses wondering whether the duke kept the actress or vice versa. But despite Mrs. Jordan's noble efforts, the pile of ducal debt mounted inexorably. Following Clarence's desertion, Dorothy Jordan died abroad, alone, poverty stricken, and neglected by her children as well as by the man she had loved so tenderly and faithfully.

30 **But she was delicate** Elizabeth Clarence died at the age of three months. Her effigy is preserved at Windsor.

31 **As soon as the Duchess of Cambridge** Fulford, *The Wicked Uncles*, p. 299.

31 **For twenty-seven years** Many legends grew up about Madame Saint Laurent, especially in Canada, where she was credited with noble birth, several illegitimate children, and marriage to a nobleman after her separation from the Duke of Kent. Finally, a Canadian scholar, Mollie Gillen, turned up the documents that proved that the Duke of Kent's mis-

tress came from a comfortable bourgeois family in Provence, that she had no children, and that she lived the rest of her life unmarried and in obscurity. See Gillen, *The Prince and His Lady*, Toronto: Griffin House, 1970.

32 **Prince Leopold had a sister** Queen Victoria's mother was christened Marie Luise Victoire, but was known by family in Germany as "Victoire." In England, she anglicized her name to Maria Louisa Victoria.

32 **This meant that "they could contract** *The Letters of Queen Victoria*,1837–1861, ed. Arthur Christopher Benson and Viscount Esher, London: John Murray, 1908, vol. 1, p. 3.

33 **He knew that gentleman** Mollie Gillen chastises the standard biographies of the Duke of Kent for claiming that he was a vicious martinet on the parade ground and drove men and officers to mutiny by his sadistic intransigence. Gillen says that she could find no evidence that Kent was any more cruel than most high officers of his time, and her discussion of the Canadian episodes is persuasive. However, there is no getting around the fact that the Duke of Kent, unlike his brothers York and Cumberland, was systematically barred from military command after he returned from Canada, and that there was something about his use of military authority that went against the grain with the military powers that be.

33 **More troubling was the fact** Gillen discovered that Kent did have one illegitimate daughter by a Geneva woman before he began his liaison with Saint Laurent.

33 **Vigorously lobbied** According to Harald Bachmann, the person who managed to persuade Victoire of Leiningen to accept Edward of Kent was her intimate friend in Amorbach, Polyxena (Pauline) von Tubeuf Wagner. (See Harald Bachmann, pp. 15–16.) Pauline as a young teenager had exchanged passionate letters and embraces with the young Prince Leopold, but their mothers were opposed to their marriage, and Pauline had to settle for marriage with Herr Hofrat Wagner, tutor to Victoire of Leiningen's son Charles. It is unclear from Bachmann's account, and so presumably from the archival sources, whether Leopold and Pauline were lovers either before or after her marriage of convenience.

33 **Thus, within six weeks** Adelaide, who was quite intelligent, had learned some English before her marriage, but Victoire had not and needed the vows spelled out to her phonetically. All the royal English dukes, whose mother was German, spoke fluent German. This was essential when they were sent over to Hanover for military service and diplomatic work, and when they were alone with their German wives.

33 **Dynastic strategy, not elective affinity** After her mother died in 1861, Queen Victoria read with great emotion the letters her parents had exchanged in their brief marriage.

33 **As a little girl, Victoire** In her memoirs, Caroline Bauer tells how her mother, Christina Bauer, was able to mend the torn Sunday dress of her playmate, Antoinette of Saxe-Coburg, Victoire's older sister, and thus avert the wrath of Antoinette's mother.

34 **The legitimacy of his child** The issue of substitute babies was a delicate one in the history of the English royal family. In 1688, after many years of marriage, Mary of Modena, the Catholic second wife of the unpopular King James II, gave birth to a baby son, who became heir apparent to the throne, displacing his Protestant half sisters Mary and Anne. It was widely believed in England that Queen Mary of Modena had had a phantom pregnancy, and that a male baby had been smuggled into the royal bedroom in a warming pan by the Catholic faction, determined to prevent a Protestant succession. The child was almost certainly the King's, but his birth did seem excessively providential, and radically changed the whole political situation in England. In short order, James II was deposed, and, in what history knows as the Glorious Revolution, his daughter Mary and her husband, William of Orange, were installed as joint monarchs. James II's son, known to history as the Old Pretender, made one attempt to take back the throne, as did his more famous and colorful son Charles, Bonnie Prince Charlie.

36 **He allowed the child only two** For example, Prince Albert's mother, a princess of Saxe-Gotha, was baptized Dorothy Louise Pauline Charlotte Frederica Augusta.

36 **Instead she had names so foreign** See Benson-Esher, p. 55.

36. **The Duchess of Kent had been allowed** As Princess of Leiningen, Victoire breast-fed her first child, Charles, for five months. However, when her second child, a girl, was born, the princess fed the child for only two months. I found this information in a letter from Victoire's eldest brother, Ernest, Duke of Saxe-Coburg, to his mistress Pauline Panam, advising her to stop suckling their illegitimate child (Pauline Panam, *Mémoires d'une jeune Grecque*, London: Sherwood Jones and Co., 1823, p. 139).

37. **When the second most senior doctor** To the end of his life, this same famous physician would give it as his opinion that the Duke of Kent died because he had not been sufficiently bled. There is a horrid fascination in seeing how little actual clinical outcomes influenced medical practice at the highest professional level during this period.

Chapter 3: THE WIFE TAKES THE CHILD

38. **If the father died** The plots of many nineteenth-century novels, such as *Vanity Fair* and *Little Lord Fauntleroy*, center on the legal tragedy of the widow of blameless virtue who must give up her adored child to the nasty old paternal grandfather.

38. **As the Duchess of Kent boasted** Quoted in *Memoirs of Baron Stockmar*, ed. Ernest Stockmar, London: Longman's, 1873, vol. 1, p. 375.

38. **As a ward of the Crown** When the Princess Charlotte's parents separated in her infancy, she became the ward of her grandfather, King George III, who, according to Caroline Bauer, "was just and kind enough to ordain that the up-bringing of the Princess Charlotte till her eighth year should devolve on the mother" (*Caroline Bauer and the Coburgs*, London: Vizetelly, 1885, p. 308). At eight, Charlotte was given her own household of governor, governess, tutors, and servants at Lower Lodge in Windsor Park, and visits to her mother were rare and carefully supervised.

39. **The Duke of Kent's will** See David Duff, *Edward of Kent—The Life Story of Queen Victoria's Father*, London: Stanley Paul, 1938, p. 283; also, Dorothy Margaret Stuart, *The Mother of Victoria: A Period Piece*, London: Macmillan, 1941, p. 98.

39. **Apprised of the Duke of Kent's** See King Leopold's letter to Queen Victoria of Jan. 22, 1841, *Queen Victoria's Early Letters*, ed. John Raymond, New York: Macmillan, 1907/1963, p. 47.

39. **The trustee named under the will** Stuart, p. 98.

40. **The King's only comfort came** For an excellently researched and argued account of the Queen Caroline affair and its political significance, see *Rebel Queen* by Jane Robins, New York: Simon & Schuster, 2006.

40. **The Duke of Kent and Strathearn** The Duke of Kent went into the red as a boy of sixteen, and by 1807 he already owed 200,000 pounds (40 million in today's dollars). From then on, things went from bad to worse, and in 1815 he was obliged to flee to Brussels and attempt, quite unsuccessfully, to live on 7,000 pounds a year.

41. **if Edward, Duke of Kent** The Duke of Kent wrote from Sidmouth in the winter of 1819–20 to the philanthropist Robert Owen: "I am satisfied that to continue to live in England, even in the quiet way in which we are going on, *without splendour*, and *without show*, *nothing short of doubling the 7,000 pounds* will do REDUCTION BEING IMPOSSIBLE" (David Duff, *Edward of Kent*, p. 280).

42. **George IV was bent on driving** George IV went so far as to refuse the Duchess of Kent the rangership of the Home Park, Hampton Court, a sinecure the Duke of Kent had held that brought in 800 pounds per year. It would have cost the King nothing to allow the Duchess of Kent that income, as he allowed his other sister-in-law, the Duchess of Clarence, to have the income from the rangership of Bushey Park. But, spitefully, George IV gave the rangership of the Home Park to the wife of one of his gentlemen-in-waiting.

42. **"Remember that it was not I** Cecil Woodham-Smith, *Queen Victoria from Her Birth to the Death of the Prince Consort*, New York: Knopf, 1972, p. 51.

43. **It was xenophobic enough** In the letters he wrote to Queen Victoria in the weeks immedi-

ately following her accession in 1837, King Leopold was still worried that the Duke of Cumberland and the extreme faction of the Tory Party of which Cumberland was the leader would challenge Victoria's right to the throne of Great Britain. Leopold had seen long civil wars break out in both Spain and Portugal when paternal uncles refused to accept the rights to the throne of the two child queens, Isabella and Maria da Glória. Leopold therefore advised Victoria to stress in her public utterances that she—unlike her two male cousins, George Cumberland and George Cambridge—was born in England and had never in her life left its shores.

44   **A mistress was essential to Leopold** King Leopold I of the Belgians had a series of liaisons throughout his first widowhood and during and after his second marriage. In 1849 he selected the wife of an officer as his "maitresse en titre," coldly informing Queen Louise that he was obliged to do so, as illness and religious devotions had led her to neglect her duties as a wife. The queen meekly accepted the rebuke and the mistress. She died in October 1850, probably of consumption, aged thirty-nine. See Richardson, chapter 26.

46   **Victoria never bore them a grudge** Prince Albert was characteristically more censorious, blaming his uncle for failing in his duty toward Queen Victoria as a child. "Mama here," wrote Prince Albert years later, referring to the Duchess of Kent, "would never have fallen into the hands of Conroy if uncle Leopold had taken the trouble to guide her" (Dorothy Margaret Stuart, *The Mother of Victoria*, p. 106).

46   **He believed he could trace** The key work on Sir John Conroy is *A Royal Conflict: Sir John Conroy and the Young Victoria* by Katherine Hudson (London: Hodder and Stoughton, 1994). Hudson, with John Jones, edited the Conroy Papers for Balliol College, Oxford.

47   **Though always happier in German** Elizabeth Longford quotes an 1818 document in the Royal Archives in which someone has spelled out phonetically a little speech for the Duchess of Kent to deliver on her arrival in England. "Ei hoeve tu regrétt, biing *aes yiett* so little conversant in this Inglisch lênguetsch uitsch obleitsches—miy, to seh, in *averi fiu* words, theat ei em môhst gretful for yur congratuleschens end gud uishes" (Elizabeth Longford, *Victoria R.I.*, London: Pan Books, 1964, p. 23).

47   **She also gave him money** Hudson clarifies Conroy's extremely murky finances. From the early 1820s on, Conroy lived an increasingly opulent life, even though he drew no salary from the Duchess of Kent and earned only a thousand pounds from his position at the Colonial Audit Office. His chief source of income was the Princess Sophia, though this was kept a close secret. Following John Conroy's death, his heirs estimated that between 1820 and her death in 1848, Princess Sophia gave Conroy 148,000 pounds, a house in Kensington, and an estate in Wales that included lucrative mines. That sum was almost certainly a low estimate. When Conroy finally was persuaded to leave the service of the Duchess of Kent in 1840, Princess Sophia, now blind and deaf, remained his loyal friend. To salve his wounded pride and keep him in England, she gave him a superb English country estate called Arborfield and 3,000 pounds a year. When Princess Sophia died, she was virtually penniless. From 1837 to his death in 1854, Conroy also received some 51,000 pounds from the Queen's privy purse and 25,500 from the Duchess of Kent's parliamentary allowance. Whether Conroy or his shifty underling William Rea also embezzled large sums of money from the Duchess of Kent between 1831 and 1837, when she started to receive generous parliamentary grants, was widely alleged but never proven. Conroy and Rea were careful either to keep no accounts or to lose them. To the rage and astonishment of his heirs, Conroy managed to die deeply in debt. His wife and children, who had lived off the royal largesse all their lives, continued to pester Queen Victoria for financial assistance and did not come away empty handed. If one wonders just how Queen Victoria managed to spend her huge income, it is important to remember that she felt financially responsible even for people like the daughter-in-law of her former archenemy John Conroy.

48   **He once mystified Victoria** Hudson, p. 74, quoting Queen Victoria's unpublished journal entry of January 21, 1839. Hudson's revelation about Elizabeth Fisher Conroy's supposed

kinship to the Duke of Kent is based on an entry in a little leather notebook of Conroy's that was carefully preserved by his descendents.

48   **It was only after Victoria became** See Hudson for the various unflattering names that King Leopold in later years was to apply to Sir John Conroy.

48   **As Victoria edged closer** Hudson, p. 61.

Chapter 4: THAT DISMAL EXISTENCE

51   **When Uncle York died** *Queen Victoria in Her Letters and Journals*, ed. Christopher Hibbert, New York: Viking, 1984, pp. 9–11.

51   **After one stormy episode** Elizabeth Longford, *Victoria R.I.*, p. 33.

51   **As Victoria moved out of infancy** Queen Victoria's half sister, the second child of the Duchess of Kent by Emich Charles, Prince of Leiningen-Dachburg-Hadenburg, was christened Feodorowna but was known as Feodora or Feodore.

51   **Over the years, Victoria amply repaid** It was impossible for Victoria and Feodora to correspond freely before Victoria's accession, but Feodora understood better than anyone what Conroy was capable of. From Germany, she tried to keep informed about the situation at Kensington Palace, and she wrote to King William IV and to King Leopold to seek their protection for Victoria when Conroy's dictatorship seemed to threaten Victoria's happiness or even her life.

52   **Louise Lehzen became Victoria's mother** This is the report from biographers such as Longford, who have read the full transcripts of the Queen's diaries in the Royal Archives. The published sections of the diaries systematically omit references to Baroness Lehzen. The editors, writing in the early part of the twentieth century, were anxious to conceal the fact that Queen Victoria had been abused by her mother in her youth and was barely on speaking terms with her between 1837 and 1840.

52   **At Amorbach Castle, her recent home** Stuart, *The Mother of Queen Victoria*, p. 6.

52   **Lehzen once told a member** Katherine Hudson, *A Royal Conflict*, p. 19.

52   **More controversially** Davys was made a bishop as a reward for his work as Queen Victoria's tutor.

53   **However, in the documentation** For the upbringing of Queen Victoria's eldest children, the Princess Royal and the Prince of Wales (Vicky and Bertie), see chapters 24 and 25.

54   **She went pink with delight** There is some discussion in the literature as to whether Queen Victoria is correct in assigning this event to 1826.

55   **Who knew, whispered Conroy** Ernest Cumberland (later king of Hanover) was always at daggers drawn with Queen Victoria and Prince Albert over matters of precedence, and the prince was inclined to share the Duchess of Kent's paranoia about Cumberland. However, as Woodham-Smith shows in an appendix, Queen Victoria in her private papers scrupulously insisted that Conroy had been quite wrong to claim that Cumberland attempted to harm her as a child.

55   **At Amorbach, Victoire** For more on this incident, see chapter 8.

55   **The duchess herself had fortunately arrived** Caroline Bauer recounts this incident in her memoirs. Just as Victoria was gazing at Fräulein Bauer and her mother, Frau Christina Bauer, the Duchess of Kent (who had known Christina since childhood) rode up and hurried her daughter away.

56   **"I must unequivocally state to you** Woodham-Smith, p. 60.

56   **"When I look back upon** Woodham-Smith, pp. 55 and 62.

56   **But he was only thirty-two** Princess Feodora's marriage to Prince Ernest of Hohenlohe-Langenburg was generally seen in English court circles as a mésalliance, the crowning proof that the Duchess of Kent placed her own interests and pleasures ahead of her elder daughter's. The families of the two sisters were assiduously intertwined. Queen Victoria married her granddaughter Alexandra of Edinburgh and Saxe-Coburg to Feodora's son, also named

Ernest of Hohenlohe. Ernest and Alexandra's son Gottfried married his cousin Margarita of Greece, another direct descendent of Queen Victoria and Prince Albert. Most important, Augusta of Schleswig-Holstein-Sonderburg-Glücksburg, one of Feodora's granddaughters, was the bride chosen by Victoria's eldest grandson, Kaiser William II of Germany.

57 **"He [Conroy] has never lived** Woodham-Smith, p. 72.

Chapter 5: THE KENSINGTON SYSTEM

59 **The Kensington System, as it later came** The term "the Kensington System" seems to have been coined by Charles von Leiningen, Queen Victoria's half brother, who, at the request of Prince Albert, wrote up a long account of Conroy's role in his sister's life before her accession. Prince Leiningen first came to England in 1824 and was initially impressed by Conroy's affability and his devotion to the Duchess of Kent. Conroy counted Leiningen as an ally. The prince's account is now in the Royal Archives at Windsor (M.7/67). See Longford, p. 69.

59 **The Kensington System became more oppressive** The facts about Queen Victoria's difficult childhood and the Duchess of Kent's blind deference to the abusive Conroy were hidden from the public for some thirty years after the Queen's death in 1901. The Conroy story was first pieced together in the 1930s by Kurt Jagow, using German archival sources. It was taken up for the English public by Woodham-Smith in the late 1950s, and amply confirmed in 2000 with materials from the Royal Archives in Christopher Hibbert's magisterial biography *Queen Victoria: A Personal History*, New York: Harper Collins, 2001.

59 **At four, Vickelchen** The expression is the Queen's own, from the recollections of her childhood she set down in 1872.

62 **Darnley called her "unexampled** Alison Plowden, *The Young Victoria*, New York: Sutton, 2000 (first published 1981), p. 61.

62 **Unsurprisingly, the King was outraged** According to Philip Ziegler, "The Duchess of Kent seemed to have considered [William IV's] reign as an undesirable and inconsiderately protracted interregnum between the black wickedness of the Georges and the radiant paradise to open with the accession of Queen Victoria" (*King William IV*, London: Fontana, 1973, p. 277).

63 **The duchess replied that the Princess** Sir Walter Scott was permitted to meet the Princess Victoria in May 1828, around the time of her ninth birthday. Scott wrote in his diary: "This little lady is educating with much care, and watched so closely that no busy maid has a moment to whisper 'You are heir to England.' I suspect if we could dissect the little heart we should find some pigeon or other bird of the air had carried the matter" (quotation from Sir Walter Scott's diary, Theodore Martin, *The Life of the Prince Consort*, vol. 1, New York: Appleton, 1875, p. 23). Queen Victoria insisted that Scott was wrong, and that she did not know that she would be "heir to England." It is interesting that the great novelist in a brief and formal visit was impressed by how closely the Princess Victoria was watched and kept even from conversing with the maids.

63 **The conversation went as follows** Woodham-Smith, p. 76. This is the account given by Baroness Lehzen in 1867 in a private letter to Queen Victoria. The Queen annotated the letter in the margins and confirmed its accuracy. She remembered how much she cried to hear of what the future held for her and how much she prayed that her aunt Adelaide would indeed have children.

Chapter 6: FIGHTING BACK

65 **As Queen Victoria recalled** *Dearest Child: Letters Between Queen Victoria and the Princess Royal, 1858–1861*, ed. Roger Fulford, New York: Holt, Rinehart and Winston, 1964, p. 72.

66 **As she understood very well** Just after her newly married daughter Vicky had left for Prus-

sia, Queen Victoria wrote to tell Vicky how much affectionate interest had been shown in the marriage by people of every class in England. "People are so kind about you! . . . Lord Shaftesbury said, there was nothing in history like the feeling shown on this occasion—and the great affection, not for us only—but for you personally . . . Tell this to Fritz [soon to be Crown Prince of Prussia] for you know (and he ought to know) that such a feeling in England is worth a great deal—as it is the real feeling of the people, not merely a sense of respect—which can be put on, for you cannot force people here to be enthusiastic if they don't choose" (*Dearest Child,* p. 63).

66   **Her voice was her greatest beauty** The great nineteenth-century actress Fanny Burney once remarked on the Queen's marvelous voice as one professional performer to another.

66   **It was warm, clear, ringing** By contrast, Victoria's own children, especially the four eldest who were brought up mainly by their German father, apparently retained slight traces of German pronunciation. Vicky, the eldest child and her father's favorite, was equally at home in English and German but was said to have a German accent in English and an English accent in German.

67   **Nonetheless, in one of the many** Charlot, p. 65.

68   **Amenorrhea is a common symptom** The letters between King Leopold and Baroness Lehzen point to amenorrhea, though, of course, such intimate female matters could not be discussed with medical accuracy.

69   **As she later told Lord Melbourne** Charlot, p. 66, who cites "RA, Queen Victoria's Journal, 26 February 1838." This entry is not included in Esher's edition of Queen Victoria's Journal.

69   **However, Queen Victoria herself was told** Just before the prince consort died of typhoid, Queen Victoria wrote to her uncle Leopold: "It is the first time I ever witnessed anything of this kind although I suffered from the same at Ramsgate and was much worse" (*Queen Victoria in Her Letters and Journals,* ed. Hibbert, p. 155).

70   **"I talk to you at length** The quotations in this and the following paragraph are taken from Woodham-Smith, pp. 122–123.

71   **"I trust in God that my life** Woodham-Smith pp. 126–127, quoting apparently from the account left by Lord Adolphus FitzClarence, one of the King's illegitimate sons, who heard the whole tirade and immediately set down an account for the history books.

72   **"The Monster and Demon Incarnate"** The quotations are from the Queen's diary of 1842 and 1843, when she was at last free to write frankly about her life under Conroy. See Hibbert, *Queen Victoria in Her Letters and Journals,* pp. 42 and 71.

73   **"Her feelings seem** Woodham-Smith, p. 136. Woodham-Smith gives an unequaled blow-by-blow account of the days just preceding the accession of Queen Victoria, full of hitherto unpublished quotations from archival sources.

73   **Despite everything her mother claimed** According to Katherine Hudson, Conroy himself left a different account of the medical crisis in Ramsgate, which puts the blame for neglecting the princess's serious condition on the duchess and on Dr. Clark.

74   **Conroy gave Stockmar a list** Longford, p. 82.

75   **"Tuesday, 20th June** *The Childhood of Queen Victoria,* ed. Esher, vol. 1, pp. 196–197. Let me repeat that this entry forms part of that section of Queen Victoria's diaries that was transcribed by Esher before Princess Beatrice could take her scissors to it and is therefore pretty close to what the Queen actually wrote.

Chapter 7: VICTORIA, VIRGIN QUEEN

77   **At last Victoria was permitted** Alan Hardy, *Queen Victoria Was Amused,* London: John Murray, 1976, p. 164.

78   **"I felt for the first time** Esher, *The Girlhood of Queen Victoria,* vol. 1, p. 227. This vision of the young Queen Victoria on horseback will stir the memories of elderly Britons like myself. I remember well from my youth the seductive images of Queen Elizabeth II as a young

woman reviewing the household cavalry on horseback, riding sidesaddle, marvelously elegant in her cocked hat and tightly fitting military uniform.

79 **"Everything is new and delightful** Woodham-Smith, p. 141.

79 **To her half sister Feodora** Charlot, p. 101.

79 **To her uncle King Leopold** Benson and Esher, *The Letters of Queen Victoria*, vol. 1, p. 79.

81 **She had an exceptional memory** For the fact that the Queen in private called Lehzen "Daisy" or "Mother" see Longford, p. 107, quoting an unpublished section from the Queen's journal.

82 **She paid her personal servants** Vera Watson found the Queen's annotations on bills in the records of the Lord Chamberlain's department. See *A Queen at Home: An Intimate Account of the Social and Domestic Life of Queen Victoria's Court*, London: Allen, 1952.

82 **King Leopold had fully expected** Stockmar arrived in England just a month before the death of William IV and remained in England, in close communication with the Queen and with Melbourne, for some fifteen months. Stockmar came back to London, at the request of Prince Albert, a month before the prince himself arrived for his wedding in February 1840 (see *Memoirs of Baron Stockmar*, vol. ii, chapter XVIII).

83 **In the evenings and at weekends** According to Clare Jerrold, at least six members of the Paget family were at the court of the young Queen Victoria. Matilda and Laura were maids of honor, Lady Sandwich was a lady-in-waiting, Lord Alfred Paget (who fell madly and very publicly in love with Victoria) was an equerry, the Earl of Uxbridge was Lord Chamberlain, following a Paget in-law, Lord Conyngham. Lady Constance Paget was also at court in some capacity (*The Married Life of Queen Victoria*, London: Eveleigh Nash, 1913, p. 53).

85 **As the second Lord Melbourne once remarked** Lord David Cecil, *Lord Melbourne: The Later Life*, London: Constable, 1954, pp. 177–178. The English oligarchs of the late eighteenth and early nineteenth centuries led lives quite as sexually innovative as the Bloomsbury group in the early twentieth, but they were careful not to leave anything on paper that could affect their own social standing and political careers, or the inheritance rights of their children. Thus whereas contemporaries gossiped in letters and diaries, and historians have speculated that the first Lady Melbourne, her son Lord Melbourne, her daughter Emily, Lady Cowper, and her daughter's second husband Lord Palmerston all had numerous affairs, there is no documentary proof. Lord Palmerston was rumored to have slept with at least three of the famous patronesses of Almacks—Lady Cowper and her friends Lady Jersey and Princess Lieven—but biographers have been unable to confirm this.

85 **The young Lambs were brought up** See Amanda Foreman, *Georgiana, Duchess of Devonshire*, Random House, 1998.

86 **She expected Victoria to pay** Charlot, p. 109.

87 **By the summer of 1839** Hibbert, *Queen Victoria in Her Letters and Journals*, p. 55.

87 **Melbourne agreed** Charlot, p. 149.

PART ONE: THE YEARS APART | *Albert: A Motherless Prince*

92 **Queen Victoria's crest appears** I am describing the 1867 Harpers American edition of the Grey book, which I have in my possession.

93 **The regular correspondence between** Hector Bolitho, in preparation for his 1932 biography of the prince consort, was by his own account, the first person allowed to see the brothers' correspondence. Duke Ernest II of Saxe-Coburg and Gotha wrote a two-volume memoir, but it deals almost exclusively with the years after his brother left for England.

Chapter 8: THE COBURG LEGACY

95 **"I shall, while tirelessly striving** *Early Years of the Prince Consort*, p. 335, my own translation. At the back of this volume, Queen Victoria gives an invaluable selection of her husband's early letters, in the original German.

96 **Coburg, the state where Prince Albert** German historians have recently begun to comb through the archives of the city of Coburg and of the Saxe-Coburg family. They question, politely, the claims of the Saxe-Coburg dynasty in Germany to have been a force for liberalism. They cast a severe eye on the relationship between the dukes and their Coburg and Gotha citizens. In the account of Coburg I give here and in succeeding chapters, I am deeply indebted to the following works that, unfortunately, have not yet been translated: *Das Haus von Sachsen-Coburg und Gotha 1826 bis 2001* (The House of Saxe-Coburg and Gotha from 1826 to 2001) by Harald Sandner (Coburg: Neue Presse, undated but around 2002); *Die Coburger Jahre des Prinzen Leopold bis zu seiner Englischen Heirat 1816* (The Coburg Years of Prince Leopold up to His English Marriage 1816) by Harald Bachmann (Jahrbuch der Coburger Landesstiftung, 2005); *Zwei Herzöge und eine Primadonna* (Two Dukes and a Diva) by Gertraude Bachmann, (Jahrbuch der Coburger Landesstiftung, 2003).

96 **At the time of his birth, Coburg** See Stanley Weintraub, *Uncrowned King: The Life of Prince Albert*, New York: Free Press, 1997, p. 2. Coburg and Gotha today are two little German cities off the main tourist map. They suffered little damage during two world wars and are still recognizably the cities that Prince Albert saw in his youth. Anyone interested in Queen Victoria and Prince Albert should spend some time savoring the charming medieval city centers nestled among wooded hills that the prince remembered with such passionate fondness. Formerly part of Communist East Germany, Gotha is at best ambivalent about its ducal heritage. To this day, however, Coburg advertises itself as the cradle of the English, Russian, Spanish, Romanian, Greek, and Albanian royal houses. My Coburg guide alleged that the town emerged intact from World War II because of Coburg's strong ties to the English royal family. The Saxe-Coburg family still makes its main residence near Coburg and owns large estates in the area.

99 **Charlotte took her dowry** See Flora Fraser, *Princesses*.

100 **The army was the only career** Hessians, for example, formed an important part of the British army fighting in the American War of Independence.

100 **The empress intended to choose** Grand Duke Constantine was heir to the Russian throne until he yielded his claims to his younger brother Alexander in order to marry his mistress. She was of inferior rank, so their marriage was morganatic. A morganatic marriage fulfills the usual requirements for legal union, but any children are debarred from inheriting their father's titles and estates because of their mother's low rank. Louis XIV's marriage to Madame de Maintenon was morganatic. The Duke of Sussex's marriage to Lady Cecilia Buggin (see chapter 2, note to p. 29) was morganatic. Some children of morganatic unions have succeeded in erasing the taint on their family, notably the German family of Battenberg. This branch of the Hesse family married two of its sons to a daughter and granddaughter of Queen Victoria. In 1914, at a moment of immense anti-German feeling in England, the English Battenbergs metamorphosed into the Mountbattens just as the reigning house of Saxe-Coburg and Gotha metamorphosed into the house of Windsor. Queen Elizabeth II's husband, Philip, is a Mountbatten.

101 **"That's the one," said Catherine** Caroline Bauer is the origin of this strange and oft-repeated story. It seems probable that she or her mother, who as a child played with the ducal children of Coburg, was told it by one of the sisters themselves.

101 **"The brutal Constantine treated** Bauer, p. 22.

101 **After some eight years, Juliana fled** Constantine did his best to make his estranged wife's life difficult until it suited him to get a divorce. Juliana, it seems, led a fairly irregular life once she went into exile, and efforts were made by her brothers and nephews to keep the facts about her from Queen Victoria and the respectable English branch of the family.

101 **Intimate and lasting connections** King Leopold maintained good relations with his former brother-in-law Grand Duke Constantine to the end, and defended him to posterity. In the Coburg family memoir he wrote for inclusion in Queen Victoria's book on the early years

of Prince Albert, King Leopold represents Constantine as a wild youth who just needed a firm female hand.

101 **Thanks to the good offices** Richardson, *My Dearest Uncle*, p. 18.

103 **De Pouilly was largely responsible** The wartime diaries of Duchess Augusta of Saxe-Coburg document how much the whole family was inspired and supported by the brave and intransigent de Pouilly. Sophia adored him. Augusta relied on him. Ferdinand followed him to Vienna. Leopold aspired to be like him. See *Napoleonic Days: Extracts from the Private Diaries of Augusta, Duchess of Saxe-Coburg-Saalfeld, Queen Victoria's Maternal Grandmother, 1806–1821*, selected and translated by HRH the Princess Beatrice, London: John Murray, 1941.

104 **With her he founded a new dynasty** To recapitulate, Ferdinand of Coburg-Kohary married his eldest son, also named Ferdinand, to Maria da Glória, the queen of Portugal, founding a dynasty there. Another son and a daughter married children of King Louis Philippe of France.

105 **Duke Francis of Saxe-Coburg** A Coburg blacksmith once threatened to kill Duke Francis of Saxe-Coburg-Saalfeld, Prince Albert's grandfather, for harassing his womenfolk. This incident was probably remembered because most citizens did not dare to protest their liege lord's predatory ways.

105 **The sexual mores that prevailed** Panam's *Mémoires d'une jeune Grecque: Madame Pauline Adélaïde Alexandre Panam contre son Altesse Sérénissime le Prince Régnant de Saxe-Cobourg* appeared in 1823. Bauer's *Nachgelassene Memoiren von Karoline Bauer* appeared after the author's death in 1876 but was probably written twenty years or more earlier. I consulted the original French text for Panam, and *Caroline Bauer and the Coburgs* (London: Vizetelly), translated and edited by Charles Nisbet, the 1885 English abridged version of Bauer's three-volume work. Rage and hatred against the Coburg family fill the pages of both memoirs, but the writers are intelligent, write well, and quote extensively from their correspondence with Coburg family members. These memoirs constitute an essential primary source on the Coburgs of the beginning of the nineteenth century.

105 **As the girls stood gazing** Caroline Bauer's description of Schloss Ehrenburg bears no resemblance to the handsome free-standing edifice, surrounded by gardens, that we see in Coburg today. But during the Napoleonic wars, the palace was uninhabitable, and Prince Albert's paternal grandparents lived and had all their children in a modest town house around the corner. After the Coburg family started to move up the royal hierarchy in Europe, both Prince Albert's father and his brother made it a priority to enlarge, remodel, and restore Schloss Ehrenburg, at one point employing the famous Berlin architect Karl Friedrich Schinkel.

107 **As Grand Duke Constantine once sneered** *Mémoires d'une jeune Grecque*, p. 211.

107 **Caroline Bauer was a native Coburger** Caroline Bauer wrote three sets of memoirs; two (*From My Life on the Stage* and *Theatrical Tours*) were published during her lifetime, and the third, and most famous, the 1876 *Nachgelassene Memoiren von Karoline Bauer*, was at once translated in whole or part in various languages. There is no doubt that Bauer gives a very slanted account of her relationship with King Leopold. Her protestations of sexual innocence were probably an attempt to protect her reputation posthumously. It is possible that she and Leopold, in fact, continued their relationship for some years after she returned to Germany. The Coburg Tourist Office guide who showed me around the city took me to a charming little country house where, he said, Leopold and Caroline met. There is no doubt that Bauer was close to Coburg all her life and obsessively collected every piece of information that came her way about the ducal family.

108 **This, with a characteristic mixture** For an excellent description of "drizzling," or "parfilage," as it was first known at the court of Louis XV, see Bauer, pp. 261–263.

109 **Father, uncle, and counselor** Monica Charlot in her biography of the young Queen Victoria notes Prince Albert's "capacity for reconstructing reality" (Charlot, p. 216) and how

he manipulated the Queen by questioning her memories of her youth, and by feeding her the story of his own moral superiority from early childhood.

Chapter 9: A DYNASTIC MARRIAGE

110 **Louise's mother, a princess of** Duchess Caroline was born in 1768 and died in 1848. If Duke Augustus married soon after the birth of his daughter Louise in December 1800, Caroline would have been about thirty-three at her wedding, old for a princess bride but still presumably capable of having children. .

110 **Under Salic law, Louise could not** The fact that (a) between them the brothers Augustus and Frederick of Gotha had only one legitimate child, (b) Augustus had to make do with a woman past her reproductive prime as his second bride and sired no children by her, (c) Frederick could never get any eligible girl to marry him, and (d) both gentlemen died suddenly in their forties suggests to me that they were infected with venereal disease. The remarks made by contemporaries about Augustus's "eccentricity" and invalidism, and about Frederick's moral turpitude, are probably couched in a genteel code, easily cracked at the time. Venereal disease of various kinds was rampant among the European aristocracy in the eighteenth and early nineteenth centuries, and people understood that there was a link to infertility. Early stage syphilis and gonorrhea were not well distinguished, and the standard treatments involved mercury and arsenic, which certainly did not improve fertility. In its tertiary stage, the ravages of syphilis are hard to miss. A German aristocratic father, keen to see grandchildren, might marry his daughter to a drunken brute but would need compelling reasons to accept a man as his son-in-law who bore the marks of syphilis on his face.

110 **Frederick had made various attempts** At the time of Louise's marriage, her uncle Frederick renewed his efforts to find a bride and make an heir, but again he failed. See D. A. Ponsonby, *The Lost Duchess*, London: Chapman and Hall, 1958, pp. 121–122. This is still the standard biography available in English. Duchess Louise of Coburg indicated to Augusta von Studnitz (who herself was on Prince Frederick's list of possible wives) that she had once aroused her uncle's sexual interest. "I, too, had the good fortune to appear pleasing to him, but that signifies little, as I am his submissive niece" (Ponsonby, quoting Louise's letter, p. 121). The idea of Frederick marrying his niece Louise seems grotesque except that, some ten years later, Duke Ernest I of Coburg, after his divorce from Duchess Louise, actually did marry one of his nieces, Marie of Württemberg.

111 **Tall, athletic, and dashing** Duchess Louise gives a rapturous description of an actual tourney arranged by her husband in which he and other young men dressed in medieval armor and jousted. Duke Ernest appeared to perfection on horseback and in armor.

112 **The two sons were known as** The order of Prince Albert's given names is in some dispute. I use the order given in *Early Years*, p. 34. However, Ponsonby (*The Lost Duchess*, p. 106) says the prince's birth entry in the *Almanach de Gotha* is Albert Francis Augustus Charles Emanuel. The prince consort was named Albrecht at birth, after his distant ancestor, but early on his name changed to the more modern Albert, and this is the name that appears on his German monuments.

112 **Yet from Albert's birth** In a letter solicited by Queen Victoria, King Leopold noted that he had seen Prince Albert in Coburg in 1822, 1823, 1824, 1826, 1827, and 1829, and that Albert "held a certain sway over his elder brother, who rather kindly submitted to it" *Early Years*, p. 46.

112 **In letters, his mother and grandmother** Roger Fulford says that as an adult, Duke Ernest "was as unattractive as Prince Albert was attractive. His complexion was sallow with liver spots, his eyes were bloodshot and his lower teeth, like those of a bulldog, protruded far above his upper ones" (Fulford, *The Prince Consort*, London: Macmillan, 1949, p. 22). The many extant paintings of Ernest as a child and as an adult currently on display in Coburg and in Gotha barely indicate these defects.

112 **Louise of Gotha wrote to her friend** *Early Years*, pp. 85–86.

113 **He learned to submit** In one of her memoranda in the book on the prince consort's early years, Queen Victoria notes that as an adult, Prince Albert still had the scars from the leeches applied during his childhood. It is moving to see the Queen recalling every detail of that beloved body.

113 **Once his mother had him dressed up** This event occurred after the boy had been entrusted to Herr Florschütz, and Duchess Louise seems to have blamed the tutor for Albert's gauche conduct. She remarked: "This comes of his *good* education." Quoted from Florschütz's recollections, *Early Years*, p. 97

113 **According to the testimony submitted** *Early Years*, p. 90.

113 **He spoke haltingly** Pauline Panam casually remarks on the duke's stammer. She also says how frustrated the duke was because he had been ignored and snubbed during the peace negotiations following the close of the Napoleonic wars.

114 **When he saw the teenage Prince** *Memoirs of Baron Stockmar*, vol. II, p. 6.

114 **He reported that whereas Albert** Richard Rhodes James, *Prince Albert: A Biography*, New York: Knopf, 1983, p. 26, apparently citing some unnamed archival source.

114 **"Even as a child," the Queen** *Early Years*, p. 42.

115 **After some negotiation, Duchess Louise** The terms of the "Trennungvertrag" (separation agreement) are given in *Das Haus vob Sachsen-Coburg und Gotha 1826 bis 2001* by Harald Sandner, p. 59.

116 **In some aristocratic circles** See, for example, the careers of the first Lady Melbourne, of Georgiana, Duchess of Devonshire, and of Madame de Pompadour.

116 **Then the crowd demanded** D. A. Ponsonby, the English biographer of Duchess Louise, suggests that Duke Ernest was not just a womanizer but a practicing homosexual, and that the men who served over the years as his personal aides were also his lovers. Ponsonby argues that when Duchess Louise discovered that Duke Ernest and Maximilian von Szymborski were lovers, she was revolted and felt obliged to leave her husband, even at the cost of losing her sons. When Szymborski took an active role in ending the duchess's marriage and sending her into exile, the local people turned into what we might now call an antihomosexual lynch mob (Ponsonby, pp. 155–156). Ponsonby was writing in the 1950s, when homosexuality had been isolated from the sexual continuum and was commonly seen as pathological. Her main evidence for the assertion that Ernest and Szymborski were lovers is that, in her letter to Augusta von Studnitz at the time of her separation, Louise refers to Szymborski as Ernest's "darling" (*Liebling*). Another translation for *Liebling* would be "favorite," but, of course, some version of the word *favorite* has been used in many languages to refer discreetly to the men with whom European kings such as James I of England or Henri II of France enjoyed especially intimate relations. I would doubt that Louise left Ernest because she could not stomach his homosexuality. The vast majority of gay men in the past married, and many had successful marriages. All the same, I think Ponsonby is to be trusted about Duke Ernest's sexual proclivities. Her family had been associated with the English Crown for at least 150 years, and she would not launch an accusation of homosexuality against Prince Albert's father casually at a time when to be called gay was a slur. Second, it seems to me that Pauline Panam's *Memoirs* support Ponsonby's assertion that Duke Ernest II was bisexual. It is surely suggestive that Duke Ernest asked his teenage mistress Panam to travel as a boy and to maintain male dress for some months after her arrival in Coburg. When describing her first meeting with Duke Ernest's then chief aide, Baron Fichler, the predecessor to Szymborski, Panam refers to him as "Ami du Prince"— capital letters and underlined, as if it were a title. She mocks Fichler's mincing walk, high, squeaky voice, exaggeratedly fashionable dress, and blinking eyes—in other words, his obvious effeminacy. Panam was a successful courtesan when she wrote her memoirs, and she had needed to acquire a sophisticated understanding of male sexual patterns and practices.

116   In the final letter to her friend Ponsonby, p. 151.

116   Louise never again saw Duke Ernest first exiled his wife and a few attendants he had chosen as his spies to St. Wendel in his personal fief (*Furstentum*) of Lichtenberg. There she acted for a time as a kind of regent and proved immensely popular with the people who were beginning to show signs of rebellion against their absent and exploitative duke. Duchess Louise's body was first kept in a house in St. Wendel. A street, a pharmacy, and a restaurant in the town are named for her. See Sandner, pp. 61–62 and also p. 47. Prussia purchased Lichtenberg from the Duke of Coburg in 1833 for 2.1 million talers.

116   In 1825 Louise's uncle The year 1826 saw a complicated reshuffling of the Ernestine domains between the five branches of the Thuringian Wettins. To gain Gotha, Duke Ernest had to give up the territory of Saalfeld and renounce any claim to Altenburg.

117   Others, of an anti-Semitic bent According to royal biographer Hector Bolitho, who was himself Jewish, in 1921 Herr Max W. L. Voss, author of *England als Erzieher* (England As Educator) wrote, "Prince Albert of Coburg, the Prince Consort, is to be described without contradiction as a half Jew, so that, since his time, Jewish blood has been circulating in the veins of the English royal family." See the introduction to Hector Bolitho's *Albert—Prince Consort*, New York: Bobbs-Merrill, 1964, p. 11. Also, in 1921 Lytton Strachey suggested more discreetly and sympathetically that Baron Mayern, "a charming and cultivated man, of Jewish extraction, was talked of" as the prince's father.

117   He accused royal historian Theodore Martin David Duff, *Victoria and Albert*, New York: Berkeley Medallion Book, 1972, pp. 30–35. Duff wrote a series of books on members of the English royal family and seems to have become progressively more disenchanted. No biographer has written a more scathing, or better referenced, indictment of the prince consort.

117   It is a canard that Prince Albert In the recent book on the house of Saxe-Coburg that received the current duke's imprimatur, Harald Sandner once again points to the enormous difference in character and looks among Prince Albert and his father and brother, and strongly suggests that Albert was not the Duke of Coburg's son. Sandner has gone through the Coburg state archives with care, but he does not identify Duchess Louise's supposed lover of 1818.

119   All the same, for a sensitive These were among the documents that Queen Victoria collected, or had copied, after her husband's death and that she had translated and published in her book *The Early Years*.

119   If they confided them to anyone Frank Eyck, Prince Albert's most informed and serious biographer, in his brief account of the prince's youth, states: "The loss of his mother and the break-up of his home . . . had a profound influence on him. He still remembered vividly many years later what a shock it had been for him to have suddenly lost his mother, for whom he always kept an affection" (*The Prince Consort: A Political Biography*, Houghton Mifflin, 1959, p. 14). Eyck cites as support for this statement a letter written to Queen Victoria by Christoph Florschütz, January 7, 1863 (Royal Archives Z. 272.6). This letter has never been published.

120   "It is a satisfaction to me *Early Years*, pp. 90–91. Florschütz's testimony as to Albert's happiness as a child has been cited as definitive by most of the prince's subsequent biographers, but to me it seems self-evidently unreliable. The tutor wrote from memory in the mid-1860s, he was deeply implicated in his own narrative, and he needed to protect his relations with the house of Coburg. When he arrived in Coburg in 1823, his position in the ducal household was, as he says, fraught with difficulties and stresses. Florschütz was a poor man who took no holidays, ate and slept with his pupils, and had barely a moment to himself. Until the princes came of age, his personal life was on hold, and his future depended on the bonds he could forge with the two boys. He and Duchess Louise were rivals for the affections of her sons. Seeing which way his bread was buttered, Florschütz gave his allegiance to the tall, manly, imposing man who employed him. After his fifteen years

of service to the princes, Florschütz retired on a pension and took up life in Coburg. He attended court, enjoyed the patronage of the dukes, and basked in the reflected glory of his famous pupil. Asked about the childhood of Albert, the Prince Consort, Florschütz unsurprisingly testified to an idyll.

Chapter 10: THE PARADISE OF OUR CHILDHOOD

122   **The older ladies would provide** Prince Albert to his father, 1826, *Early Years*, p. 52.

122   **Grandmother Augusta was a sharp** Queen Victoria experienced her grandmother's sharp tongue when Duchess Augusta paid a visit to Kensington Palace in 1826. "[Grandmama] was excessively kind to children, but could not bear naughty ones—and I shall never forget her coming into the room where I had been crying and naughty at my lessons and scolding me severely, which had a very salutary effect" (Hibbert, *Queen Victoria in Her Letters and Journals*, p. 11).

122   **The boys soon learned** The prince was known for his devotion to his stepgrandmother, Duchess Caroline, and he corresponded with her faithfully until her death. Duchess Caroline's extravagant grief when Prince Albert left Gotha to be married features in many biographies. And yet, between 1835 and 1839, Albert spent little more than hours with the Duchess of Gotha, as she notes unhappily in her letters. She was one of the people of whom absence made his heart grow fonder.

122   **As a result, in comparison** For example, the Darwins, Priestleys, Wedgwoods, Macaulays, Nightingales, Emersons, Beechers, Alcotts, or Peabodys. Queen Victoria was extremely impressed by a program of study that Prince Albert laid out for himself, though she admits he had little opportunity to pursue it. "The amount of work which the Prince thus traces for himself would probably not only seem excessive to the most studious English schoolboy . . . but was such as a hard-reading man at our universities might almost have shrunk from" (*Early Years*, p. 88). Maybe!

122   **Florschütz himself did much** Eyck reports that some notables in the German duchies believed that Florschütz had radical political ideas and proselytized to his pupils (*The Prince Consort: A Political Biography*, p. 16).

123   **From the little attic bedroom** When Queen Victoria first visited the Rosenau in 1844, she was struck by the extreme modesty of the attic sleeping quarters the princes Albert and Ernest had shared with their tutor as boys. Unfortunately, despite the recent renovations, this section of the house is still not opened to the public.

124   **His native landscapes were etched** In *Early Days*, Queen Victoria devotes several pages to describing the countryside around the cities of Coburg and Gotha.

125   **This was excellent revenge** The first edition of Grimms' folk tales appeared in 1812, and Prince Albert read them as a child. In one tale, a princess is obliged to marry an ugly frog. When she finds the creature in her bed, she smashes it against the wall in fury and discovers that the frog is a handsome prince under a spell.

125   **"Is it not too long** *Early Days*, p. 60.

125   **In his memoir, Duke Ernest II** Stanley Weintraub, *Uncrowned King: The Life of Prince Albert*, p. 33.

126   **Florschütz, who also had to** *Early Years*, p. 46.

126   **But only by taking part** Biographers of Prince Albert have tended to assume that he could not have loved his father when he was a boy and that the constant expressions of love that appear in Prince Albert's letters to Duke Ernest were insincere or coached. I take his letters at face value. Just because a parent is abusive does not mean that a child does not love that parent.

126   **The letters and journals** Even in childhood, Albert seems to have taken "Discretion is the better part of valor" for his motto. From the age of eleven until his death, he kept a diary, but not for the purposes of confession or self-analysis. All Albert's correspondence as a boy

was subject to review by his father and his tutor. For eighteen years, he and his brother were never apart and so had no need to write until Albert went to Bonn. The most candid extant letters were written to his stepmother and his stepgrandmother. The letters between the two brothers are presumably still in the private archives of the Coburg family. Hector Bolitho was allowed to see the letters for his 1932 biography and was then permitted to edit and publish a small selection. Bolitho's 1934 volume *The Prince Consort and His Brother* is a model of discretion—in other words, it gives us frustratingly little that was not available to Queen Victoria and Grey. Nothing would advance our knowledge of Prince Albert more than a new, uncensored edition of his correspondence with his brother.

126 **In sympathetic response** Weintraub, *Uncrowned King*, p. 36.

126 **In youth, he suffered** In their private correspondence, Stockmar and Leopold drop the occasional casual remark about the execrable moral tone of the people around Duke Ernest, although they offer no details. It is clear that they both agreed that it was essential to remove Albert from Coburg as a teenager to prevent him from being corrupted.

126 **"From our earliest years," wrote** *Early Years*, p. 213.

127 **"You well knew the events and scandals** Hector Bolitho, *The Prince Consort and His Brother,* New York: Appleton, 1934, p. 17.

127 **"I longed to be with you** Ibid, p. 173.

127 **In short order, the new king** Louise, first queen of the Belgians, wept uncontrollably at the time of her marriage, and her life was tragic and short. Queen Louise was another Coburg woman victim.

127 **"I wish I was with you** *Early Years*, p. 82.

128 **It says something of the unhappy** According to Monica Charlot, several French newspapers reported that the new king of the Belgians planned to marry his niece, the Princess Victoria of Kent (Charlot, p. 75). Given the fact that his older brother Ernest did marry their niece Marie of Württemberg, it is not inconceivable that Leopold may at one point have entertained the idea of marrying his darling niece Victoria.

128 **She bore him no children** By 1843, Duchess Marie had adopted a child of humble parentage and was bringing him or her up as her own. Prince Albert wrote to her, agreeing on the pleasures of seeing a child grow up, but cautioning her on giving the child expectations that could not be realized. "I wish you more success than generally attends the education of poor children of the lower ranks by persons of our own," remarked Albert pompously (*The Letters of the Prince Consort 1831–1861*, ed. Kurt Jagow, trans. E.T.S Dugdale, New York: Dutton, 1938, p. 83). The definitive book on Marie, based on extensive research in the Coburg state archives, is *Herzogin Marie von Sachsen-Coburg und Gotha* by Gertraude Bachmann (Historischen Gesellschaft Coburg, 1999).

128 **History has been grateful for this.** Duchess Marie decamped to Paris soon after her husband died, returning to Coburg mainly to see her visiting English relatives. Prince Albert continued to correspond with her until her death. These letters are often quoted, but Prince Albert's biographers in English at least have not probed the relationship between the two. Bolitho in Germany was shown an interesting letter from Marie to Albert, written probably when the Coburg princes had left Coburg for Brussels and Bonn, which indicates that the cousins were at one time close allies. Marie wrote: "You think of me no more; you do not love me properly; and you do not consider my advice as being well intentioned." Albert replied: "This doubt of our enormous love for you, and our gratitude, downright affection and care, cannot do otherwise than disturb us" (Bolitho, *Albert—Prince Consort*, p. 19).

128 **"So you go to England** *Early Years*, p. 145. Duchess Marie was Victoria's first cousin too, before becoming her stepmother-in-law.

129 **They went first to Mecklenburg** Queen Charlotte, the wife of King George III and mother to his fifteen children, was a princess of Mecklenburg-Strelitz, which gave her paternal family a luster it had hitherto lacked.

129   To his stepmother/cousin *Early Years*, p. 113.

129   **Duke Ernest could afford** At this time, virtually all army officers in England as well as in Germany came from the ranks of the aristocracy or landed gentry, and officers generally had to find the money to buy their commissions and to maintain themselves in the service.

130   **Victoria dreamed of a partner** Queen Victoria confided as much to Lord Melbourne in the week of her engagement.

Chapter 11: TRAINING FOR THE BIG RACE

131   **His older brother, Ernest** Duke Ernest of Württemberg married Princess Marie of Bourbon, another of the sisters of Queen Louise of the Belgians. The two cousins called Ernest were also in the late 1850s rivals for the love of the German opera star known as Natalie Frassini. See Gertraude Bachmann, *Zwei Herzöge und eine Primadonna* (*Two Dukes and a Diva*), Sonderdruck aus Jahrbuch der Coburger Landesstiftung, 2003.

131   **Feodora of Hohenlohe-Langenburg** See *Memoirs of Baron Stockmar,* vol. 1, pp. 364–365.

131   **Ernest had not inherited** King Leopold until early 1836 favored the marriage of his nephew Albert to another of his nieces, also, confusingly, called Victoire/Victoria but three years younger than Victoria Kent. Victoria Coburg-Kohary was the daughter of Leopold's brother Ferdinand and of Maria Antoinette Gabriella Kohary. Victoire Kohary's mother was a Hungarian princess who, through some legal hocus-pocus, had been declared a male and thus enabled to inherit the estates of her fabulously wealthy father. The family took the name Coburg-Kohary, and Ferdinand had higher ambitions for his children than marriage to an impoverished Coburg cousin like Albert. In due course, Leopold and Stockmar successfully negotiated the marriage of the eldest Kohary son, also named Ferdinand, with the queen of Portugal. The second Kohary son married Clementine of Bourbon, younger daughter of King Louis Philippe of France and sister of Queen Louise of the Belgians. In 1840 Victoire Coburg-Kohary married another Bourbon, Louis, Duc de Nemours, Queen Louise's brother, the young man who found Queen Victoria's table manners unacceptable.

132   **"If simply to fill** *Memoirs of Baron Stockmar,* vol. 1, pp. 336–337.

133   **For decades, long before** I am greatly simplifying the congruence in views between Leopold and Stockmar, especially after Leopold went to Brussels in 1831. Frank Eyck, the most sober and lucid guide to Coburg political ideas, notes how different the two men were both in personal morality and in political worldview.

133   **At the same time** The evidence on Stockmar's astonishing influence over the lives of both Queen Victoria and Prince Albert can be gained from his memoirs, his correspondence with King Leopold, the Queen's own testimony, and an unpublished memorandum by Prince Albert's private secretary, Sir George Anson (Royal Archives, Y.54.15).

133   **Wiechmann was a tedious old soldier** Prince William of Löwenstein wrote to Queen Victoria: "The somewhat stiff military nature of the princes' governor, Colonel von Wiechmann, gave occasion to many disputes with the young princes, and frequently led to most comical scenes. It is impossible to give an idea in writing of the many trifling occurrences of this kind, for the ludicrous effect depended more on the mimicry and accentuation than upon the subject itself" (*Early Years*, p. 147).

134   **The mathematician Adolphe Quetelet** Quetelet once observed that whereas Prince Albert did not think enough of his own talents, King Leopold never forgot his.

134   **"Such an expedition would require** *Early Years*, p. 126.

134   **Berlin, Stockmar informed King Leopold,** *Memoirs of Baron Stockmar,* p. 369. In *Strangers* (New York: Norton, 2003), his book on nineteenth-century homosexuals, Graham Robb notes that Berlin was famous for its male prostitutes.

135   **As Prince Albert wrote** *Early Years*, pp. 154–155.

135   **Faced with the mass of evidence** Lytton Strachey, in his biography of the Queen, com-

ments: "In one particular, it was observed, [PA] did not take after his father; *owing either to his peculiar upbringing or to a more fundamental idiosyncrasy he had a marked distaste for the opposite sex* [my italics]" (*Queen Victoria*, New York: Barnes and Noble Books, 1998/1921, p. 88). Strachey offers a sympathetic portrait of the prince as, implicitly, a gay man like himself; a brilliant, sensitive intellectual tragically immolated on the altar of his family's dynastic ambitions and his wife's predatory sexuality. Edward. F. Benson (*Queen Victoria*, New York: Longmans, 1935) comments over and again on Prince Albert's feminine traits and the reversal of roles between him and the Queen. Discussing Prince Albert's decision to fire the tutor whom his eldest son Bertie had begun to trust and obey, Benson asserts that Albert "remembered his own affection for Herr Florschütz, a disordered unnatural fancy" (Benson, p. 190). Benson gives no supporting reference for this assertion, but it was taken up and cited in 1972 by maverick royal historian David Duff. He accuses the prince of having had "strange and unnatural feelings" for his tutor that had to be "sternly repressed" (Duff, *Victoria and Albert*, p. 70). Monica Charlot, in her 1991 biography of Queen Victoria, notes that Florschütz was "obviously attracted" to the boy Albert, repeats Duff's assertion of an improper relationship between the two, and concludes that given the traumatic incidents in the boy's early childhood and the fact that tutor and pupils lived together in close quarters night and day for fifteen years, it would be "scarcely abnormal" if indeed they had developed some kind of homosexual relationship (*Victoria: The Young Queen*, pp. 153–154).

136 **Bonn in the early nineteenth century** For a fascinating account of Cambridge student life for Prince Albert's English contemporaries, see James Pope-Hennessy's two-volume biography of Richard Monckton Milnes.

136 **Very, very occasionally men were** See Graham Robb, *Strangers: Homosexual Love in the Nineteenth Century.*

136 **As the writer and critic J. M. Coetzee has put it** J. M. Coetzee, "Love and Walt Whitman," the *New York Review of Books*, September 22, 2005, p. 24.

137 **It contained an edelweiss** The Queen kept and treasured the flower, and she notes that, thanks to the scrapbook and to a diary kept by Florschütz, her younger son, Prince Arthur, was able to retrace his father's steps exactly in 1865.

137 **All the same, the grandsons spent** *Early Years*, p. 137.

137 **Prince Albert had seriously injured** Again, in a note that allows her to remember each tiny feature of her husband's body, Queen Victoria reports that Albert had a large scar on his knee from this accident.

137 **The visit would give him** *Letters of the Prince Consort*, ed. Jagow, p. 15.

138 **"The chief question," wrote Prince Albert** Ibid, p. 144.

138 **As soon as the academic semester** Within months of saying good-bye to his ducal charges, Rath Christopher Florschütz, aged forty, married the daughter of Herr Superintendent Genzler, a Coburg divine. Prince Albert was astonished at the marriage, as he told his brother.

139 **As Albert wrote to Ernest** *The Prince Consort and His Brother*, ed. Bolitho, p. 11.

139 **On this occasion, as on many** Astonishingly, another fire broke out at the Ehrenburg Palace a year later, when, during the feast to celebrate Albert's betrothal, the gauzy curtains in the great hall blew into the candles and went up in flames. Such minor accidents were taken in stride.

139 **Now I am quite alone** *Early Years*, pp. 156–157. I have preferred to do my own translation from the German text Queen Victoria included in appendix C to her book, rather than cite the overly cautious translation done by her daughter that appears on pp. 156–157. In general Albert has not been well served by his translators.

140 **No one better than Stockmar** King Leopold wrote to Queen Victoria on April 13, 1838: "Concerning the education of our friend Albert, it has been the best plan you could have fixed upon, to name Stockmar your commissary-general; it will give *unité d'action et de*

l'ensemble . . . I have communicated to him what your uncle [Duke Ernest], and the young gentleman seem to wish, and what strikes me as best for the moment. Stockmar will make a regular report to you on this subject" (Raymond, *Queen Victoria's Early Letters*, p. 29).

140 **"In many, many respects** Eyck, p. 18.

140 **In Florence at a ball** "Voilà un prince don't nous pouvons être fiers. La belle danseuse l'attend—le savant l'occupe." *Early Years*, p. 120

141 **"[Prince Albert] had been accustomed** *Early Years*, pp 164–165.

141 **Albert himself paints** *Early Years*, pp. 166–167.

141 **In the same bitter vein** Cecil Woodham-Smith, *Queen Victoria*, p. 186.

141 **He opined that the prince would** *Memoirs of Baron Stockmar*, vol. ii, p. 7. It was presumably the publication of comments like this about the young Albert that led Queen Victoria to deplore the publication of the baron's memoirs.

141 **"Then I must go** *Early Years*, p. 326.

142 **The visit may have been** Harald Sandner reports a fascinating rumor that Albert in Carlsbad had an affair with a certain Countess Resterlitz, but he offers no supporting evidence (see Sander, p. 70).

142 **This fact is established conclusively** Guardians of the reputation of the English royal family, notably Hector Bolitho, editor of the brothers' correspondence, successfully kept this incriminating letter out of print. The quoted passage was published only in 1959 by Frank Eyck, one of the rare British historians capable of reading nineteenth-century German handwriting.

142 **I am deeply distressed and grieved** *The Prince Consort: A Political Biography*, Frank Eyck, p. 19.

143 **In 1844 Alexandrine officially adopted** Sandner, p. 106.

143 **He had a succession of** According to Harald Sandner, these illegitimate children were Helene von Sternheim, born around 1839, of Fräulein Steinpflug; Karl Raymond, Freiherr von Ketschendorff, born of the opera singer Victorine Noel; and Graf Razumofsky von Wigstein, born 1852 of Baroness Rosa Löwenstein (Sander, p. 103).

143 **Either Albert's purity or his authority** Even the most loyalist of English royal biographers have been obliged to admit, when pressed, that Duke Ernest II of Saxe-Coburg and Gotha, Prince Albert's brother, had a scandalous private life, but it was a subject they preferred to avoid. Facts were hard to come by until the German scholars Harald Sandner, Harald Bachmann, and Gertraude Bachmann explored the Coburg state archives in the late 1990s. Anecdotal attacks on Duke Ernest II are found scattered in various English memoirs. Lt. Col. Arthur Haig, in a letter written in the early 1880s to Henry Ponsonby, one of Queen Victoria's most trusted aides, was scathing: "Ernest the Great, the Good, the Chaste, the Second, the Father, the Grandfather now of many of his subjects, will appear in state. His Consort and all his other Consorts will be there—all those that have been—that are—and that are going to be—all . . . Send out a Hogarth quick to paint the picture of 'La Famille ducale et demi-ducale.' " Haig then goes on to say that the duke had found a bourgeois husband for his most recent *maitresse en titre* at the lady's own request. She had decided that she needed a respectable exit from Coburg, since her lover the duke seemed likely to die soon and his heir, Alfred, Duke of Edinburgh, Queen Victoria's second son, was sure to send her packing (Arthur Ponsonby, *Henry Ponsonby*, London: Macmillan, 1942, p. 350). Dean Stanley, an intimate of Queen Victoria accompanying the Prince of Wales on a tour of the Near East following the death of the prince consort, met the Duke of Saxe-Coburg in Egypt in 1862 and confided to his diary: "If anything could increase the respect for Prince Albert and the thankfulness for what he has been to England, it may be the reflection of what would have been the difference had the Queen married the older brother. He [Ernest II] is going to hunt in Abyssinia and I trust I may never set eyes on him again" (Bolitho, *Albert—Prince Consort*, p xi). Lady Marie Mallet wrote around 1890: "The old Duke of Saxe-Coburg has been here [Balmoral] today with his wife. He is the Prince Consort's only brother and an awful-looking man, the Queen dislikes him particularly. He is

always writing anonymous pamphlets against the Queen and the Empress Frederick [Queen Victoria's eldest daughter] which naturally cause a great deal of annoyance in the family" (*Life With Queen Victoria: Letters from Court*, ed. Victor Mallet, Boston: Houghton Mifflin, 1968, p. 52).

PART TWO: TOGETHER

Chapter 12: VICTORIA PLANS HER MARRIAGE

147 **He called her *Vortrefflichste*** This may have been less extravagant a compliment than it seems. Extracts from the correspondence and journals of members of the Coburg family show that *vortrefflich* was a favorite adjective rather like the English "delightful," used to describe almost anything enjoyable.

148 **"An experienced man** John Plunkett, *Queen Victoria, First Media Monarch*, Oxford University Press, 2003, p. 213.

149 **These were the facts** After his marriage, Albert received tuition in the English constitution from Mr. William Selwyn, an acknowledged English legal expert. See Martin, vol. i, p. 87. This older gentleman shocked the prince by daring to sit down in "the presence" without authorization and delivering long, rather meandering and haphazard lectures, sadly lacking in the kind of abstract political principles the prince admired. See Fulford, *The Prince Consort*, p. 65. Also in 1842, the Queen and the prince together read Hallam, a standard authority on the English constitution.

150 **He would leave her queen** A good example of the advice given to the prince is the following remark by King Leopold recorded by Prince Albert's private secretary George Anson at Windsor in August 1840: "The Prince ought in business as in everything to be necessary to the Queen, he should be to her a walking dictionary for reference on any point which her own knowledge or education have not enabled her to answer. There should be no concealment from him on any subject" (quoted by Frank Eyck, p. 22, from a memorandum by Anson, Royal Archives Y.54.8).

151 **There, according to Stockmar's memoirs** Stockmar, *Memoirs*, vol. ii, p. 18.

152 **The Coburg party, which comprised** For a brief summary of these events (which are covered in detail in all biographies of Queen Victoria), see chapter 7, p. 87.

153 **It was a point of honor** In the fifteenth century, Frederick the Wise, elector of Saxony, one of Prince Albert's ancestors, took up the cause of Martin Luther, and suffered a permanent loss of land, wealth, and status as a result. See the opening section of *Early Years*.

154 **She duly issued letters patent** This is the version I have found in standard biographies, but Stockmar in his memoirs claims to have advised the Queen to issue the letters patent establishing Albert's precedence.

154 **As a loyal wife-to-be** She raised the issue on at least three separate occasions: with her Whig prime minister Melbourne before her marriage and with her Tory prime minister Peel in late 1841 and again in 1845. Though Peel was a close ally of the prince's, he saw quite as clearly as Melbourne that a motion to make Albert king consort was doomed to fail in parliament and risked bringing down the monarchy if it were made public.

154 **"For God's sake, say no more** Jerrold, *The Married Life of Queen Victoria*, p. 43.

155 **The Tories unearthed their social conscience** A general dislike of the Coburg family among the British ruling classes was more probably the reason for the cut in Prince Albert's appanage than the poverty of the masses. Leopold, by clinging to his parliamentary income even after he was given the Belgian throne, had queered the pitch for his nephew, and both knew it.

155 **They laid the blame squarely** Stockmar, who was in London as the Coburg family's agent during the time of the engagement, blamed Melbourne's careless handling of the negotiations with parliament for the slights suffered by Prince Albert. He also believed that the

opposition to the prince expressed by the High Tory faction had been fomented by Victoria's senior uncle, Ernest, Duke of Cumberland, king of Hanover. Whether or not this allegation was true, Albert believed it, and his relations with Cumberland were always extremely hostile.

155 **In fact, the Tories could afford** As Prince Albert recalled to Baron Stockmar in 1854: "When I first came [to England], I was met by this want of knowledge and unwillingness to give a thought to the position of this luckless personage [the husband of a queen regnant]. Peel cut down my income, Wellington refused me my rank, the Royal family cried out against the foreign interloper, the Whigs in office were only inclined to concede to me just as much space as I could stand upon" (Jagow, *Letters of the Prince Consort*, p. 205).

156 **Determined that this money at least** David Duff gives a detailed analysis of the correspondence between Victoria and Albert during the engagement period. He quotes the following unpublished letter from Albert: "As the Queen's husband, I shall be in a dependent position, more dependent than any other husband in my circumstances. My private fortune is all that is left to me to dispose of. I am therefore not unfair in requesting that that which has belonged to me since I came of age a year ago shall be left under my control" (Duff, *Victoria and Albert*, p. 182). Duff says that Albert gave Ernest the money he had inherited from their mother. My reading of the published letters between the two brothers leads me to believe that Albert merely designated Ernest to act for him in the matter of the property.

157 **Charles Greville, a cynical man** See Fulford, p. 81, citing Greville, vol. v, p. 229.

157 **No Tories, not even the Duke** Hibbert, *Queen Victoria: A Personal Biography*, p. 116. Lord Ashley was the husband of Minnie Cowper, the elder daughter of Lady Emily Cowper, Lord Melbourne's sister. Ashley succeeded to his father's title and became the Seventh Earl of Shaftesbury, the name by which he is known to history.

159 **Thereupon, as she recorded later** One of Queen Victoria's bridesmaids remembered Albert's look of panic when, after the wedding ceremony, the bridesmaids went away, leaving him in charge of getting his wife and her long train into the carriage for the ride back to the palace.

160 **Bride and groom did not get** All this we know because, day by day, Victoria recorded the events of her betrothal and marriage at length in her journal. Frank yet maidenly, factual yet superficial, fascinating yet free of literary artifice, these pages of Queen Victoria's journal form a key document in Victorian social history. After February 1840, a veil is drawn over the intimate side of the royal marriage. We hear no more from Queen Victoria about the delights of watching Albert bare that beautiful white neck to shave or letting him help her put on her stockings. As a token of love and trust in the early days of the marriage, Victoria allowed Albert to read the entries she had written at the time of their engagement and wedding. She does not say how he reacted, but it seems likely that he was horrified by his wife's frankness and begged her to be more discreet in the future. It is possible that the Queen continued to be frank in her journal but that, after her death and on her instructions, all the intimate passages were cut by her daughter Princess Beatrice.

160 **The experienced men of her court** There are comments to this effect by Greville, Wellington, Stockmar, and King Leopold. Lord Melbourne, who saw the Queen every day, was obviously aware of her emotional state.

160 **None of this bodes well** John Ruskin married late in life and on his wedding night was overcome by the sight of his wife Effie's naked body. The two were finally divorced, on the grounds of nonconsummation. The Ruskin divorce case was one of the most sensational of the Victorian era.

161 **Now, as if by a miracle** I seem to be the only biographer who finds it remarkable that the self-professed sexual neophyte Prince Albert performed so superbly on his wedding night. This to me is *prima facie* evidence that, in fact, he had explored his sexuality before marriage with consenting partners, probably males.

161 **However, from the beginning, erotic passion** As Hector Bolitho, perhaps the most pam-

pered and prolific of twentieth-century royal biographers tactfully puts it: "Love, in the terms that appealed to [the Queen,] was alien to [the prince's] almost celibate nature" (Hector Bolitho, *Albert-Prince Consort*, p. viii). This book is a revised version of the 1932 *Albert the Good*. Bolitho, a New Zealander of Jewish background, managed in the 1920s to establish a close relationship with the descendents of Queen Victoria and was given extraordinary access to archival sources and to personal reminiscences in Germany as well as Great Britain. His most interesting and enlightened source was Queen Marie of Romania, daughter of Alfred, Duke of Edinburgh, Queen Victoria's second son.

161 **As Victoria wrote in heartbroken fragments** Queen Victoria to her daughter Vicky, then Crown Princess of Prussia, letter of December 18, 1861 (*Dearest Mama*, ed. Roger Fulford, New York: Holt, Rinehart and Winston, 1969, p. 23).

Chapter 13: BEARING THE FRUITS OF DESIRE

163 **In a letter to his university** To Prince William of Löwenstein, Albert wrote in May 1840: "In my home life, I am very happy and contented; but the difficulty in filling my place with the proper dignity is, that I am only the husband, and not the master in the house" (Jagow, *Letters of the Prince Consort*, p. 69).

164 **As one of Queen Victoria's ladies** Charlot, *Victoria—The Young Queen*, p. 188.

164 **She wrote forthrightly** Charlot, p. 191.

165 **To Uncle Leopold she was** Charlot, p.192.

165 **Albert wrote to Stockmar** Charlot, p. 193.

166 **This birth was too important** In 1838 it was Clark, examining Lady Flora through her clothes, as was usual at the time, who made the disastrous diagnosis that she was pregnant (she was, in fact, in the final stages of liver cancer), informed the Queen of this, and provoked a huge scandal.

166 **Albert wrote enigmatically** Bolitho, *The Prince Consort and His Brother*, p. 34.

167 **Lord Clarendon, writing to Lord Granville** Woodham-Smith, p. 217.

167 **The Queen was sharply taken aback** Hibbert, *Queen Victoria*, p. 133.

167 **"My sufferings were really** Charlot, p. 207.

169 **When she was carrying Leopold** She was able to admit this to her daughter after Vicky had undergone her first pregnancy.

169 **"Now to reply to your observation** *Dearest Child*, pp. 77–78.

170 **Virtuous husbands like Albert** The Calvinist divine Lyman Beecher lost two young wives, worn out by childbearing, and married a third who survived him. Beecher had some eleven children in all. A generation later, Lord Shaftesbury and Patrick Bronte, to take only two famous examples, were deeply in love with their wives and felt fully entitled to the pleasures of the marital bed. When their wives died after bearing many children in quick succession, the husbands suffered but accepted the deaths as God's will. Traditionally, a husband's right to virtuous (that is, vaginal) sex trumped a wife's right to life.

Chapter 14: WHIGS AND TORIES

172 **And whereas Albert, a married man** The scandal in the divorce courts over Melbourne's relationship with Lady Caroline Norton occurred in 1835, only two years before Queen Victoria's accession.

173 **But under Albert's influence** On October 1, 1842, just after Lehzen's departure, Queen Victoria reread the diary entries for the first years of her reign when she and Lord Melbourne had been so close. She wrote: "Wrote & looked over & corrected one of my old journals, which do not *now* awake very pleasant feelings. The life I led then was so artificial & superficial & yet I thought I was happy. Thank God! I know now what real happiness means" (Longford, *Victoria R.I.* p. 207).

173 **"A worse school for a young** Quoted from *Early Years*, p. 220, in Stockmar's *Memoirs*, vol. ii, p. 4.

174 **Albert had become so identified** Greville, vol. III, p. 129.

175 **In token of his regard** When Wellington died in 1852, he was given a state funeral that cost the Treasury 29,968 pounds eighteen shillings and ninepence. Such an immense expenditure aroused no protests in press or parliament, and the whole country, including the Queen and the prince, engaged in a long period of extravagant mourning for the duke. At the Queen's command, the court went into full black, and when the duke's body was lying in state at Chelsea Hospital, she herself went to pay her respects. Rarely, if ever, had royalty paid such homage to a commoner. See Vera Watson, *A Queen at Home*, pp. 118–120.

175 **The consort to the Queen of England** Jagow, *Letters of the Prince Consort*, pp. 156–157. The expression "peculiar and delicate role" is Prince Albert's own from this letter.

Chapter 15: DEAREST DAISY

179 **He convinced himself** Charlot, pp. 208–209.

181 **This process would shape the young** Stockmar's influence on the parenting of Queen Victoria and Prince Albert is laid out in detail in his *Memoirs*, vol. ii, p. 48. Stockmar claimed that the organization of the royal nursery occupied a great deal of his time and "gives me more trouble than the government of a kingdom."

181 **The prince had no use** Quoted from Melbourne's correspondence with Queen Victoria by Giles St. Aubyn (*Edward VII, Prince and King*, New York: Athenaeum, 1979, p. 17).

181 **Far more fatefully** This incident is reported, I believe for the first time, by Daphne Bennett, who was given full access to the Windsor Archives and has interesting new information about life in the royal nurseries. See *Queen Victoria's Children*, New York: St. Martins, 1980, p. 34.

183 **The note read: "Dr. Clark** Charlot, p. 209.

184 **On one occasion, Victoria reportedly** Strachey, *Queen Victoria*, p. 93, citing Jerrold. Strachey comments that the story "survives, ill authenticated, and perhaps mythical, yet summing up . . . , the central facts of the case."

185 **When apart, the two men corresponded** Prince Albert probably confided more in Stockmar than anyone else, and our understanding of the prince is due in no small part to the parts of that correspondence that have been published. Neither Windsor nor Coburg was able to censor the Stockmar–Prince Albert letters directly, which is an advantage. Nonetheless, as is the case with all the prince consort's papers, we have only a tiny, heavily edited, and quite possibly misleading selection. When Stockmar's son Ernest prepared his father's papers for publication, he was extremely careful to protect the baron's reputation and avoid the wrath of the Saxe-Coburgs. Ernest Stockmar ends his biographical sketch of his father with these enigmatic words: "[Baron Christian Stockmar] was content to remain always half hidden before the eyes of posterity. Faithful to his spirit, this book also lifts the veil but a little" (vol. 1, p. cx). All the same, when *Memoirs* was published in 1873, it caused quite a sensation, and Queen Victoria was very displeased at what she regarded as a betrayal of confidence.

186 **The German title of baron** In 1821 the then Prince Leopold secured a Saxon barony for his friend Stockmar. This was raised to Baron of Bavaria in 1831 and then Baron of Austria in 1840 (*Memoirs*, vol. 1, p. liv).

186 **In their private letters** "Nowhere in the records of history has Royalty been served with a devotion so purely noble and unselfish as that of this remarkable man [Stockmar] to the Queen and the Prince," writes Martin, clearly expressing the judgment of his employer and collaborator, Queen Victoria (vol. i. p. 72). The encomium continues for three long pages.

186 **This passage from one of his last** *Memoirs*, vol. i, p. civ.

187   **He sired three children** Ibid, p. lv.

187   **"[The Queen] was quite a girl** Stockmar confided this in a conversation with the Prince of Wales's admiring young tutor, Frederick Gibbs, whom Stockmar had been instrumental in engaging. See "The Education of a Prince: Extracts from the Diaries of Frederick Weymouth Gibbs 1851–1856, *Cornhill Magazine*, spring 1951, p. 117.

188   **"I expressed [to Peel, the new** Charlot, p. 208.

188   **According to the memoirs** Bauer claimed that Stockmar's wife was a miser as well as a harridan who actually kept her husband short of food. This may simply be malicious gossip, but Bauer lived in Coburg during her cousin Stockmar's last years and had ample opportunity to observe him and his family. As editor of his father's memoirs, Stockmar's son says nothing about his mother and the relations between his parents.

190   **They would be a formidable team** In the memoir she cowrote with General Grey, Queen Victoria describes this turning point in her relations with her husband thus: "Thanks to the firmness, but, at the same time, gentleness with which the Prince insisted on filling his proper position as head of the family—thanks also to the clear judgment and right feeling of the Queen, as well as her singularly honest and straightforward nature—but thanks, more than all, to the mutual love and perfect confidence which bound the Queen and the Prince to each other, it was impossible to keep any separation or difference of interests or duties between them. To those who would urge upon the Queen that, as sovereign, she must be head of the house and the family, as well as of the state, Her Majesty would reply that she had solemnly engaged at the altar to 'obey' as well as to 'love and honor,' [sic] and this sacred obligation she could consent neither to limit nor refine away" (*Early Years*, p. 256).

Chapter 16: ALBERT TAKES CHARGE

191   **He said he "was desirous** Woodham-Smith, pp. 217–18. Jones was finally sent away to sea, where he drowned.

192   **The result was a lengthy** For a published extract of this document, see Stockmar's *Memoirs*, vol. 2, pp. 116–125.

193   **The Queen had her own stable** *The Private Life of the Queen by a Member of the Royal Household*, New York: Appleton, 1897, p. 13. Originally the author of this book was not identified, but it is now known that he was C. Arthur Pearson.

193   **Due to the fabulous extravagance** Queen Victoria's income from the civil list remained the same until her death, but this fact is somewhat misleading, since Prince Albert pioneered new methods of getting money out of the Treasury.

194   **Victoria was quite sure** Vicky, as Princess Frederick of Prussia, was amazed to view the collection of jewelry that the dowager Empress Charlotte (born a Hohenzollern princess, widow of Tsar Nicholas I) traveled with. "Hers are huge things and really in such profusion that it seems almost magic—sapphires, emeralds, pearls, rubies, etc., but the quality is not very fine—her diamonds excepted which are magnificent" (Hannah Pakula, *An Uncommon Woman: The Empress Frederick, Daughter of Queen Victoria, Wife of the Crown Prince of Prussia, Mother of Kaiser Wilhelm*, New York: Simon & Schuster, 1995, p. 137). English diplomats at the height of the power of the British Empire were at times struck dumb by the glittering profusion of gold and precious stones on display in foreign courts. For example, at the coronation of the tsar in 1883, the diplomat Everard Primrose wrote to his friend Mary Ponsonby: "The blaze of jewels was astonishing. The Archduchess from Austria glittered like the spray of a beautiful fountain, the Grand Duchess Constantine could scarcely support the weight of countless precious stones, while Princess Kotsoubey wore a wig of pearls" (Magdalen Ponsonby, *Mary Ponsonby: A Memoir and a Journal*, London: John Murray, 1927, p. 166). The Russian tsars, meanwhile, were competing with the fabulous heaps of jewels and gold and silver ornaments, including jewel-encrusted thrones, owned

by the sultan of Turkey, the emperors of China and Japan, and several Indian maharajahs. The wonders Aladdin discovers in a cave were not simply a fairy tale.

194 **One of Victoria's bridesmaids** Longford, p. 213.

194 **Victoria did have a crown** The crown traditionally placed upon the head of a British monarch during the coronation ceremony is the massive St. Edward's crown, containing elements that date back to the Middle Ages but first used in 1661 for the coronation of Charles II. This crown appears for a brief time only once in every reign. However, from the images taken of Victoria even at the actual moment of coronation, she was crowned not with St. Edward's crown but with the crown that was made for her. This crown is an early version of what is now known as the imperial state crown.

194 **The gallant Victoria allowed herself** Betty Askwith, *The Lytteltons: A Family Chronicle of the Nineteenth Century*, London: Chatto and Windus, 1975, p. 65.

194 **However, by the early 1850s** George IV found the coronet too effeminate, but both Queen Victoria and her successor, Queen Elizabeth II, loved to wear it as young women. We see Victoria with this coronet in the blurred image taken at her daughter Vicky's wedding, and again in the famous 1859 portrait of her in state robes, with the imperial state crown on a small table behind her. The coronet is familiar to us today from many photographs of Elizabeth as a dazzlingly beautiful queen and from the image chosen for the postage stamps early in her reign.

194 **The British government decided** Queen Victoria kept the family jewels long enough to wear them at the brilliant festivities marking the Princess Royal's wedding to Prince Frederick of Prussia in January 1858. But immediately thereafter, she sent the Guelph treasure to Hanover. The princess, on her honeymoon journey through Germany, attended a state banquet in Hanover and was horrified to find that she was eating off the gold dinner service she knew so well from Windsor. She kept this mortifying piece of information from her mother, but this German slight to English power was an early sign of the ferocious hostility that Vicky was to experience in her life abroad. See Pakula, pp. 88–89.

195 **The 385,000 pounds a year** See Vera Watson, *A Queen at Home: An Intimate Account of the Social and Domestic Life of Queen Victoria's Court*, p. 22. Watson based her valuable book on extensive research into the records of the Lord Chamberlain's Department 1837–1885.

195 **The royal household was a division** The areas of authority of the four departments in charge of the royal household were, it seems, divided up topologically. Both the Lord Chamberlain and the Lord Stewart ruled "inside" the royal residences, with the Lord Chamberlain "upstairs," dealing with the members of the royal family in their official and ceremonial capacity. The Lord Steward conducted affairs "downstairs," notably in regard to feeding the whole household. The Commissioners of Woods and Forests and the Master of the Horse had dominion "outside." The commission was responsible not only for the gardens, parks, and farms surrounding the royal residences but also with the physical structure of the buildings. The Master of the Horse, the smallest of the departmental units, looked after the Queen's horses and carriages, and supervised her travel, which, over the years, became more and more extensive.

195 **Queen Victoria referred to them once** Queen Victoria to King Leopold, March 25, 1845, Martin, vol. i, p. 209.

196 **Answer: because the Lord Chamberlain's men** *Memoirs of Baron Stockmar*, vol. 11, pp. 118–125.

196 **No wonder the official name** See Watson, p. 19.

197 **After the coronation, a decorous tussle** Watson, pp. 37–38.

197 **His campaign for domestic reform** Martin, vol. ii, p. 5.

198 **The butler was under notice** On her first visit to Germany, Queen Victoria expressed her delight in drinking beer. How much she drank at home is not clear.

199 **By 1845, Albert had wrapped** In a speech in the Commons in 1845, Sir Robert Peel opined that in governing its finances the country could do no better than follow the example of

the Queen's household. He noted that three great monarchs had visited Great Britain in one year, all were entertained magnificently, and all without incurring any debt or requesting any additional funds under the civil list (see Martin, vol. i, p. 213).

199 **When the prince cut the wages** Queen Victoria was aware of the criticisms aimed at her husband and felt obliged to counter them in the biography of the prince she commissioned from Theodore Martin. "The Prince," wrote Martin, "possessed no independent authority by right of his position, and could exercise none, even within his own household, without trenching on the privileges of others, who were not always disposed to admit of interference. This could scarcely fail to embarrass his position in the midst of a vast royal establishment, which had inherited many of the abuses of former reigns and where he could find much of which he could not approve, yet was without the power to rectify. And as behind every abuse there is always someone interested in maintaining it, he could not but be aware that he was regarded with no friendly eyes by those who were in that position, and who naturally dreaded the presence among them of one so visibly intolerant of worthlessness and incapacity" (Martin, vol. i, p. 68).

199 **Judge published a stream of articles** Jasper Tomsett Judge of Windsor seems to be the source of many of the unflattering anecdotes about Prince Albert that are reported by negative biographers, notably David Duff in his *Victoria and Albert*. Clare Jerrold gives a long and admiring account of Judge and his associates in her invaluable book *The Married Life of Queen Victoria*.

Chapter 17: THE COURT OF ST. ALBERT'S

202 **The traditional qualifications** The Duchess of Sutherland, Queen Victoria's first mistress of the robes, did not have any obvious need of the Lord Chamberlain's salary, but as the reign proceeded, and the political power of the Crown waned, the wives of England's greatest lords were apparently less and less inclined to serve in the royal household. Membership had ceased to be a passport to influence and wealth as it had been in the reign of Charles II. The issue of financial need is carefully skirted in the memoirs of nineteenth-century courtiers. Even the Ponsonbys in the correspondence the family chose to publish do not discuss money. Queen Victoria confirms that money was key. Hearing from her daughter Vicky in Prussia that it was very difficult to find any suitable people to form part of her household, Queen Victoria answered: "What you say about needy gentlemen and ladies wanting to be about the Court is the case everywhere. The nice ones are always more difficult to get" (*Dearest Child*, p. 254).

203 **After Albert's death, she chose** Queen Victoria's close relationship in old age to her Indian servant Abdul Karim, often referred to as the Munshi, is fascinating.

203 **As his brother, Ernest, would later** See Fulford, p. 99, citing Duke Ernest's *Memoirs* without page reference. Fulford, pp. 90–100, is very good on why Prince Albert was so unpopular in England, and I am indebted to his analysis.

204 **What kind of man was beholden** To quote one of the anonymous rhymes published in the English press at the time of the royal marriage, and which Prince Albert, apparently, collected: "Quoth Hudibras of old 'a thing / Is worth as much as it will bring.' / How comes it then that Albert clear / Has thirty thousand pounds a year?" (Clare Jerrold, *The Married Life of Queen Victoria*, p. 11).

205 **He surely anticipated that these skills** An example of Albert's passion for hunting occurred on a trip by yacht around the coast of Wales. Albert and his brother-in-law Charles Leiningen spotted a small island covered with sea birds, and rushed down for their guns only to discover to their dismay that the birds were out of range. One of Albert's technical passions over the years was to find guns that were more accurate and had a longer range. Though she hated guns, Victoria gave them to her husband as presents.

206 **To ensure that the numbers were impressive** The battue system had been in operation in Germany for centuries, as we can see from a precious set of seventeenth-century marquetry pictures that paneled the walls of a room at the Ehrenburg Palace in Coburg during Prince Albert's youth. These great works of art, probably the most expensive things in his collection, were transferred by Duke Ernest I to the Veste fortress in Coburg sometime after his younger son's marriage.

206 **He claimed in his fifty-six years** See Sandner, *Das Haus Sachsen-Coburg und Gotha, 1826–2001*, p. 52 and p. 96.

207 **Sing a song of Gotha** Clare Jerrold, *The Married Life of Queen Victoria*, p. 320. Queen Victoria in her journal says that she took no pleasure in the Gotha battue, which family courtesy obliged her to attend, and that the English gentlemen in her party thought it a slaughter, not a sport.

207 **Albert learned that battues** Some hostile biographers like Duff report that Albert organized a battue on his Osborne estate because the deer were destroying his shrubs.

208 **By 1844, the prince had set** Frank Eyck cites an egregious example of the royal intransigence in regard to persons who failed to meet the prince's standards of personal morality. When the Tory Lord Derby became prime minister, he begged that the wife of his lord chancellor, Sir Edward Sugden (later Lord St. Leonards), should be received at court. The Sugdens had been married for fifty years, but they began their relationship as teenagers, when Lady Sugden ran away with her then schoolboy lover. The two lived together for a few years before they could be married. The Queen declined to lower her standards for Lady Sugden, and so, as Eyck remarks, "The faithful old husband requested that he should not be asked to Court as long as the prohibition on his wife continued" (*The Prince Consort: A Political Biography*, p. 192).

208 **The result was that** This estrangement with members of her own family persisted throughout the prince's lifetime, and even beyond. In her letters to her daughter in Berlin, Victoria constantly advised Vicky not to become close to her (QV's) first cousin Augusta, by this point Duchess of Mecklenburg-Strelitz, who was often at the Prussian court. Augusta, wrote Victoria, reported everything back to her mother, the Duchess of Cambridge—which, of course, was just what Victoria expected Vicky to do.

209 **The Cambridges were furious** See Longford, p. 181.

209 **Today these rules seem** Note that Greville's diaries were published only after his death. Two of the most celebrated memoirists of the Victorian court, Mary Ponsonby and Marie Mallett, obeyed the royal rules while in waiting. However, they kept their letters, and in later life set down memories of life at court and the royal family that their children were able to discover after their deaths and eventually publish in the twentieth century. Tina Brown, in her 2007 book on Diana, Princess of Wales, asserts that the old compact of privacy and confidentiality between the royal family and members of the British aristocracy held until the late 1960s or early 1970s.

210 **At his first dinner** Arthur Ponsonby, *Henry Ponsonby: His Life from His Letters*, London: Macmillan, 1943, p. 26.

210 **The new maid of honor** Mary Ponsonby describes "the excitement and pleasurable mystery . . . in the first arriving into waiting; was it likely I should see the Queen alone and get to know her well?" (*Mary Ponsonby: A Memoir and a Journal*, p. 2).

211 **"For the Household appointments** Eyck, pp. 191–192.

212 **The prince "was in ability** For the lengthy dissection of the prince consort, see *Mary Ponsonby*, pp. 2–6. Magdalen Ponsonby's 1927 memoir of her mother was followed in 1943 by Arthur Ponsonby's memoir of their father (*Henry Ponsonby: His Life from His Letters*). Henry was a consummate courtier and royal official, as Mary was not, and in his references to Prince Albert, he is much more circumspect. However, he does call the prince "the Snark," a reference to the creature in Lewis Carroll's poem who is "slow in taking a jest"

and "always looks grave at a pun," and makes it delicately clear that he and the prince were never friends.

213 **"It was a fine and gratifying** *Queen Victoria in Her Letters and Journals,* ed. Hibbert, p. 73.

213 **He risked appearing** The hypocritical and villainous Mr. Pecksniff appears in *Martin Chuzzlewit.* The accusation of sanctimonious hypocrisy was peculiarly damaging in English high society, as Victoria's father, the Duke of Kent, discovered in his dealings with ministers, parliament, the army top brass, and his family. The Duke of Kent was known to his mother and siblings as Joseph Surface, a reference to the hypocritical seducer and social climber in Richard Brinsley Sheridan's play *The School for Scandal.*

Chapter 18: FINDING FRIENDS

214 **assassins might lurk in the crowd** Five assassination attempts were made on the Queen during Prince Albert's lifetime: in June 1840, May 1842, July 1842, May 1849, and May 1850. In 1840, when she was pregnant with her first child, the Queen was shot at twice as she drove in an open phaeton through Hyde Park. (See the prince's own account of this event to his stepgrandmother; Jagow, p. 70.) In 1842, when a man shot at his wife on the mall, with extraordinary bravado Prince Albert deliberately provoked the unknown assassin to make a second attempt, and this led to the man's arrest. (See the prince's narration to his father; Jagow, pp. 76–79.) In 1850, two weeks after the birth of her seventh child, a man fired at the Queen as she drove up Constitution Hill. Eight days later, a man came up and struck her on the face with the brass knob of his cane. Fortunately, the deep brim of her bonnet cushioned the blow.

214 **As the Queen later wrote** *Dearest Child,* p. 77.

215 **He not infrequently attended** Jerrold reports that in August 1840 the prince was given the freedom of the city and made a member of the Goldsmiths and Fishmongers Companies, the greatest honors in the gift of the City of London. He was scheduled to receive the freedom of the city at a splendid banquet given by the Lord Mayor. Only hours before the event, the prince wrote saying he could not attend the banquet, rode over to the Guildhall, where he received the freedom of the city, apologized verbally, drove back to Buckingham Palace for dinner, and then drove out to Windsor, where Queen Victoria, heavily pregnant, was awaiting him. This debacle in public relations was possibly the Queen's fault, but it was blamed upon the prince (*The Married Life of Queen Victoria,* p. 76).

216 **For her part, Victoria admitted** Elizabeth Longford gives the most detailed account of this rapprochement. See *Victoria R.I.* pp. 145–148.

221 **Queen Victoria described Skerrett** *My Mistress the Queen: The Letters of Frieda Arnold, Dresser to Queen Victoria,* ed. Benita Storey and Heinrich C. Weltzien, London: Weidenfeld & Nicolson, 1994, p. 8.

223 **She says how delighted she was** *My Mistress the Queen,* p. 24.

223 **As the documented examples** One of the insights that Tina Brown in *The Diana Chronicles* provides about the British aristocracy is that, until the 1970s, girls of that class were given a minimum of formal education. The miseducation of the famous Mitford sisters in the 1930s was, it appears, more typical than exceptional.

223 **They were cultured but not intellectual** Arnold's letters, written in the mid-1850s and illustrated by the author's own drawings, bear a distinct resemblance to the *Leaves from a Journal of our Life in the Highlands* that Victoria herself would publish in the 1860s. Like Victoria, Arnold says a great deal but leaves out a lot more.

224 **"While I was dressing," wrote the Queen** Cecil Woodham-Smith, *Queen Victoria,* p. 395.

224 **Reportedly Isaac Cart was a Swiss** Queen Victoria, *The Early Years,* p. 95. Some biographers say that Cart used to carry Albert upstairs at night when he was very little, but this seems not to be true.

224 **In October 1838, when Albert** Prince Albert to his stepgrandmother; Jagow, *Letters of the Prince Consort*, p. 17.

224 **In August 1840, Albert's first year** Bolitho, *The Prince Consort and His Brother*, p. 25.

Chapter 19: A HOME OF OUR OWN

225 **As he wrote to his stepgrandmother** Jerrold, p. 61.

226 **The Duke of Wellington, now in** The Cinque Ports were an ancient confederation of southern seaports, originally composed of Hastings, Romney, Dover, Hyde, and Sandwich. The wardenship of the Cinque Ports was a lucrative sinecure.

227 **This was a bureaucratic revolution** Before the telegraph, the railway, and the steamship, communications between London and Paris took a minimum of two days; London to Moscow, Rome, or Lisbon, ten to fourteen days; London to Washington or Constantinople, four weeks; London to Canton, five to seven months (Jasper Ridley, *Lord Palmerston*, p. 107).

228 **Above all, what Prince Albert called** Prince Albert to his brother, October 18, 1844, Bolitho, p. 73.

228 **After bearing two children** The Queen's Scottish journals are full of quotations from and references to Walter Scott.

229 **What if the Scots proved** See David Duff's introduction to his excellent edition of selections from the Queen's journals, *Victoria in the Highlands*, New York: Taplinger, 1968.

230 **To his Scottish hosts, he felt** Alan Hardy, *Queen Victoria Was Amused*, p. 39, quoting the book on Queen Victoria written by her Scottish son-in-law, the Duke of Argyll.

231 **"Here we were with only** Duff, *Victoria in the Highlands*, p. 55.

232 **As for Victoria, it would be** Osborne House is testimony to the love of Indian architecture and Indian people that Queen Victoria developed after the death of her husband. The Durbar Room, partly designed by Princess Beatrice, is rather a monstrosity, but the painted portraits the Queen commissioned of ordinary Indian folk are superb.

232 **One of the jewels of Regency** George IV's architectural legacy relies heavily on the Royal Pavilion at Brighton, since Carlton House, his fabulously expensive London residence as Prince of Wales and Regent, was torn down when he came to the throne.

233 **By 1850, the Queen could leave** In 1855 Frieda Arnold traveled with her mistress Queen Victoria from Osborne to Windsor and noted that the journey took only three hours (*My Mistress the Queen*, p. 34).

234 **With the technical assistance** See Martin, *Life of the Prince Consort*, vol. ii, p. 208.

234 **For the Queen, with her long** A visitor to the Ehrenburg Palace in Coburg today is shown Queen Victoria's water closet, the first ever to be installed in the building.

235 **In this, their first real home** The statues were commissioned from Mary Thorneycroft, and in 1858 the same artist produced a study of the youngest child, Beatrice, in a shell. Another specially commissioned piece was John Gibson's statue of the Queen in classical robes with a wreath in her hand, "set in a niche like a shrine," as Frieda Arnold aptly notes (*My Mistress, the Queen*, p. 32).

235 **There were also a number** Ibid, p. 32.

237 **The prince consort, critics contend** See Mark Girouard on Osborne House in *The Victorian Country House*, pp. 147–153, New Haven: Yale University Press, 1979.

237 **"Dear Madam, you really must** Mary Ponsonby, p. 8.

238 **Then the two could retire** Victoria's eldest son, the sophisticated, sybaritic Bertie, spent far too many of his days kicking his heels at Osborne in his mother's last decades, and as Edward VII, he could hardly wait to get rid of it. His sisters, who adored Osborne and had separate properties on the estate, were most upset. Today Victoria and Albert's first home belongs to the nation and is open to the public most of the year. To find Prince Albert's

original Osborne, one must subtract the significant additions and alterations that the Queen made in the thirty years after her husband's death.

238 **The royal family's first visit** All of these properties now form an integral part of the Balmoral estate. Prince Albert first purchased the lease on Balmoral for 2,000 pounds and then bought the property outright in 1852 for 30,000 guineas (a guinea was one pound and one shilling), apparently in his own name. In 1848 he bought Birkhall and its 6,500 acres in his son Bertie's name. (See the letter to his brother, Ernest, of December 12, 1848: "I did not buy the estate in the Highlands, but Bertie. It seems to us to be a desirable purchase for him." Bolitho, *The Prince Consort and His Brother*, p. 106.) According to David Duff, Queen Victoria acquired Ballochbuie some years after her husband's death, but Abergeldie is still technically owned by the Gordon family, which leases it to the monarch (*Victoria in the Highlands*, pp. 84–85).

239 **When Lord Canning almost shot** Fulford, *The Prince Consort*, p. 92.

239 **But as a woman and a landowner** The 2007 movie *The Queen* shows that deerstalking is still a key sport for the men of the British royal family. When the princes William and Henry lose their mother in a tragic accident, their paternal grandfather, Prince Philip, can think of nothing better than a day of deerstalking to distract them.

239 **The negotiations with the Fife trustees** There was a seventeenth-century tower, but otherwise the house dated to the 1830s.

239 **In 1855 Queen Victoria was able** Duff, *Victoria in the Highlands*, p. 151.

240 **On her six-hour carriage journey** *My Mistress the Queen*, p. 125.

240 **On a grander scale** On her first visit to Coburg in 1844, the Queen was ecstatic about everything at the Rosenau except the chamber-pots that she was obliged to use there and indeed in palaces throughout Germany.

Chapter 20: THE GREATEST SHOW ON EARTH

245 **The idea of the Great Exhibition** Other accounts credit John Scott Russell with having the big idea and selling it to the prince.

246 **In the end, parliament voted** This is the account given by Martin in *Life of the Prince Consort*, vol. ii.

247 **Never one to let the grass** The precious piece of blotting paper is now preserved at the Victoria and Albert Museum.

247 **Amazingly, its fan of intersecting ribs** An etching of Paxton's daughter standing on the lily pad appeared in the *Illustrated London News*.

248 **The memory of the great revolutions** In 1858 England and France came close to war when a group of Italian revolutionaries tried to blow up the Emperor Napoleon III, and the grenades were found to have been built in Great Britain. Karl Marx, of course, found refuge in England in 1849 and wrote much of *Das Kapital* in the British Museum.

248 **As the prince wrote to his** Prince Albert to Marie, dowager Duchess of Coburg, April 1851, Martin, *Life of the Prince Consort*, vol. ii, pp. 293–294.

248 **Three years after the end** See Kingsley Martin, *The Triumph of Lord Palmerston: A Study of Public Opinion in England Before the Crimean War*, London: Hutchison, 1963.

249 **"Mathematicians have calculated** Jagow, *Letters of the Prince Consort*, pp. 176–177.

250 **"The tremendous cheers** Martin, *Life of the Prince Consort*, vol. ii, p. 299.

250 **As Victoria herself noted** Martin, vol. ii, p. 314.

253 **And the building was pulled down** The enlarged and re-created Crystal Palace was destroyed by fire in 1934.

254 **The frantic months of activity** All of these expressions come from the Queen's journal.

254 **When the prince met such men** Lyon Playfair, who collaborated closely with Prince Albert on many public and private projects and admired him very much, once commented that never in all their dealings did the prince ever ask him to sit down.

254 **Albert could preside** Several of the men associated with the Great Exhibition were subsequently knighted by Queen Victoria—Henry Cole, Joseph Paxton, Charles Fox. Lyon Playfair ended his life as Lord Playfair.

Chapter 21: LORD PALMERSTON SAYS NO

255 **By November 1853, he was** This is what Prince Albert told Stockmar in a long letter of January 24, 1854; Jagow, ed., p. 207.

255 **She frankly admitted this** *Queen Victoria's Early Letters*, ed. Raymond, p. 188.

256 **In the face of the vitriolic** Albert to Stockmar: "As for the calumnies themselves, I look upon them as a fiery ordeal that will serve to purge away impurities . . . Everyone who has been able to express or surmise any ill of me has conscientiously contributed his faggot to burn the heretic, and I may say with pride, that not the veriest tittle of a reproach can be brought against me *in truth*" (Jagow, p. 206). Yet in 1860 Prince Albert was still sending to his "Dear Cousin" William, the prince regent (soon to be king) of Prussia, an exact account of the recent and secret negotiations of the Emperor Napoleon III with Russia and Austria, which he had heard of from the foreign office papers or discussions. Albert begins this brief note: "It may not be uninteresting to you to hear something that I will beg you to regard as strictly confidential" (Jagow, p. 349). The letter of February 8, 1859, to Prince William's wife, Augusta, makes clear that Prince Albert also communicated on foreign policy issues with the Prussian court by trusted private emissaries such as Count Perponcher, who would convey information and opinions without committing any of it to paper.

256 **If any one man was responsible** In my account of Prince Albert's foreign policy, my key source is the five-volume biography of the prince that Queen Victoria commissioned from Theodore Martin. Frank Eyck's *The Prince Consort: A Political Biography* (Boston: Houghton Mifflin, 1959) was also very important in forming my opinions of Prince Albert's geopolitical ideas and diplomatic initiatives. Eyck was a naturalized Englishman born in Germany and a scholar of acumen and probity. He was given unusually complete access to the archives at Windsor and Coburg, and, almost alone among biographers of Prince Albert publishing in English, he was able to read the unpublished papers written in German. Eyck seeks to present Prince Albert in as positive a light as possible, but, unlike Hector Bolitho, he was more interested in the historical record than in hobnobbing with Prince Albert's descendents. His work is all the more damning for being sober, scrupulously documented, and based on wide knowledge of nineteenth-century German history. For my account of Lord Palmerston, I rely mainly on Jasper Ridley's *Lord Palmerston* (London: Macmillan, 1971) and Kingsley Martin's *The Triumph of Lord Palmerston: A Study of Public Opinion Before the Crimean War* (London: Hutchison, 1963). After completing this chapter, I came upon a copy of Anthony Trollope's 1882 contribution to the "English Political Leaders Series" (*Lord Palmerston*, London: Isbister) and was delighted to find the great novelist endorsing my account of the struggle between prince and foreign secretary. Trollope writes stalwartly in his introduction: "With the verdict of the Prince . . . in regard to Lord Palmerston [as revealed in the recently published biography of the prince consort by Theodore Martin] I am compelled to differ . . . I think that I shall be able to show that England has disagreed with his Royal Highness, and that England is right" (p. 2).

257 **They fought any measure likely** In her official capacity as commander in chief, Queen Victoria put her signature on every army commission. This inevitably resulted in a backlog of commissions and was hardly conducive to army efficiency. However, when the practical suggestion was made that commissions should be certified in some other way, Victoria refused.

258 **The famine in Ireland** For a brief summary of the issues involved in the repeal of the Corn Laws, see chapter 14.

261 **In the words of novelist** Trollope, *Lord Palmerston*, London: Isbister, 1882, p. 26.

262 **Mrs. Brand resisted** There are at least three versions of this affair: Greville (vol. vi, p. 441) and two memoranda in the Royal Archives by Prince Albert and by his secretary George Anson. Greville says that Queen Victoria knew about the event at the time. Albert and Anson believe that she did not and that she was horribly shocked when her husband told her about in 1850. My guess is that Victoria, in fact, did know in 1840, since the Brand affair would certainly have come to the ears of Baroness Lehzen, reputed to be a great gossip and a favorite with Melbourne and Palmerston. Court gossip between Lehzen and Victoria was one of the things that Prince Albert held against the baroness.

262 **Back in 1810, when Emily** Gossips claimed that both Emily Cowper and her mother, the first Lady Melbourne, had an amorous liaison with the prince regent (later George IV). One of Emily's younger brothers was reputedly the prince regent's child.

262 **As the husband of a beautiful** Lady Palmerston had three brothers, but none of them had any children when he died, so she inherited all the Melbourne estates.

265 **But on certain key issues** See Prince Albert's letter to Stockmar of August 20, 1850, soon after the Peace of Olmutz kept Prussia from going to war with Austria over Schleswig-Holstein: "The fixed idea here [essentially in Lord Palmerston's foreign office] is, that Germany's only object in separating Holstein with Schleswig from Denmark is to incorporate them with herself and then to draw them from the English into the Prussian commercial system. Denmark will then become a State too small to maintain a separate independence, and so the division of European territory and the balance of power will be disturbed. I grant that this is a tenable view, and that Germany (especially Prussia) has given cause for it; but assuredly this affords no ground for doing violence to law, to honour, to equity, to morality, in order to defeat an eventuality which has not been brought about by ambition or caprice, but by the nature of things" (Martin, *The Life of the Prince Consort*, vol. ii, p. 259). In 1864, three years after the prince's death, Prussia under Bismarck crushed Austria and Denmark and absorbed not only Schleswig and Holstein but also Hanover, Hesse, Nassau, and Frankfurt am Main. In 1870 Prussia went to war with France and inflicted a stunning defeat. The Emperor Napoleon III was deposed and fled to England. Prussia, which by this point already had two-thirds of the population of Germany, acquired the French border provinces of Alsace and Lorraine. Suffice it to say that ambition and caprice, to say nothing of an obsession with military might, accounted far better for Prussia's foreign affairs strategy than Prince Albert's law, honor, equity, and morality.

265 **Reports that the tsar of Russia** One ambassador claimed to have read the whole of *Clarissa*—then the longest novel in the English language—while waiting for Lord Palmerston.

266 **While giving lip service** In 1848 a popular insurrection forced the Austrian emperor to agree formally to certain democratic reforms, including some form of elected assembly to which the executive arm of government would be responsible. The emperor, who believed that he was appointed by God to rule, never had any intention of respecting these agreements. By 1851, he felt strong enough to renounce them publicly, declaring, "Henceforth [Austrian] Ministers should be responsible solely to the Crown, as the center of all authority" (Martin, *Life of the Prince Consort*, vol. ii, p. 321).

267 **"Osborne, 20th August** *Queen Victoria's Early Letters*, ed. Raymond, pp. 147–148.

268 **It begins: "I said to Lord** For the full text, ibid., pp. 148–150.

268 **According to the memorandum** Frank Eyck, *The Prince Consort: A Political Biography*, p. 139. Eyck notes that Prince Albert also dug out the file of old grievances in 1848, when his wife's half brother, Charles Leiningen, disagreed with him over German politics. He accused Leiningen of having "intrigued with Sir John Conroy against Queen Victoria before her accession" (Eyck, p. 92). This was both unfair and irrelevant.

269 **In August 1850, the Queen specified** *Queen Victoria's Early Letters*, ed. Raymond, pp. 172–173.

270   **Victoria wrote to her uncle Leopold** *Queen Victoria's Early Letters*, ed. Raymond, p. 188. Prince Albert in a January 1852 letter to Prince William, the de facto ruler of Prussia, was smugly pleased that Palmerston's affronts to Austria and support of Hungary were at an end: "Since then he has himself made it easy for his colleagues by suddenly becoming Louis Napoleon's accomplice. That was too much of a good thing, and the pitcher broke at last after too many journeys to the well. There is no doubt that now he is thinking solely of revenge, but I think him less dangerous in opposition than he would be in power, for there are not at his disposal those vast possibilities of doing harm, which the Foreign Office gave him" (*Letters of the Prince Consort*, ed. Jagow, p. 181).

270   **But once a respected statesman** Lord Palmerston wrote: "The real ground for my dismissal [in 1851] was a weak truckling to the hostile intrigues of the Orléans family, Austria, Russia, Saxony, and Bavaria and in some degree the present Prussian government. All these parties found their respective views and systems of policy thwarted by the course pursued by the British Government, and they thought that if they could move the Minister they would change the policy. They had for a long time past effectually poisoned the mind of the Queen and Prince against me, and John Russell giving way, rather encouraged than discountenanced the desire of the Queen to remove me from the Foreign Office." Quoted in vol. ii of Martin's *Life of the Prince Consort*, where Queen Victoria does her best to defend her dead husband against the charge that he unfairly conspired against Lord Palmerston as foreign secretary.

272   **But he was not an aggressive** Trollope writes of Palmerston: "He could fight and would fight as long as he could stand; but as a conqueror he could be thoroughly generous" (p. 9).

274   **One crucial source of information** The Hampshire property of William Nightingale, Florence Nightingale's father, abutted on Broadlands, Lord Palmerston's country estate. The two men were allies in local politics and went hunting together. On one occasion, Florence was invited to spend the weekend at Broadlands and met Lady Palmerston and her daughters. Florence Nightingale had strong ties to Palmerston's stepson-in-law, the reforming Tory politician Lord Shaftesbury who, like Nightingale herself and Palmerston, was a convinced sanitarian—in other words, supporter of public health policy.

274   **When the Queen asked specifically** In my book *Nightingales*, I give a thorough account of the origins and conduct of the Crimean War. For the condition of the troops during the winter of 1854–1855 and Nightingale's correspondence on the soldiers' needs, see especially chapter 16.

275   **Two more such tassels decorated** *My Mistress the Queen*, p. 19.

275   **In April 1856, the Queen** *Queen Victoria in Her Letters and Journals*, ed. Hibbert, p. 135.

276   **His struggle with Prince Albert** Attempts have been made by historians, especially in Germany, to establish Prince Albert's importance as a statesman. Kurt Jagow, who edited the major collection of Prince Albert's letters, wrote: "When all is considered, it is in essence due to the merits of the German prince, who for less than two decades sat upon, or rather stood by, the throne of England as a faithful guardian of the Crown, that today the British monarchy is able to command the power, prestige, and internal strength, required by the British Empire to hold together its self-governing members, and to take rank as a World Power." Unfortunately, Jagow was writing this in 1938, as an adherent of Adolf Hitler's National Socialist Party.

276   **That the new prime minister** In their biography of the prince, Queen Victoria and Theodore Martin offer detailed evidence of what they regard as Lord Palmerston's sins at the foreign office and of Prince Albert's strenuous efforts to get him sacked. They then choose to interpret the subsequent cooperation between the Crown and Lord Palmerston as prime minister not to Palmerston's graciousness in victory but to Albert's greatness. Albert, as Victoria sees it, could not be wrong. "In the discussions which ensued in the public journals and in society upon Lord Palmerston's removal from office [in 1851], it was often broadly hinted by his supporters that the Prince Consort had been the chief instrument of his fall.

Whether Lord Palmerston encouraged this view, or not, is now of little moment. This much is certain, however, that in after years no man spoke more warmly of the Prince, or was readier to acknowledge his services to this country" (Martin, vol. ii, p. 348–349).

277 **The Queen recorded in her journal** *Queen Victoria in Her Letters and Journals*, ed. Hibbert, p. 134.

Chapter 22: BLUE BLOOD AND RED

278 **The Queen was due to give** Longford p. 315, quoting the Queen's journal of 1855.

278 **They then communicated** See Cecil Woodham-Smith, chapter 11, for the most detailed and insightful account of the evolving relationship between the Queen and the prince.

278 **She claimed that, like most men** "Oh! If those selfish men—who are the cause of all one's misery, only knew what their poor slaves go through! What suffering—what humiliation to the delicate feelings of a poor woman, above all a young one—especially with those nasty doctors" (Hibbert, *Queen Victoria in Her Letters and Journals*, p. 115).

278 **Pregnant, Victoria felt less like** Queen Victoria to Vicky, expecting her first child: "What you say of the pride of giving life to an immortal soul is very fine, dear, but I own I cannot enter into that. I think much more of our being like a cow or a dog at such moments." (*Dearest Child*, p. 115).

279 **There is no doubt that Queen Victoria** In deciding whether husband or wife had the most to bear in the royal marriage, the Queen's many biographers have been swayed more by their personal experience and the period they lived in than by the available documentation. Writing around the time of the First World War, Lytton Strachey, a gay man in hot rebellion against the Victoria era, sympathizes deeply with Albert and implies that Victoria harried her husband into an early grave. Fifty years later, Elizabeth Longford, herself a devoted wife and mother to a large family, assumes that Victoria was right to fulfill the traditional female role and obey her husband. Monica Charlot, writing in the 1990s, sees Victoria as a woman struggling against a misogynist society and a repressive husband.

280 **In fact, the pregnancy proceeded** This is the same John Snow famous in the annals of epidemiology for disconnecting the Broad Street pump in London and thus proving that cholera was caused by infected water.

280 **Her fourth son** "Leopold" was in affectionate remembrance of "dearest uncle," and "Duncan" a gracious gesture toward the royal couple's increasingly beloved Scotland. Queen Victoria gave all her sons the name Albert. Two of the five daughters received the name Victoria, and the fourth was called Louise Alberta. She gave her name to the Canadian province of Alberta and to Lake Louise.

280 **Remembering the recent fire** Longford, *Victoria R.I.*, p. 294.

280 **Thus when Albert went to Ipswich** Martin, *Life of the Prince Consort*, vol. II, p. 310.

281 **"Du, du liegst mir im Herzen** Ibid, p. 495.

281 **As Victoria once told her friend** Hibbert, *Queen Victoria in Her Letters and Journals*, p. 100.

281 **To her daughter Vicky, Queen Victoria** *Dearest Child*, p. 112.

281 **Deprived of Albert, her ideal companion** This point emerges clearly from Queen Victoria's letters to her daughter Vicky, as editor Roger Fulford points out in his introduction to *Dearest Child*, p. 10.

282 **To convey just how busy** Martin and *Dearest Child*, p. 386.

283 **She was unhappy about this** See *Dearest Child*, p. 104.

283 **"Abstractedly, I have no tender for them** *Dearest Child*, p. 191.

283 **She told Princess Augusta of Prussia** Hibbert, *Queen Victoria in Her Letters and Journals*, pp. 99–100.

283 **Albert, to the contrary, reveled** When her daughter Vicky wrote about how enchanted her husband Fritz was by their first baby, Queen Victoria remarked that Prince Albert "cannot enter into [Fritz's] ecstasy about him [baby Willy]; he has never felt it himself. After a cer-

tain age if they are nice (and not like Bertie and Leopold were) he is very fond of playing with them" (*Dearest Child*, p. 191).

284 **She made their father's perfection** Queen Victoria wrote to her daughter Vicky soon after Vicky's wedding: "You know my dearest, that I will never admit any other wife can be as happy as I am—so I can admit no comparison for I maintain Papa is unlike anyone who lives or ever lived or will live . . . Dear Papa has always been my oracle" (*Dearest Child*, pp. 45–46).

284 **A full understanding of hemophilia** Hemophilia is a genetic disease that afflicts males. Today it can be treated effectively through blood transfusions and can be eliminated by genetic counseling, but it is still incurable. Hemophiliac patients have a defective copy of the gene that codes a key component in blood coagulation, usually factor VIII, rarely factor IX. This defective gene is carried on the X chromosome, and so boys inherit it from their mothers. Each woman has two X chromosomes, receiving an X from each parent. Even if one X has the factor VIII defect, a woman's blood will clot normally. There are almost no cases of hemophilia in women, as a girl would need to inherit a defective chromosome from both parents. The few hemophiliac girls known in medical literature died when they began to menstruate. When she reproduces, a woman passes one of her two X chromosomes to her child. Each male child receives an X from his mother and a Y from his father. Thus the male child of a woman carrying the genetic defect has a 50 percent chance of receiving her defective X chromosome and suffering from hemophilia. Each female child of a woman carrying the genetic defect also has a 50 percent chance of inheriting the defective X chromosome. Like her mother, she will be symptom free, but each male child she has will run a 50 percent risk of being hemophiliac and each daughter a 50 percent risk for being a carrier. On average, one in two of the sons of a female carrier will get the disease, and one in two of the daughters of a carrier will become carriers in their turn.

The science of hemophilia has advanced enormously since 1950, and certain advances in genetic testing date only from the last decade or so. Information on the disease in books written before 1990 is incomplete and often incorrect. Even Robert K. Massie's deservedly famous *Nicholas and Alexandra* (1967) does not have the facts on hemophilia quite right.

284 **However, even in 1854** Jewish doctors who practiced ritual male circumcision were among the first to report on the phenomenon of baby boys whose blood kept flowing and occasionally bled to death. Before the second half of the twentieth century, the ravages on male children ensured that families afflicted by the disease tended to disappear within two or three generations. However, the disease did not die out. New cases of hemophilia occur regularly because clotting factor VIII is on a large, complex gene, highly subject to random mutation. One-third of all cases of hemophilia are the result of new mutations—that is to say there is no previous history of the disease in the family—contributing to an incidence of 1 in 5,000 males born with hemophilia worldwide, or approximately 1 in 10,000 persons overall.

286 **Even a suggestion that** Historians of the British royal family have been intrigued by the question of how Queen Victoria became a carrier for hemophilia. Her father was certainly not hemophiliac, and all available evidence shows that her mother was not a carrier. The overwhelming probability is that hemophilia entered the British royal family as a result of a spontaneously mutated gene. But random mutation is an unexciting solution to a famous historical puzzle and a few historians in recent years have found it seductive to suggest that Leopold's hemophilia proved that Queen Victoria was not her father's daughter. This is a recent and apparently more scientific counterpart to the old rumor that, since Prince Albert bore no resemblance either to his "father," or to his elder brother, he must have been a bastard (see chapter 9). In 1997 two eminent British doctors, the brothers D. M. and W.T.W. Potts, published a sensational book called *Queen Victoria's Gene: Haemophilia in the Royal Family* (Alan Sutton, 1995), in which they purport to examine all the possible explanations

for how the hemophilia gene came into the royal family. Potts and Potts unearthed an unpublished study that traced both the Hanoverians and the Coburgs back for many generations and found no evidence that there had ever been a bleeder in the family before Leopold, Duke of Albany. Could it be, then, they hypothesize, that Queen Victoria was a bastard, foisted on the English people by her mother, an unscrupulous and immoral intrigant who despaired of ever conceiving a child with the aging duke she had just been persuaded to marry? For this theory to work, the unknown lover selected within weeks of marriage by the Duchess of Kent to father the royal baby would most probably be a hemophiliac who had survived to reproductive age. Every daughter of a hemophiliac carries the defective gene, inherited from her father. Unfortunately, the duchess's phantom lover has never been glimpsed, much less identified. In the end, Potts and Potts admit that a spontaneously occurring genetic mutation in one of her parents is most probably how Queen Victoria came to carry the gene for hemophilia. However, they spend so many pages working through the more interesting (and wildly improbable) theories that historians such as Jerrold M. Packer in his book *Queen Victoria's Daughters* have failed to follow the medical argument to its conclusion. They cite the worthy doctors as authorities for the hypothesis that Queen Victoria's gene for hemophilia proves that she was not the granddaughter of George III. It is ironic that so much respectable historiographic ink has been spilled arguing that the great dynasts Victoria and Albert were, in fact—both of them—illegitimate.

286 **What doctor, or indeed what husband** Before genetic analysis, it was impossible for a woman or her doctor to know for sure that she was *not* a carrier. The birth of a hemophiliac son proved that she was. Had Queen Victoria decided to stop having babies after the birth of three "normal" sons, the presumption would have been that she was not a carrier.

287 **Leopold was a plucky, willful child** Leopold's hemophiliac nephew Frederick ("Frittie"), the second son of his sister Alice, was not so fortunate. The wife of a mere duke of Hesse, Alice could not afford a large staff. One day she was in her rooms sewing as her favorite child Frittie, three years old, played. Hearing his older siblings outside, Frittie ran to the window, tumbled out onto the stone courtyard below, and was soon dead of a cerebral hemorrhage. Head injuries were almost invariably fatal for hemophiliacs. Queen Victoria mourned darling Frittie but also reproached her daughter for not looking after the child properly. Alice of Hesse never recovered from the sorrow and guilt she felt at the death of her son. She died at the age of thirty-five, leaving one son and four daughters, the latter largely educated by their grandmother Queen Victoria. Alice of Hesse was a woman of high intelligence and conscience, a skilled nurse and an expert on women's health issues. She was the person in the family who might have unearthed the medical facts about hemophilia, seen its long-term significance for women like herself and her daughters, and explained them to her mother, Queen Victoria.

288 **She liked pretty, obedient, healthy children** Victoria makes regular mentions of Leopold in her letters to her daughter in Prussia and is severe about his physical handicaps and odd character.

288 **Perhaps a kingdom would be found** In the last half of the nineteenth century, countries in need of a new king turned reflexively to Saxe-Coburgs. This is how one of the many Ferdinands ("Foxy") became, for a while, king of Bulgaria.

288 **He not only survived childhood** Prince Leopold, created Duke of Connaught by his mother to improve his chances of finding a wife, married in his late twenties and quickly sired a daughter and a son. But Leopold never knew his son, as in 1884, aged thirty-one, he fell on some steps, took massive doses of alcohol and opium to kill the pain, and hemorrhaged to death. Since the X or female chromosome is responsible for clotting, Leopold's son Charles, who inherited a healthy X from his mother, Princess Helene of Pyrmont Waldeck, and a healthy Y from his father, was not a hemophiliac. Leopold's daughter Alice inherited her father's defective X chromosome and was thus necessarily a carrier. She married

Prince Alexander of Teck (later Earl of Athlone) and had a daughter and two sons who were both hemophiliac. One died in early childhood, but the other lived to adulthood and even served in the First World War.

289   **However, Ella's sister Irene** Stephanie Coontz, in her *Marriage—A History: How Love Conquered Marriage* (Penguin Books, 2005), shows that once biological science established the deleterious effects of inbreeding, the marriage of first cousins became increasingly frowned upon in advanced European cultures. In this regard, the Saxe-Coburgs were a throwback to an earlier age, since they were intermarrying at an even higher rate at the end of the nineteenth century than at the beginning.

289   **The men of the far-flung** The family also spawned a psychopath (Kaiser Wilhelm II), a cretin (Edward VII's eldest son Albert Victor, who could barely read or tell the time), an idiot-epileptic (George V's son John, who died at nineteen after a secluded life on the Sandringham estate), several social deviants (including Alfred, only son of the Duke of Edinburgh and Saxe Coburg, who died paralyzed and raving mad from syphilis at age twenty-five), and a fascist (Charles Edward, second Duke of Albany, Duke of Saxe-Coburg) who fought in the kaiser's army in World War I and was a Nazi sympathizer in World War II. On the other hand, the family produced at least three women of outstanding brilliance: Queen Victoria's two eldest daughters, Victoria (the Princess Royal, Empress Frederick of Prussia) and Alice (Duchess of Hesse-Darmstadt), and her granddaughter Marie (queen of Romania). Queen Victoria's fourth daughter, Louise (Duchess of Argyll), was also a very bright woman and, as her statue of her mother in Kensington Gardens proves, an artist of some standing.

294   **She had passed to her son** The Empress Alexandra of Russia was only thirty-two when she gave birth to her fifth child and first son, Alexei, and discovered to her horror that he was hemophiliac. Unlike her cousin Ena, queen of Spain, who kept having children until she produced a healthy boy, Alexandra lapsed into chronic invalidism and religious mania. She concentrated all her energies on her son's survival, kept his hemophilia a secret even from other members of the family, and resisted all democratic reforms that might lead to a republic and thus deprive "Baby," as she called Alexei, of his divine right to rule. Convinced that God was punishing her, Alexandra went mad from guilt and remorse, and her four daughters were the innocent victims of her obsession with Alexei's illness.

294   **As the medical historians** *Queen Victoria's Gene: Haemophilia and the Royal Family*, D. M. Potts and W.T.W. Potts, Phoenix Mill: Alan Sutton Publishing, 1995, p. 82.

294   **Alfonso XIII trusted his eyes** Unlike her cousin Alix, Victoria Eugenie (Ena), Queen of Spain, was a survivor. She can be seen in the pictures of the coronation of her great-great-niece Elizabeth II. Ena was at first in love with her husband King Alfonso XIII, but he turned against her when their first child was a hemophiliac boy. Despite the bitter relations with his wife, Alfonso was determined on having more sons, since under Spanish law only a healthy heir could inherit the throne. Jaime, Ena's second child, became blind and deaf after an attack of meningitis, so he also was barred from the succession. She then produced two girls, a healthy boy, and another hemophiliac boy. In Spain, news of the hemophiliac princes leaked out, and the public was fed fantastic rumors that they survived by drinking the blood of young soldiers. Alfonso was an ineffective and highly promiscuous ruler, but it was at least in part because of his sons' ill health that he was deposed in 1930. The interregnum in the Spanish monarchy ended when Ena's grandson Juan Carlos was recalled to the throne in 1975.

294   **As their first cousin Marie** Julia P. Gelardi, *Born to Rule: Five Reigning Consorts, Granddaughters of Queen Victoria*, New York: St Martin's Press, 2005, p. 14.

294   **By the early twentieth century** For my information on hemophilia in the Saxe-Coburg family, I have relied on the book by Potts and Potts and also on the following two articles in the medical literature: An Historical Review by Richard F. Stevens, "The History of

Haemophilia in The Royal Families of Europe," *British Journal of Haematology*, 1999, 105, 25–32; and "Historical and political implications of Haemophilia in the Spanish royal family," by C. Ojeda-Thies and E. C. Rodriguez-Merchan, *Haemophilia* (2003), 9, 153–156.

Chapter 23: FRENCH INTERLUDE

295 **He was a supreme political opportunist** "[Napoleon III] was described as having the 'appearance of an opium eater' " (Woodham-Smith, p. 346).

295 **In smooth charm he was not unlike** Benjamin Disraeli (1804–1881) was born into the brilliant and cosmopolitan D'Israeli family. He became an Anglican at the age of thirteen, a conversion that allowed him to go into English politics while pursuing a highly successful career as a novelist. He was prime minister from 1874 to 1880 and became close friends with the Queen. Victoria had many prejudices, but she was not a racist.

295 **As a lengthy memorandum** Martin, vol. 3, pp. 98–109.

297 **Three years later, he suspended** This was the coup d'état of the 18th Brumaire in 1851, which sent a number of important republicans into exile in Britain, including Victor Hugo, France's greatest poet. From his place of exile on the Island of Jersey, Hugo launched an excoriating set of political satires called "Les Châtiments" [Chastisements], which presents Napoleon III as the vile merchandiser of his uncle's great legend.

297 **In 1853, having failed** Napoleon III made determined efforts to win the hand of Queen Victoria's niece Adelaide of Hohenlohe Langenburg (third daughter of the Queen's half sister Princess Feodora), among others. Adelaide was a young sixteen, and both her mother and aunt felt the hot-house atmosphere of the French court would be too much for her happiness and her morals.

297 **In 1840 he had paid forty pounds** Martin, vol. 3, p. 211.

297 **"How strange to think," Victoria confided** Martin, vol. 3, p. 205.

297 **"I felt that I was possibly** Ibid. p. 211.

298 **The two women would be friends** After her husband was deposed in 1870, the Empress Eugenie (1826–1920) spent the rest of her life in England. A Spaniard by birth, she is said to have promoted the marriage of Queen Victoria's granddaughter Princess Victoria Eugenie of Battenburg (Ena) to King Alfonso XIII of Spain. Ena was the empress's goddaughter and namesake.

298 **"Altogether I am delighted** Martin, vol. 3, p. 209.

299 **"In spite of the great heat** Tisdall, p. 34.

299 **If Prince Albert, in his capacity** As Queen Victoria once remarked in a letter to her daughter Vicky, she never chose so much as a bonnet without consulting her husband. Victoria had little interest in fashion and was quite aware that, as a small, plump woman with a plain face, she was hard to dress. As an unmarried woman, the Queen got good fashion advice from other women, notably her mother, her aunt Louise in Belgium, and court ladies such as the Duchess of Sutherland, her first mistress of the robes. For her wedding, the simple dresses Victoria chose for herself and her bridesmaids got excellent press. But once she was married, Victoria cared only for Albert's approval, and apparently he made time to supervise her choice of dresses and hats. The results were spectacularly bad. Even the English wondered why their Queen looked so much less chic in her day outfits than the average middle-class woman dressed for town.

300 **Victoria was determined to return** Queen Victoria devoted pages of her journal to the visit of Napoleon III and his wife to Windsor in April 1855, and to her visit to Paris with the prince and their two eldest children five months later. The Queen allowed sections of her journals to be published—I believe her first move into print—and critics have found it interesting to compare this, as it were, self-edited version to the bowdlerized one produced by Princess Beatrice two generations later. We also have immediate, first-person accounts of the state visit to France in the letters written from France to her family in England by Mary

Bulteel Ponsonby, who attended the Queen as a maid of honor, and to her family in Germany from Frieda Arnold, who attended the Queen as a dresser. All three ladies were overwhelmed by the superb preparations the French had made for the visit.

300 **On her last night in Paris** Woodham-Smith, p. 361.

300 **To her diary she confided** Longford, p. 316, quoting Queen Victoria's journal.

302 **When she politely said** Woodham-Smith, p. 361.

302 **Like his mother, the Prince of Wales** In her letters to her daughter Vicky, Queen Victoria comments over and again on how miserable and bored she is by court life at Windsor and Buckingham Palace.

302 **Here was diplomatic tact and womanly sympathy** On the relations between the French imperial couple and the Princess Royal (Vicky), see Pakula, chapter 4, pp. 54–59.

Chapter 24: THE PRUSSIAN ALLIANCE

304 **The idea that Victoria, Princess Royal** At three, already fluent in German and English, "Pussette," as Vicky was then known to her family, impressed her French governess one day when out on her pony ride. Looking at the landscape, Vicky quoted a line from a poem she had just memorized by the poet Alphonse de Lamartine: "le tableau se déroule à mes pieds" (the scene unfolds at my feet) (Pakula, p. 37, quoting Queen Victoria's letter to King Leopold).

304 **His personal mission as a diplomat** The business and professional classes in Prussia were essentially excluded from political power, which was wielded by a small, entrenched landed aristocracy represented by the court party, often called the camarilla. The camarilla, in turn, was supported by the large, well-financed, and superbly trained army, which, unlike the British army that was scattered all over the globe, saw its mission to lie in Europe. The social classes were kept rigorously separate, and it was rare for a Prussian merchant or intellectual to have connections at court or a relationship with a member of the royal family. When Victoria's daughters Vicky and especially Alice tried to move across class lines in Prussia and Hesse, they met with savage criticism. The Prussian merchants and intellectuals were eager to follow the example of Britain and take control of the nation's politics and administration, but they failed. In the first half of the nineteenth century, occasional uprisings would force some movement toward democratic reforms and the formation of elected assemblies. But as soon as the rioters returned to their homes and things quieted down, the army would assert its grip, the king and his government would renege on all their promises of reform, the assemblies were dismissed, and the camarilla came down hard on political dissidents, the press, and the courts. In the second half of the century, the army's success in military campaigns against Austria, France, and Denmark—and Prussia's reunification of the nation—kept protest in check.

304 **Prince Albert wrote, begging** As many people in Great Britain remarked with indignation, the Prince of Wales had many baptismal sponsors, all but two of them German.

305 **He also welcomed the Prussian minister** Thus, in the memoirs she prepared of her dead husband, Baroness Bunsen describes the masque of the four seasons that the royal children performed to celebrate the wedding anniversary of their parents in 1854 (*Bunsen's Life*, vol. II, p. 328, quoted in Martin's *Life of the Prince Consort*, vol. III, pp. 16–17).

305 **There King Frederick William IV** E. F. Benson, *Queen Victoria*, p. 145.

305 **In a telling little scene** See Woodham-Smith, p. 250. In Martin's *Life of the Prince Consort*, a whole chapter of volume II is devoted to the 1845 visit to Germany, based largely on the Queen's diary, and detailing every step of the way. There is, however, no hint of a disagreement with the Prussians.

306 **Frederick William himself, the eldest** Roger Fulford, introduction to *Dearest Child*, p. 17.

307 **"Your Majesty, I must begin** Jagow, p. 108. When thanking the king of Prussia for a gift to the Prince of Wales, Prince Albert is even more gushing: "When I think that this princely

gift springs not only from the hands, but also from the brain of Your Majesty . . . and when I think also of all the treasure of the messages contained in your recent letters to us, I am obliged to say to myself: No man has ever in a single present had showered upon him by another so incalculable a wealth of gifts" (Jagow, p. 114).

308 **Learning of the speech, Prince Albert** Jagow, p. 113.

309 **"That every good German desires** Martin, *Life of the Prince Consort*, vol. III, p. 24.

310 **She failed to win his love** As a young man, Prince William fell passionately in love with a Polish aristocrat, Eliza Radziwill, but his parents refused to countenance their marriage. William married Augusta of Saxe-Weimar, a woman seventeen years his junior. The two proved to be incompatible. After two difficult births, which produced the requisite healthy male heir, Augusta refused to have marital relations with her husband (Pakula, p. 104). From then on, the two were locked in constant combat until, under the guidance of Bismarck, William became emperor of Prussia. Then he and his wife united in opposition to their heir and his English wife.

311 **As Queen Victoria wrote** Pakula, p. 51.

311 **It was unfortunate, in the prince's** Members of the Prussian royal family prided themselves on being tall. King Frederick William IV collected a personal guard of men over six feet in height. One of the many reasons for Kaiser Wilhelm II's massive insecurity was that he was a small man in comparison with his father and grandfather. Soon after her daughter Vicky went to Berlin as a bride, Queen Victoria received a copy of a private letter describing Vicky's reception by the court of Berlin. "Only one thing I can't understand she [the Grand Duchess of Mecklenburg-Schwerin] says 'She [Vicky] is very small' which considering that you are a great deal taller than me, and I am not a dwarf, is rather hard" (Hibbert, *Queen Victoria in Her Letters and Journals*, p. 102).

312 **It was true that** Mary Bulteel (later Ponsonby), as a maid of honor to the Queen who spoke excellent German, had good opportunities to observe her friend the Princess Royal's German suitor and was not impressed. She summed up Fritz as "a good-humoured . . . lieutenant with large hands and feet, but not in the least clever" (Pakula, p. 71). Apparently Fritz was quite unable to master the simple rules of the parlor game vingt-et-un.

313 **His uncles wanted nothing better** When the Prince of Wales was permitted to pay a visit to his sister in Berlin in 1859, Vicky and Fritz had to exert all their influence to keep Bertie from being led astray by Fritz's debauched uncles and cousins.

313 **He had found her perfection** As Crown Prince Fritz once wrote of his wife: "You cannot form an idea what a sweet little thing [Vicky] was at the time [of their first meeting in 1851]; such childlike simplicity combined with a woman's intellect . . . and dignity . . . She seemed almost too perfect, so perfect, indeed, that I often caught myself wondering whether she was really a human being" (Pakula, p. 50).

313 **"It is *not* politics** Pakula, p. 68.

313 **"[Fritz] is a dear, excellent** Hibbert, *Queen Victoria In Her Letters and Journals*, p. 98.

313 **As Albert expressed it** Jagow, p. 236.

314 **The Queen recorded the scene** Part of the Queen's journal entry for September 29, 1855. Hibbert, *Queen Victoria In Her Letters and Journals*, p. 98.

314 **The *Times* newspaper wrote a series** Pakula, p. 77.

315 **He hurried the match in 1855** Feeling the need to defend his dead brother against the charge that he had sacrificed his daughter to further his geopolitical designs, Duke Ernest of Saxe-Coburg and Gotha wrote in his *Memoirs:* "My brother loved his eldest daughter much too tenderly, to be influenced *entirely* [my italics] by political considerations in respect of her marriage. For many years . . . his heart's desire had been to see his favourite child . . . in a great position. He took a paternal delight in imagining his promising, talented, and precocious daughter on a powerful throne, but, above all, I knew how much he also desired to render her inwardly happy . . . the son of the Prince of Prussia, above all

other scions of reigning houses, afforded the greatest hopes for the future" (Pakula, p. 83, collating the texts of two separate published works by Duke Ernest). This is Saxe-Coburg casuistry.

315 **The attraction between Vicky and Fritz** That Prince Albert sought to convince himself that Vicky was marrying Fritz because she loved him, not because her family wished for a dynastic alliance with Prussia, is shown clearly in the letter he wrote on March 27, 1856, attempting to explain to Prince William of Prussia why England was in an uproar over the engagement: "British feeling rises against the conception of a young person being promised away long before the proper time into strange hands for political or family reasons. This not taking place in our case could only be demonstrated to the public by letting them know more of the story of the young people's love affair. And this is not advisable, if only because the very causes which made it originally desirable to us that a proposal should not be made before her Confirmation must now cause us to desire not to have to explain to the public that the proposal really took place before the Confirmation" (Jagow, p. 259). More casuistry!

315 **The Queen received a disturbing** Pakula, p. 71.

315 **Once Vicky was confirmed at sixteen** Queen Victoria wrote to Lord Palmerston on March 24, 1856: "According to *established rule* in *Prussia, no* such *private family* agreement *can* take place, without being *officially* announced as a '*betrothal*' to the Royal Family, & published in the *Gazette* there" (Woodham-Smith, p. 373.)

316 **Cut to the quick, Queen Victoria** Woodham-Smith, p. 373.

316 **"From her youth onwards** Pakula, p. 72.

316 **Deeply invested in Prince Albert's dream** Fulford, *Dearest Child*, p. 77.

317 **How, Victoria wondered** Prince Albert wrote to his brother that Queen Victoria "cannot imagine that the child can arouse such feelings" in her fiancé (Bolitho, *The Prince Consort and His Brother*, p. 160). Things went better for the young couple when the Queen detailed Bertie to keep an eye on them for her. Bertie moved into the next room and played with the younger children, giving Vicky and Fritz some private time.

317 **"We dined with Vicky, who generally** Pakula, p. 76.

318 **The Princess Royal had always had** As a little girl, the Princess Royal was not infrequently whipped or subjected to such harsh punishments as being locked up or having her hands bound behind her. Her temper tantrums improved when she was five and placed under the authority of an intelligent and gifted governess. In 1858 Queen Victoria told Vicky, "Your saying you thought a young girl was not in an enviable position comes I think a little from that proud, high spirit which you will remember we did all we could to check and which it would have been so wrong in us to have tolerated. I am sure you feel now my dear child how right and wise we were. But you were trying" (*Dearest Child*, p. 78).

318 **The Queen, in turn, complained bitterly** Queen Victoria wrote to her daughter Vicky: "A more insubordinate and unequal-tempered child and girl I think I never saw! I must say so, honestly, now, dear, The tone you used to me, you know, shocked all who heard you . . . You and Bertie (in very different ways) were indeed great difficulties" (*Dearest Child*, p. 124).

318 **As Queen Victoria remembered** Ibid, p. 96.

319 **He refused to confer** Elisabeth, queen of Prussia, was born a princess of Bavaria. Her life in Prussia was difficult, as she had no children, and she was at daggers drawn with her sister-in-law and presumed successor, Augusta of Saxe-Weimar. She was at first deeply suspicious of and hostile toward her nephew Fritz's English wife. However, after the death of her husband, Frederick William IV, Elisabeth was surprised and touched by the genuine affection and understanding that Vicky showed her. When Elisabeth died, she left her extensive collection of jewelry to Vicky, then crown princess, not to Queen Augusta. Sadly, this only caused a rift between Vicky and her mother-in-law.

319 **However, she must find the money** For example, Vicky was obliged to use her English parliamentary income to buy all her clothes for her father-in-law's coronation.

319 **"I resent bitterly** Pakula, quoting Queen Victoria's diary, p. 71.

319 **Prince Albert wrote back reprovingly** Pakula, p. 77.

319 **The wedding, to be held** The wedding and honeymoon of Victoria, Princess Royal of England, and Prince Frederick William of Prussia is attested by an astonishing array of documents. As soon as the young couple had driven off to Windsor, Queen Victoria sat down to write a lengthy account of the day in her diary. Prince Albert started a letter to Stockmar in the morning and concluded it in the evening. On arriving with her bridegroom at Windsor Castle, the bride took off her bonnet and sat down at once to pen a note of love and thanks to her parents. At breakfast the next day, she received an answer from her mother. And so it went on.

320 **After seventeen years as a wife** Queen Victoria wrote to Vicky: "I think people really marry far too much . . . [Marriage] is such a lottery after all, and for a poor woman a very doubtful happiness" (*Dearest Child*, p. 99).

320 **"Vicky is very reasonable"** Bolitho, *Albert, Prince Consort*, p. 160.

321 **"My heart was very full** Martin, *Life of the Prince Consort*, vol. IV, p. 169.

Chapter 25: FATHER AND SON

322 **"It is a strange omission** Hibbert, *Queen Victoria in Her Letters and Journals*, p. 152. For more on the issue of title and precedence for Prince Albert in 1839–1840, see chapter 12.

323 **"Today I will write** Bolitho, *The Prince Consort and His Brother*, p. 177.

324 **Queen Victoria followed** Queen Victoria wrote to her daughter Vicky, pregnant with her first child: "I hope you will have no chance of two for some time and not of three for a long time. Bertie and I both suffered (and the former will ever suffer) from coming so soon after you" (*Dearest Child*, p. 147).

325 **A few weeks after** Hibbert, *Queen Victoria in Her Letters and Journals*, p. 93.

325 **Two years later, even more ominously** Martin, vol. I, p. 193.

325 **Instead Bertie turned out** This is what Stockmar confided to Frederick Gibbs ("The Education of a Prince," p. 110). Queen Victoria, ever self-deprecating, told her daughter Vicky that Bertie "is my caricature, and that is the misfortune, and in a man—this is so much worse. You are quite your dear beloved Papa's child!" (*Dearest Child*, p. 187).

326 **When Bertie was seventeen** *Dearest Child*, p. 147.

326 **In 1861 she found him** Woodham-Smith, p. 414.

326 **Fed, according to his father's instructions** A Welsh nurse hired by the prince was surprised to find that her little brothers and sisters were better fed than the royal children.

327 **He wrote to his own** Bolitho, *Albert, Prince Consort*, p. 109. Bolitho dates this quotation to 1846, but it must be later if the reference to six children is correct. Louise, the sixth child, was born in March 1848.

327 **This last statement** From the account given by Cecil Woodham-Smith, Queen Victoria and Lady Lyttelton had a good understanding, and both saw the need not to pressure or overwork the Prince of Wales. However, once Birch was appointed, Prince Albert had total supervision of his son, and the Queen ceased to intervene.

328 **"I seem," Birch told Baron Stockmar** St. Aubyn, p. 28. Himself a master at Eton, the Hon. Giles St. Aubyn thoroughly detests both Prince Albert and Baron Stockmar, considering them sanctimonious humbugs. He is quite clear that Henry Birch was dismissed because he had managed to win the affection of his pupil.

328 **He was realistic about the Prince** This is what St. Aubyn writes, p. 28. Unfortunately he sloppily conflates reports on the Prince of Wales contributed by Birch and by Gibbs. Philip Magnus's 1964 biography of Edward VII is less class obsessed and more scholarly than St.

Aubyn's, but he has little to say about his subject's youth, apart from noting: "The treadmill devised for the future Edward VII was a vicarious atonement for the wickedness of George IV." The fullest account of Henry Birch's relationship with Bertie comes in Hector Bolitho's biography of the prince consort. By his own account, Bolitho had unrivaled access not only to the material in the Windsor Archives but to stories about Prince Albert passed down in the royal family. He claims that Prince Albert at first liked the "young, good-looking, amiable" master from Eton, and thought Bertie was likely to become "attached" to him. But when the boy did become attached, Prince Albert decided "that the degree of attachment was dangerous . . . The kind sympathetic tutor became a symbol of romantic fondness that the boy did not seem to feel for his parents. The young Prince wrote affectionate letters to Birch, and, stealing into his bedroom, placed them on his pillow. Sometimes there was a present to prove his devotion" (Bolitho, *Albert, Prince Consort*, p. 110).

329 **Gibbs, he wrote, was "exempt from reproach"** Ibid., p. 29.

329 **The baron's historical anecdotes** Until quite recently, the diaries of royal servants have been rare. However, in spring 1951, an article entitled "The Education of a Prince: Extracts from the Diaries of Frederick Weymouth Gibbs, 1851–1856," was published in *Cornhill*. The magazine did not divulge who had submitted the article and, presumably, owned or found the diaries.

329 **He was deeply affected** Lady Canning, an intelligent woman at the court, watched the parting and wrote, "It has been a trouble and sorrow to the Prince of Wales, who has done no end of touching things since he heard he was to lose [Birch]" (Bolitho *Albert, Prince Consort*, p. 110).

330 **He developed a passion for sticks** "The Queen & Prince sent to ask me if the Prince of Wales was unwell. He had behaved rudely to his sister in their presence," wrote Frederick Gibbs in his diary. "I told them he had been so to me—that he had thrown dirt and swung a large stick at me, and had struck me with a stick in a passion. The Prince told me not to allow this—that if he did so I must box his ears or take the same stick and rap his knuckles sharply" ("The Education of a Prince," p. 111).

330 **Tens of thousands of boys** Lord Shaftesbury's brother, a scion of one of England's oldest families, got into a fight at Eton with an older boy, was beaten, knocked out, and died before anyone thought to intervene.

332 **It was only when Bertie approached** Longford, quoting an archival document, p. 348.

332 **Lord Valletort was chosen** Fulford, *The Prince Consort*, p. 258.

332 **In his leisure, the Prince of Wales** Woodham-Smith, p. 404.

332 **The Queen and her beloved doctor** Longford, p. 345.

332 **Colonel Lindsay, one of the equerries** St. Aubyn, p. 30.

332 **Queen Victoria reported to Vicky** *Dearest Child*, p. 144.

333 **"The only use for Oxford** St. Aubyn, p. 45.

335 **"It is very difficult** Letter of June 4, 1861 (*Dearest Child*, pp. 337–338). The future Queen Alexandra was indeed one of the great beauties of the age and a fashion plate. Her one blemish was a scar on her neck, and she became famous for her high chokers as well as her legendary wasp waist. Her three daughters disciplined their bodies to produce the waist, but did not inherit their mother's beauty.

335 **When reports came in** Princess Dagmar, Alexandra's younger sister, married Tsar Alexander III and became known as Tsaritsa Maria Fedorovna. Much against her will, since she hated Germans with a passion, her son, Tsar Nicholas II, married Princess Alix of Hesse.

335 **He did, however, repair immediately** *Dearest Child*, p. 353.

336 **Usually a loyal defender** Ibid., p. 356.

336 **It would, in his view** Sandringham was acquired by Queen Victoria for her son Bertie in 1862, soon after the prince consort's death. In the end, both the Prince and the Princess of Wales loved Sandringham, which they remodeled to suit themselves.

Chapter 26: PROBLEMS IN A MARRIAGE

337 **Victoria began to write** In preparation for his biography of the Empress Frederick (*The English Empress*, English edition, 1957), Count Egon Corti apparently counted the letters that
had been preserved in the Windsor and Kronberg archives from the mother (3,707) and
the daughter (4,161) (Woodham-Smith, p. 389). Roger Fulford, in *Dearest Child*, the first
volume of his edition of the letters between the Queen and the princess, says that the
bound volumes of the letters numbered eight from Vicky to her mother, four from Vicky to
her father, and thirteen from Queen Victoria to her daughter. Fulford does not say how
many volumes there are of letters from Prince Albert to his daughter. Fulford says that he
chose to publish about a fifth of the Queen's letters. Even in the published selection of the
correspondence, the number of letters passed between the mother in England and the
daughter in Berlin just from January to May of 1858 is astonishing.

338 **"I wish you for the future** *Dearest Child*, p. 35.

338 **At once, the Queen was all** Ibid, p. 96.

339 **She wrote to Vicky in June** Ibid, p. 120. "Annoyance" does not begin to describe the birth
of Vicky's first child. Almost pathologically modest, Vicky refused any physical exami-
nations during her pregnancy, and thus no one was able to establish that her baby was
in the breech position. Queen Victoria longed to attend her daughter's first delivery but
could not leave England when parliament was in session. However, the Queen sent from
England her personal physician Sir James Clark, a trusted nurse, and a supply of chloroform. The princess went into labor on schedule one evening, but after some twelve hours
of increasing agony, the baby remained stuck in the birth canal. The lives of the princess
and her baby were in jeopardy, and Clark begged the Prussian physicians in attendance
to intervene with forceps or at least dull the young mother's pain. They refused, preferring to begin writing the official death notice. Finally, Dr. Eduard Martin, the competent
obstetrician expected to preside over the birth, received word that the princess was in
labor. Mysteriously, the message to Martin had been delivered to the wrong address.
When Martin got to the palace, he insisted on doing a vaginal examination, directed
Clark to administer the chloroform, and pulled out the baby with forceps. The facts surrounding the birth of future Kaiser Wilhelm II were long shrouded in mystery, and, as
one reads the version that emerged decades later, it is hard not to think that a faction in
the Prussian court would have been happy to see the English princess die in childbirth.
The princess's husband failed lamentably to protect the wife he adored by taking control
of the birth as his father-in-law, Prince Albert, had done in similar circumstances.
Vicky's own reaction was strange. She acknowledged that Martin had saved her but was
still repulsed by the liberty he had taken by thrusting his hand into her vagina, and
in her subsequent, and fortunately uneventful pregnancies, she continued to use Dr.
Wegner, the court-appointed doctor who had stood by while she and her first baby
fought for life.

Unsurprisingly, the baby who emerged after this birth trauma was not breathing, and
it took great efforts to revive him. None of the attending doctors reported that there was
anything wrong with the child. However, some days later, the English nurse sent by Queen
Victoria reported that the baby's left arm had been torn out of its socket and was dangling
and useless. It proved that his ear had also been permanently injured and the hours in the
birth canal probably damaged his brain. As an adult, the emperor of Germany had a left
arm some eight inches shorter than the right and virtually useless, and was psychopathic.
History might have been different and Vicky's life less tragic if Dr. Martin had arrived in
time to save her but failed to resuscitate the child.

339 **As the Queen told her daughter** *Dearest Child*, p. 184.

339 **"My heart requires sympathy"** Pakula, p. 133.

339 **On her return to Berlin** *Dearest Child*, p.181 .

339 **The Queen and her daughter became** Mother and daughter died within months of each other. In her final years, Vicky, by this time the dowager Empress Frederick, had inoperable breast cancer and lived in an agony of pain for which her German doctors, on her son the emperor's instructions, refused to give her more than tiny doses of opium. Vicky held on to life in part to save her mother sorrow. When Queen Victoria died, ironically in Kaiser Wilhelm's arms, Vicky set all her affairs in order, got her personal papers out of the country, and died. See Sir Frederick Ponsonby, *Letters of the Empress Frederick*, London: Macmillan, 1928.

340 **"Dear Papa has always been** *Dearest Child*, pp. 45–46.

341 **The prince consort at once planned** It was on this occasion that Prince Albert told his brother that he would be traveling with "only Colonel Ponsonby, and Dr. Becker [his German librarian], besides one courier, a valet de chamber, and three men servants" (Bolitho, *The Prince Consort and His Brother*, p. 185). This was Albert's idea of a minimal staff.

341 **Victoria told Vicky** Ibid, p. 91.

341 **"I assure you dear** Ibid, p. 104.

341 **Writing of the disappointment** Ibid, p. 123.

341 **Queen Victoria liked Louis of Hesse** Prince Louis of Hesse and Prince Frederick William of Prussia were not dissimilar in looks, but Alice was not nearly as happy with her Louis as Vicky was with her Fritz. Alice, like her older sister, thought that her father was the ideal man and wanted to marry someone just like him. She soon discovered that her husband was a vain, stupid, and sensual man.

342 **On October 4, 1858** *Dearest Child*, p. 135.

342 **"Papa is much pleased** Ibid, pp. 292–293.

343 **"One becomes so worn out** *Dearest Child*, p. 192.

343 **"I really think those ladies** *Dearest Child*, p. 191.

343 **"No father, no man** Ibid, p. 182. In this same letter, Queen Victoria notes that Alice has picked up on some things (presumably relating to sex and reproduction) and is beginning to dread marriage.

343 **After Vicky wrote in disgust** Ibid, p. 205.

343 **Weary of congratulating young ladies** Ibid, p. 269.

343 **Victoria is not known to have** Beatrice, referred to in the family as "Baby" until she was at least five, was allowed to watch her father shave and cheek her mother at mealtimes. The Queen's letters have many references to Baby's darling new outfits and her cunning little sayings. One wonders how Alice, Helena, and Louise reacted to such favoritism.

343 **In November 1857, they gazed** See the prince's letter describing this tragic event that occurred at Claremont, to his uncle Leopold, Jagow, p. 284.

344 **Given the same advice** In her fascinating little book (*Queen Victoria. The Woman, the Monarchy, The People* (New York: Pantheon, 1990, p. 43), Dorothy Thompson relates this story, noting that it crops up a lot in the literature, mostly without attribution. Thompson apparently found the story in Barry St. John Neville's *Life at the Court of Queen Victoria: Illustrated from the Collections of Lord Edward Pelham-Clinton, Master of the Household, with Selections from the Journal of Queen Victoria* (Salem, New Hampshire: Salem House, 1984, introduction, p. 13, no attribution).

344 **As he once confided** Roger Fulford, *The Prince Consort*, citing the Royal Archives, p. 265.

345 **If pregnancy was the price** Elizabeth Longford claims that Victoria told her daughter Vicky just after Prince Albert's death that she bitterly regretted not having another child (Longford, pp. 389–390). Longford acknowledges that this is odd given the Queen's "violent attitude toward childbearing." My interpretation would be that Victoria wished that, in their final years together, she and her husband had enjoyed conjugal relations, even at the risk of another pregnancy.

345 **Her feelings for him were** *Dearest Mama*, p. 106.

345 **I and the girls** *Dearest Child*, p. 131–139.

Chapter 27: "I DO NOT CLING TO LIFE AS YOU DO"

346 **"To my imagination it appears** Letter to King Frederick William II of Prussia, Jagow p. 81.

347 **"God have mercy on us!"** Woodham-Smith, p. 402 and note p. 468, quoting *Memoirs* of Ernest II, Duke of Saxe-Coburg and Gotha, 1888, vol. IV, p. 55.

347 **Such remarks would make** *Dearest Mama,* p. 30.

348 **Prince Albert aged so fast** When it became clear to Queen Victoria that she must intervene, it was too late. On December 7, 1861, Queen Victoria talked with doctors Clark and Jenner "over what could have caused" her husband's illness. "Great worry and far too hard work for long!" she concluded. "*That* must be stopped" (Woodham-Smith, p. 425).

348 **"Were there not so many things** Jagow, p. 347.

350 **Gastric problems troubled Albert** In *Uncrowned King,* Stanley Weintraub suggests that Prince Albert had stomach cancer, and Christopher Hibbert in his biography of Queen Victoria hints at the same thing. Since Queen Victoria refused to allow an autopsy on her husband's body, it is impossible to substantiate this hypothesis.

351 **Her diagnosis was** Two weeks before her husband died, Queen Victoria was writing to her daughter in Berlin: "I can begin by saying that dear Papa is in reality much better—only so much reduced and as usual desponding as men really only are—when unwell" (Hibbert, *Queen Victoria in Her Letters and Journals,* p. 153).

352 **On one of his visits to London** Measles is highly contagious but dangerous mainly to children who are undernourished and to adults who have never acquired any immunity. In 1861 almost everybody in Europe contracted measles in early childhood and was thereafter immune, with mothers conferring initial immunity on their infants up to about the age of one. It is possible that royal persons were less exposed to common childhood ailments like measles and thus did not acquire immunity. In the nineteenth century, measles was often confused with the less serious rubella (German measles). That Prince Louis was able to travel to England when he had measles and then infected only his future mother-in-law and one of her children seems unlikely. That Queen Victoria claimed she caught measles twice is another indication that on at least one occasion she came down with rubella, not measles.

352 **"You say no one is perfect** *Dearest Child,* p. 354.

353 **In his diary he wrote in June** Woodham-Smith, p. 414.

354 **Victoria had the most fun ever** Victoria published an account of these "Great Expeditions" in her first volume of Highland memoirs. See David Duff, *Victoria in the Highlands,* pp. 172–192.

355 **On his occasional meetings** Historians have had little good to say about King Pedro, or his father.

355 **"The death of poor, good Pedro** Fulford, *The Prince Consort,* p. 264.

355 **Queen Victoria confided to her diary** Jagow, p. 370.

355 **"If you were to try and deny it** I paraphrase here the account of the letter given by Cecil Woodham-Smith, pp. 416–417, the only one with quotations. The full text of this letter has never been published.

357 **He was suffering from typhoid fever** According to the death certificate made out by his eldest son, the prince consort contracted the typhoid fever that killed him on November 22. This date was no doubt supplied by one of his attendant physicians, Dr William Jenner. Such dates were necessarily approximate at a time when blood tests for pathogens were unknown. It seems far from unlikely that the prince in fact contracted typhoid some weeks earlier, soon after his return to Windsor Castle. If so, the news of the deaths of Pedro and Ferdinand, ironically from typhoid, and the letter from Stockmar came when the prince consort was already suffering from the disease that would kill him. Well or sick, the prince would certainly have reacted with deep disappointment and rage to the news of Bertie's dalliance with Nellie Clifden. But if Albert's reaction to his son's fall from grace has always

seemed so extreme, it may have been in no small part because he was suffering the effects of a life-threatening fever. The exploit of the Prince of Wales clearly exacerbated his father's mental disarray. But Bertie was not responsible for his father's death, as Queen Victoria fervently believed for many years.

359 **Though he was a fervent advocate** Let me cite just two instances of the prince consort's work as a sanitarian. At the Great Exhibition, Albert constructed in Hyde Park model working-class houses that featured indoor plumbing. At this time, a water closet and running water were considered to be luxuries. When Florence Nightingale returned from the Crimea in 1856, she was invited to stay with the Queen and the prince at Balmoral and had long conversations with them about how and why so many men had died of infectious disease in the recent war. At the prince's strong recommendation, the Queen authorized a royal commission to examine the issues. The resulting report, that Nightingale supervised and wrote, was a major step toward protecting the lives of British soldiers.

359 **By December 1** The death of the prince consort was an important and dramatic event. It was observed by a number of people, several of whom left detailed accounts of what they had seen. Many letters—between the Queen and her various relatives, between the Queen and Lord Palmerston, between Palmerston and Sir George Phipps—are extant, and many have been published. Every book on Queen Victoria and Prince Albert gives an account of the prince's death. I have relied especially on those by Woodham-Smith, Longford, and Fulford. Victoria continued to write her journal every day until December 13. The journal started up again after two weeks. In 1872, after several unsuccessful attempts, the Queen was finally able to give her own account of her husband's last days, which, she says, were engraved upon her memory.

360 **"Albert is a little rheumatic** This and subsequent quotations in this paragraph are from *The Letters of Queen Victoria, 1837–1861*, ed. Benson and Esher, vol. III, pp. 468–471.

361 **"You did wrong," he commented** Longford, p. 374.

361 **This was especially true** This was not the view of contemporaries. Lord Clarendon famously remarked that Sir James Clark and Sir Henry Holland could not be trusted to look after a sick cat. Florence Nightingale remarks in her private papers that the prince consort could have been saved had he received proper nursing.

Chapter 28: MOURNING A PRINCE

365 **Dissatisfied by such ephemeral tributes** For my discussion here and below of the memorials and monuments erected by the nation, I am indebted to *The Cult of the Prince Consort* by Elisabeth Darby and Nicola Smith, New Haven and London: Yale University Press, 1983.

365 **the Earl of Oxford exclaimed** Duff, *Victoria and Albert*, p. 297, citing Jerrold. Other sources ascribe this anecdote to the Earl of Oxford.

367 **In a private conversation** Lytton Strachey, *Queen Victoria*, p. 186, citing the 1886 memoir of his years as Prussia's representative in London, 1852–1864, by Carl Friedrich Graf Vitzhum von Eckstadt.

368 **This was the view** "If there comes a real collision between the Queen and the House of Commons," wrote Mary Ponsonby in 1878 to her husband, who was then Queen Victoria's private secretary, "it is quite possible she would turn restive . . . and then her reign will end in a fiasco or she prepares one for the Prince of Wales; for I do think in a tussle of that sort, and I do hope and pray it should be so, that the People win the day" *Mary Ponsonby*, pp. 144–145.

368 **Jane Ely and Jane Churchill** Duff, *Victoria and Albert*, p. 19.

368 **"I feel right well"** "Biographical Sketch" of his father by Ernest Stockmar, introduction to *Memoirs of Baron Stockmar*, vol. 1, p. xcviii.

368 **Albert had been dearer to him** Fulford, *The Prince Consort*, p. 273.

370 **"Oh! That boy** *Dearest Mama*, p. 30.

373 **Then she took to sleeping** The Princess Royal (Vicky) wrote to her husband from Osborne in March 1862: "Mama is dreadfully sad . . . always sleeps with Papa's coat over her and his dear red dressing gown beside and some of his clothes in her bed! . . . [She is] as much in love with Papa as though she had married him yesterday . . . she feels the same as your little Fräuchen . . . and is always consumed with longing for her husband" (Hibbert, *Queen Victoria: A Personal History*, New York: Basic Books, 2000, p. 271).

373 **"I never dreamt** *Dearest Mama*, p. 23.

373 **"I am alas! not old** Nina C. Epton, *Victoria and Her Daughters*, New York: Norton, 1971, p. 102.

373 **Even in her first letter** *Letters of Queen Victoria*, vol. iii, p. 473.

374 **The loneliness and longing** Queen Victoria, in a letter to her daughter when Vicky was in despair over the death of her husband, volunteered that she had once been tempted "to put an end to my life *here*, but a *voice* told me for *His* sake—no! Still Endure." Longford, p. 426, citing Kronberg Letters, October 2, 1888.

374 **"I can so well understand** *Dearest Mama*, p. 35.

375 **"I am also anxious to repeat** Benson and Esher, *Letters of Queen Victoria 1837–1861*, vol. III, p. 476.

381 **Hibbert, a scrupulous scholar** Hibbert, Queen Victoria, chapter 42, "John Brown," especially pp. 321–323.

381 **Longford declared** *Victoria R.I*, p. 417.

381 **Hibbert drily confirms** Thompson, *Queen Victoria: The Woman, the Monarchy and the People*, p. 77, and Hibbert, *Queen Victoria*, p. 497.

383 **Her harshest judgment** Queen Victoria reportedly told Lord Derby that the prince consort "would die—he seemed not to care to live . . . He died from want of what they call pluck." Longford, quoting Disraeli, p. 391.

$\mathcal{I}llustration\ \mathcal{C}redits$

Bridgeman Art Archive

INSERT

p. 6 bottom, FC 12259

p. 7 bottom, STC 61533

The illustration on p. 275 first appeared in the *Illustrated London News* of April 26, 1856.

Special thanks to Karen Lawson, senior picture library assistant at the Royal Collection, and to Matthew Bailey, assistant picture library manager at the National Gallery.

$\mathcal{I}ndex$

We Two

GILLIAN GILL

A Reader's Guide

WHEN I WAS GROWING UP in South Wales, the part of Great Britain best known for coal mines, people like me did not write about royalty. We left that to "nobs" like Countess (Elizabeth) Longford, who were actually invited to coronations, or to people like Cecil Woodham-Smith, who had double-barreled surnames and weird given names that proclaimed their membership in the elite public (i.e. private) school set. My family was the kind that lined the route of a rare royal visit to our provincial city and waved tiny union jacks.

My sister, Rose, and I were reared jointly by our mother and our grandmother until I was a teenager. Mummy and Nana lived together all their lives and quarreled every day but shared a passion for the British royal family. In our house, the pantheon of royals was worshipped with more fervor and regularity than we mustered at the plain little branch of the Church of Wales just around the corner. The royals were glamour and romance, items severely rationed in post-war Britain.

The year of Queen Elizabeth II's coronation, 1953, was a banner year for our family. My mother bought a television set and invited her humbler relatives over to squint at the magnificent event on our twelve-inch, black and white set. There followed a street party and my grandmother, who had once apprenticed as a milliner, contrived marvelous costumes for Rose and me. I was queen for the day with a long white dress, purple robe, crown, orb, and scepter.

But once my father retired from the Merchant Navy and took his place in the family, his carefully informed left-wing politics took hold of me, and my grandmother's reverence for the royal family began to seem silly and ignorant. When I was about seventeen, I made some flip remark about the abdication of King Edward VIII, which so infuriated Nana that she slapped my face. At the time I was shocked and wholly at a loss. Now I think I understand. A handsome and engaging young king had once come to South Wales and spoken movingly of the plight of the miners. Women of my grandmother's generation had never forgotten it. Like the rest of the general public in Britain, she had been carefully shielded by the press from any knowledge of Edward VIII's prenuptial dalliances and fascist opinions.

By 1965 I was a graduate of Cambridge University, the first of my family to attend university and a budding academic. When it was announced that the Queen Mother would come to New Hall, my Cambridge college, to open the new buildings, I was blasé to the point of disdain. But when I found myself curtseying and carefully shaking the tips of Her Majesty's gloved fingers, I was swept away by the mystique of royalty. How delightful she was in person and how proud my grandmother would be when she saw the photo of me with the Queen Mum.

All of which is to explain why my book about Queen Victoria is prefaced by the old English saying: "A cat may look at a king."

QUESTIONS AND TOPICS FOR DISCUSSION

1. Movies about princesses are perennial favorites. Many little girls love to play pretend, trailing around in long dresses and wearing plastic tiaras. How does the reality of Queen Victoria's youth complicate this modern fantasy?

2. Gillian Gill claims that we can learn a lot about the real lives of queens and princesses from traditional fairy stories like "Snow White," "Donkey Skin," and "Sleeping Beauty." Do you agree? Why or why not?

3. Until the death of her husband when she was forty-two, Queen Victoria was probably never on her own either indoors or out. Would you like it or hate it if you were never alone?

4. What motivated Queen Victoria to choose her cousin Albert as her husband? Was it family loyalty? Romantic ideas? Raging hormones? Social pragmatism? A sense of isolation?

5. Unlike the married English queens who were her predecessors (Mary Tudor, Mary Stuart, and Anne Stuart) Victoria had no difficulty producing the heirs that her nation and her husband required. How did she handle having nine children in seventeen years and seeing them all reach adulthood? Do you think she was a good mother?

6. Did you agree with the way Queen Victoria and Prince Albert actively promoted the engagement of their eldest daughter, Vicky, to Prince Frederick William of Prussia, when Vicky was just shy of her fifteenth birthday?

7. Hemophilia has been called the royal malady because it afflicted three or more generations of the Saxe-Coburg and Gotha families, beginning with Queen Victoria's fourth son, Prince Leopold, Duke of Albany. How did the royal family cope with their hemophiliac sons? What policy did they follow with their daughters who, even in the nineteenth century, were known by medical science to run a significant risk of carrying the terrible disease on to the next generation?

8. Why do you think Prince Albert reacted so violently when he heard the news that his eldest son, nineteen-year-old Bertie, had had a brief liaison with an actress?

9. What factors were involved in the death of Prince Albert at the early age of forty-two? Do you think he wanted to die, as Queen Victoria sometimes seems to have believed?

10. Why do you think the widowed Queen Victoria never considered remarriage? Do you think she should have abdicated in favor of her son Bertie when he was still a young man?

11. Queen Victoria and Prince Albert put the British monarchy on such a firm foundation that it survives to this day. Do you think Great Britain would be better off without a king or queen?

PHOTO: © LINDA CROSSKEY

GILLIAN GILL, who holds a Ph.D. in modern French literature from Cambridge University, has taught at Northeastern, Wellesley, Yale, and Harvard. She is the author of *Nightingales: The Extraordinary Upbringing and Curious Life of Miss Florence Nightingale; Agatha Christie: The Woman and Her Mysteries;* and *Mary Baker Eddy.* She lives in suburban Boston.